SOCIOLOGICAL THEORY

Present-Day Sociology

from the Past

SOCIOLOGICAL THEORY

Present-Day Sociology
from the Past

EDITED BY

EDGAR F. BORGATTA

RUSSELL SAGE FOUNDATION

AND

HENRY J. MEYER

NEW YORK UNIVERSITY

ALFRED A. KNOPF   NEW YORK
1 9 5 6

L.C. catalog card number: 56–6940

© Edgar F. Borgatta and Henry J. Meyer, 1956

THIS IS A BORZOI BOOK
PUBLISHED BY ALFRED A. KNOPF, INC.

FIRST EDITION

To

DON, SLATS, AND WELLMAN

WHAT'S PAST IS PROLOGUE.

SHAKESPEARE, The Tempest

PREFACE

THE FORMATIVE STATE OF SOCIOLOGICAL THEORY TODAY ALLOWS us a privilege which more mature sciences cannot enjoy. In the absence of a highly developed formal theory, speculation and, indeed, even "arm chair" theorizing may on occasion have the force of study based on the optimum data necessary for generalization. Such speculations and generalizations are not necessarily wrong nor are they necessarily correct. What is important is that occasionally some scholar summarizes his own reflections in what turns out in time to be the most appropriate way. He may, for example, observe only his own children and, because he *sees* them as they are behaving, he can propose generalizations about the socialization process which require little modification half a century later. Wisdom, as well as science, has played an important part in the unfolding of generalized knowledge about social behavior. Some of the most important ideas of relevance to sociological theory and research today were developed by clear-eyed observers willing to look at the world they could see from their study windows, unhampered by compulsions to elaboration and having sufficient leisure and self-confidence to fondle thoughts into mature ideas.

We may easily overestimate how much of the knowledge we have about social behavior has been discovered within our own generation. A modern textbook may be a marvel of sophistication, but we should never lose sight of the fact that our current work is inevitably an extension of the past. This should not lead to a worship of prior work, but to a recognition of what in the past is suitable for use in the present. In this sense, an examination of contributions of the past which are modern today serves a multiple purpose. It encourages the economy of continuity in the development of the discipline, it requires recognition in small part of our present limitations, and it can help to develop a balanced attitude toward our accomplishments, whatever they may be.

Many contemporary social and behavioral scientists seem to sense that the dismissal of early theorists is too quick among the students in training today. Particularly in sociology and psychology, the accumulation of a literature of rigorous description and experimentation commands a considerable portion of the attention of the student. There is a tendency to think that ideas begin with their last statement, or with the testing of an experimental hypothesis. This often leads to neglect of the fact that thoughtful observations about the ways people have dealt with people have probably been made as long as there have been people. On the other hand, a healthy respect for the thinking of our predecessors does not mean that the student of today should relax from his concern with the more recent and more rigorous experimental and descriptive literature and begin to create "theories." On the contrary, attentive recourse to our predecessors should indicate that ideas, sophisticated extrapolation, and the experience of generations is not lacking. What is necessary at this point *is* rigor in the considered thought given to a problem and in the design of hypotheses for experiment and research. The availability of developed tools of research, of statistics and "gadgets," makes possible the rigor of technique, but these cannot be substituted for intelligent and imaginative thinking. The application of scientific method begins with an idea.

In viewing the early sociological theorists we may have a tendency to dismiss them because they do not use the same language we do, or because we are not interested in some of the problems that interested them. Looking at their work more closely, however, we find that differences of language frequently mask great similarities of interest in work of the present and the past. Furthermore one should be careful not to overlook important contributions in the work of an author merely because one aspect of his work is not satisfactory by modern standards. The keen discernment of variables useful for the description and interpretation of behavior to be found, for example, in the work of such authors as Spencer and Morgan, is often ignored because of their "evolutionary bias." We may grant that there is serious bias in the perspective of some social theorists of the past as there most certainly is among social theorists of the present. But we should not overemphasize the error to the point of overlooking the truth. Sociology and psychology have had many biases—usually called schools of thought—and yet, through time, a core of knowledge appears to have accumulated.

In this connection, however, the student of sociological theory who works with materials from the past, including those in this particular volume, is cautioned to remember that the meanings and the overtones of language change. Thus, for example, recent concern with problems of "race" prejudice has led to the development of specific meanings associated with the concept of race which are quite different from those it had at the turn of the century. At one level, race is today identified as a biological concept; at another, it refers to categorical distinctions between groups on visibly identifiable bases, with a "cultural" overtone to the distinction. But in the earlier writing, some of which is represented in this volume, no such narrow meanings were attached to the concept, and it was sometimes used as a generalized and unspecific classificatory term. So it is also with several other concepts, and the student should be careful not to miss the meaning by failure to enter the language of the author.

The selection of materials for inclusion in this book was governed by several criteria. In the first place, we did not choose any writing merely because of its historical importance to sociology. For example, Franklin H. Giddings' concept of "consciousness of kind," Lester F. Ward's of "social telesis," and William G. Sumner's of "folkways" are important historically but not especially fruitful for contemporary theory. It is our hope that this book of readings will spur the interest of teachers and students alike in theory itself as distinguished from the history of theory, interesting and important as the latter may be for the scholar.

A second criterion led us to exclude contributions essentially methodological in character. This is not because such contributions are irrelevant today for the thinking of sociologists, and it is certainly not for want of excellent writings from which to choose. We would strongly recommend to serious students of sociology today much of Emile Durkheim's *Rules of Sociological Method* or Giddings' keen methodological exhortations. But in our arbitrary definition, considerations of methodology are not sociological theory. At the one extreme they are philosophy, and at the other tools and technical instructions. Furthermore, they are implicit in theory.

By the same token, we have omitted general philosophical discussions of the nature of society and such generalized concepts as culture, language and communication, and interaction. Important as these are, we deem them for our present purposes to be outside of—perhaps even more basic than—sociological theory. The acceptance of such concepts as culture, symbolic communication, observability of social relations, and the like are assumed rather than elaborated. So, too, is the applicability of the common method of science to the data of sociology.

With reference to our positive criteria, we sought to include selections which were not only of relevance today, but which were, in a sense, fresh and suggestive. To be sure, any creative literature of the past concerned with people is relevant and suggestive to responsive imaginations today. But we have tried to apply this criterion to the writings of earlier sociologists in such a way that their work from the past could be expected to compete in stimulation with that which appears today in textbooks and journal articles.

As we review our work, we feel our selections have on the whole satisfied this criterion. Some of the selections are more dated by language and concept than others. Some are deceptively simple and others deceptively difficult. But we feel emphatically that some of the selections are unsurpassed today.

In the selection process we favored clarity of expression, and in those cases in which the earliest exponent of an idea has been surpassed by a student, a disciple, or even a competitor who "said it better," we have preferred the follower to the originator. In fact, we acknowledge a certain conspicuous naïvete in some of the selections we have chosen. If conclusions have been so well stated and in such obvious conformity to the empirical situation that they appear at times to be self-evident, we may suggest that the theorists have properly done their jobs.

The theoretical passages included in this volume are written at differing levels of generality. Sociological theory need not always be of the highest abstraction nor must it always refer to all groups and all societies. Because of the multiplicity of factors involved in sociological phenomena, one should not hesitate to restrict the sphere of generalization, acknowledging that it is "culturally" or "societally" bound. If operative theories can be constructed for restricted units, we may be assured that more general theory will not be long in coming.

In editing some of the selections, we have occasionally removed passages from their contexts. The selection from Herbert Spencer is an extreme example. This was necessary to meet our objective of reducing the materials to generalized description or to principle. Therefore, we wished to omit as much as possible the illustrations and side excursions of the authors. In this respect we have taken editorial liberties rather freely. In some cases this has involved deleting sentences; in others it has meant taking the key sentences in a series of paragraphs spread out over a large segment of a work; and in still others it has involved picking out an occasional paragraph. In presenting the materials we have not indicated directly what the editing has been, because the use of a series of dots interferes with reading. We hope that the notice here served will be sufficient to warn those who are interested in quoting the materials to check them in their original contexts.

We acknowledge that since we have used materials out of context we may have inadvertently altered their meanings. We have tried to avoid this, but surely some change of meaning must be expected. Where it occurs we hope it will reflect a change in the direction of more sophisticated interpretation of the materials. The advantage of the present-day reader over past writers is that he may view their ideas in a modern context and free them from their own time. It may be argued that such editing does not do justice to a writer's place in history because it may omit his contributions as well as his errors. We do not mean to minimize or to exaggerate the modernity of earlier sociological work. But when salient ideas appear along with negligible ones there is little reason to conceal the former out of a pedantic respect for the latter. In all our editing our concern has been to present such generalizations as are capable of generating ideas for serious sociologists in their theory and research. If this is rewriting the ideas of the past in contemporary terms, it is only in such fashion that a body of theory, as distinguished from mere history, can accumulate.

Such editing has removed much of the polemic and the topical which was associated with the period in which these selections were written. We have used ideas which are suggestive, if not acceptable, today. In so doing we have taken some of the sparkle of the writing and placed it in a clearing where it might attract the eye. But if these writings have sparkle in this edited form, the serious student will find the reading of the originals even more rewarding. Even where our text is the original as it appeared, in no case is the entirety of a man's work included. For each item which the reader finds stimulating and illuminating in this text, many others are to be found in the original sources. This book is not a substitute for more extensive reading. But until the student is moved to such reading, this collection of materials will, we hope, indicate that a worthwhile experience is available.

In our editing, we have not taken so rigid a point of view that all with which we have disagreed has been deleted. Rather, we have retained much speculative richness and, in many cases, competing points of view are evident. In uncertain areas of knowledge, firmly based theory can develop only in the constant testing of competing ideas. In this sense, aside from its pedagogical utility, a real value of this volume should be to provide a reference point for alternative theories and to point to some hypotheses and hunches which need research exploration.

This volume of readings is necessarily incomplete. No book could include everything from the past that is useful to the contemporary sociological theorist. But if the text must be incomplete it can provide at least a set of useful starting points. We have not forced the inclusion of sections merely to round out the materials and produce a synthetic, systematic theory. Yet, most of the major topics of sociology are touched on in this volume, and there is a common frame of reference. Thus some of the selections could be placed almost anywhere in the outline of the volume. Similarly, the range of ideas in a given selection may cut across other topics.

The materials of this volume have been arranged into parts and chapters according to major theoretical problems. Thus, the central five parts of the book deal with (a) the person as a social unit, or the problems of socialization and transmission of social patterns through the generations; (b) social forms and processes, or generalizations which can be made about social behavior at the highest levels of abstraction; (c) societal structures, or manifestations of crystallized patterns and regularities in society; (d) the persistence of social structures, or the ways in which society maintains itself and its identity; and (e), social change, or the way in which society evolves through time. Obviously, even as stated in these broad terms, we would expect the parts to overlap. Our arrangement is not intended to confine the rich contributions contained in this collection to a limited conceptual structure. Rather, it should be viewed as one of convenience which grew out of the materials. We have accordingly written short introductions for the parts, and within these, let the sociologists speak for themselves.

The time span which these selections cover extends roughly from the last quarter of the 19th century to the 1930's. We chose to start after the emergence of the field of sociology under that name. Our terminal date was set rather naturally at the threshold of the resurgence of interest in the making of sociological theory which has characterized the last fifteen or so years.

In the preparation of this volume, we are of course grateful to authors and publishers who have given us permission to reproduce their materials. We must also express appreciation to our editor and publisher who have encouraged us to include whatever materials we thought necessary. The authors owe a debt to Donald Young, Leonard S. Cottrell, Jr., and Wellman J. Warner whose wealth of learning has been exploited more than they realize. In another sense, the exploitation of our families is also most gratefully acknowledged. Most of all, however, we are grateful to those men of ideas whose theories we are privileged to present again to another generation of sociologists.

Finally, if any atrocities have occurred in the handling of these materials, we claim full credit for them.

New York, N.Y.   E. F. B.
October 20, 1955   H. J. M.

CONTENTS

PART SIX: SOCIAL CHANGE
page 445

SOCIOLOGICAL THEORY

Present-Day Sociology
from the Past

Society and Knowledge of Society

O NE DOES NOT BECOME CONSCIOUS OF HIS OWN VALUES UNTIL they are contrasted with values which are different. Within any relatively homogeneous value system it is possible to be entirely unaware of the habitual and common ways of thinking and acting because the system may not provide a means of examining itself. Whether the system is a family group, a religious organization, a society, an historical epoch, or even science, the boundaries of the system determine the development of ideas and what is named knowledge. Thus, examining the bases of ideas and knowledge and their relationship to the group in which they exist is a fundamental prerequisite for a social science. The social science must examine its own roots in society.

It is appropriate that a volume of selections of sociological theory should begin with a passage from Karl Mannheim's *Ideology and Utopia*. With lucid detail, Mannheim considers, in the context of the historical development of social systems, the relationship of ideas and knowledge to the social group within which they arise.

CHAPTER 1

The Sociology of Ideas

---◦•●•◦---

THE SOCIOLOGY OF IDEAS

BY

KARL MANNHEIM

THE principal thesis of the sociology of knowledge is that there are modes of thought which cannot be adequately understood as long as their social origins are obscured. It is indeed true that only the individual is capable of thinking. There is no such metaphysical entity as a group mind which thinks over and above the heads of individuals, or whose ideas the individual merely reproduces. Nevertheless it would be false to deduce from this that all the ideas and sentiments which motivate an individual have their origin in him alone, and can be adequately explained solely on the basis of his own life-experience.

Just as it would be incorrect to attempt to derive a language merely from observing a single individual, who speaks not a language of his own but rather that of his contemporaries and predecessors who have prepared the path for him, so it is incorrect to explain the totality of an outlook only with reference to its genesis in the mind of the individual. Only in a quite limited sense does the single individual create out of himself the mode of speech and of thought we attribute to him. He speaks the language of his group; he thinks in the manner in which his group thinks. He finds at his disposal only certain words and their

From *Ideology and Utopia* by Karl Mannheim. Reprinted by permission of Harcourt, Brace and Company, Inc.
Abridged from: Mannheim, Karl, *Ideology and Utopia: An Introduction to the Sociology of Knowledge* (Translated by L. Wirth and E. A. Shils) New York: Harcourt, Brace and Company, 1936.

meanings. These not only determine to a large extent the avenues of approach to the surrounding world, but they also show at the same time from which angle and in which context of activity objects have hitherto been perceptible and accessible to the group or the individual.

The first point which we have to emphasize is that the approach of the sociology of knowledge intentionally does not start with the single individual and his thinking in order then to proceed directly in the manner of the philosopher to the abstract heights of "thought as such." Rather, the sociology of knowledge seeks to comprehend thought in the concrete setting of an historical-social situation out of which individually differentiated thought only very gradually emerges. Thus, it is not men in general who think, or even isolated individuals who do the thinking, but men in certain groups who have developed a particular style of thought in an endless series of responses to certain typical situations characterizing their common position.

Strictly speaking it is incorrect to say that the single individual thinks. Rather it is more correct to insist that he participates in thinking further what other men have thought before him. He finds himself in an inherited situation with patterns of thought which are appropriate to this situation and attempts to elaborate further the inherited modes of response or to substitute others for them in order to deal more adequately with the new challenges which have arisen out of the shifts and changes in his situation. Every individual is therefore in a two-fold sense predetermined by the fact of growing up in a society: on the one hand he finds a ready-made situation and on the other he finds in that situation preformed patterns of thought and of conduct.

The second feature characterizing the method of the sociology of knowledge is that it does not sever the concretely existing modes of thought from the context of collective action through which we first discover the world in an intellectual sense. Men living in groups do not merely coexist physically as discrete individuals. They do not confront the objects of the world from the abstract levels of a contemplating mind as such, nor do they do so exclusively as solitary beings. On the contrary they act with and against one another in diversely organized groups, and while doing so they think with and against one another. These persons, bound together into groups, strive in accordance with the character and position of the groups to which they belong to change the surrounding world of nature and society or attempt to maintain it in a given condition. It is the direction of this will to change or to maintain, of this collective activity, which produces the guiding thread for the emergence of their problems, their concepts, and their forms of thought. In accord with the particular context of collective activity in which they participate, men always tend to see the world which surrounds them differently. Just as pure logical analysis has severed individual thought from its group situation, so it also separated thought from action. It did this on the tacit assumption that those inherent connections which always exist in reality between thought on the one hand, and group and activity on the other, are either insignificant for "correct" thinking or can be detached from these foundations without any resultant difficulties. But the fact that one ignores something by no means puts an end to its existence. Nor can anyone who has not first given himself whole-heartedly to the exact observation of the wealth of forms in which men really think decide *a priori* whether this severance from the social situation and context of activity is always realizable. Nor indeed can it be determined offhand that such a complete dichotomy is fully desirable precisely in the interest of objective factual knowledge.

It may be that, in certain spheres of knowledge, it is the impulse to act which first makes the objects of the world accessible to the acting subject, and it may be further that it is this factor which determines the selection of those elements of reality which enter into thought. And it is not inconceivable that if this volitional factor were entirely excluded (in so far as such a thing is possible), the concrete content would completely disappear from the concepts, and the organizing principle which first makes possible an intelligent statement of the problem would be lost.

But this is not to say that in those domains where attachment to the group and orientation towards action seem to be an essential element in the situation, every possibility of intellectual, critical self-control is futile. Perhaps it is precisely when the hitherto concealed dependence of thought on group existence and its rootedness in action becomes visible that it really becomes possible for the first time, through becoming aware of them, to attain a new mode of control over previously uncontrolled factors in thought.

It is, of course, true that in the social sciences, as elsewhere, the ultimate criterion of truth or falsity is to be found in the investigation of the object, and the sociology of knowledge is no substitute for this. But the examination of the object is not an isolated act; it takes place in a context which is coloured by values and collective-unconscious, volitional impulses. In the social sciences it is this intellectual interest, oriented in a matrix of collective activity, which provides not only the general questions, but the concrete hypotheses for research and the thought-models for the ordering of experience. Only as we succeed in bringing into the area of conscious and explicit observation the various points of departure and of approach to the facts which are current in scientific as well as popular discussion, can we hope, in the course of time, to control the unconscious motivations and presuppositions which, in the last analysis, have brought these modes of thought into existence. A new type of objectivity in the social sciences is attainable not through the exclusion of evaluations but through the critical awareness and control of them.

It is one of the fundamental insights of the sociology of knowledge that the process by which collective-unconscious motives become conscious cannot operate in every epoch, but only in a quite specific situation. This situation is sociologically determinable. One can point out with relative precision the factors which are inevitably forcing more and more persons to reflect not merely about the things of the world, but about thinking itself and even here not so much about truth in itself, as about the alarming fact that the same world can appear differently to different observers.

It is clear that such problems can become general only in an age in which disagreement is more conspicuous than agreement. One turns from the direct observation of things to the consideration of ways of thinking only when the possibility of the direct and continuous elaboration of concepts concerning things and situations has collapsed in the face of a multiplicity of fundamentally divergent definitions. Now we are enabled to designate more precisely than a general and formal analysis makes possible, exactly in which social and intellectual situation such a shift of attention from things to divergent opinions and from there to the unconscious motives of thought must necessarily occur. In what follows we wish to point out only a few of the most significant social factors which are operating in this direction.

Above all, the multiplicity of ways of thinking cannot become a problem in periods when social stability underlies and guarantees the internal unity of a world-view. As long as the same meanings of words, the same ways of deducing ideas, are inculcated from childhood on into every member of the group, divergent thought-processes cannot exist in that society. Even a gradual modification in ways of thinking (where it should happen to arise), does not become perceptible to the members of a group who live in a stable situation as long as the tempo in the adaptations of ways of thinking to new problems is so slow that it extends over several generations. In such a case, one and the same generation in the course of its own life span can scarcely become aware that a change is taking place.

But in addition to the general dynamics of the historical process, factors of quite another sort must enter before the multiplicity of the ways of thinking will become noticeable and emerge as a theme for reflection. Thus it is primarily the intensification of social mobility which destroys the earlier illusion, prevalent in a static society, that all things can change, but thought remains eternally the same. And what is more, the two forms of social mobility, horizontal and vertical, operate in different ways to reveal this multiplicity of styles of thought. Horizontal mobility (movement from one position to another or from one country to another without changing social status) shows us that different peoples think differently. As long, however, as the traditions of one's national and local group remain unbroken, one remains so attached to its customary ways of thinking that the ways of thinking which are perceived in other groups are regarded as curiosities, errors, ambiguities, or heresies. At this stage one does not doubt either the correctness of one's own traditions of thought or the unity and uniformity of thought in general.

Only when horizontal mobility is accompanied by intensive vertical mobility, i.e. rapid movement between strata in the sense of social ascent and descent, is the belief in the general and eternal validity of one's own thought-forms shaken. Vertical mobility is the decisive factor in making persons uncertain and sceptical of their traditional view of the world. It is, of course, true that even in static societies with very slight vertical mobility, different strata within the same society have had different ways of experiencing the world. It is the merit of Max Weber to have clearly shown in his sociology of religion how often the same religion is variously experienced by peasants, artisans, merchants, nobles, and intellectuals. In a society organized along the lines of closed castes or ranks the comparative absence of vertical mobility served either to isolate from each other the divergent world-views or if, for example, they experienced a common religion, according to their different contexts of life, they interpreted it in a different way. This accounts for the fact that the diversity of modes of thought of different castes did not converge in one and the same mind and hence could not become a problem. From a sociological point of view, the decisive change takes place when that stage of historical development is reached in which the previously isolated strata begin to communicate with one another and a certain social circulation sets in. The most significant stage of this communication is reached when the forms of thought and experience, which had hitherto developed independently, enter into one and the same consciousness impelling the mind to discover the irreconcilability of the conflicting conceptions of the world.

In a well stabilized society the mere infiltration of the modes of thought of the lower strata into the higher would not mean very much since the bare perception by the dominant group of possible variations in thinking would not result in their being intellectually shaken. As long as a society is stabilized on the basis of authority, and social prestige is accorded only to the achievements of the upper stratum, this class has little cause to call into question its own social existence and the value of its achievements. Apart from a considerable social ascent, it is not until we have a general democratization that the rise of the lower strata allows their thinking to acquire public significance. This process of democratization first makes it possible for the ways of thinking of the lower strata, which formerly had no public validity, to acquire validity and prestige. When the stage of democratization has been reached, the techniques of thinking and the ideas of the lower strata are for the first time in a position to confront the ideas of the dominant strata on the same level of validity. And now, too, for the first time these ideas and modes of thought are capable of impelling the person who thinks within their framework to subject the objects of his world to a fundamental questioning. It is with this clashing of modes of thought, each of which has the same claims to representational validity, that for the first time there is rendered possible the emergence of the question which is so fateful, but also so fundamental in the history of thought, namely, how it is possible that identical human thought-processes concerned with the same world produce divergent conceptions of that world. And from this point it is only a step further to ask: Is it not possible that the thought-processes which are involved here are not at all identical? May it not be found, when one has examined all the possibilities of human thought, that there are numerous alternative paths which can be followed?

In addition to those social factors which account for the early unity and subsequent multiplicity in the dominant forms of thought, another important factor should be mentioned. In every society there are social groups whose special task it is to provide an interpretation of the world for that society. We call these the "intelligentsia." The more static a society is, the more likely is it that this stratum will acquire a well-defined status or the position of a caste in that society. Thus the magicians, the Brahmins, the medieval clergy are to be regarded as intellectual strata, each of which in its society enjoyed a monopolistic control over the moulding of that society's world-view, and over either the reconstruction or the reconciliation of the differences in the naïvely formed world-views of the other strata. The sermon, the confession, the lesson, are, in this sense, means by which reconciliation of the different conceptions of the world takes place at less sophisticated levels of social development.

This intellectual stratum, organized as a caste and monopolizing the right to preach, teach, and interpret the world is conditioned by the force of two social factors. The more it makes itself the exponent of a thoroughly organized collectivity (e.g. the Church), the more its thinking tends towards "scholasticism." It must give a dogmatically binding force to modes of thought which formerly were valid only for a sect and thereby sanction the ontology and epistemology implicit in this mode of thought. The necessity of having to present a unified front to outsiders compels this transition. The same result may also be brought about by the possibility that the concentration of power within the social structure will be so pronounced that uniformity of thought and experience can be imposed upon the members of at least one's own caste with greater success than heretofore.

The second characteristic of this monopolistic type of thought is its relative remoteness from the open conflicts of everyday life; hence it is also "scholastic" in this sense, i.e. academic and lifeless. This type of thought does not arise primarily from the struggle with concrete problems of life nor from trial and error, nor from experiences in mastering nature and society, but rather much more from its own need for systematization, which always refers the facts which emerge in the religious as well as in other spheres of life back to given traditional and intellectually uncontrolled premises. The antagonisms which emerge in these discussions do not embody the conflict of various modes of experience so much as various positions of power within the same social structure, which have at the time identified themselves with the different possible interpretations of the dogmatized traditional "truth." The dogmatic content of the premises with which these divergent groups start and which this thought then seeks in different ways to justify turns out for the most part to be a matter of accident, if judged by the criteria of factual evidence. It is completely arbitrary in so far as it depends upon which sect happens to be successful, in accordance with historical-political destiny, in making its own intellectual and experiential traditions the traditions of the entire clerical caste of the church.

When one considers that with the renunciation of the monopolistic privileges of a caste type of existence, free competition began to dominate the modes of intellectual production, one understands why, to the extent that they were in competition, the intellectuals adopted in an ever more pronounced fashion the most various modes of thought and experience available in society and played them off against one another. They did this inasmuch as they had to compete for the favour of a public which, unlike the public of the clergy, was no longer accessible to them without their own efforts. This competition for the favour of various public groups was accentuated because the distinctive modes of experiencing and thinking of each attained increasing public expression and validity.

In this process the intellectual's illusion that there is only one way of thinking disappears. The intellectual is now no longer, as formerly, a member of a caste or rank whose scholastic manner of thought represents for him thought as such. In this relatively simple process is to be sought the explanation for the fact that the fundamental questioning of thought in modern times does not begin until the collapse of the intellectual monopoly of the clergy. The almost unanimously accepted world-view which had been artificially maintained fell apart the moment the socially monopolistic position of its producers was destroyed. With the liberation of the intellectuals from the rigorous organization of the church, other ways of interpreting the world were increasingly recognized.

PART II

The Person as a Social Unit

WHATEVER ELSE SOCIETY MAY BE, IT IS COMPOSED OF PEOPLE. Assumptions about the nature of persons as elementary units of social life underlie all theories of social behavior. The need to examine the basis of these assumptions has been an important focus in sociology, and the preoccupation of a distinguished group of earlier sociologists with "human nature" has left an exceptionally rich theoretical literature. The point of view thus developed has become central in the theory which deals with the nature of the human being, of socialization and of personality.

In opposition to more restrictive, biologically oriented influences, a continuous line of philosophers, psychologists, and sociologists strove to develop the idea that the person is himself a social entity and that the unit of meaningful study of social behavior must be the person-in-society. The present-day point of view was already well worked out around the turn of the century in the writings of the philosophers John Dewey and Josiah Royce, the psychologists, William James and James Mark Baldwin, and the sociologists, Charles Horton Cooley and George H. Mead. With respect to this common problem, the classification of these writers in different disciplines is a matter of academic history because, as selections from their work in this book clearly show, their approaches to the problem of the social and the personal unit were similar. There is perhaps no area of sociological theory in which so integrated a viewpoint is to be found. Taken together Baldwin's *Social and Ethical Interpretations in Mental Development*, Cooley's *Human Nature and the Social Order* and Mead's *Mind, Self and Society*, from which selections have been chosen for Part II, represent a remarkable consistency of theoretical analysis.

The selections in Part II can be read with profit in any order. In the present arrangement Chapter 2 presents statements of the general theory of the self as social, and of the central place of the social self in personality. This theme is further elaborated in the more detailed analysis of the socialization process in Chapter 3. The emergence of the social person through the imaginative interplay of self and other roles is described by Cooley in the selection on sociability and personal ideas. The selection from Mead examines the processes of role taking, the experiencing of social norms through play and the game, and the internalization of the generalized other as a part of the individualized self. The selection from Baldwin entitled "Society as an Organization of Selves" makes explicit the conclusion that the end process of socialization is society as well as personality.

This conclusion is further clarified in Chapter 4 by the materials taken from Baldwin and from Jean Piaget's study of the social development of the child in his book, *The Moral Judgement of the Child*. In these selections the social sources of crucial attributes of personality such as conscience, morality and the sense of justice are examined. The discussion is pointed primarily toward the individual but it is equally pertinent to the consideration of social norms and values. This is not surprising in view of the essential unity which this theory finds for the social and the personal.

Selections in the final chapter of this part, Chapter 5, consider questions of the limits of personality. In his search for ex-planations of suicide, Emile Durkheim, in his most famous book, *Suicide,* calls attention to the fact that the social personality op-erates within the boundaries both of human needs and collective requirements. He further considers the stabilizing effects of such limits and the consequences of their breakdown. The two selec-tions from Ralph Linton's *The Study of Man* deal with the limits which arise from the fact that socialization always has a cultural content. A culture provides, therefore, the boundaries within which the social self develops. Indeed, as the final selection by Linton points out, participation in culture actually means par-ticipation in subcultures and hence the cultural boundaries of personality are further narrowed.

CHAPTER 2

The Person as a Self

———•◦•———

THE PERSON AS A SELF

BY

JAMES MARK BALDWIN

IF it be true, as much evidence goes to show, that what the person thinks of as himself is a pole or terminus at one end of an opposition in the sense of personality generally, and that the other pole or terminus is the thought he has of the other person, the "alter," then it is impossible to isolate his thought of himself at any time and say that in thinking of himself he is not essentially thinking of the alter also. What he calls himself now is in large measure an incorporation of elements that, at an earlier period of his thought of personality, he called some one else. The acts now possible to himself, and so used by him to describe himself in thought to himself, were formerly only possible to the other; but by imitating that other he has brought them over to the opposite pole, and found them applicable, with a richer meaning and a modified value, as true predicates of himself also. If he thinks of himself in any particular past time, he can single out what was then he, as opposed to what has since become he; and the residue, the part of him that has since become he, that was then only thought of—if it was thought of as an attribute of personality at all—as attaching to some one with whom he was acquainted.

So the truth we now learn is this: that very many of the particular

Abridged from: Baldwin, James M., *Social and Ethical Interpretations in Mental Development*, New York: The Macmillan Co., 1897.

marks which I now call mine, when I think of myself, have had just this origin. I have first found them in my social environment, and by reason of my social and imitative disposition, have transferred them to myself by trying to act as if they were true of me, and so coming to find out that they are true of me. And further, all the things I hope to learn, to acquire, to become, all—if I think of them in a way to have any clear thought of my possible future—are now, before I acquire them, possible elements of my thought of others, of the social alter, or of what considered generally we may call the "socius."

But we should also note that what has been said of the one pole of this dialectical relation, the pole of self, is equally true of the other also—the pole represented by the other person, the alter. What do I have in mind when I think of him as a person? Evidently I must construe him, a person, in terms of what I think of myself, the only person whom I know in the intimate way we call "subjective."

So the dialectic may be read thus: my thought of self is in the main, as to its character as a personal self, filled up with my thought of others, distributed variously as individuals; and my thought of others, as persons, is mainly filled up with myself. In other words, but for certain minor distinctions in the filling, and for certain compelling distinctions between that which is immediate and that which is objective, *the ego and the alter are to our thought one and the same thing.*

To bring our development of the sense of personality into view let us inquire briefly into one of the main points in the theory of society which recent discussion has tended to formulate. This point is that which concerns the "interests" of the individual. What are the interests of the individual, and how do they stand related to the interests of the community, state, social group, in which the individual lives?

Popularly, a man's interests are those aspects of possible fortune which are best for him. What is thus best for him is in the main what he wants; but the two classes are not always identical. Yet for the sake of making our point more plain in the sequel, suppose we begin by defining a man's interest as that which he wants, and is willing to put forth some endeavour to obtain. Then let us see how this tends to involve the man's self, and the selves of those who are associated with him.

If the analysis given above be true, then what a man thinks of as himself, is in large measure identical with what he thinks of as another, or the others in general. So the ejecting of the thought of "person," which, when looked at subjectively, he calls "myself," into "another,"—this qualifies that other to be clothed on with all the further predicates found to attach to the self. The so-called love of self, it is evident, is such a predicate; it is a description of the attitude which the man takes to himself; a sort of reaction of part of his nature upon another part. When he is proud, it is because the qualities by which he represents himself to himself are such that they arouse his approbation. When he thinks, therefore, of the other in terms of the same predicates, he has to react, in some degree, with the same sense of approval.

When, likewise, I go farther in thought and say, "being such and such a person, it is my interest to have such or such a fate," I must *perforce*—that is, by the very same mental movement which gives the outcome in my own case—attribute to the other the same deserts and the same fate. Viewed psychologically, we should say that the predicate is a function of the content which we call self, and that, so far as the content is the same, the predicate must be the same. But this sense of equal interest, desert, because of identical position in the evolution of selves, what is this but, in the abstract, the sense of justice, and in the concrete, the feeling of sympathy with the other? The very concept of interests, when one considers it with reference to himself, necessarily involves others, therefore, on very much the same footing as oneself. One's interests, the things he wants in life, are the things which, by the very same thought, he allows others, also, the right to want; and if he insists upon the gratification of his own wants at the expense of the legitimate wants of the "other," then he in so far does violence to his sympathies and to his sense of justice. And this in turn must impair his satisfaction. For the very gratification of himself thus secured must, if it be accompanied with any reflection at all, involve the sense of the other's gratification also; and since this conflicts with the fact, a degree of discomfort must normally arise in mind varying with the development which the self has attained in the dialectical process described above.

Let us say that the sense of self always involves the sense of the other. And this sense of the other is but that of another "self," where the word "self" is equivalent to myself, and the meaning of the word "other" is that which prevents it from being myself. Now my point is that much of what I fancy, hope, desire holds for self in general, without distinction as to which self it is; it remains the same whether I do actually qualify it by the word "my" or by the word "your." Psychologically there is a great mass of motor attitudes and reactive expressions, felt in consciousness as emotion and desire, which are common to the self-thought everywhere.

This is true just in so far as there is a certain typical other self whose relation to me has been that of the give-and-take by which the whole development of a sense of self of any kind has been made possible. And we find certain distinctions at different stages of the development which serve to throw the general idea of the social relationship into clearer light.

Let us look at the life of the child with especial reference to his attitudes to those around him; taking the most common case, that of a child in a family of children. We find that such a child shows, in the very first stages of his sense of himself as a being of rights, duties, etc., a very imitative nature. He is mainly occupied with the business of learning about himself, other people, and nature. He imitates everything, being a veritable copying-machine. He spends the time not given to imitating others very largely in practising in his games what he has picked up by his imitations, and in the exploiting of these accomplishments. His two dominating characteristics are a certain slavishness, on the one hand, in following all examples set around him; and then, on the other hand, a certain bold aggressiveness, inventiveness, a showing-off, in the use he makes of the things he learns.

But it does not take very extended observation to convince us that this difference in his attitudes is not a contradiction: that the attitudes themselves terminate upon different determinations of self. The child imitates his elders, not from choice, but from his need of adaptation to the social environment; for it is his elders who know more than he does, and who act in more complex ways. But he is less often aggressive toward his elders; that is, toward those who have the character of command, direction, and authority over him. His aggressions are directed mainly toward his brothers and sisters; and even as toward them, he shows very striking discriminative selection of those upon whom it is safe to aggress. In short, it is plain that the difference in attitude really indicates differences in his thought, corresponding to differences in the elements of the child's social environment. We may suppose the persons about him divided roughly into two classes: those from whom he learns, and those on whom he practises; and then we see that his actions are accounted for as adaptations toward these, in his personal development.

The facts covered by this distinction—probably the first general social distinction in the child's career—are very interesting. The stern father of the family is at the extreme end of the class he reveres with a shading of fear. The little brother and sister stand at the other extreme; they are the fitting instruments of his aggression, the practise of his strength, the assertion of his agency and importance. The mother usually stands midway, it seems, serving to unite the two aspects of personality in the youngster's mind. And it is pretty clear, when the case is closely studied, that the child has, as it were, two ways of thinking of her, according as she on occasion falls into one or the other of these classes. He learns when, in what circumstances, she will suffer him to assert himself, and when she will require him to be docile and teachable. And although she is for the most part a teacher and example, yet on occasion he takes liberties with the teacher.

The child's sense of himself is, as we have seen, one pole of a relation; and which pole it is to be, depends on the particular relation which the other pole, over which the child has no control, calls on it to be. If the other person involved presents uncertain, ominous, dominating, instructive features, or novel imitative features, then the self is "subject" over against what is "projective." He recognizes new elements of personal suggestion not yet accommodated to. His consciousness is in the learning attitude; he imitates, he serves, he trembles, he is a slave. But on the other hand, there are persons to whom his attitude has a right to be different. In the case of these the dialectic has gone further. He has mastered all their features, he can do himself what they do, he anticipates no new developments in his intercourse with them; so he "ejects" them, as the psychological expression is: for an "eject" is a consciousness thought of as having only those elements in it which the individual who thinks of that consciousness is able, out of his own store of experience, to read into it. It is ejective to him, for he makes it what he will, in a sense. Now this is what the brothers and sisters, notably the younger ones, are to our youthful hero. They are his "ejects"; he knows them by heart, they have no thoughts, they do no deeds, which he could not have read into them by anticipation. So he despises them, practises his superior activities on them, tramples them under foot.

Now at this earliest stage in his unconscious classification of the elements of his personal world, it is clear that any attempt to describe the child's interests—the things which he wants, as we have agreed to define "interests"—as selfish, generous, or as falling in any category of developed social significance, is quite beside the mark. If we say that to be selfish is to try to get all the personal gratification possible, we find that he does this only part of the time; and even on these occasions, not because he has any conscious preference for that style of conduct, but merely because his consciousness is then filled with the particular forms of personal relationship—the presence of his little sister, etc.—which normally issue in the more habitual actions which are termed "aggressive" in our social terminology. His action is only the motor side of a certain collection of elements. He acts that way, then, simply because it is natural for him to practise the functions which he has found useful.

But that this is arguing beyond our facts—really arguing on the strength of the psychological ignorance of our hearers, and our own—

is clear when we turn the child about and bring him into the presence
of the other class of persons to whom we have seen him taking up a
special attitude. We have but to observe him in the presence of his
father, usually, or of some one else whom he habitually imitates and
from whom he learns the lessons of life, to find out that he is just as
pre-eminently social, docile, accommodating, centred-outwardly, so to
speak, as before we considered him unsocial, aggressive, and self-
centred. If we saw him only in these latter circumstances, we should
say possibly that he was by nature altruistic, most responsive to generous suggestion, teachable in the extreme. But here the limitation is
the same as in the former case. He is not altruistic in any high social
sense, nor consciously yielding to suggestions of response which require
the repression of his selfishness. As a matter of fact, he is simply acting
himself out; and in just the same natural way as on the occasion of his
apparent selfishness. But it is now a different thought which is acting
itself out. The self is now at the receptive pole. It is made up of elements which are inadequate to a translation of the alter at the other
pole of the relationship now established. The child's sense of self is
now not that of a relatively completed self in relation to the alter before him; it was that in the earlier case, and the aggression of which
he was then guilty showed as much. Now he feels his lack of adequate
means of response to the personality before him. He cannot anticipate
what the father will do next, how long approbation will smile upon
him, what the reasons are for the changes in the alter-personality. So
it is but to state a psychological truism to say that his conduct will be
different in this case. Yet from the fact that the self of this social state
is also in a measure a regular pole of the dialectic of personal growth,
it often tempts the observer to classify the whole child, on the strength
of this one attitude, in some one category of social and political description.

I do not see, in short, how the personality of this child can be expressed in any but social terms; nor how, on the other hand, social
terms can get any content of value but from the understanding of the
developing individual. This is a circle in the process of growth. On the
one hand, we can get no doctrine of society but by getting the psychology of the "socius" with all his natural history; and on the other hand,
we can get no true view of the "socius" at any time without describing
the social conditions under which he normally lives, with the history
of their action and reaction upon him. Or to put the outcome in the
terms of the restriction which we have imposed upon ourselves,—the
only way to get a solid basis for social theory based upon human want
or desire, is to work out first a descriptive and genetic psychology of
desire in its social aspects; and on the other hand, the only way to get

an adequate psychological view of the rise and development of desire in its social aspects, is by a patient tracing of the conditions of social environment in which the child and the race have lived and which they have grown up to reflect.

But the observation of the child shows us that we may carry our discrimination of his personal attitudes farther along the same lines. We have found him classifying his companions and associates by the shadings of conduct which his spontaneous adaptations of himself show; yielding to some and studying them mainly by imitation, abusing others and asserting himself against them aggressively. This distinction gets a wider development as his experience goes on accumulating. As was hinted in the case of his attitude to his mother, one person may come to have for him the force of several, or of both of the two great classes of persons. Sometimes he tyrannizes over his mother and finds her helpless; at other times he finds her far from submitting to tyranny, and then he takes the role of learner and obedient boy. Now the further advance which he makes in the general sense of the social situation as a whole, is in the line of carrying the same adaptability of attitude into his relation to each of the persons whom he knows. Just as he himself is sometimes one person and again another, sometimes the learner, the altruist, the unselfish pupil, and then again the egoist, the selfish aggressor; so he continues the dialectical process by making this also "ejective" to him. He reads the same possibility of personal variation back into the alter also. He comes to say to himself in effect: he, my father, has his moods just as I have. He, no less than I, cannot be adequately considered all-suffering or all-conquering. Sometimes he also is at one pole of the self-dialectic, sometimes at the other. And so is my mother, and my brother and sister, as they grow older,—indeed, so are all men.

So it then becomes his business not to classify persons, but to classify actions. He sees that any person may, with some few exceptions, act in either way: any person may be his teacher or his slave, on occasion. So his next step in social adaptation is his adaptation to *occasions;* to the groups of social conditions in which one or the other class of actions may be anticipated from people generally. And he makes great rough classes in which to put his "ejects"—the read-out personalities about him—according to his expectations of treatment from them. He learns the signs of wrath, of good humour, of sorrow; of joy, hope, love, jealousy; giving them the added interpretation all the time which his own imitation of them enables him to make by realizing what they mean in his own experience. And so he gets himself equipped with that extraordinary facility of transition from one attitude to another in his responses to those about him, which all who are familiar with children will have remarked.

Now all these changes have meaning only as we realize the fact of the social dialectic, which is the same through it all. There are changes of attitude simply and only because there are changes in the content of his sense of self. In more popular terms: he changes his attitude in each case because the thing called another, the alter, changes. His father is his object; and the object is the "father," *as the child thinks him,* on this occasion and under these circumstances, *right out of his own consciousness.* The father-thought is a part of the child's present social situation; and this situation in the child's mind issues in the attitude which is appropriate to it. If it be the father in wrath, the situation produces such a father out of the child's available social thought-material; and the presence of the combination in the child's mind itself issues in the docile, fearful attitude. But if it then turn into the jovial father, the child does not then himself set about reversing his attitude. No, the father-thought is now a different father-thought, and of itself issues in the child's attitude of playful aggression, rebellion, or disobedience. The growing child is able to think of self in varying terms as varying social situations impress themselves upon him; so these varying thoughts of self, when made real in the persons of others, call out, by the regular process of motor discharge, each its own appropriate attitude.

But see, in this more subtle give-and-take of elements for the building up of the social sense, how inextricably interwoven the ego and the alter really are! The development of the child's personality could not go on at all without the constant modification of his sense of himself by suggestions from others. So he himself, at every stage, is really in part some one else, even in his own thought of himself. And then the attempt to get the alter stript from elements contributed directly from his present thought of himself is equally futile. He thinks of the other, the alter, as his *socius,* just as he thinks of himself as the other's *socius:* and the only thing that remains more or less stable, throughout the whole growth, is the fact that there is a growing sense of self which includes both terms, the ego and the alter.

If we think it worth while again to raise the question as to what such a self pursues when, as we say, he identifies his interests with his wants, the answer is just as before. The growing subtlety of the dialectical process has not changed the values which the elements represent to the child. What he wants in each circumstance is expressed by his attitude in that circumstance. It changes with change of circumstance. He is now a creature of burning self-assertion, eager to "kill and destroy in all God's holy mountain"; and presto! change, he is now the "lion lying down beside the lamb." His wants are not at all consistent. They are in every case the outcome of the social situation; and it is absurd to endeavour to express the entire body of his wants as a fixed quantity under such a term of description as "selfish," or "generous," or other, which has reference to one class only of the varied situations of his life.

So far, therefore, in our search for a definition of the interests of the individual, in relation to his social environment, we find a certain outcome. His wants are a function of the social situation as a whole. The social influences which are working in upon him are potent to modify his wants, no less than are the innate tendencies of his personal nature to issue in such wants. The character which he shows actively at any time is due to these two factors in union. One of them is no more himself than the other. He is the outcome of "habit" and "suggestion," as psychology would say in its desire to express everything by single words. Social suggestion is the sum of the social influences which he takes in and incorporates in himself when he is in the receptive, imitative, attitude to the alter; habit is the body of formed material, already cast in the mould of a self, which he brings up for self-assertion and aggression, when he stands at the other pole of the relation to the alter, and exhibits himself as a bully, a tyrant, or at least, as master of his own conduct. Of course his personal hereditary characteristics are on this latter side in so far as they are of an anti-social sort. And the social unit of desire, as far as the individual is taken as the measure of it, in any society, is the individual's relatively fixed conduct, considered as reflecting his interpretation of the current social modes of life.

It is easy to discern in the behavior of the child, from about five years old, the blending of these two influences. Two children in the same family may differ possibly by all the width of the distinction current in psychology by the terms "sensory *versus* motor" in their types or dispositions; and yet we may see in them the influence of the common environment. One acts at once on the example of the father; the other reflects upon it, seems to understand it, and then finally acts upon what he thinks it means. The motor child learns by acting; the sensory child learns and tests his learning by subsequent action. But both end by getting the father's essential conduct learned. Both modify the thought of self by the new elements drawn from the father; and act out the new self thus created; but each shows the elements differently interpreted in a synthesis with the character which he already had.

Or take the same process of incorporating elements of social suggestion as they are absorbed respectively by a boy and a girl of about the same age. The difference of sex is a real and fundamental difference, so we should expect that the same social suggestions given the two would be taken up differently by them, and show different interpretations when the child of one sex or the other comes to act upon them. The boy is generally more aggressive, more prone to fall into the self-pole of high confidence in his own abilities. We find him refusing certain forms of suggestion—say those coming from a female nurse—which the little girl readily responds to. Furthermore, the boy is capable, just for the same reason, of standing up to the rougher elements of his social *milieu* which only frighten and paralyze his sister. And when the same suggestion is given to the boy and girl together, the former is likely to use it wherewith to exercise himself upon animals, etc., while the girl is more likely to use the new act strictly in an imitative way, repeating the actual conduct of others.[1]

But apart from the attempt to reduce the forms of active interpretation to general classes, it is enough here to point out the extraordinary variety which the same suggestions take on in the active interpretations by different children; and to point out with it the need of recognizing the fact that in this interpretation by the child there is always the fusion of the old self with the new elements coming in from the selves external to it. Every conscious interpretation of human action is, I think, essentially of this kind. We think the deeds of others as we bring ourselves up to the performance of similar deeds; and we do the deeds of others only as we ourselves are able to think them. In the case of the young child in the family, we may often tell how far he is learning correctly; also the particular alter from whom he has taken his lesson. But in the larger social whole of adult life both elements are so complex—the solidified self of the individual's history is so fixed, and the social suggestions of the community are so varied and conflicting—that the outcome of the fusion, in a particular instance, is a thing which no man can prophesy.

Waiving the inquiry into the interests of the family group as a whole, that is, the question of objective interests apart from actual want or desire (as we did in the earlier case), our question is now about this: What can be said of the wants of the other individuals of the family in which the young hero, whose life we have so far described, lives and exploits himself? This seems to be answered, certainly in part, by the consideration that they have each been through the same process of growth in securing the notion of self, both the ego-self and the alter-self, that he has. Each has been a child. Each has imitated

---

[1] Of course, we can only say "more likely" in any single instance, and in the other distinctions between boys and girls as well.

some persons and assaulted others. So, of course, of the other children in the family; for they are the very specimens of the alter which have furnished to the hero his "socii" all the way through. So we have only to make them one by one hero in turn to see that then all the others become "socii"; and the group development replaces the individual development. Even the parents are in great measure capable of the same interpretation; since they have furnished the largest amount of personal suggestion to all the children: and the children, in imitating one another, aggressing upon one another, etc., are really perpetuating the features of social life which characterize the parents' lives. No family, of course, lives in such isolation as to be in any sense obliged to support itself upon its own social stock from one generation to another; and there is the further modifying influence spoken of above of the peculiar interpretations given to his social suggestions by each child. But apart from the personal form in which the family suggestions are worked over by each child, we may say that the material of the social life of the family is largely common stock for all the members of the family.

This means that the alter to each ego is largely common to them all; and that what has been said of the wants of the ego being not egoistic in the selfish sense, nor generous in the altruistic sense, but general in the social sense, holds of the family group as a whole. What each child wants for himself, he wants more or less consciously for each member of his family. While he may assault his brother, viewing him as an alter to practise on in certain circumstances, how soon he turns in his defence in the presence of the alter foreign to them both, when the larger social ego of both swells within his breast! What boy among boys, what school-fellow among his companions, what Rob Roy surrounded by the clan has not felt the socius, the common self of the group, come in to drive out the narrower ego of his relatively private life within the group? This is not to say that the interests of the group may not be more clearly seen by one member than by others, nor that direct conflicts may not arise in which some one ego will refuse to yield to the demands of the socius of the group. Those things may well be, and are. To say the contrary would be to say that the development of all the individuals was equal. For if each has his ego and his alter only by the assimilation of suggestions, then the amount of assimilation, of progressive learning of the possibilities and relationships of conduct, must indicate what the sense of social good is to each. His insistence on his interpretation, however, is no more egoistic and selfish than is the insistence by the other members of the family on a different line of conduct. His double self, giving the socius, may be in advance of theirs or behind, but it arises in just the same way; and it is just his social

nature which may compel him to fight for what seems to be a private
and selfish interest.

Apart from the apparent exceptions—not really such—now noted,
we may say, therefore, that the interests of the family group are reflected in the wants of each member of the group. Hatred of society,
in this primitive form of society, is pathological,—if indeed it be
possible. Nothing but an upheaval of the foundations of personality
can eradicate the sense of social solidarity in every child in a family.
And the ultimate sanction for family life and its only permanent safeguard is here. No legal provisions could have originated the family,
no personal conventions advanced it, nor can it be endangered by foes
from without. Nothing but the kind of suggestion in education which
would replace the sort of socius represented in the family, by another
sort, through the same process of identification of the self with its alter
all the way through the history of the growth of personality, could
affect it materially one way or the other.

The family is, of course, the first place in which the child finds food
for his own personal assimilation; but he does not long limit himself
to the family diet. Nor is he from his early months entirely shut up to
suggestions from within the family circle. His nurse comes in to stand
as a member of his social company, and often the most important
member from the point of view of the regularity and intimate character of her ministrations. She is part of the family to all intents and
purposes. And other children from abroad who come often or at critical
times to play, etc., are also "in it." Then again certain actual members
of the home circle may see the child so seldom or in such a passing way
that they practically are not, as far as the child's personal growth is
concerned. So while the family is the theatre of this first stage of his
growth, it still represents a rather flexible set of personal influences.

And his circle grows as he comes to have other relationships than
those of his immediate and domestic life. When he begins to go to the
kindergarten or school, the teacher in the first instance, then the pupils
beside him there, or some of them, come to bear on his life in the
same way that his family companions do. So gradually he widens out
the sphere of the exploitation of his two selves—the receptive self, and
no less, the aggressive self. In all the stretch of early childhood, pet
animals, dolls, toys, etc., also play a part, especially as giving him now
and then a more or less complete alter on which to wreak the performance of the new acts recently learned. And as he grows a little
older, and the sense of personal agency arises to play its great part in
the development of his activities, all mechanical tools, contrivances,
building-blocks, sliced animals, etc., are valuable aids to the exercise
of his understanding of the powers of himself and of others.

In this expansion of his interests—and with it, his enlarging sense of the sphere of personality realized in himself and in others, gradual as it is—we may mark off certain dividing lines. We may always say, no matter what the details of the boy's daily life are, that there is a circle within which his socius resides. His socius is the higher sense of commonalty, personal implication, mutual interest, which social intercourse arouses in him. This is always alive when events occur which involve persons in a larger or smaller circumference drawn about him.

* * *

There are two general principles apparently involved in all a child's originalities; these two principles have grown up in my own mind as necessary interpretations of the observations which I have made of children in the last few years, and in the course of the meditating which I have done on the varied doings of childhood. I shall venture to state one of these principles at a time, in the form of a somewhat dogmatic-sounding opinion, and then go on to cite the evidence and give the illustrations upon which it is based, as far as space may permit.

1. *The child's originalities are in great part the new ways in which he finds his knowledges falling together in consequence of his attempts to act to advantage on what he already knows.* Or, made more brief, his originalities arise through his action, struggle, trial of things for himself in an imitative way.

2. *The child's originalities, further, are in great measure the combinations of his knowledges which he feels justified in expecting to hold for others to act on also.*

These two statements I do not mean to make as two distinct principles operative apart or in opposition to each other, nor are they the expression of a chronological order in the child's development; they rather present phases of the one fact of invention, and for convenience for reference we may call them respectively the "personal phase" and the "social phase."

The child's inventions are, in these two phases, reflections of the twofold aspects of his own personal growth: by the imitative absorption of material from the persons about him, in the first instance; and then, in the second instance, by legislating his own personal growth—the facts which he has found out about himself as a personal being—back into the persons around him again. Now the first phase of his inventive activity is shown in connection with the first of these personal movements: *he is original in the way he learns from others* by taking in personal elements from them. And the second phase of his originality is a function of the other process of his personal growth, *he is original in the way he treats others,* the way he disports himself in his intercourse with them. And the latter is a sort of test or proof of the value of the former to the child himself.

In order to avoid repetition, use may be made of the results of the earlier pages devoted to the development of the child's sense of his ego or personal self; and we may draw from the details the great fact that all his personal absorption from his immediate associates is through his tendency to imitate. The interesting character which draws him to this element or that in the man, woman, or child from whom he learns, is itself due to imitation; for his interests are really only the intellectual reflection of his habits, and his habits are the motor phenomena which have resulted from his earlier activities of the same imitative type. But quite apart from theory, we are constrained by the facts to say that the method of his personal progress is imitation. For if we say that he cannot do anything without some approximate ability to apprehend what he is to do—that is, without a content of revival of something already apprehended on an earlier occasion; and if we go on to enforce the other psychological truth put in evidence just above—that no action can take place which is not, in greater or less degree, the proper outcome of the motor energies of the revived content: admitting these two points, then the action which the child performs in any case must have an imitative character just in so far as the habit which it tends to stimulate is true to the situation outside him which the child observes; that is, in so far as he succeeds in learning.

For example, say a child sees me finger a ring. He has certain habits of action. The content of his consciousness—my fingers—tends to start the one of his habits of action which is attached to other contents most nearly like this one, i.e., his own fingers. But this movement of his fingers thus brought about is imitative; and the fact that it is imitative, that is, that it is the motor expression of a presentation like the one set before him—his finger substituted for mine—this is the reason, and the only reason, that a movement takes place by which he learns. In other words, he can only learn by imitating; for if he only acts strictly on the revived elements of content which come up in his own consciousness from within, then he is acting strictly as he has acted before, and that teaches him nothing. On the other hand, he cannot act in ways absolutely new, for they come into his consciousness with no tendency to stir up any appropriate kinds of action. He cannot act suitably upon them at all. Hence it is only new presentations which are assimilable to old ones that can get the benefit of the habits already attached to the old ones, and so lead to actions more or less suited to the new. But this is imitation.

We have just been giving, as may have been evident, the basis of what is usually called the "instinct of imitation." The instinct to imitate operates by the use of the movements required to do the thing imitated. But unless the child has a sense of what movements will do it, he cannot produce them. This sense of the proper movements can only have come from the earlier performance of those movements in connection with some other mental content. And the movements associated with another mental content can be available for this content only if this new content can take the place of the old one in the motor scheme.

We must at once see that his own movements, his imitative actions, bring new elements into the situation. He has, just after he acts, three things in his mind—let us say in the case of the imitation of the movements of the fingers. First, he sees the movements of the other person; then he has the memory of his own finger-movements (probably indeed both of his fingers as they look and of the movements of them as felt); then finally, the sight of his own finger-movements. Now two different things may happen, and which of the two it is to be will depend largely on the age of the child. He may learn something, and he may not. If he has already attained what is called "persistent imitation"—the try-try-again tendency—or the more developed exercise of volition which comes through the exercise of persistent imitation, then he will learn. Indeed, then he cannot help learning.

Apart from the acquisition of the finger-combination which is his immediate object, he has learned a variety of things. Only the principal features of his learning may be mentioned here: the essentials of the fact of learning itself apart from the details of this particular finger-exercise. He learns we may say, first, a great number of combinations which are not those he is after. Each of the single efforts which he makes is a novelty to him, and each has its interesting features. Indeed, if we watch him, and especially if we withdraw the "copy" which our finger-combination sets before him, we may find his becoming so absorbed in the single efforts which he makes, the partial successes which crown his efforts, that he forgets to go on trying. He begins to reproduce his own combinations again and again, and so to learn them. So in each of his efforts, no matter how far removed it may be from the copy he sets out to imitate, in each of them he finds a possible combination of fruitful pursuit for his training and in many cases also fruitful for his utilities of movement.

Then, again, another very valuable lesson; he learns the method of all learning. He begins to see that it is he who varies the copy by trying to reproduce it; that he turns out interesting combinations which are his own peculiar property. He stops in wonder before his own doings, and runs again to his elders or to his companions saying, "See what I can do." He thus grows to recognize himself as more than a mere imitator. He begins to see that it is just by this method of exercising themselves that the other persons from whom he is accustomed to learn get their facility in giving him new things to learn; and so he gradually apprehends that after all he is not entirely dependent upon them for the setting of new lessons to himself. He begins to be in a measure self-regulative in the tasks of his daily life.

We have already seen how it is that his sense of himself grows by these accretions from the elements of personality taken in by imitation. It is thus that the projective in the personal life of father, mother, etc., are incorporated in his thought of his own subjective self. This new self, at each new plane, is also a real invention. The child not only becomes a self, not only acquires the sense of higher power, mastery, goodness, or whatever aspect of his personal growth the particular instance may illustrate; he does more. He makes it; he gets it for himself by his own action; he achieves, invents it. And the same is true of all his knowledges. He never simply takes the knowledge of some one else. This it would be impossible for him to do. Even the weak-minded of whom I have spoken must have enough self-control to imitate, and enough assimilative capacity to hold together, in a new form, the elements which surge into his consciousness through and with his imitative act. But the active healthy child brings a new self up to a new object every time he acts in a way not entirely dictated by habit; and the result ensuing, the second construction which then again follows his new act, is another invention for him to take delight in. The growth of self is seen in the growth of his demand that his results shall show constantly more independence of the external copy. The growing complexity and utility of the invention which he turns out is a new premium put in his thought upon the need of considering himself more than an imitator. So he comes to view himself as a free man who, in an ever-increasing degree, bends nature and his fellow-man to his will, and to view what he does as a contribution to the arrangements and utilities of things.

Coming to take up the so-called "social" aspects of this question, we may again state the general principle which the following pages are to illustrate: the principle that the child now, after having made his discovery, does not treat it as an individual possession, but considers it common property, for others as for himself, and then, withal, considers others subject to the same need of finding it true that he is.

The first phase of originality we have found to have its mental motive in the child's absorption of new elements of the personal and generally projective environment; he imitates, as has been made clear, and proves himself an inventor in the very midst of his imitations.

The process is that of the first movement described in the theory of a "dialectic of personal growth." The projective becomes subjective, and by so doing it becomes in each event an invention. But it will be remembered that the child understands others better by coming to better knowledge of himself. He reads out of himself the facts learned of himself; and so lodges the richer thought of self also in the persons of others. This has been enlarged upon sufficiently in the earlier connection.

Now this second aspect of his treatment of the material of his personal thought adds an interesting phase also to the meaning of his originalities. Whatever his constructions are, he reads them into the appropriate escort, connection, setting, in the world of persons and things around him. And the degree of success in this process, the degree of what we call truth which he finds his new syntheses attaining under this exaction, this is the measure of his learning.

Let me explain a little further what I conceive this second factor in invention to be. We may get at it possibly better by looking at the child's mental constructions negatively. Let us ask what distinguishes his inventions, his originalities, the things of some dignity and worth and truth, from mere imaginations or fancies as such? Certainly he has vain imaginations, no less than we adults; and the real originalities, the truthful ones, must have some distinguishing mark.

This question presents itself in a very broad way to general psychology; and I may at once assume the result that in the criterion established by our first principle—*i.e.*, that it is by action and thought upon real things, copies, events, that the true inventions arise—we have confirmed the conclusion reached theoretically above, which rules out the vagaries of mere fancy, or so-called "passive" imagination. The outcome of fancy, or in general of imagination uncontrolled by present reality or by the attitude of strenuous thinking and action upon a real situation, is generally worthless. So when I ask how the ordinary creations of the mind, in its normal pursuit of truth, and in the midst of its full struggles for consistent and enlightened conduct, fall short of being true inventions, it is a closer question, the very necessity for which is often overlooked. It is this, in the terms of my child's lie: what is the value, to the child's construction, of the further acceptance of it by me which she tells the "lie" to secure? Is it a true invention before this, or does the child's sense that I must accept it illustrate a real and necessary requirement?

I think it does represent a real requirement, and this because this factor, when it is secured, *brings into the very construction itself new elements, the assimilation of which revises and purifies the construc-*

tion itself. To deny this would be to surrender, it seems to me, one of the main lessons which we seemed to learn from the growth of the personal and social sense; the lesson that the suggestions constantly received from the persons around us are elements in the thought of self, and through the thought of self, elements also in the valuation passed on all persons and things.

While we cannot say that the construction which the child makes, considered simply for himself, is not in a sense an invention, still we can say that it is not a complete invention. The very attempt to put the question in that way is mistaken. The child himself never attempts to make this artificial distinction between what he is and what he does, and again between what he does altogether alone and what he does with the help of others. His world of reality is one, and he is there in the midst of it. He knows only the one personal experience in which the two phases are united in one superb series of progressive advances. To stop him off short without the social confirmation for his constructions is to leave him in that condition of permanent hesitation, doubt, and anxiety, which produces, when forced, all sorts of personal isolations and often, as a matter of fact in the cases of adult patients, ends in certain forms of mania known as the "insanities of doubt."

The relative importance of the two factors now described—that called "personal" and that called "social"—differs greatly in different children, and also at different periods in the life of the same child. We find the one child at times—some children constitutionally—developing very fast in the direction of an exaggerated sense of personal agency, independence, self-confidence, trust in the outcome of his own processes of thought with a minimum of social confirmation. This tendency is seen in the phenomenon which has been lately called "contrary suggestion." The child seems to rebel against instruction, to insist upon his own understanding and use of things, and to try to impose his individual thought, whether or no, upon the persons who touch his life. This is, when not too insistent, a healthy sign. It betokens the rapid progress of the assimilation of elements to his nucleus of "subject," which carries with it the sense of agency, power, and freedom. The "contrary" boy is a very promising boy, provided he be not allowed to domineer when he should be made to obey. But this spirit should be confined within very strait limits; for it is evident that the indulgence, in the boy or girl, of the sense of self-sufficiency, will itself tend to dwarf and impoverish that very sense of self on which it is based. For the stopping up of the avenues of imitation which it involves, cuts off the supply of higher personal suggestion upon which the growth of the self-sense depends. For instance, how can the ethical sense, which is essentially a subordination of all private thoughts of self, grow more competent, when the suggestions which stand for law are not humbly received, nor obediently?

On the other hand, also, there are many—and periods again in the life of all—in whom the second aspect of the whole process of invention takes on an exaggerated importance. The need of social confirmation becomes so great to the child that his distrust of his single-handed performances becomes excessive and abnormal. He meets so often the overriding lessons of the alter, finds his small meed of understanding so insufficient for his life, grows so accustomed to see the larger wisdom of his adults victorious over the objects and events of nature by which, when alone, he is piteously overcome, that he dare not stand up without a social arm about him. This period of timidity in most children follows that of aggression.

THE SOCIAL SELF

B Y

CHARLES HORTON COOLEY

IT is well to say at the outset that by the word "self" in this discussion is meant simply that which is designated in common speech by the pronouns of the first person singular, "I," "me," "my," "mine," and "myself." "Self" and "ego" are used by metaphysicians and moralists in many other senses, more or less remote from the "I" of daily speech and thought, and with these I wish to have as little to do as possible. What is here discussed is what psychologists call the empirical self, the self that can be apprehended or verified by ordinary observation. I qualify it by the word social not as implying the existence of a self that is not social—for I think that the "I" of common language always has more or less distinct reference to other people as well as the speaker—but because I wish to emphasize and dwell upon the social aspect of it.

The distinctive thing in the idea for which the pronouns of the first person are names is apparently a characteristic kind of feeling which may be called the my-feeling or sense of appropriation. Almost any sort of ideas may be associated with this feeling, and so come to be named "I" or "mine," but the feeling, and that alone it would seem, is the determining factor in the matter. As Professor James says in his admirable discussion of the self, the words "me" and "self" designate "all the things which have the power to produce in a stream of consciousness excitement of a certain peculiar sort."

The emotion or feeling of self may be regarded as instinctive, and was doubtless evolved in connection with its important function in stimulating and unifying the special activities of individuals.[1] It is thus very profoundly rooted in the history of the human race and apparently indispensable to any plan of life at all similar to ours. It seems to exist in a vague though vigorous form at the birth of each individual, and like other instinctive ideas or germs of ideas, to be defined and developed by experience, becoming associated, or rather incorporated, with muscular, visual, and other sensations; with perceptions, apperceptions, and conceptions of every degree of complexity and of infinite variety of content; and, especially, with personal ideas. Meantime the feeling itself does not remain unaltered, but undergoes differentiation and refinement just as does any other sort of crude innate feeling. Thus, while retaining under every phase its characteristic tone or flavor, it breaks up into innumerable self-sentiments. And concrete self-feeling, as it exists in mature persons, is a whole made up of these various sentiments, along with a good deal of primitive emotion not thus broken up. It partakes fully of the general development of the mind, but never loses that peculiar gusto of appropriation that causes us to name a thought with a first-personal pronoun. The other contents of the self-idea are of little use, apparently, in defining it, because they are so extremely various. It would be no more futile, it seems to me, to attempt to define fear by enumerating the things that people are afraid of, than to attempt to define "I" by enumerating the objects with which the word is associated. Very much as fear means primarily a state of feeling, or its expression, and not darkness, fire, lions, snakes, or other things that excite it, so "I" means primarily self-feeling, or its expression, and not body, clothes, treasures, ambition, honors, and the like, with which this feeling may be connected. In either case it is possible and useful to go behind the feeling and inquire what ideas arouse it and why they do so, but this is in a sense a secondary investigation.

As many people have the impression that the verifiable self, the object that we name with "I," is usually the material body, it may be well to say that this impression is an illusion, easily dispelled by any one who will undertake a simple examination of facts. It is true that when we philosophize a little about "I" and look around for a tangible

[1] It is, perhaps, to be thought of as a more general instinct, of which anger, etc., are differentiated forms, rather than as standing by itself.

object to which to attach it, we soon fix upon the material body as the most available *locus;* but when we use the word naïvely, as in ordinary speech, it is not very common to think of the body in connection with it; not nearly so common as it is to think of other things. There is no difficulty in testing this statement, since the word "I" is one of the commonest in conversation and literature, so that nothing is more practicable than to study its meaning at any length that may be desired. One need only listen to ordinary speech until the word has occurred, say, a hundred times, noting its connections, or observe its use in a similar number of cases by the characters in a novel. Ordinarily it will be found that in not more than ten cases in a hundred does "I" have reference to the body of the person speaking. It refers chiefly to opinions, purposes, desires, claims, and the like, concerning matters that involve no thought of the body. *I* think or feel so and so; *I* wish or intend so and so; *I* want this or that; are typical uses, the self-feeling being associated with the view, purpose, or object mentioned. It should also be remembered that "my" and "mine" are as much the names of the self as "I," and these, of course, commonly refer to miscellaneous possessions.

As already suggested, instinctive self-feeling is doubtless connected in evolution with its important function in stimulating and unifying the special activities of individuals. It appears to be associated chiefly with ideas of the exercise of power, of being a cause, ideas that emphasize the antithesis between the mind and the rest of the world. The first definite thoughts that a child associates with self-feeling are probably those of his earliest endeavors to control visible objects—his limbs, his playthings, his bottle, and the like. Then he attempts to control the actions of the persons about him, and so his circle of power and of self-feeling widens without interruption to the most complex objects of mature ambition. Although he does not say "I" or "my" during the first year or two, yet he expresses so clearly by his actions the feeling that adults associate with these words that we cannot deny him a self even in the first weeks.

"I" is not all of the mind, but a peculiarly central, vigorous, and well-knit portion of it, not separate from the rest but gradually merging into it, and yet having a certain practical distinctness, so that a man generally shows clearly enough by his language and behavior what his "I" is as distinguished from thoughts he does not appropriate. It may be thought of, as already suggested, under the analogy of a central colored area on a lighted wall. It might also, and perhaps more justly, be compared to the nucleus of a living cell, not altogether separate from the surrounding matter, out of which indeed it is formed, but more active and definitely organized.

The reference to other persons involved in the sense of self may be distinct and particular, as when a boy is ashamed to have his mother catch him at something she has forbidden, or it may be vague and general, as when one is ashamed to do something which only his conscience, expressing his sense of social responsibility, detects and disapproves; but it is always there. There is no sense of "I," as in pride or shame, without its correlative sense of you, or he, or they.

In a very large and interesting class of cases the social reference takes the form of a somewhat definite imagination of how one's self—that is any idea he appropriates—appears in a particular mind, and the kind of self-feeling one has is determined by the attitude toward this attributed to that other mind. A social self of this sort might be called the reflected or looking-glass self:

> "Each to each a looking-glass
> Reflects the other that doth pass."

As we see our face, figure, and dress in the glass, and are interested in them because they are ours, and pleased or otherwise with them according as they do or do not answer to what we should like them to be; so in imagination we perceive in another's mind some thought of our appearance, manners, aims, deeds, character, friends, and so on, and are variously affected by it.

A self-idea of this sort seems to have three principal elements: the imagination of our appearance to the other person; the imagination of his judgment of that appearance, and some sort of self-feeling, such as pride or mortification. The comparison with a looking-glass hardly suggests the second element, the imagined judgment, which is quite essential. The thing that moves us to pride or shame is not the mere mechanical reflection of ourselves, but an imputed sentiment, the imagined effect of this reflection upon another's mind. This is evident from the fact that the character and weight of that other, in whose mind we see ourselves, makes all the difference with our feeling. We are ashamed to seem evasive in the presence of a straightforward man, cowardly in the presence of a brave one, gross in the eyes of a refined one, and so on. We always imagine, and in imagining share, the judgments of the other mind. A man will boast to one person of an action —say some sharp transaction in trade—which he would be ashamed to own to another.

The tendency of the self, like every aspect of personality, is expressive of far-reaching hereditary and social factors, and is not to be understood or predicted except in connection with the general life. Although special, it is in no way separate—speciality and separateness are not only different but contradictory, since the former implies connection with a whole.

Habit and familiarity are not of themselves sufficient to cause an idea to be appropriated into the self. Many habits and familiar objects that have been forced upon us by circumstances rather than chosen for their congeniality remain external and possibly repulsive to the self; and, on the other hand, a novel but very congenial element in experience, like the idea of a new toy, or, if you please, Romeo's idea of Juliet, is often appropriated almost immediately, and becomes, for the time at least, the very heart of the self. Habit has the same fixing and consolidating action in the growth of the self that it has elsewhere, but is not its distinctive characteristic.

I imagine, that as a rule the child associates "I" and "me" at first only with those ideas regarding which his appropriative feeling is aroused and defined by opposition. He appropriates his nose, eye, or foot in very much the same way as a plaything—by antithesis to other noses, eyes, and feet, which he cannot control. It is not uncommon to tease little children by proposing to take away one of these organs, and they behave precisely as if the "mine" threatened were a separable object—which it might be for all they know. And, as I have suggested, even in adult life, "I," "me," and "mine" are applied with a strong sense of their meaning only to things distinguished as peculiar to us by some sort of opposition or contrast. They always imply social life and relation to other persons. That which is most distinctively mine is very private, it is true, but it is that part of the private which I am cherishing in antithesis to the rest of the world, not the separate but the special. The aggressive self is essentially a militant phase of the mind, having for its apparent function the energizing of peculiar activities, and, although the militancy may not go on in an obvious, external manner, it always exists as a mental attitude.

In some of the best-known discussions of the development of the sense of self in children the chief emphasis has been placed upon the speculative or quasi-metaphysical ideas concerning "I" which children sometimes formulate as a result either of questions from their elders, or of the independent development of a speculative instinct. The most obvious result of these inquiries is to show that a child, when he reflects upon the self in this manner, usually locates "I" in the body. Interesting and important as this juvenile metaphysics is, as one phase of mental development, it should certainly not be taken as an adequate expression of the childish sense of self.

The process by which self-feeling of the looking-glass sort develops in children may be followed without much difficulty. Studying the movements of others as closely as they do they soon see a connection between their own acts and changes in those movements; that is, they perceive their own influence or power over persons. The child appropriates the visible actions of his parent or nurse, over which he finds he has some control, in quite the same way as he appropriates one of his own members or a plaything, and he will try to do things with this new possession, just as he will with his hand or his rattle. A girl six months old will attempt in the most evident and deliberate manner to attract attention to herself, to set going by her actions some of those movements of other persons that she has appropriated. She has tasted the joy of being a cause, of exerting social power, and wishes more of it. She will tug at her mother's skirts, wriggle, gurgle, stretch out her arms, etc., all the time watching for the hoped-for effect. These performances often give the child, even at this age, an appearance of what is called affectation, that is, she seems to be unduly preoccupied with what other people think of her. Affectation, at any age, exists when the passion to influence others seems to overbalance the established character and give it an obvious twist or pose.

The young performer soon learns to be different things to different people, showing that he begins to apprehend personality and to foresee its operation. If the mother or nurse is more tender than just she will almost certainly be "worked" by systematic weeping. It is a matter of common observation that children often behave worse with their mother than with other and less sympathetic people. Of the new persons that a child sees it is evident that some make a strong impression and awaken a desire to interest and please them, while others are indifferent or repugnant. Sometimes the reason can be perceived or guessed, sometimes not; but the fact of selective interest, admiration, prestige, is obvious before the end of the second year. By that time a child already cares much for the reflection of himself upon one personality and little for that upon another. Moreover, he soon claims intimate and tractable persons as *mine*, classes them among his other possessions, and maintains his ownership against all comers.

I doubt whether there are any regular stages in the development of social self-feeling and expression common to the majority of children. The sentiments of self develop by imperceptible gradations out of the crude appropriative instinct of new-born babes, and their manifestations vary indefinitely in different cases. Many children show "self-consciousness" conspicuously from the first half-year; others have little appearance of it at any age. Still others pass through periods of affectation whose length and time of occurrence would probably be found to be exceedingly various. In childhood, as at all times of life, absorption in some idea other than that of the social self tends to drive "self-consciousness" out.

CHAPTER 3

The Self and the Other

SOCIABILITY AND PERSONAL IDEAS

B Y

CHARLES HORTON COOLEY

To any but a mother a new-born child hardly seems human. It appears rather to be a strange little animal, wonderful indeed, exquisitely finished even to the finger-nails; mysterious, awakening a fresh sense of our ignorance of the nearest things of life, but not friendly, not lovable. It is only after some days that a kindly nature begins to express itself and to grow into something that can be sympathized with and personally cared for. The earliest signs of it are chiefly certain smiles and babbling sounds, which are a matter of fascinating observation to any one interested in the genesis of social feeling.

When a child is, say, five months old, no doubt can remain, in most cases, that the smile has become an expression of pleasure in the movements, sounds, touches, and general appearance of other people. It would seem, however, that personal feeling is not at first clearly differentiated from pleasures of sight, sound, and touch of other origin, or from animal satisfactions having no obvious cause. The general impression left upon one is that the early manifestations of sociability indicate less fellow feeling than the adult imagination likes to impute, but are expressions of a pleasure which persons excite chiefly because they offer such a variety of stimuli to sight, hearing, and touch; or, to put it otherwise, kindliness, while existing almost from the first, is vague and undiscriminating, has not yet become fixed upon its proper objects, but flows out upon all the pleasantness the child finds about him. Indeed, there is nothing about personal feeling which sharply marks it off from other feeling; here as elsewhere we find no fences, but gradual transition, progressive differentiation.

A baby does not smile by imitation, but because he is pleased; and what pleases him in the first year of life is usually some rather obvious stimulus to the senses. If you wish a smile you must earn it by acceptable exertion; it does no good to smirk. The belief that many people seem to have that infants respond to smiling is possibly due to the fact that when a grown-up person appears, both he and the infant are likely to smile, each at the other; but although the smiles are simultaneous one need not be the cause of the other, and many observations lead me to think that it makes no difference to the infant whether the grown-up person smiles or not. He has not yet learned to appreciate this rather subtle phenomenon.

At this and at all later ages the delight in companionship so evident in children may be ascribed partly to specific social emotion or sentiment, and partly to a need of stimulating suggestions to enable them to gratify their instinct for various sorts of mental and physical activity. The influence of the latter appears in their marked preference for active persons, for grown-up people who will play with them— provided they do so with tact—and especially for other children. It is the same throughout life; alone one is like fireworks without a match: he cannot set himself off, but is a victim of *ennui,* the prisoner of some tiresome train of thought that holds his mind simply by the absence of a competitor. A good companion brings release and fresh activity, the primal delight in a fuller existence. So with the child: what excitement when visiting children come! He shouts, laughs, jumps about, produces his playthings and all his accomplishments. He needs to express himself, and a companion enables him to do so. The shout of another boy in the distance gives him the joy of shouting in response.

But the need is for something more than muscular or sensory activities. There is also a need of feeling, an overflowing of personal emotion and sentiment, set free by the act of communication. By the time a child is a year old the social feeling that at first is indistinguishable from sensuous pleasure has become much specialized upon persons, and from that time onward to call it forth by reciprocation is a chief aim of his life.

I take it that the child has by heredity a generous capacity and need for social feeling, rather too vague and plastic to be given any specific name like love. It is not so much any particular personal emotion or sentiment as the undifferentiated material of many: perhaps sociability is as good a word for it as any.

And this material, like all other instinct, allies itself with social experience to form, as time goes on, a growing and diversifying body of personal thought, in which the phases of social feeling developed correspond, in some measure, to the complexity of life itself. It is a process of organization, involving progressive differentiation and integration, such as we see everywhere in nature.

In children and in simple-minded adults, kindly feeling may be very strong and yet very naïve, involving little insight into the emotional states of others. A child who is extremely sociable, bubbling over with joy in companionship, may yet show a total incomprehension of pain and a scant regard for disapproval and punishment that does not take the form of a cessation of intercourse. In other words, there is a sociability that asks little from others except bodily presence and an occasional sign of attention, and often learns to supply even these by imagination. It seems nearly or quite independent of that power of interpretation which is the starting-point of true sympathy.

When left to themselves children continue the joys of sociability by means of an imaginary playmate. Although all must have noticed this who have observed children at all, only close and constant observation will enable one to realize the extent to which it is carried on. It is not an occasional practice, but, rather, a necessary form of thought, flowing from a life in which personal communication is the chief interest and social feeling the stream in which, like boats on a river, most other feelings float. Some children appear to live in personal imaginations almost from the first month; others occupy their minds in early infancy mostly with solitary experiments upon blocks, cards, and other impersonal objects, and their thoughts are doubtless filled with the images of these. But, in either case, after a child learns to talk and the social world in all its wonder and provocation opens on his mind, it floods his imagination so that all his thoughts are conversations. He is never alone. Sometimes the inaudible interlocutor is recognizable as the image of a tangible playmate, sometimes he appears to be purely imaginary.

The main point to note here is that these conversations are not occasional and temporary effusions of the imagination, but are the naïve expression of a socialization of the mind that is to be permanent and to underlie all later thinking. The imaginary dialogue passes beyond the thinking aloud of little children into something more elaborate, reticent, and sophisticated; but it never ceases. Grown people, like children, are usually unconscious of these dialogues; as we get older we cease, for the most part, to carry them on out loud, and some of us practise a good deal of apparently solitary meditation and experiment. But, speaking broadly, it is true of adults as of children, that the mind lives in perpetual conversation. It is one of those things that we seldom notice just because they are so familiar and involuntary; but we can perceive it if we try to. If one suddenly stops and takes note of his thoughts at some time when his mind has been running free, as when he is busy with some simple mechanical work, he will be likely to find them taking the form of vague conversations. This is particularly true when one is somewhat excited with reference to a social situation. If he feels under accusation or suspicion in any way he will probably find himself making a defense, or perhaps a confession, to an imaginary hearer. A guilty man confesses "to get the load off his mind"; that is to say, the excitement of his thought cannot stop there but extends to the connected impulses of expression and creates an intense need to tell somebody. Impulsive people often talk out loud when excited, either "to themselves," as we say when we can see no one else present, or to any one whom they can get to listen. Dreams also consist very largely of imaginary conversations; and, with some people at least, the mind runs in dialogue during the half-waking state before going to sleep. There are many other familiar facts that bear the same interpretation—such, for instance, as that it is much easier for most people to compose in the form of letters or dialogue than in any other; so that literature of this kind has been common in all ages.

Every one, in proportion to his natural vigor, necessarily strives to communicate to others that part of his life which he is trying to unfold in himself. It is a matter of self-preservation, because without expression thought cannot live. Imaginary conversation—that is, conversation carried on without the stimulus of a visible and audible response —may satisfy the needs of the mind for a long time. There is, indeed, an advantage to a vigorously constructive and yet impressible imagination in restricting communication; because in this way ideas are enabled to have a clearer and more independent development than they could have if continually disturbed by criticism or opposition. Thus artists, men of letters, and productive minds of all sorts often find it better to keep their productions to themselves until they are fully matured. But, after all, the response must come sooner or later or thought itself will perish. The imagination, in time, loses the power to create an interlocutor who is not corroborated by any fresh experience. If the artist finds no appreciator for his book or picture he will scarcely be able to produce another.

People differ much in the vividness of their imaginative sociability. The more simple, concrete, dramatic, their habit of mind is, the more their thinking is carried on in terms of actual conversation with a visible and audible interlocutor. Women, as a rule, probably do this more vividly than men, the unlettered more vividly than those trained to abstract thought, and the sort of people we call emotional more vividly than the impassive. Moreover, the interlocutor is a very mutable person, and is likely to resemble the last strong character we have been in contact with. I have noticed, for instance, that when I take up a book after a person of decided and interesting character has been talking with me I am likely to hear the words of the book in his voice. The same is true of opinions, moral standards, and the like, as well as of physical traits. In short, the interlocutor, who is half of all thought and life, is drawn from the accessible environment.

It is worth noting here that there is no separation between real and imaginary persons; indeed, to be imagined is to become real, in a social sense, as I shall presently point out. An invisible person may easily be more real to an imaginative mind than a visible one; sensible presence is not necessarily a matter of the first importance. A person can be real to us only in the degree in which we imagine an inner life which exists in us, for the time being, and which we refer to him. The sensible presence is important chiefly in stimulating us to do this. All real persons are imaginary in this sense. If, however, we use imaginary in the sense of illusory, an imagination not corresponding to fact, it is easy to see that visible presence is no bar to illusion. Thus I meet a stranger on the steamboat who corners me and tells me his private history. I care nothing for it, and he half knows that I do not; he uses me only as a lay figure to sustain the agreeable illusion of sympathy, and is talking to an imaginary companion quite as he might if I were elsewhere. So likewise good manners are largely a tribute to imaginary companionship, a make-believe of sympathy which it is agreeable to accept as real, though we may know, when we think, that it is not. To conceive a kindly and approving companion is something that one involuntarily tries to do, in accordance with that instinctive hedonizing inseparable from all wholesome mental processes, and to assist in this by at least a seeming of friendly appreciation is properly regarded as a part of good breeding. To be always sincere would be brutally to destroy this pleasant and mostly harmless figment of the imagination.

Thus the imaginary companionship which a child of three or four years so naïvely creates and expresses is something elementary and almost omnipresent in the thought of a normal person. In fact, thought and personal intercourse may be regarded as merely aspects of the same thing: we call it personal intercourse when the suggestions that keep it going are received through faces or other symbols present to the sense; reflection when the personal suggestions come through memory and are more elaborately worked over in thought. But both are mental, both are personal. Personal images, as they are connected with nearly all our higher thought in its inception, remain inseparable from it in memory. The mind is not a hermit's cell, but a place of hospitality and intercourse. We have no higher life that is really apart from other people. It is by imagining them that our personality is built up; to be without the power of imagining them is to be a low-grade idiot; and in the measure that a mind is lacking in this power it is degenerate. Apart from this mental society there is no wisdom, no power, justice, or right, no higher existence at all. The life of the mind is essentially a life of intercourse.

Apparently, voice, facial expression, gesture, and the like, which later become the vehicle of personal impressions and the sensible basis of sympathy, are attractive at first chiefly for their sensuous variety and vividness, very much as other bright, moving, sounding things are attractive; and the interpretation of them comes gradually by the interworking of instinct and observation. This interpretation is nothing other than the growth, in connection with these sensuous experiences, of a system of ideas that we associate with them. The interpretation of an angry look, for instance, consists in the expectation of angry words and acts, in feelings of resentment or fear, and so on; in short, it is our whole mental reaction to this sign. It may consist in part of sympathetic states of mind, that is of states of mind that we suppose the other to experience also; but it is not confined to such. These ideas that enrich the meaning of the symbol—the resentment or fear, for instance—have all, no doubt, their roots in instinct; we are born with the crude raw material of such feelings. And it is precisely in the act of communication, in social contact of some sort, that this material grows, that it gets the impulses that give it further definition, refinement, organization. It is by intercourse with others that we expand our inner experience. In other words, and this is the point of the matter, the personal idea consists at first and in all later development, of a sensuous element or symbol with which is connected a more or less complex body of thought and sentiment; the whole social in genesis, formed by a series of communications.

An infant's states of feeling may be supposed to be nearly as crude as his ideas of the appearance of things; and the process that gives form, variety, and coherence to the latter does the same for the former. It is precisely the act of intercourse, the stimulation of the mind by a personal symbol, which gives a formative impulse to the vague mass of hereditary feeling-tendency, and this impulse, in turn, results in a larger power of interpreting the symbol. It is not to be supposed, for instance, that such feelings as generosity, respect, mortification, emulation, the sense of honor, and the like, are an original endowment of the mind. Like all the finer and larger mental life these arise in conjunction with communication and could not exist without it. It is these finer modes of feeling, these intricate branchings or differentiations of the primitive trunk of emotion, to which the name sentiments is usually applied. Personal sentiments are correlative with personal symbols, the interpretation of the latter meaning nothing more than that the former are associated with them; while the sentiments, in turn, cannot be felt except by the aid of the symbols.

Thus no personal sentiment is the exclusive product of any one influence, but all is of various origin and has a social history. The more clearly one can grasp this fact the better, at least if I am right in supposing that a whole system of wrong thinking results from overlooking it and assuming that personal ideas are separable and fragmentary elements in the mind.

Facial expression, tone of voice, and the like, the sensible nucleus of personal and social ideas, serve as the handle, so to speak, of such ideas, the principal substance of which is drawn from the region of inner imagination and sentiment. The personality of a friend, as it lives in my mind and forms there a part of the society in which I live, is simply a group or system of thoughts associated with the symbols that stand for him. To think of him is to revive some part of the system—to have the old feeling along with the familiar symbol, though perhaps in a new connection with other ideas. The real and intimate thing in him is the thought to which he gives life, the feeling his presence or memory has the power to suggest. This clings about the sensible imagery, the personal symbols already discussed, because the latter have served as bridges by which we have entered other minds and therein enriched our own. We have laid up stores, but we always need some help to get at them in order that we may use and increase them; and this help commonly consists in something visible or audible, which has been connected with them in the past and now acts as a key by which they are unlocked. Thus the face of a friend has power over us in much the same way as the sight of a favorite book, of the flag of one's country, or the refrain of an old song; it starts a train of thought, lifts the curtain from an intimate experience. And his presence does not consist in the pressure of his flesh upon a neighboring chair, but in the thoughts clustering about some symbol of him, whether the latter be his tangible person or something else. If a person is more his best self in a letter than in speech, as sometimes happens, he is more truly present to me in his correspondence than when I see and hear him. And in most cases a favorite writer is more with us in his book than he ever could have been in the flesh; since, being a writer, he is one who has studied and perfected this particular mode of personal incarnation, very likely to the detriment of any other. I should like as a matter of curiosity to see and hear for a moment the men whose works I admire; but I should hardly expect to find further intercourse particularly profitable.

The world of sentiment and imagination, of all finer and warmer thought, is chiefly a personal world—that is, it is inextricably interwoven with personal symbols. If you try to think of a person you will find that what you really think is chiefly sentiments which you connect with his image; and, on the other hand, if you try to recall a sentiment you will find, as a rule, that it will not come up except along with symbols of the persons who have suggested it.

So far as the study of immediate social relations is concerned the personal idea is the real person. That is to say, it is in this alone that one man exists for another, and acts directly upon his mind. My association with you evidently consists in the relation between my idea of you and the rest of my mind. If there is something in you that is wholly beyond this and makes no impression upon me it has no social reality in this relation. *The immediate social reality is the personal idea;* nothing, it would seem, could be much more obvious than this.

Society, then, in its immediate aspect, *is a relation among personal ideas.* In order to have society it is evidently necessary that persons should get together somewhere; and they get together only as personal ideas in the mind. Where else? What other possible *locus* can be assigned for the real contact of persons, or in what other form can they come in contact except as impressions or ideas formed in this common *locus?* Society exists in my mind as the contact and reciprocal influence of certain ideas named "I," Thomas, Henry, Susan, Bridget, and so on. It exists in your mind as a similar group, and so in every mind. Each person is immediately aware of a particular aspect of society: and so far as he is aware of great social wholes, like a nation or an epoch, it is by embracing in this particular aspect ideas or sentiments which he attributes to his countrymen or contemporaries in their collective aspect. In order to see this it seems to me only necessary to discard vague modes of speech which have no conceptions back of them that will bear scrutiny, and look at the facts as we know them in experience.

Yet most of us, perhaps, will find it hard to assent to the view that the social person is a group of sentiments attached to some symbol or other characteristic element, which keeps them together and from which the whole idea is named. The reason for this reluctance I take to be that we are accustomed to talk and think, so far as we do think in this connection, as if a person were a material rather than a psy-

chical fact. Instead of basing our sociology and ethics upon what a
man really is as part of our mental and moral life, he is vaguely and
yet grossly regarded as a shadowy material body, a lump of flesh, and
not as an ideal thing at all. But surely it is only common sense to hold
that the social and moral reality is that which lives in our imaginations and affects our motives. As regards the physical it is only the
finer, more plastic and mentally significant aspects of it that imagination is concerned with, and with them chiefly as a nucleus or centre
of crystallization for sentiment. Instead of perceiving this we commonly make the physical the dominant factor, and think of the mental
and moral only by a vague analogy to it.

Persons and society must, then, be studied primarily in the imagination. It is surely true, *prima facie,* that the best way of observing things
is that which is most direct; and I do not see how any one can hold
that we know persons directly except as imaginative ideas in the
mind. These are perhaps the most vivid things in our experience, and
as observable as anything else, though it is a kind of observation in
which accuracy has not been systematically cultivated. The observation of the physical aspects, however important, is for social purposes
quite subsidiary: there is no way of weighing or measuring men which
throws more than a very dim side-light on their personality. The physical factors most significant are those elusive traits of expression already
discussed, and in the observation and interpretation of these physical
science is only indirectly helpful. What, for instance, could the most
elaborate knowledge of his weights and measures, including the anat-
omy of his brain, tell us of the character of Napoleon? Not enough,
I take it, to distinguish him with certainty from an imbecile. Our real
knowledge of him is derived from reports of his conversation and
manner, from his legislation and military dispositions, from the impression made upon those about him and by them communicated to
us, from his portraits and the like; all serving as aids to the imagina
tion in forming a system that we call by his name. I by no means aim
to discredit the study of man or of society with the aid of physical
measurements, such as those of psychological laboratories; but I think
that these methods are indirect and ancillary in their nature and are
most useful when employed in connection with a trained imagination.

I conclude, therefore, that the imaginations which people have of
one another are the *solid facts* of society, and that to observe and
interpret these must be a chief aim of sociology. I do not mean merely
that society must be studied *by* the imagination—that is true of all
investigations in their higher reaches—but that the *object* of study is
primarily an imaginative idea or group of ideas in the mind, that we

have to imagine imaginations. The intimate grasp of any social fact will be found to require that we divine what men think of one another. Charity, for instance, is not understood without imagining what ideas the giver and recipient have of each other; to grasp homicide we must, for one thing, conceive how the offender thinks of his victim and of the administrators of the law; the relation between the employing and hand-laboring classes is first of all a matter of personal attitude which we must apprehend by sympathy with both, and so on. In other words, we want to get at motives, and motives spring from personal ideas. There is nothing particularly novel in this view; historians, for instance, have always assumed that to understand and interpret personal relations was their main business; but apparently the time is coming when this will have to be done in a more systematic and penetrating manner then in the past. Whatever may justly be urged against the introduction of frivolous and disconnected "personalities" into history, the understanding of persons is the aim of this and all other branches of social study.

Society is simply the collective aspect of personal thought. Each man's imagination, regarded as a mass of personal impressions worked up into a living, growing whole, is a special phase of society; and Mind or Imagination as a whole, that is human thought considered in the largest way as having a growth and organization extending throughout the ages, is the *locus* of society in the widest possible sense.

It may be objected that society in this sense has no definite limits, but seems to include the whole range of experience. That is to say, the mind is all one growth, and we cannot draw any distinct line between personal thought and other thought. There is probably no such thing as an idea that is wholly independent of minds other than that in which it exists; through heredity, if not through communication, all is connected with the general life, and so in some sense social. What are spoken of above as personal ideas are merely those in which the connection with other persons is most direct and apparent. This objection, however, applies to any way of defining society, and those who take the material standpoint are obliged to consider whether houses, factories, domestic animals, tilled land, and so on are not really parts of the social order. The truth, of course, is that all life hangs together in such a manner that any attempt to delimit a part of it is artificial. Society is rather a phase of life than a thing by itself; it is life regarded from the point of view of personal intercourse. And personal intercourse may be considered either in its primary aspects, such as are treated in this book, or in secondary aspects, such as groups, institutions, or processes. Sociology, I suppose, is the science of these things.

THE SELF, THE GENERALIZED OTHER
AND THE INDIVIDUAL

BY

GEORGE H. MEAD

THE problem now presents itself as to how, in detail, a self arises. We have to note something of the background of its genesis. First of all there is the conversation of gestures between animals involving some sort of co-operative activity. There the beginning of the act of one is a stimulus to the other to respond in a certain way, while the beginning of this response becomes again a stimulus to the first to adjust his action to the oncoming response. Such is the preparation for the completed act, and ultimately it leads up to the conduct which is the outcome of this preparation. The conversation of gestures, however, does not carry with it the reference of the individual, the animal, the organism, to itself. It is not acting in a fashion which calls for a response from the form itself, although it is conduct with reference to the conduct of others. We have seen, however, that there are certain gestures that do affect the organism as they affect other organisms and may, therefore, arouse in the organism responses of the same character as aroused in the other. Here, then, we have a situation in which the individual may at least arouse responses in himself and reply to these responses, the condition being that the social stimuli have an effect on the individual which is like that which they have on the other. That, for example, is what is implied in language; otherwise language as significant symbol would disappear, since the individual would not get the meaning of that which he says.

The peculiar character possessed by our human social environment belongs to it by virtue of the peculiar character of human social activity; and that character, as we have seen, is to be found in the process of communication, and more particularly in the triadic relation on which the existence of meaning is based: the relation of the gesture of one organism to the adjustive response made to it by another organism, in its indicative capacity as pointing to the completion or resultant of the act it initiates (the meaning of the gesture being thus the response of the second organism to it as such, or as a gesture).

Abridged from: Mead, George H. (edited by Charles W. Morris), *Mind, Self and Society,* Chicago: University of Chicago Press, 1934. Reprinted by permission of the University of Chicago Press.

What, as it were, takes the gesture out of the social act and isolates it as such—what makes it something more than just an early phase of an individual act—is the response of another organism, or of other organisms, to it. Such a response is its meaning, or gives it its meaning. The social situation and process of behavior are here presupposed by the acts of the individual organisms implicated therein. The gesture arises as a separable element in the social act, by virtue of the fact that it is selected out by the sensitivities of other organisms to it; it does not exist as a gesture merely in the experience of the single individual. The meaning of a gesture by one organism, to repeat, is found in the response of another organism to what would be the completion of the act of the first organism which that gesture initiates and indicates.

In a thought process there has to be some sort of a symbol that can refer to this meaning, that is, tend to call out this response, and also serve this purpose for other persons as well. It would not be a thought process if that were not the case. Our symbols are all universal.[1] You cannot say anything that is absolutely particular; anything you say that has any meaning at all is universal. You are saying something that calls out a specific response in anybody else provided that the symbol exists for him in his experience as it does for you. Thinking always implies a symbol which will call out the same response in another that it calls out in the thinker. Such a symbol is a universal of discourse; it is universal in its character. We always assume that the symbol we use is one which will call out in the other person the same response, provided it is a part of his mechanism of conduct. A person who is saying something is saying to himself what he says to others; otherwise he does not know what he is talking about.

What is essential to communication is that the symbol should arouse in one's self what it arouses in the other individual. It must have that sort of universality to any person who finds himself in the same situation. There is a possibility of language whenever a stimulus can affect the individual as it affects the other.

Another set of background factors in the genesis of the self is represented in the activities of play and the game.

Among primitive people the necessity of distinguishing the self

[1] Thinking proceeds in terms of or by means of universals. A universal may be interpreted behavioristically as simply the social act as a whole, involving the organization and interrelation of the attitudes of all the individuals implicated in the act, as controlling their overt responses. This organization of the different individual attitudes and interactions in a given social act, with reference to their interrelations as realized by the individuals themselves, is what we mean by a universal; and it determines what the actual overt responses of the individuals involved in the given social act will be, whether that act be concerned with a concrete project of some sort (such as the relation of physical and social means to ends desired) or with some purely abstract discussion, say the theory of relativity or the Platonic ideas.

and the organism was recognized in what we term the "double": the individual has a thing-like self that is affected by the individual as it affects other people and which is distinguished from the immediate organism in that it can leave the body and come back to it. This is the basis for the concept of the soul as a separate entity.

We find in children something that answers to this double, namely, the invisible, imaginary companions which a good many children produce in their own experience. They organize in this way the responses which they call out in other persons and call out also in themselves. Of course, this playing with an imaginary companion is only a peculiarly interesting phase of ordinary play. Play in this sense, especially the stage which precedes the organized games, is a play at something. A child plays at being a mother, at being a teacher, at being a policeman; that is, it is taking different roles, as we say. We have something that suggests this in what we call the play of animals: a cat will play with her kittens, and dogs play with each other. Two dogs playing with each other will attack and defend, in a process which if carried through would amount to an actual fight. There is a combination of responses which checks the depth of the bite. But we do not have in such a situation the dogs taking a definite role in the sense that a child deliberately takes the role of another. This tendency on the part of the children is what we are working with in the kindergarten where the roles which the children assume are made the basis for training. When a child does assume a role he has in himself the stimuli which call out that particular response or group of responses. He may, of course, run away when he is chased, as the dog does, or he may turn around and strike back just as the dog does in his play. But that is not the same as playing at something. Children get together to "play Indian." This means that the child has a certain set of stimuli which call out in itself the responses that they would call out in others, and which answer to an Indian. In the play period the child utilizes his own responses to these stimuli which he makes use of in building a self. The response which he has a tendency to make to these stimuli organizes them. He plays that he is, for instance, offering himself something, and he buys it; he gives a letter to himself and takes it away; he addresses himself as a parent, as a teacher; he arrests himself as a policeman. He has a set of stimuli which call out in himself the sort of responses they call out in others. He takes this group of responses and organizes them into a certain whole. Such is the simplest form of being another to one's self. It involves a temporal situation. The child says something in one character and responds in another character, and then his responding in another character is a stimulus to himself in the first character, and so the conversation goes on. A certain organized structure arises in him and in his other which replies to it, and these carry on the conversation of gestures between themselves.

If we contrast play with the situation in an organized game, we note the essential difference that the child who plays in a game must be ready to take the attitude of everyone else involved in that game, and that these different roles must have a definite relationship to each other. Taking a very simple game such as hide-and-seek, everyone with the exception of the one who is hiding is a person who is hunting. A child does not require more than the person who is hunted and the one who is hunting. If a child is playing in the first sense he just goes on playing, but there is no basic organization gained. In that early stage he passes from one role to another just as a whim takes him. But in a game where a number of individuals are involved, then the child taking one role must be ready to take the role of everyone else. If he gets in a ball nine he must have the responses of each position involved in his own position. He must know what everyone else is going to do in order to carry out his own play. He has to take all of these roles. They do not all have to be present in consciousness at the same time, but at some moments he has to have three or four individuals present in his own attitude, such as the one who is going to throw the ball, the one who is going to catch it, and so on. These responses must be, in some degree, present in his own make-up. In the game, then, there is a set of responses of such others so organized that the attitude of one calls out the appropriate attitudes of the other.

This organization is put in the form of the rules of the game. Children take a great interest in rules. They make rules on the spot in order to help themselves out of difficulties. Part of the enjoyment of the game is to get these rules. Now, the rules are the set of responses which a particular attitude calls out. You can demand a certain response in others if you take a certain attitude. These responses are all in yourself as well. In his game he has to have an organization of these roles; otherwise he cannot play the game. The game represents the passage in the life of the child from taking the role of others in play to the organized part that is essential to self-consciousness in the full sense of the term.

The fundamental difference between the game and play is that in the latter the child must have the attitude of all the others involved in that game. The attitudes of the other players which the participant assumes organize into a sort of unit, and it is that organization which controls the response of the individual. The illustration used was of a person playing baseball. Each one of his own acts is determined by his assumption of the action of the others who are playing the game.

What he does is controlled by his being everyone else on that team, at least in so far as those attitudes affect his own particular response. We get then an "other" which is an organization of the attitudes of those involved in the same process.

The organized community or social group which gives to the individual his unity of self may be called "the generalized other." The attitude of the generalized other is the attitude of the whole community. Thus, for example, in the case of such a social group as a ball team, the team is the generalized other in so far as it enters—as an organized process or social activity—into the experience of any one of the individual members of it.

If the given human individual is to develop a self in the fullest sense, it is not sufficient for him merely to take the attitudes of other human individuals toward himself and toward one another within the human social process, and to bring that social process as a whole into his individual experience merely in these terms: he must also, in the same way that he takes the attitudes of other individuals toward himself and toward one another, take their attitudes toward the various phases or aspects of the common social activity or set of social undertakings in which, as members of an organized society or social group, they are all engaged; and he must then, by generalizing these individual attitudes of that organized society or social group itself, as a whole, act toward different social projects which at any given time it is carrying out, or toward the various larger phases of the general social process which constitutes its life and of which these projects are specific manifestations. This getting of the broad activities of any given social whole or organized society as such within the experiential field of any one of the individuals involved or included in that whole is, in other words, the essential basis and prerequisite of the fullest development of that individual's self: only in so far as he takes the attitudes of the organized social group to which he belongs toward the organized, co-operative social activity or set of such activities in which that group as such is engaged, does he develop a complete self or possess the sort of complete self he has developed. And on the other hand, the complex co-operative processes and activities and institutional functionings of organized human society are also possible only in so far as every individual involved in them or belonging to that society can take the general attitudes of all other such individuals with reference to these processes and activities and institutional functionings, and to the organized social whole of experiential relations and interactions thereby constituted—and can direct his own behavior accordingly.

It is in the form of the generalized other that the social process influences the behavior of the individuals involved in it and carrying it on, i.e., that the community exercises control over the conduct of its individual members; for it is in this form that the social process or community enters as a determining factor into the individual's thinking. In abstract thought the individual takes the attitude of the generalized other toward himself, without reference to its expression in any particular other individuals; and in concrete thought he takes that attitude in so far as it is expressed in the attitudes toward his behavior of those other individuals with whom he is involved in the given social situation or act. But only by taking the attitude of the generalized other toward himself, in one or another of these ways, can he think at all; for only thus can thinking—or the internalized conversation of gestures which constitutes thinking—occur. And only through the taking by individuals of the attitude or attitudes of the generalized other toward themselves is the existence of a universe of discourse, as that system of common or social meanings which thinking presupposes at its context, rendered possible.

The self-conscious human individual, then, takes or assumes the organized social attitudes of the given social group or community (or of some one section thereof) to which he belongs, toward the social problems of various kinds which confront that group or community at any given time, and which arise in connection with the correspondingly different social projects or organized co-operative enterprises in which that group or community as such is engaged; and as an individual participant in these social projects or co-operative enterprises, he governs his own conduct accordingly. In politics, for example, the individual identifies himself with an entire political party and takes the organized attitudes of that entire party toward the rest of the given social community and toward the problems which confront the party within the given social situation; and he consequently reacts or responds in terms of the organized attitudes of the party as a whole. He thus enters into a special set of social relations with all the other individuals who belong to that political party; and in the same way he enters into various other special sets of social relations, with various other classes of individuals respectively, the individuals of each of these classes being the other members of some one of the particular organized subgroups (determined in socially functional terms) of which he himself is a member within the entire given society or social community. In the most highly developed, organized, and complicated human social communities—those evolved by civilized man—these various socially functional classes or subgroups of individuals to which any given individual belongs (and with the other individual members of which he thus enters into a special set of social relations) are of two kinds. Some of them are concrete social classes or subgroups, such as political parties, clubs, corporations, which are all actually functional social units, in terms of which their individual members are directly related to one another. The others are abstract social classes or subgroups, such as the class of debtors and the class of creditors, in terms of which their individual members are related to one another only more or less indirectly, and which only more or less indirectly function as social units, but which afford or represent unlimited possibilities for the widening and ramifying and enriching of the social relations among all the individual members of the given society as an organized and unified whole. The given individual's membership in several of these abstract social classes or subgroups makes possible his entrance into definite social relations (however indirect) with an almost infinite number of other individuals who also belong to or are included within one or another of these abstract social classes or subgroups cutting across functional lines of demarcation which divide different human social communities from one another, and including individual members from several (in some cases from all) such communities. Of these abstract social classes or subgroups of human individuals the one which is most inclusive and extensive is, of course, the one defined by the logical universe of discourse (or system of universally significant symbols) determined by the participation and communicative interaction of individuals; for of all such classes or subgroups, it is the one which claims the largest number of individual members, and which enables the largest conceivable number of human individuals to enter into some sort of social relation, however indirect or abstract it may be, with one another—a relation arising from the universal functioning of gestures as significant symbols in the general human social process of communication.

I have pointed out, then, that there are two general stages in the full development of the self. At the first of these stages, the individual's self is constituted simply by an organization of the particular attitudes of other individuals toward himself and toward one another in the specific social acts in which he participates with them. But at the second stage in the full development of the individual's self that self is constituted not only by an organization of these particular individual attitudes, but also by an organization of the social attitudes of the generalized other or the social group as a whole to which he belongs.

What goes to make up the organized self is the organization of the attitudes which are common to the group. A person is a personality because he belongs to a community, because he takes over the institutions of that community into his own conduct. He takes its language as a medium by which he gets his personality, and then through a process of taking the different roles that all the others furnish he comes to get the attitude of the members of the community. Such, in a certain sense, is the structure of a man's personality. There are certain common responses which each individual has toward certain common things, and in so far as those common responses are awakened in the individual when he is affecting other persons he arouses his own self. The structure, then, on which the self is built is this response which is common to all, for one has to be a member of a community to be a self. Such responses are abstract attitudes, but they constitute just what we term a man's character. They give him what we term his principles, the acknowledged attitudes of all members of the community toward what are the values of that community. He is putting himself in the place of the generalized other, which represents the organized responses of all the members of the group. It is that which guides conduct controlled by principles, and a person who has such an organized group of responses is a man whom we say has character, in the moral sense.

*　　　　*　　　　*

The fact that all selves are constituted by or in terms of the social process, and are individual reflections of it—or rather of this organized behavior pattern which it exhibits, and which they prehend in their respective structures—is not in the least incompatible with, or destructive of, the fact that every individual self has its own peculiar individuality, its own unique pattern; because each individual self within that process, while it reflects in its organized structure the behavior pattern of that process as a whole, does so from its own particular and unique standpoint within that process, and thus reflects in its organized structure a different aspect or perspective of this whole social behavior pattern from that which is reflected in the organized structure of any other individual self within that process. In other words, the organized structure of every individual self within the human social process of experience and behavior reflects, and is constituted by, the organized relational pattern of that process as a whole; but each individual self-structure reflects, and is constituted by, a different aspect or perspective of this relational pattern, because each reflects this relational pattern from its own unique standpoint; so that the common social origin and constitution of individual selves and their structures does not preclude wide individual differences and variations among them, or contradict the peculiar and more or less distinctive individuality which each of them in fact possesses. Every individual self within a given society or social community reflects in its organized structure the whole relational pattern of organized social behavior which that society or community exhibits or is carrying on, and its organized structure is constituted by this pattern; but since each of these individual selves reflects a uniquely different aspect or perspective of this pattern in its structure, from its own particular and unique place or standpoint within the whole process of organized social behavior which exhibits this pattern—since, that is, each is differently or uniquely related to that whole process, and occupies its own essentially unique focus of relations therein—the structure of each is differently constituted by this pattern from the way in which the structure of any other is so constituted.

The individual, as we have seen, is continually reacting back against this society. Every adjustment involves some sort of change in the community to which the individual adjusts himself. These changes are changes that take place gradually and more or less imperceptibly. We know that as we pass from one historical period to another there have been fundamental changes, and we know these changes are due to the reactions of different individuals. It is only the ultimate effect that we can recognize, but the differences are due to the gestures of these countless individuals actually changing the situation in which they find themselves, although the specific changes are too minute for us to identify. As I have pointed out, the ego or "I" that is responsible for changes of that sort appears in experience only after its reaction -has taken place. It is only after we have said the word we are saying that we recognize ourselves as the person that has said it, as this particular self that says this particular thing; it is only after we have done the thing that we are going to do that we are aware of what we are doing. However carefully we plan the future it always is different from that which we can previse, and this something that we are continually bringing in and adding to is what we identify with the self that comes into the level of our experience only in the completion of the act.

In some respects, of course, we can determine what that self is going to do. We can accept certain responsibilities in advance. One makes contracts and promises, and one is bound by them. The situation may change, the act may be different from that which the individual himself expected to carry out, but he is held to the contract which he has made. He must do certain things in order to remain a member of the community. In the duties of what we call rational conduct, in adjusting ourselves to a world in which the laws of nature and of economics and of political systems obtain, we can state what is going to happen and take over the responsibility for the thing we are going to do, and yet the real self that appears in that act awaits the completion of the act itself. Now, it is this living act which never gets directly into reflective experience. It is only after the act has taken place that we can catch it in our memory and place it in terms of that which we have done. It is that "I" which we may be said to be continually trying to realize, and to realize through the actual conduct itself. One does not ever get it fully before himself. Sometimes somebody else can tell him something about himself that he is not aware of. He is never sure about himself, and he astonishes himself by his conduct as much as he astonishes other people.

The possibilities in our nature, those sorts of energy which William James took so much pleasure in indicating, are possibilities of the self that lie beyond our own immediate presentation. We do not know just what they are. They are in a certain sense the most fascinating contents that we can contemplate, so far as we can get hold of them. We get a great deal of our enjoyment of romance, of moving pictures, of art, in setting free, at least in imagination, capacities which belong to ourselves, or which we want to belong to ourselves. Inferiority complexes arise from those wants of a self which we should like to carry out but which we cannot—we adjust ourselves to these by the so-called inferiority complexes. The possibilities of the "I" belong to that which is actually going on, taking place, and it is in some sense the most fascinating part of our experience. It is there that novelty arises and it is there that our most important values are located. It is the realization in some sense of this self that we are continually seeking.

There are various ways in which we can realize that self. Since it is a social self, it is a self that is realized in its relationship to others. It must be recognized by others to have the very values which we want to have belong to it. It realizes itself in some sense through its superiority to others, as it recognizes its inferiorities in comparison with others. The inferiority complexes are the reverse situations to those feelings of superiority which we entertain with reference to ourselves as over against people about us. It is interesting to go back into one's inner consciousness and pick out what it is that we are apt to depend upon in maintaining our self-respect. There are, of course, profound and solid foundations. One does keep his word, meet his obligations; and that provides a basis for self-respect. But those are characters which obtain in most of the members of the community with whom we have to do. We all fall down at certain points, but on the whole we always are people of our words. We do belong to the community and our self-respect depends on our recognition of ourselves as such self-respecting individuals. But that is not enough for us, since we want to recognize ourselves in our differences from other persons. We have, of course, a specific economic and social status that enables us to so distinguish ourselves. We also have to some extent positions in various groups which give a means of self-identification, but there is back of all these matters a sense of things which on the whole we do better than other people do. It is very interesting to get back to these superiorities, many of them of a very trivial character, but of great importance to us. We may come back to manners of speech and dress, to a capacity for remembering, to this, that, and the other thing—but always to something in which we stand out above people. We are careful, of course, not directly to plume ourselves. It would seem childish to intimate that we take satisfaction in showing that we can do something better than others. We take a great deal of pains to cover up such a situation; but actually we are vastly gratified.

This sense of superiority does not represent necessarily the disagreeable type of assertive character, and it does not mean that the person wants to lower other people in order to get himself into a higher standing. That is the form such self-realization is apt to appear to take, to say the least, and all of us recognize such a form as not simply unfortunate but as morally more or less despicable. But there is a demand, a constant demand, to realize one's self in some sort of superiority over those about us. It appears, perhaps, more definitely in such situations as those to which I have referred, and which are the hardest things to explain. There is a certain enjoyableness about the misfortunes of other people, especially those gathered about their personality. It finds its expression in what we term gossip, even mischievous gossip. We have to be on our guard against it. We may relate an event with real sorrow, and yet there is a certain satisfaction in something that has happened to somebody else but has not happened to us.

This is the same attitude that is involved in the humor of somebody else tumbling down. In such laughter there is a certain release from the effort which we do not have to make to get up again. It is a direct response, one that lies back of what we term self-consciousness, and the humor of it does not go along with the enjoyment of the other person's suffering. If a person does actually break a leg we can sympathize with him, but it was funny, after all, to see him sprawling out. This is a situation in which there is a more or less identification of the individual with the other. We do, so to speak, start to fall with him, and to rise up after he has fallen, and our theory of laughter is that it is a release from that immediate tendency to catch ourselves under those conditions. We have identified ourselves with the other person, taken his attitude. That attitude involves a strenuous effort which we do not have to carry out, and the release from that effort expresses itself in laughter. Laughter is the way in which the "I," so to speak, responds under those conditions. The individual probably sets to work helping the other person to get up, but there was an element in the response which expressed itself in the sense of the superiority of the person standing toward the person on the sidewalk. Now, that general situation is not simply found under physical situations, but is equally evident in the community in which a person commits a *faux pas;* we have here the same sense of amusement and of superiority.

The sense of superiority is magnified when it belongs to a self that identifies itself with the group. It is aggravated in our patriotism, where we legitimize an assertion of superiority which we would not admit in the situations to which I have been referring. It seems to be perfectly legitimate to assert the superiority of the nation to which one belongs over other nations, to brand the conduct of other nationalities in black colors in order that we may bring out values in the conduct of those that make up our own nation. It is just as true in politics and religion in the putting of one sect over against the others. It is not, of course, confined to nationalism and patriotism. We all believe that the group we are in is superior to other groups. We can get together with the members in a bit of gossip that with anyone else or any other group would be impossible. Leadership, of course, plays its part, since the enthusiasm for those who have a high standing among us aids in the organization of the group; but on the whole we depend upon a common recognition that other people are not quite as good as we are.

The feeling of group superiority is generally explained in terms of the organization of the group. Groups have survived in the past in so far as they have organized against a common enemy. They maintain themselves because they have acted as one against the common enemy—such is the explanation, from the standpoint of the survival of the fittest, of the community which is most satisfactorily organized. It certainly is the easiest way of getting together, and it may be that it is an adequate explanation.

If one does have a genuine superiority it is a superiority which rests on the performance of definite functions. One is a good surgeon, a good lawyer, and he can pride himself on his superiority—but it is a superiority which he makes use of. And when he does actually make use of it in the very community to which he belongs it loses that element of egoism which we think of when we think of a person simply pluming himself on his superiority over somebody else. When the sense of superiority goes over into a functional expression, then it becomes not only entirely legitimate, but it is the way in which the individuals do change the situations in which they live. We change things by the capacities which we have that other people do not have. Such capacity is what makes us effective. The immediate attitude is one which carries with it a sense of superiority, of maintaining one's self. The superiority is not the end in view. It is a means for the preservation of the self. We have to distinguish ourselves from other people and this is accomplished by doing something which other people cannot do, or cannot do as well.

SOCIETY AS AN ORGANIZATION OF SELVES

BY

JAMES MARK BALDWIN

The matter of social organization consists of thoughts—by which is meant intellectual states—which are socially available in the way now to be considered. These thoughts, or knowledges or informations, originate in the mind of the individuals of the group, as inventions, more or less novel conceptions; what we have called "particularizations." At their origin there is no reason for calling them social matter, since they are particular to the individual. They become social only when society—that is, the other members of the social group, or some of them—also thinks them, knows them, is informed of them. This reduces them, from the individual and particular form to a general or social form, and it is only in this form that they furnish social material, through what has been called, again, the "generalizations" effected by society. It is evident that these positions are not at all new; our main interest in presenting them, as well as the points of evidence which follow, lies in the advantage of having them definitely formulated about the present topic, and also as bringing us to a characterization of the *sort of thought* which is socially available.

The general considerations upon which this opinion is based may be given in contradistinction from special lines of evidence. These general considerations will be seen to arise in connection with the general requirements of social theory.

(1) It is only thoughts or knowledges which are imitable in the fruit-

Abridged from: Baldwin, James M., *Social and Ethical Interpretations in Mental Development*, New York: The Macmillan Co., 1897.

ful way required by a theory of progressive social organization. It has been said by some that beliefs and desires are thus imitable. It is clear, however, to the psychologist that beliefs and desires are functions of the knowledge-contents about which they arise. No belief can be induced in one individual by another except as the fact, truth, information, believed is first induced. The imitator must first get the thought before he can imitate belief in the thought. So of a desire. I cannot desire what you do except as I think the desirable object somewhat as you do. Both belief and desire are, as has been argued above, functions of thought-content.

If it be a question of imitative propagation or reproduction from one member of a social group to another, the vehicle of such a system of reproductions must be thought or knowledge. The only other psychological alternative is to say that the imitative propagation takes place by the simple contagion of feeling and impulse. This, however, takes us back to a question already raised, *i.e.*, the question of possible progress by society. We found that the reign of imitative feeling and impulse, whether it be by instinct or by suggestion, would make possible only the form of organization in which fixed habit is all, and in which no accommodation, movement, progress, would take place. This we found to characterize certain animal companies, and mobs of persons, in distinction from true societies.[1]

(2) It is only in the form of thoughts, conceptions, or inventions that new material, new "copies for imitation," new schemes of modified organization, can come into a society at any stage of its development. This seems evident from the mere statement of it. If we ask how a new measure of legislation, a new scheme of reform, a new opinion about style, art, literature, even a new cut to our coats or a changed height of hat—how any one of these originates, we are obliged to say that some one first *thought of it. Thought* of it, that is the important thing. Feeling and desire might have impelled to thought; urgent need may have prompted the invention; decaying modes may have made reform a matter of necessity; but with all the urgency that we may conceive, the measure, the reform, the new style, has to originate somewhere in the form of a concrete device, which society may take up and spread abroad. This particular form is then—apart from

---

[1] The biological view which considers the unit-person as such the material of social organization may be refuted in a word. It is as *persons* that persons come into social relationships, and the differences of persons are just in the psychological part. One physical body is as good as another before social law, unless indeed by reason of its colour, etc., it becomes a matter to arouse *psychological* attitudes: a point suggested above *apropos* of "social forces." The distinction between things in groups and persons in society is that there is a "give-and-take" in the latter case. The object of social study is thus the "giving and taking," and the material is that which is "given and taken."

happy accidents of discovery [2]—the thought of some one; and society afterwards "generalizes" the thought.

Of all the individual's doings, therefore, it is his thoughts which are the socially available factors of his life. Of course there is a form of social propagation which takes its origin in the actions alone of this man or that, whether any thought be discoverable in the actions or not. But apart from the fact that such actions have to be thought by the imitators, however spontaneous or accidental they may have been on the part of the original actor, it is evident that this form of social origination is on the side of mere accident, and reduces itself to repetition, social convention, or mob-action, and is lacking in itself of any fruitfulness in the production of new phases of social progress. It is thus even with the cases of contagion of crime. However much we deplore them and lament the victims, we do not fear that the crimes may become recognized social modes of conduct.

With these general considerations in mind,—which are enough in themselves to justify a close examination of the position that thought or knowledge is the matter of social organization,—we may proceed to cite two lines of evidence which support this view. One of them is drawn from the facts of the child's social development, as already depicted, and the other from the corresponding facts of the social and ethical man's relations to the historical institutions of society. These are the two spheres in which the consideration of the psychological factors involved in social organization leads us to reliable results.

A further development of the line of thought suggested in our consideration of social interests leads us to the view that the so-called "dialectic," whereby the child comes to a knowledge of himself by building up a sense of his social environment, may also be looked at from the side of social organization. If we grant that the thought of self takes its rise as a gradual achievement on the part of the child by means of his constant experience of the personalities about him, and that he has not two different thoughts for himself and the other, —the *ego* and the *alter*,—but one thought common in the man for both; then it becomes just as impossible to construe the social factor, the organized relationships between him and others, without taking account of his and their thoughts of self, as it is to construe the thoughts of self without taking account of the social relationships. The thought of self arises directly out of certain given social relationships; indeed, it is the form which these actual relationships take on in the organization of a new personal experience. The ego of which he thinks at any time is not the isolated-and-in-his-body-alone-situated

---

[2] And, of course, the happy accidents have to be *re-thought*.

abstraction which our theories of personality usually lead us to think. It is rather a sense of a network of relationships among you, me, and the others, in which certain necessities of pungent feeling, active life, and concrete thought require that I throw the emphasis on one pole sometimes, calling it me; and on the other pole sometimes, calling it you or him. The social meaning of this state of things comes out when we look into its psychological presuppositions in the whole group. Let us then call the child's sense of the entire personal situation in which he finds himself at any time in his thought, his *self-thought-situation*. This phrase, which I use simply for shorthand, may be expanded always into: *"the social situation implicated in the thought of self."*

Now, whatever is true of one individual's growth by imitative appropriation of personal material, is true of all; and we have the giver turned into the taker and the taker into the giver everywhere. The growing sense of a "self-thought-situation" in each is, *just to the extent that the social bonds are intimate and intrinsic, the same for all.* The possibility of co-operation—as, for example, the co-operations of children's games—depends upon this essential sameness of the personal thoughts of the whole circle in each situation. My action depends upon my understanding of your thought and his, and your action depends upon your understanding of my thought and his, and so on. Looked at objectively, we say that the children are in social relationship; looked at subjectively, the truth is that they are thinking the same thoughts of the personal-social situation, and this thought is just the "self-thought" in the stage of development which it has reached in this little mind or that, to be brought out on this or that occasion. H. understands E. in terms of her own motives, desires, tendencies, likes and dislikes, and, acting on this understanding, finds that it works; so E. treats her self-thought as true to H.'s thought, and it works; to find that either of these expectations did not work in the great run of cases of action would be to say, from the objective point of view, that the social relationship was dissolved. But this could not be without at the same time disintegrating, so far as the factors are intrinsic, the sense of personal self in each of the children, or taking it back toward the beginning of its development.

The question of the material of social organization comes up here as soon as we ask what it is that the children pass about, give and take, in this interplay with one another. And we find here just the distinction which occurred from the consideration of the difference between human and animal co-operations. We find the child at first largely organic, instinctive, directly emotional, under the influence of pleasures and pains. His sympathy is at first organic, and his antipathies likewise. But close observation shows that it is largely by the growing realization of personal distinctions, on the basis of which his thought of self develops, that he comes to have conscious imitations, original interpretations, hesitations, inhibitions, volitions. At first the relation is one of direct stimulation and direct response. If this state of things continued, men would form "companies," not "societies." Direct suggestion, emotional reaction, as much co-operation as heredity might give consistently with the other features—that would be the state of things. But now let the child begin to think, and we find certain great features of social import springing up in his life. First, a distinction in the elements of his environment according as they are personal or not; second, a difference of attitude toward persons, and toward different persons, according as the elements of personal suggestion become assimilated to this group of experiences or to that; third, the interpretation of the other persons in the same terms as himself, *i.e.,* as having attitudes like his in similar circumstances, and as thinking of him as he thinks of them. But all this is due to thought, involves knowledges, and the sorting of them out. The emotions now spring from thought-experiences, and the attitudes, actions, responses now take on the character of means to a personal end, the end being the thought which issues in this or that attitude or action. This development has been all along the burden of our song.

We may say then, as a first gain, from the consideration of the children, that what we call *objective social relationships are the objective manifestations to the on-looker of a common self-thought-situation in the different individuals, together with the movements of its growth in each as the immediate situation calls it out.*

We have now found so much justification for two positions: first, that the material of social organization must be considered as thought; thoughts which arise in individual minds and are then re-thought imitatively by others, and so carried on through a social career; and second, that the child's social sense, that is, his sense of social situations, however meagre and contracted or however full and rich, arises and grows as a function of his thought of himself. In other words, society to the child—society from the private subjective point of view —is a concrete situation involving related changes among the elements and attitudes which constitute his self-thought. The further question remains: given this objective social material—thought—and given also this subjective sense of society in the individual, *what then is the objective character of social organization?* For, of course, the question of science is just this objective question; not only what does each individual think of the social situation when he thinks of it at all, but what must the observer think of it after he finds out scientifically all about it? His question, then, in view of the two earlier determinations, is this: is the thought which constitutes the material of social organization any thought at random, thought X, thought Y, thought Z, these and others? Or must it be some particular sort of thought? And again, if the latter, must it be the sort of thought which the individual thinks when he reaches his sense of social situations as functions of his thought of himself? To come right to the conclusion, I think the last is true; and its truth appears, again, in what was called the *Publicity* of all social truth. What, then, is this publicity when considered from the objective point of view of social science? It may be stated in a sentence (which we go on to illustrate and explain): *every socially available thought implies a public "self-thought-situation" which is strictly analogous in its rise and progress to the self-thought-situation of the individual member of society.*

We may take an illustration from the ordinary attitude which society takes toward human life, in contrast with the attitude which the individual might sometimes think himself justified in taking toward his own life, in case he succeeded in stripping from his thought its "publicity," and acted on the lower unethical sanctions alone.

Let us say that there is a question in the mind of Mr. A as to whether he shall put a barrier across his hay-field to protect himself from injury at the point at which a railroad crosses the field. He says to himself: "I have crossed that field many times; I have never been struck by a train; the chances are that I never shall be; it would be useless trouble and expense." So he takes the risk of his life, and is probably justified by the event in doing so. So the sanctions of a private kind, mainly that of his intelligence, seem to sustain him in this decision.

But now let us suppose that Mr. A is also a public official and has to consider the question of putting up barriers at railway crossings generally. He is then told that at each place at which a railway crosses a road, a certain proportion of the pedestrians who go that way are killed each year. He might say of each of these what he had before said of himself, that the chances were in favour of safety. But now that he takes a *public* point of view, this is no longer sanctioned in his thought. It is no longer the question of the continuance of the life of this one man or that. It is now the question of the greatest possible safety to the collective or entire life of the community. To put up barriers at all the crossings would undoubtedly prevent the loss of many citizens a year. The social or public sanction, then, impels him in just the opposite direction; and he not only votes for the measure, but bears a share of the taxation and *allows the barrier to be put up in his own hay-field.*

If now we take this situation at its lowest terms and attempt to analyze it we find that it implies certain things:

(1) A shifting of the individual's point of view, in such a way that *the earlier private thought of self is held in check* before a higher or ideal thought of self; the self of the man acting in public is different; if he be true to it, he can no longer act out his private thought. (2) There is in his mind a sense of the *reciprocity of action of all the individuals* with reference to one another under this larger self-thought; and the actual social situation, involving all the individuals, is possible because this reciprocity and sameness of attitude are actually real. This, then, constitutes the *public self-thought-situation or the social situation implicated in the public thought of self.*

It is only through the reality of the first of these movements in Mr. A's mind that the second becomes possible, and has its value for objective science. The public or reciprocal reference of the judgment in each case arises only through the assimilation of the private and ejective self-thoughts in a larger whole of the same kind. The constituting of the larger self is just the evidence of the integrating of the more partial selves; and if the public reference is due to the common element in the different individuals' self-thoughts, then each individual must get the growth which the assimilation represents, and *all the individuals must construct somewhat the same ideal.* The former is secured in the normal growth of the "self-thought-situation" in each, and the latter through their actual life in a common social tradition and heritage.

Taking the point of view of society, therefore, in contrast with that of the individual, we find the state of things which social science is led to recognize, *i.e.,* an actual integration of individuals just through the identical higher self which their life together makes it possible for them to set up. From this point of view, therefore, we may call this a public "self-thought-situation,"—a social situation which is implicated in a public thought of self—and go on to inquire into the laws of progress and development which it shows, always with reference to the individuals of whose growth it is a function. It is interesting to note that in this public self thus understood, we have reached a measure of genetic justification for a position taken up by Aristotle and so often reasserted in the history of ethical discussion: the position which finds itself obliged to fall back upon a hypothetical "best man" or oracle, whose judgment would be correct if it could be had. In our development, however, this public self is the objective form of organization into which growing personalities normally fall, and its meaning will grow clearer, I trust, as we proceed.

But it may be said, surely it is not necessary that all thoughts, inventions, schemes, ideas, reforms, etc., should have this quality which we have called "publicity" to be available for the instruction or reforming of society. Yes, they must have it; that is just the point which I wish to urge. No knowledge, simply as knowledge, can be social knowledge or become the instrument of social advance until it be made over to the public self, by becoming in the minds of the individuals who think it *a public thing,* in contradistinction to the private thoughts which they entertain simply as individuals. Whatever the thought is, however great the invention, however pregnant the suggestion of reform, it is not of social value until I am justified in thinking it as also thought by the ideal self whose entertainment of it gives it validity and general authority to all the other individuals of the group. I may, from my private judgment, discount this further development of my thought beforehand; that is, I may confidently expect that my invention will be ratified by society, and so come to have the requisite publicity; but I then only do so as I appeal just to that higher self already formed in my breast through social experience, and through it anticipate the fate of the thought which I thus value. This is when the invention is looked at subjectively. As soon as we look at it objectively,—that is, from the point of view of the science of social organization,—we have to say that no thought is social or socially available which is still in the mind of an individual awaiting that generalization by the public which will give it the character of publicity by reason of the essential attribution of it to a public and general self.

In other words, my private thought, in order to be social matter, must enter into that organization or integration of the public "self-thought-situation" which is reflected more or less adequately in every adult; it is thus thought by that higher self which imposes law upon all; with this goes the thought by me that all men agree with me in thinking it, and that they will give the enforcement of it the same recognition (including its enforcement upon me) that I give it (including its enforcement upon them). The thought thus becomes involved in the growth of the personal self, and just by this becomes public also. Without this connection it cannot be social. *The ultimate subjective criterion of social thought is the self-thought,* with all its wealth of implication as to the social situation. And *the ultimate objective criterion is the actual ratification of the thought by the individuals through common action upon the situation which their self-thoughts mutually implicate.* By this they show their common integration in a public "self-thought-situation."

We come, therefore, in closing in upon our question as last stated to see that the growing "self-thought-situation" in the mind of the individual is, when viewed in its mutual interactions and correlations in the group, *just the material of social organization itself.* For nowhere else can we find the requisites for public availability fulfilled. Thus arises *ipso facto* a public "self-thought-situation"; on no other view can we account for the response of individuals to the organization which society shows. So both from the side of the child's and man's growth, and from the side of society considered objectively, we are led to identify the organization of the individual's personality directly with that of society, in respect both to its material and to its method of acting.

CHAPTER 4

The Social Character of Personality

THE ETHICAL SELF AND CONSCIENCE

BY

JAMES MARK BALDWIN

TURNING to the child and observing him in the period when his personal relationships are becoming complex, say along through the third year, the dawning moral sense is then caught as it were in the process of making. And in it we have a right to see, as I have had occasion to say in regard to other of the child's processes, the progress of the race depicted with more or less adequacy of detail.

The child begins to be dimly aware of such a presence, in his contact with others, as that which has been called in the abstract the *socius*. What this is to him is, of course, at this early stage simply an element of personal quality in the suggestions which he now gets from others; an element which is not done justice to by either of the thoughts of self to which he is accustomed on occasion to react. He notes in the behaviour of his father and mother, whenever certain contingencies of the social situation present themselves, a characteristic which, in the development of "personality-suggestion," was termed the "regularity of personal agency." He sees the father pained when he has to administer punishment; and he hears the words, "Father does not like to punish his little boy." He finds the mother reluctantly

Abridged from: Baldwin, James M., *Social and Ethical Interpretations in Mental Development*, New York: The Macmillan Co., 1897.

refusing to give a biscuit when it is her evident desire to give it. He sees those around him doing gay things with heavy hearts, and forcing themselves to be cheerful in the doing of things which are not pleasant. He sees hesitations, conflicts, indecisions, and from the bosom of them all he sees emerge the indications of something beyond the mere individual attitudes of the actor, something which stands toward these higher persons from whom he learns, as the family law, embodied possibly in the father, stands toward him.

Now I do not mean that the child sees all this in the terms in which I have described what he "sees." He does not see anything clearly. He simply feels puzzled at the richness of the indications of personal behaviour which pour in upon him. But the very puzzle of these situations is just the essential thing. It means that the categories of personality which he has so far acquired, the two selves which exhaust the possible modes of behaviour he is able to depict to himself in thought, are really inadequate. Here in these situations of his father and mother is more personal suggestion, which is still quite "pro- jective." It is personal; things do not show it. But it is not yet under- stood. The self of habit, no less than the self of accommodation, is thrust aside, as he sees his mother's sorrow when she refuses him the biscuit; he cannot act aggressively toward her nor yet sympathetically. There must needs be some other type of personal behaviour, *some other thought of a self;* for if not, then character must after all remain to him a chaotic, capricious thing.

We may ask, before we attempt to find a way for the child to extri- cate himself from this confusion in his thoughts of personality, whether he have in his own experience any analogies which will help him to assimilate the new suggestive elements. And our observation is very superficial if we do not light upon an evident thing in his life; the thing he has come to understand something about every time he *obeys.*

Whenever he obeys, the boy has forced in upon him a situation which his thoughts of himself are not adequate to interpret. He is responding neither to his habitual self nor to his accommodating self. Not to the former, for if the thing he is told to do is something he does not want to do, his habits, his private preferences, are directly vio- lated. And on the other hand he is not acting out his accommodating self simply, just in proportion as he is unwilling to do what he is told to do. If this self held all the room in his consciousness, then obedience would be companionship, and compliance would be no more than approval. No, it is really his private habitual self that is mainly present; the other being a forced product, unless by dint of schooling in sub- mission his obedience has become free and unconstrained.

Besides these elements, his two selves, then, what more is there to the child? This: *a dominating other self, a new alter,* is there; that is the important thing. And what does it mean? It means, in the first instance, a line of conduct on his part which the obedience represents. It is just by it that he learns more about character, precisely as, by his spontaneous imitations at the earlier stage, he established lines of conduct which taught him more about character. At this stage also, his intelligence is not so rudimentary as at the earlier one. It does not take him long to learn certain great things. By the action he performs through obedience, he learns the meaning of these actions: how they feel, what good or evil results they lead to. And in all his learning by this agency, he learns above all the great lesson essential to the development of his thought of self: that there is a something always present, an atmosphere, a circle of common interest, a family propriety, a mass of accepted tradition. *This is his first realization to himself of what the socius means.* It comes by his growth as a personal self, but the process of obedience greatly abbreviates his growth. For a long time it is embodied as a matter of course in the persons whom he obeys. But the social limitations which these persons respectively represent are not always coextensive or parallel. His father and mother often embody very different family spirits to him. And it is only after many tentative adjustments, mistaken efforts to please, excesses of duty in one direction, and instances of rebellion in other directions, that he learns the essential agreements of the different persons who set law to him.

Now this is a new thought of self. How can it be otherwise when all its origin is from persons, and all its characters are learned only by the efforts of the struggling hero to realize their meaning by his own actions? Apart from the elements of a possible self, there is absolutely nothing. It is his own actions felt, then added to imitatively and made to illustrate the actions of others, with which he fills his consciousness when he thinks of it. And in each of his straining efforts to obey, to do what he is told to do, his success or failure is a further defining of the limitations of one or the other of his old selves, and in so far the creation of a new self which sets law to both of them.

Now this new self arises right out of the competitions, urgencies, inhibitions of the old. Suppose a boy who has once obeyed the command to let an apple alone, coming to confront the apple again, when there is no one present to make him obey. There is his private, greedy, habitual self, eying the apple; there is also the spontaneously suggestible, accommodating, imitative self over against it, mildly prompting him to do as his father said and let the apple alone; and there is—or would be, if the obedience had taught him no new thought of self—the quick victory of the former. But now a lesson had been learned. There arises a thought of one who obeys, who has no struggle in carrying out the behests of the father. This may be vague; his habit may be yet weak in the absence of persons and penalties, but it is there, however weak. And it is no longer merely the faint imitation of an obedient self which he does not understand. It carries within it, it is true, all the struggle of the first obedience, all the painful protests of the private greedy self, all the smoke of the earlier battlefield. But while he hesitates, it is now not merely the balance of the old forces that makes him hesitate; it is the sense of the new, better, obedient self hovering before him. A few such fights and he begins to grow accustomed to the presence of something in him which represents his father, mother, or in general, *the lawgiving personality*. So, as he understands the meaning of obedience better, through his own acting out of its behests in varied circumstances, the projective elements of the alter which thus sets law to him become subjective. The socius becomes more and more intimate as a law-abiding self of his own.

Then, with this self in him, he proceeds to do with it what we always do with our thoughts of self; he "ejects" it into all the other members of the family and of his social circle. He expects, and rightly too, that each brother and sister will have the same responsibility to the *Zeitgeist* that he has—will reverence the same Penates. He exacts from them the same obedience to father and mother that he himself renders. It is amusing to see the jealousy with which one child in a family will watch the others, and see that they do not transgress the law of the family. If the father makes an exception of one little being, he is quickly "brought up" by the protests of other little beings. This is a pertinent piece of evidence to the essential truthfulness of the process depicted above, where it was said that the alter is one with the ego as a self, and that it is impossible for the child to attach predicates to the one without, *ipso facto,* attaching the same predicates to the other. To say that little brother need not obey, when I am called on to obey, is to say that little brother is in some way not a person, that is all. So we constantly have to explain to our children "the dollie cannot feel," "the leather elephant cannot eat," "the woolly dog need not be beaten when he gets in the way." "These things," in short, we say to our children, "are not selves; they have the shapes of possible selves, it may be, and they have so far served as convenient alters for you to practise on, but they need not be expected to take up with you the responsibilities of family life."

Taking up the sense of morality, therefore,—the sense that we mean when we use the word "ought,"—we now have it. Let the child continue to act by the rule of either of his former partial selves,—the private habitual self or the accommodating capricious self of impulse and sympathy,—and this new ideal of a self, a self that fulfils law, comes up to call him to account. My father, says the child, knows and would say "what" and "how"; and later, when the father-self has proved not to know all "whats" and all "hows," then my teacher, my book, my inspired writer, my God, knows "what" and "how" still. In so far as I have learned from him, I also know; and this I expect you, my brother, my friend, my alter, to know too, for our common life together. And the sense of this my self-of-conformity-to-what-he-teaches and would have me do—*this is, once for all, my conscience.*

We do not need to develop in this place a complete theory of the adult conscience; that would be outside our topic. But no account of the development of the sense of self, or of the social conditions under which the sense of self arises and grows, as the later developments of our work go on to depict them, would be adequate which left out this highest reach of the child's constructiveness. We are wont to think that we can draw lines in the attainments of mind, interpret so far and leave the rest over; but the surging activities of stimulation and response pass right over our boundary lines, and we find the germs of the higher impregnating the lower stages. The child, when once this sense of a self which is not but ought to be, comes to him, does everything under its law—whether his action conform to what he understands of it or whether he disobey and offend it. He is henceforth never innocent with the innocence of neutrality. He must think of the better with sorrow if he choose the worse, and of the worse with joy if he choose the better; and when he makes his act only in response to the measure of good which he sees, taking a step in the dark, still there is with him the necessary conviction of a self that he groped for, but did not find,—a law behind the chaos of his struggle.

It is enough, in this connection, that one or two truths regarding the nature of this ethical self should remain in mind. It is, first of all, a slow social attainment on the part of the child. He gets it only by getting certain other thoughts of self first. Then it takes on various forms, each held to only to be superseded in turn by something higher and richer. The obligation to obey it is also slow in its rise. It is a function of the self—this self, the socius—just as the tendency to yield to the behests of habit or of sympathy are simply functions, the motor side of their respective contents. The "ought" comes right up out of the "must." Transfer the self to be obeyed from the environment to the inner throne, make it an ego instead of an alter, and its authority is not a whit changed in nature. Something of its executive compulsion is gone; it is one of the very intimate differences between an ego and an alter, that the ego is its own impulsion while the alter brings compulsion; and as the alter aspect of the new self becomes more and more adequately assimilated, this difference grows more emphatic. The developed ethical sense needs less and less to appeal to an alter self, an authority, a holy oracle, to sanction the ought of conscience; it gets itself more and more promptly executed by its own inner impulsion.

And a second point to be borne in mind: that as the socius expands in the mind of the child, there is the constant tendency to make it real —to eject it—in some concrete form in the social group. The father, mother, nurse, are apt to be the first embodiment of social law, and their conduct, interpreted through obedience and imitation, the first ethical standard. And as the child finds one man or woman inadequate to the growing complications of the case, other concrete selves are erected in the same way. The popular voice, the literature of the period, the king, the state, the church,—all these are choice repositories of the ejected ethical self. Public opinion is our modern expression for the purely social form of this spirit.

Then a third point: we may ask what the law is which we find this self embodying. And we get a two-fold answer. Most comprehensively it may be said that the law is in one sense always the realized self of somebody. Apart from a self it can be nothing, because nobody would understand it. It must come out of somebody's apprehension of the social situation and the requirements of the case. The parents themselves are usually the source of family law over against the rest of the family. But that they are held to the actual socius—to the relationships existing between them and the others—is seen in any attempts they make to transcend these relationships. Suppose that the father commands each of the family to dance the highland fling and then to write a book. Whether the first of these commands be obeyed, would depend upon whether he has had a right to include in his sense of the alter personalities of the family the accomplishment in question. And, as to the second, it is likely that he would get a laugh for his pains.

But further, the law, thus tempered by the thought of the other selves involved, is a function of the socius-consciousness in each of its two aspects. It is "projective" to the child when he first receives it and submits himself to it. He does not yet understand it; it requires him to act blindly. He, in his individual capacity, is not a judge of the wisdom or appropriateness of it. The other person sets it, the self in whom he is then finding his socius realized; and the child is properly social only if he submit, even if he have to be made properly social by being compelled to submit. And the other aspect of the law is equally important, that set by the other thought of self which the socius includes, the "ejective" embodiment of the law. After the child has obeyed, and learned by obedience, he himself sets the law of the house for the other members of it. And the law then becomes "common law," inasmuch as it is engrained in the very thought of the better self of every member of the social group. All commands and behests which are not thus embodied in the spirit of the whole, are yet to a degree really only the reflection of the highest thought of self in the group, that of the father; if to the others these have not yet become "common law," the common dictates of the common social self, that is because the individuals are yet immature members of the circle or family. Put briefly, all law must arise somewhere in the family from the legitimate development of the social self; and it is realized, or obeyed as law, only as the members of the family come, each in his turn, to mould his social self into intelligent observance of it, and intelligent enforcement of it. And the family is typical of the community.

A final observation is this: there is, as was intimated above, a sense in which the socius, the social self, and with it the ethical self, is a self of habit. If this thought of self which we are calling the "socius" really be, in so far as the child understands his own thought of it, a sense of his denials of both his lower and less social selves—the self of private habit and the self of accommodation—in favour of a law set him by an alter, then this very attitude must become in some degree a habit, a tendency to look for a higher law, a moving toward a higher authority. But it is a habit of *acting*, not a habit of *action*. It involves the most acutely painful and difficult violations of old habits of action. *It is a habit of violating habits*—that is the relation of morality to habit. And it is an interesting side-light on the method of the rise of the successive selves by imitation and submission, that in the lower stages of evolution we find the organism working under the same subtlety. The organism develops only by cultivating the habit of imitating; while the very value of imitation is that by it the organism acquires new accommodations by breaking up habits already acquired. The organism must be ready, by a habit of acting, to impair the habits of action it already has. And the origin of the moral sense by this method shows it to be an imitative function. We do right by habitually imitating a larger self whose injunctions run counter to the tendencies of our partial selves.

*   *   *

We have seen the child's mind showing a finer sort of appreciation of the meaning of the actions of his social fellows, as he grows into the more adequate realization of personality; and we have found him gradually forming a thought of self which is above the examples of personality which men as individuals show. He reaches on to an ideal self, which represents his best accommodation to self in general; the regular, law-abiding, sanction-bringing, duty-observing self hovers over his thought, inspires it, and regulates its tendencies to action. I say that it represents his accommodations, since, as we have been seeing all along, it is by his action on the "copies" which he gets that he realizes and interprets their meaning in his own growth. This general notion of self is, like all general notions considered as general, not a presentation, not a mental content, but an attitude, a way of acting; and the child has to bring all the partial personal tendencies to action which spring up on the thought of the partial more isolated selves of his habit, into the way of action which we call ethical conduct. The growth of the ethical sense is a growth in motor accommodation. Viewed on the side of what it has already hardened into, on the side of habit, it shows the man's or the child's actual morality, his degree of actual conformity to the ethical ideal; and, viewed on the side of the ideal itself, its unrealized part, its tendency to perfect lawfulness and complete submission without revolt, it shows his obligation.

Of course both of these phases tend to terminate on actual persons; all attitudes have to have objective termini. The child's actual mental picture of what is good in a person is made up from his own acts and the acts which he conceives as possibly his own; this is the concrete body of his ethical ideal. And then, so far as he feels it to be inadequate, he seeks to find, in the persons projective to him, some one or more whose actions are better than his. This means "better" in the vague undefined way that all "projective" experience must be. He knows that the father, for example, is good in the way that he understands goodness; but he feels that the father is also better, in the goodness which is his alone, *i.e.,* which the child cannot yet understand nor illustrate by his own acts or thought.

Now this latter aspect of his attitude is, I think, what we mean by sentiment: it is the emotional or active tendency of consciousness away beyond the confines of its actual interpretations. It represents the further drift of habit toward its own completion; it is the way we discount, in feeling, our own future progress in personal attainment and growth. It is essentially "prospective" in its nature. Just as we get the thought of the ego as a fact, as a thing which is, by a growth upon which we are able to look back in retrospect, and say, "this is my history; here is the road which I have travelled up to personality, and to my social place;" so we get the ego that is to be, that "ought to be," by a prophecy of similar growth along the same path. We hie us onward by anticipation. We long to think of other men as being further on, and we give them reverence by turning toward them the sentiments which stand in us as the guerdon of our hopes. Imitation runs through it all; imitation is, indeed, the essential method of growth in this active stretch of our energies toward the ideal. For the interpretations which our past actions express were secured by the imitative absorption of the personal suggestive copies of the social environment; and the pro-jective part of the ideal set us by others is, in so far as we picture it at all, a reconstruction, in an imitative way, of the same material. And when the actor goes on to attain the new growth which brings him further towards the ideal, it is again by actually finding in the social circle better illustrations of righteousness, beauty, etc., which he takes to himself by imitation. This I need not enlarge upon. But the actual phases of the sentiments which thus arise about the ideal growth of personality may now claim some attention; since they will be seen in the sequel to be factors of the greatest importance in the organization and progress of society.

The most general and important phase of ethical sentiment is that known in theoretical ethics as the sense of obligation. Defining this sense, as the sense of the lack of unity in the highest region of motor function, we may point out a little more fully its mode of working and its bearings in the mental and social life.

The growing habit which is seen in the thought of an ideal self stands as the goal of assimilation for the partial expressions of per-sonality issuing in particular selfish or generous actions. The fact, how-ever, that these particular actions are not inhibited or modified in view of the ideal, but get performed in spite of the need of further co-ordination and assimilation to the ideal copy, is felt as a state of tension and lack of equilibrium, which accounts for the real antithesis of tendencies which appears in every ethical situation. The sense of obli-gation brings to consciousness two antithetical thoughts of personal-ity: that of the self as it stands, more or less complete in habit, with its well-known tendencies to action; and over against this the sense of the ideal self, the being perhaps temporarily embodied in father, priest, or whoever-else, the better self from whose actions the copy is to come for the further reduction of the selfishly or generously capricious self to order and goodness. I feel that I ought to be like the better person; and even though I cannot see how this better person will act in this case or that, yet I have enough of a habit of submission to him, or enough reverence for his ideals, to feel my personal actions tending to lose their independence and their adequacy in my own eyes. In the mind of the child, this sense of "oughtness" arises in a very interesting way, as soon as he has learned to obey in measure sufficient to set the habit of submission on its feet; for, in so doing, the beginning of assimilation to the larger copy set by the injunction of another is secured; and on that basis, the further growth may be expected to proceed by the internal injunction which this very tendency to a larger assimilation creates.

The leading-string in the child's ethical growth is, all the time, the presence of other persons from whom the "word of command" and the suggestion and example of goodness, directly come. The very strenuousness of command at first breaks in upon his personal capricious reactions, and so starts his sense of a larger order. Then the constant teachings of the actions of others, their conduct toward each other, to which the child comes as a curious spectator, their ways of leading him out into his imitations, and their comments upon the interpretations which he makes when he comes to act more complexly for himself, all this—in this sphere as in the wider sphere of personal attainment in general, in which we have already traced the influences which he experiences—stimulates, confirms, and controls his growth. Further, he finds two social ways of showing his progress. He constantly exhibits his attainments in this direction, as in others—that first; and then he lays down the crude law of his own righteousness to the other children, and even seeks occasion to find his elders violating what they have taught him. This is a natural and necessary movement in the growth of the ethical sense. It indicates that the child's sense that my assimilation of the self of habit, the self which he has ejected outward and lodged in me, must go on just as his does; and that the conduct of this myself-of-habit which does not show proper reduction to the growing ideal of a self "ought" not to act as it does. The two applications of this "ought not"—that to me and that to him—are not really two; they are one; for the very exhibition of self to which the ought-not applies is the same in me as in him.

This latter it is which gives its social value to the experience. It elevates the social basis of the emotions, and attitudes generally, right up into the ethical sphere, and shows the moral sense to be essentially a social thing. The child's exhibitions of his morality, and his requirement that we shall recognize and confirm them by ourselves conforming to them, is an outlet for the intimate and hidden movement of his growth. Without this social appeal and its consequences, he could not be sure of his progress, or have that sense of social security in his judgments which makes his morality really a part of the world morality. In short, what, on this subjective side, is a spontaneous appeal of the child to the social environment for confirmation and support, is on the objective side evidence that the child is growing under direct social control.

The second general social feature of the child's subjective ethical experience is seen in the possibility of his further progress at any time. As he gets more adequate views of morality, and incorporates them in his own self-sense, under stress of the sense of obligation, his sense of the ideal grows too. His obligations, instead of diminishing, only increase.

As the child grows up under the influence of teacher, friend, companion, his spontaneous reflections and judgments agree, in the main, with those of his social *milieu*. His ethical insight, as his intellectual inventiveness,—only much more,—is limited by his limitations of social growth. And since these limitations are set by the system of influences which bear in upon him in the social group, and which he cannot transcend, his own opinions and judgments are as strictly a matter of general acceptance as if he and others had been born with a set of ready-made ethical intuitions in common. But it is because these so-called intuitions are progressive things, that society and the individual in society do not stand still in the ethical life any more absolutely than in the intellectual, or in the purely social life. Ethical phenomena are phenomena of organization,—that is, in their origin,—and the solidarity of the results, the apparent universality of ethical sentiment, is due to the fact that this sentiment is a thing of common and united attainment. It is in society because it is in all the individuals; but it is in each individual because it is already in society. It is one of those genetic circles by which nature so often works out her development problems. Of course we must not leave out the actual increments of progress which the individuals make, the ways in which the best individuals improve upon the lessons which they learn from society, and so go on, in turn, to teach society; but that is apart from the topic of our present interest,—the topic which we set ourselves when we inquire into the individual's method of attaining to ethical sentiment and character. The point here is that he learns his ethical lessons from society; and that means that he learns them from his ancestors to the same extent that he would if they were knit into his original endowment; and further, that they are of the same general and universal character as if they had been imposed by some authority upon both the individual and society, instead of coming by the natural process of learning and growth.

The child feels the impulsion of all examples, both the selfish and the social, and if this impulsion were the "ought," then indeed he would have two "oughts," as on occasion he has two "musts"; but he now feels—after the ideal thought of personality has a good beginning in him—that some of these actions on both sides will assimilate to this ideal, are called for by this, will strengthen and reinforce this, while others will not; then comes the sense that these are good and the rest in comparison with them are bad. He says: "I ought to do *this,* since the good man, my ideal personality, does this; I ought not to do *that,* because he does it not." And further, the reason that he does it not, is just because the action which he does not do represents one of the lower concrete habits, one whose indulgence would tend to set more firmly the antithesis between the partial selves on the one hand, and between them and the higher ideal self on the other hand. To act selfishly—or to act capriciously, even though the action be a generous one—is to undo my growth toward a law-abiding, reasonable, and, in its highest sense, *social* person.

The sense of a self that is good, regular, law-abiding, ethical, the standard of all my judgments of right and wrong, must be, in my consciousness of it, a public self. This means that when I think of this ideal, when I bring a given action to the test of assimilation to it,—for I cannot think of it in any circumstances which do not call for its application to a concrete case of action,—a part of the content of my thought is necessarily the thought that the judgment is one of social generality, that others are also making the same assimilation of this act to the same ideal. In case, then, I know that the action is quite private, quite secret, absolutely unknown to anybody else, then the full reinstatement of the conditions of an ethical judgment are, *ipso facto,* not present. My ideal category of action is not brought out; for to bring it out requires the very sense of *publicity* which my knowledge of privacy contradicts.

My thought of the ideal self is general; it must apply in all the particular cases. Whatever mental movement it gives rise to, must be present in all the particular cases. I find it giving rise to a feeling of condemnation, in my case, when a certain action is before me. It must give rise to the same condemnation in the mind of each of them. But, it is said, this is very different from saying that I must think that it is actually present to them. Certainly; but we must remember that I cannot think of myself with anything reflectively before me without in the act thinking ejectively on the same content; hence, to think of myself with this case before me is to think of other men also with this case before them. To fall short of this is to think, not in terms of the general thought of self, not with reference to the ideal; but in reference to some particular partial self to whose knowledge the case before me is restricted. So it is not enough that I feel what others would say if they knew; *I must feel that others are judging because I judge.*

If this is so, then in the case in which I am conscious that no one but myself knows the act which I am committing, this consciousness really contradicts an element in the mental psychosis which arouses the ethical sentiment; and as long as I fully assure myself of this, I cannot get a completely moral judgment. Of course it is impossible to maintain this state of mind in its purity; the drift toward the general statement of the case in social terms tends to establish the proper ethical sense, and imagination supplies the needed elements by whispering what my friends would say if they knew my conduct. But this does not take the place of actual knowledge; although it often brings on most tragic illusions and hallucinations of persecution, discovery, pursuit by priests, bodily occupation by devils, etc. These latter cases indeed would serve, I think, if adequately investigated by ethical writers who give themselves to casuistry, to show two very instructive points in the social nature of the ethical sense: first, the point that hallucinations of social opinion may come to take the place of personal social thought and of real social tests; and second, that actual social opinion may create illusions of conscience where the personal ego thought is weak or deranged. In other words, there are necessarily the two ingredients, the subjective and the ejective ingredients, in the general thought of personality; either may be deranged, to the extent which we describe as hallucination, in different types of real moral insanity.

There can be no opposition between society and the individual in the matter of the essential demands of the moral and religious consciousness. The fact of "publicity" in all religious and ethical thought makes it necessary that the same ideal should be erected in the individual and in the community in which the individual is reared, since the growth of the ideal self-thought in the individual depends constantly upon the absorption of moral and religious suggestions from the social environment. Both the individuals and society must be moral and religious, and similarly moral and religious. Speaking, then, of the "matter" of the ideal consciousness, as it is realized in the "ought" judgments, on the one hand, and in the feelings of dependence and mystery, on the other hand, we may say that opposition does not normally arise between society and the man. Their sanction is the same,— a function of the necessary movement of the human mind in its development toward an ideal self-thought. In the ethical judgments this sanction is administered exclusively by the individual conscience. It is a personal sanction; yet the "publicity" of it makes it also a matter of mutual judgment, to which each individual is, as we have seen, peculiarly sensitive.

As far as there is in informal urgency about religious conformity,— a sort of sanction exerted upon the individual through the social usages and strenuous beliefs of his community,—this comes under the head of pedagogical sanction of the more conventional type seen in public opinion, of which we have already said enough. The average man yields so readily to suggestion in this sphere, and goes, indeed, so readily to extremes in his suggestibility, that the sphere of religion becomes and has always been a stronghold of the conservative spirit. This is the more emphasized in history by the dogmatic claims of religious systems, which amount to civil sanctions of a supernatural kind, so to speak, coming to reinforce the pedagogical sanctions, and so to create what may be called a new sanction altogether,—that of divine authority.

The content of religious sentiment takes on, by the very conditions of its rise in and with the individual's personal growth, certain forms of rational statement. The categories of personality, cause, and design are among these constant intelligent moulds of the religious ideal; and the concrete filling which they get, once and again, has its character from the degree of refinement which the personality constructions, sustaining the ideal, show at this epoch or that. *There must always arise, religious doctrines in the individual and religious dogmas in society.*

There is a necessary *ejective postulation* of the intellectual content of the ideal; in this case, of the religious formulation. The existence of the object of worship is a function of its very thought; for there is no divorce between personal thought and personal belief. Reality comes only by an artificial abstraction from thought. So there is al- ways a direct objectifying of religious sentiment in the world. Men are theists in some form.

And man is not isolated. His sense of the publicity of his beliefs makes him, in a sense, a legislator for others. His own sense of ethical obligation is just this element of publicity itself reflected subjectively. So the obligation to do what he ought and to make others do what they ought is never absent from his sense of the divine being who is the embodiment of what ought to be done, and the source of its sanction.

There arises, therefore, *ipso facto,* with the religious sentiment, some public religious institution. It is a social institution. In early times, before the differentiation of the sentiments, it is also a political in- stitution. This institution becomes, from the element of publicity, more a rallying-place for conservatism than any other institution. It has the supernatural sanction direct from the personal divinity. The individual who is so far exceptional in his personal growth as to reach an intellectual construction of the religious ideal different in its form from the form thus divinely sanctioned, is a rebel against society and against God. And it is only a step for society to conclude, in such a case, as it concludes in all the cases of anti-social individuals who are harmful to established institutions, that such an individual should be suppressed.

THE DEVELOPMENT OF MORALITY
IN THE CHILD

BY

JEAN PIAGET

ONE may say that in a certain sense neither logical nor moral norms
are innate in the individual mind. We can find, no doubt, even before
language, all the elements of rationality and morality. Thus sensori-
motor intelligence gives rise to operations of assimilation and construction, in which it is not hard to see the functional equivalent of the
logic of classes and of relations. Similarly the child's behaviour towards persons shows signs from the first of those sympathetic tendencies and affective reactions in which one can easily see the raw material
of all subsequent moral behaviour. But an intelligent act can only be
called logical and a good-hearted impulse moral from the moment
that certain norms impress a given structure and rules of equilibrium
upon this material. Logic is not co-extensive with intelligence, but
consists of the sum-total of rules of control which intelligence makes
use of for its own direction. Morality plays a similar part with regard
to the affective life. Now there is nothing that allows us to affirm the
existence of such norms in the pre-social behaviour occurring before
the appearance of language. The control characteristic of sensori-
motor intelligence is of external origin: it is things themselves that
constrain the organism to select which steps it will take; the initial
intellectual activity does actively seek for truth. Similarly, it is persons
external to him who canalize the child's elementary feelings, those
feelings do not tend to regulate themselves from within.

This does not mean that everything in the *a priori* view is to be
rejected. Of course the *a priori* never manifests itself in the form of
ready-made innate mechanisms. The *a priori* is the obligatory element,
and the necessary connections only impose themselves little by little, as
evolution proceeds. It is at the end of knowledge and not in its beginnings that the mind becomes conscious of the laws immanent to it.
Yet to speak of directed evolution and asymptotic advance towards a
necessary ideal is to recognize the existence of a something which acts
from the first in the direction of this evolution. But under what form

does this "something" present itself? Under the form of a structure that straightway organizes the contents of consciousness, or under the form of a functional law of equilibrium, unconscious as yet because the mind has not yet achieved this equilibrium, and to be manifested only in and through the multitudinous structures that are to appear later? There seems to us to be no doubt about the answer. There is in the very functioning of sensori-motor operations a search for coherence and organization. Alongside, therefore, of the incoherence that characterizes the successive steps taken by elementary intelligence we must admit the existence of an ideal equilibrium, indefinable as structure but implied in the functioning that is at work. Such is the *a priori:* it is neither a principle from which concrete actions can be deduced nor a structure of which the mind can become conscious as such, but it is a sum-total of functional relations implying the distinction between the existing states of disequilibrium and an ideal equilibrium yet to be realized.

How then will the mind extract norms in the true sense from this functional equilibrium? It will form structures by means of an adequate conscious realization (*prise de conscience*). To ensure that the functional search for organization exhibited by the initial sensori-motor and affective activity give rise to rules of organization properly so called, it is sufficient that the mind should become conscious of this search and of the laws governing it, thus translating into structure what till then had been function and nothing more.

But this coming into consciousness or conscious realization is not a simple operation and is bound up with a whole set of psychological conditions. It is here that psycho-sociological research becomes indispensable to the theory of norms and that the genetic parallelism existing between the formation of the logical and of the moral consciousness can be observed.

In the first place it should be noticed that the individual is not capable of achieving this conscious realization by himself, and consequently does not straight away succeed in establishing norms properly so-called. It is in this sense that reason in its double aspect, both logical and moral, is a collective product. This does not mean that society has conjured up rationality out of the void, nor that there does not exist a spirit of humanity that is superior to society because dwelling both within the individual and the social group. It means that social life is necessary if the individual is to become conscious of the functioning of his own mind and thus to transform into norms properly so called the simple functional equilibria immanent to all mental and even all vital activity.

For the individual, left to himself, remains egocentric. By which we mean simply this—Just as at first the mind, before it can dissociate what belongs to objective laws from what is bound up with the sum of subjective conditions, confuses itself with the universe, so does the individual begin by understanding and feeling everything through the medium of himself before distinguishing what belongs to things and other people from what is the result of his own particular intellectual and affective perspective. At this stage, therefore, the individual cannot be conscious of his own thought, since consciousness of self implies a perpetual comparison of the self with other people. Thus from the logical point of view egocentrism would seem to involve a sort of alogicality, such that sometimes affectivity gains the ascendant over objectivity, and sometimes the relations arising from personal activity prove stronger than the relations that are independent of the self. And from the moral point of view, egocentrism involves a sort of anomy such that tenderness and disinterestedness can go hand in hand with a naïve selfishness, and yet the child not feel spontaneously himself to be better in one case than the other. Just as the ideas which enter his mind appear from the first in the form of beliefs and not of hypotheses requiring verification, so do the feelings that arise in the child's consciousness appear to him from the first as having value and not as having to be submitted to some ulterior evaluation. It is only through contact with the judgments and evaluations of others that this intellectual and affective anomy will gradually yield to the pressure of collective logical and moral laws.

In the second place, the relations of constraint and unilateral respect which are spontaneously established between child and adult contribute to the formation of a first type of logical and moral control. But this control is insufficient of itself to eliminate childish egocentrism. From the intellectual point of view this respect of the child for the adult gives rise to an "annunciatory" conception of truth: the mind stops affirming what it likes to affirm and falls in with the opinion of those around it. This gives birth to a distinction which is equivalent to that of truth and falsehood: some affirmations are recognized as valid while others are not. But it goes without saying that although this distinction marks an important advance as compared to the anomy of egocentric thought, it is none the less irrational in principle. For if we are to speak of truth as rational, it is not sufficient that the contents of one's statements should conform with reality: reason must have taken active steps to obtain these contents and reason must be in a position to control the agreement or disagreement of these statements with reality. Now, in the case under discussion, reason is still very far removed from this autonomy: truth means whatever conforms with the spoken word of the adult. Whether the child has himself discovered the propositions which he asks the adult to sanction with his authority, or whether he merely repeats what the adult has said, in both cases there is intellectual constraint put upon an inferior by a superior, and therefore heteronomy. Thus, far from checking childish egocentrism at its source, such a submission tends on the contrary partly to consolidate the mental habits characteristic of egocentrism. Just as, if left to himself, the child believes every idea that enters his head instead of regarding it as a hypothesis to be verified, so the child who is submissive to the word of his parents believes without question everything he is told, instead of perceiving the element of uncertainty and search in adult thought. The self's good pleasure is simply replaced by the good pleasure of a supreme authority. There is progress here, no doubt, since such a transference accustoms the mind to look for a common truth, but this progress is big with danger if the supreme authority be not in its turn criticized in the name of reason. Now, criticism is born of discussion, and discussion is only possible among equals: cooperation alone will therefore accomplish what intellectual constraint failed to bring about. And indeed we constantly have occasion throughout our schools to notice the combined effects of this constraint and of intellectual egocentrism. What is "verbalism," for example, if not the joint result of oral authority and the syncretism peculiar to the egocentric language of the child? In short, in order to really socialize the child, co-operation is necessary, for it alone will succeed in delivering him from the mystical power of the word of the adult.

An exact counterpart of these findings about intellectual constraint is supplied by the observations on the effect of moral constraint. Just as the child believes in the adult's omniscience so also does he unquestioningly believe in the absolute value of the imperatives he receives. This result of unilateral respect is of great practical value, for it is in this way that there is formed an elementary sense of duty and the first normative control of which the child is capable. But it seemed to us clear that this acquisition was not sufficient to form true morality. For conduct to be characterized as moral there must be something more than an outward agreement between its content and that of the commonly accepted rules: it is also requisite that the mind should tend towards morality as to an autonomous good and should itself be capable of appreciating the value of the rules that are proposed to it. Now in the case under discussion, the good is simply what is in conformity with heteronomous commands. And as in the case of intellectual development, moral constraint has the effect of partly consolidating the habits characteristic of egocentrism. Even when the child's behaviour is not just a calculated attempt to reconcile his individual interest with the letter of the law, one can observe (as we had occasion to do in the game of marbles) a curious mixture of respect for the law and of caprice in its application. The law is still external to the mind, which cannot therefore be transformed by it. Besides, since he regards the adult as the source of the law, the child is only raising up the will of the adult to the rank of the supreme good after having previously accorded this rank to the various dictates of his own desires. An advance, no doubt, but again an advance charged with doubtful consequences if cooperation does not come and establish norms sufficiently independent to subject even the respect due to the adult to this inner ideal. And indeed so long as unilateral respect is alone at work, we see a "moral realism" developing which is the equivalent of "verbal realism." Resting in part on the externality of rules, such a realism is also kept going by all the other forms of realism peculiar to the egocentric mentality of the child. Only cooperation will correct this attitude, thus showing that in the moral sphere, as in matters of intelligence, it plays a liberating and a constructive role.

Hence a third analogy between moral and intellectual evolution: cooperation alone leads to autonomy. With regard to logic, cooperation is at first a source of criticism; thanks to the mutual control which it introduces, it suppresses both the spontaneous conviction that characterizes egocentrism and the blind faith in adult authority. Thus, discussion gives rise to reflection and objective verification. But through this very fact cooperation becomes the source of constructive values. It leads to the recognition of the principles of formal logic in so far as these normative laws are necessary to common search for truth. It leads, above all, to a conscious realization of the logic of relations, since reciprocity on the intellectual plane necessarily involves the elaboration of those laws of perspective which we find in the operations distinctive of systems of relations.

In the same way, with regard to moral realities, cooperation is at first the source of criticism and individualism. For by comparing his own private motives with the rules adopted by each and sundry, the individual is led to judge objectively the acts and commands of other people, including adults. Whence the decline of unilateral respect and the primacy of personal judgment. But in consequence of this, cooperation suppresses both egocentrism and moral realism, and thus achieves an interiorization of rules. A new morality follows upon that of pure duty. Heteronomy steps aside to make way for a consciousness of good, of which the autonomy results from the acceptance of the norms of reciprocity. Obedience withdraws in favour of the idea of justice and of mutual service, now the source of all the obligations which till then had been imposed as incomprehensible commands. In a word, cooperation on the moral plane brings about transformations exactly parallel to those of which we have just been recalling the existence in the intellectual domain.

Is there any need, by way of conclusion, to point to the educational consequences of such observations? If education claims to be the direct application of what we know about Child Psychology, it would not be necessary. It is obvious that our results are as unfavourable to the method of authority as to purely individualistic methods. It is absurd and even immoral to wish to impose upon the child a fully worked-out system of discipline when the social life of children amongst themselves is sufficiently developed to give rise to a discipline infinitely nearer to that inner submission which is the mark of adult morality. It is idle, again, to try and transform the child's mind from outside, when his own taste for active research and his desire for cooperation suffice to ensure a normal intellectual development. The adult must therefore be a collaborator and not a master, from this double point of view, moral and rational. But conversely, it would be unwise to rely upon biological "nature" alone to ensure the dual progress of conscience and intelligence, when we realize to what extent all moral as all logical norms are the result of cooperation.

RETRIBUTIVE AND DISTRIBUTIVE JUSTICE

BY

JEAN PIAGET

LET us distinguish retributive from distributive justice, for the two go together only when reduced to their fundamental elements, and let us begin with distributive judgment, whose fate in the course of mental development seems to indicate that it is the most fundamental form of justice itself.

Distributive justice can be reduced to the ideas of equality or equity. From the point of view of epistemology such notions cannot but be regarded as *a priori*, if by *a priori* we mean, not of course an innate idea, but a norm, towards which reason cannot help but tend as it is gradually refined and purified. For reciprocity imposes itself on practical reason as logical principles impose themselves morally on theoretical reason. But from the psychological point of view, which is that of what is, not of what should be, an *a priori* norm has no existence except as a form of equilibrium. It constitutes the ideal equilibrium towards which the phenomena tend, and the whole question is still to know why, the facts being what they are, their form of equilibrium is such and no other. This last problem, which is of a causal order, must not be confused with the first, which can be solved only by abstract reflection. The two will coincide only when mind and reality become coextensive. In the meantime let us confine ourselves to psychological analysis, it being understood that the experimental explanation of the notion of reciprocity can in no way contradict its *a priori* aspect.

From this point of view it cannot be denied that the idea of equality or of distributive justice possesses individual or biological roots which are necessary but not sufficient conditions for its development. One can observe in the child at a very early stage two reactions which will play a very important part in this particular elaboration. Jealousy, to begin with, appears extremely early in babies: infants of 8 to 12 months often give signs of violent rage when they see another child seated on their mother's knees, or when a toy is taken from them and given to another child. On the other hand, one can observe in conjunction with imitation and the ensuing sympathy, altruistic reactions and a tendency to share, which are of equally early date. An infant of 12 months will hand his toys over to another child, and so on. But it goes without saying that equalitarianism can never be regarded as a sort of instinct or spontaneous product of the individual mind. The reactions we have just alluded to lead to a capricious alternation of egoism and sympathy. It is true, of course, that jealousy prevents other people from taking advantage of us, and the need to communicate prevents the self from taking advantage of others. But for true equality and a genuine desire for reciprocity there must be a collective rule which is the *sui generis* product of life lived in common. There must be born of the actions and reactions of individuals upon each other the consciousness of a necessary equilibrium binding upon and limiting both "alter" and "ego." And this ideal equilibrium, dimly felt on the occasion of every quarrel and every peace-making, naturally presupposes a long reciprocal education of the children by each other.

But between the primitive individual reactions, which give the need for justice a chance of showing itself, and the full possession of the idea of equality, our enquiry shows the existence of a long interval in time. For it is not until about 10–12, at the age where children's societies attain to the maximum of organization and codification of rules, that justice really frees herself from all her adventitious trappings. Here, as before, we must therefore distinguish constraint from cooperation, and our problem will then be to determine whether it is unilateral respect, the source of constraint, or mutual respect, the source of co-operation, that is the preponderating factor in the evolution of equalitarian justice.

Now on this point the results of our analysis seem to leave no room for doubt. Authority as such cannot be the source of justice, because the development of justice presupposes autonomy. This does not mean, of course, that the adult plays no part in the development of justice, even of the distributive kind. In so far as he practises reciprocity with the child and preaches by example rather than by precept, he exercises here, as always, an enormous influence. But the most direct effect of adult ascendancy is the feeling of duty, and there is a sort of contradiction between the submission demanded by duty and the complete autonomy required by the development of justice. For, resting as it does on equality and reciprocity, justice can only come into being by free consent. Adult authority even if it acts in conformity with justice, has therefore the effect of weakening what constitutes the essence of justice. Hence those reactions which we observed among the smaller children, who confused what was just with what was law, law being whatever is prescribed by adult authority. Justice is identified with formulated rules—as indeed it is in the opinion of a great many adults, of all, namely, who have not succeeded in setting autonomy of conscience above social prejudice and the written law.

Thus adult authority, although perhaps it constitutes a necessary moment in the moral evolution of the child, is not in itself sufficient to create a sense of justice. This can develop only through the progress made by cooperation and mutual respect—cooperation between children to begin with, and then between child and adult as the child approaches adolescence and comes, secretly at least, to consider himself as the adult's equal.

In support of these hypotheses, one is struck by the extent to which, in child as well as in adult society, the progress of equalitarianism goes hand in hand with that of "organic" solidarity, i.e. with the results of cooperation. For if we compare the societies formed by children of 5–7 with those formed at the age of 10–12, we can observe four interdependent transformations. In the first place, while the little ones' society constitutes an amorphous and unorganized whole, in which all the individuals are alike, that of the older children achieves an organic unity, with laws and regulations, and often even a division of social work (leaders, referees, etc.). In the second place, there exists between the older children a far stronger moral solidarity than among the younger ones. The little ones are simultaneously egocentric and impersonal, yielding to every suggestion that comes along and to every current of imitation. In their case the group feeling is a sort of communion of submission to seniors and to the dictates of adults. Older children, on the contrary, ban lies among themselves, cheating, and everything that compromises solidarity. The group feeling is therefore more direct and more consciously cultivated. In the third place, personality develops in the measure that discussion and the interchange of ideas replace the simple mutual imitation of the younger children. In the fourth place, the sense of equality is, as we have just seen, far stronger in the older than in the younger children, the latter being primarily under the domination of authority. Thus the bond between equalitarianism and solidarity is a universal psychological phenomenon, and not, as might appear to be the case in adult society, dependent only upon political factors. With children as with adults, there exist two psychological types of social equilibrium—a type based on the constraint of age, which excludes both equality and "organic" solidarity, but which canalizes individual egocentrism without excluding it, and a type based on cooperation and resting on equality and solidarity.

Let us pass on to retributive justice. In contrast to the principles of distributive justice, there does not seem to be in the ideas of retribution or punishment any properly rational or *a priori* element. For while the idea of equality gains in value as intellectual development proceeds, the idea of punishment seems actually to lose ground. To put things more precisely, we must, as we have already done, distinguish two separate elements in the idea of retribution. On the one hand there are the notions of expiation and reward, which seems to constitute what is most specific about the idea of punishment, and on the other, there are the ideas of "putting things right" or making reparation, as well as the measures which aim at restoring the bond of solidarity broken by the offending act. These last ideas, which we have grouped under the title of "punishment by reciprocity," seem to draw only on the conceptions of equality and reciprocity. It is the former set of ideas that tends to be eliminated when the morality of heteronomy and authority is superseded by the morality of autonomy. The second set are of far more enduring stuff, precisely because they are based upon something more than the idea of punishment.

Whatever may be said of this evolution of values, it is possible here, as in connection with distributive justice, to assign three sources to the three chief aspects of retribution. Certain individual reactions condition the appearance of retribution; adult constraint explains the formation of the idea of expiation, and cooperation accounts for the eventual fate of the idea of punishment.

It cannot be denied that the idea of punishment has psycho-biological roots. Blow calls for blow and gentleness moves us to gentleness. The instinctive reactions of defence and sympathy thus bring about a sort of elementary reciprocity which is the soil that retribution demands for its growth. But this soil is naturally not enough in itself, and the individual factors cannot of themselves transcend the stage of impulsive vengeance without finding themselves subject—at least implicitly—to the system of regulated and codified sanctions implied in retributive justice.

Things change with the intervention of the adult. Very early in life, even before the infant can speak, its conduct is constantly being subjected to approval or censure. According to circumstances people are pleased with baby and smile at it, or else frown and leave it to cry, and the very inflections in the voices of those that surround it are alone sufficient to constitute an incessant retribution. During the years that follow, the child is watched over continuously, everything he does and says is controlled, gives rise to encouragement or reproof, and the vast majority of adults still look upon punishment, corporal or otherwise, as perfectly legitimate. It is obviously these reactions on the part of the adult, due generally to fatigue or impatience, but often, too, coldly thought out on his part, it is obviously these adult reactions, we repeat, that are the psychological starting-point of the idea of expiatory punishment. If the child felt nothing but fear or mistrust, as may happen in extreme cases, this would simply lead to open war. But as the child loves his parents and feels respect for their actions, punishment appears to him as morally obligatory and necessarily connected with the act that provoked it. Disobedience—the principle of all "sin"—is a breach of the normal relations between parent and child; some reparation is therefore necessary, and since parents display their "righteous anger" by the various reactions that take the form of punishments, to accept these punishments constitutes the most natural form of reparation. The pain inflicted thus seems to re-establish the relations that had momentarily been interrupted, and in this way the idea of expiation becomes incorporated in the values of the morality of authority. In our view, therefore, this "primitive" and materialistic conception of expiatory punishment is not imposed as such by the adult upon the child, and it was perhaps never invented by a psychologically adult mind; but it is the inevitable product of punishment as refracted in the mystically realistic mentality of the child.

If, then, there is such close solidarity between the idea of punishment and unilateral respect *plus* the morality of authority, it follows that all progress in cooperation and mutual respect will be such as to gradually eliminate the idea of expiation from the idea of punishment, and to reduce the latter to a simple act of reparation, or a simple measure of reciprocity. And this is actually what we believe we have observed in the child. As respect for adult punishment gradually grows less, certain types of conduct develop which one cannot but class under the heading of retributive justice. We see an example of this in the judgments made by our subjects on the topic of "hitting back"; the child feels more and more that it is fair that he should defend himself and to give back the blows he receives. This is retribution without doubt, but the idea of expiation seems not to play the slightest part in these judgments. It is entirely a matter of reciprocity. So-and-so takes upon himself the right to give me a punch, he therefore gives me the right to do the same to him. Similarly, the cheat gains a certain advantage by the fact of cheating; it is therefore legitimate to restore equality by turning him out of the game or by taking back the marbles he has won.

It may be objected that such a morality will not take one very far, since the best adult consciences ask for something more than the practice of mere reciprocity. Charity and the forgiving of injuries done to one are, in the eyes of many, far greater things than sheer equality. In this connection, moralists have often laid stress on the conflict between justice and love, since justice often prescribes what is reproved by love and *vice versa*. But in our view, it is precisely this concern with reciprocity which leads one beyond the rather short-sighted justice of those children who give back the mathematical equivalent of the blows they have received. Like all spiritual realities which are the result, not of external constraint but of autonomous development, reciprocity has two aspects: reciprocity as a fact, and reciprocity as an ideal, as something which ought to be. The child begins by simply practising reciprocity, in itself not so easy a thing as one might think. Then, once he has grown accustomed to this form of equilibrium in his actions, his behaviour is altered from within, its form reacting, as it were, upon its content. What is regarded as just is no longer merely reciprocal action, but primarily behaviour that admits of indefinitely sustained reciprocity. The motto "Do as you would be done by," thus comes to replace the conception of crude equality. The child sets forgiveness above revenge, not out of weakness, but because "there is no end" to revenge (a boy of 10). Just as in logic, we can see a sort of reaction of the form of the proposition upon its content when the principle of contradiction leads to a simplification and purification of the initial definitions, so in ethics, reciprocity implies a purification of the deeper trend of conduct, guiding it by gradual stages to universality itself. Without leaving the sphere of reciprocity, generosity—the characteristic of our third stage—allies itself to justice pure and simple, and between the more refined forms of justice, such as equity and love properly so called, there is no longer any real conflict.

In conclusion, then, we find in the domain of justice, as in other domains, that opposition of two moralities to which we have so often drawn the reader's attention. The ethics of authority, which is that of duty and obedience, leads, in the domain of justice, to the confusion of what is just with the content of established law and to the acceptance of expiatory punishment. The ethics of mutual respect, which is that of good (as opposed to duty), and of autonomy, leads, in the domain of justice, to the development of equality, which is the idea at the bottom of distributive justice and of reciprocity. Solidarity between equals appears once more as the source of a whole set of complementary and coherent moral ideas which characterize the rational mentality. The question may, of course, be raised whether such realities could ever develop without a preliminary stage, during which the child's conscience is moulded by his unilateral respect for the adult. As this cannot be put to the test by experiment, it is idle to argue the point. But what is certain is that the moral equilibrium achieved by the complementary conceptions of heteronomous duty and of punishment properly so called, is an unstable equilibrium, owing to the fact that it does not allow the personality to grow and expand to its full extent. As the child grows up, the subjection of his conscience to the mind of the adult seems to him less legitimate, and except in cases of arrested moral development, caused either by decisive inner submission (those adults who remain children all their lives), or by sustained revolt, unilateral respect tends of itself to grow into mutual respect and to the state of cooperation which constitutes the normal equilibrium. It is obvious that since in our modern societies the common morality which regulates the relations of adults to each other is that of cooperation, the development of child morality will be accelerated by the examples that surround it. Actually, however, this is more probably a phenomenon of convergence than one simply of social pressure. For if human societies have evolved from heteronomy to autonomy, and from gerontocratic theocracy in all its forms to equalitarian democracy, it may very well be that the phenomena of social condensation so well described by Durkheim have been favourable primarily to the emancipation of one generation from another, and have thus rendered possible in children and adolescents the development we have outlined above.

CHAPTER 5

Social and Cultural Limits
of Personality

———◦•◦———

THE SOCIAL SHAPING OF HUMAN NEEDS

B Y

EMILE DURKHEIM

No living being can be happy or even exist unless his needs are sufficiently proportioned to his means. In other words, if his needs require more than can be granted, or even merely something of a different sort, they will be under continual friction and can only function painfully. Movements incapable of production without pain tend not to be reproduced. Unsatisfied tendencies atrophy, and as the impulse to live is merely the result of all the rest, it is bound to weaken as the others relax.

In the animal, at least in a normal condition, this equilibrium is established with automatic spontaneity because the animal depends on purely material conditions. All the organism needs is that the supplies of substance and energy constantly employed in the vital process should be periodically renewed by equivalent quantities; that replacement be equivalent to use. When the void created by existence in its own resources is filled, the animal, satisfied, asks nothing further. Its power of reflection is not sufficiently developed to imagine other ends than those implicit in its physical nature. On the other hand, as the work demanded of each organ itself depends on the general state of vital energy and the needs of organic equilibrium, use is regulated in turn by replacement and the balance is automatic. The limits of one are those of the other; both are fundamental to the constitution of the existence in question, which cannot exceed them.

This is not the case with man, because most of his needs are not dependent on his body or not to the same degree. Strictly speaking, we may consider that the quantity of material supplies necessary to the physical maintenance of a human life is subject to computation, though this be less exact than in the preceding case and a wider margin left for the free combinations of the will; for beyond the indispensable minimum which satisfies nature when instinctive, a more awakened reflection suggests better conditions, seemingly desirable ends craving fulfillment. Such appetites, however, admittedly sooner or later reach a limit which they cannot pass. But how determine the quantity of well-being, comfort or luxury legitimately to be craved by a human being? Nothing appears in man's organic nor in his psychological constitution which sets a limit to such tendencies. The functioning of individual life does not require them to cease at one point rather than at another; the proof being that they have constantly increased since the beginnings of history, receiving more and more complete satisfaction, yet with no weakening of average health. Above all, how establish their proper variation with different conditions of life, occupations, relative importance of services, etc.? In no society are they equally satisfied in the different stages of the social hierarchy. Yet human nature is substantially the same among all men, in its essential qualities. It is not human nature which can assign the variable limits necessary to our needs. They are thus unlimited so far as they depend on the individual alone. Irrespective of any external regulatory force, our capacity for feeling is in itself an insatiable and bottomless abyss.

But if nothing external can restrain this capacity, it can only be a source of torment to itself. Unlimited desires are insatiable by definition and insatiability is rightly considered a sign of morbidity. Being unlimited, they constantly and infinitely surpass the means at their command; they cannot be quenched. Inextinguishable thirst is constantly renewed torture. It has been claimed, indeed, that human activity naturally aspires beyond assignable limits and sets itself unattainable goals. But how can such an undetermined state be any more reconciled with the conditions of mental life than with the demands of physical life? All man's pleasure in acting, moving and exerting himself implies the sense that his efforts are not in vain and that by walking he has advanced. However, one does not advance when one walks toward no goal, or—which is the same thing—when his goal is infinity. Since the distance between us and it is always the same, whatever road we take, we might as well have made the motions without progress from the spot. Even our glances behind and our feeling of pride at the distance covered can cause only deceptive satisfaction, since the remaining distance is not proportionately reduced. To pursue a goal which is by definition unattainable is to condemn oneself to a state of perpetual unhappiness. Of course, man may hope contrary to all reason, and hope has its pleasures even when unreasonable. It may sustain him for a time; but it cannot survive the repeated disappointments of experience indefinitely. What more can the future offer him than the past, since he can never reach a tenable condition nor even approach the glimpsed ideal? Thus, the more one has, the more one wants, since satisfactions received only stimulate instead of filling needs. Shall action as such be considered agreeable? First, only on condition of blindness to its uselessness. Secondly, for this pleasure to be felt and to temper and half veil the accompanying painful unrest, such unending motion must at least always be easy and unhampered. If it is interfered with only restlessness is left, with the lack of ease which it, itself, entails. But it would be a miracle if no insurmountable obstacle were never encountered. Our thread of life on these conditions is pretty thin, breakable at any instant.

To achieve any other result, the passions first must be limited. Only then can they be harmonized with the faculties and satisfied. But since the individual has no way of limiting them, this must be done by some force exterior to him. A regulative force must play the same role for moral needs which the organism plays for physical needs. This means that the force can only be moral. The awakening of conscience interrupted the state of equilibrium of the animal's dormant existence; only conscience, therefore, can furnish the means to re-establish it. Physical restraint would be ineffective; hearts cannot be touched by physio-chemical forces. So far as the appetites are not automatically restrained by physiological mechanisms, they can be halted only by a limit that they recognize as just. Men would never consent to restrict their desires if they felt justified in passing the assigned limit. But, for reasons given above, they cannot assign themselves this law of justice. So they must receive it from an authority which they respect, to which they yield spontaneously. Either directly and as a whole, or through the agency of one of its organs, society alone can play this moderating role; for it is the only moral power superior to the individual, the authority of which he accepts. It alone has the power necessary to stipulate law and to set the point beyond which the passions must not go. Finally, it alone can estimate the reward to be prospectively offered to every class of human functionary, in the name of the common interest.

As a matter of fact, at every moment of history there is a dim perception, in the moral consciousness of societies, of the respective value of different social services, the relative reward due to each, and the consequent degree of comfort appropriate on the average to workers in each occupation. The different functions are graded in public opinion and a certain coefficient of well-being assigned to each, according to its place in the hierarchy. According to accepted ideas, for example, a certain way of living is considered the upper limit to which a workman may aspire in his efforts to improve his existence, and there is another limit below which he is not willingly permitted to fall unless he has seriously bemeaned himself. Both differ for city and country workers, for the domestic servant and the day-laborer, for the business clerk and the official, etc. Likewise the man of wealth is reproved if he lives the life of a poor man, but also if he seeks the refinements of luxury overmuch. Economists may protest in vain; public feeling will always be scandalized if an individual spends too much wealth for wholly superfluous use, and it even seems that this severity relaxes only in times of moral disturbance. A genuine regimen exists, therefore, although not always legally formulated, which fixes with relative precision the maximum degree of ease of living to which each social class may legitimately aspire. However, there is nothing immutable about such a scale. It changes with the increase or decrease of collective revenue and the changes occurring in the moral ideas of society. Thus what appears luxury to one period no longer does so to another; and the well-being which for long periods was granted to a class only by exception and supererogation, finally appears strictly necessary and equitable.

Under this pressure, each in his sphere vaguely realizes the extreme limit set to his ambitions and aspires to nothing beyond. At least if he respects regulations and is docile to collective authority, that is, has a wholesome moral constitution, he feels that it is not well to ask more. Thus, an end and goal are set to the passions. Truly, there is nothing rigid nor absolute about such determination. The economic ideal assigned each class of citizens is itself confined to certain limits, within which the desires have free range. But it is not infinite. This relative limitation and the moderation it involves, make men contented with their lot while stimulating them moderately to improve it; and this average contentment causes the feeling of calm, active happiness, the pleasure in existing and living which characterizes health for societies as well as for individuals. Each person is then at least, generally speaking, in harmony with his condition, and desires only what he may legitimately hope for as the normal reward of his activity. Besides, this does not condemn man to a sort of immobility. He may seek to give beauty to his life; but his attempts in this direction may fail without causing him to despair. For, loving what he has and not fixing his desire solely on what he lacks, his wishes and hopes may fail of what he has happened to aspire to, without his being wholly destitute. He has the essentials. The equilibrium of his happiness is secure because it is defined, and a few mishaps cannot disconcert him.

But it would be of little use for everyone to recognize the justice of the hierarchy of functions established by public opinion, if he did not also consider the distribution of these functions just. The workman is not in harmony with his social position if he is not convinced that he has his desserts. If he feels justified in occupying another, what he has would not satisfy him. So it is not enough for the average level of needs for each social condition to be regulated by public opinion, but another, more precise rule, must fix the way in which these conditions are open to individuals. There is no society in which such regulation does not exist. It varies with times and places. Once it regarded birth as the almost exclusive principle of social classification; today it recognizes no other inherent inequality than hereditary fortune and merit. But in all these various forms its object is unchanged. It is also only possible, everywhere, as a restriction upon individuals imposed by superior authority, that is, by collective authority. For it can be established only by requiring of one or another group of men, usually of all, sacrifices and concessions in the name of the public interest.

Some, to be sure, have thought that this moral pressure would become unnecessary if men's economic circumstances were only no longer determined by heredity. If inheritance were abolished, the argument runs, if everyone began life with equal resources and if the competitive struggle were fought out on a basis of perfect equality, no one could think its results unjust. Each would instinctively feel that things are as they should be.

Truly, the nearer this ideal equality were approached, the less social restraint will be necessary. But it is only a matter of degree. One sort of heredity will always exist, that of natural talent. Intelligence, taste, scientific, artistic, literary or industrial ability, courage and manual dexterity are gifts received by each of us at birth, as the heir to wealth receives his capital or as the nobleman formerly received his title and function. A moral discipline will therefore still be required to make those less favored by nature accept the lesser advantages which they owe to the chance of birth. Shall it be demanded that all have an equal share and that no advantage be given those more useful and deserving? But then there would have to be a discipline far stronger to make these accept a treatment merely equal to that of the mediocre and incapable.

But like the one first mentioned, this discipline can be useful only if considered just by the peoples subject to it. When it is maintained only by custom and force, peace and harmony are illusory; the spirit of unrest and discontent are latent; appetites superficially restrained are ready to revolt. This happened in Rome and Greece when the faiths underlying the old organization of the patricians and plebeians were shaken, and in our modern societies when aristocratic prejudices began to lose their old ascendancy. But this state of upheaval is exceptional; it occurs only when society is passing through some abnormal crisis. In normal conditions the collective order is regarded as just by the great majority of persons. Therefore, when we say that an authority is necessary to impose this order on individuals, we certainly do not mean that violence is the only means of establishing it. Since this regulation is meant to restrain individual passions, it must come from a power which dominates individuals; but this power must also be obeyed through respect, not fear.

It is not true, then, that human activity can be released from all restraint. Nothing in the world can enjoy such a privilege. All existence being a part of the universe is relative to the remainder; its nature and method of manifestation accordingly depend not only on itself but on other beings, who consequently restrain and regulate it. Here there are only differences of degree and form between the mineral realm and the thinking person. Man's characteristic privilege is that the bond he accepts is not physical but moral; that is, social. He is governed not by a material environment brutally imposed on him, but by a conscience superior to his own, the superiority of which he feels. Because the greater, better part of his existence transcends the body, he escapes the body's yoke, but is subject to that of society.

But when society is disturbed by some painful crisis or by beneficent but abrupt transitions, it is momentarily incapable of exercising this influence; thence come the sudden rises in the curve of suicides.

In the case of economic disasters, indeed, something like a declassification occurs which suddenly casts certain individuals into a lower state than their previous one. Then they must reduce their requirements, restrain their needs, learn greater self-control. All the advantages of social influence are lost so far as they are concerned; their moral education has to be recommenced. But society cannot adjust them instantaneously to this new life and teach them to practice the increased self-repression to which they are unaccustomed. So they are not adjusted to the condition forced on them, and its very prospect is intolerable; hence the suffering which detaches them from a reduced existence even before they have made trial of it.

It is the same if the source of the crisis is an abrupt growth of power and wealth. Then, truly, as the conditions of life are changed, the standard according to which needs were regulated can no longer remain the same; for it varies with social resources, since it largely determines the share of each class of producers. The scale is upset; but a new scale cannot be immediately improvised. Time is required for the public conscience to reclassify men and things. So long as the social forces thus freed have not regained equilibrium, their respective values are unknown and so all regulation is lacking for a time. The limits are unknown between the possible and the impossible, what is just and what is unjust, legitimate claims and hopes and those which are immoderate. Consequently, there is no restraint upon aspirations. If the disturbance is profound, it affects even the principles controlling the distribution of men among various occupations. Since the relations between various parts of society are necessarily modified, the ideas expressing these relations must change. Some particular class especially favored by the crisis is no longer resigned to its former lot, and, on the other hand, the example of its greater good fortune arouses all sorts of jealousy below and about it. Appetites, not being controlled by a public opinion become disoriented, no longer recognize the limits proper to them. Besides, they are at the same time seized by a sort of natural erethism simply by the greater intensity of public life. With increased prosperity desires increase. At the very moment when traditional rules have lost their authority, the richer prize offered these appetites stimulates them and makes them more exigent and impatient of control. The state of de-regulation or anomy is thus further heightened by passions being less disciplined, precisely when they need more disciplining.

But then their very demands make fulfillment impossible. Overweening ambition always exceeds the results obtained, great as they may be, since there is no warning to pause here. Nothing gives satisfaction and all this agitation is uninterruptedly maintained without appeasement. Above all, since this race for an unattainable goal can give no other pleasure but that of the race itself, if it is one, once it is interrupted the participants are left empty-handed. At the same time the struggle grows more violent and painful, both from being less controlled and because competition is greater. All classes contend among themselves because no established classification any longer exists. Effort grows, just when it becomes less productive. How could the desire to live not be weakened under such conditions?

This explanation is confirmed by the remarkable immunity of poor countries. Poverty protects against suicide because it is a restraint in itself. No matter how one acts, desires have to depend upon resources to some extent; actual possessions are partly the criterion of those aspired to. So the less one has the less he is tempted to extend the range of his needs indefinitely. Lack of power, compelling moderation, accustoms men to it, while nothing excites envy if no one has superfluity. Wealth, on the other hand, by the power it bestows, deceives us into believing that we depend on ourselves only. Reducing the resistance we encounter from objects, it suggests the possibility of unlimited success against them. The less limited one feels, the more intolerable all limitation appears. Not without reason, therefore, have so many religions dwelt on the advantages and moral value of poverty. It is actually the best school for teaching self-restraint. Forcing us to constant self-discipline, it prepares us to accept collective discipline with equanimity, while wealth, exalting the individual, may always arouse the spirit of rebellion which is the very source of immorality. This, of course, is no reason why humanity should not improve its material condition. But though the moral danger involved in every growth of prosperity is not irremediable, it should not be forgotten.

CULTURE AND PERSONALITY

BY

RALPH LINTON

THE first requirement for a discussion of the relation between culture and personality is to find a satisfactory definition for the latter. Here *personality* has been used to designate the whole of the individual's mental qualities, i.e., the sum total of his rational faculties, perceptions, ideas, habits, and conditioned emotional responses. Although some investigators may protest that such a definition is too inclusive, these qualities together form a single configuration all of whose parts function in constant relation to each other. To exclude some of them from consideration may appear to simplify the study of personality, but it simultaneously diminishes the value of the results of such study.

That there is a close relation between this personality configuration and the culture of the society to which the individual belongs cannot be doubted. Culture, in so far as it is anything more than an abstrac-

Abridged from: Linton, Ralph, *The Study of Man*, New York: Appleton-Century, 1936. Reprinted by permission of Appleton-Century-Crofts, Inc.

tion made by the investigator, exists only in the minds of the individuals who compose a society. It derives all its qualities from their personalities and the interaction of these personalities. Conversely, the personality of every individual within the society develops and functions in constant association with its culture.

The process of personality formation seems to be primarily one of integrating the individual's experience with his constitutional qualities to form a mutually adjusted, functional whole. This process continues throughout life but seems to be most active during the earlier years. Experience derives from the individual's contacts with his environment, but it is a result of the interaction of this environment with his constitutional qualities.

In spite of its constant interaction with constitutional qualities, environment dominates experience. The term *environment* is here used in its widest sense to include the whole of the individual's surroundings; the personalities as well as the objects and natural phenomena with which he is in contact. It is through its effects upon the environment that culture is able to influence experience and through this the personality. Although the individual's environment is not entirely a product of the culture of his group, it is influenced by it at many points. Even the natural environment provided by a particular geographic area impinges upon the individual only after it has been filtered through the screen which culture interposes between man and nature.

We have said that the individual's environment includes not only objects and natural phenomena but also other persons. In determining the qualities of these and the nature of the individual's interactions with them cultural factors are again of tremendous importance. All the other persons with whom he normally comes in contact are like himself participants in the culture of his particular society. Through them he is brought into contact with its accumulated knowledge, its attitudes toward the things to which it attaches symbolic value, and its emotional reactions to particular acts or situations. Although the individual's contact with these elements of culture is through the medium of the other individuals who share them, the very fact that they are shared gives them an impersonal quality. They are as real and effective parts of his environment as trees and chairs. Common contacts with them give the members of any society a fund of common experience varied only in so far as it has been influenced by their constitutional qualities as individuals.

At least the more formal aspects of the individual's relations with other members of his society are also controlled by culture. Every society has its patterns for behavior between individuals occupying particular statuses such as the old and the young, husband and wife, and employer and employee. However, the influence of culture upon personal relationships does not end with these. Thus culture delimits the size and nature of the group of persons with whom the individual is brought into close contact. The degree to which children or women or old people are segregated by the society will have an important effect both upon the contacts of individuals belonging to these categories and upon the opportunities which individuals of other categories have for contact with them and the types of experience resulting from it.

All these general environmental influences are continuous in their operation and result in similar experiences either for all the members of a society or for all those who belong to one of its recognized categories. One other source of individual experience should be mentioned at this time. This is the atypical and more or less accidental incidents which may befall the individual. Being caught in a burning house or stepping on a snake would be cases in point. However, the potentialities of such experiences for affecting the personality are probably determined quite as much by the attitudes of other individuals toward the incident as by any intrinsic qualities of the incident itself. Since these attitudes are primarily determined by culture, even this type of experience is culturally influenced.

Whether culture shapes the experience of the individual through the medium of his physical environment or through the medium of other individuals and the patterns which it establishes for their behavior toward him is not of paramount importance to the present discussion. Suffice it to say that it does influence this experience so profoundly that it may be said to dominate most of it. However, culture does not affect all individuals within a given society in the same ways. From this point of view culture influences may be divided into two groups, the general and the specific. The general influences are those which culture exerts upon the developing personalities of all members of the society which bears it. The specific influences are those which it exerts upon persons belonging to particular, socially recognized groups or categories of individuals within the society. Thus among ourselves boys and girls are subject to the same general influences deriving from life in houses of the same sort, going to the same schools, eating meals at the same hours, and receiving instruction in the same ethical ideas. However, each of these groups is further subject to a series of specific influences which are no less derivatives of our culture. Thus boys and girls are dressed differently almost from infancy, are taught to perform different tasks, and are encouraged to behave in different ways in many of the same situations.

From the point of view of the person who is influenced there is no particular difference between these general and specific factors. Both of them affect his experience, and through this his personality, in much the same way. The intensity of these influences derives not from whether they are general or specific but from the degree to which the particular element of culture is participated in by the rest of the society and the intensity of its emotional connotations. Thus many of the specific influences to which girls are subjected in any society derive from elements which, in spite of their limited application, are Universals in our classification of culture content. While only girls are expected to act in certain ways, every one in the group will believe that they should act in these ways, and the influence deriving from this pattern will be exerted upon them through the medium of men and boys as well as other women and girls. The real importance for our study of this differentiation between general and specific influences is that the presence of specific influences does much to increase the diversity of experience among individuals reared within the frame of a single culture and society. It means that the environment which a given culture provides is actually different for males and females, for members of different social classes, and even for members of different families. Any attempt to establish valid correlations between culture and personality type must take this fact into account.

Although the general influences provide the members of any society with a fund of common experience, it goes without saying that such influences will differ profoundly from one society to another. Every culture is responsible for a different set of them. Man has come so far from his animal beginnings that practically everything he does is shaped by culture. Even such elementary and vitally necessary activities as the nursing and care of infants are controlled by culture patterns, not by instinct. Proof of this is afforded by the wide variations with regard to these which we find in different societies. Thus in some, infants are given the breast whenever they cry for it. In others they are fed on a regular schedule. In some they will be nursed by any woman who happens to be at hand, in others only by their mothers. In some the process of nursing is a leisurely one, accompanied by many caresses and a maximum of sensuous enjoyment for both mother and child. In others it is hurried and perfunctory, the mother regarding it as an interruption of her regular activities and urging the child to finish as rapidly as possible. Some groups wean infants at a very early age; other continue nursing for years.

In the techniques of caring for infants there is an even greater cultural range. One society may make the baby the center of attention for the entire family, various adults constantly carrying it about, playing with it, and giving it anything it wants. Another society may regard infants as a nuisance and pay little attention to them outside the satisfaction of their physical needs. In some societies the child is in almost constant bodily contact with its mother during the first two years. In other societies this constant bodily contact is lacking, but the child is handled frequently. In still others it is rarely touched except at feeding time. In some societies the child is allowed to tumble about without interference. In others it spends its first eighteen months bound to a board, even its arms sometimes being confined.

Psychologists have written a good deal about the presumed effects of infantile experience upon the adult personality. It would seem that a study of individuals from societies with markedly different patterns of infant care could provide proof or disproof of many current theories, but this work has barely been begun.

As the child grows older, the general influences which his culture exerts upon him become increasingly numerous and complex. We have already spoken of the possible effects of various patterns of family organization on the individual's personal-social relations. The spacing of births which is characteristic of many societies would also affect these. Thus in a society where children were born at fairly regular eighteen-month intervals, the child would be in contact with at least two others near his own age. In societies where children were normally born at intervals of anywhere from three to six years, age differences between brothers and sisters would be marked and would affect general experience. Such intentional spacing of births is much commoner than is generally supposed. Turning to the more direct effects of culture patterns upon the developing individual, we have an almost infinite range of variations in the degree to which he is consciously trained, discipline or lack of it, and responsibilities imposed upon him. Society may take the child in hand almost from infancy and deliberately train him for his adult status, or it may permit him to run wild until the age of puberty. He may receive corporal punishment for even the smallest offenses or never be punished at all. As a child he may have a claim upon the time and attention of all adults with whom he comes in contact or, conversely, all adults may have a claim upon his services. He may be put to work and treated as a responsible contributing member of the family group almost from the moment that he is able to walk and have it constantly impressed upon him that life is real and earnest.

Examples of cultural differences in the treatment of children could be multiplied indefinitely. The important point is that every culture exerts a series of general influences upon the individuals who grow up under it. These influences differ from one culture to another, but they provide a common denominator of experience for all persons belonging to any given society. This common experience provides the background against which the specific influences of the culture operate. These vary not only from culture to culture but also within each culture. The individual's exposure to certain of them and not to others is determined primarily by the social units or categories of persons to which he belongs. Thus, to begin with the smallest recognized social unit, every family has certain distinctive habits. Since these are shared by its members, they must be considered a part of culture.

All societies are quite unconscious of the general influences which their culture exerts upon their members. They are somewhat more conscious of the specific influences, especially of those associated with differences in sex or social position, since the contrasts serve to bring them to attention. Thus any one can see that the environment which our culture provides for boys and for girls is different in each case and can even list offhand several of the ways in which it differs.

One other category of specific influences remains to be mentioned: those which derive from the society's more or less conscious attempts to train the individual to occupy a particular place in its system. This training always looms large in the minds of the society's members. The general influences and the other categories of specific ones are taken so much for granted that their possible effects are ignored or at least greatly underestimated. The conscious training of the individual undoubtedly influences the content of his personality, making for the establishment of particular habits and attitudes. It also influences the more superficial aspects of personality organization by setting certain concrete goals for the individual's attainment and directing his energies toward these. However, its influence is too intermittent and forms too small a part of the total influences to which the individual is subjected for it to have much effect on the deeper organization of personality. To put it concretely, conscious training can develop almost any one into a fairly successful business man or craftsman, but it cannot make him an extrovert.

Of course societies do not think of the training process in psychological terms. All they attempt to do is to fit the individual for the occupation of certain ascribed statuses, i.e., those positions in the social structure which he will, in the normal course of events, come to occupy. The occupation of any status enjoins upon its holder not simply certain duties but also certain emotional attitudes. The latter provide the individual with his main incentive for the constant and conscientious performance of his roles. Their presence makes it possible for the entire system to function without the exercise of direct social compulsion.

It is thus vitally necessary to the functioning of a society that the personalities of its members be at least superficially adapted to their statuses. Each society approves and rewards certain combinations of qualities when they appear in individuals occupying particular statuses. Furthermore, it tries to develop these qualities in all the individuals for whom the particular statuses can be forecast. In other words, each society has a series of ideal personalities which correspond to the various statuses which it recognizes. Such status personalities are not to be confused with psychological types. In their delimitation societies do not go far below the surface. The status personality does not correspond to the total personality but simply to certain aspects of the content and more superficial orientations of the latter, i.e., to those elements of the total personality which are immediately concerned with the successful performance of the individual's roles. The status personality is a social phenomenon, the psychological type an individual phenomenon. There can be do doubt that certain psychological types are better adapted to particular status personalities than others, but individuals of more than one psychological type can usually assume the same status personality and perform the roles associated with the status at least adequately.

Since every social system includes numerous statuses, the status personalities toward which any society tries to shape its members are numerous and varied. Moreover, the qualities which it considers appropriate to one of these status personalities may be strongly disapproved for another.

In general, the ideal personalities for individuals in complementary statuses are mutually adjusted. Otherwise the reciprocal relationships which are the essence of the whole system of statuses and roles could hardly be maintained. However, many societies reveal a curious lack of correlation in their ideal personalities for statuses which the same individual may be expected to occupy at different periods in his life.

In our earlier discussion of status we pointed out that every social system includes achieved statuses as well as ascribed ones. The former are usually of little importance as regards the society's conscious efforts to form personality, but they are of great importance as regards the social adjustment and utilization of individuals. Achieved statuses are those which are not forecast for particular categories of individuals. For the most part, the roles associated with these statuses are of such a nature that their successful performance cannot be assured by training alone. Thus, as many nations have learned to their cost, a military education will not in itself produce an able general. By leaving such statuses open to individuals who reveal the necessary qualities, the society is able to utilize the special abilities of some of its members. It also provides a place for individuals whose characteristics are incompatible with the ideal personalities for its ascribed statuses, turning them into a social asset instead of a liability.

Achieved statuses are often of great functional importance to a society, and those who come to occupy them may be liberally rewarded. However, the qualities, especially the psychological type, which will make a man a success in one of them are very frequently of a sort which militate against his success in ordinary life. The achieved status is thus desired by the individual both because of the rewards which it brings and because it offers him an alternative to the ascribed status which he finds uncongenial. It seems that from this point of view achieved statuses could be arranged in a graded series ranging from those which are highly desirable in themselves to those which could be considered desirable only as an alternative to failure in the individual's ascribed status.

The special qualities or psychological types which various societies approve and reward in connection with their achieved statuses are highly diverse. Some societies even provide in this way for persons whom we would consider pathological. Thus some groups not only tolerate individuals who suffer from epilepsy, hallucinations, or hysterical seizures, but encourage these abnormalities and give those who manifest them an honored position. In a very large number of societies hallucinations and hysterical seizures are taken as signs of the individual's close contact with the supernatural. Since easy access to this is felt to be necessary to the society's well-being, persons who suffer from such conditions are assigned a special status as intermediaries between it and the Beings who are powerful to help or harm. It is felt that such individuals' vagaries of conduct are more than compensated for by their usefulness, and they are often accorded a high measure of prestige and power. Many an individual who is at present an inmate of one of our asylums would be not only free but "sitting on top of the world" if he had happened to be born into some other society.

This brings us at once to the problem of individual maladjustment, which must not be confused with that of incomplete or faulty personality organization. Even among the insane there are many personalities which are thoroughly organized and well integrated. The same holds for a large proportion of even acutely maladjusted individuals. In fact a too complete and thorough integration of the personality may in itself be a source of maladjustment, since it interferes with the individual's easy assumption of the required status personality. The maladjusted individual is simply one who has difficulty in assuming the status personality which his society requires, irrespective of what the causes of this difficulty may be. The condition represents a lack of adjustment to environment and cannot be satisfactorily studied except in relation to environment.

In its ascribed and achieved statuses every society provides congenial settings for a particular series of psychological types, but the range of these statuses is never extensive enough to provide for all possible types. Moreover, any individual in any society is automatically debarred from certain of even its achieved statuses. For example, some of these are open only to men, others only to women. We therefore have maladjusted individuals in all societies. Some of these are debarred from statuses which would be congenial to their actual personalities, although such statuses are present in the system, while the system provides no statuses which would be congenial to the actual personalities of others. Since status personalities differ from one society to another, it is obvious that the individual who is badly maladjusted in one group might be fairly well adjusted in another.

It seems probable that there is some status in some society which would be completely congenial to any given psychological type. However, it is very rarely that status personality and actual personality happen to coincide exactly for any individual. In spite of the psychologist's delimitation of types, individual personalities are infinitely varied, and the theoretical types represent at most greater frequencies of occurrence at certain points in the total range of variation. The average individual in all societies is able to reach a working adjustment between his actual personality and his status personality. Maladjustment is, after all, a matter of degree. The person who has been unable to make any adjustment is never encountered. Society eliminates him before he reaches that point. The individual who is perfectly adjusted does not appear once in a million times.

Actually, this condition is never found. It is unfortunate that we have no exact, objective techniques for identifying psychological types, but general observations lead to the conclusion that the total range of these types is much the same in all societies. Due to the superficial adjustments which individuals make to status personalities and to the great extent to which the content of personality is controlled by culture, an investigator's initial impression of the members of an alien society is that all those in any particular status are much alike in personality. This is quite on a par with his other initial impression that they all look very much alike. In other words, as soon as he penetrates the screen of cultural difference he finds that these people are fundamentally like ourselves. At the same time, different societies seem to show differences in the relative frequency of occurrence of the various psychological types. There can be little doubt that some of them show a higher proportion of introverts or megalomaniacs or paranoids than others.

The fact that the same psychological types seem to appear, at least sporadically, in all societies, is a fairly clear indication that some factors other than cultural ones are at work in their production. It further indicates that these factors must be of such a sort that they recur in all societies. The first and most obvious explanation of the observed conditions would be that psychological type is determined by physiological qualities. We have spoken of the individual variations with respect to these and of their constant influence upon experience. On purely biological grounds we would expect all the possible variations to appear at one time or another in every human group, leading to the eventual repetition in all of them of all known psychological types. This theory might even explain the varying frequencies of these types in different societies. The average tribal society is composed of closely related individuals. If the physiological factors responsible for various types follow the ordinary Mendelian laws of dominance and recession, the majority of the members of such an inbred group might very well have a hereditary predisposition to a particular psychological type, resulting in a greater frequency for the type.

Merely because it is so attractive the physiological theory of personality determination should be handled with caution. At the present time its validity can be neither proved nor disproved. Moreover, in view of the dominant influence which experience certainly exerts upon the content of personality and upon the superficial aspects of its organization, it is hard to believe that this influence does not extend to the deeper levels as well. Actually there are a series of what we may term sub-cultural experiences which recur in all societies, although with varying frequencies in different ones, and which might thus account for the observed conditions. Although all societies have formal, culturally determined patterns governing the interrelations of persons in particular statuses, the actual relations always include a factor which is not culturally determined. The interactions take place not between abstract statuses but between the individuals who occupy those statuses, and they derive much of their quality from the personalities involved. This is especially true as regards the relations of the child with his parents or other persons who are in close and continuous contact with him. Thus in one household the father may be an irritable tyrant exercising all the prerogatives with respect to his children which the pattern for the relationship allows him and keeping them in a constant state of fear and uncertainty. In another he may be good-natured and easy-going, exercising his prerogatives only in public. In one family the mother may be a docile, sweet-tempered individual and in another a shrew. In one the child may be dominated and bullied by an older one, in another he may be helped and cared for by his older brothers and sisters and develop a strong feeling of dependence upon them. Each of these situations will result in a different basal experience for the child.

Moreover, the same sort of personal-social relationships, as Dr. Kimball Young calls them, recur in practically all societies in spite of the differences in formal culture patterns. It makes very little difference whether masculine authority over the growing boy is exercised by his father, as among ourselves, or by his mother's brother, as in many other societies. In either case the boy may find himself dominated by a tyrant or in an easy, friendly relation with an adviser and helper. The personal aspects of the situation will far outweigh the cultural ones. Again, in all societies there are certain individuals who, through lack of physical strength or intelligence, are dominated by other children and more or less abused by them. Such situations repeat themselves in spite of culture and, because of the strong emotional elements involved, might be expected to influence the development of particular psychological types as profoundly as any sort of experience could.

It seems fairly certain that the observed conditions with regard to psychological types cannot be explained entirely on the basis of cultural influence. They can be almost completely explained on the basis of this influence working in combination with either the constitutional qualities of the individual or his personal-social relations. However, it seems most probable that psychological types are really a result of the interaction of factors of all three sorts and that the relative importance of at least the last two may vary with the individual. Thus the personal-social factors might be dominant in forming the personality of an individual who had no outstanding constitutional qualities, or strong and atypical qualities might dominate the process of personality formation in an individual who possessed them. Personalities, like cultures, derive their qualities from the interaction of numerous and varied factors, and it is unsafe to assume that any one of these factors exerts a dominant influence under all conditions.

PARTICIPATION IN CULTURE

B Y

RALPH LINTON

IT is the possession of a common culture which gives a society its *esprit de corps* and makes it possible for its members to live and work together with a minimum of confusion and mutual interference. At the same time, the society gives culture overt expression in its behavior, and hands it on from generation to generation. However, societies are so constituted that they can only express culture through the medium of their component individuals and can only perpetuate it by the training of these individuals. It is with the participation of these individuals in the total culture of their society that we will deal here.

It has been pointed out that no one individual is ever familiar with the total content of the culture of the society to which he belongs. Even in the simplest cultures the content is too rich for any one mind to be able to apprehend the whole of it. The patterns of division of and specialization in activities make it possible for the individual to function successfully as a member of his society without such complete knowledge. He learns and employs certain aspects of the total culture and leaves the knowledge and exercise of other aspects to other individuals. At the same time, every person is usually familiar with elements of his society's culture which he will never be called upon to express in action.

These factors increase the degree of the individual's participation in culture, but it never reaches completeness. If we observe the culture of any homogeneous society, we will find that the content of this culture can be divided into three categories, these being derived from the extent to which the elements within each category are shared by the society's members. As in all classifications, there may be some difficulty in assigning certain elements to their places in this three-fold division, but the position of most of them will be plain enough.

First, there are those ideas, habits, and conditioned emotional responses which are common to all sane, adult members of the society. We will call these the *Universals*. It must be understood that this terminology applies only to the content of a particular culture. An

Abridged from: Linton, Ralph, *The Study of Man,* New York: Appleton-Century, 1936. Reprinted by permission of Appleton-Century-Crofts, Inc.

element classed as a Universal in one culture may be completely lacking in another. To this category belong such elements as the use of a particular language, the tribal patterns of costume and housing, and the ideal patterns for social relationships. This category also includes the associations and values which lie, for the most part, below the level of consciousness but which are, at the same time, an integral part of culture.

Second, we have those elements of culture which are shared by the members of certain socially recognized categories of individuals but which are not shared by the total population. We will call these the *Specialties*. Under this head come the patterns for all those varied but mutually interdependent activities which have been assigned to various sections of the society in the course of its division of labor. In all societies certain things are done by or known to only a designated part of the population, although they contribute to the well-being of the whole. Thus all the women within a tribe will be familiar with certain occupations and techniques, while the men will be familiar with a different series. As a rule, the men will only have a rather vague general knowledge of the things which belong in the women's province and vice versa. Under this head there can also be classed the activities which the society has assigned to special craftsmen or functionaries such as the smith, carpenter, doctor, and priest.

The cultural elements which fall into this class are, for the most part, manual skills and technical knowledge. The greater part of them are concerned with the utilization and control of the natural environment. Although such elements are not shared by the entire society, the benefits arising from them are shared, and all members of the society will have a fairly clear idea as to what the end product of each specialized activity should be. Thus a husband may have only a general idea of the processes involved in making bread, but he will be keenly conscious of whether it has been made properly or not. Again, the average man does not know the techniques of the smith and regards his skill in metalworking with some awe, but he has a clear mental picture of what constitutes a good knife or hoe and will be both resentful of inferior workmanship and suspicious of innovations. The same thing holds for the activities of the doctor or priest. The uninstructed do not know the full details of their procedure, but every one has a general knowledge of how healing or sacrificing should be done and of the results to be expected from it. Any departure from the accustomed procedure or failure to achieve the expected results brings an emotional reaction.

Third, there are in every culture a considerable number of traits which are shared by certain individuals but which are not common

to all the members of the society or even to all the members of any one
of the socially recognized categories. We will call these *Alternatives*.
The elements of culture which may be included in this class have a
very wide range, varying from the special and often quite atypical
ideas and habits of a particular family to such things as different
schools of painting or sculpture. Aside from the nature of the participation in them, all these Alternatives have this in common: they represent different reactions to the same situations or different techniques
for achieving the same ends. The cultures of small societies living
under primitive conditions usually include only a moderate number
of such Alternatives, while in such a culture as our own they are very
plentiful. Examples of such Alternatives for ourselves would be such
things as the use of horses, bicycles, railroads, automobiles, and air-
planes for the single purpose of transportation overland; our variety
of teaching techniques; or our wide range of beliefs and attitudes toward the supernatural.

Beyond the limits of culture there lies still a fourth category of
habits, ideas and conditioned emotional responses; that of *Individual
Peculiarities*. These include such things as one person's abnormal fear
of fire, due perhaps to some accident of his early experience, a craftsman's individual tricks of technique or characteristic muscular habits,
or a purely personal doubt regarding some generally accepted article
of faith. Every individual has certain peculiarities of this sort whether
he is a member of a primitive tribe or a modern urban community, and
the sum total of such individual differences within any society is
enormous.

Individual Peculiarities cannot be classed as a part of culture, in the
sense in which the term is ordinarily used, since they are not shared
by any of a society's members. At the same time they are of extreme
importance in cultural dynamics since they are the starting point of
everything which later becomes incorporated into culture. There is
always some one individual in a community who is the first to discover,
invent, or adopt a new thing. As soon as this new thing has been
transmitted to and is shared by even one other individual in the society, it must be reckoned a part of culture. Individual Peculiarities
occupy somewhat the same position with regard to culture that individual mutations occupy with regard to a biological species. Most
Individual Peculiarities, like most physical variations, are never transmitted at all or are transmitted to only a few individuals and ultimately disappear. However, if the Peculiarity is of a sort advantageous
to its possessor, it may be transmitted to an ever-widening circle of individuals until it is accepted by the whole society.

It is easiest to apply the foregoing classification to elements within cultures of the sort carried by small, closely integrated social units such as the local groups. When we turn to larger units such as tribes, or more especially modern states, we find a vastly more complex situation. While ethnologists have been accustomed to speak of tribes and nationalities as though they were the primary culture-bearing units, the total culture of a society of this type is really an aggregate of sub-cultures. Within tribes or unmechanized civilizations these sub-cultures are normally carried by the various local groups which go to make the total society and are transmitted within these groups. In a few cases there may also be sub-cultures which are characteristic of particular social classes and which are transmitted within them, but this arrangement is much less characteristic than the local one. Every sub-culture always differs in some respects from all the rest, and the total culture consists of the sum of its sub-cultures plus certain additional elements which are a result of their interaction.

If we attempt to apply our three-fold classification to a tribal culture we will find that, in comparison with any of the sub-cultures which compose it, it shows fewer Universals and a marked increase in Specialties. The peculiarities of the various sub-cultures must be listed as Specialties rather than Alternatives since they are not presented to the individual as traits toward which he can exercise choice. Each individual accepts the patterns of his own sub-culture as proper guides to behavior and rarely attempts to imitate the patterns of other sub-cultures even when he is familiar with them. In fact, the presence of such differences usually makes him cling more tenaciously to the habits of his particular sub-culture, since these become a symbol of his membership in his particular social unit.

When we take such a culture as a whole, the number of Alternatives will also show some increase over those within a given sub-culture, since all the Alternatives within all the sub-cultures will be included. However, as long as the contacts between the social units which bear the sub-cultures are not very close or frequent, the total number of these Alternatives will bear little relation to the number of them which are submitted to any given individual for choice.

The sub-cultures within a tribal culture must of necessity be adapted to each other and have a considerable number of elements in common, else it will be impossible to maintain a feeling of tribal unity or for the tribe to function as a unit. However, the degree of adaptation necessary will depend largely upon the amount of contact between the units bearing the sub-cultures and especially upon the degree to which they are interdependent. When, on the other hand, the groups which bear the sub-cultures are in close and frequent contact, or when the products of certain of these groups are necessary to the rest, there will have to be a much greater degree of adjustment. In particular, changes in any one of the sub-cultures will be strongly influenced by the situation existing in the rest.

Even when there is close contact and marked interdependence between the groups which bear sub-cultures, it is still possible for the sub-cultures to maintain their integrity. They become adapted to each other and to the total social structure, each of them performing certain functions with relation to the whole. Once a satisfactory adaptation has been achieved, there is no incentive for the individuals who share a particular sub-culture to give up their distinctive habits. These habits constitute Specialties, from the point of view of the culture as a whole, and are an integral part of it. While they may subject those who share them to jests and good-natured ridicule, as when the peasants of one village laugh at the costume of those in the next, they have the reinforcement of general recognition. As long as the groups which bear the sub-cultures remain conscious of themselves as distinct entities and retain their hold on the individuals who compose them, the sub-cultures will persist.

It is only when the hold of the local group or social class upon its members is broken, as it is beginning to be in our own society, that the sub-cultures tend to merge and disappear. The first effect of this merging is that the distinctive features of the sub-cultures cease to be Specialties and become Alternatives, i.e., are thrown open to individual choice. As competing Alternatives, most of them will finally be eliminated, with a consequent loss to the total content of the culture. However, until this elimination has taken place there will be a marked increase in the number of culture elements made available to any individual within the society.

The incomplete participation of all individuals in the culture of their societies is reflected in the presence within all societies of differential lines for the transmission of various culture elements. These lines correspond not only to the membership of the social units which carry particular sub-cultures but also to the various socially established categories of individuals within each of the functional social units. Thus certain elements are transmitted in family lines. Similarly, in all cultures the knowledge of the Specialties assigned to women will be transmitted almost entirely in the female line, while knowledge of those assigned to men will be transmitted in the male line.

One of the most interesting aspects of this differentiation of lines of cultural transmission, and one very frequently overlooked, is that the various age categories within a society also correspond to lines of cultural transmission. While the growing individual learns much from his elders, he learns even more from his contemporaries, as many baffled parents can attest. His contacts with his contemporaries are normally closer and less formal, and the heroes whom he strives to imitate are usually not adults, whose interests and activities lie largely beyond his ken, but individuals within his own general age category. In particular he will copy those who are slightly older than himself and more expert in the activities socially ascribed to the particular category. Even in our own culture there are many elements which are transmitted almost exclusively within certain age brackets. For example, adults very rarely teach children to play marbles, this particular item being transmitted from boy to boy. Similarly, the techniques employed by adolescents in their first romantic advances to each other are constantly transmitted from older to younger adolescents without penetrating either the adult level or the child level. Although individuals naturally carry a knowledge of these techniques with them when they pass into the higher age groups, they would never think of employing them, still less of teaching them to their offspring. It seems quite possible that even the antagonism between adolescents and their elders and those questionings of certain values which we call "the revolt of youth" represent simply culture elements which are differentially transmitted in the adolescent line.

While the Universals and Specialties within any culture normally form a fairly consistent and well-integrated unit, the Alternatives necessarily lack such consistency and integration. Many of them are in opposition to each other, and some of them may even be at variance with elements in the first two categories. Actually, all cultures consist of two parts, a solid, well-integrated, and fairly stable core, consisting of the mutually adapted Universals and Specialties, and a fluid, largely unintegrated, and constantly changing zone of Alternatives which surrounds this core. It is the core which gives a culture its form and basic patterns at each point in its history, while the presence of the fluid zone gives it its capacity for growth and adaptation. If we study any culture continuum we will be able to detect a constant process of give-and-take between these two parts, with traits moving from one to the other. New traits, beginning as Individual Peculiarities, gain adherents, rise to the status of Alternatives, and finally pass into the core as they achieve general recognition. Old ones, as soon as they are brought into competition with new ones, are drawn into the zone of Alternatives and, if they are inferior, finally drop out of the culture. This exit, in turn, takes place by way of the Individual Peculiarities. Some die-hard individual may insist on driving a horse and buggy after all the rest of his society have automobiles, and the trait will not finally disappear until his death.

The proportion which each of these two parts of a culture bears to its total content may vary greatly at different points in its history. In general, the more rapid the contemporary rate of change, the higher the proportion of Alternatives. The proposition is stated in this form simply because most of the stimuli to change, as well as the bulk of the new traits by the acceptance of which it is accomplished, normally originate outside the culture. When a culture is changing very rapidly, as our own is at present, the Alternatives may become so numerous that they quite overshadow the Universals and Specialties. Each new trait, as soon as it is accepted by any part of the society, draws certain traits which were formerly Universals or Specialties out of the core of the culture into the fluid zone. As the content of the core is reduced, the culture increasingly loses pattern and coherence.

Such a fluid, disorganized condition within culture has inevitable repercussions upon the society which bears it. It is the common adherence of a society's members to the elements which form the core of their culture which makes it possible for them to function as a society. Without a wide community of ideas and habits the members of the group will not react to particular stimuli as a unit, nor will they be able to cooperate effectively. Such cooperation really rests upon the predictability of the other individuals' behavior. When there are very few elements of culture in which all the members of a society participate, i.e., when the proportional size of the culture core has been greatly reduced, the group tends to revert to the condition of an aggregate. The society is no longer able to feel or act as a unit. Its members may continue to live together, but many forms of social intercourse will be hampered by the impossibility of predicting the behavior of individuals on any basis other than that of their known personalities.

PART III

Social Forms and Processes

EVEN TO IDENTIFY SUCH SOCIAL UNITS AS CHURCHES, POLITICAL parties and the like in categorical terms is already to achieve a rudimentary degree of abstraction. But to speak of such units at this level involves content which delimits the scope of the generalization. To speak about social groups *in general* is, in a sense, at the heart of sociology. Ultimately a scientific theory of society must be stated at its most abstract level, in terms of *all* social groups. The efforts of sociological theorists to achieve such a level is represented in the selections which make up Part III.

Georg Simmel oriented his analyses of social phenomena around what have been called the social *forms* and processes. His approach to the subject matter was most general, and he dealt with content areas only as they related to his general analysis. In Chapter 6 we present a major portion of his famous essay concerning the size of the group and its influence on the processes and relationships which may develop within the group. In this essay Simmel deals with *large* and *small groups* and the limits of size on the character of interaction which is possible. Unique features are associated with large groups not to be found with small ones, and vice versa, and processes which are common to both large and small groups may be manifest in similar or different ways. At bottom, the processes to be found in groups of different size are tied to the nature of the social person. The single-person unit is either not social or is isolated and the latter implies a group. The dyad must then be viewed as the smallest unity which is social in this sense, and it may take particular forms and have particular properties. The differences between a dyad and a triad are radical in implication, as will be seen in Simmel's text. In addition to Simmel's essay we have included in Chapter 6 a section from Gustave Le Bon's *The Crowd.* This particular section supplements Simmel's essay and stands as a classic statement of the "psychological crowd."

The essence of social behavior is that relationships are ordered, and this is the concern of Chapter 7. In the development of social relationships there are in general but two ways in which statuses and roles are parceled out among the members, through ascription and through achievement. The notion underlying this distinction is to be found in Sir Henry S. Maine's section in *Ancient Law* on status and contract in which he delineates historically and in a comparative sense the development of relationships based on contract. Competition may be seen to be an important process in the differentiation of statuses and roles in terms of achievement. Charles Horton Cooley develops this analysis in his essay on personal competition. Then, Ralph Linton, in a section on status and role in *The Study of Man,* succinctly summarizes the distinction between status and role, between ascription and achievement. It is a truism that in differentiation some persons should be successful or ascendant and others not. Cooley considers the concept of leadership or personal ascendancy in his volume on *Human Nature and the Social Order,* taking largely the personality view of the problem. Georg Simmel, on the other hand, in his essay on superiority and subordination, systematically considers the ordering of power relationships in terms of both individuals and groups. Whether one person, or two, or a small group are in the superior position may determine the limits of power of leader and led, or the character of the entire social structure, but the ramifications of the analysis are much broader than this.

In Chapter 8 the two selections deal with knowledge about the other and the form of the social relationship. Georg Simmel's materials are taken from his essay on secrecy and the secret society in which he considers the question of the nature of the relationship and the kinds of information the members must have concerning each other. Basically, his work focuses on the communication nexus, and points to the kinds of realities to which one responds in any social relationship. One responds to what *he* knows of the other, not to some externally defined reality. Knowledge of the other, or ignorance of the other, thus, is a vital determiner of the nature of the social relationship, just as the social relationship which is defined may dispose towards learning certain kinds of knowledge about the other. Charles Horton Cooley's passage, taken from *Social Organization*, concerns the primary group and primary ideals. The face-to-face relationship requires development of knowledge of the other, of intimacy, in fact. When the primary group is considered a generic unit of society, certain distinctive qualities appear to be associated with it.

CHAPTER 6

The Form of the Group: Size and Character

THE NUMBER OF PERSONS AS DETERMINING THE FORM OF THE GROUP

BY

GEORG SIMMEL

IN respect to the fundamental problem which appears to me solely to form the basis of a sociology as a distinct science, I indicate here merely that this problem rests upon the distinction between the content or purpose of socializations, and the form of the same. The content is economic or religious, domestic or political, intellectual or volitional, pedagogic or convivial. That these purposes and interests, however, attain to realization in the form of a society, of the companionship and the reciprocity of individuals, is the subject-matter of special scientific consideration. That men build a society means that they live for the attainment of those purposes in definitely formed interactions. If there is to be a science of society as such, it must therefore abstract those forms from the complex phenomena of societary life, and it must make them the subject of determination and explanation. Those contents are already treated by special sciences, historical and systematic; the relationships, however, of men to each other, which in the case of the most diverse purposes may be the same, and in the

Abridged from: Simmel, Georg, The Number of Members as Determining the Sociological Form of the Group (translated by Albion W. Small), *American Journal of Sociology*, 1902, 8, 1–46 and 158–196. Reprinted by permission of the University of Chicago Press.

case of like purposes may be most various—these have not as yet been the subject-matter of a particular science; and yet such a science, when constituted, would for the first time make manifest what it is which makes the society—that is, the totality of historical life—into society.

It will be conceded at the first glance, without hesitation, that the sociological structure of a group is essentially modified by the number of the individuals that are united in it. It is an everyday experience— yes, it is almost to be construed from the most general social-psychological presuppositions—that a group of a certain extent and beyond a certain stage in its increase of numbers must develop for its maintenance certain forms and organization which it did not previously need; and that, on the other hand, more restricted groups manifest qualities and reciprocal activities which, in the case of their numerical extension, inevitably disappear. A double significance attaches itself to the quantitative determination: first, the negative significance that certain forms which are necessary or possible from the contents or the conditions of life can come to realization only before or after a certain numerical extension of the elements; the positive significance that other forms are promoted directly through definite and purely quantitative modifications of the group. As a matter of course, these do not emerge in every case, but they depend upon other social circumstances in the group. The decisive matter, however, is that the forms in question never spring from these latter conditions alone, but are produced from them only through the accompanying numerical factor. Thus it may be demonstrated that quite or nearly communistic formations have up to the present day been possible only in relatively small circles, while they have always failed in large groups. The presumption of such socialistic groups—namely, justice in the distribution of effort and of enjoyment—can no doubt be established in a small group, and, what is at least quite as important, it can be observed and controlled by the individuals. What each does for the totality, and wherewith the totality rewards him, is in such cases close at hand, so that comparison and equalization easily occur. In a great group this practice is hindered, particularly by the unavoidable differentiation of persons within it, of their functions and of their claims. A very large number of people can constitute a unity only with decisive division of labor, not merely on the obvious grounds of economic technique, but because this alone produces that interpenetration and interdependence of persons which puts each through innumerable intermediaries in combination with each, and without which a widely extended group would break apart on every occasion. Consequently the more intimate the unity demanded in the same, the more exact must be the specialization of individuals, in order that the individuals may be the more immediately responsible to the whole, and the whole may be dependent upon the individuals. The communism of a great community would thus promote the sharpest differentiation of the personalities, which would naturally extend over and beyond their labor, to their feeling and desiring. Hence a comparison of services with each other, of rewards with each other, and equilibration of the two, is infinitely difficult; but upon this the feasibility of approximate communism for small, and therefore undifferentiated, circles rests. What limits such circles, under advanced culture, by a sort of logical necessity, so to speak, to restricted numerical extent, is their dependence upon goods which under their peculiar productive conditions can never be furnished.

A previously calculated, mechanically working life-system, in which every detail is regulated according to general principles, can be applied, to be sure, in a small circle which can draw from a greater one whatever it requires for the establishment of its internal equilibrium. But human needs appear to contain an accidental or incalculable element, and this fact permits their satisfaction only at the cost of carrying on parallel activities which produce countless irrational and unavailable by-products. A circle, therefore, which avoids this, and confines itself to complete responsibility and utility in its activities, must always remain minute, because it has need of a greater group in order to be reinforced with the requisite capacity for life.

Small and centripetally organized groups usually call out and employ to their full extent the energies available within them; in greater groups, on the other hand, much more energy, not merely absolutely but also relatively, remains in a latent condition. The demand of the whole does not seize upon every member constantly and completely, and it permits much power to remain unused which then, in extreme cases, may be mobilized and actualized. The decisive thing in this case is, as indicated, the social centripetalism, that is, the ratio in which the energies present in the society are harnessed for its purposes. When it, therefore, occurs that a lower and smaller group allows its members much autonomy and independence, the latter then often develop energies which are not used socially, and, therefore, in case the appeal to the common interests occurs, they represent a considerable available recourse. This was for a long time the case, for example, with the nobility of the Scotch highlands. Likewise, on the other hand, where dangers, which demand an unused quantity of social energy, are excluded by the circumstances, means of numerical limitation, which extend even beyond endogamy, may be quite appropriate. The dangers of the quantitative limitation are provided against by the external conditions of the life of the group, and their consequences for its inner structure.

Where the small group absorbs the personalities in considerable
measure into its unity, especially in political groups, it strives, precisely
for the sake of its unity, for definiteness of status toward persons,
material tasks, and other societies. The large group, with the number
and variety of its elements, demands or tolerates such definiteness much
less. It is precisely that absence of organs, of reserves, of undefined and
transitional elements, which makes modification and adaptation difficult for them, and, apart from their external conditions, forces them,
on account of their fundamental sociological configuration, much
oftener to confront the question, "To be or not to be?"

By the side of such tendencies in smaller circles I cite, with the same
unavoidable arbitrary selection from innumerable cases, the following
for the sociological characterization of greater circles. I start from the
fact that these, compared with smaller circles, seem to show an inferior
degree of radicalism and obstinacy of attitude. This, however, requires
a limitation. Precisely where great masses must be set in motion in
political, social, and religious movements, they show a ruthless radicalism, a victory of the extreme parties over the mediating. This is
primarily for the reason that great masses are always filled merely with
simple ideas, and can be led by such only. What is common to many
must for that reason be of a sort which the lowest, most primitive
minds among them can entertain. And even higher and more differentiated personalities will approach each other in great numbers, not
in the more complicated and highly elaborated, but only in the relatively simple universal human conceptions and impulses. Since, however, the actualities in which the ideas of the mass strive to become
practical are always articulated in a very multifold way, and are composed of a great assemblage of very divergent elements, it follows that
simple ideas can work only in an entirely one-sided, ruthless, and
radical fashion. This fact is accentuated in case the behavior of a
crowd in actual physical contact is in question. Under such circumstances, the innumerable suggestions working back and forth produce
an extraordinarily intense nervous excitement, which often deprives
the individual of his senses, and drags him along as though he were
unconscious. It inflates every impulse, often in a freakish manner, and
makes the mob the prey of the most passionate personality in its number. This melting of masses into *one* feeling, in which all peculiarity
and reserves of personalities are suspended, is naturally in its content
so thoroughgoing, so radical, so alien to all mediation and consideration, that it would lead to sheer impracticabilities and destructions, if
it did not usually find its end at an earlier stage from inner wearinesses
and reactions, the consequence of this one-sided exaggeration. More
than that, the masses, in the sense now in mind, have little to lose. On

the contrary, they believe, so to speak, that they have everything to gain. This is the situation in which most of the restraints of radicalism habitually fall away; in this unorganized mass which consists of human beings with their immediate reciprocities, without a super-individual unity and form, those indefinitenesses, many-sidednesses, and mediatorial phenomena are lacking through which the great community ordinarily is distinguished from the small one. In order to form themselves upon the periphery of a community, they need precisely a stable center of the same, an objective social form and interest, in excess of the merely subjective and momentary unification of the elements.

Thus it is to be observed in general that small parties are more radical than large ones, of course within the limits which the ideas constituting the party prescribe. The radicalism here meant is immediately sociological; that is, it is marked by the unreserved dedication of the individual to the tendency of the group, by the sharp delimitation of the same against neighboring structures which is necessary to the self-preservation of the group, by the impossibility of taking up into the externally narrow frame a multitude of far-reaching endeavors and thoughts. The radicalism which is peculiarly such in its content is to a considerable degree independent of the sort here in mind. The unqualified coherence of the elements, upon which the possibility of radicalism rests sociologically, loses power to maintain itself as more and more varied individual elements are introduced with numerical accretion. For that reason professional labor coalitions, whose purpose is the improvement of the conditions of labor in detail, know very well that they lose in actual coherence with increase of extent. In this case, however, numerical extension has, on the other hand, the tremendous significance that every added member frees the coalition from a competitor, perhaps underbidding and thereby threatening it in its existence. There occur evidently quite special life-conditions for a group which constitutes itself inside of a large group, and subordinate to its idea, and when its idea realizes its purpose only in so far as it unites in itself all elements which fall under its presuppositions. In such cases the rule usually holds: "He that is not for me is against me"; the personality outside of the group to which it, in accordance with the claims of the latter, so to speak, ideally belongs, does the group a very positive injury, through the mere indifference of non-attachment. This is the case whether, as among labor coalitions, through competition, or when it reveals to those standing outside of the group the boundaries of its power, or when the group only comes to real existence by the inclusion of all the elements concerned, as in the case of many industrial syndicates. In case, therefore, the question of completeness, which is by no means always in point, confronts a group—that is, the question whether all elements to which its principle extends are also actually included in it—then the consequences of this *completeness* must be carefully distinguished from those consequences which follow from its size alone. To be sure, the group will also be larger if it is complete than if it is incomplete; but not this association as a quantity, but the problem dependent immediately upon that, viz., whether with that quantity the group fills out therewith a prescribed scheme, may be so important for the group that, as in the case of labor coalitions, the disadvantages in cohesion and unity, following from mere increase of numbers, may stand in direct antagonism and counterpoise with the advantages of increasing completeness.

In general we may, in a very essential degree, explain the structures which are peculiar to large communities, as such, from the fact that they produce with these structures a substitute for the personal and immediate cohesion which is peculiar to the smaller circles. In the case of the large group, the question is one of correlating centers which are channels and mediators of the reciprocal action of the elements, and which thus operate as independent bearers of the societary unity, after this is no longer produced by immediate relationship of person to person. For this purpose magistracies and representatives grow up, laws and symbols of the group-life, organizations and social generalizations. At this point I have only to emphasize their connection with the numerical point of view. They all occur purely and maturely, so far as the main point is concerned, only in large circles, *i. e.*, as the abstract form of group-dependence, whose concrete form can no longer exist after a certain extension of the community has been reached. Their utility, ramifying into a thousand social qualities, rests in the last analysis upon numerical presuppositions. The character of the superpersonal and objective with which such incorporations of the group-energies face the individual is derived directly from the *multiplicity* of the variously operative individual elements; for only through their multiplicity is the individual element in them paralyzed, and from the same cause the universal mounts to such a distance from the individual that it appears as something existing entirely by itself, not needing the individual, and possibly even antagonistic to the individual—somewhat as the *concept,* which, composed of singular and various phenomena of the common, is the higher above everyone of these details, the more it includes; so that precisely the universal ideas which rule the greatest circumference of particulars—the abstractions with which metaphysics reckons—attain a life apart, whose norms and developments are often alien, or hostile, to those of the tangible particulars. The great group thus gains its unity—as it expresses itself in its organs and in its law, in its political ideas and in its ideals—only at the price of a wide distance of all those structures from the individual, his views and needs, which find immediate activity and consideration in the social life of a small circle. From this relation there arises the typical difficulty of organizations in which a series of minor combinations are included within a larger one; viz., the fact is that the situations can be readily seen, and treated with interest and care, only close at hand; while, on the contrary, only from the distance which the central position holds can a just and regular relation of all the details to each other be established. The relationships of person to person, which constitute the life-principle of smaller circles, are not easily compatible with the distance and coolness of the objective-abstract norms without which the great group cannot exist.

The unity and the correlating form of the great group, as contrasted with its elements and their primary socializations, come into existence only through negations. Social actions and regulations evolve in many ways the character of negativity in the degree of their numerical inclusiveness. In the case of mass actions, the motives of individuals are often so different that their unification is possible in the degree in which their content is merely negative and destructive. The unrest which leads to great revolutions is always nursed from so many, and often directly opposing, sources that their focalization upon a positive aim would be impossible. The erection of the latter is usually the task then of the smaller circles, and of the energy of individuals who separate from each other in countless private undertakings, while these individuals united in a mass have worked in sweeping and destructive fashion. The same trend appears in the results of wide appeals to popular suffrage, which are so often, and almost incomprehensively, negative.

The negative character of the bond which unites the great area into a unit appears primarily in its norms. This is prepared for by the phenomenon that, other things being equal, combining determinations of every sort must be the more simple and the less comprehensive, the larger the circumference of their application. Illustrations might extend from the rules of "international courtesy," which are much fewer in number than those to be observed in every narrower circle; to the fact that the individual states of the German empire have, as a rule, a less comprehensive constitution the larger they are. Expressed in the form of a theorem: With increasing extent of the circle, the common elements which bind each with each into the social unity are decreasingly circumstantial. It is consequently (although at first paradoxical) possible to hold a great circle together with a smaller minimum of norms than would be required for a small circle. Of course, the aggregate of norms will be greater in the former than in the latter, but it consists of the special norms of the subdivisions of the circle, whereas the circle as a totality makes up for its size by deficit of many generally applicable norms. In qualitative respects, moreover, the modes of conduct which a community, in order to exist as such, must demand of its members are usually the more prohibitive and limiting in nature as extension increases. The positive combinations which, proceeding from element to element, give the group-life its proper content must at last be left to the individuals. The manifoldness of the persons, the interests, the occurrences, becomes too great to be regulated from one center. To this center, therefore, there is left only the prohibitive function, the determination of those things which *under no circumstances* may be done; the bounding of freedom rather than the direction of it—wherewith, of course, is meant only the trend of a development which is perpetually crossed and turned aside by other tendencies. Thus, where a great number of divergent circles of religious feeling or interest are to be composed into a unity. That which especially fits prohibitions to generalize smaller circles into a larger one is the circumstances that the counterpart of the forbidden is by no means always the forbidden, but often only the allowed. Thus, if in the circle A no a may occur, but β, γ, δ; in B no β, but a, γ, δ; in C no γ, but a, β, δ, etc., the unified structure may be formed from A, B, and C, upon the prohibition of a, β, γ. The unity is only possible if in A β and γ are not forbidden, but merely allowed, so that it also may be omitted. If, instead of that, β and γ are as positively forbidden as is a, and correspondingly in B and C, the consequence would be that no unit could be created which included all the positive group-limitations, because then there would always be on the one side direct prescription of that which on the other side is directly forbidden.

Perhaps the connection between the enlargement of the circle and the negative character of its determinations shows itself most decisively in the following: The more generally, that is, for the greater circle, the norm is applicable, the less is its observance characterizing and significant for the individual; while the failure to observe it is usually accompanied by especially severe and notable consequences. This is particularly the case, in the first place, in the intellectual realm. The theoretical understanding, without which there could be no human society, rests upon a small number of generally recognized, although of course not abstractly conscious, norms which we designate as logical principles. They constitute the minimum of that which must be recognized by all who want to hold commerce with each other. Upon this basis rests the most fleeting consensus of individuals least acquainted with each other, as well as the daily association of the most intimate.

Intellectual observance of these simplest norms, without which there could be no reckoning with experienced reality, is the most inexorable and most universal condition of all sociological life; for with all variety of the subjective and objective world-view, logic produces a certain common ground, departure from which must destroy all intellectual community in the broadest sense of the term. But logic, however, strictly speaking, neither means nor produces any positive possession whatever. It is only the norm against which we may not sin, while at the same time obedience to it does not afford any distinction, any specific good or quality. All attempts to win a specific cognition with the help of mere logic fail, and their sociological significance is consequently quite as negative as that of the criminal statute book. On the other hand, only failure to observe produces a special and classified situation, while remaining within the norm affords to the individual nothing else than the possibility of remaining, theoretically or practically, in the generality. To be sure, from thousandfold divergence of content, the intellectual nexus itself may fail, even with strict observance of logic; but with disregard of logic it *must* fail—precisely as the moral-social community, even with the most exact avoidance of everything criminally forbidden, may go to pieces; while with disobedience of these norms it *must* go to pieces. The case is not different with the societary forms in the more restricted sense, so far as they are actually general in a community. Although their observance is distinctive for nobody, transgression of them is in the highest degree distinctive, for the most universal laws of a community are merely not to be transgressed, while the special norms which hold together restricted circles, in the degree of their specialization, lend to the individual a positive shading and difference. The disobedience of these latter norms may destroy such a circle, but the larger comprehending group, in which the elements of the smaller belong in addition, remains still intact, and does not dissolve until its elements transgress that minimum of norms the essence of which is, in the ratio of their generality, merely prohibitive. Upon this relationship rests also the great practical utility of the quite empty societary forms of courtesy. Upon the positive existence of respect and loyalty of which they testify to us we may not count, even from their most accurate observance; on the other hand, the slightest failure to observe them proves that those feelings are *not* present. The salute upon the street by no means demonstrates respect; the omission of the same, however, gives very decided evidence of the contrary. As symbols of positive subjective attitude, these forms completely fail to be of service. The negative, however, they advertise in a most useful way, since a quite easy negligence may radically and definitely determine the relation to a given person—and indeed in the degree in which the form of courtesy is quite universal and conventional, that is, a part of the essential nature of a relatively large circle.

This form-difference of the life-conditions which attaches itself to the social quantity-difference is, in the large, denoted also by the antithesis between custom and law. It appears as though in the case of the Aryan peoples the first attachments of the individual to a super-individual life-order proceeded from a quite general instinct or concept, which signified the categorical, the appropriate, the should-be in general. The particular regulations in the realms of religion, morality, conventions, law, are not details in the sense that from them that concept could have proceeded as that which was common to them all, but they are the ramifications which rest undifferentiated in it. The concept is the original, not the later abstracted unity. In contrast now to the opinion in accordance with which morality, custom, and law have developed, so to speak, as pendants from that germ-condition, the germ seems to me rather to persist still in that which we call custom, and to represent the indifference-condition which puts forth from itself from different sides the form of law and of morality. Custom as a form of sociological combination seems to me scarcely to be capable of positive definition, but it can properly be defined only through the antithesis to those two forms which develop themselves from it— here also betraying its quite primary and general character. All three forms serve to assure the demeanor of the individual in accordance with the demands of social utility. Law has in statute and in its executive agencies the differentiated organs through which it can first precisely circumscribe its contents and, second, control them externally. Hence, however, it limits itself for utilitarian purposes to the quite essential conditions of the group-life. The free morality of the individual, on the other hand, possesses no other law than that which it gives itself autonomously from within, and no other executive than conscience. Hence its scope embraces, to be sure, in principle, the totality of action; it has, however, visibly, in its external practice, in every individual case, special accidental and varying boundaries.[1]

---

[1] That law and morality thus alike spring *pari passu* from *one* variation of societary development appears in the teleological significance of the two, which, more than the first appearance betrays, connote each other. If the restricted leading of the individual, which includes a life regulated altogether by custom, gives place to the universal legal norm, which has a much wider distance from everything individual, yet in the social interest the therewith attained freedom may still not remain responsible to itself alone. Through the moral imperative the juristic demands are enlarged, and the gaps in the regulations of life are filled, which are produced by defect of universally regulating custom. Regulation is now at the same time transferred much higher above the individual and much deeper within him, for whatever personal and metaphysical values conscience and the autonomous morality may

Through custom, then, a community assures to itself the appropriate conduct of its members, where the pressure of the law is inadequate, and the superindividual morality is not to be relied upon. Thus custom works today as complement of these two institutions, as it was the sole regulator of life at a time when these differentiated forms of norm existed either not at all or merely in the germ. Therewith is the sociological place of custom sufficiently indicated. It stands between the largest circle, as a member of which the individual is subordinate to the law, and absolute individuality, which is the sole bearer of free morality. Custom belongs, therefore, to the narrower circles, the intermediate structures between the individual and the greater community. Almost all custom is that of a rank or class; its manners of expression, such as external behavior, fashion, honor, control always only a subordinate division of the largest circle to which the law applies, and they have in the contiguous subdivisions a different content. Against failures to observe good customs reaction is produced on the part of the narrower circle of those who are in some way affected by it, or are witnesses of it, while a violation of the legal order calls out the reaction of the totality. Since custom has as its executive only public opinion, and certain reactions of individuals immediately attached to it, it is evident that a great circle, as such, is excluded from administering it. There is no need of expanding the observation that the customs of trade, as such, permit or command something different from those of the aristocracy; those of a religious circle, again, something different from those of a literary body; etc. In this connection it is obvious that the content of custom consists of the special limitations which a narrower circle needs, which circle has at its disposal for the guarantee of the limitations neither the power of civic law nor entirely trustworthy autonomous moral impulses. What is common to these circles and the most primitive, with

---

represent, their social value, which concerns us here alone, lies in their enormous prophylactic utility. Law and custom seize upon the activities of the will in their external manifestation and their realization; they operate, purely as such, in a compulsory way, at the utmost through fear. Morality, however, stands at the roots of the deed; it thus reconstructs the subjectivity of the agent until, of his own accord, he permits only the right action to proceed from himself, without needing the support of those relatively external forces. But society has no interest in the purely subjective moral perfecting of the agent. This is important to society only, and is only cultivated by society, in so far as it results in the utmost guarantee for the socially useful actions of precisely this agent. In the morality of the individual, society creates for itself an organ which is not only more fundamentally operative than law and custom, but which also spares society the different sorts of cost involved in these institutions. Hence the tendency of society to satisfy its demands as cheaply as possible results in appeals to "good conscience," through which the individual pays to himself the wages for his righteousness, which otherwise would probably have to be assured to him in some way through law or custom.

which for us social history begins, is nothing else than numerical paucity. The life-forms which earlier sufficed for the entire community-circle have, with the growth of the latter, withdrawn themselves to its subordinate divisions, for these contain now the possibilities of personal relationships, the approximate equality of level of the members, the common interests and ideals, in the presence of which one may confide social regulation to so precarious and ambiguous a species of norm as customary morality is. With increasing quantity of the elements, and of the therewith unavoidable independence of the same, these limitations disappear for the circle as a whole. The peculiar constraining power of custom becomes for the state too little, and for the individual too much. The former demands greater guarantees, the latter greater freedom; and only with those sides with which each element belongs to intermediate circles is it still socially controlled through custom.

To this correlation which attaches the difference of the social form of custom from that law, to the quantitative variation of the communities, there are obvious exceptions. Within the particular state many modes of action are established as law which in external relationships, that is, within the largest circle, must be consigned to the looser form of custom. The resolution of the contradiction is very simple: The size of the circle demands the legal form naturally only in that relation in which the manifoldness of its elements *is composed into a unity.* The social unity is a graduated idea; the spirit and purpose of various circles demand various degrees in the closeness and strength of their unity; so that the social form of regulation which is demanded by a certain quantity of the circle, with respect to the degree of the unity which it is to achieve may still be the same with different quantities. The significance of the numerical conditions is thus not impaired if a greater circle, on account of its special tasks, may or must content itself without giving legal forms to its rules, just as in other cases is possible only to a smaller circle.

It is evident that the concepts "greater and smaller circle" are of a very crude scientific order, entirely indefinite and fluctuating, and properly applicable in general only in order to point out the dependence of the sociological form-character of a group upon its quantitative limitations. It cannot serve in any way to show more exactly the actual proportion which exists between the former and the latter. Nevertheless it is perhaps not in all cases impossible to make out this proportion more exactly. In the thus far observed formations and relationships any attempt to assign precise numerical values would evidently be, for any stage of our knowledge that can be foreseen, a completely fantastic undertaking. But within certain limits even now traits of those socializations may be cited which exist between a limited number of persons, and which are characterized by this limitation.

THE ISOLATE

The numerically simplest formations which can at all be designated as social reciprocities appear to occur in the case of reactions between two elements. Yet there is a structure still simpler in external appearance, which belongs in sociological categories, namely, however paradoxical and essentially contradictory it seems, the isolated individual man. As a matter of fact, the processes which produce formations in the case of a duality of elements are often simpler than those necessary for the sociological characterization of the integer. In the case of these latter we have to do chiefly with two here pertinent phenomena: isolation and freedom. The mere fact that an individual is in no sort of reciprocal relationship with other individuals is, of course, not sociological, but it also does not fill out the entire concept of isolation. This concept rather, in so far as it is emphasized and is essentially significant, signifies by no means merely the absence of all society, but rather the existence of society in some way represented and afterward inhibited. Isolation receives its unequivocal positive meaning as long-distance effect of society—whether as echo of past or anticipation of future relationships; whether as longing after society or as voluntary turning away from it. The isolated man has not the same characteristics as if he had been from the beginning the only inhabitant of the world; but socialization, even if it is only that with the negative coefficient, determines *his* condition also. The whole joy and the whole bitterness of isolation are merely various reactions upon socially experienced influences. Either is a reciprocal effect from which the one member, after production of definite consequences, is really excluded and further lives and further works only ideally in the mind of the other member. In this connection there is decided significance in the well-known psychological fact that the feeling of loneliness seldom occurs so decidedly and importunately in actual physical isolation as when one is conscious of being a stranger and without attachments among many physically quite adjacent people. For the configuration of a group much depends upon whether it favors or even renders possible such loneliness within its limits. Close and intimate communities do not permit such intercellular vacuums in their structure. As we speak, however, of a social deficit, which is produced in fixed proportions to the societary conditions—the anti-social phenomena of the miserable, the criminal, the suicides—in like manner a given quantity and quality of societary life produces a certain number of temporarily or chronically solitary existences, which, to be sure, the statistician cannot so exactly as in these other cases express in arithmetical terms. In another way isolation becomes sociologically significant, so soon as it ceases to consist in a relationship which is a play within an individual between himself and another definite group, or group-life in general; but is rather a pause or a periodic differentiation within one and the same relationship. This is important in relationships which from their fundamental idea are aimed at permanent negation of isolation, as in the chief instance of monogamous marriage. So far as in the structure of this relation the finest subjective shadings express themselves, there is an essential difference whether man and wife, with the complete happiness of life in common, have still preserved for themselves the pleasure in isolation, or whether their relation is never interrupted by devotion to solitude—either because the habit of being together has taken from solitude its charm, or because an absence of essential assurance of love makes such interruptions feared as dangers or as infidelities. Thus isolation, apparently confined to a single person, consisting in the negation of sociality, is really a phenomenon of very positive sociological significance; not merely from the side of the agent, in whom it presents, as a conscious affection, an entirely determinate relation to society, but also through the decisive characteristic which its occurrence, both as cause and as effect, lends to large groups as well as to the most intimate relationships.

THE DYAD

The sociological formation which is *methodologically* simplest is that between *two* elements. It furnishes the scheme, the germ, and the material for countless more complex formations; although its sociological significance by no means rests merely upon its extensions and its multiplications. It is rather itself a socialization, in which not only many forms of socialization realize themselves, purely and characteristically, but the limitation to a duality of the elements is, indeed, the condition under which alone a certain series of forms of relationship can emerge. The typically sociological nature of the same appears then not only in the fact that the greatest manifoldness of the individualities and of the combining motives does not alter the similarity of these formations, but rather that these sometimes occur quite as typically between pairs of groups—families, states, combinations of various sorts—as between pairs of single persons.

The peculiar conferring of characteristics upon a relationship through the duality of persons concerned in it is exhibited by everyday experiences. For instance, how differently a common lot, an undertaking, an agreement, a shared secret binds each of two sharers, from the case when even only three participate. The specific character of this difference is determined by the fact that the relationship, as a unity composed of its individuals, as a special structure beyond these, has a different bearing upon each of its participants from that of a more complicated structure to each of its members. However it may appear to third parties as an independent, superindividual unity, yet, as a rule, that is not the case for its participants, but each regards himself in antithesis only with the other, but not with a collectivity extending beyond him. The social structure rests immediately upon the one and the other. The departure of each single individual would destroy the whole, so that it does not come to such a superpersonal life of the whole that the individual feels himself independent; whereas, even in the case of an association of only three, if one individual departs, a *group* may still continue to exist.

There are, nevertheless, exceptions to this character of the dual groupings, the most decisive of which seems to appear in the case of that relationship which depends most definitely upon the dyad type, that is, monogamous marriage. The by no means rare fact that among thoroughly worthy persons decidedly unfortunate marriages occur, and very fortunate ones between defective persons, points at once to the fact that this structure, however *dependent* it is upon each of the members, still may have a character which coincides with that of neither associate. If, for example, each of the wedded pair suffers from vagaries, difficulties, and unavailabilities, but at the same time understands how to localize these upon himself, while he invests in the marital relationship only his best and purest, and thus holds the relationship free from all the discounts which affect himself as a person, this may immediately be to the credit merely of the partner in marriage as a person, but nevertheless arises from it the feeling that marriage is something superpersonal, something in itself worthy and sacred, which stands over and above the unsanctity of each of its elements. Since within a relationship the one is sensitive only on the side toward the other, and behaves only with regard to him, his qualities, although they are, of course, always his own, nevertheless attain a quite different shading, status, and meaning from that which they have when, referring only to the proper *ego,* they weave themselves into the total complexity of the *ego.* Hence for the consciousness of each of the two the relationship may crystallize to an entity outside of himself, which is more and better—under certain circumstances also worse—than himself; something toward which he has obligations, and from which there come to him, as from an objective existence, benefits and injuries.

Something sociologically similar might be pointed out, furthermore, in the duality of partners in a business. Although the formation and operation of the partnership rest, perhaps, exclusively upon the cooperation of these two personalities, yet the subject-matter of this co-operation, the business or the firm, is an objective structure, toward which each of its components has rights and duties—in many respects not otherwise than any third party. Yet this has a sociological meaning different from that in the case of marriage; for the business is something from the beginning separated from the persons of those who carry it on, and indeed in the case of a duality of such persons this is not otherwise true than in the case of one alone or many. The reciprocal relationship of the business associates has its purpose outside of itself; whereas in the case of marriage it is within itself. In the former instance the relationship is the means for the gaining of certain objective results; in the latter everything objective appears really only as a means for the subjective relationship. It is the more observable that in marriage, nevertheless, the objectivity and self-reliance of the group-structure, which are otherwise more foreign to groups of two, psychologically increase in contrast with immediate subjectivity.

One constellation, however, of extreme sociological importance is wanting in every grouping of two, while it is in principle open to every group of larger numbers, namely, the *shifting* of duties and responsibilities upon the impersonal structure, which so often, and not to its advantage, characterizes social life. This occurs in two directions. Every totality which is more than a mere juxtaposition of given individuals has an indefiniteness of its boundaries and of its power which easily tempts us to expect from it all sorts of achievements that really belong to the separate members. We turn them over to the society, as we very often, in pursuance of the same psychological tendency, postpone them to our own future, whose nebulous possibilities give room for everything, or will accomplish, by spontaneously growing strength, everything which the present moment is not willing to take upon itself. In the precise circumstances in question, the power of the individual is transparent, but for that very reason it is also clearly limited, while in contrast with it is always the somewhat mystical power of the totality, of which we therefore easily expect, not only what the individual cannot perform, but also what he would not care to perform, and, moreover, with the feeling of the full legitimacy of this transfer. Quite as dangerous, however, as on the side of omission is membership in a totality also on the side of commission. Here the point is not merely the increase of impulsiveness and the exclusion of moral restraint, as they appear in the case of the individual in a crowd, and lead to those mass-crimes in which even the legal responsibility of the participants is debatable, but the point is that the true or the ostensible interest of a community justifies or constrains the individual in undertakings for which he would not be willing to bear the responsibility as an individual. Economic combinations make demands of such shameless egoism, colleagues in office wink at such crying malfeasances, corporations of political or of scientific nature exercise such monstrous suppressions of individual rights, as would be impossible in the case of an individual if he were responsible for them as a person, or at least they would put him to shame. As a member of a corporation, however, he does all this with untroubled conscience, because in that case he is anonymous and feels himself covered and, as it were, concealed by the totality. There are few cases in which the distance of the social unity from the elements which constitute it is so great. It is perceptible and operative to a degree which descends almost to caricature.

It was necessary to indicate this reduction of the practical worth of personality, which inclusion in a group often occasions for the individual, in order that, by exclusion of this factor, we might characterize the dyad-group. Since in this case each element has only another individual by its side, but not a multiplicity which ultimately constitutes a higher unity, the dependence of the whole upon himself, and consequently his co-responsibility for all collective action, is made perfectly visible. He can, to be sure, as happens frequently enough, shift responsibility upon his associate, but the latter will be able to decline the same much more immediately and decisively than can often be done by an anonymous whole, which lacks the energy of personal interest or the legitimate representation requisite for such cases. Moreover, just as the one of two constituting a group cannot hide himself behind the group in cases of positive action, no more can he claim the group for his excuse in cases of culpable inaction. The energies with which the group very indefinitely and very partially, to be sure, but still very perceptibly, overtops the individual cannot in this instance reinforce the individual inadequacy, as in the case of larger combinations; for, however manifoldly two combined individuals accomplish more than two that are isolated, yet the decisive factor in this case is that each must actually perform something, and that, when he refuses to do this, only the other remains, without any superindividual energy such as, even in the case of a combination of only three, is in some measure present. The significance of this detail resides, however, by no means merely in the negative, in that which it excludes; from it grows rather a close and special modulation of the union of two. Precisely the fact that each knows he can depend only upon the other, and upon nobody else, gives to such a combination— for example, marriage, friendship, and even more external combinations up to political adjustment of two groups—a special consecration; each element in them is, in respect to its sociological destiny and everything dependent upon this, much more frequently made to confront the alternative of all or nothing than in other associations. This peculiar intimacy appears most simply in the contrast between it and combinations of three. In such a case each individual element operates as a court of appeal between the two others, and exhibits the double function of such an organ. It operates both in combining and separating. Where three elements, A, B, C, constitute a community, there is added to the immediate relationship which exists, for example, between A and B, the immediate relationship which they gain by their common relation to C. This is unquestionably a sociological enrichment, apart from the bond by the straight and shortest line; each pair of elements are now joined by a broken line. Points upon which the pair could find no immediate contact are put in reciprocal relationship by the third element, which offers to each another side, and joins these, nevertheless, in the unity of its personality. Separations which the parties could not of themselves reconcile are accommodated by the third, or by their being included in a comprehensive whole. On the other hand, the direct union is not merely strengthened by the indirect, but it may also be destroyed. There is no relationship so complete between three that each individual may not, under certain circumstances, be regarded by the other two as an intruder, even if it is only to the extent of sharing in certain moods, which can develop their concentration and timid tenderness only with undisturbed glance from eye to eye. It may also be observed how extraordinarily rare and difficult it is for three people, even in the case of a visit to a museum or in the presence of a landscape, to come into a really united state of feeling, which, however, may occur with relative ease between two. A and B may emphasize the μ which they have in common and may feel it undisturbed, because the ν which A does not share with B and the ξ which B does not share with A are felt immediately as an individual reserve, and as located in another story of one's being. If, however, a C joins the company, who shares the ν with A and the ξ with B, the result is that even under this scheme, which is still favorable to the unity of the whole, the unification of feeling is in principle arrested. While two may actually be *one* party, or may stand quite beyond the party question, it is usual in precisely such finely tuned combinations for three to constitute at the same time three parties, and consequently to terminate the unified relation of each to every other. The sociological structure of the combination in twos is consequently distinguished by the fact that both phenomena are lacking: both the strengthened attachment through a third, or, it may be, through a social frame reaching out over both, and also the interruption and distraction of pure and immediate reciprocation. But in many cases this lack makes the relationship more intensive and strong, for in the feeling of being thrown exclusively upon each other, and of having no hope of recourse to cohesive forces which do not spring from immediate reciprocity, many otherwise undeveloped energies, which have their source in remoter psychical reservoirs, will become vital in the community, and many disturbances and threatenings into which there might be betrayal, under confidence in the third party and in a totality, are carefully avoided. This intimacy, to which the circumstances existing between *two* people incline them, furnishes the reason why precisely these constitute the chief seat of jealousy.

Merely another variation of the same fundamental sociological constellation may be expressed in the observation that relationships of twos, composition of a whole out of only two participants, must presuppose a higher degree of individualization on the part of each of these than, *caeteris paribus,* in the case of combinations of many elements. In the present instance the essential factor is that in a combination of two there is no majority which can override the individual, and that occasion for such a majority is given so soon as a single unit is added. Relationships, however, in which the domination of an individual by a majority is possible, not merely depress the individuality, but, so far as they are voluntary, they will not be readily entered upon by very decided individualities. In this connection, nevertheless, we must distinguish two frequently interchanged concepts; namely, the decided and the strong individuality. There are persons and collective structures of the extremest individualization that, however, have not the energy to protect this peculiarity against suppressions or leveling forces. On the contrary, the strong personality may confirm its formation in reaction with these very contrasts, in struggle for its peculiarity, and in opposition to all temptations to smoothing and mixture. The former, the merely qualitative individuality, will shun unions in which it finds itself in antithesis with an eventual majority; it is, on the contrary, as it were, predestined to the manifold unions in pairs, because, by reason of its differentiation, as well as its susceptibility to attack, reinforcement by another is its indicated recourse. The other type, the more intensive individuality, rather courts, on the other hand, the opposition of others against whose quantitative excess it can preserve its dynamic superiority. Technical grounds, so to speak, will justify this preference: the triple consulate of Napoleon was decidedly more convenient for him than a duality would have been, for he needed to gain over only the *one* colleague (which is very easy for the stronger nature among three) in order to dominate the other; that is, in fact, to dominate the other two in the most legal form. On the whole, it may be said that unions in pairs, as contrasted with those of larger numbers, favor a relatively higher individuality of the participants, while, on the other hand, they presuppose that the restraint of peculiarity through the social articulation to an average level is lacking.

That combinations of two in general have, as such, specific traits is shown not merely by the fact that the entrance of a third modifies them entirely, but still more the variously observed fact that the still further extension to four or more by no means modifies the nature of the combination to a correspondingly wide degree. For example, a marriage union resulting in a single child has a quite different character from a childless union, while there is not an equally significant difference between it and the union resulting in two or more children. To be sure, the difference in its essential nature which the second child produces is again much greater than that springing from the arrival of the third. But this simply follows the above rule; for a family with one child is still, in many respects, a relationship between two members; namely, the parents as a unity, on the one hand, the child on the other. The second child is then in fact not merely a fourth, but, sociologically considered, at the same time also a third member in a relationship, and it exerts the peculiar influences of such third members; for within the family, so soon as the actual age of minority is passed, the parents constitute much more frequently a working unity than do the children as a totality.

Furthermore, in the realm of the forms of marriage the decisive difference is whether, on the one hand, monogamy prevails, or, on the other, the man has a second wife. If the latter is the case, the third or the twentieth wife is relatively without significance for the structure of the union. Within the boundaries of such a structure, the step to the second wife is here also, at least in *one* direction, richer in consequences than that to a still larger number, for precisely the duality of wives may give occasion, in the life of the man, to the sharpest conflicts and profoundest perplexities, which, in general, do not arise in the case of each higher number. For in the latter instance such a fundamental declassing and deindividualizing of the wives is involved, there is so decided reduction of the relationship to its sensuous basis (since every more spiritual union is always of a more individual nature), that in general it cannot lead to those profounder disturbances for the man which may flow directly and only from a dual relationship.

It is the same fundamental motive which reappears in the assertion of Voltaire about the utility of religious anarchy; that is, two rival sects within a state produce, unavoidably, disturbances and difficulties such as never could arise in the case of two hundred. The meaning which the dualism of the one element in a combination of several members possesses, is, of course, not less specific and significant when it serves to secure, rather than disturb, the total relationship. Thus it is asserted that the collegiate relationship of the two Roman consuls perhaps operated more effectively against monarchical ambitions than the system of the nine highest functionaries in Athens. It is the same tension of dualism which works, now destructively, now conservatively, according to the other circumstances of the total association. The essential thing here is that this total association receives a totally different sociological character so soon as the performance in question is the work either of a single person, on the one hand, or of more than two, on the other.

In addition, now, to the type which presented the duality of the elements in general as so decisive that further numerical increase did not change it in a marked degree, I mention furthermore two very singular, but nevertheless, as sociological types, highly important facts. The political status of France in Europe was immediately modified most significantly when it entered into a close relationship with Russia. A third and fourth member of the alliance would produce no further essential variation after the principal change had once occurred. The contents of human life vary to a considerable degree in accordance with whether the first step is the most difficult and decisive, and all later steps have in comparison with it secondary importance, or whether the first step in itself means nothing, but its continuations and advances realize the modifications toward which it merely points. The numerical relationships of socialization furnish, as will later appear more and more, abundant examples for both forms. For to the state which has lost its political prestige by isolation, the fact of any alliance at all is the decisive matter, whereas perhaps definite economic or military advantages may be reached only when a circle of combinations is realized, from which not even *one* may be lacking without totally preventing the success of the whole. Between these two types there is evidently, then, the one into which the definite character and result of the combination enter, in direct ratio with the number of the elements; for example, as a rule in the case of the unification of great masses. The second type comprises the experience that relationships of command and assistance change their character in principle when, instead of *one* servant, assistant, or other subordinate, there are two in the same relationship. Housekeepers often prefer, entirely apart from the question of expense, to get along with a single servant, on account of the peculiar difficulties that come with an increase of the number. From the natural need of attachment the single servant will seek to approach and identify himself with the personal sphere and the circle of interests of his employer. Precisely the same cause will influence him, however, to compose, with a possible second servant, a party against the employer, for now each has a recourse in the other. The class feeling, with its latent or conscious opposition against the employer, does not become effective until there are two, because it emerges as the common element between them. In short, the sociological situation between the superior and the inferior is absolutely changed so soon as the third element is added. Instead of solidarity, party formation is rather the more natural tendency. Instead of emphasis upon that which is a bond of union between servant and master, the emphasis is rather put on that which divides them, because community is now sought on the side of the associate, and is, of course, found precisely in that which constitutes the antithesis between the two and the superior. Moreover, the transformation of the numerical into a qualitative difference remains not less fundamental when it shows the reverse result for the controlling element of the association. It is easier to hold at the desired distance two subordinates than one, and their superior possesses, in their jealousy and competition, an instrument for keeping each down and making him obedient, for which there is no equivalent to be used in the case of a single inferior. In a formally similar sense, an old proverb says: "He that hath one child is its slave; he that hath more is their master." In each case the combination of threes is distinguished as a completely new structure from that of twos. The latter are characterized by the fact that the former are specifically differentiated, only backward, in contrast with the dual combinations, but not forward, by contrast with those which are composed of four and more elements.

In transition to the special forms of the tripartite combination of elements, attention must be called to the variety of group characters which their division into two or into three chief parties announces. Periods of excitement habitually place the whole of public life under the motto: "He that is not for me is against me." The consequence must be a division of the elements into two parties. In such case the duality appears, not as the point of departure of sociological formations, but as result and expression of them. We cannot make the tremendous variety of the forms of relationship, and of the degrees of repulsion and attraction within them, more evident than in the application of that principle; for all interests, convictions, impulses, which place us in any positive or negative relationship whatsoever to others, are differentiated by the extent to which the principle applies to them, and they may be arranged in a series, starting from the radical exclusion of all mediation and nonpartisanship and extending to tolerance for the contrasted standpoint, as one that is also legitimate and, up to a certain gradation of *more-or-less,* in agreement with the peculiar standpoint. Every decision which has a relationship to the narrower or wider circle that surrounds us, which assigns us a station in it, which includes a subjective or external co-operation, a well-wishing or a mere acquiescence, a magnifying of self, or a positive imperiling of self, occupies a definite degree in such a scale. Each draws an ideal line around us which definitely includes or excludes every other with finality, or it has gaps to which the question of inclusion or exclusion is not proposed, or the line is so drawn that it makes possible a mere tangency, or a merely partial inclusion and partial exclusion. Whether and with what decisiveness the question "for me or against me" is raised, is determined by no means merely by the logical precision of its content, nor by the passion with which the soul insists upon this content, but rather by the relation of the questioner to his social circle. The narrower and more compact this circle is, the less can the agent coexist with others than those who are of entirely similar minds; and the more his ideal demand synthesizes the totality of all the latter as a unity, the more uncompromising will be, in each case, the pressing of the question "for or against." The radicalism with which Jesus formulates this alternative rests upon the unlimited strength of the feeling of the peculiar unity of all those to whom his message has come. That there can be, with reference to this message, not merely acceptance or rejection, but only acceptance or hostility, this is the strongest expression of the unlimited unity of those who belong with him and of the unlimited externality of those who do not belong with him. The struggle, the being against me, is always a decisive relationship; it proclaims a still stronger subjective unity, although perverse in its tendency, than the indifferent standing by, and the compromising half-and-half doing. The basal sociological feeling will consequently impel to the division of the whole complex of elements into two parties. Where, on the contrary, that passionate, comprehensive feeling with reference to the whole is lacking, which constrains each to take a positive attitude of acceptance or of attack with reference to the emerging idea or demand; where every fractional group contents itself essentially with its existence as a partial group, without taking seriously the demand for inclusion of the whole, there a platform is given for a multiplicity of party structures, for tolerance, for intermediate parties, for a scale of graded changes. That epochs in which great masses are set in motion closely correspond with the dualism of parties, exclude indifferentism, and degrade the influence of mediating parties, is intelligible from the radicalism which we have observed as the character of mass movements. The *simplicity* of the ideas by which these are led demands a decisive yes or no. In the presence of the fundamental practical problems, there are, as a rule, only those two simple standpoints, while there may be innumerable that are mixed and thus mediating. In the same way, as a rule every *energetic* movement within a group, from the domestic group through the whole series of interest communities up to the political, will tend to promote stratification into a pure dualism. The accelerated tempo in the evolution of interests in the progress through stages of development, urges constantly toward more definitive decisions and separations. All mediations require time and leisure; quiet and stagnant epochs, in which the live questions are not stirred up, but are left covered by the regularity of the everyday interests, easily permit unobserved transitions to occur, and they give room for indifferent personalities which a more energetic tendency would necessarily drag into the antithesis of the principal parties. The typical difference of the sociological constellation remains thereby evidently always that of the two or of three chief parties. In the function of the third, namely, that of mediating between two extremes, several may share in graded degrees. This function is, so to speak, only a sort of extension or refinement in the technical equipment of the principle. This mediation itself, however, the decisive modification of the configuration from within, occurs only through the addition of the *third* party.

THE TRIAD

The role which the third party plays, and the configurations which result between *three* social elements, are herewith already indicated in large measure. The two presented both the first synthesis and unification and also the first separation and antithesis. The appearance of the third denotes transition, conciliation, abandonment of the absolute antithesis—sometimes, indeed, also the founding of such an antithesis. The tri-unity as such appears to me to produce three sorts of typical group-forms, which on the one hand are not possible with two elements, on the other hand, in case of a number greater than three, are either likewise excluded, or are merely extended quantitatively without changing their form-type.

1. *The unpartisan and the mediator.*—It is a highly effective sociological fact that the common relationship of isolated elements to a potentiality existing outside of themselves produces a unification between them.

In the most significant case of bipartite combinations, namely, monogamous marriage, the child or the children, as a third element, may often exercise the function of holding the whole together. In the case of many nature peoples, the marriage is only considered actually complete or as indissoluble when a child is born. The ground for this rests, of course, in the value which the child has for the man, and in his inclination, sanctioned by statute or custom, to disown a childless wife. The actual result, however, is that this third additional element really for the first time closes the circle by binding the two others together. This may occur in two forms. Either the existence of the third element immediately produces or strengthens the attachment of the two, as for example, when the birth of a child increases the love of the parents for each other, or, at least, that of the man for the wife, or the relation of each one of the two to the third produces a new and *indirect* attachment between them, as the common cares of parents for a child universally signify a bond which must always lead beyond this child, and does not consist of sympathies which could spare this intermediate station. This coming into existence of essential socialization out of three elements, while the two elements of themselves offer resistance to socialization, is the reason why many essentially disharmonious married pairs wish for no children. It is the instinct that therewith a circle would be closed, within which they would be bound closer together—and that not externally alone, but also in the profounder psychic strata—than they are inclined to be. It is by no means a contradictory case if sometimes very intimate and passionate unions prefer to be childless. In such instances the immediate attachment is so strong that if a third element were to enter the circle, even though it is indirectly an element of cohesion, it would stimulate consciousness not so much of the attachment, which already exists in its highest degree, but rather of the indirectness of the relation through the third factor, which would thus operate relatively as an interruption. We must not overlook the fact, which is of the highest importance for all human attachment, that every mediation inserts itself *between* the elements which are to be combined, and thus separates in the very act of uniting them. When mediation is no longer necessary, this factor of interposition and separation, latent in every mediation, is accentuated: where mediation is superfluous, it is for that very reason worse than superfluous, and becomes quite as obnoxious as where its unifying function as such is not desired.

Another variation of mediation occurs when the third element functions as a nonpartisan. In that case the mediator will either secure a consensus of the other two colliding elements, in which instance the mediator seeks to eliminate himself, and only to bring to pass that the two disunited or ununited parties may unite directly; or he acts as arbitrator and attempts to reconcile to each other the conflicting claims, and to eliminate whatever in them is irreconcilable. We find boards of conciliation in which the parties, under the presidency of a nonpartisan, put an end to quarrels by conferences. The mediator in this form brings about reconciliation, to be sure, only when, in the belief of both parties, the circumstances in themselves indicate the advantage of peace; in a word, when the real situation in itself justifies peace. Apart from matter-of-course removal of misunderstandings, appeals to good intentions, etc., the way is prepared for progress of this belief among the parties, through the mediation of the nonpartisan, somewhat in the following manner: While the nonpartisan holds the claims and the arguments of the one party before the other, they lose the tone of that subjective passion which produces the like on the other side. Here appears, in a wholesome way, what is so often to be regretted; namely, that the feeling which accompanies a psychic content within its first agent, within a second, to whom this content is transferred, is considerably weakened. For that reason recommendations and testimonials which must first pass several intermediate persons are so often impotent, even if their objective content comes with no real diminution to the person who is to give the final decision. In the transfer affective imponderabilities are lost which not only insufficient actual reasons replace, but even sufficient ones supply with the impulse for realization. This fact, which is highly significant for the development of purely psychical influences, brings to pass, in the simple case of a third mediating social element, that the modulations of feeling which accompany the demand, because they are formulated from one unpartisan side and represented to the other, suddenly fall away from the material content, and thus the circle fatal to all conciliation is avoided, viz., that the intensity of the one provokes that of the other, and then the latter reacts to increase the violence of the first, and so on until there is no stopping-place. More than this, each party not merely hears more objective statement, but each must also express himself more objectively than in the case of immediate confronting of the contestant. For now it is an object to each party to win over the mediator also to its standpoint. Where the third party is not arbitrator, but merely the leader of the attempted reconciliation, and must constantly hold himself this side of actual decision, whereas the arbitrator finally takes a decided position on one side, this winning of the mediator's approval can be hoped for only on the basis of the most real grounds. Within the range of sociological technique there is nothing which so effectively promotes the uniting of conflicting parties as their objectivity; that is, the attempt to let the bare material-content underneath the complaints and demands speak for itself—to put it in philosophic terms, to let the objective spirit of the party standpoint speak—so that the persons appear only as the irrelevant vehicles of the same. The personal form in which objective contents are subjectively living must pay for its warmth, its shading, its depth of feeling, with the keenness of the antagonism which it produces in cases of conflict; the toning down of this personal factor is the condition upon which agreement and understanding are attainable between the opponents; and this is the case especially because only under such conditions does each party actually perceive what the other *must* insist upon. Psychologically expressed, the problem is that of reducing the volitional form of antagonism to the intellectual: the understanding is everywhere the principle of consensus; upon it as a basis there may be accommodation of those things which, upon the basis of feeling and of final appeal to the will, irreconcilably repel each other. The mediator's office is, then, to promote this reduction, to represent it at the same time in himself, or, otherwise expressed, to constitute a sort of central station which, in whatever form the controverted material may come in from one side, may give it out to the other side only in objective form, and may hold back everything over and above the objective which needlessly encourages strife carried on without mediation.

For the analysis of community life it is important to make clear that the constellation just characterized constantly occurs in all groups which count more than two elements, even where the mediator is not specially chosen, and is not, as such, particularly known or designated. The group of three is here only type and scheme. All cases of mediation finally reduce to its form. There is no community of threes, from the conversation for an hour up to family life, in which there does not presently occur dissension, now between this pair, now between that, harmless or acute, momentary or permanent, of theoretical or practical nature, and in which the third does not exercise a mediatorial function. This occurs countless times in quite rudimentary ways, perhaps only in suggestive fashion, mixed with other actions and reciprocal relationships from which it is impossible to abstract the mediating function distinctly. Such mediations need not occur in words: a gesture, a way of listening, the quality of feeling which proceeds from a person, suffices to give to this dissent between two others a direction toward consensus, to make the essentially common underneath an acute difference of opinion perceptible, to bring this into the form in which it will most easily exert its proper influence. The issue need by no means be a real strife or struggle. It is rather the thousand easy varieties of opinion, the jarring of an antagonism of natures, the emergence of quite momentary antitheses of interest or feeling, which color the fluctuating form of every association, and is constantly modified in its course by the presence of the third party, who almost of necessity exercises the mediatorial function. This function passes around among the three elements in rotation, so to speak, since the ebb and flow of associated life constantly realize this form in the case of every possible combination of the elements.

The nonpartisanship demanded for mediation may have two sorts of pre-condition. The third party is nonpartisan if he is either beyond the interests and opinions which separate the others and is thus untouched by them, or if he shares in *both* in equal degrees. The former case is the simplest, and it involves the smallest number of complications.

The position of the nonpartisan tends to more complicated formation when he owes his position to equal participation in the contradictory interests instead of to indifference to both. A mediatorial status upon this basis is often made possible when a personality belongs locally to another circle of interests from that which is immediately concerned with the material question. The difficulty of such position of mediator usually consists in the fact that the equality of his interest for both parties, his essential equilibrium of interest, is not securely demonstrable, and is often enough suspected by *both* parties. A still more difficult and often tragic situation occurs, however, when it is not such separated interest-provinces of the third party with which he is attached to each of the others, but when his *whole* personality is close to both. This case is most sharply defined when the object of struggle cannot be distinctly objectified, and the essential significance of the struggle is only an excuse or an accidental occasion for deeper personal incompatibilities. In such a case the third party, who is intimately united by love or duty, by destiny or habit, with each of the two in equal degrees, will be directly consumed by the conflict much more than if he placed himself upon one of the two sides. This is all the more the case since in these instances the equilibrium of his interests, which permits no one-sided decision, usually leads to no successful mediation, because reduction to a merely material antithesis is impossible. This is the type of very many family conflicts. Whereas the mediator who is nonpartisan through equal distance from the contestants can with relative ease do justice to both, he who is mediator by reason of equal nearness to both will find it very much more difficult, and will come personally into the most painful dualism of feeling.

Herewith is the transition given to the second form of unification by means of the nonpartisan: that is, to arbitration. So long as the third party works as a real mediator, the ending of the conflict rests finally in the hands of the parties themselves. By choice of the arbitrator they have put this ultimate decision out of their own hands.

They have at the same time projected their purpose of conciliation beyond themselves. It has become a person in the arbitrator, whereby it attains special distinctness and energy in contrast with the antagonistic forces. The voluntary appeal to an arbitrator, to whom the parties subordinate themselves *a priori,* presupposes a greater subjective confidence in the objectivity of the judgment than any other form of decision, for even before the civic court the action of the appellant only proceeds from confidence in the justness of the decision (since he regards that decision as just which is favorable to himself); the respondent must take part in the process, whether he believes in the nonpartisanship of the judge or not. Arbitration, however, occurs, as was said, only through this belief on *both* sides. In principle mediation is differentiated from arbitration very sharply by the difference thus pointed out, and the more official the conciliatory action is, the more tenaciously will this differentiation be kept in mind, from the conflicts between capitalists and laborers mentioned above, to those of high politics, in which the "friendly offices" of a government, for the adjustment of a conflict between two others, are something quite different from the function of arbitrator which the ruler of a third land is sometimes invited to undertake.

On the whole, in accordance with all the foregoing, the existence of the nonpartisan serves to promote the stability of the group; as provisional representative of the intellectual energy, in contrast with the momentary disposition of the parties to be controlled more by will and feeling, he reinforces these parties, so to speak, to completeness of the psychic unity which resides in the life of the group. He is, on the one side, the retarding factor opposed to the impulsiveness of the other, while, on the contrary, he may carry and lead the movement of the whole group in case the antagonism of the two other elements would paralyze its energy. Nevertheless, this result may be transformed into its opposite. In case of the assumed correlation the elements of the group that are intellectually most endowed will especially incline to nonpartisanship, because cool intelligence is likely to find light and shade on both sides, and is not likely to find objective equity wholly on either side. Consequently the most intelligent elements are often unable to exert influence upon the decision of conflicts, although such influence from precisely such a quarter were highly to be wished. Just such elements as these should throw their weight into the balance when the group must choose between yes and no, since with their help the balance would be the more likely to incline toward the right side. If, therefore, nonpartisanship does not contribute to practical mediation, the consequence will be that through its connection with the intellectuality of the group the decision will be left to the play of the more foolish, or at least the more prejudiced, forces of the group.

2. *The tertius gaudens.*—The nonpartisanship of the third element has benefited or injured the group as a whole, in the combinations thus far discussed. The mediator and the arbitrator alike wish to preserve the group unity against the danger of disruption. The nonpartisan, however, may use his relatively superior status in a purely egoistic interest. While in the former cases he acted as a means to the ends of the group, in this case, on the contrary, he makes the reciprocal occurrences between the parties and between himself and the parties a means for his own ends. Here we have to do not always with previously consolidated structures, in the social life of which this occurrence emerges by the side of others, but now the relationship between the parties and the nonpartisan is often formed *ad hoc.* Elements which otherwise constitute no reciprocal unity may come into conflict; a third, previously unattached to both alike, may seize, by means of a spontaneous action, the opportunities which this conflict gives to him, the nonpartisan, and thus may set up a purely precarious reciprocity, whose vitality and richness of forms may for each element be entirely out of proportion to the fluidity of its constitution.

I note, without further discussion, two forms of the *tertius gaudens,* because the reciprocity within the tetrad, with the typical forms of which we are here concerned, does not appear very characteristically in these instances. Rather is the significant thing in these cases a certain passivity, which rests either upon the two contestants or upon the third element. The forms are these: In the first place the advantage of the third may be produced by the fact that the two others hold each other reciprocally in check, and he can now make a gain which one of these two would otherwise contest with him. The quarrel brings about in this instance merely a paralyzing of forces which, if they could, would turn against the third. The situation in this case thus really suspends the reciprocity between the three elements, instead of establishing it, without on that account, it must be added, excluding the most appreciable results for all three. We have to treat the intentional production of this situation in the case of the next configuration of threes. In the second place, advantage may accrue to the third party merely because the action of the one contending party realizes this advantage for purposes of its own, and without the necessity of using any initiative on the part of the person reaping the advantage. The type for this form is furnished by the benefactions and the promotions which a party may confer upon a third, merely for the sake of thereby embarrassing the opposing party.

The formations of this type which are more essential at this point, result when the third party, for reasons of prudence respecting his own interests, adopts an attitude of practical support toward the one party (that is, not merely by way of intellectual decision, as in the case of the arbitrator) and from this attitude derives his mediate or immediate gain. Within this form there are two chief variations; namely, two parties are hostile to each other, and for that reason compete for the favor of a third; or two parties compete for the favor of a third, and are for that reason hostile to each other. This difference has specially important bearings upon the further development of the constellation. If an already existing hostility makes in the direction of an attempt by each party to get the favor of the third, the decision of this competition, that is, the attachment of the third to the one party, will really mean the beginning of the conflict. On the other hand, in case the two elements independent of each other seek the favor of a third, and this constitutes the ground of their hostility, of their partisanship, the final assignment of this favor, which is in this case end, not means, of the strife, will terminate the same. The decision is reached, and further hostility is therewith made meaningless. In both cases the advantage of nonpartisanship, with which the *tertius* originally stood in antithesis with the other two, consists in the fact that he can set his own *conditions* for the decision. Where, for any reason, this assignment of conditions is denied to him, the situation does not bring to him the complete advantage.

3. *Divide et impera.*—In these combinations of the triad scheme we have to do with an existing or an emerging conflict of two elements, from which the third derives an advantage; it is now a variation to be regarded as separate, although it is in reality not always separable, that the third instigates the difference intentionally, in order to gain a controlling situation. It is also to be premised in this case that the triple number is, as a matter of course, only the minimum number of the elements requisite for this formation, and consequently it may serve as the most simple scheme. The essential fact here in question is that two elements are opposed to a third, and in this opposition they are either combined with each other or dependent upon each other, and that the third is able to set in motion *against each other* the two powers which are combined *against him*. The consequence is, then, that they either hold the balance against each other, so that he, undisturbed by the two, may follow his advantage, or that they reciprocally so weaken each other that neither of them can withstand the superior power of the third. I proceed to characterize a few steps of the scale in which one may arrange the phenomena here in question. The most simple occurs when a superior power prevents the uniting of elements which

do not positively attempt to form such a union, but still *might* perhaps make such an attempt. The prophylactic prevention of unification operates more distinctly in case there exists a direct endeavor for union. This preventing of combination between the elements attains, instead of a merely prohibitive, an active form in case the third party instigates jealousy between them. We have not here in mind the cases in which he instigates hostilities between the other two in order to produce at their cost a new order of things; but the facts here in question are frequently conservative tendencies, the third party tries to maintain his already existing prerogative through preventing a dreaded coalition of the two others, by means of jealousy between them, at the beginning or at least early in the course of the development of the combination beyond its first elements. There is especial likelihood of utilizing this constellation in case the two personalties to be restrained from combination already possess certain competencies. These furnish the appropriate objects of jealousy. For that reason this technique of *divide et impera* is not easily applicable in the case of personalities low in the social scale or without property. The baldest form of *divide et impera,* the instigation of positive struggle between two elements, may have its purpose in the relation of the third party either to these two, or to an object existing outside of them. The latter occurs in case one of three candidates for an office understands how to instigate the two others against each other, in such a way that by gossip and slander, which each of them sets in motion against the other, they spoil each other's chances.

In case, finally, the purpose of the third does not reside in an object, but in the immediate control of the two other elements, two sociological points of view are essential.

(1) Certain elements are so formed that they can be successfully opposed only by similar elements. The will to subjugate them finds no proper point of attack in themselves, so that the only thing remaining is, as it were, to divide them against themselves, and to maintain between the divisions a struggle which they now can carry on with homogeneous weapons, until they are sufficiently weakened, and so may fall a prey to the third party. Precisely those who by likeness of interests are brought together best know reciprocally each other's weaknesses and their vulnerable points, so that the principle of *similia similibus*—the annihilation of a condition by producing a similar condition—may here be produced in the widest degree. Although reciprocity and unification may best be obtained with a certain degree of qualitative variation, because reinforcement, consolidation, organically differentiated life can thus result, reciprocal disturbance seems to succeed best in case of qualitative likeness, apart, of course, from so great

quantitative superiority in the energy of the one party that the terms of correlation are a matter of utter indifference. The whole category of enmities of which fraternal strife is the extreme derives its radically destructive character precisely from the fact that experience and knowledge, just like the instincts which have their source in the same radical unity, place in the hands of each the most deadly weapon against this very opponent. That which constitutes the basis of the relationship of similars to each other—namely, knowledge of the external situation, and ability to enter sympathetically into the subjective situation—this is evidently quite as much the means of the deepest wounds, which do not allow any opportunity for attack to escape, and it leads, since by its very nature it is reciprocal, to the most utter destruction. Consequently struggle of like against like, the division of the enemy into two, qualitatively homogeneous parties, is one of the most thorough realizations of *divide et impera*.

(2) Where it is not possible for the oppressor to have his purposes carried out so exclusively by his victims themselves, where he must himself enter into their struggle, the scheme is very simple. He simply supports the one until the other is a practically eliminated factor, whereupon the former is his easy prey. This support is most advantageously given to the one who of himself is the stronger. This policy may be carried out in the more negative form, that the more powerful, in a complex of elements which is to be suppressed, may merely be protected.

THE CROWD

BY

GUSTAVE LE BON

IN its ordinary sense the word "crowd" means a gathering of individuals of whatever nationality, profession, or sex, and whatever be the chances that have brought them together. From the psychological point of view the expression "crowd" assumes quite a different signification. Under certain given circumstances, and only under those circumstances, an agglomeration of men presents new characteristics very different from those of the individuals composing it. The sentiments and ideas of all the persons in the gathering take one and the same direction, and their conscious personality vanishes. A collective mind is formed, doubtless transitory, but presenting very clearly defined

Abridged from: Le Bon, Gustave, *The Crowd*, London: Unwin, 1896.

characteristics. The gathering has thus become what, in the absence of a better expression, I will call an organised crowd, or, if the term is considered preferable, a psychological crowd. It forms a single being, and is subjected to the *law of the mental unity of crowds.*

A psychological crowd once constituted, it acquires certain provisional but determinable general characteristics. To these general characteristics there are adjoined particular characteristics which vary according to the elements of which the crowd is composed, and may modify its mental constitution. Psychological crowds, then, are susceptible of classification; and when we come to occupy ourselves with this matter, we shall see that a heterogeneous crowd—that is, a crowd composed of dissimilar elements—presents certain characteristics in common with homogeneous crowds—that is, with crowds composed of elements more or less akin (sects, castes, and classes)—and side by side with these common characteristics particularities which permit of the two kinds of crowds being differentiated.

But before occupying ourselves with the different categories of crowds, we must first of all examine the characteristics common to them all.

It is not easy to describe the mind of crowds with exactness, because its organisation varies not only according to race and composition, but also according to the nature and intensity of the exciting causes to which crowds are subjected. The same difficulty, however, presents itself in the psychological study of an individual. It is only in novels that individuals are found to traverse their whole life with an unvarying character. It is only the uniformity of the environment that creates the apparent uniformity of characters. I have shown elsewhere that all mental constitutions contain possibilities of character which may be manifested in consequence of a sudden change of environment.

It being impossible to study here all the successive degrees of organisation of crowds, we shall concern ourselves more especially with such crowds as have attained to the phase of complete organisation. In this way we shall see what crowds may become, but not what they invariably are. It is only in this advanced phase of organisation that certain new and special characteristics are superposed on the unvarying and dominant character of the race; then takes place that turning already alluded to of all the feelings and thoughts of the collectivity in an identical direction. It is only under such circumstances, too, that what I have called above the *psychological law of the mental unity of crowds* comes into play.

Among the psychological characteristics of crowds there are some that they may present in common with isolated individuals, and others, on the contrary, which are absolutely peculiar to them and are only to be met with in collectivities. It is these special characteristics that we shall study, first of all, in order to show their importance.

The most striking peculiarity presented by a psychological crowd is the following: Whoever be the individuals that compose it, however like or unlike be their mode of life, their occupations, their character, or their intelligence, the fact that they have been transformed into a crowd puts them in possession of a sort of collective mind which makes them feel, think, and act in a manner quite different from that in which each individual of them would feel, think, and act were he in a state of isolation. There are certain ideas and feelings which do not come into being, or do not transform themselves into acts except in the case of individuals forming a crowd. The psychological crowd is a provisional being formed of heterogeneous elements, which for a moment are combined, exactly as the cells which constitute a living body form by their reunion a new being which displays characteristics very different from those possessed by each of the cells singly.

It is easy to prove how much the individual forming part of a crowd differs from the isolated individual, but it is less easy to discover the causes of this difference.

To obtain at any rate a glimpse of them it is necessary in the first place to call to mind the truth established by modern psychology, that unconscious phenomena play an altogether preponderating part not only in organic life, but also in the operations of the intelligence. The conscious life of the mind is of small importance in comparison with its unconscious life. The most subtle analyst, the most acute observer, is scarcely successful in discovering more than a very small number of the unconscious motives that determine his conduct. Our conscious acts are the outcome of an unconscious substratum created in the mind in the main by hereditary influences. This substratum consists of the innumerable common characteristics handed down from generation to generation, which constitute the genius of a race. Behind the avowed causes of our acts there undoubtedly lie secret causes that we do not avow, but behind these secret causes there are many others more secret still which we ourselves ignore. The greater part of our daily actions are the result of hidden motives which escape our observation.

Men the most unlike in the matter of their intelligence possess instincts, passions, and feelings that are very similar. From the intellectual point of view an abyss may exist between a great mathematician and his bootmaker, but from the point of view of character the difference is most often slight or non-existent.

It is precisely these general qualities of character, governed by forces of which we are unconscious, and possessed by the majority of the normal individuals of a race in much the same degree—it is precisely these qualities, I say, that in crowds become common property. In the collective mind the intellectual aptitudes of the individuals, and in consequence their individuality, are weakened. The heterogeneous is swamped by the homogeneous, and the unconscious qualities obtain the upper hand.

Different causes determine the appearance of these characteristics peculiar to crowds, and not possessed by isolated individuals. The first is that the individual forming part of a crowd acquires, solely from numerical considerations, a sentiment of invincible power which allows him to yield to instincts which, had he been alone, he would perforce have kept under restraint. He will be the less disposed to check himself from the consideration that, a crowd being anonymous, and in consequence irresponsible, the sentiment of responsibility which always controls individuals disappears entirely.

The second cause, which is contagion, also intervenes to determine the manifestation in crowds of their special characteristics, and at the same time the trend they are to take. Contagion is a phenomenon of which it is easy to establish the presence, but that it is not easy to explain. It must be classed among those phenomena of a hypnotic order, which we shall shortly study. In a crowd every sentiment and act is contagious, and contagious to such a degree that an individual readily sacrifices his personal interest to the collective interest. This is an aptitude very contrary to his nature, and of which a man is scarcely capable, except when he makes part of a crowd.

A third cause, and by far the most important, determines in the individuals of a crowd special characteristics which are quite contrary at times to those presented by the isolated individual. I allude to that suggestibility of which, moreover, the contagion mentioned above is neither more nor less than an effect.

To understand this phenomenon it is necessary to bear in mind certain recent physiological discoveries. We know to-day that by various processes an individual may be brought into such a condition that, having entirely lost his conscious personality, he obeys all the suggestions of the operator who has deprived him of it, and commits acts in utter contradiction with his character and habits. The most careful observations seem to prove that an individual immerged for some length of time in a crowd in action soon finds himself—either in consequence of the magnetic influence given out by the crowd, or from some other cause of which we are ignorant—in a special state, which much resembles the state of fascination in which the hypnotised individual finds himself in the hands of the hypnotiser. The activity of the brain being paralysed in the case of the hypnotised subject, the latter becomes the slave of all the unconscious activities of his spinal cord, which the hypnotiser directs at will. The conscious personality has entirely vanished; will and discernment are lost. All feelings and thoughts are bent in the direction determined by the hypnotiser.

Such also is approximately the state of the individual forming part of a psychological crowd. He is no longer conscious of his acts. In his case, as in the case of the hypnotised subject, at the same time that certain faculties are destroyed, others may be brought to a high degree of exaltation. Under the influence of a suggestion, he will undertake the accomplishment of certain acts with irresistible impetuosity. This impetuosity is the more irresistible in the case of crowds than in that of the hypnotised subject, from the fact that, the suggestion being the same for all the individuals of the crowd, it gains in strength by reciprocity. The individualities in the crowd who might possess a personality sufficiently strong to resist the suggestion are too few in number to struggle against the current. At the utmost, they may be able to attempt a diversion by means of different suggestions. It is in this way, for instance, that a happy expression, an image opportunely evoked, have occasionally deterred crowds from the most bloodthirsty acts.

We see, then, that the disappearance of the conscious personality, the predominance of the unconscious personality, the turning by means of suggestion and contagion of feelings and ideas in an identical direction, the tendency to immediately transform the suggested ideas into acts; these we see, are the principal characteristics of the individual forming part of a crowd. He is no longer himself, but has become an automaton who has ceased to be guided by his will.

He possesses the spontaneity, the violence, the ferocity, and also the enthusiasm and heroism of primitive beings, whom he further tends to resemble by the facility with which he allows himself to be impressed by words and images—which would be entirely without action on each of the isolated individuals composing the crowd—and to be induced to commit acts contrary to his most obvious interests and his best-known habits.

It is for these reasons that juries are seen to deliver verdicts of which each individual juror would disapprove, that parliamentary assemblies adopt laws and measures of which each of their members would disapprove in his own person. Taken separately, the men of the Convention were enlightened citizens of peaceful habits. United in a crowd, they did not hesitate to give their adhesion to the most savage proposals, to guillotine individuals most clearly innocent, and, contrary to their interests, to renounce their inviolability and to decimate themselves.

It is not only by his acts that the individual in a crowd differs essentially from himself. Even before he has entirely lost his independence, his ideas and feelings have undergone a transformation, and the transformation is so profound as to change the miser into a spendthrift, the sceptic into a believer, the honest man into a criminal, and the coward into a hero. The crowd may, according to circumstances, be better or worse than the individual. All depends on the nature of the suggestion to which the crowd is exposed.

CHAPTER 7

The Ordering of Relationships

———— ◦•◦ ————

FROM STATUS TO CONTRACT

BY

HENRY S. MAINE

THE movement of the progressive societies has been uniform in one respect. Through all its course it has been distinguished by the gradual dissolution of family dependency and the growth of individual obligation in its place. The Individual is steadily substituted for the Family, as the unit of which civil laws take account. The advance has been accomplished at varying rates of celerity, and there are societies not absolutely stationary in which the collapse of the ancient organisation can only be perceived by careful study of the phenomena they present. But, whatever its pace, the change has not been subject to reaction or recoil, and apparent retardations will be found to have been occasioned through the absorption of archaic ideas and customs from some entirely foreign source. Nor is it difficult to see what is the tie between man and man which replaces by degrees those forms of reciprocity in rights and duties which have their origin in the Family. It is Contract. Starting, as from one terminus of history, from a condition of society in which all the relations of Persons are summed up in the relations of Family, we seem to have steadily moved towards a phase of social order in which all these relations arise from the free agreement of Individuals. In Western Europe the progress achieved in this direction has been considerable. Thus the status of the Slave has disappeared—it has

Abridged from: Maine, Henry S., *Ancient Law*, 1861. (Currently available in an edition published by the Oxford University Press, 1931.)

been superseded by the contractual relation of the servant to his master. The status of the Female under Tutelage, if the tutelage be understood of persons other than her husband, has also ceased to exist; from her coming of age to her marriage all the relations she may form are relations of contract. So too the status of the Son under Power has no true place in the law of modern European societies. If any civil obligation binds together the Parent and the child of full age, it is one to which only contract gives its legal validity. The apparent exceptions are exceptions of that stamp which illustrate the rule. The child before years of discretion, the orphan under guardianship, the adjudged lunatic, have all their capacities and incapacities regulated by the Law of Persons. But why? The reason is differently expressed in the conventional language of different systems, but in substance it is stated to the same effect by all. The great majority of Jurists are constant to the principle that the classes of persons just mentioned are subject to extrinsic control on the single ground that they do not possess the faculty of forming a judgment on their own interests; in other words, that they are wanting in the first essential of an engagement by Contract.

The word Status may be usefully employed to construct a formula expressing the law of progress thus indicated, which, whatever be its value, seems to me to be sufficiently ascertained. All the forms of Status taken notice of in the Law of Persons were derived from, and to some extent are still coloured by, the powers and privileges anciently residing in the Family. If then we employ Status, agreeably with the usage of the best writers, to signify these personal conditions only, and avoid applying the term to such conditions as are the immediate or remote result of agreement, we may say that the movement of the progressive societies has hitherto been a movement *from Status to Contract*.

THE EARLY HISTORY OF CONTRACT

There are few general propositions concerning the age to which we belong which seem at first sight likely to be received with readier concurrence than the assertion that the society of our day is mainly distinguished from that of preceding generations by the largeness of the sphere which is occupied in it by Contract. Some of the phenomena on which this proposition rests are among those most frequently singled out for notice, for comment, and for eulogy. Not many of us are so unobservant as not to perceive that in innumerable cases where old law fixed a man's social position irreversibly at his birth, modern law allows him to create it for himself by convention; and indeed several of the few exceptions which remain to this rule are constantly denounced with passionate indignation. The point, for instance, which is really debated in the vigorous controversy still carried on upon the subject of negro servitude, is whether the status of the slave does not belong to bygone institutions, and whether the only relation between employer and labourer which commends itself to modern morality be not a relation determined exclusively by contract. The recognition of this difference between past ages and the present enters into the very essence of the most famous contemporary speculations. It is certain that the science of Political Economy, the only department of moral inquiry which has made any considerable progress in our day, would fail to correspond with the facts of life if it were not true that Imperative Law had abandoned the largest part of the field which it once occupied, and had left men to settle rules of conduct for themselves with a liberty never allowed to them till recently. The bias indeed of most persons trained in political economy is to consider the general truth on which their science reposes as entitled to become universal, and, when they apply it as an art, their efforts are ordinarily directed to enlarging the province of Contract and to curtailing that of Imperative Law, except so far as law is necessary to enforce the performance of Contracts. The impulse given by thinkers who are under the influence of these ideas is beginning to be very strongly felt in the Western world. Legislation has nearly confessed its inability to keep pace with the activity of man in discovery, in invention, and in the manipulation of accumulated wealth; and the law even of the least advanced communities tends more and more to become a mere surface-stratum having under it an ever-changing assemblage of contractual rules with which it rarely interferes except to compel compliance with a few fundamental principles or unless it be called in to punish the violation of good faith.

Social inquiries, so far as they depend on the consideration of legal phenomena, are in so backward a condition that we need not be surprised at not finding these truths recognised in the commonplaces which pass current concerning the progress of society. These commonplaces answer much more to our prejudices than to our convictions. The strong disinclination of most men to regard morality as advancing seems to be especially powerful when the virtues on which Contract depends are in question, and many of us have an almost instinctive reluctance to admitting that good faith and trust in our fellows are more widely diffused than of old, or that there is anything in contemporary manners which parallels the loyalty of the antique world. From time to time, these prepossessions are greatly strengthened by the spectacle of frauds, unheard of before the period at which they were observed, and astonishing from their complication as well as shocking from criminality. But the very character of these frauds shows clearly that, before they became possible, the moral obligations of which they are the breach must have been more than proportionately developed. It is the confidence reposed and deserved by the many which affords facilities for the bad faith of the few, so that, if colossal examples of dishonesty occur, there is no surer conclusion than that scrupulous honesty is displayed in the average of the transactions which, in the particular case, have supplied the delinquent with his opportunity. If we insist on reading the history of morality as reflected in jurisprudence, by turning our eyes not on the law of Contract but on the law of Crime, we must be careful that we read it aright. The only form of dishonesty treated of in the most ancient Roman law is Theft. At the moment at which I write, the newest chapter in the English criminal law is one which attempts to prescribe punishment for the frauds of Trustees. The proper inference from this contrast is not that the primitive Romans practised a higher morality than ourselves. We should rather say that, in the interval between their days and ours, morality has advanced from a very rude to a highly refined conception—from viewing the rights of property as exclusively sacred, to looking upon the rights growing out of the mere unilateral reposal of confidence as entitled to the protection of the penal law.

COMPETITION AND SOCIAL PLACEMENT

B Y

CHARLES HORTON COOLEY

THE function of personal competition, considered as a part of the social system, is to assign to each individual his place in that system. If "all the world's a stage," this is a process that distributes the parts among the players. It may do it well or ill, but, after some fashion, it does it. Some may be cast in parts unsuited to them; good actors may be discharged altogether and worse ones retained; but nevertheless the thing is arranged in some way and the play goes on.

That such a process must exist can hardly, it seems to me, admit of question: in fact I believe that those who speak of doing away with competition use the word in another sense than is here intended. Within the course of the longest human life there is necessarily a complete renewal of the persons whose communication and cooperation make up the life of society. The new members come into the world

Abridged from: Cooley, Charles H., Personal Competition, *Economic Studies* (American Economic Association) 1899, 4, no. 2.

without any legible sign to indicate what they are fit for, a mystery to others from the first and to themselves as soon as they are capable of reflection: the young man does not know for what he is adapted, and no one else can tell him. The only possible way to get light upon the matter is to adopt the method of experiment. All I wish to say here is that the necessity of some selective process is inherent in the conditions of social life.

It will be apparent that, in the sense in which I use the term, competition is not necessarily a hostile contention, nor even something of which the competing individual is always conscious. It is eligibility to perform some social function that makes a man a competitor, and he may or may not be aware of it, or, if aware of it, he may or may not be consciously opposed to others. I trust that the reader will bear in mind that I always use the word competition in the sense here explained.

There is but one alternative to competition as a means of determining the place of the individual in the social system, and that is some form of *status*, some fixed, mechanical rule, usually a rule of inheritance, which decides the function of the individual without reference to his personal traits, and thus dispenses with any process of comparison.[1] It is possible to conceive of a society [2] organized entirely upon the basis of the inheritance of functions, and indeed societies exist which may be said to approach this condition. In India, for example, the prevalent idea regarding the social function of the individual is that it is unalterably determined by his parentage, and the village blacksmith, shoemaker, accountant or priest has his place assigned to him by a rule of descent as rigid as that which governs the transmission of one of the crowns of Europe. If all functions were handed down in this way, if there were never any deficiency or surplus of children to take the place of their parents, if there were no progress or decay in the social system, making necessary new activities or dispensing with old ones; then, there would be no use for a selective process. But precisely in the measure that a society departs from this condition, that individual traits are recognized and made available, or social change of any sort comes to pass, in that measure must there be competition.

Status is not an active process as competition is; it is simply a rule of conservation, a makeshift to avoid the inconveniences of continual readjustment in the social structure. Competition or selection is the only constructive principle, and everything worthy the name of organization had at some time or other a competitive origin.

[1] The principle of length of service, so widely recognized in making promotions, is an example of a form of *status* unconnected with inheritance.

[2] As there has been much discussion concerning the meaning of this word it may be well to say that I use it, with conscious vagueness, to mean a totality of social relations. I also use the terms "social order" and "social system" in the same sense.

Sir Henry Maine has pointed out that the increase of competition is a characteristic trait of modern life, and that the powerful ancient societies of the old world were for the most part non-competitive in their structure. While this is true, it would be a mistake to draw the inference that *status* is a peculiarly natural or primitive principle of organization and competition a comparatively recent discovery. On the contrary the spontaneous relations among men, as we see in the case of children, and as we may infer from the life of the lower animals, are highly competitive, personal prowess and ascendency being everything and little regard being paid to descent simply as such. The *régime* of inherited *status,* on the other hand, is a comparatively complex and artificial product, necessarily of later growth, whose very general prevalence among the successful societies of the old world is doubtless to be explained by the stability and consequently the power which it was calculated to give to the social system. It survived because under certain conditions it was the fittest. It was not and is not universally predominant among savage or barbarous peoples. With the American Indians, for example, the definiteness and authority of *status* were comparatively small, personal prowess and initiative being correspondingly important.

Throughout history there has been a struggle between the principles of *status* and competition regarding the part that each should play in the social system. Generally speaking the advantage of *status* is in its power to give order and continuity. The chief danger of *status* is that of suppressing personal development, and so of causing social enfeeblement, rigidity and ultimate decay. On the other hand competition develops the individual and gives flexibility and animation to the social order; its danger being chiefly that of disintegration in some form or other. The general tendency in modern times has been toward the relative increase of the free or competitive principle, owing to the fact that the rise of other means of securing stability has diminished the need for *status.* The latter persists, however, even in the freest countries, as the method by which wealth is transmitted, and also in social classes, which, so far as they exist at all, are based chiefly upon inherited wealth and the culture and opportunities that go with it. The ultimate reason for this persistence—without very serious opposition—in the face of the obvious inequalities and limitations upon liberty that it perpetuates, is perhaps the fact that no other method of transmission has arisen that has shown itself capable of giving continuity and order to the control of wealth.

Generally speaking the world requires of a man two classes of faculties, which may be roughly described as the special and the social. The first distinguish him from other men and enable him to perform some more or less peculiar function; the second unite him to other men and enable him to put his more special aptitudes into a wholesome and fruitful relation to the world at large. It is very well if nature and education have made one a master of the technique of carpentry, or banking, or medicine, or law, or any other specialty; but as a rule this will do little for a man if he does not add to it those social and moral qualities which enable him to place and keep himself where his gift is available, and to exercise it in such a manner as to make it an effectual working piece of the general mechanism. Special ability is a helpless thing unless it is supplemented by general ability.

These two requirements evidently arise out of the very nature of organization. Just as the special structure of the eye is meaningless and dead without the nervous mechanism that unifies it with the whole, so, I may also say, is a man who has special faculties without social faculties. Moreover since these two requirements spring from the same root, the need of organic life, they do or should develop equally. The more highly specialized a social system becomes the greater should be the development of the unifying and co-ordinating activities of every kind: and as regards the individual this means that more and more will be required of him in the way of intelligence, morality, self-reliance, and the like. Under favorable conditions individualization and socialization proceed *pari passu;* and I recommend this suggestion to the consideration of those who believe that the increasing specialization which marks our time necessarily involves the narrowing and dwarfing of personality. On the contrary it calls for a larger, richer personality; and that is what must in the end prevail.

In every social career a prime demand is steadiness: it matters little what the task is, the incumbent must be faithful to it, he must be one upon whom the world can depend to be at his post doing work of standard quality. To illustrate this in detail and to show that unreliability spells failure would be superfluous. The demand for this trait is steadily upon the increase; since the greater the complexity and interdependence of the social order the greater the need of soundness in all parts of its structure. The unreliable man is a public nuisance; and the wider the relations in which he is involved the more intolerable he becomes: there is really no use for him, and he inevitably falls into the class of those who can expect only casual employment. The moral quality underlying steadiness is of course self-control, the power to subordinate passing impulses to a rational rule and purpose; the lack of this is social degeneracy, and is perhaps the most common cause of failure.

Enterprise may be described as a disposition to make experiments upon life, and perseverance as a disposition to make those experiments conclusive. From earliest infancy, as any observer of children may see, the method by which we advance in knowledge and power is what Professor Baldwin calls the try-try-again method, the only one, indeed, by which progress is achieved in any sort of endeavor. In social life this becomes enterprise, aggressiveness, a habit of making intelligent plans and of actively attempting to carry them out. In a competitive society every one must undertake and execute a voyage of discovery whose object is to find out his own proper relation to the world; and if he is to accomplish anything much above the common he may need as much courage as Columbus. The leaders of men, the successful innovators of every sort, are first of all explorers; and in this regard the requisites for success are much the same in science, in literature, in war, business and politics, as they are in navigation. The wider the field of opportunity, the more necessary it becomes to explore it, the greater the need for that self-knowledge and self-reliance that can only come by bold experimentation. Accordingly the standard of courage and enterprise up to which men must come if they are to hold their own increases with the growth of liberty.

Perseverance is required to make this experimentation thorough. In the prosecution of all endeavors there are times of doubt and discouragement, dead-centers at which the propelling forces cease to act. At such times the whole matter of success or failure usually hangs upon the question whether the person has formed that *habit of keeping-on* that constitutes perseverance and gives momentum to his undertakings, or whether, on the contrary, he is a victim to the fatal *habit of leaving-off*, which will condemn the most exceptional talents to futility. And the need for thoroughness undoubtedly increases with the advance of civilization: "the fields for long-ranged, cumulative efforts, are wider, more numerous and far more needy" at the present time than they have ever been in the past.

Address or *savoir-faire* appears to be based upon a sympathetic insight into human nature, guided by intelligence and steadied by a natural coolness or phlegm. It is also closely connected with the qualities mentioned above, since it is developed or educated only by practical endeavor to further one's purposes in the world. It is social facility in the largest sense, skill and efficiency in dealing with the infinitely variegated forces of the social environment. It is a faculty that is necessary to every one in the early part of his career, or at times of change, in order to make his way through the social medium to the place where he can bring his special abilities into play.

If it were true, as some persons seem to believe, that immorality is on the whole more favorable to success than morality, the outlook for the future would be dark indeed; for it seems to me that practices which tend, on the whole and in the long run, to produce success, to achieve the ends of endeavor, must inevitably be adopted. And if these practices, instead of being difficult, like self-denial, faith in the unseen and perseverance in the face of discouragements, were such as our lower nature is naturally prone to, like violence and deceit, their spread would be rapid and ruinous.

The forces that cause success to be associated with morality, or the reverse, may profitably be considered, it seems to me, under two heads: (1) Social Conditions, dealing with the forces of custom, opinion and law that impose moral or immoral conditions upon the aspirant for success; and (2) Psychical Correlation, dealing with conditions imposed by the fact that the mind of each man is a whole, so that certain qualities and activities of the individual imply others as their necessary correlates.

I shall assume that any one who reads this essay is enough of a sociologist to understand that the moral standards which the individual applies to his own conduct are always the reflection, more or less individualized, of those of his social environment, of the group, or complex of groups, of which he forms a part; that, to be specific, a lawyer necessarily accepts, with more or less modification, the moral standards of that great social group the legal profession; and so with the physician, the mechanic, the clergyman, the schoolboy, even the criminal. Every group, in the measure of its organization, controls its members and exacts from them conformity to certain standards of conduct. If they do not conform to these standards the group inflicts failure upon them and casts them out. This control or casting out is accomplished in a great variety of ways—most of which do not imply deliberate purpose—which it would be out of place to discuss in this connection. I would refer those who wish a full exposition to the lucid articles of Professor Ross on "Social Control."

In every career, therefore, in which success is pursued the aspirant finds himself conditioned by certain standards more or less peculiar to the group and different from those of other groups. The army officer cannot hope to rise unless he comes up to standards peculiar to the army; the clergyman finds that a somewhat different set of qualities conduce to success in his profession. At the same time, beside these special conditions, there are more general conditions imposed by public sentiment and by the law upon all men, or at least upon all who share in the normal life of the community. In other words, except in some inconceivable condition of anarchy, success is always conditioned by social forces, both general and special, some of them acting through definite command and penalty, like the law, but most of them of a less definite, though not necessarily less efficacious character, working through social feeling, ambition, the dread of disapproval and the like.

The reason why each group imposes special conditions of success upon its members is, of course, that its interests as a group require that certain standards be maintained, their precise character depending upon the activities which the group performs, so that custom and sentiment, re-enforced often by definite social machinery, very naturally take a form tending to enforce these standards.

From this follows a corollary that is very important to sound notions of the relation of success to morality, namely, that the morality inculcated by each specialized group is, as a rule, superior in some respects and inferior in others to the more general standards current in the society as a whole. As regards the virtues particularly important to the prosperity of the social group its standard will be higher than that of the people in general, while other sorts of morality will be correspondingly neglected.

The result of this is that the young man entering upon almost any recognized social career will find his new surroundings elevating in some respects and demoralizing in others, judged by his previous standards. If he goes into the army he will find required of him a promptness, a regularity, a submission to discipline, which is in most cases extremely good for him: on the other hand he will find little opportunity or encouragement for individual enterprise or intellectual culture, and may fall into certain vices which are less reprobated in armies than in civilian life. Of course the higher, from a moral standpoint, the activities of the group the more moral the conditions of success in it become; and *vice versa*. In a criminal organization crime is a condition of success; while on the other hand there are careers in which honesty is unquestionably the best policy.

Again, since every person is involved in several or many social groups and seeks more than one sort of success, each man's mind is the theatre of a conflict of standards: we are continually called upon to choose between different kinds of success, or between a temporary and a durable success in any particular direction.

STATUS AND ROLE

B Y

RALPH LINTON

THE functioning of societies depends upon the presence of patterns for reciprocal behavior between individuals or groups of individuals. The polar positions in such patterns of reciprocal behavior are technically known as *statuses*. The term *status*, like the term *culture*, has come to be used with a double significance. *A status,* in the abstract, is a position in a particular pattern. It is thus quite correct to speak of each individual as having many statuses, since each individual participates in the expression of a number of patterns. However, unless the term is qualified in some way, *the status* of any individual means the sum total of all the statuses which he occupies. It represents his position with relation to the total society.

A status, as distinct from the individual who may occupy it, is simply a collection of rights and duties. Since these rights and duties can find expression only through the medium of individuals, it is extremely hard for us to maintain a distinction in our thinking between statuses and the people who hold them and exercise the rights and duties which constitute them.

A *role* represents the dynamic aspect of a status. The individual is socially assigned to a status and occupies it with relation to other statuses. When he puts the rights and duties which constitute the status into effect, he is performing a role. Role and status are quite inseparable, and the distinction between them is of only academic interest. There are no roles without statuses or statuses without roles. Just as in the case of *status,* the term *role* is used with a double significance. Every individual has a series of roles deriving from the various patterns in which he participates and at the same time *a role,* general, which represents the sum total of these roles and determines what he does for his society and what he can expect from it.

Although all statuses and roles derive from social patterns and are integral parts of patterns, they have an independent function with relation to the individuals who occupy particular statuses and exercise their roles. To such individuals the combined status and role represent the minimum of attitudes and behavior which he must assume if he is

Abridged from: Linton, Ralph, *The Study of Man,* New York: Appleton-Century, 1936. Reprinted by permission of Appleton-Century-Crofts, Inc.

to participate in the overt expression of the pattern. Status and role serve to reduce the ideal patterns for social life to individual terms. They become models for organizing the attitudes and behavior of the individual so that these will be congruous with those of the other individuals participating in the expression of the pattern.

It is obvious that, as long as there is no interference from external sources, the more perfectly the members of any society are adjusted to their statuses and roles the more smoothly the society will function. In its attempts to bring about such adjustments every society finds itself caught on the horns of a dilemma. The individual's formation of habits and attitudes begins at birth, and, other things being equal, the earlier his training for a status can begin the more successful it is likely to be. At the same time, no two individuals are alike, and a status which will be congenial to one may be quite uncongenial to another. Also, there are in all social systems certain roles which require more than training for their successful performance. Perfect technique does not make a great violinist, nor a thorough book knowledge of tactics an efficient general. The utilization of the special gifts of individuals may be highly important to society, as in the case of the general, yet these gifts usually show themselves rather late, and to wait upon their manifestation for the assignment of statuses would be to forfeit the advantages to be derived from commencing training early.

Fortunately, human beings are so mutable that almost any normal individual can be trained to the adequate performance of almost any role. Most of the business of living can be conducted on a basis of habit, with little need for intelligence and none for special gifts. Societies have met the dilemma by developing two types of statuses, the *ascribed* and the *achieved*. *Ascribed* statuses are those which are assigned to individuals without reference to their innate differences or abilities. They can be predicted and trained for from the moment of birth. The *achieved* statuses are, as a minimum, those requiring special qualities, although they are not necessarily limited to these. They are not assigned to individuals from birth but are left open to be filled through competition and individual effort. The majority of the statuses in all social systems are of the ascribed type and those which take care of the ordinary day-to-day business of living are practically always of this type.

LEADERSHIP OR PERSONAL ASCENDENCY

B Y

CHARLES HORTON COOLEY

IT is plain that the theory of ascendancy involves the question of the mind's relative valuation of the suggestions coming to it from other minds; leadership depending upon the efficacy of a personal impression to awaken feeling, thought, action, and so to become a cause of life. While there are some men who seem but to add one to the population, there are others whom we cannot help thinking about; they lend arguments to their neighbors' creeds, so that the life of their contemporaries, and perhaps of following generations, is notably different because they have lived. The immediate reason for this difference is evidently that in the one case there is something seminal or generative in the relation between the personal impression a man makes and the mind that receives it, which is lacking in the other case. If we could go farther than this and discover what it is that makes certain suggestions seminal or generative, we should throw much light on leadership, and through that on all questions of social tendency.

It must be evident that we can look for no cut-and-dried theory of this life-imparting force, no algebraic formula for leadership. We know but little of the depths of human tendency; and those who know most are possibly the poets, whose knowledge is little available for precise uses. Moreover, the problem varies incalculably with sex, age, race, inherited idiosyncrasy, and previous personal development. The general notions of evolution, however, lead us to expect that what awakens life and so gives ascendancy will be something important or functional in the past life of the race, something appealing to instincts which have survived because they had a part to perform; and this, generally speaking, appears to be the case.

The prime condition of ascendancy is the presence of undirected energy in the person over whom it is to be exercised; it is not so much forced upon us from without as demanded from within. The mind,

Abridged from: Cooley. Charles H., *Human Nature and the Social Order*, New York: Charles Scribner's Sons, 1922 (Revised edition).

having energy, must work, and requires a guide, a form of thought, to facilitate its working. All views of life are fallacious which do not recognize the fact that the primary need is the need to do. Every healthy organism evolves energy, and this must have an outlet.

We are born to action; and whatever is capable of suggesting and guiding action has power over us from the first. The attention of the new-born child is fixed by whatever exercises the senses, through motion, noise, touch, or color. Persons and animals interest him primarily because they offer a greater amount and variety of sensible stimulus than other objects. They move, talk, laugh, coax, fondle, bring food, and so on. The prestige they thus acquire over the child's mind is shared with such other stimulating phenomena as cars, engines, windmills, patches of sunlight, and bright-colored garments. A little later, when he begins to acquire some control over his activities, he welcomes eagerly whatever can participate in and so stimulate and guide them. The playthings he cares for are those that go, or that he can do something with—carts, fire-engines, blocks, and the like. Persons, especially those that share his interests, maintain and increase their ascendancy, and other children, preferably a little older and of more varied resources than himself, are particularly welcome. Among grown-ups he admires most those who do something that he can understand, whom he can appreciate as actors and producers—such as the carpenter, the gardener, the maid in the kitchen.

It will be observed that at this stage a child has learned to reflect upon action and to discriminate that which is purposeful and effective from mere motion; he has gained the notion of power. Himself constantly trying to do things, he learns to admire those who can do things better than himself, or who can suggest new things to do. His father sitting at his desk probably seems an inert and unattractive phenomenon, but the man who can make shavings or dig a deep hole is a hero; and the seemingly perverse admiration which children at a later age show for circus men and for the pirates and desperadoes they read about, is to be explained in a similar manner. What they want is *evident* power. The scholar may possibly be as worthy of admiration as the acrobat or the policeman; but the boy of ten will seldom see the matter in that light.

If we ask what are the mental traits that distinguish a leader, the only answer seems to be that he must, in one way or another, be a great deal of a man, or at least appear to be. He must stand for something to which men incline, and so take his place by right as a focus of their thought.

Evidently he must be the best of his kind available. It is impossible that he should stand forth as an archetype, unless he is conceived as superior, in some respect, to all others within range of the imagination. Nothing that is seen to be second-rate can be an ideal; if a character does not bound the horizon at some point we will look over it to what we can see beyond. The object of admiration may be Cæsar Borgia, or Napoleon, or Jesse James the train-robber, but he must be typical, must stand for something. No matter how bad the leader may be, he will always be found to owe his leadership to something strong, affirmative, and superior, something that appeals to onward instinct.

To be a great deal of a man, and hence a leader, involves, on the one hand, a significant individuality, and, on the other, breadth of sympathy, the two being different phases of personal caliber, rather than separate traits.

It is because a man cannot stand for anything except as he has a significant individuality, that self-reliance is so essential a trait in leadership: except as a person trusts and cherishes his own special tendency, different from that of other people and usually opposed by them in its inception, he can never develop anything of peculiar value. He has to free himself from the domination of purposes already defined and urged upon him by others, and bring up something fresh out of the vague underworld of subconsciousness; and this means an intense self, a militant, gloating "I."

On the other hand, success in unfolding a special tendency and giving vogue to it, depends upon being in touch, through sympathy, with the current of human life. All leadership takes place through the communication of ideas to the minds of others, and unless the ideas are so presented as to be congenial to those other minds, they will evidently be rejected. It is because the novelty is not alien to us, but is seen to be ourself in a fresh guise, that we welcome it.

It has frequently been noticed that personal ascendancy is not necessarily dependent upon any palpable deed in which power is manifested, but that there is often a conviction of power and an expectation of success that go before the deed and control the minds of men without apparent reason. There is something fascinating about this immediate and seemingly causeless personal efficacy, and many writers of insight lay great stress upon it. Most men of executive force possess something of this direct ascendancy, and some, like Napoleon, Cromwell, Bismarck, and Andrew Jackson, have had it in pre-eminent measure. It is not confined to any class, however, but exists in an infinite variety of kinds and degrees; and men of thought may have it as well as men of action. Dante, Milton, Goethe, and their like, bear the authority to dominate the minds of others like a visible mantle upon their shoulders, inspiring a sense of reverence and a tendency to believe and follow in all the impressionable people they meet. Such men are only striking examples of what we are all familiar with in daily life, most persons of decided character having something imposing about them at times. Indeed, there is hardly any one so insignificant that he does not seem imposing to some one at some time.

Notwithstanding the mystery that is often made of this, it appears to be simply a matter of impulsive personal judgment, an impression of power, and a sense of yielding due to interpretation of the visible or audible symbols of personality. Another may impress us with his power, and so exercise ascendancy over us, either by grossly performing the act, or by exhibiting traits of personality which convince our imaginations that he can and will do the act if he wishes to. It is in this latter way, through imaginative inference, that people mostly work upon us in ordinary social intercourse. It would puzzle us, in many cases, to tell just how we know that a man is determined, dauntless, magnanimous, intrinsically powerful, or the reverse.

In face-to-face relations, then, the natural leader is one who always has the appearance of being master of the situation. He includes other people and extends beyond them, and so is in a position to point out what they must do next. Intellectually his suggestion seems to embrace what is best in the views of others, and to embody the inevitable conclusion; it is the timely, the fit, and so the prevalent. Emotionally his belief is the strongest force present, and so draws other beliefs into it. Yet, while he imposes himself upon others, he feels the other selves as part of the situation, and so adapts himself to them that no opposition is awakened; or possibly he may take the violent method, and browbeat and humiliate a weak mind: there are various ways of establishing superiority, but in one way or another the consummate leader always accomplishes it.

It is a very natural result of the principles already noted that the fame and power of a man often transcend the man himself; that is to say, the personal idea associated by the world with a particular name and presence has often little basis in the mind behind that name and presence, as it appears to cool and impartial study. The reason is that the function of the great and famous man is to be a symbol, and the real question in other minds is not so much, What are you? as, What can I believe that you are? What can you help me to feel and be? How far can I use you as a symbol in the development of my instinctive tendency? The scientific historian may insist on asking, What are you? because the instinct he is trying to gratify is the need to make things consistent to the intelligence. But few persons have this need strongly developed, in comparison with those of a more emotional character;

and so most will care more for the other questions. The scientific point
of view can never be that of the most of mankind, and science, it seems
to me, can hardly be more than the critic and chastener of popular
faith, not its leader.

SUPERIORITY AND SUBORDINATION[1] IN
SOCIAL RELATIONSHIPS

B Y

GEORG SIMMEL

I UNDERSTAND the task of sociology to be description and determination
of the historico-psychological origin of those forms in which interactions take place between human beings.[2] The totality of these interactions, springing from the most diverse impulses, directed toward the
most diverse objects, and aiming at the most diverse ends, constitutes
"society." Those different contents in connection with which the forms
of interaction manifest themselves are the subject-matter of special
sciences. These contents attain the character of social facts by virtue of
occurring in this particular form in the interactions of men. We must
accordingly distinguish two senses of the term "society:" first, the
broader sense, in which the term includes the sum of all the individuals concerned in reciprocal relations, together with all the interests
which unite these interacting persons; second, a narrower sense, in
which the term designates the society or the associating as such, that is
the interaction itself which constitutes the bond of association, in
abstraction from its material content—the subject-matter of sociology
as the doctrine of society *sensu stricto*.

Thus, for illustration, we designate as a cube on the one hand any
natural object in cubical form; on the other hand the simple form
alone, which made the material contents into a "cube" in the former
sense, constitutes of itself, independently and abstractly considered, an
object for geometry. The significance of geometry appears in the fact

---

Abridged from: Simmel, Georg, "Superiority and Subordination as Subject-matter
of Sociology" (translated by Albion W. Small), *American Journal of Sociology*, 1896,
2, 167–189 and 392–415.
[1] *Ueberordnung und Unterordnung. Superordination and Subordination* would
be a more precise rendering, but above appears on the whole preferable. Tr. [ALBION
W. SMALL]
[2] *Cf.* my paper, "The Problem of Sociology," in *Annals of the American Academy*, November 1895, Vol. VI, No. 3.

that the formal relations which it determines hold good for all possible objects formed in space. In like manner it is the purpose of sociology to determine the forms and modes of the relations between men which, although constituted of entirely different contents, material, and interests, nevertheless take shape in formally similar social structures. If we could exhibit the totality of possible forms of social relationship in their gradations and variations we should have in such exhibit complete knowledge of "society" as such. We gain knowledge of the forms of socialization by bringing together inductively the manifestations of these forms which have had actual historical existence. In other words we have to collect and exhibit that element of form which these historical manifestations have in common, abstracted from the variety of material—economical, ethical, ecclesiastical, social, political, etc.— with respect to which they differ.

Now geometry has the advantage of finding within its field very simple figures to which the most complicated forms may be reduced. Truths respecting these simple figures are therefore very widely applicable. From relatively few fundamental truths all possible arrangements of form may be interpreted. In the case of social forms, on the contrary, an approximate reduction to simple elements has not been made. Social phenomena are too immeasurably complicated, and the methods of analysis are too incomplete. The consequence is that if sociological forms and names are used with precision they apply only within a relatively contracted circle of manifestations. Long and patient labor will be necessary before we can understand the concrete historical forms of socialization as the actual compounds of a few simple fundamental forms of human association.

When one says, for example, that superiority and inferiority is a formation to be found in every human association, though the proposition certainly involves very profound insight into the essence of human nature and human relationship, yet the assertion is so general that it affords little knowledge of particular societary formations. In order to reach such particular knowledge we must study separate types of superiority and inferiority, and we must master the special features of their formation, which in proportion to their definiteness of course lose generality of application.

In what follows I will exhibit some of the typical species of superiority and inferiority, in so far as they construct forms of association between individuals. For we must observe that superiority and inferiority is by no means a formation necessarily subsequent to the existence of "society." It is rather one of the forms in which "society" comes into being. It is one of the manifold interactions between individuals, the sum of which we designate as the socialization of the indi-

viduals concerned. The sociological task is therefore to interpret historical examples so as to show, first, from what material or formal conditions this form of society, in its different variations, takes its rise, and,
on the other hand, what material or formal consequences attach themselves to the relation so discovered.

*   *   *

Every social occurrence as such, consists of an interaction between
individuals. In other words, each individual is at the same time an
active and a passive agent in a transaction. In case of superiority and
inferiority, however, the relation assumes the appearance of a one-
sided operation; the one party appears to exert, while the other seems
merely to receive an influence. Such, however, is not in fact the case.
No one would give himself the trouble to gain or to maintain superiority, if it afforded him no advantage or enjoyment. This return to
the superior can be derived from the relation, however, only by virtue
of the fact that there is a reciprocal action of the inferior upon the
superior. The decisive characteristic of the relation at this point is this,
that the effect which the inferior actually exerts upon the superior is
determined by the latter. The superior causes the inferior to produce
a given effect which the superior shall experience. In this operation, in
case the subordination is really absolute, no sort of spontaneity is present on the part of the subordinate. The reciprocal influence is rather
the same as that between a man and a lifeless external object with
which the former performs an act for his own use. That is, the person
acts upon the object in order that the latter may react upon himself. In
this reaction of the object no spontaneity on the part of the object is
to be observed, but merely the further operation of the spontaneity of
the person. Such an extreme case of superiority and inferiority will
scarcely occur among human beings. Rather will a certain measure of
independence, a certain direction of the relation proceed also from the
self-will and the character of the subordinate. The different cases of
superiority and inferiority will accordingly be characterized by differences in the relative amount of spontaneity which the subordinates
and the superiors bring to bear upon the total relation. In exemplification of this reciprocal action of the inferior, through which superiority and inferiority manifests itself as proper socialization, I will
mention only a few cases, in which the reciprocity is difficult to discern.

When in the case of an absolute despotism the ruler attaches to his
edicts the threat of penalty or the promise of reward, the meaning is
that the monarch himself will be bound by the regulation which he
has ordained. The inferior shall have the right on the other hand to

demand something from the lawgiver. Whether the latter subsequently grants the promised reward or protection is another question. The spirit of the relation as contemplated by the law is that the superior completely controls the inferior, to be sure, but that a certain claim is assured to the latter, which claim he may press or may allow to lapse, so that even this most definite form of the relation still contains an element of spontaneity on the part of the inferior.

Still farther; the concept *law* seems to connote that he who gives the law is in so far unqualifiedly superior. Apart from those cases in which the law is instituted by those who will be its subjects, there appears in lawgiving as such no sign of spontaneity on the part of the subject of the law.

Once more, the orator who confronts the assembly, or the teacher his class, seems to be the sole leader, the temporary superior. Nevertheless every one who finds himself in that situation is conscious of the limiting and leading reaction of the mass which is apparently merely passive and submissive to his guidance. This is the case not merely when the parties immediately confront each other. All leaders are also led, as in countless cases the master is the slave of his slaves.

When we advance from this preliminary question, to the particular differentiations of the relation with which we are concerned, three possible types of superiority at once present themselves. Superiority may be exercised (*a*) by an individual (*b*) by a group (*c*) by an objective principle higher than individuals. I proceed to notice some of the sociological significance of these three cases.

The subordination of a group to a single person has in the first place as a consequence a very decided unification of the group, and this is equally the case with both the characteristic forms of this subordination: viz., (1) when the group with its head constitutes a real internal unity; when the superior is more a leader than a master, and only represents in himself the power and the will of the group; (2) when the group is conscious of opposition between itself and its head, when a party opposed to the head is formed. In both cases the unity of the supreme head tends to bring about an inner unification of the group. The elements of the latter are conscious of themselves as belonging together, because their interests converge at one point. Moreover the opposition to this unified controlling power compels the group to collect itself, to condense itself into unity.

This unification may present itself in two different forms, viz., as a leveling, or a gradation. In case a collection of human beings are alike subordinate to a single individual, they are in so far equal. The correlation between despotism and equality has long been recognized. On that account, from the other point of view, the autocrat often has an interest in equalizing the differences of social classes because marked superiorities and inferiorities in the relations between subjects come into real as well as psychological competition with his own supremacy. But there is concealed in this relation between autocracy and the leveling of the ruled another social factor of great significance. This factor may be indicated as follows: The structure of a society in which a single person rules and the great mass obeys is to be understood only through the consideration that the mass, that is the ruled, includes only a portion of the personality belonging to the individuals concerned, while the ruler invests his whole personality in the relationship. Lordship over a developed society does not consequently differ so very much from rule over a horde, since the individuals build into the structure of the mass only fragments of their personality and reserve the remainder. There are wanting therefore in the mass, as the ruled subject, the resources, adaptabilities, the accommodations, the developments of power which the whole individual possesses through the unity and presence of his total psychical energy. Apart from consideration of this difference, this devotion of a mere fraction of individuality to the mass, the frequent facility of its subserviency is not to be understood.

Wonder has often been felt over the irrationality of the condition in which a single person exercises lordship over a great mass of others. The contradiction will be modified when we reflect that the ruler and the individual subject in the controlled mass by no means enter into the relationship with an equal *quantum* of their personality. The mass is composed through the fact that many individuals unite fractions of their personality—one-sided purposes, interests and powers, while that which each personality as such actually is towers above this common level and does not at all enter into that "mass," *i.e.,* into that which is really ruled by the single person. Hence it is also that frequently in very despotically ruled groups individuality may develop itself very freely, in those aspects particularly which are not in participation with the mass. It is one of the highest tasks of administrative art to distinguish properly between those characteristics of men with respect to which they may be included in a leveled mass, and those other characteristics which may be left to free individual development. For this distinction there is needed the most accurate knowledge of what is common to the mass, and what consequently is the material for the establishment of a common level, upon which the subjects may stand at a constantly equal height, while that in which the individuals composing the mass cannot be unified must be left outside the circuit of superiority and subordination. This is a formal sociological demand and arrangement which is by no means valid in political autocracies alone, but in every possible autocracy as well. It is therefore in this more exact sense that the leveling must be understood which corresponds with the superiority of a single person.

In the second place the group may assume the form of a pyramid. In this case the subordinates stand over against the superior not in an equalized mass, but in very nicely graded strata of power. These strata grow constantly smaller in extent but greater in significance. They lead up from the inferior mass to the head, the single ruler.

This form of the group may come into existence in two ways. It may emerge from the autocratic supremacy of an individual. The latter often loses the substance of his power, and allows it to slip downwards, while retaining its form and titles. In this case more of the power is retained by the orders nearest to the former autocrat than is acquired by those more distant. Since the power thus gradually percolates, a continuity and graduation of superiority and inferiority must develop itself. This is in fact the way in which in oriental states the social forms often arise. The power of the superior orders disintegrates, either because it is essentially incoherent, and does not know how to attain the above emphasized proportion between subordination and individual freedom; or because the persons comprising the administration are too indolent or too ignorant of governmental technique to preserve supreme power. For the power which is exercised over a large circle is never a constant possession. It must be constantly acquired and defended anew if anything more than its shadow and name is to remain.

The other way in which a scale of power is constructed up to a supreme head is the reverse of that just described. Starting with a relative equality of the social elements, certain elements gain greater significance; within the circle of influence thus constituted certain especially powerful individuals differentiate themselves, until this development accommodates itself to one or to a few heads. The pyramid of superiority and inferiority is built in this case from below upward, while in the former case the development was from above downward. This second form of development is often found in economic relationships, where at first there exists a certain equality between the persons carrying on the work of a certain industrial society. Presently some of the number acquire wealth; others become poor; others fall into intermediate conditions which are as dependent upon an aristocracy of property as the lower orders are upon the middle strata; this aristocracy rises in manifold gradations to the magnates, of whom sometimes a single individual is appropriately designated as the "king" of a branch of industry.[3]

[3] Of course such developments take place not in clear cut form nor in strict accordance with a scheme of explanation, but always in devious courses and obscured by all sorts of collateral phenomena. The sociological type which we derive from all

So much with reference to the forms which the group assumes in subordination to an individual, which forms, either in clear exhibit or as elements of a complicated manifestation, are to be found in the structure of the most various groups, ecclesiastical not less than political, military as well as relationships which receive their structure entirely from the traits of character of those who compose them. It goes without saying that similar phenomena may occur in case of subordination to a numerous body. The numerical composition of the superior power is not always characteristic of it. In the sociological respect thus far referred to it may be a matter of indifference if the superior position of the one person happens to be occupied by a number of persons.

In reference to those social structures which are characterized by the superiority of a number of persons, a social totality over individuals or other totalities, it is to be noticed at once that the consequences for the subordinates are very unequal. At the same time the contrary may be observed. The chief consideration is that the point in which all the members of a large group securely coincide is very low in the scale of the moral; that consideration and delicacy is always of an individual and personal nature; that it will not usually be possible to unite a great number upon the same personal considerations; and that, especially in an association for economic ends, unlimited egoism in pursuit of material advantage and in saving cost is the one interest to be unqualifiedly accredited to all.

But subordination to a single individual may be preferred to that under a body of persons upon more ideal grounds, viz., when the superiority and inferiority bears a personal character, when it is a relation of fidelity, and the superior appears rather as a leader than a ruler. In that case there is in subordination a certain freedom and dignity which disappears when one is subordinate to a number of persons.

Of great importance for the outline of the sociological picture is the question whether and in what degree the lordship of a numerous body is exercised directly or through agents. The "agent" is a very peculiar phenomenon, emerging in every highly developed form of intercourse. This phenomenon manifests its genuinely sociological character in the fact that it occurs in the most diverse sorts of groups and in the service of the most varied interests, everywhere exhibiting however certain

---

this is always an abstraction, but not other than those at the basis of every science. The object of a special science seldom occurs in the purity and isolation in which it is scientifically treated, but in reality always mixed and entangled with phenomena to which other branches of science are devoted, so that each special science treats only an abstraction. It is therefore better to acknowledge freely that this is the case with the new science of sociology.

similar formal traits. This common fundamental characteristic consists in the transference of responsibility. The real consequences of his
action do not fall upon the agent, as they do upon every one who
pursues his own proper interests. The affair itself does not make him
responsible. Only because the consequences of his procedure fall upon
another, and this latter has some sort of power over him, can the
agent's action produce pleasure or pain in himself. This circumstance
must make the essential relationship between the agent and the object
of his action take a shape quite different from that which appears
when the action is direct, without transference to the agency of another. On account of the greater distance of personal interest from the
object the requirements of the agent may be less immediate and precise, and on that account very wide scope is often present for personal
differences, especially where a totality is represented by a single individual. Here is room for hard-heartedness and pleasure in cruelty,
which assumes the appearance of rigorous care for the interests of the
principal; for pedantry or actual conscientiousness, which, in effect,
amounts to the same thing; for negligence and complaisance, which
tolerates lax discharge of duty on the part of the subordinate on the
ground that the generality can easily bear the injury. This wide scope
which the vicarious principle gives to personal tendencies, that are
often little restrained by the requirements of the action concerned, is
evidently one ground for the fact that subjection to a totality may have
such widely contrasted consequences for the subordinate.

A peculiar form of subordination to a number of individuals is determination by vote of a majority. The presumption of majority rule
is that there is a collection of elements originally possessing equal
rights. In the process of voting the individual places himself in subordination to a power of which he is a part, but in this way, that it is
left to his own volition whether he will belong to the superior or the
inferior, *i.e.*, the outvoted party. We are not now interested in cases of
this complex problem in which the superiority is entirely formal, as,
for example, in resolves of scientific congresses, but only with those in
which the individual is constrained to an action by the will of the
party outvoting him, that is, in which he must practically subordinate
himself to the majority. This dominance of numbers through the fact
that others, though only equal in right, have another opinion, is by
no means the matter of course which it seems to us today in our time
of determinations by masses. Ancient German law knew nothing of it.
If one did not agree with the resolve of the community he was not
bound by it. As an application of this principle unanimity was later
necessary in the choice of king, evidently because it could not be expected or required that one who had not chosen the king would obey

him. The English baron who had opposed authorizing a levy, or who had not been present, often refused to pay it. In the tribal council of the Iroquois, as in the Polish Parliament, decisions had to be unanimous. There was therefore no subordination of an individual to a majority, unless we consider the fact that a proposition was regarded as rejected if it did not receive unanimous approval, a subordination, an outvoting, of the person proposing the measure.

When, on the contrary, majority rule exists, two modes of subordination of the minority are possible, and discrimination between them is of the highest sociological significance. Control of the minority may, in the first place, arise from the fact that the many are more powerful than the few. Although, or rather because the individuals participating in a vote are supposed to be equals, the majority have the physical power to coerce the minority. The taking of a vote and the subjection of the minority serves the purpose of avoiding such actual measurement of strength, but accomplishes practically the same result through the count of votes, since the minority is convinced of the futility of such resort to force. There exist in the group two parties in opposition as though they were two groups, between which relative strength, represented by the vote, is to decide.

Quite another principle is in force, however, in the second place, where the group as a unity predominates over all individuals, and so proceeds that the passing of votes shall *merely give expression to the unitary group will.* In the transition from the former to this second principle the enormously important step is taken from a unity made up merely of the sum of the individuals to recognition and operation of an abstract objective group unity. In case the group, however, is a self-existent structure—whether consciously or merely in point of fact —in case the group organization effected by union of the individuals remains along with and in spite of the individual changes, this self-existent unity—state, community, association for a distinctive purpose —must surely will and act in a definite manner. Since, however, only one of two contradictory opinions can ultimately prevail, it is assumed as more probable that the majority knows or represents this will better than the minority. According to the presumptive principle involved the minority is, in this case, not excluded but included. The subordination of the minority is thus in this stage of sociological development, quite different from that in case the majority simply represents the stronger power. In the case in hand the majority does not speak in its own name, but in that of the ideal unity and totality. It is only to this unity, which speaks by the mouth of the majority, that the minority subordinates itself.

To these must be joined, third, those formations in which subordination is neither to an individual nor yet to a majority, but to an impersonal objective principle. Here, where we seem to be stopped from speaking of a *reciprocal influence* between the superior and the subordinate, a sociological interest enters in but two cases: first, when this ideal superior principle is to be interpreted as the psychological consolidation of a real social power; second, when the principle establishes specific and characteristic relationships between those who are subject to it in common. The former case appears chiefly in connection with the moral imperatives. In the moral consciousness we feel ourselves subject to a decree which does not appear to be issued by any personal human power; we hear the voice of conscience only in ourselves, although with a force and definiteness in contrast with all subjective egoism, which, as it seems, could have had its source only from an authority outside the subject. As is well known the attempt has been made to resolve this contradiction by the assumption that we have derived the content of morality from social decrees. Whatever is serviceable to the species and to the group, whatever on that account is demanded of the members for the self-preservation of the group, is gradually bred into individuals as an instinct, so that it asserts itself as a peculiar autonomous impression by the side of the properly personal, and consequently often contradictory impulses. Thus would be explained the double character of the moral command. On the one side it appears to us as an impersonal order to which we have simply to yield. On the other side, however, no visible external power, but only our own most real and personal instinct enforces it upon us. Sociologically this is of interest as an example of a wholly peculiar form of reaction between the individual and his group. The social force is here completely grown into the individual himself. The result of this process often continues itself in the acts of the individual, by which he exerts an influence on the group. The influence of the group upon the individual, and that of the individual upon the group, in the case of these ethical occurrences, are far removed in time from each other. The former influence, through the transformation just indicated, is changed into a subjective imperative, which thus presents subordination of the individual to the conditions of the life of his group, in the form of obedience to an ideal impersonal principle.

We now turn to the second sociological question raised by the case of subordination to an impersonal ideal principle, viz., how does this subordination affect the reciprocal relation of the persons thus subordinated in common? Here again it should in the outset be observed that before this ideal subordination came into existence it was preceded by various kinds of actual subordination. We frequently observe the exercise of superiority by a person or a class in the name of an ideal principle, to which the thus prevailing personality is itself ostensibly subject. It appears to be the logical course for this relationship to precede and for the real organization of authority among men to develop itself in consequence of this ideal dependence. Historically, however, the way is as a rule the reverse. From interrelations of very real personal power there arise coordinations of superiority and inferiority, over which gradually, through spiritualization of the dominant power, or through extension and de-personalization (*Entpersonalisirung*) of the whole relationship, an ideal objective power grows up. When this stage has been reached the superior, the immediate representative of the power so derived, exercises only the authority of this objective power. The development of the position of the *pater familias* among the Aryans exhibits this clearly. The power of the *pater familias* was originally unlimited and entirely subjective; that is, his momentary desire, his personal advantage was permitted to give the decision upon all regulations. But this arbitrary power gradually became limited by a feeling of responsibility. The unity of the domestic group, embodied in the *spiritus familiaris,* grew into the ideal power in relation to which the lord of the whole came to regard himself as merely an obedient agent. Accordingly it follows that morals and custom, instead of subjective preference, determine his acts, his decisions, his judicial judgments; that he no longer behaves as though he were absolute lord of the family property, but rather the manager of it in the interest of the whole; that his position bears more the character of an official station than that of an unlimited right. Thus the relation between superiors and inferiors is placed upon an entirely new basis. While in the first stage the latter constitute only a personal competence, so to speak, of the former, the objective idea of the family is now created. The family is thought of as standing above all the individual members. The guiding patriarch himself is, like every other member, subordinate to the family idea. He may give directions to the other members of the family only in the name of the higher ideal unity.

An example of formally similar development is furnished by the most recent times with their increasing preponderance of the objective and technical element over the personal. Many sorts of superiority and inferiority which formerly bore a personal character, so that in a given relation one party was plainly the superior and the other the inferior, are now so changed that they are both and equally subject to an objective purpose, and the subordination of the one to the other persists only as a *technical necessity* within this common relationship to the higher principle. So long as the relation of the wage-worker is looked on as a rental contract—the laboring man is hired or *rented*—so long does the relationship contain essentially an element of sub-ordination of the laborer to the employer. This element is excluded however so soon as we regard the labor compact not as rental but as purchase of labor as an economic good. Then is the subordination which the relation demands of the laborer, as has been said, only a subordination "to cooperative progress, which for the entrepreneur, in so far as he performs any activity, is as essential as for the laborer." The increased self-consciousness of the modern laborer must in part at least be credited to this perception. He has no longer the feeling that he is a subject person. He regards himself only as servant of an objective economic *technique,* within which the element that as entre-preneur or leader is superior to himself works no longer as a personal superior, but simply as a technical necessity. Inasmuch as the laborer is no longer hired as an entire person, but rather a quantitatively de-fined service is stipulated, he is freed as a man from the relation of inferiority. He now belongs to the relationship only as a factor of the process of production, *thus in so far coordinate with the leader.*

In what manner the relation between superiority and subordination is modified by the fact that in its entirety it is subsidiary to an ideal purpose, depends upon the question, is the person in the superior station the representative of the higher objective principle as against the subordinate, or have they a similar relation to this principle, so that the gradation between them is a matter of technique and organiza-tion? The former case occurs in the relation of an official to the public; the second in his relation to subordinate officials. In the former in-stance the official represents the whole idea and power of the state over against the citizen, who by transgression of law, may have placed him-self outside of normal civic relations. The power which the official exercises flows from that higher civic principle to which, to be sure, the citizen belongs, yet for the moment this power confronts the latter as an external constraint, and asserts itself as superior to him. In the relation of the higher to the lower official on the other hand, the civic principle, the superior idea, is alike present in both. The one represents this idea as well as the other. Superiority and subordination between them are not produced by the antithesis of two principles, but by organization within one and the same principle.

These two forms of superiority and subordination dominated by a higher principle, with their very different consequences, emerge in the most various social spheres and with the most manifold complications. In all the countless cases in which an objective idea, an abstract unity, manifests itself in hierarchical organization, this double relationship of the individual is to be found. He is clothed with the dignity and importance of that principle, and he therewith enters into a relationship of superiority to all those over whom the principle has power. This occurs most obviously in the case of civic officials, who by no means owe their superiority over the citizens to the power of their own personality, but only to that of the principle of which they are the exponents. The same is often the case with a member of a priestly order, in short, in all those social structures in which each individual member, *even when he occupies a very subordinate place within the structure,* yet towards those without represents the whole power and importance of the principle. On the other hand, such attachment to an organization may give rise to a certain subordination to those without.

We thus see the most remarkable complications emerge where superiority and inferiority between individuals is limited and crossed by the subordination of the whole relationship to a higher principle. From such a very special example it may be evident that only the most accurate analysis of the forms of the relations which occur among men may gradually lead at last to an actual understanding of the complicated structure of human society. For "society" means that these countless bonds, dependences, relations of equilibrium or preponderance establish themselves between individuals. It is evident that we can reach an understanding of these relationships only by casting the sum of a great number of real historical cases; that is, by leaving out of consideration the differences in the material content of these relations, and by making only the forms of the relations, in all their modifications, crossings and complications the object of our investigations, just as logic becomes a science when we disregard all defined and specific contents of thought and consider only the forms in which single representations are so combined as to form truths.

*   *   *

In the case of subordination to a numerous superior, of which I have so far spoken, the separate elements of this superior order are coordinated with each other—or at least they work, in the relation that comes here into view, as though they were coordinated. New appearances occur so soon as the numerous superior ceases to act as a unity of similar elements. In this event the superiors may be either opposed to each other or they may compose a series in which the superior is in his turn subordinate to a higher. I will now consider the former case, which may have very different consequences for the subordinates.

When it occurs that one is totally subject to a number of mutually opposed persons or groups, that is, in such manner that the subject brings no spontaneity into the relation, but rather is completely dependent upon each of the superiors, he will suffer severely under their opposition. In the first place, each of the superiors will demand his entire strength and service, and on the other hand will hold him as responsible for everything which he does under the compulsion of the others as though it were of his own motion. This is the typical situation of him who "serves two masters." It is to be seen in the case of children whose parents are inharmonious, and likewise in that of a petty state which is equally dependent on two powerful neighbors, and consequently in the event of conflict between the superiors the inferior will be held responsible by the one for that to which it was forced by its inferiority to the other. If this conflict of the individuals or groups is completely subjectified in the inferior, if the contestants operate as ideal moral forces which set up their demands within the inferior person, the case is "a conflict of duties." Here, as in those external cases which still compose the type for the latter, a smooth solution of the difficulty is in most cases out of the question. On the contrary the subordinate will often enough be crushed between the colliding interests of his superiors.

This result, as was said, presupposes that the subordinate himself exercises no spontaneity in the relation, but is entirely dependent. A wholly contrasted result appears so soon as the subordinate himself has any power to exert in the relation, with any degree of freedom in its application. Then occurs the case of such extreme sociological significance—*duobus litigantibus tertius gaudet*. In departments of activity concerned with the most widely different material interests, in the most manifold often concealed combinations, the significance of the *tertius gaudens* comes into effect. It is one of the typical forms of the attitude of human beings toward each other. It becomes actual equally in connection with the most wildly contrasted provinces of interests.

When subordination means not merely inferiority in power, but direct obligation to obey, this position between opposed superiors, so soon at least as the slightest independence in relation to the latter exists, may lead to entire emancipation from inferiority.

Finally, this consequence may result not alone from the opposition of contemporary superior powers, but also from that of unlike powers that supersede each other. The progress is formally the same—*i. e.*, the growing independence (*Verselbständigung*) of the subordinate through the position as *tertius gaudens*—the difference being that the superiors are not contemporary but successive.

Equally different consequences for the inferior result in the second case, viz., when the superiors themselves stand in the relation of superiority and inferiority. In this case the decisive consideration is whether the subordinate possesses an immediate relation to the highest in rank of his superiors, or whether the intermediate authority, which while superior to the subordinate is also inferior to the highest in rank, separates the subordinate in question from the supreme authority, and thus *de facto* alone represents the superior elements over against that particular subordinate.

Thus the lot of an inferior with reference to a superior is a favorable one, if this superior in turn is inferior to a higher authority to whom the lowest in rank has recourse. This is also the peculiar natural consequence of the sociological configuration here under discussion. Since as a rule some sort of rivalry and conflict of authority arises between contiguous elements in the scale of superiority, the intermediate is often in conflict with the higher as well as with the lower in rank. Common opposition is however a strong bond of union—one of the most typical of formal rules, which applies in all existing departments of social life. Through this relation a coalition is established between the highest element of this series and the lowest, and this connection affords to the latter a strong security against his immediate superior.

If however this direct connection is interrupted, if the intermediate stratum has inserted itself so extensively and powerfully between the higher and the lower strata that all initiative of the highest in favor of the lowest can be mediated only through the middle stratum, there result conversely very unfavorable consequences for the inferior. Thus in case the organization consists of three elements, a highest central power, an extended lowest stratum, and a middle stratum, which exercises toward the lowest stratum a portion of the governmental functions, either from original and free right, or by virtue of transference from the supreme power—then is the working of this middle stratum not so much a connection as a separation of the two others.

This combination, the erection of different superiors the one above the other, exhibits a very important sociological formation: elements which are at once superior and inferior. This is the characteristic form of the hierarchy, upon which every highly elaborated organization of a group is based. Wherever the realization of an objective purpose is concerned, the personal cooperation of the elements which are to produce the result will take place for the most part in the form of a stratified numerously articulated superiority and inferiority. I would refer to the constitution of every factory, of every enterprise on a large scale, and especially of every army. That through the simultaneous superiority and inferiority of each element in the hierarchy, its position, both with reference to the higher and the lower elements, is accurately defined, must lead the individual to a high degree of stability in his feeling about life (*Lebensgefühl*), in so far as this is at all socially determinable. It must thereby assure to the whole organization a much closer coherence than if the individual regards himself as either exclusively superior or exclusively inferior.

In case very numerous and energetic superiorities and inferiorities are present in a group, whether in the form of the hierarchic structure or in parallel collocation, the group as a whole will derive its character essentially from subordination. This results from the fact that the strata extend themselves downward in rapid progression, so that the quantitatively preponderant is always the subordinate; and consequently the whole produces the impression of universal subordination. If we take a purely æsthetic view of the case we may, to be sure, through quite special combinations, get the impression of universal superiority in a group. In general the antithesis of universal subordination appears to be not so much universal superiority as universal freedom. If we look closer it appears almost always that liberation from inferiority means at the same time the gain of a superiority, either over against the hitherto superior, or to a stratum henceforth destined to more definite inferiority.

Moreover this sociological type, viz., that liberation from inferiority at once enlarges itself by effort after or gain of superiority—exhibits itself in somewhat more complicated manifestations. In case the whole lowest strata sought to gain an absolute elevation of their position, a lessening of the quantum of their inferiority, the consequence has often been that a certain portion of the group uniformly seeking elevation reaches the higher plane, which, however, only means that these become a part of the previously superior strata, while the rest remain inferior. This is especially the case, and very naturally, wherever within the aspiring strata there is already a division of superiors and inferiors. In this case, after the end of the rebellion against the stratum which is superior to them all, the difference between the rebels, which during the commotion fell into the background, will at once appear again, and will bring it to pass that the formerly more eminent now assimilate themselves to that higher stratum, while their former associates in effort become so much the more degraded.

Both socialism and anarchism will allege that liberation from inferiority will no longer thus enlarge itself by immediate endeavor after superiority, so soon as social organization in general is no longer effected in the form of superiority and inferiority, and these gradations are no more to be encountered at any point. Both theories contradict the above emphasized significance of the hierarchy for associated production, and they presuppose the belief that economy is possible in the life and activity of the group along with complete coordination of its members. For so long in the future as prevision can reach, however, we may contest the possibility of a social constitution without superiority and inferiority, just as we may assert that the natural differences between human beings, which no common education can remove, will press for expression in external gradations of ranks, in differences of superordination and subordination. A tendency of culture is nevertheless thinkable which, in spite of the persistence of superordination and subordination, approximates in result to that which socialism and anarchism want to reach by doing away with social ranks. The way to this would be through such psychical development that the individual's consciousness of life (*Lebensgefühl*) would become less dependent upon external activity and the position assigned to the individual within the same. It is quite conceivable that in the progress of civilization productive activity may become more and more technique, and may at last lose practically all its consequences for that which is essential and personal in man. As a matter of fact we find the approach to this separation as the sociological type of numerous phases of development. While personality and performance (*Leistung*) were in the beginning closely mingled, the division of labor and the production of commodities for the market, *i. e.*, for wholly unknown and indifferent consumers, brings it about that personality tends to withdraw from industrial performance and to find recourse in itself. This tendency is promoted by advances in technique, in consequence of which productive activity is constantly acquiring a more mechanical and objective character.

We may think of an ideal constitution, in which in one respect or at one time A is superior to B; in another respect or at another time, however, B is superior to A. In such case the value of superordination and subordination as elements of organization would be preserved, while their oppressiveness, one-sidedness and injustice would disappear. In point of fact there are very many phenomena of life in society in which this form-type is realized, although it may be in partial, mangled and obscured fashion. All groups in which the leader changes, either through frequent choice or according to regular term, down to the case of chairman of a social union, seek in this way to gain the technical advantage of superiority and subordination while avoiding its personal disadvantages. Simultaneous superordination and subordination is one of the most decisive forms of reciprocity, and, if properly disposed throughout the various departments of activity, may, by virtue of this very intimate reciprocity which it signifies, constitute a most powerful bond between individuals. The matrimonial relation owes its external and internal stability (*Festigkeit*), at least in part, to the fact that it encompasses a great number of departments of interest, with reference to many of which the one party is superior, while with respect to many others the other party is foremost. There arises from this fact a growing together (*Ineinanderwachsen*), a oneness, and at the same time such essential vitality of the relation as is hardly to be attained in the case of other sociological forms. What we call "equality of right" between husband and wife in marriage will doubtless turn out to be such an alternating superordination and subordination. At least this would be a much more organic and centripetal relation than would result from a mechanical equality in the immediate sense of the word.

It must be observed further that this advantageous consequence of the form of association under discussion depends upon provision that the sphere within which the one social element is superior is very accurately and unequivocally delimited from those spheres in which the other is superior. Whenever this is not the case conflicts of authority will incessantly arise, and the consequence will be not strengthening but weakening of the relationship. Especially in the event that one who is generally subordinate by some peculiar turn of affairs reaches a superiority which remains within the province of his previous inferiority, it follows that partly through the character of rebellion which the condition will then usually bear, partly through the inadequate qualification of the always subordinate for superiority in the same sphere, the stability of the group will suffer.

*   *   *

I come now to the discussion of a further characteristic of relations of superiority and inferiority, viz., that which is imparted to the group by subsidiary relations between the elements so connected. Whether the persons so connected are near to each other or far apart, whether they manifest likenesses or unlikenesses, imparts to the superiority and inferiority existing between them definite consequences and shadings. Thus among the essential distinguishing signs of sociological formations is whether a group preferably subordinates itself to a stranger or to one of its own members. Subordination to one who has emerged from the same circle, and is essentially no more than the equal of those subordinated to him, is sometimes regarded as more tolerable, more useful, more desirable, and again as more oppressive, more obstructive, and more unworthy. In a precisely corresponding way is subordination to a stranger, or a person outside the group, contradictorily valued. In Germany in the Middle Ages the feudal lords at first had the right to name at will judges and leaders from abroad for the people attached to their estate. At length, however, the latter often won the concession that the official should be taken from within their own circle. At the same time Italian cities, on the contrary, followed the principle of procuring their judges from distant cities. This divergence, viz., estimate of control by a stranger, now as lighter, now as severer, than control by one who is nearer, has certain utilitarian justifications. The stranger is less partisan, the member of the group is more intelligent about its conditions. But these consciously rational grounds not only fail entirely in many cases, but, since they are in principle of equal value, the *decision between them* requires a higher ground, which is always instinctive. This is due to the fact that this question is a side issue of the great psychical dualism—the equality of both attraction and repulsion by like and by unlike. According as the one tendency or the other is psychically predominant, will the group prefer to subordinate itself to one of its own or to a stranger. As a matter of fact it is wholly an affair of feeling, which cannot be rationalized, whether one seems to himself more humiliated by subordination to one who is near or to one farther removed. In general we may say that the lower a group stands as a whole, the more each individual member is accustomed to subordination, the less willingly will they suffer themselves to be controlled by one of their own; the higher the group stands, the more likely it will be to subordinate itself to one of its peers alone.

Just as in this case a relation of such definite inferiority as that of an accused to his judge may still be regarded as placing the two upon a certain level of equality, so on the contrary may equality be sometimes regarded as subordination. Sir Henry Maine once said that the principle of nationality, as it is often presented, appears to assert that men of one race suffer an invasion of their rights, if they are obliged to have political arrangements in common with men of another race. Thus if two different social characters are in consideration, A and B, A appears to be subordinated to B, so soon as a constitution is thought of for the former like that belonging to the latter; although this constitution may contain nothing which connotes such lower standing or subordination.

Finally there belongs under this rubric the very important observation that subordination under a somewhat remotely stationed personage seems to be most serviceable when the group itself consists of heterogeneous and dissimilar elements. In this case the members of a group that is subordinated to a superior personage are related to each other precisely as the particular representations, which go to make up a general conception, are related to each other. That is to say, this conception must be the higher and the more abstract, in other words it must stand at the greater distance from each particular representation, the more unlike each other these latter are, which the general conception must comprehend. The most familiar and typical case of this sort, which recurs with formal similarity in a thousand spheres,

is that of rival parties that come together for the purpose of choosing
an arbiter, and very properly fix their choice upon one who is standing completely apart from both. The more the latter is the case the
more willingly will both submit to his decision. It is to be kept in
mind as decisive in this case that the contending parties must be co-
ordinate, if the type is to appear in its purity. If there already rules
between them any sort of superiority and inferiority, this will all too
easily create a special connection of the judge with the one party, and
to that extent non-partisanship will be destroyed. Even when the
referee is quite removed from either contestant's circle of specific
interests, he will often nevertheless bring to his judgment a prejudice
in favor of the superior, in many cases also in favor of the inferior.
From the other point of view the nomination of an unpartisan arbiter
is, for the reason just mentioned, a sign that the contestants concede
to each other a certain coordination.

*   *   *

I come now to the last sociological problem which I will connect
with the fact of superiority and inferiority. On the one hand superiority and inferiority constitute a form of the objective organization
of society. On the other hand they are an expression of differences in
the personal quality of men. What now is the relation of these two
determinations to each other, and how is the form of socialization affected by the variations of this relation?

In the beginning of social development superordination of one
person over others must have been the adequate expression and consequence of personal superiority. There is no visible reason why, in a
social condition without firm organization which *a priori* assigns to the
individual his station, anybody should subordinate himself to another,
unless force, piety, mental superiority, suggestion, in short the relation
of his personal qualities to those of the other, determined him to such
submission. From this origin of superordination and subordination,
which of course is at every moment operative within society, and
continually founds new relations, there develop permanent organizations of superordination and subordination into which individuals are
born, or in which they gain specific positions on the ground of quite
other qualities than those which established in the first place the
superordination and subordination in question. While at first there
were simply human beings with their peculiarities, and their relations
grew out of these, later the relations themselves were given as objective
forms, "stations," empty spaces and boundaries as it were, thenceforth
to be "filled out" by individuals. The more firmly and technically the
organization of the group is elaborated, the more objectively and for-

mally will the schemes of superordination and subordination present themselves. Then, as a supplementary matter, the proper persons are selected for these relationships, or they are filled out by the mere accidents of birth and other chances. In this connection we are by no means to think merely of the hierarchy of civil positions. Financial economy creates within the spheres of its control a wholly similar formation of society. Possession or lack of a determined sum of money signifies a determined social station almost entirely independent of the personal qualities of the individual concerned. This is thrown out into bold relief by the fact that money is a possession not in any necessary connection with personality, but possible to everyone who may earn or inherit it. People traverse the positions corresponding with possession of determined sums of money, just as purely fortuitous substances find their way through rigidly fixed forms.

This analysis brings us to a sociological perception of the very highest significance: that superordination and subordination are a formal structural (*organisatorische*) necessity for the continuance of the group. In comparison with this necessity, what persons shall be the superiors or inferiors is a secondary question. As a demand of social self-preservation this necessity confronts us in very primitive conditions. At the time when in Germany the earliest constitution of complete personal and property equality within the community had become obsolete, the landless man found himself without the active rights of a freeman. If he did not wish to remain without any connection with the community, it was necessary for him to attach himself to a lord, in order thus, as entitled to protection (*Schutzgenosse*), to participate indirectly in the public associations. The community had an interest in his doing this, for it could not tolerate an unattached man within its circuit; consequently Anglo-Saxon law expressly made it the duty of the landless man to attach himself to a lord. Likewise in mediæval England the interest of the community demanded that the stranger should place himself under a protecting lord. From such very simple points of departure the conviction grew that men must in general be governed—better by unfit persons than not at all—that in general only the group must assume the form of superordination and subordination, so that it is consequently only a desirable accident if, in the objectively necessary position, the subjectively suitable individual has his place. As explanations or justifications of this order, which is supposed to be immanent in the nature of social beings, all the theories appear which, since Aristotle, teach that there are φύσει δοῦλοι who in general could not bear another kind of life than that of subordination, and that the organization of society after the form of superordination and subordination is merely an expression of this fact. At the same time the converse possibility is often overlooked, viz., that the actual subordination, resting upon quite other grounds than personal qualifications, has led to an adaptation of individuals and classes to this condition, i. e., to the now evidently actual quality and disposition for subordination.

Two lines of thought stand here over against each other, each of which may cite for itself a long series of facts from every department of social life, so that each represents a significant sociological formation.

In consideration of the actual unlikeness in the qualities of human beings—to be removed only in a Utopia—the aristocracy of the best is surely the sort of constitution in which the external relationship between men is the most exact and efficient expression of their subjective relation. But an aristocracy of the best, such as Plato wanted, can never be fully realized, because there is no infallible means of recognizing the best. Even if it could be realized it would not exist permanently, since the possession of power unquestionably corrupts not always individuals but corporate bodies and classes. The aristocracy of the best lies therefore in close proximity to the aristocracy of the worst. Consequently the condition of universal equality seems to be the *lesser evil*, which may gradually attain to the dignity of an absolutely good condition. The peculiar difficulties then which the formal fact of superordination entails, produce the advantage of an external constitution which stands in direct antithesis with the subjective qualifications of the individuals.

And yet, the corresponding pessimistic temper may deny the necessity of this result, and may hold that which here appears the lesser evil to be the greater. This may be plausible from the point of view that, should rigid superordination and subordination disappear, there would go with it the compulsion, which human nature now at all events needs, to avoid falling into complete aimlessness and formlessness of conduct. Thus for many historical epochs one may cite the advantage of established hereditary despotism, which forces wide territories together in unity, in comparison with free federation of the same. There is the same presumption in favor of despotism that there is in favor of marriage as contrasted with "free love." Marriage often holds the parties together by force, when from passion, or anger or indifference they would separate if they could. But what blessing there is in this compulsion! How it helps over disturbances of the relation, to which it would be irreparable injury to yield. Only subordination could accomplish this—either to a person or to a law. It is as though there existed in our soul two strata or tendencies, differentiated from each other in principle; the one bearing the real meaning and purpose and substance of our lives, while the other is made up of momentary impulses and isolated irritations. The latter would still oftener conquer the former if the inconsistencies and perversities in its variations were not broken up by objective regularities, through which the abiding undercurrent repeatedly recovers its power. Since now the objective and ideal constraint must, as a rule, be borne by superordinated persons, so in the most complicated relations, those of the family, of the class (*ständischen*), of politics, of the church, of social intercourse in the restricted sense (*geselligen*)—personal superordination seems to be the necessary form of coherence of the elements. Here also adaptation of the superordinated or subordinated position to the individual qualification is not a necessary element. It is only the universally human qualification which, in the sociological form of organized constraint, finds its adequate expression.

More than this, such correspondence of personal qualifications and social position in the series of superordinations and subordinations is *in general and on principle impossible,* no matter what sort of organization may be proposed for this purpose. With this perception we encounter the last and most radical complication which connects itself with the problem of the correspondence of these factors. It consists in the fact that there are always more persons qualified for superior positions than there are positions of that order. Of the millions subject to a prince there are surely a great number who would be equally good and perhaps better princes. Of the workmen in a factory there are many who would be equally good managers or at least foremen. Among the common soldiers of an army are many who possess full, though perhaps latent, qualifications to be officers. This unquestioned fact is not done away with by the contrasted fact that there are also many people in superior positions who do not possess sufficient qualifications for the same. In the first place such an occurrence is very conspicuous. Incapacity in a position from which others must be led is less easily concealed than other incapacities. It consequently seems to occur with special frequency, precisely *because* so many others really fitted for the superior station occupy contiguous inferior positions. As a matter of fact the purely individual incompetency of the persons in controlling positions is relatively infrequent. A German proverb says, "When God gives an office he gives the brains for it." The truth of the observation herein contained rests upon the fact that the intelligence requisite for occupancy of superior positions exists in many people, but it may exert and develop and reveal itself only when they assume the position. When we think of the ridiculous and uncontrollable accidents by which men in all departments of life reach their positions, it would seem a miracle that the number of incompetents in responsible positions is so small, if we were not obliged to assume that latent qualifications for the positions are very extensively present.

This incommensurability between the quantum of qualification for superior stations and the quantum of their possible exercise is perhaps to be explained by the difference between the character of men as members of groups and as individuals. The group as such is low and in need of guidance. The peculiarities which the group develops as simply common characteristics of the group are only those of subordination. So soon, however, as combinations of groups occur, that is, a formation of larger circles comes into being, it is necessary for the whole mass to organize itself in the form of subordination to a few. This does not prevent the possession of higher and finer characteristics by each person in this mass. These, however, are individual. In *various* respects they extend beyond the common possession, and consequently they do not raise from their low plane those qualities which are common to the members of the group as such. From this relation it follows, on the one hand, that the group as a whole needs a leader, and there must be many subordinate and few superiors; on the other hand, however, each individual of the group is more highly qualified, that is, as element of the group and as subordinate.

This enormous difficulty, which presents the sting and the most radical incommensurability in all social formations, this antinomy between the just claim to superior relation and the technical impossibility of satisfying it, is overcome in the sociological respect by the principle of rank (*ständische Princip*), and the existing social order, by erecting classes pyramidally one above the other, with constantly diminishing numbers of members, and thereby *a priori* diminishing the number of those "qualified" for leading positions. Since in case of the equal right of all to all positions it would be impossible to satisfy every legitimate claim, the social order which includes ranks and classes provides at the outset for a limiting selection which pays no attention to the individual, but rather on the contrary determines the individual. In a multitude *a priori* equal, it is impossible to bring each to a suitable position; consequently this social arrangement might be considered as an attempt, on the contrary, from the point of view of the previously determined position, to discipline men for this preordained station. Whether a socialistic constitution, without such a prejudice for superordination and subordination, could fulfill its promises is to me doubtful. Under socialism, on the one hand, with removal of every accidental chance, only talent shall determine the attainment of position. On the other hand every talent shall find its appropriate station; that is, shall bring its highest potency to development, in consequence of which, according to the above explanations, there must be more superiors than inferiors, more to give orders than to execute them. By no means political organizations alone, but group formations of every kind and of every content labor under this difficulty, which rests in the last analysis upon the conflict between the individual totality of men and their character as an element of the group. The inferiority (*Niedrigkeit*) of the latter (group element) in comparison with the former (total individual) brings about the necessity that there shall be many subordinates and few superiors. The eminence of the former (total individual) in comparison with the latter (group element) amounts to necessity that there shall be incomparably more persons essentially and potentially qualified for superior positions than there are such positions to be filled.

CHAPTER 8

Knowledge About Others and Social Relationships

KNOWLEDGE AND IGNORANCE

BY

GEORG SIMMEL

ALL relationships of people to each other rest, as a matter of course, upon the precondition that they know something about each other. The merchant knows that his correspondent wants to buy at the lowest price and to sell at the highest price. The teacher knows that he may credit to the pupil a certain quality and quantity of information. Within each social stratum the individual knows approximately what measure of culture he has to presuppose in each other individual. In all relationships of a personally differentiated sort there develop, as we may affirm with obvious reservations, intensity and shading in the degree in which each unit reveals himself to the other through word and deed. How much error and sheer prejudice may lurk in all this knowing is immaterial. Just as our apprehension of external nature, along with its elusions and its inaccuracies, still attains that degree of truth which is essential for the life and progress of our species, so each knows the other with whom he has to do, in a rough and ready way, to the degree necessary in order that the needed kinds of intercourse may proceed. That we shall know with whom we have to do, is the

Abridged from: Simmel, Georg, "The Sociology of Secrecy and of Secret Societies" (Translated by Albion W. Small), *American Journal of Sociology*, 1906, 11, 441–498. Reprinted by permission of the University of Chicago Press.

first precondition of having anything to do with another. The customary reciprocal presentation, in the case of any somewhat protracted conversation, or in the case of contact upon the same social plane, although at first sight an empty form, is an excellent symbol of that reciprocal apprehension which is the presumption of every social relationship. The fact is variously concealed from consciousness, because, in the case of a very large number of relationships, only the quite typical tendencies and qualities need to be reciprocally recognized. Their necessity is usually observed only when they happen to be wanted. It would be a profitable scientific labor to investigate the sort and degree of reciprocal apprehension which is needed for the various relationships between human beings. It would be worth while to know how the general psychological presumptions with which each approaches each are interwoven with the special experiences with reference to the individual who is in juxtaposition with us; how in many ranges of association the reciprocal apprehension does or does not need to be equal, or may or may not be permitted to be equal; how conventional relationships are determined in their development only through that reciprocal or unilateral knowledge developing with reference to the other party. The investigation should finally proceed in the opposite direction; that is, it should inquire how our objectively psychological picture of others is influenced by the real relationships of practice and of sentiment between us. This latter problem by no means has reference to falsification. On the contrary, in a quite legitimate fashion, the theoretical conception of a given individual varies with the standpoint from which it is formed, which standpoint is given by the total relationship of the knower to the known. Since one never can absolutely know another, as this would mean knowledge of every particular thought and feeling; since we must rather form a conception of a personal unity out of the fragments of another person in which alone he is accessible to us, the unity so formed necessarily depends upon that portion of the other which our standpoint toward him permits us to see. These differences, however, by no means spring merely from differences in the quantity of the apprehension. No psychological knowledge is a mere mechanical echo of its object. It is rather, like knowledge of external nature, dependent upon the forms that the knowing mind brings to it, and in which it takes up the data. When we are concerned with apprehension of individual by individual, these forms are individually differentiated in a very high degree. They do not arrive at the scientific generality and supersubjective conclusiveness which are attainable in our knowledge of external nature, and of the typically individual psychic processes. If A has a different conception of M from that of B, this does not necessarily mean incompleteness or deception. On the contrary, the personality of A and the total circumstances of his relation to M being what they are, his picture of M is for him true, while for B a picture differing somewhat in its content may likewise be true. It is by no means correct to say that, over and above these two pictures, there is the objectively correct apprehension of M, by which the two are to be corrected according to the measure of their agreement with it. Rather is the ideal truth which, to be sure, the actual picture of M in the conception of A approaches only asymptotically, that is as ideal, something different from that of B. It contains, as integrating organizing precondition, the psychical peculiarity of A and the special relationship into which A and M are brought, by virtue of their characteristics and their fortunes. Every relationship between persons causes a picture of each to take form in the mind of the other, and this picture evidently is in reciprocal relationship with that personal relationship. While this latter constitutes the presupposition, on the basis of which the conceptions each of the other take shape so and so, and with reference to which these conceptions possess actual truth for the given case, on the other hand the actual reciprocity of the individuals is based upon the picture which they derive of each other. Here we have one of the deep circuits of the intellectual life, inasmuch as one element presupposes a second, but the second presupposes the first. While this is a fallacy within narrow ranges, and thus makes the whole involved intellectual process unreliable, in more general and fundamental application it is the unavoidable expression of the unity in which these two elements coalesce, and which cannot be expressed in our forms of thought except as a building of the first upon the second, and at the same time of the second upon the first. Accordingly, our situations develop themselves upon the basis of a reciprocal knowledge of each other, and this knowledge upon the basis of actual situations, both inextricably interwoven, and, through their alternations within the reciprocal sociological process, designating the latter as one of the points at which reality and idea make their mysterious unity empirically perceptible.

In the presence of the total reality upon which our conduct is founded, our knowledge is characterized by peculiar limitations and aberrations. We cannot say in principle that "error is life and knowledge is death," because a being involved in persistent errors would continually act wide of the purpose, and would thus inevitably perish. At the same time, in view of our accidental and defective adaptations to our life-conditions, there is no doubt that we cherish not only so much truth, but also so much nescience, and attain to so much error as is useful for our practical purposes. We may call to mind in this connection the vast sums of human knowledge that modify human life, which, however, are overlooked or disregarded if the total cultural situation does not make these modifications possible and useful. At the other extreme, we may refer to the *Lebenslüge* of the individual, so often in need of illusion as to his powers and even as to his feelings, of superstition with reference to God as well as men, in order to sustain himself in his being and in his potentialities. In this psycho-biological respect error is co-ordinated with truth. The utilities of the external, as of the subjective, life provide that we get from the one as well as from the other precisely that which constitutes the basis of the conduct which is essential for us. Of course, this proposition holds only in the large, and with a wide latitude for variations and defective adaptations.

But there is within the sphere of objective knowledge, where there is room for truth and illusion, a definite segment in which both truth and illusion may take on a character nowhere else observed. The subjective, internal facts of the person with whom we are in contact present this area of knowledge. Our fellow-man either may voluntarily reveal to us the truth about himself, or by dissimulation he may deceive us as to the truth. No other object of knowledge can thus of its own initiative, either enlighten us with reference to itself or conceal itself, as a human being can. No other knowable object modifies its conduct from consideration of its being understood or misunderstood. This modification does not, of course, take place throughout the whole range of human relations. In many ways our fellow-man is also in principle only like a fragment of nature, which our apprehension, so to speak, holds fast in its grasp. In many respects, however, the situation is different, and our fellow-man of his own motion gives forth truth or error with reference to himself. Every lie, whatever its content, is in its essential nature a promotion of error with reference to the mendacious subject; for the lie consists in the fact that the liar conceals from the person to whom the idea is conveyed the true conception which he possesses. The specific nature of the lie is not exhausted in the fact that the person to whom the lie is told has a false conception of the fact. This is a detail in common with simple error. The additional trait is that the person deceived is held in misconception about the true intention of the person who tells the lie. Veracity and mendacity are thus of the most far-reaching significance for the relations of persons with each other. Sociological structures are most characteristically differentiated by the measure of mendacity that is operative in them. To begin with, in very simple relationships a lie is much more harmless for the persistence of the group than in complex associations. Primitive man, living in communities of restricted extent, providing for his needs by his own production or by direct cooperation, limiting his spiritual interests to personal experience or to simple tradition, surveys and controls the material of his existence more easily and completely than the man of higher culture. In the latter case life rests upon a thousand presuppositions which the individual can never trace back to their origins, and verify; but which he must accept upon faith and belief. In a much wider degree than people are accustomed to realize, modern civilized life—from the economic system which is constantly becoming more and more a credit-economy, to the pursuit of science, in which the majority of investigators must use countless results obtained by others, and not directly subject to verification—depends upon faith in the honor of others.

Human intercourse rests normally upon the condition that the mode of thought among the persons associated has certain common characteristics; in other words, that objective spiritual contents constitute the common material, which is developed in its individual phases in the course of social contacts. The type and the most essential vehicle of this community of spiritual content is common language. If we look a little closer, however, the common basis here referred to consists by no means exclusively of that which all equally know, or, in a particular case, of that which the one accepts as the spiritual content of the other; but this factor is shot through by another, viz., knowledge which the one associate possesses, while the other does not. If there were such a thing as complete reciprocal transparency, the relationships of human beings to each other would be modified in a quite unimaginable fashion. The dualism of human nature, by reason of which every manifestation of it has its sources in numerous origins that may be far distant from each other, and every quantity is estimated at the same time as great or small, according as it is contemplated in connection with littleness or greatness, makes it necessary to think of sociological relationships in general dualistically; that is, concord, harmony, mutuality, which count as the socializing forces proper, must be interrupted by distance, competition, repulsion, in order to produce the actual configuration of society. The strenuous organizing forms which appear to be the real constructors of society, or to construct society as such, must be continually disturbed, unbalanced, and detached by individualistic and irregular forces, in order that their reaction and development may gain vitality by alternate concession and resistance. Relationships of an intimate character, the formal vehicle of which is psycho-physical proximity, lose the charm, and even the content, of their intimacy, unless the proximity includes, at the same time and alternately, distance and intermission. Finally—and this is the matter with which we are now concerned—

the reciprocal knowledge, which is the positive condition of social relationships, is not the sole condition. On the contrary, such as those relationships are, they actually presuppose also a certain nescience, a ratio, that is immeasurably variable to be sure, of reciprocal concealment. The lie is only a very rude form, in the last analysis often quite self-contradictory, in which this necessity comes to the surface. However frequently lying breaks up a social situation, yet, so long as it existed, a lie may have been an integrating element of its constitution. We must take care not to be misled, by the ethically negative value of lying, into error about the direct positive sociological significance of untruthfulness, as it appears in shaping certain concrete situations. Moreover, lying in connection with the elementary sociological fact here in question—viz., the limitation of the knowledge of one associate by another—is only one of the possible means, the positive and aggressive technique, so to speak, the purpose of which in general is obtained through sheer secrecy and concealment. The following discussion has to do with these more general and negative forms. Before we come to the question of secrecy as consciously willed concealment, we should notice in what various degrees different circumstances involve disregard of reciprocal knowledge by the members of associations. Among those combinations which involve some degree of direct reciprocity on the part of their members, those which are organized for a special purpose are first in eliminating this element of reciprocal knowledge. Among these purposeful organizations, which in principle still involve direct reciprocity, the extreme in the present particular is represented by those in which utterly objective performances of the members are in view. This situation is best typified by the cases in which the contribution of so much cash represents the participation of the individuals in the activities of the group. In such instances reciprocity, coherence, and common pursuit of the purpose by no means rest upon psychological knowledge of the one member by the others. As a member of the group the individual is exclusively the agent of a definite performance; and whatever individual motive may impel him to this activity, or whatever may be the total characteristics of his conduct as a whole, is in this connection a matter of complete indifference. The organization for a special purpose (*Zweckverband*) is the peculiarly discreet sociological formation; its members are in psychological respects anonymous; and, in order to form the combination, they need to know of each other only *that* they form it. Modern culture is constantly growing more objective. Its tissues grow more and more out of impersonal energies, and absorb less and less the subjective entirety of the individual. In this respect the hand laborer and the factory laborer furnish the antithesis which illustrates the difference between past and present social structure. This objective character impresses itself also upon sociological structure, so that combinations into which formerly the entire and individual person entered, and which consequently demanded reciprocal knowledge beyond the immediate content of the relationship, are now founded exclusively on this content in its pure objectivity.

By virtue of the situation just noticed, that antecedent or consequent form of knowledge with reference to an individual—viz., confidence in him, evidently one of the most important synthetic forces within society—gains a peculiar evolution. Confidence, as the hypothesis of future conduct, which is sure enough to become the basis of practical action, is, as hypothesis, a mediate condition between knowing and not knowing another person. The possession of full knowledge does away with the need of trusting, while complete absence of knowledge makes trust evidently impossible. Whatever quantities of knowing and not knowing must commingle, in order to make possible the detailed practical decision based upon confidence, will be determined by the historic epoch, the ranges of interests, and the individuals. The objectification of culture referred to above has sharply differentiated the amounts of knowing and not knowing essential as the condition of confidence. The modern merchant who enters into a transaction with another, the scholar who undertakes an investigation with another, the leader of a political party who makes an agreement with the leader of another party with reference to an election, or the handling of a proposed bill—all these, with exceptions and modifications that need not be further indicated, know, with reference to their associates, precisely what it is necessary to know for the purposes of the relationship in question. The traditions and institutions, the force of public opinion, and the circumscription of the situation, which unavoidably prejudice the individual, are so fixed and reliable that one only needs to know certain externalities with reference to the other in order to have the confidence necessary for the associated action. The basis of personal qualities, from which in principle a modification of attitude within the relationship could spring, is eliminated from consideration. The motivation and the regulation of this conduct has become so much a matter of an impersonal program that it is no longer influenced by that basis, and confidence no longer depends upon knowledge of that individual element. In more primitive, less differentiated relationships, knowledge of one's associates was much more necessary in personal respects, and much less in respect to their purely objective reliability. Both factors belong together. In order that, in case of lack in the latter respect, the necessary confidence may be produced, there is need of a much higher degree of knowledge of the former sort.

That purely general objective knowledge of a person, beyond which everything that is strictly individual in his personality may remain a secret to his associates, must be considerably reinforced in the knowledge of the latter, whenever the organization for a specific purpose to which they belong possesses an essential significance for the total existence of its members. The merchant who sells grain or oil to another needs to know only whether the latter is good for the price. The moment, however, that he associates another with himself as a partner, he must not merely know his standing as to financial assets, and certain quite general qualities of his make-up, but he must see through him very thoroughly as a personality; he must know his moral standards, his degree of companionability, his daring or prudent temperament; and upon reciprocal knowledge of that sort must depend not merely the formation of the relationship, but its entire continuance, the daily associated actions, the division of functions between the partners, etc. The secret of personality is in such a case sociologically more restricted. On account of the extent to which the common interest is dependent upon the personal quality of the associates, no extensive self-existence is in these circumstances permitted to the personality of the individual.

Beyond the organizations for distinct purposes, but in like manner beyond the relationships rooted in the total personality, stands the relationship, highly significant sociologically, which is called, in the higher strata of culture, "acquaintance." That persons are "acquainted" with each other signifies in this sense by no means that they know each other reciprocally; that is, that they have insight into that which is peculiarly personal in the individuality. It means only that each has, so to speak, taken notice of the existence of the other. As a rule, the notion of acquaintanceship in this sense is associated only with mere mentioning of the name, the "presentation." Knowledge of the *that,* not of the *what,* of the personality distinguishes the "acquaintanceship." In the very assertion that one is acquainted with a given person, or even well acquainted with him, one indicates very distinctly the absence of really intimate relationships. In such case one knows of the other only his external characteristics. These may be only those that are on exhibit in social functions, or they may be merely those that the other chooses to exhibit to us. The grade of acquaintanceship denoted by the phrase "well acquainted with another" refers at the same time not to the essential characteristics of the other, not to that which is most important in his inmost nature, but only to that which is characteristic in the aspect presented to the world. On that account, acquaintanceship in this polite sense is the peculiar seat of "discretion." This attitude consists by no means merely in respect for the secret of the other—that is, for his direct volition to conceal from us this or that. It consists rather in restraining ourselves from acquaintance with all of those facts in the conditions of another which he does not positively reveal. In this instance the particulars in question are not in principle distinctly defined as forbidden territory. The reference is rather to that quite general reserve due to the total personality of another, and to a special form of the typical antithesis of the imperatives; viz.: what is not forbidden is permitted, and, what is not permitted is forbidden. Accordingly, the relationships of men are differentiated by the question of knowledge with reference to each other: what is not concealed may be known, and what is not revealed may yet not be known. The last determination corresponds to the otherwise effective consciousness that an ideal sphere surrounds every human being, different in various directions and toward different persons; a sphere varying in extent, into which one may not venture to penetrate without disturbing the personal value of the individual. Honor locates such an area. Language indicates very nicely an invasion of this sort by such phrases as "coming too near" (zu nahe treten). The radius of that sphere, so to speak, marks the distance which a stranger may not cross without infringing upon another's honor. Another sphere of like form corresponds to that which we designate as the "significance" (Bedeutung) of another personality. Towards the "significant" man there exists an inner compulsion to keep one's distance. Even in somewhat intimate relationships with him this constraint does not disappear without some special occasion; and it is absent only in the case of those who are unable to appreciate the "significance." Accordingly, that zone of separation does not exist for the valet, because for him there is no "hero." This, however, is the fault, not of the hero, but of the valet. Furthermore, all intrusiveness is bound up with evident lack of sensitiveness for the scale of significance among people. Whoever is intrusive toward a significant personality does not, as it might superficially appear, rate that person high or too high; but on the contrary, he gives evidence of lacking capacity for appropriate respect. As the painter often emphasizes the significance of one figure in a picture that includes many persons, by grouping the rest at a considerable distance from the important figure, so there is a sociological parallel in the significance of distance, which holds another outside of a definite sphere filled by the personality with its power, its will, and its greatness. A similar circuit, although quite different in value, surrounds the man in the setting of his affairs and his qualities. To penetrate this circuit by curiosity is a violation of his personality. As material property is at the same time an extension of the ego—property is precisely that which obeys the will of the possessor, as, in merely graduated difference, the body is our first "property" (*Besitz*)—and as on that account every invasion of this possession is resented as a violation of the personality; so there is a spiritual private property, to invade which signifies violation of the ego at its center. Discretion is nothing other than the sense of justice with respect to the sphere of the intimate contents of life. Of course, this sense is various in its extension in connection with different personalities, just as the sense of honor and of personal property has a quite different radius with reference to the persons in one's immediate circle from that which it has toward strangers and indifferent persons. In the case of the above-mentioned social relationships in the narrower sense, as most simply expressed in the term "acquaintanceship," we have to do immediately with a quite typical boundary, beyond which perhaps no guarded secrets lie; with reference to which, however, the outside party, in the observance of conventional discretion, does not obtrude by questions or otherwise.

The question where this boundary lies is, even in principle, by no means easy to answer. It leads rather into the finest meshes of social forms. The right of that spiritual private property just referred to can no more be affirmed in the absolute sense than that of material property. We know that in higher societies the latter, with reference to the three essential sides, creation, security, and productiveness, never rests merely upon the personal agency of the individual. It depends also upon the conditions and powers of the social environment; and consequently its limitations, whether through the prohibitions that affect the mode of acquiring property, or through taxation, are from the beginning the right of the whole. This right, however, has a still deeper basis than the principle of service and counterservice between society and the individual. That basis is the much more elementary one, that the part must subject itself to so much limitation of its self-sufficiency as is demanded by the existence and purposes of the whole. The same principle applies to the subjective sphere of personality. In the interest of association, and of social coherence, each must know certain things with reference to the other; and this other has not the right to resist this knowledge from the moral standpoint, and to demand the discretion of the other; that is, the undisturbed possession of his being and consciousness, in cases in which discretion would prejudice social interests. The business man who enters into a contractual obligation with another, covering a long future; the master who engages a servant; and, on the other hand, this latter, before he agrees to the servile relationship; the superintendent who is responsible for the promotion of a subordinate; the head of a household who admits a new personality into her social circle—all these must have the right to trace out or to combine everything with reference to the past or the present of the other parties in question, with reference to their temperament, and their moral make-up, that would have any relation to the conclusion or the rejection of the proposed relationship. These are quite rough cases in which the beauty of discretion—that is, of refraining from knowledge of everything which the other party does not voluntarily reveal to us —must yield to the demands of practical necessity. But in finer and less simple form, in fragmentary passages of association and in unuttered revelations, all commerce of men with each other rests upon the condition that each knows something more of the other than the latter voluntarily reveals to him; and in many respects this is of a sort the knowledge of which, if possible, would have been prevented by the party so revealed. While this, judged as an individual affair, may count as indiscretion, although in the social sense it is necessary as a condition for the existing closeness and vitality of the interchange, yet the legal boundary of this invasion upon the spiritual private property of another is extremely difficult to draw. In general, men credit themselves with the right to know everything which, without application of external illegal means, through purely psychological observation and reflection, it is possible to ascertain. In point of fact, however, indiscretion exercised in this way may be quite as violent, and morally quite as unjustifiable, as listening at keyholes and prying into the letters of strangers. To anyone with fine psychological perceptions, men betray themselves and their inmost thoughts and characteristics in countless fashions, not only in spite of efforts not to do so, but often for the very reason that they anxiously attempt to guard themselves. The greedy spying upon every unguarded word; the boring persistence of inquiry as to the meaning of every slight action, or tone of voice; what may be inferred from such and such expressions; what the blush at the mention of a given name may betray— all this does not overstep the boundary of external discretion; it is entirely the labor of one's own mind, and therefore apparently within the unquestionable rights of the agent. This is all the more the case, since such misuse of psychological superiority often occurs as a purely involuntary procedure. Very often it is impossible for us to restrain our interpretation of another, our theory of his subjective characteristics and intentions. However positively an honorable person may forbid himself to practice such cogitation with reference to the unrevealed traits of another, and such exploiting of his lack of foresight and defenselessness, a knowing process often goes on with reference to another so automatically, its result often presents itself so suddenly and unavoidably, that the best intention can do nothing to prevent it. Where the unquestionably forbidden may thus be so unavoidable, the division line between the permitted and the non-permitted is the more indefinite. To what extent discretion must restrain itself from mental handling "of all that which is its own," to what extent the interests of intercourse, the reciprocal interdependence of the members of the same group, limits this duty of discretion—this is a question for the answer to which neither moral tact, nor survey of the objective relationships and their demands, can alone be sufficient, since both factors must rather always work together. The nicety and complexity of this question throw it back in a much higher degree upon the responsibility of the individual for decision, without final recourse to any authoritative general norm, than is the case in connection with a question of private property in the material sense.

In contrast with this preliminary form, or this attachment of secrecy, in which not the attitude of the person keeping the secret, but that of a third party, is in question, in which, in view of the mixture of reciprocal knowledge or lack of knowledge, the emphasis is on the amount of the former rather than on that of the latter—in contrast with this, we come to an entirely new variation; that is, in those relationships which do not, like those already referred to, center around definitely circumscribed interests; but in relationships which, at least in their essential idea, rest upon the whole extension of the personalities concerned. The principal types in this category are friendship and marriage. The ideal of friendship that has come down from antique tradition, and singularly enough has been developed directly in the romantic sense, aims at absolute spiritual confidence, with the attachment that material possession also shall be a resource common to the friends. This entrance of the entire undivided ego into the relationship may be the more plausible in friendship than in love, for the reason that, in the case of friendship, the one-sided concentration upon a single element is lacking, which is present in the other case on account of the sensuous factor in love. To be sure, through the circumstance that in the totality of possible grounds of attachment one assumes the headship, a certain organization of the relationship occurs, as is the case in a group with recognized leadership. A single strong factor of coherence often blazes out the path along which the others, otherwise likely to have remained latent, follow; and undeniably in the case of most men, sexual love opens the doors of the total personality widest; indeed, in the case of not a few, sexuality is the sole form in which they can give their whole ego; just as, in the case of the artist, the form of his art, whatever it may be, furnishes the only possibility of presenting his entire nature. This is to be observed with special frequency among women—to be sure, the same thing is to be asserted in the case of the quite different "Christian love"—namely, that they not only, because they love, devote their life and fortune without reserve; but that this at the same time is chemically dissolved in love, and only and entirely in its coloring, form, and temperature flows over upon the other. On the other hand, however, where the feeling of love is not expansive enough, where the other contents of the soul are not flexible enough, it may take place, as I indicated, that the predominance of the erotic nexus may suppress not only the practically moral, but also the spiritual, contacts that are outside of the erotic group. Consequently friendship, in which this intensity, but also this inequality of devotion, is lacking, may more easily attach the whole person to the whole person, may more easily break up the reserves of the soul, not indeed by so impulsive a process, but throughout a wider area and during a longer succession. This complete intimacy of confidence probably becomes, with the changing differentiation of men, more and more difficult. Perhaps the modern man has too much to conceal to make a friendship in the ancient sense possible; perhaps personalities also, except in very early years, are too peculiarly individualized for the complete reciprocality of understanding, to which always so much divination and productive phantasy are essential. It appears that, for this reason, the modern type of feeling inclines more to differentiated friendships; that is, to those which have their territory only upon one side of the personality at a time, and in which the rest of the personality plays no part. Thus a quite special type of friendship emerges. For our problem, namely, the degree of intrusion or of reserve within the friendly relationship, this type is of the highest significance. These differentiated friendships, which bind us to one man from the side of sympathy, to another from the side of intellectual community, to a third on account of religious impulses, to a fourth because of common experiences, present, in connection with the problem of discretion, or self-revelation and self-concealment, a quite peculiar synthesis. They demand that the friends reciprocally refrain from obtruding themselves into the range of interests and feelings not included in the special relationship in each case. Failure to observe this condition would seriously disturb reciprocal understanding. But the relationship thus bounded and circumscribed by discretion nevertheless has its sources at the center of the whole personality, in spite of the fact that it expresses itself only in a single segment of its periphery. It leads ideally toward the same depths of sentiment, and to the same capacity to sacrifice, which undifferentiated epochs and persons associate only with a community of the total circumference of life, with no question about reserves and discretions.

Much more difficult is measurement of self-revelation and reserve, with their correlates intrusiveness and discretion, in the case of marriage. In this relationship these forms are among the universal problems of the highest importance for the sociology of intimate associations. We are confronted with the questions, whether the maximum of reciprocality is attained in a relationship in which the personalities entirely resign to each other their separate existence, or quite the contrary, through a certain reserve—whether they do not in a certain qualitative way belong to each other more if they belong to each other less quantitatively. These questions of ratio can of course, at the outset, be answered only with the further question: How is the boundary to be drawn, within the whole area of a person's potential communicability, at which ultimately the reserve and the respect of another are to begin? The advantage of modern marriage—which, to be sure, makes both questions answerable only one case at a time—is that this boundary is not from the start determined, as was the case in earlier civilizations. In these other civilizations marriage is, in principle, as a rule, not an erotic phenomenon, but merely a social-economic institution. The satisfaction of the instincts of love is only accidentally connected with it. With certain exceptions, the marriage is not on grounds of individual attraction, but rather of family policy, labor relationships, or desire for descendants. The Greeks, for example, carried this institution to the most extreme differentiation. Thus Demosthenes said: "We have *hetaerae* for our pleasure, concubines for our daily needs, but wives to give us lawful children and to care for the interior of the house." The same tendency to exclude from the community of marriage, *a priori,* certain defined life-contents, and by means of super-individual provisions, appears in the variations in the forms of marriage to be found in one and the same people, with possibility of choice in advance on the part of those contracting marriages. These forms are differentiated in various ways with reference to the economic, religious, legal, and other interests connected with the family. We might cite many nature-peoples, the Indians, the Romans, etc. No one will, of course, fail to observe that, also within modern life, marriage is, probably in the majority of cases, contracted from conventional or material motives; nevertheless, entirely apart from the frequency of its realization, the sociological idea of modern marriage is the community of all life-contents, in so far as they immediately, and through their effects, determine the value and the destiny of the personalities. Moreover, the prejudice of this ideal demand is by no means ineffective. It has often enough given place and stimulus for developing an originally very incomplete reciprocation into an increasingly comprehensive attachment. But, while the very indeterminateness of this process is the vehicle of the happiness and the essential vitality of the relationship, its reversal usually brings severe disappointments. If, for example, absolute unity is from the beginning anticipated, if demand and satisfaction recognize no sort of reserve, not even that which for all fine and deep natures must always remain in the hidden recesses of the soul, although they may think they open themselves entirely to each other—in such cases the reaction and disillusionment must come sooner or later.

In marriage, as in free relationships of analogous types, the temptation is very natural to open oneself to the other at the outset without limit; to abandon the last reserve of the soul equally with those of the body, and thus to lose oneself completely in another. This, however, usually threatens the future of the relationship. Only those people can without danger give themselves entirely to each other who *cannot possibly* give themselves entirely, because the wealth of their soul rests in constant progressive development, which follows every devotion immediately with the growth of new treasures. Complete devotion is safe only in the case of those people who have an inexhaustible fund of latent spiritual riches, and therefore can no more alienate them in a single confidence than a tree can give up the fruits of next year by letting go what it produces at the present moment. The case is quite different, however, with those people who, so to speak, draw from their capital all their betrayals of feeling and the revelations of their inner life; in whose case there is no further source from which to derive those elements which should not be revealed, and which are not to be disjoined from the essential ego. In such cases it is highly probable that the parties to the confidence will one day face each other empty-handed; that the Dionysian free-heartedness may leave behind a poverty which—unjustly, but not on that account with less bitterness—may so react as even to charge the enjoyed devotion with deception. We are so constituted that we not merely, as was remarked, need a certain proportion of truth and error as the basis of our life, but also a similar mixture of definiteness and indefiniteness in the picture of our life-elements. That which we can see through plainly to its last ground shows us therewith the limit of its attraction, and forbids our phantasy to do its utmost in adding to the reality. For this loss no literal reality can compensate us, because the action of the imagination of which we are deprived is self-activity, which cannot permanently be displaced in value by any receptivity and enjoyment. Our friend should not only give us a cumulative gift, but also the possibility of conferring gifts upon him, with hopes and idealizations, with concealed beauties and charms unknown even to himself. The manner, however, in which we dispose of all this, produced by ourselves, but for his sake, is the vague horizon of his personality, the intermediate zone in which faith takes the place of knowledge. It must be observed that we have here to do by no means with mere illusions, or with optimistic or infatuated self-deception. The fact is rather that, if the utmost attractiveness of another person is to be preserved for us, it must be presented to us in part in the form of vagueness or impenetrability. This is the only substitute which the great majority of people can offer for that attractive value which the small minority possess through the inexhaustibility of their inner life and growth. The mere fact of absolute understanding, of having accomplished psychological exhaustion of the contents of relationship with another, produces a feeling of insipidity, even if there is no reaction from previous exaltation; it cripples the vitality of the relationship, and gives to its continuance an appearance of utter futility. This is the danger of that unbroken, and in a more than external sense shameless, dedication to which the unrestricted possibilities of intimate relationships seduce, which indeed is easily regarded as a species of obligation in those relationships. Because of this absence of reciprocal discretion, on the side of receiving as well as of giving, many marriages are failures. That is, they degenerate into vulgar habit, utterly bereft of charm, into a matter-of-course which retains no room for surprises. The fruitful depth of relationships which, behind every latest revelation, implies the still unrevealed, which also stimulates anew every day to gain what is already possessed, is merely the reward of that tenderness and self-control which, even in the closest relationship, comprehending the whole person, still respect the inner private property, which hold the right of questioning to be limited by a right of secrecy.

All these combinations are characterized sociologically by the fact that the secret of the one party is to a certain extent recognized by the other, and the intentionally or unintentionally concealed is intentionally or unintentionally respected. The intention of the concealment assumes, however, a quite different intensity so soon as it is confronted by a purpose of discovery. Thereupon follows that purposeful concealment, that aggressive defense, so to speak, against the other party, which we call secrecy in the most real sense. Secrecy in this sense—i. e., which is effective through negative or positive means of concealment—is one of the greatest accomplishments of humanity. In contrast with the juvenile condition in which every mental picture is at once revealed, every undertaking is open to everyone's view, secrecy procures enormous extension of life, because with publicity many sorts of purposes could never arrive at realization. Secrecy secures, so to speak, the possibility of a second world alongside of the obvious world, and the latter is most strenuously affected by the former. Every relationship between two individuals or two groups will be characterized by the ratio of secrecy that is involved in it. Even when one of the parties does not notice the secret factor, yet the attitude of the concealer, and consequently the whole relationship, will be modified by it. The historical development of society is in many respects characterized by the fact that what was formerly public passes under the protection of secrecy, and that, on the contrary, what was formerly secret ceases to require such protection and proclaims itself. This is analogous with that other evolution of mind in which movements at first executed consciously become unconsciously mechanical, and, on the other hand, what was unconscious and instinctive rises into the light of consciousness. How this development is distributed over the various formations of private and public life, how the evolution proceeds toward better-adapted conditions, because, on the one hand, secrecy that is awkward and undifferentiated is often far too widely extended, while, on the other hand, in many respects the usefulness of secrecy is discovered very late; how the quantum of secrecy has variously modified consequences in accordance with the importance or indifference of its content—all this, merely in its form as questions, throws a flow of light upon the significance of secrecy for the structure of human reciprocities. In this connection we must not allow ourselves to be deceived by the manifold ethical negativeness of secrecy. Secrecy is a universal sociological form, which, as such, has nothing to do with the moral valuations of its contents. On the one hand, secrecy may embrace the highest values: the refined shame of the lofty spirit, which covers up precisely its best, that it may not seem to seek its reward in praise or wage; for after such payment one retains the reward, but no longer the real value itself. On the other hand, secrecy is not in immediate interdependence with evil, but evil with secrecy. For obvious reasons, the immoral hides itself, even when its content encounters no social penalty, as, for example, many sexual faults. The essentially isolating effect of immorality as such, entirely apart from all primary social repulsion, is actual and important. Secrecy is, among other things, also the sociological expression of moral badness, although the classical aphorism, "No one is so bad that he also wants to seem bad," takes issue with the facts. Obstinacy and cynicism may often enough stand in the way of disguising the badness. They may even exploit it for magnifying the personality in the judgment of others, to the degree that sometimes immoralities which do not exist are seized upon as material for self-advertising.

The application of secrecy as a sociological technique, as a form of commerce without which, in view of our social environment, certain purposes could not be attained, is evident without further discussion. Not so evident are the charms and the values which it possesses over and above its significance as a means, the peculiar attraction of the relation which is mysterious in form, regardless of its accidental content. In the first place, the strongly accentuated exclusion of all not within the circle of secrecy results in a correspondingly accentuated feeling of personal possession. For many natures possession acquires its proper significance, not from the mere fact of having, but besides that there must be the consciousness that others must forego the possession. Evidently this fact has its roots in our stimulability by contrast. Moreover, since exclusion of others from a possession may occur especially in the case of high values, the reverse is psychologically very natural, viz., that what is withheld from the many appears to have a special value. Accordingly, subjective possessions of the most various sorts acquire a decisive accentuation of value through the form of secrecy, in which the substantial significance of the facts concealed often enough falls into a significance entirely subordinate to the fact that others are excluded from knowing them. Among children a pride and self-glory often bases itself on the fact that the one can say to the others: "I know something that you don't know." This is carried to such a degree that it becomes a formal means of swaggering on the one hand, and of de-classing on the other. This occurs even when it is a pure fiction, and no secret exists. From the narrowest to the widest relationships, there are exhibitions of this jealousy about knowing something that is concealed from others. The sittings of the English Parliament were long secret, and even in the reign of George III reports of them in the press were liable to criminal penalties as violations of parliamentary privilege. Secrecy gives the person enshrouded by it an exceptional position; it works as a stimulus of purely social derivation, which is in principle quite independent of its casual content, but is naturally heightened in the degree in which the exclusively possessed secret is significant and comprehensive. There is also in this connection an inverse phenomenon, analogous with the one just mentioned. Every superior personality, and every superior performance, has, for the average of mankind, something mysterious. To be sure, all human being and doing spring from inexplicable forces. Nevertheless, within levels of similarity in quality and value, this fact does not make the one person a problem to another, especially because in respect to this equality a certain immediate understanding exists which is not a special function of the intellect. If there is essential inequality, this understanding cannot be reached, and in the form of specific divergence the general mysteriousness will be effective—somewhat as one who always lives in the same locality may never encounter the problem of the influence of the environment, which influence, however, may obtrude itself upon him so soon as he changes his environment, and the contrast in the reaction of feeling upon the life-conditions calls his attention to this causal factor in the situation. Out of this secrecy, which throws a shadow over all that is deep and significant, grows the logically fallacious, but typical, error, that everything secret is something essential and significant. The natural impulse to idealization, and the natural timidity of men, operate to one and the same end in the presence of secrecy; viz., to heighten it by phantasy, and to distinguish it by a degree of attention that published reality could not command.

Singularly enough, these attractions of secrecy enter into combination with those of its logical opposite; viz., treason or betrayal of secrets, which are evidently no less sociological in their nature. Secrecy involves a tension which, at the moment of revelation, finds its release. This constitutes the climax in the development of the secret; in it the whole charm of secrecy concentrates and rises to its highest pitch— just as the moment of the disappearance of an object brings out the feeling of its value in the most intense degree. The sense of power connected with possession of money is most completely and greedily concentrated for the soul of the spendthrift at the moment at which this power slips from his hands. Secrecy also is sustained by the consciousness that it *might be* exploited, and therefore confers power to modify fortunes, to produce surprises, joys, and calamities, even if the latter be only misfortunes to ourselves. Hence the possibility and the temptation of treachery plays around the secret, and the external danger of being discovered is interwoven with the internal danger of self-discovery, which has the fascination of the brink of a precipice. Secrecy sets barriers between men, but at the same time offers the seductive temptation to break through the barriers by gossip or confession. This temptation accompanies the psychical life of the secret like an overtone. Hence the sociological significance of the secret, its practical measure, and the mode of its workings must be found in the capacity or the inclination of the initiated to keep the secret to himself, or in his resistance or weakness relative to the temptation to betrayal. From the play of these two interests, in concealment and in revelation, spring shadings and fortunes of human reciprocities throughout their whole range. If, according to our previous analysis, every human relationship has, as one of its traits, the degree of secrecy within or around it, it follows that the further development of the relationship in this respect depends on the combining proportions of the retentive and the communicative energies

—the former sustained by the practical interest and the formal attractiveness of secrecy as such, the latter by inability to endure longer the tension of reticence, and by the superiority which is latent, so to speak, in secrecy, but which is actualized for the feelings only at the moment of revelation, and often also, on the other hand, by the joy of confession, which may contain that sense of power in negative and perverted form, as self-abasement and contrition.

All these factors, which determine the sociological role of secrecy, are of individualistic nature, but the ratio in which the qualities and the complications of personalities form secrets, depends at the same time upon the social structure upon which its life rests. In this connection the decisive element is that the secret is an individualizing factor of the first rank, and that in the typical double role; i. e., social relationships characterized by a large measure of personal differentiation permit and promote secrecy in a high degree, while, conversely, secrecy serves and intensifies such differentiation. In a small and restricted circuit, construction and preservation of secrets are technically difficult from the fact that each is too close to the circumstances of each, and that the frequency and intimacy of contacts carry with them too great temptation to disclose what might otherwise be hidden. But in this case there is no need of secrecy in a high degree, because this social formation usually tends to level its members, and every peculiarity of being, acting, or possessing the persistence of which requires secrecy, is abhorrent to it. That all this changes to its opposite in case of large widening of the circle is a matter-of-course. In this connection, as in so many other particulars, the facts of monetary relationships reveal most distinctly the specific traits of the large circle. Since transfers of economic values have occurred principally by means of money, an otherwise unattainable secrecy is possible in such transactions. Three peculiarities of the money form of values are here important: first, its compressibility, by virtue of which it is possible to make a man rich by slipping into his hand a check without attracting attention; second, its abstractness and absence of qualitative character, in consequence of which numberless sorts of acquisitions and transfers of possessions may be covered up and guarded from publicity in a fashion impossible so long as values could be possessed only as extended, tangible objects; third, its long-distance effectiveness, by virtue of which we may invest it in the most widely removed and constantly changing values, and thus withdraw it utterly from the view of our nearest neighbors. These facilities of dissimulation which inhere in the degree of extension in the use of money, and which disclose their dangers particularly in dealings with foreign money, have called forth, as protective provisions, publicity of the financial operations of corporations. This points to a closer definition of the formula of evolution discussed above; viz., that throughout the form of secrecy there occurs a permanent in- and out-flow of content, in which what is originally open becomes secret, and what was originally concealed throws off its mystery. Thus we might arrive at the paradoxical idea that, under otherwise like circumstances, human associations require a definite ratio of secrecy which merely changes its objects; letting go of one, it seizes another, and in the course of this exchange it keeps its quantum unvaried. We may even fill out this general scheme somewhat more exactly. It appears that with increasing telic characteristics of culture the affairs of people at large become more and more public, those of individuals more and more secret. In less developed conditions, as observed above, the circumstances of individual persons cannot protect themselves in the same degree from reciprocal prying and interfering as within modern types of life, particularly those that have developed in large cities, where we find a quite new degree of reserve and discretion. On the other hand, the public functionaries in undeveloped states envelop themselves in a mystical authority, while in maturer and wider relations, through extension of the range of their prerogatives, through the objectivity of their technique, through the distance that separates them from most of the individuals, a security and a dignity accrue to them which are compatible with publicity of their behavior. That earlier secrecy of public functions, however, betrayed its essential contradictoriness in begetting at once the counter-movements of treachery, on the one hand, and of espionage, on the other.

To what extent this development is to be regarded as advantageous depends upon social standards of value. Democracies are bound to regard publicity as the condition desirable in itself. This follows from the fundamental idea that each should be informed about all the relationships and occurrences with which he is concerned, since this is a condition of his doing his part with reference to them, and every community of knowledge contains also the psychological stimulation to community of action. It is immaterial whether this conclusion is entirely binding. If an objective controlling structure has been built up, beyond the individual interests, but nevertheless to their advantage, such a structure may very well, by virtue of its formal independence, have a rightful claim to carry on a certain amount of secret functioning without prejudice to its *public* character, so far as real consideration of the interests of all is concerned. A logical connection, therefore, which would necessitate the judgment of superior worth in favor of the condition of publicity, does not exist. On the other hand, the universal scheme of cultural differentiation puts in an appearance here: that which pertains to the public becomes more public, that which belongs to the individual becomes more private. Moreover, this historical development brings out the deeper real significance: that which in its nature is public, which in its content concerns all, becomes also externally, in its sociological form, more and more public; while that which in its inmost nature refers to the self alone—that is, the centripetal affairs of the individual—must also gain in sociological position a more and more private character, a more decisive possibility of remaining secret.

While secrecy, therefore, is a sociological ordination which characterizes the reciprocal relation of group elements, or rather in connection with other forms of reaction constitutes this total relation, it may further, with the formation of "secret societies," extend itself over the group as a whole. So long as the being, doing, and having of an individual persist as a secret, his general sociological significance is isolation, antithesis, egoistic individualization. In this case the sociological meaning of the secrecy is external; as relationship of him who has the secret to him who does not have it. So soon, however, as a group as such seizes upon secrecy as its form of existence, the sociological meaning of the secrecy becomes internal. It now determines the reciprocal relations of those who possess the secret in common. Since, however, that relation of exclusion toward the uninitiated exists here also with its special gradations, the sociology of secret societies presents the complicated problem of ascertaining the immanent forms of a group which are determined by attitudes of secrecy on the part of the same toward other elements.

PRIMARY GROUPS AND PRIMARY IDEALS

BY

CHARLES HORTON COOLEY

By primary groups I mean those characterized by intimate face-to-face association and cooperation. They are primary in several senses, but chiefly in that they are fundamental in forming the social nature and ideals of the individual. The result of intimate association, psycho-

From *Social Organization* by Charles Horton Cooley; copyright 1909 by Charles Scribner's Sons, 1937 by Elsie Jones Cooley. Reprinted by permission of the publishers.
Abridged from: Cooley, Charles H., *Social Organization*, New York: Charles Scribner's Sons, 1909.

logically, is a certain fusion of individualities in a common whole, so that one's very self, for many purposes at least, is the common life and purpose of the group. Perhaps the simplest way of describing this wholeness is by saying that it is a "we"; it involves the sort of sympathy and mutual identification for which "we" is the natural expression. One lives in the feeling of the whole and finds the chief aims of his will in that feeling.

It is not to be supposed that the unity of the primary group is one of mere harmony and love. It is always a differentiated and usually a competitive unity, admitting of self-assertion and various appropriative passions; but these passions are socialized by sympathy, and come, or tend to come, under the discipline of a common spirit. The individual will be ambitious, but the chief object of his ambition will be some desired place in the thought of the others, and he will feel allegiance to common standards of service and fair play. So the boy will dispute with his fellows a place on the team, but above such disputes will place the common glory of his class and school.

The most important spheres of this intimate association and co-operation—though by no means the only ones—are the family, the play-group of children, and the neighborhood or community group of elders. These are practically universal, belonging to all times and all stages of development; and are accordingly a chief basis of what is universal in human nature and human ideals.

Primary groups are primary in the sense that they give the individual his earliest and completest experience of social unity, and also in the sense that they do not change in the same degree as more elaborate relations, but form a comparatively permanent source out of which the latter are ever springing.

These groups, then, are springs of life, not only for the individual but for social institutions. They are only in part moulded by special traditions, and, in larger degree, express a universal nature. The religion or government of other civilizations may seem alien to us, but the children or the family group wear the common life, and with them we can always make ourselves at home.

By human nature, I suppose, we may understand those sentiments and impulses that are human in being superior to those of lower animals, and also in the sense that they belong to mankind at large, and not to any particular race or time. It means, particularly, sympathy and the innumerable sentiments into which sympathy enters, such as love, resentment, ambition, vanity, hero-worship, and the feeling of social right and wrong.

Human nature in this sense is justly regarded as a comparatively permanent element in society. Always and everywhere men seek honor and dread ridicule, defer to public opinion, cherish their goods and their children, and admire courage, generosity, and success. It is always safe to assume that people are and have been human.

To return to primary groups: the view here maintained is that human nature is not something existing separately in the individual, but a *group-nature or primary phase of society,* a relatively simple and general condition of the social mind. It is something more, on the one hand, than the mere instinct that is born in us—though that enters into it—and something less, on the other, than the more elaborate development of ideas and sentiments that makes up institutions. It is the nature which is developed and expressed in those simple, face-to-face groups that are somewhat alike in all societies; groups of the family, the playground, and the neighborhood. In the essential similarity of these is to be found the basis, in experience, for similar ideas and sentiments in the human mind. In these, everywhere, human nature comes into existence. Man does not have it at birth; he cannot acquire it except through fellowship, and it decays in isolation.

Life in the primary groups gives rise to social ideals which, as they spring from similar experiences, have much in common throughout the human race.

The ideal that grows up in familiar association may be said to be a part of human nature itself. In its most general form it is that of a moral whole or community wherein individual minds are merged and the higher capacities of the members find total and adequate expression. And it grows up because familiar association fills our minds with imaginations of the thought and feeling of other members of the group, and of the group as a whole, so that, for many purposes, we really make them a part of ourselves and identify our self-feeling with them.

The ideal of moral unity I take to be the mother, as it were, of all social ideals.

Among the ideals inseparable from loyalty are those of truth, service, and kindness, always conceived as due to the intimate group rather than to the world at large.

Truth or good faith toward other members of a fellowship is, so far as I know, a universal human ideal. It does not involve any abstract love of veracity, and is quite consistent with deception toward the outside world, being essentially "truth of intercourse" or fair dealing among intimates. There are few, even among those reckoned lawless, who will not keep faith with one who has the gift of getting near to them in spirit and making them feel that he is one of themselves.

The ideal of service likewise goes with the sense of unity. If there is a vital whole the right aim of individual activity can be no other than to serve that whole. And this is not so much a theory as a feeling that will exist wherever the whole is felt.

All mankind acknowledges kindness as the law of right intercourse within a social group. By communion minds are fused into a sympathetic whole, each part of which tends to share the life of all the rest, so that kindness is a common joy, and harshness a common pain. It is the simplest, most attractive, and most diffused of human ideals. The golden rule springs directly from human nature.

Every intimate group, like every individual, experiences conflicting impulses within itself, and as the individual feels the need of definite principles to shape his conduct and give him peace, so the group needs law or rule for the same purpose. It is not merely that the over-strong or the insubordinate must be restrained, but that all alike may have some definite criterion of what the good member ought to do. It is a mere fact of psychology that where a social whole exists it may be as painful to do wrong as to suffer it—because one's own spirit is divided—and the common need is for harmony through a law, framed in the total interest, which every one can and must obey.

No doubt every one remembers how the idea of justice is developed in children's games. There is always something to be done, in which various parts are to be taken, success depending upon their efficient distribution. All see this and draw from experience the idea that there is a higher principle that ought to control the undisciplined ambition of individuals.

The law or rule that human nature demands has a democratic principle latent in it, because it must be one congenial to general sentiment. Explicit democracy, however—deciding by popular vote and the like—is not primary and general like the need of law, but is rather a mechanism for deciding what the rule is to be, and no more natural than the appeal to authority. Indeed, there seems to be, among children as among primitive peoples, a certain reluctance to ascribe laws to the mere human choice of themselves and their fellows. They wish to assign them to a higher source and to think of them as having an unquestionable sanction. So far as my own observation goes, even American boys prefer to receive rules from tradition or from their elders, when they can. Nothing is easier than for a parent, or mentor of any kind, to be a lawgiver to children, if only he has their confidence, and if the laws themselves prove workable. But the test of law is social and popular; it must suit the general mind.

PART IV

Societal Structures

THE STRUCTURAL CHARACTERISTICS WHICH SOCIOLOGISTS FRE-
quently identify in societies include patterns of conduct, associations of persons cooperating to achieve common objectives,
communities, and social strata or classes. These are the subject
matter of Part IV. Sociologists have long recognized that social
processes produce societal structures which can be identified. Indeed, Herbert Spencer, in *The Principles of Sociology* from which
the first selection of Chapter 9 is taken, states the general principle
of differentiation which underlies such structures.

The selections of Chapter 9 have in common the recognition
that structural patterns can be understood only as they function
within the larger society. Thus the two essays by Edward Sapir
treat custom and fashion as they have meaning for social structure.
Similarly, Charles Horton Cooley's conceptions of institutions and
of public opinion, as found in his *Social Organization,* see these
structures within what he calls the "organic unity" of society. So,
also, does Ralph Linton conceive, in the selection from *The Study
of Man,* what he calls "social systems." The final selection in Chapter 9 is a discussion of precisely this functional point of view, as
presented by A. R. Radcliffe-Brown. So central is the discussion of
the structural-functional conception to the analysis of societal phenomena that it could serve to introduce this part of the book.

Of the many associations in which sociologists have been interested, the family, the state, the economy and the religious organization are considered in Chapter 10. The analysis of the family by George F. Vincent and Albion W. Small is taken from their textbook, or manual, entitled *An Introduction to the Study of Society*. It is concise and descriptive but presents a rounded consideration of the many aspects of the family which make it a central or primary association in any society. Robert M. MacIver's discussion of the political and economic associations, taken from his textbook, *Society,* is less a description than an analysis of the methods of action which characterize these associations. The selection from Emile Durkheim's *Elementary Forms of the Religious Life* emphasizes the experience which underlies the religious association and hence suggests the personal as well as the societal needs for which associations function. The integrating role of the association is suggested by another selection by Durkheim, taken from his study of *Suicide* and entitled "The Occupational Group." Edward A. Ross' essay on "The Organization of Effort" is applicable to all associations as a consideration in considerable detail of the determinants and consequences of bureaucratic organization.

Perhaps no concept has been more elusive in sociological theory than that of the community. Sociologists have sensed the meaningfulness of locality, but they have rarely been able to go beyond a static description of the externals of community structure or a sentimental appreciation of community spirit. The conception of the urban community which Robert E. Park presents in Chapter 11 is a bold attempt to suggest the dynamic consequences of living in close proximity. Associated with such ideas is the study of human ecology. The insights which Park presented in this article have been only partially explored.

The idea of social stratification is considered in Chapter 12. The selection on class and caste from Charles Horton Cooley's *Social Organization* identifies the operation of the caste principle and discusses the conditions in societies which encourage development of caste or of open classes. The selection from Thorstein Veblen's *Theory of the Leisure Class* illustrates the way in which the emergence and persistence of stratification, as represented by the existence of a leisure class can be analyzed. Finally, the selection by Max Weber on "Class, Status and Party" presents a view of social stratification as a phenomenon of the distribution of power within a society.

CHAPTER 9

Structural Patterns

———◆◦◆———

SOCIAL STRUCTURES AND THEIR
DIFFERENTIATION

B Y

HERBERT SPENCER

IN societies, as in living bodies, increase of mass is habitually accompanied by increase of structure. Along with that integration which is the primary trait of evolution, both exhibit in high degrees the secondary trait, differentiation. As we progress from small groups to larger; from simple groups to compound groups; from compound groups to doubly compound ones; the unlikenesses of parts increase. The social aggregate, homogeneous when minute, habitually gains in heterogeneity along with each increment of growth; and to reach great size must acquire great complexity.

This increase of heterogeneity, which in both classes of aggregates goes along with growth, presents another trait in common. Beyond unlikenesses of parts due to development of the co-ordinating agencies, there presently follow unlikenesses among the agencies co-ordinated.

The advance of organization which thus follows the advance of aggregation, conforms to the general law: differentiations proceed from the more general to the more special. First broad and simple contrasts of parts; then within each of the parts primarily contrasted, changes which make unlike divisions of them; then within each of these unlike divisions, minor unlikenesses; and so on continually.

Abridged from: Spencer, Herbert. *The Principles of Sociology.* New York: D. Appleton and Company, 1897 (Authorized edition).

Changes of structures cannot occur without changes of functions. Much that was said above might, therefore, be said here with substituted terms. Indeed, as in societies many changes of structure are more indicated by changes of function than directly seen, it may be said that these last have been already described by implication.

There are, however, certain functional traits not manifestly implied by traits of structure.

If organization consists in such a construction of the whole that its parts can carry on mutually-dependent actions, then in proportion as organization is high there must go a dependence of each part upon the rest so great that separation is fatal; and conversely. This truth is equally well shown in the individual organism and in the social organism.

The *consensus* of functions becomes closer as evolution advances. In low aggregates, both individual and social, the actions of the parts are but little dependent on one another; whereas in developed aggregates of both kinds, that combination of actions which constitutes the life of the whole, makes possible the component actions which constitute the lives of the parts.

Another corollary must be named. Where parts are little differentiated, they can readily perform one another's functions; but where much differentiated they can perform one another's functions very imperfectly, or not at all.

In proportion as the units forming any part of an individual organism are limited to one kind of action, as that of absorbing, or secreting, or contracting, or conveying an impulse, and become adapted to that action, they lose adaptation to other actions; and in the social organism the discipline required for effectually discharging a special duty, causes unfitness for discharging special duties widely unlike it.

While the society as a whole has the character of its sustaining system determined by the character of its environment, inorganic and organic, the respective parts of this system differentiate in adaptation to local circumstances; and, after primary industries have been thus localized and specialized, secondary industries dependent on them arise in conformity with the same principle. Further, as fast as societies become compounded and re-compounded, and the distributing system develops, the parts devoted to each kind of industry, originally scattered, aggregate in the most favourable localities; and the localized industrial structures, unlike the governmental structures, grow regardless of the original lines of division.

Increase of size, resulting from the massing of groups, necessitates means of communication; both for achieving combined offensive and defensive actions, and for exchange of products. Faint tracks, then paths, rude roads, finished roads, successively arise; and as fast as intercourse is thus facilitated, there is a transition from direct barter to trading carried on by a separate class; out of which evolves a complex mercantile agency of wholesale and retail distributors. The movement of commodities effected by this agency, beginning as a slow flux to and re-flux from certain places at long intervals, passes into rhythmical, regular, rapid currents; and materials for sustentation distributed hither and thither, from being few and crude become numerous and elaborated. Growing efficiency of transfer with greater variety of transferred products, increases the mutual dependence of parts at the same time that it enables each part to fulfil its function better.

I have used the analogies elaborated, but as a scaffolding to help in building up a coherent body of sociological inductions. Let us take away the scaffolding: the inductions will stand by themselves.

CUSTOM

B Y

EDWARD SAPIR

THE word custom is used to apply to the totality of behavior patterns which are carried by tradition and lodged in the group, as contrasted with the more random personal activities of the individual. It is not properly applicable to those aspects of communal activity which are obviously determined by biological considerations. The habit of eating fried chicken is a custom, but the biologically determined habit of eating is not.

Custom is a variable common sense concept which has served as the matrix for the development of the more refined and technical anthropological concept of culture. It is not as purely denotative and objective a term as culture and has a slightly affective quality indicated by the fact that one uses it more easily to refer to geographically remote, to primitive or to bygone societies than to one's own. When applied to the behavior of one's own group the term is usually limited to relatively unimportant and unformalized behavior patterns which

Sapir, Edward, "Custom," *Encyclopedia of the Social Sciences*, New York: The Macmillan Co., 1933. Reprinted by permission of The Macmillan Company.

lie between individual habits and social institutions. Cigarette smok-
ing is more readily called a custom than is the trial of criminals in
court. However, in dealing with contemporary Chinese civilization,
with early Babylonian culture or with the life of a primitive Australian
tribe the functional equivalent of such a cultural pattern as our court
trial is designated as custom. The hesitation to describe as custom
any type of behavior in one's own group that is not at once collective
and devoid of major importance is perhaps due to the fact that one
involuntarily prefers to put the emphasis either on significant individualism, in which case the word habit is used, or on a thoroughly
rationalized and formalized collective intention, in which case the
term institution seems in place.

Custom is often used interchangeably with convention, tradition
and mores, but the connotations are not quite the same. Convention
emphasizes the lack of inner necessity in the behavior pattern and
often implies some measure of agreement, express or tacit, that a
certain mode of behavior be accepted as proper. The more symbolic
or indirect the function of a custom, the more readily is it referred to
as a convention. It is a custom to write with pen and ink; it is a
convention to use a certain kind of paper in formal correspondence.
Tradition emphasizes the historic background of custom. No one
accuses a community of being wanting in customs and conventions,
but if these are not felt as possessed of considerable antiquity a community is said to have few if any traditions. The difference between
custom and tradition is more subjective than objective, for there
are few customs whose complete explanation in terms of history does
not take one back to a remote antiquity. The term mores is best reserved for those customs which connote fairly strong feelings of the
rightness or wrongness of modes of behavior. The mores of a people
are its unformulated ethics as seen in action. Such terms as custom,
institution, convention, tradition and mores are, however, hardly
capable of a precise scientific definition. All of them are reducible to
social habit or, if one prefers the anthropological to the psychological
point of view, to cultural pattern. Habit and culture are terms which
can be defined with some degree of precision and should always be
substituted for custom in strictly scientific discourse, habit or habit
system being used when the locus of behavior is thought of as residing
in the individual, cultural pattern or culture when its locus is thought
of as residing in society.

From a biological standpoint all customs are in origin individual
habits which have become diffused in society through the interaction
of individual upon individual. These diffused or socialized habits,
however, tend to maintain themselves because of the unbroken con-

tinuity of the diffusion process from generation to generation. One more often sees custom helping to form individual habit than individual habit being made over into custom. In the main, group psychology takes precedence over individual psychology. In no society, however primitive or remote in time, are the interactions of its members not controlled by a complex network of custom. Even at an early stage of the palaeolithic period human beings must have been ruled by custom to a very considerable extent, as is shown by the rather sharply delimited types of artifacts that were made and the inferences that can be drawn from some of these as to beliefs and attitudes.

The crystallization of individual habit into custom is a process that can be followed out theoretically rather more easily than illustrated in practise. A distinction can be made between customs of long tenure and customs of short tenure generally known as fashions. Fashions are set by a specific individual or group of individuals. When they have had a long enough lease of life to make it seem unimportant to recall the source or original locality of the behavior pattern, they have become customs. The habit of wearing a hat is a custom, but the habit of wearing a particular style of hat is a fashion subject to fairly rapid change. In the sphere of language custom is generally referred to as usage. Uncrystallized usages of speech are linguistic fashions, of which slang forms a particular variety. Food habits too form a well recognized set of customs, within which arise human variations that may be called fashions of food and that tend to die out after a brief period. Fashions are not to be considered as additions to custom but rather as experimental variations of the fundamental themes of custom.

In course of time isolated behavior patterns of a customary nature tend to group themselves into larger configurations which have a formal cohesion and which tend to be rationalized as functional units whether they are such historically or not. The whole history of culture has been little more than a ceaseless effort to connect originally independent modes of behavior into larger systems and to justify the secondary culture complexes by an unconscious process of rationalization. An excellent example of such a culture complex, which derives its elements from thousands of disparate customs, is the modern musical system, which is undoubtedly felt by those who make use of it to be a well compacted functional whole with various elements that are functionally interdependent. Historically, however, it is very easy to prove that the system of musical notation, the rules of harmony, the instrumental techinques, the patterns of musical composition and the conventional uses of particular instruments for specific purposes are independently derivable from customs of very different provenience and of very different age, and that it is only by slow processes of transfer of use and progressive integration of all these socialized modes of behavior that they have come to help each other out in a complex system of unified meanings. Hundreds of parallel instances could be given from such diverse fields of social activity as language, architecture, political organization, industrial technique, religion, warfare and social etiquette.

The impermanence of custom is a truism. Belief in the rapidity of change of custom is exaggerated, however, because it is precisely the comparatively slight divergences from what is socially established that arouse attention. A comparison of American life today with the life of a mediaeval English town would in the larger perspective of cultural anthropology illustrate rather the relative permanence of culture than its tendency to change.

The disharmony which cumulatively results from the use of tools, insights or other manipulative types of behavior which had enriched the cultural stock in trade of society a little earlier results in change of custom. The introduction of the automobile, for instance, was not at first felt as necessarily disturbing custom, but in the long run all those customs appertaining to visiting and other modes of disposing of one's leisure time have come to be seriously modified by the automobile as a power contrivance. Amenities of social intercourse felt to be obstructive to the free utilization of this new source of power tend to be dismissed or abbreviated. Disharmony resulting from the rise of new values also makes for change in custom. For example, the greater freedom of manner of the modern woman as contrasted with the far more conventionally circumscribed conduct of women of generations ago has come about because of the rise of a new attitude toward woman and her relation to man. The influences exerted by foreign peoples, e.g. the introduction of tea and coffee in occidental society and the spread of parliamentary government from country to country, are stressed by anthropologists more than by the majority of historians and sociologists as determinants of change. Most popular examples of the imposition of fashions which proceed from strategic personalities are probably fanciful and due to a desire to dramatize the operation of the more impersonal factors, which are much more important in the aggregate than the specific personal ones. With the gradual spread of a custom that is largely symbolic and characteristic of a selected portion of the population, the fundamental reason for its continuance weakens, so that it either dies out or takes on an entirely new function. This mechanism is particularly noteworthy in the life of language. Locutions which are considered smart or chic because they are the property of privileged circles are soon taken up by the masses and then die because of their banality. A much more powerful and exact knowledge of the nature of individual interaction, particularly as regards the unconscious transfer of feeling, is needed before a really satisfying theory of cultural change can be formulated.

Those customs survive the longest which either correspond to so basic a human need that they cannot well be seriously changed or else are of such a nature that they can easily be functionally reinterpreted. An example of the former type of persistence is the custom of having a mother suckle her child. There are numerous departures from this rule, yet both modern America and the more primitive tribes preserve as a custom a mode of behavior which obviously lies close to the life of man in nature. An example of the latter type of persistence, which may be called adaptive persistence, is language, which tends to remain fairly true to set form but which is constantly undergoing reinterpretation in accordance with the demands of the civilization which it serves. For example, the word robin refers in the United States to a very different bird from the English bird that was originally meant. The word could linger on with a modified meaning because it is a symbol and therefore capable of indefinite reinterpretation.

The word survival should not be used for a custom having a clearly defined function which can be shown to be different from its original place and significance in culture. When used in the latter, looser sense the word survival threatens to lose all useful meaning. There are few customs among us today which are not survivals in this sense. There are, however, certain customs which it is difficult to rationalize on any count and which may be looked upon as analogous to rudimentary organs in biology. The useless buttons in modern clothing are often cited as an example of such survivals. The use of Roman numerals alongside of Arabic numerals may also be considered a survival. On the whole, however, it seems safest not to use the word too freely, for it is difficult to prove that any custom, no matter how apparently lacking in utility or how far removed from its original application, is entirely devoid of at least symbolic meaning.

Custom is stronger and more persistent in primitive than in modern societies. The primitive group is smaller, so that a greater degree of conformity is psychologically necessary. In the more sophisticated community, which numbers a far larger total of individuals, departure from custom on the part of a few selected individuals, who may in turn prove instrumental for a change of culture in the community at large, does not matter so much for the solidarity of the group to begin with, because the chance individual of the group finds himself reinforced by the vast majority of his fellow men and can do without the further support of the deviants. The primitive community has also no written tradition to appeal to as an impersonal arbiter in matters of custom and therefore puts more energy into the conservation of what is transmitted through activity and oral tradition. The presence of documents relieves the individual from the necessity of taking personal responsibility for the perpetuation of custom. Far too great stress is usually laid on the actually conserving, as contrasted with the symbolically conserving, power of the written word. Custom among primitive peoples is apt to derive some measure of sacredness from its association with magical and religious procedures. When a certain type of activity is linked with a ritual which is in turn apt to be associated with a legend that to the native mind explains the activity in question, a radical departure from the traditionally conserved pattern of behavior is felt as blasphemous or perilous to the safety of the group. There is likewise a far lesser division of labor in primitive communities than in our own, which means that the forces making for experimentation in the solution of technical problems are proportionately diminished.

In the modern world custom tends to be much more conservative in the rural districts than in the city, and the reasons are similar to those given for the greater persistence of custom among primitive peoples. The greater scatter of the rural population does not generally mean the more intensive individual cultivation of the forms of custom but rather a compensatory effort to correct the threats of distance by conformity.

Within a complex community, such as is found in modern cities, custom tends to be more persistent on the whole in the less sophisticated groups. Much depends on the symbolism of a custom. There are certain types of custom, particularly such as are symbolic of status, which tend to be better conserved in the more sophisticated or wealthy groups than in the less sophisticated. The modern American custom, for instance, of having a married woman keep her maiden name is not likely soon to take root among the very wealthy, who here join hands with the unsophisticated majority, while the custom is being sparsely diffused among the intellectual middle class.

The varying degrees of conservatism in regard to custom can be illustrated in the behavior of a single individual because of the different types of social participation into which he enters. In England, for instance, the same individual may be in the vanguard of custom as a Londoner but insistent on the preservation of rural custom as a country squire. An American university man may be disdainful of customary opinion in his faculty club but be meekly observant of religious custom on Sunday at church. Loyalty or departure from custom is not a simple function of temperament or personality but part and parcel of the symbolism of multiple participation in society.

Custom is generally referred to as a constraining force. The conflict of individual will and social compulsion is familiar, but even the most forceful and self-assertive individual needs to yield to custom at most points in order that he may gain leverage, as it were, for the imposition of his personal will on society, which cannot be conquered without the implicit capture of social consent. The freedom gained by the denial of custom is essentially a subjective freedom of escape rather than an effective freedom of conquest. Custom makes for a powerful economy in the learning of the individual; it is a symbolic affirmation of the solidarity of the group. A by-product of these fundamental functions of custom is the more sentimental value which results from an ability to link the present and the past and thus to establish a larger ego in time, which supplements with its authority the larger ego represented by the community as it functions in the present.

The formulation of customs in the sphere of the rights and duties of individuals in their manifold relations leads to law. It is not useful to use the term law, as is often vaguely done in dealing with primitive societies, unless the enforcement of customary activity be made explicit, being vested in particular individuals or bodies of individuals. There are no societies that are wholly free from the binding force of implicit law, but as there are also many primitive societies which recognize some type of legal procedure it seems much better to speak of law only in the latter case. There are, for instance, few American Indian tribes in which customary obligations are recognized as a system of law that is capable of enforcement by the community. Psychologically law prevails, but not institutionally. This is in rather sharp contrast to the legal procedure which has been developed by the majority of African tribes. Here there is not merely the law of custom in an implicit sense but the perfectly explicit recognition of rules of conduct and of punishment for their infringement, with an elaborate method of discovering guilt and with the power of inflicting punishment vested in the king. The example of African law indicates that the essential difference between custom and law does not lie in the difference between oral tradition and the written formulation of custom. Law can emerge from custom long before the development of writing and has demonstrably done so in numerous cases. When custom has the psychological compulsion of law but is not controlled by society through the imposition of explicit penalties it may be called ethics or, more primitively, mores. It is difficult to distinguish law and ethics in the more simple forms of society. Both emerge from custom but in a somewhat divergent manner. Mundane or human sovereignty becomes progressively distinguished from socially diffused or supernatural or impersonal sovereignty. Custom controlled by the former is law; custom controlled by the latter is ethics.

The agencies instrumental in the formation of custom are for the most part quite impersonal in character and implicit in the mere fact of human interrelationships. There are also more self-conscious agencies for the perpetuation of custom. Among these the most important are law and religion, the latter particularly in the form of an organized church and priesthood. There are also organizations which are sentimentally interested in the conservation of customs which threaten to go out of use. In the modern world one often sees a rather weak nationalistic cause bolstered up by the somewhat artificial fostering of archaic custom. Much of the ritualism of the modern Scottish clans is secondarily rather than lineally conservative.

If complicated forms of conscious manipulation of ideas and techniques which rule the modern world are excluded from the range of the term custom, the force of custom may be said to be gradually lessening. The factors which favor this weakening of custom are: the growing division of labor with its tendency to make society less and less homogeneous; the growing spirit of rationalism, in the light of which much of the justification of custom fades away; the growing tendency to break away from local tradition; and, finally, the greater store set by individuality. The ideal which is latent in the modern mind would seem to be to break up custom into the two poles of individually determined habit on the one hand and of large scale institutional planning for the major enterprises of mankind on the other.

FASHION

B Y

EDWARD SAPIR

THE meaning of the term fashion may be clarified by pointing out how it differs in connotation from a number of other terms whose meaning it approaches. A particular fashion differs from a given taste in suggesting some measure of compulsion on the part of the group as contrasted with individual choice from among a number of possibilities. A particular choice may of course be due to a blend of fashion and taste.

Sapir, Edward, "Fashion," *Encyclopedia of the Social Sciences*, New York: The Macmillan Co., 1933. Reprinted by permission of The Macmillan Company.

Thus, if bright and simple colors are in fashion, one may select red as more pleasing to one's taste than yellow, although one's free taste unhampered by fashion might have decided in favor of a more subtle tone. To the discriminating person the demand of fashion constitutes a challenge to taste and suggests problems of reconciliation. But fashion is accepted by average people with little demur and is not so much reconciled with taste as substituted for it. For many people taste hardly arises at all except on the basis of a clash of an accepted fashion with a fashion that is out of date or current in some other group than one's own.

The term fashion may carry with it a tone of approval or disapproval. It is a fairly objective term whose emotional qualities depend on a context. A moralist may decry a certain type of behavior as a mere fashion but the ordinary person will not be displeased if he is accused of being in the fashion. It is different with fads, which are objectively similar to fashions but differ from them in being more personal in their application and in connoting a more or less definite social disapproval. Particular people or coteries have their fads, while fashions are the property of larger or more representative groups. A taste which asserts itself in spite of fashion and which may therefore be suspected of having something obsessive about it may be referred to as an individual fad. On the other hand, while a fad may be of very short duration, it always differs from a true fashion in having something unexpected, irresponsible or bizarre about it. Any fashion which sins against one's sense of style and one's feeling for the historical continuity of style is likely to be dismissed as a fad. There are changing fashions in tennis rackets, while the game of mah jong, once rather fashionable, takes on in retrospect more and more the character of a fad.

Just as the weakness of fashion leads to fads, so its strength comes from custom. Customs differ from fashions in being relatively permanent types of social behavior. They change, but with a less active and conscious participation of the individual in the change. Custom is the element of permanence which makes changes in fashion possible. Custom marks the highroad of human interrelationships, while fashion may be looked upon as the endless departure from and return to the highroad. The vast majority of fashions are relieved by other fashions, but occasionally a fashion crystallizes into permanent habit, taking on the character of custom.

It is not correct to think of fashion as merely a short lived innovation in custom, because many innovations in human history arise with the need for them and last as long as they are useful or convenient. If, for instance, there is a shortage of silk and it becomes customary to substitute cotton for silk in the manufacture of certain articles of dress in which silk has been the usual material, such an enforced change of material, however important economically or aesthetically, does not in itself constitute a true change of fashion. On the other hand, if cotton is substituted for silk out of free choice as a symbol perhaps of the simple life or because of a desire to see what novel effect can be produced in accepted types of dress with simpler materials, the change may be called one of fashion. There is nothing to prevent an innovation from eventually taking on the character of a new fashion. If, for example, people persist in using the cotton material even after silk has once more become available, a new fashion has arisen.

Fashion is custom in the guise of departure from custom. Most normal individuals consciously or unconsciously have the itch to break away in some measure from a too literal loyalty to accepted custom. They are not fundamentally in revolt from custom but they wish somehow to legitimize their personal deviation without laying themselves open to the charge of insensitiveness to good taste or good manners. Fashion is the discreet solution of the subtle conflict. The slight changes from the established in dress or other forms of behavior seem for the moment to give the victory to the individual, while the fact that one's fellows revolt in the same direction gives one a feeling of adventurous safety. The personal note which is at the hidden core of fashion becomes superpersonalized.

Whether fashion is felt as a sort of socially legitimized caprice or is merely a new and unintelligible form of social tyranny depends on the individual or class. It is probable that those most concerned with the setting and testing of fashions are the individuals who realize most keenly the problem of reconciling individual freedom with social conformity which is implicit in the very fact of fashion. It is perhaps not too much to say that most people are at least partly sensitive to this aspect of fashion and are secretly grateful for it. A large minority of people, however, are insensitive to the psychological complexity of fashion and submit to it to the extent that they do merely because they realize that not to fall in with it would be to declare themselves members of a past generation or dull people who cannot keep up with their neighbors. These latter reasons for being fashionable are secondary; they are sullen surrenders to bastard custom.

The fundamental drives leading to the creation and acceptance of fashion can be isolated. In the more sophisticated societies boredom, created by leisure and too highly specialized forms of activity, leads to restlessness and curiosity. This general desire to escape from the trammels of a too regularized existence is powerfully reenforced by a ceaseless desire to add to the attractiveness of the self and all other objects of love and friendship. It is precisely in functionally powerful societies that the individual's ego is constantly being convicted of helplessness. The individual tends to be unconsciously thrown back on himself and demands more and more novel affirmations of his effective reality. The endless rediscovery of the self in a series of petty truancies from the official socialized self becomes a mild obsession of the normal individual in any society in which the individual has ceased to be a measure of the society itself. There is, however, always the danger of too great a departure from the recognized symbols of the individual, because his identity is likely to be destroyed. That is why insensitive people, anxious to be literally in the fashion, so often overreach themselves and nullify the very purpose of fashion. Good hearted women of middle age generally fail in the art of being ravishing nymphs.

Somewhat different from the affirmation of the libidinal self is the more vulgar desire for prestige or notoriety, satisfied by changes in fashion. In this category belongs fashion as an outward emblem of personal distinction or of membership in some group to which distinction is ascribed. The imitation of fashion by people who belong to circles removed from those which set the fashion has the function of bridging the gap between a social class and the class next above it. The logical result of the acceptance of a fashion by all members of society is the disappearance of the kinds of satisfaction responsible for the change of fashion in the first place. A new fashion becomes psychologically necessary, and thus the cycle of fashion is endlessly repeated.

Fashion is emphatically a historical concept. A specific fashion is utterly unintelligible if lifted out of its place in a sequence of forms. It is exceedingly dangerous to rationalize or in any other way psychologize a particular fashion on the basis of general principles which might be considered applicable to the class of forms of which it seems to be an example. It is utterly vain, for instance, to explain particular forms of dress or types of cosmetics or methods of wearing the hair without a preliminary historical critique. Bare legs among modern women in summer do not psychologically or historically create at all the same fashion as bare legs and bare feet among primitives living in the tropics. The importance of understanding fashion historically should be obvious enough when it is recognized that the very essence of fashion is that it be valued as a variation in an understood sequence, as a departure from the immediately preceeding mode.

Changes in fashion depend on the prevailing culture and on the social ideals which inform it. Under the apparently placid surface of culture there are always powerful psychological drifts of which fashion is quick to catch the direction. In a democratic society, for instance, if there is an unacknowledged drift toward class distinctions fashion will discover endless ways of giving it visible form. Criticism can always be met by the insincere defense that fashion is merely fashion and need not be taken seriously. If in a puritanic society there is a growing impatience with the outward forms of modesty, fashion finds it easy to minister to the demands of sex curiosity, while the old mores can be trusted to defend fashion with an affectation of unawareness of what fashion is driving at. A complete study of the history of fashion would undoubtedly throw much light on the ups and downs of sentiment and attitude at various periods of civilization. However, fashion never permanently outruns discretion and only those who are taken in by the superficial rationalizations of fashion are surprised by the frequent changes of face in its history. That there was destined to be a lengthening of women's skirts after they had become short enough was obvious from the outset to all except those who do not believe that sex symbolism is a real factor in human behavior.

The chief difficulty of understanding fashion in its apparent vagaries is the lack of exact knowledge of the unconscious symbolisms attaching to forms, colors, textures, postures and other expressive elements in a given culture. The difficulty is appreciably increased by the fact that the same expressive elements tend to have quite different symbolic references in different areas. Gothic type, for instance, is a nationalistic token in Germany, while in Anglo-Saxon culture the practically identical type known as Old English has entirely different connotations. In other words, the same style of lettering may symbolize either an undying hatred of France or a wistful look backward at madrigals and pewter.

An important principle in the history of fashion is that those features of fashion which do not configurate correctly with the unconscious system of meanings characteristic of the given culture are relatively insecure. Extremes of style, which too frankly symbolize the current of feeling of the moment, are likely to find themselves in exposed positions, as it were, where they can be outflanked by meanings which they do not wish to recognize. Thus, it may be conjectured that lipstick is less secure in American culture as an element of fashion than rouge discreetly applied to the cheek. This is assuredly not due to a superior sinfulness of lipstick as such, but to the fact that rosy cheeks resulting from a healthy natural life in the country are one of the characteristic fetishisms of the traditional ideal of feminine beauty, while lipstick has rather the character of certain exotic ardors and goes with flaming oriental stuffs. Rouge is likely to last for many decades or centuries because there is, and is likely to be for a long time to come, a definite strain of nature worship in our culture. If lipstick is to remain it can only be because our culture will have taken on certain violently new meanings which are not at all obvious at the present time. As a symbol it is episodic rather than a part of the underlying rhythm of the history of our fashions.

In custom bound cultures, such as are characteristic of the primitive world, there are slow non-reversible changes of style rather than the often reversible forms of fashion found in modern cultures. The emphasis in such societies is on the group and the sanctity of tradition rather than on individual expression, which tends to be entirely unconscious. In the great cultures of the Orient and in ancient and mediaeval Europe changes in fashion can be noted radiating from certain definite centers of sophisticated culture, but it is not until modern Europe is reached that the familiar merry-go-round of fashion with its rapid alternations of season occurs.

The typically modern acceleration of changes in fashion may be ascribed to the influence of the Renaissance, which awakened a desire for innovation and which powerfully extended for European society the total world of possible choices. During this period Italian culture came to be the arbiter of taste, to be followed by French culture, which may still be looked upon as the most powerful influence in the creation and distribution of fashions. But more important than the Renaissance in the history of fashion is the effect of the industrial revolution and the rise of the common people. The former increased the mechanical ease with which fashions could be diffused; the latter greatly increased the number of those willing and able to be fashionable.

Modern fashion tends to spread to all classes of society. As fashion has always tended to be a symbol of membership in a particular social class and as human beings have always felt the urge to edge a little closer to a class considered superior to their own, there must always have been the tendency for fashion to be adopted by circles which had a lower status than the group setting the fashions. But on the whole such adoption of fashion from above tended to be discreet because of the great importance attached to the maintenance of social classes. What has happened in the modern world, regardless of the official forms of government which prevail in the different nations, is that the tone-giving power which lies back of fashion has largely slipped away from the aristocracy of rank to the aristocracy of wealth. This means a psychological if not an economic leveling of classes because of the feeling that wealth is an accidental or accreted quality of an individual as contrasted with blood. In an aristocracy of wealth everyone, even the poorest, is potentially wealthy both in legal theory and in private fancy. In such a society, therefore, all individuals are equally entitled, it is felt, so far as their pockets permit, to the insignia of fashion. This universalizing of fashion necessarily cheapens its value in the specific case and forces an abnormally rapid change of fashion. The only effective protection possessed by the wealthy in the world of fashion is the insistence on expensive materials in which fashion is to express itself. Too great an insistence on this factor, however, is the hall mark of wealthy vulgarity, for fashion is essentially a thing of forms and symbols not of material values.

Perhaps the most important of the special factors which encourage the spread of fashion today is the increased facility for the production and transportation of goods and for communication either personally or by correspondence from the centers of fashion to the outmost periphery of the civilized world. These increased facilities necessarily lead to huge capital investments in the manufacture and distribution of fashionable wear. The extraordinarily high initial profits to be derived from fashion and the relatively rapid tapering off of profits make it inevitable that the natural tendency to change in fashion is helped along by commercial suggestion. The increasingly varied activities of modern life also give greater opportunity for the growth and change of fashion. Today the cut of a dress or the shape of a hat stands ready to symbolize anything from mountain climbing or military efficiency through automobiling to interpretative dancing and veiled harlotry. No individual is merely what his social role indicates that he is to be or may vary only slightly from, but he may act as if he is anything else that individual phantasy may dictate. The greater leisure and spending power of the bourgeoisie, bringing them externally nearer the upper classes of former days, are other obvious stimuli to change in fashion, as are the gradual psychological and economic liberation of women and the greater opportunity given them for experimentation in dress and adornment.

Fashions for women show greater variability than fashions for men in contemporary civilization. Not only do women's fashions change more rapidly and completely but the total gamut of allowed forms is greater for women than for men. In times past and in other cultures, however, men's fashions show a greater exuberance than women's. Much that used to be ascribed to woman as female is really due to woman as a sociologically and economically defined class. Woman as a distinctive theme for fashion may be explained in terms of the social psychology of the present civilization. She is the one who pleases by being what she is and looking as she does rather than by doing what she does. Whether biology or history is primarily responsible for this need not be decided. Woman has been the kept partner in marriage and has had to prove her desirability by ceaselessly reaffirming her attractiveness as symbolized by novelty of fashion. Among the wealthier classes and by imitation also among the less wealthy, woman has come to be looked upon as an expensive luxury on whom one spends extravagantly. She is thus a symbol of the social and economic status of her husband. Whether with the increasingly marked change of woman's place in society the factors which emphasize extravagance in women's fashions will entirely fall away it is impossible to say at the present time.

There are powerful vested interests involved in changes of fashions, as has already been mentioned. The effect on the producer of fashions of a variability which he both encourages and dreads is the introduction of the element of risk. It is a popular error to assume that professional designers arbitrarily dictate fashion. They do so only in a very superficial sense. Actually they have to obey many masters. Their designs must above all things net the manufacturers a profit, so that behind the more strictly psychological determinants of fashion there lurks a very important element due to the sheer technology of the manufacturing process or the availability of a certain type of material. In addition to this the designer must have a sure feeling for the established in custom and the degree to which he can safely depart from it. He must intuitively divine what people want before they are quite aware of it themselves. His business is not so much to impose fashion as to coax people to accept what they have themselves unconsciously suggested. This causes the profits of fashion production to be out of all proportion to the actual cost of manufacturing fashionable goods. The producer and his designer assistant capitalize the curiosity and vanity of their customers but they must also be protected against the losses of a risky business. Those who are familiar with the history of fashion are emphatic in speaking of the inability of business to combat the fashion trends which have been set going by various psychological factors. A fashion may be aesthetically pleasing in the abstract, but if it runs counter to the trend or does not help to usher in a new trend which is struggling for a hearing it may be a flat failure.

The distribution of fashions is a comparatively simple and automatic process. The vogue of fashion plates and fashion magazines, the many lines of communication which connect fashion producers and fashion dispensers, and modern methods of marketing make it almost inevitable that a successful Parisian fashion should find its way within an incredibly short period of time to Chicago and San Francisco. If it were not for the necessity of exploiting accumulated stocks of goods these fashions would penetrate into the remotest corners of rural America even more rapidly than is the case. The average consumer is chronically distressed to discover how rapidly his accumulated property in wear depreciates by becoming outmoded. He complains bitterly and ridicules the new fashions when they appear. In the end he succumbs, a victim to symbolisms of behavior which he does not fully comprehend. What he will never admit is that he is more the creator than the victim of his difficulties.

Fashion has always had vain critics. It has been arraigned by the clergy and by social satirists because each new style of wear, calling attention as it does to the form of the human body, seems to the critics to be an attack on modesty. Some fashions there are, to be sure, whose very purpose it is to attack modesty, but over and above specific attacks there is felt to be a generalized one. The charge is well founded but useless. Human beings do not wish to be modest; they want to be as expressive—that is, as immodest—as fear allows; fashion helps them solve their paradoxical problem. The charge of economic waste which is often leveled against fashion has had little or no effect on the public mind. Waste seems to be of no concern where values are to be considered, particularly when these values are both egoistic and unconscious. The criticism that fashion imposes an unwanted uniformity is not as sound as it appears to be in the first instance. The individual in society is only rarely significantly expressive in his own right. For the vast majority of human beings the choice lies between unchanging custom and the legitimate caprice of custom, which is fashion.

Fashion concerns itself closely and intimately with the ego. Hence its proper field is dress and adornment. There are other symbols of the ego, however, which are not as close to the body as these but which are almost equally subject to the psychological laws of fashion. Among them are objects of utility, amusements and furniture. People differ in their sensitiveness to changing fashions in these more remote forms of human expressiveness. It is therefore impossible to say categorically just what the possible range of fashion is. However, in regard to both amusements and furniture there may be observed the same tendency to change, periodicity and unquestioning acceptance as in dress and ornament.

Many speak of fashions in thought, art, habits of living and morals. It is superficial to dismiss such locutions as metaphorical and unimportant. The usage shows a true intuition of the meaning of fashion, which while it is primarily applied to dress and the exhibition of the human body is not essentially concerned with the fact of dress or ornament but with its symbolism. There is nothing to prevent a thought, a type of morality or an art form from being the psychological equivalent of a costuming of the ego. Certainly one may allow oneself to be converted to Catholicism or Christian Science in exactly the same spirit in which one invests in pewter or follows the latest Parisian models in dress. Beliefs and attitudes are not fashions in their character of mores but neither are dress and ornament. In contemporary society it is not a fashion that men wear trousers; it is the custom. Fashion merely dictates such variations as whether trousers are to be so or so long, what colors they are to have and whether they are to have cuffs or not. In the same way, while adherence to a religious faith is not in itself a fashion, as soon as the individual feels that he can pass easily, out of personal choice, from one belief to another, not because he is led to his choice by necessity but because of a desire to accrete to himself symbols of status, it becomes legitimate to speak of his change of attitude as a change of fashion. Functional irrelevance as contrasted with symbolic significance for the expressiveness of the ego is implicit in all fashion.

INSTITUTIONS AND THE PERSON

BY

CHARLES HORTON COOLEY

AN institution is simply a definite and established phase of the public mind, not different in its ultimate nature from public opinion, though often seeming, on account of its permanence and the visible customs and symbols in which it is clothed, to have a somewhat distinct and independent existence. Thus the political state and the church, with their venerable associations, their vast and ancient power, their literature, buildings and offices, hardly appear even to a democratic people as the mere products of human invention which, of course, they are.

The great institutions are the outcome of that organization which human thought naturally takes on when it is directed for age after age upon a particular subject, and so gradually crystallizes in definite forms—enduring sentiments, beliefs, customs and symbols. And this is the case when there is some deep and abiding interest to hold the attention of men. Language, government, the church, laws and customs of property and of the family, systems of industry and education, are institutions because they are the working out of permanent needs of human nature.

These various institutions are not separable entities, but rather phases of a common and at least partly homogeneous body of thought,

From *Social Organization* by Charles Horton Cooley; copyright 1909 by Charles Scribner's Sons, 1937 by Elsie Jones Cooley. Reprinted by permission of the publishers.
Abridged from: Cooley, Charles H., *Social Organization*, New York: Charles Scribner's Sons, 1909.

just as are the various tendencies and convictions of an individual: they are the "apperceptive systems" or organized attitudes of the public mind, and it is only by abstraction that we can regard them as things by themselves. We are to remember that the social system is above all a whole, no matter how the convenience of study may lead us to divide it.

In the individual the institution exists as a habit of mind and of action, largely unconscious because largely common to all the group: it is only the differential aspect of ourselves of which we are commonly aware. But it is in men and nowhere else that the institution is to be found. The real existence of the Constitution of the United States, for example, is in the traditional ideas of the people and the activities of judges, legislators and administrators; the written instrument being only a means of communication, an Ark of the Covenant, ensuring the integrity of the tradition.

The individual is always cause as well as effect of the institution: he receives the impress of the state whose traditions have enveloped him from childhood, but at the same time impresses his own character, formed by other forces as well as this, upon the state, which thus in him and others like him undergoes change.

If we think carefully about this matter, however, we shall see that there are several somewhat different questions which might be included in a study of the relation between the individual and institutions; and these we ought to distinguish.

One of them is that of the babe to the world, or of the hereditary factor of life, existing in us at birth, to the factor of communication and influence.

Another and quite different one is that of society and personality, or of the relation between the mature individual and the whole of which he is a member.

A third is the question—again a distinct one—of the relation, not between the person and society at large, but between him and particular institutions. This last is the one with which we are more properly concerned, but it may not be amiss to offer some observations on the others.

The child at birth, when, we may suppose for convenience, society has had no direct influence upon him, represents the race stock or hereditary factor in life in antithesis of the factor of tradition, communication and social organization. He also represents an undeveloped or merely biological individuality in contrast to the developed social whole into which he comes.

In the development of the child, then, we have to do with the interaction of two types, both of which are ancient and stable, though one more so than the other. And the stir and generation of human life is precisely in the mingling of these types and in the many variations of each one. The hereditary outfit of a child consists of vague tendencies or aptitudes which get definiteness and meaning only through the communicative influences which enable them to develop. Thus babbling is instinctive, while speech comes by this instinct being defined and instructed in society; curiosity comes by nature, knowledge by life; fear, in a vague, instinctive form, is supposed to be felt even by the fœtus, but the fears of later life are chiefly social fears; there is an instinctive sensibility which develops into sympathy and love; and so on.

Nothing is more futile than general discussions of the relative importance of heredity and environment. It is much like the case of matter *versus* mind; both are indispensable to every phase of life, and neither can exist apart from the other: they are coordinate in importance and incommensurable in nature. One might as well ask whether the soil or the seed predominates in the formation of a tree, as whether nature does more for us than nurture.

As fast as a child becomes a person, he also becomes a member of the existing social order. This is simply a case of a whole and one of its differentiated parts; having so often insisted that society and the individual are aspects of the same thing, I need not enlarge upon it here. Even the degenerate, so far as they have faculty enough to be human, live in the social order and are as much one with it as the rest of mankind. We simply cannot separate the individual from society at large; to get a contrast we must pass on to consider him in relation to particular institutions, or to institutions in general as distinguished from more plastic phases of life.

An institution is a mature, specialized and comparatively rigid part of the social structure. It is made up of persons, but not of whole persons; each one enters into it with a trained and specialized part of himself. Consider, for instance, the legal part of a lawyer, the ecclesiastical part of a church member or the business part of a merchant. In antithesis to the institution, therefore, the person represents the wholeness and humanness of life; he is, as Professor Alfred Lloyd says, "a corrector of partiality, and a translator and distributor of special development." A man is no man at all if he is merely a piece of an institution; he must stand also for human nature, for the instinctive, the plastic and the ideal.

The saying that corporations have no soul expresses well enough this defect of all definite social structures, which gives rise to an irrepressible conflict between them and the freer and larger impulses of human nature. Just in proportion as they achieve an effective special mechanism for a narrow purpose, they lose humanness, breadth and adaptability. As we have to be specially on our guard against commercial corporations, because of their union of power and impersonality, so we should be against all institutions.

The institution represents might, and also, perhaps, right, but right organized, mature, perhaps gone to seed, never fresh and unrecognized. New right, or moral progress, always begins in a revolt against institutions.

Of course the institutional element is equally essential with the personal. The mechanical working of tradition and convention pours into the mind the tried wisdom of the race, a system of thought every part of which has survived because it was, in some sense, the fittest, because it approved itself to the human spirit. In this way the individual gets language, sentiments, moral standards and all kinds of knowledge: gets them with an exertion of the will trifling compared with what these things originally cost. They have become a social atmosphere which pervades the mind mostly without its active participation. Once the focus of attention and effort, they have now receded into the dimness of the matter-of-course, leaving energy free for new conquests. On this involuntary foundation we build, and it needs no argument to show that we could accomplish nothing without it.

Thus all innovation is based on conformity, all heterodoxy on orthodoxy, all individuality on solidarity. Without the orthodox tradition in biology, for instance, under the guidance of which a store of ordered knowledge had been collected, the heterodoxy of Darwin, based on a reinterpretation of this knowledge, would have been impossible.

It is from the interaction of personality and institutions that progress comes. The person represents more directly that human nature which it is the end of all institutions to serve, but the institution represents the net result of a development far transcending any single personal consciousness. The person will criticise, and be mostly in the wrong, but not altogether. He will attack, and mostly fail, but from many attacks change will ensue.

It is also true that although institutions stand, in a general way, for the more mechanical phase of life, they yet require, within themselves, an element of personal freedom. Individuality, provided it be in harness, is the life of institutions, all vigor and adaptability depending upon it.

An army is the type of a mechanical institution; and yet, even in an army, individual choice, confined of course within special channels, is vital to the machine.

The time-worn question of conservatism as against change has evidently much in common with that of personality as against institutions. Innovation, that is, is bound up with the assertion of fresh personality against mechanism. Wherever there is vigor and constructive power in the individual there is likely to be discontent with the establishment. The young notoriously tend to innovation, and so do those of a bold and restless temperament at any age; the old, on the contrary, the quiet, the timid, are conservative. And so with whole peoples; in so far as they are enfeebled by climate or other causes they become inert and incapable of constructive change.

What may not be quite so obvious, at least to those who have not read M. Tarde's work on the Laws of Imitation, is that innovation or the opposite may be a public habit, independently of differences in age or vigor. The attitude toward change is subject to the same sort of alteration as public opinion, or any other phase of the public mind. That a nation has moved for centuries in the deepest ruts of conservatism, like China or India, is no proof of a lack of natural vigor, but may mean only that the social type has matured and hardened in isolation, not encountering any influence pungent enough to pierce its shell and start a cycle of change.

Tradition comes down from the past, while convention arrives, sidewise as it were, from our contemporaries; the fireside tales and maxims of our grandparents illustrate the one, the fashions of the day the other. Both indicate continuity of mind, but tradition has a long extension in time and very little, perhaps, in place, while convention extends in place but may endure only for a day.

This seems a clear distinction, and a great deal has been made of it by some writers, who regard "custom imitation" and "fashion imitation," to use the terms of Tarde, the brilliant French sociologist, as among the primary traits that differentiate societies.

Thus mediæval society, it is said, was traditional: people lived in somewhat isolated groups and were dominated by the ideas of their ancestors, these being more accessible than those of their contemporaries. On the other hand, modern society, with its telegraphs, newspapers and migrations, is conventional. Thought is transmitted over vast areas and countless multitudes; ancestral continuity is broken up; people get the habit of looking sidewise rather than backward, and there comes to be an instinctive preference of fashion over custom.

There is, truly, a momentous difference in this regard between modern and mediæval life, but to call it a change from tradition to convention does not, I think, indicate its real character. Indeed, tradition and convention are by no means the separate and opposite things they may appear to be when we look at them in their most contrasted phases. It would be strange if there were any real separation between ideas coming from the past and those coming from contemporaries, since they exist in the same public mind. A traditional usage is also a convention within the group where it prevails. One learns it from other people and conforms to it by imitation and the desire not to be singular, just as he does to any other convention. The quaint local costume that still prevails in out-of-the-way corners of Europe is worn for the same reasons, no doubt, that the equally peculiar dress-suit and silk hat are worn by sophisticated people the world over; one convention is simply more extended than the other. In old times the conforming group, owing to the difficulty of intercourse, was small. People were eager to be in the fashion, as they are now, but they knew nothing of fashions beyond their own locality. Modern traditions are conventional on a larger scale. The Monroe Doctrine, to take a dignified example, is a tradition, regarded historically, but a convention as to the manner in which it enters into contemporary opinion.

In a similar manner we may see that conventions must also be traditions. The new fashions are adaptations of old ones, and there are no really new ideas of any sort, only a gradual transformation of those that have come down from the past.

In a large view, then, tradition and convention are merely aspects of the transmission of thought and of the unity of social groups that results from it. If our mind is fixed upon the historical phase of the matter we see tradition, if upon the contemporary phase we see convention. But the process is really one, and the opposition only particular and apparent. All influences are contemporary in their immediate origin, all are rooted in the past.

THE THEORY OF PUBLIC OPINION

B Y

CHARLES HORTON COOLEY

PUBLIC opinion is no mere aggregate of separate individual judgments, but an organization, a cooperative product of communication and reciprocal influence. It may be as different from the sum of what the individuals could have thought out in separation as a ship built by a hundred men is from a hundred boats each built by one man.

A group "makes up its mind" in very much the same manner that the individual makes up his. The latter must give time and attention to the question, search his consciousness for pertinent ideas and sentiments, and work them together into a whole, before he knows what his real thought about it is. In the case of a nation the same thing must take place, only on a larger scale. Each individual must make up his mind as before, but in doing so he has to deal not only with what was already in his thought or memory, but with fresh ideas that flow in from others whose minds are also aroused. Every one who has any fact, or thought, or feeling, which he thinks is unknown, or insufficiently regarded, tries to impart it; and thus not only one mind but all minds are searched for pertinent material, which is poured into the general stream of thought for each one to use as he can. In this manner the minds in a communicating group become a single organic whole. Their unity is not one of identity, but of life and action, a crystallization of diverse but related ideas.

It is not at all necessary that there should be agreement; the essential thing is a certain ripeness and stability of thought resulting from attention and discussion. There may be quite as much difference of opinion as there was before, but the differences now existing are comparatively intelligent and lasting. People know what they really think about the matter, and what other people think. Measures, platforms, candidates, creeds and other symbols have been produced which serve to express and assist cooperation and to define opposition. There has come to be a relatively complete organization of thought, to which each individual or group contributes in its own peculiar way.

One who would understand public opinion should distinguish clearly between a true or mature opinion and a popular impression. The former requires earnest attention and discussion for a considerable time, and when reached is significant, even if mistaken. It rarely exists regarding matters of temporary interest, and current talk or print is a most uncertain index of it. A popular impression, on the other hand, is facile, shallow, transient, with that fickleness and fatuity that used to be ascribed to the popular mind in general. It is analogous to the unconsidered views and utterances of an individual, and the more one studies it the less seriously he will take it. It may happen that ninety-nine men in a hundred hold opinions to-day contrary to those they will hold a month hence—partly because they have not yet searched their own minds, partly because the few who have really significant and well-grounded ideas have not had time to impress them upon the rest.

It is not unreasonable, then, to combine a very slight regard for most of what passes as public opinion with much confidence in the soundness of an aroused, mature, organic social judgment.

There is a widespread, but as I believe a fallacious, idea that the public thought or action must in some way express the working of an average or commonplace mind, must be some kind of a mean between the higher and lower intelligences making up the group. It would be more correct to say that it is representative, meaning by this that the preponderant *feeling* of the group seeks definite and effectual expression through individuals specially competent to give it such expression.

Public opinion is no uniform thing, as we are apt to assume, but has its multifarious differentiations. We may roughly distinguish a general opinion, in which almost everybody in the community has a part, and an infinite diversity of special or class opinions—of the family, the club, the school-room, the party, the union, and so on.

And there is an equal diversity in the kind of thought with which the public mind may be concerned: the content may be of almost any sort. Thus there are group ideals, like the American ideal of indissoluble unity among the states, the French ideal of national glory, or the ideals of honor and good-breeding cherished in many families; and there are group beliefs, regarding religion, trade, agriculture, marriage, education and the like. Upon all matters in which the mind has, in the past, taken a lively interest there are latent inclinations and prepossessions, and when these are aroused and organized by discussion they combine with other elements to form public opinion.

This diversity merely reflects the complexity of organization, current opinion and discussion being a pervasive activity, essential to growth, that takes place throughout the system at large and in each particular member. General opinion existing alone, without special types of thought as in the various departments of science and art, would indicate a low type of structure, more like a mob than a rational society. It is upon these special types, and the individuals that speak for them, that we rely for the guidance of general opinion (as, for instance, we rely upon economists to teach us what to think about the currency), and the absence of mature speciality involves weakness and flatness of general achievement. This fault is often charged to democracy, but it should rather be said that democracy is substituting a free type of speciality, based upon choice, for the old type based upon caste, and that whatever deficiency exists in this regard is due chiefly to the confused conditions that accompany transition.

General public opinion has less scope than is commonly imagined. The questions which can profitably be decided by this direct and general judgment of the public are chiefly those of organic change or readjustment, such, for instance, as the contemporary question of what part the government is to take in relation to the consolidation of industries. These the people must decide, since no lesser power will be submitted to, but routine activities, in society as in individuals, are carried on without arousing a general consciousness. The people are also peculiarly fit to make choice among conspicuous personalities.

Specialists of all sorts—masons, soldiers, chemists, lawyers, bankers, even statesmen and public officials—are ruled for the most part by the opinion of their special group, and have little immediate dependence upon the general public, which will not concern itself with them so long as their work is not palpably inefficient or in some way distasteful.

The rule of public opinion, then, means for the most part a latent authority which the public will exercise when sufficiently dissatisfied with the specialist who is in immediate charge of a particular function. It cannot extend to the immediate participation of the group as a whole in the details of public business.

The sentiment of the people is most readily and successfully exercised in their judgment of persons. Montesquieu, in discussing republican government, advocated on this ground an almost universal manhood suffrage in the choosing of representatives. "For," says he, "though few can tell the exact degree of men's capacities, yet there are none but are capable of knowing in general whether the person they choose is better qualified than most of his neighbors." The plainest men have an inbred shrewdness in judging human nature which makes them good critics of persons even when impenetrable to ideas. This shrewdness is fostered by a free society, in which every one has to make and hold his own place among his fellows; and it is used with much effect in politics and elsewhere as a guide to sound ideas.

So in answer to the question, Just what do the undistinguished masses of the people contribute to the general thought? we may say, They contribute sentiment and common-sense, which gives momentum and general direction to progress, and, as regards particulars, finds its way by a shrewd choice of leaders. It is into the obscure and inarticulate sense of the multitude that the man of genius looks in order to find those vital tendencies whose utterance is his originality. As men in business get rich by divining and supplying a potential want, so it is a great part of all leadership to perceive and express what the people have already felt.

SOCIAL SYSTEMS

B Y

RALPH LINTON

AT the very outset of any general discussion of social systems it is necessary to emphasize the distinction between such systems and societies.
Societies are groups of individuals who live and work together, their
cooperative existence being made possible by mutual adaptations in
the various members' attitudes and behavior. Social systems consist of
the mutually adjusted ideal patterns according to which the attitudes
and behavior of a society's members are organized. A society is an
organization of individuals; a social system is an organization of ideas.
It represents a particular arrangement of statuses and roles which exist
apart from the individuals who occupy the statuses and express the
roles in overt behavior.

Since patterns find expression only through the medium of the
individuals who occupy the statuses which they establish, it is the
statuses which are first brought to the attention of the investigator.
All societies have names for many of the statuses in their systems and
are accustomed to express their patterns, when these are at all conscious or verbalized, in status terms. In describing such a relationship
as that of father and son, they will tell first what one does and expects,
then what the other does and expects. As a result, most investigators
have shown a tendency to treat statuses as though they were fixed
points between which various behavioral relationships might develop.
This tendency is increased by the fact that so many statuses are ascribed
to individuals on the basis of biological relationships present in all
aggregates.

The logical starting point for investigations of society is the study
of particular social systems as wholes. The recognition of such systems
as entities distinct from societies simplifies the problem somewhat,
since it makes it possible to ignore the wide range of individual variation in the expression of the system's patterns and to concentrate upon
these patterns and their interrelations. However, the problem still remains sufficiently complex. The first task confronting the investigator
is that of ascertaining what the patterns are. Societies vary greatly in
the degree to which their patterns are conscious and verbalized.

Abridged from: Linton, Ralph, *The Study of Man*, New York: Appleton-Century,
1936. Reprinted by permission of Appleton-Century-Crofts, Inc.

Even when a complete picture of a system has been obtained, the working of the system cannot be understood unless it is studied in relation to its broader context, i.e., the environment and culture of the society. Social systems can only function as parts of a larger whole, the total culture of the society. It is possible for an investigator to isolate the social system from the rest of culture for descriptive purposes by a process of analysis and selection comparable to that by which the anatomist isolates a nervous system from the rest of an organism. However, the isolation is artificially imposed, both organisms and cultures constituting functional wholes. Viewed from this aspect, a social system is simply a segment of a culture, that fraction of the whole which provides the members of a society with designs for group living. In this respect it is on a par with those other segments of culture which provide the group with techniques for getting its food or protecting itself from enemies. Since social systems are never apprehended as wholes by those who live under them and never function except in relation to the total culture, it is an open question whether they can be considered as constituting a distinct class of phenomena. The utility of the concept for descriptive purposes is obvious, but from the standpoint of the student of function such groupings of patterns appear to be something which the investigator interposes between two genuinely operative things: the pattern, which is known to individuals and influences the behavior of individuals, and the culture, which provides for the total needs of the society.

The problem of the reality of social systems is a philosophic rather than a practical one. The important thing is that the complex of mutually adjusted patterns which we term "a social system" develops and functions in constant relation to the rest of culture and that the patterns must be adapted to this setting quite as much as to each other. The total culture, in turn, must be adapted to the natural environment of the society, since man may develop many and diverse techniques for mastering and exploiting his environment but can never escape from it. Every social system is, therefore, part of a vastly larger configuration all of whose component elements are interrelated. It can be understood only when it is studied with relation to this configuration whose other elements impose constant limits upon its growth and operation.

THE CONCEPT OF FUNCTION

B Y

A. R. RADCLIFFE-BROWN

THE concept of function applied to human societies is based on an analogy between social life and organic life. The recognition of the analogy and of some of its implications is not new. In the nineteenth century the analogy, the concept of function, and the word itself appear frequently in social philosophy and sociology.

Durkheim's definition (1895) is that the "function" of a social institution is the correspondence between it and the needs (*besoins* in French) of the social organism. This definition requires some elaboration. In the first place, to avoid possible ambiguity and in particular the possibility of a teleological interpretation, I would like to substitute for the term "needs" the term "necessary conditions of existence," or, if the term "need" is used, it is to be understood only in this sense. It may be here noted, as a point to be returned to, that any attempt to apply this concept of function in social science involves the assumption that there *are* necessary conditions of existence for human societies just as there are for animal organisms, and that they can be discovered by the proper kind of scientific enquiry.

For the further elucidation of the concept it is convenient to use the analogy between social life and organic life. Like all analogies it has to be used with care. An animal organism is an agglomeration of cells and interstitial fluids arranged in relation to one another not as an aggregate but as an integrated living whole. For the biochemist, it is a complexly integrated system of complex molecules. The system of relations by which these units are related is the organic structure. As the terms are here used the organism is *not* itself the structure; it is a collection of units (cells or molecules) arranged in a structure, i.e. in a set of relations; the organism *has* a structure. Two mature animals of the same species and sex consist of similar units combined in a similar structure. The structure is thus to be defined as a set of relations between entities. (The structure of a cell is in the same way a set of rela-

Abridged from: Radcliffe-Brown, A. R., "On the Concept of Function in Social Science," *American Anthropologist*, 1935, 37, 394–402. Reprinted in A. R. Radcliffe-Brown, *Structure and Function in Primitive Society*, London: Cohen & West, 1952. Published in U.S. by The Free Press, Glencoe, Illinois. By permission of the author.

tions between complex molecules, and the structure of an atom is a set of relations between electrons and protons.) As long as it lives the organism preserves a certain continuity of structure although it does not preserve the complete identity of its constituent parts. It loses some of its constituent molecules by respiration or excretion; it takes in others by respiration and alimentary absorption. Over a period its constituent cells do not remain the same. But the structural arrangement of the constituent units does remain similar. The process by which this structural continuity of the organism is maintained is called life. The life-process consists of the activities and interactions of the constituent units of the organism, the cells, and the organs into which the cells are united.

As the word function is here being used the life of an organism is conceived as the *functioning* of its structure. It is through and by the continuity of the functioning that the continuity of the structure is preserved. If we consider any recurrent part of the life-process, such as respiration, digestion, etc., its *function* is the part it plays in, the contribution it makes to, the life of the organism as a whole. As the terms are here being used a cell or an organ has an *activity* and that activity has a *function*. It is true that we commonly speak of the secretion of gastric fluid as a "function" of the stomach. As the words are here used we should say that this is an "activity" of the stomach, the "function" of which is to change the proteins of food into a form in which these are absorbed and distributed by the blood to the tissues. We may note that the function of a recurrent physiological process is thus a correspondence between it and the needs (i.e. necessary conditions of existence) of the organism.

If we set out upon a systematic investigation of the nature of organisms and organic life there are three sets of problems presented to us. (There are, in addition, certain other sets of problems concerning aspects or characteristics of organic life with which we are not here concerned.) One is that of morphology—what kinds of organic structures are there, what similarities and variations do they show, and how can they be classified? Second are the problems of physiology—how, in general, do organic structures function, what, therefore, is the nature of the life-process? Third are the problems of evolution or development—how do new types of organisms come into existence?

To turn from organic life to social life, we can recognise the existence of a social structure. Individual human beings, the essential units in this instance, are connected by a definite set of social relations into an integrated whole. The continuity of the social structure, like that of an organic structure, is not destroyed by changes in the unit. Individuals may leave the society, by death or otherwise; others may enter it. The continuity of structure is maintained by the process of social life, which consists of the activities and interactions of the individual human beings and of the organised groups into which they are united. The social life of the community is here defined as the *functioning* of the social structure. The *function* of any recurrent activity, such as the punishment of a crime, or a funeral ceremony, is the part it plays in the social life as a whole and therefore the contribution it makes to the maintenance of the structural continuity.

The concept of function as here defined thus involves the notion of a *structure* consisting of a *set of relations* amongst *unit entities,* the *continuity* of the structure being maintained by a *life-process* made up of the *activities* of the constituent units.

If, with these concepts in mind, we set out on a systematic investigation of the nature of human society and of social life, we find presented to us three sets of problems. First, the problems of social morphology—what kinds of social structures are there, what are their similarities and differences, how are they to be classified? Second, the problems of social physiology—how do social structures function? Third, the problems of development—how do new types of social structure come into existence?

Two important points where the analogy between organism and society breaks down must be noted. In an animal organism it is possible to observe the organic structure to some extent independently of its functioning. It is therefore possible to make a morphology which is independent of physiology. But in human society the social structure as a whole can only be *observed* in its functioning. Some of the features of social structure, such as the geographical distribution of individuals and groups can be directly observed, but most of the social relations which in their totality constitute the structure, such as relations of father and son, buyer and seller, ruler and subject, cannot be observed except in the social activities in which the relations are functioning. It follows that a social morphology cannot be established independently of a social physiology.

The second point is that an animal organism does not, in the course of its life, change its structural type. A pig does not become a hippopotamus. (The development of the animal from germination to maturity is not a change of type since the process in all its stages is typical for the species.) On the other hand a society in the course of its history can and does change its structural type without any breach of continuity.

By the definition here offered "function" is the contribution which a partial activity makes to the total activity of which it is a part. The function of a particular social usage is the contribution it makes to the total social life as the functioning of the total social system. Such a view implies that a social system (the total social structure of a society together with the totality of social usages in which that structure appears and on which it depends for its continued existence) has a certain kind of unity, which we may speak of as a functional unity. We may define it as a condition in which all parts of the social system work together with a sufficient degree of harmony or internal consistency, i.e. without producing persistent conflicts which can neither be resolved nor regulated.[1]

This idea of the functional unity of a social system is, of course, a hypothesis. But it is one which seems worth while to test by systematic examination of the facts.

There is another aspect of functional theory that should be briefly mentioned. To return to the analogy of social life and organic life, we recognise that an organism may function more or less efficiently and so we set up a special science of pathology to deal with all phenomena of disfunction. We distinguish in an organism what we call health and disease. The Greeks of the fifth century B.C. thought that one might apply the same notion to society, to the city-state, distinguishing conditions of *eunomia,* good order, social health, from *dysnomia,* disorder, social ill-health. In the nineteenth century Durkheim, in his application of the notion of function, sought to lay the basis for a scientific social pathology, based on a morphology and a physiology.

In relation to organic structures we can find strictly objective criteria by which to distinguish disease from health, pathological from normal, for disease is that which either threatens the organism with death (the dissolution of its structure) or interferes with the activities which are characteristic of the organic type. Societies do not die in the same sense that animals die and therefore we cannot define dysnomia as that which leads, if unchecked, to the death of a society. Further, a society differs from an organism in that it can change its structural type, or can be absorbed as an integral part of a larger society. Therefore we cannot define dysnomia as a disturbance of the usual activities of a social type.

Let us return for a moment to the Greeks. They conceived the health of an organism and the eunomia of a society as being in each instance a condition of the harmonious working together of its parts. Now this, where society is concerned, is the same thing as what was considered above as the functional unity or inner consistency of a social system, and it is suggested that for the degree of functional unity of a particular society it may be possible to establish a purely objective cri-

---

[1] Opposition, i.e. organised and regulated antagonism, is, of course, an essential feature of every social system.

terion. Admittedly this cannot be done at present; but the science of human society is as yet in its extreme infancy. So that it may be that we should say that, while an organism that is attacked by a virulent disease will react thereto, and, if its reaction fails, will die, a society that is thrown into a condition of functional disunity or inconsistency (for this we now provisionally identify with dysnomia) will not die, except in such comparatively rare instances as an Australian tribe overwhelmed by the white man's destructive force, but will continue to struggle toward some sort of eunomia, some kind of social health, and may, in the course of this, change its structural type. This process, it seems, the "functionalist" has ample opportunities of observing at the present day, in native peoples subjected to the domination of the civilised nations, and in those nations themselves.[2]

Space will not allow a discussion here of another aspect of functional theory, viz. the question whether change of social type is or is not dependent on function, i.e. on the laws of social physiology. My own view is that there is such a dependence and that its nature can be studied in the development of the legal and political institutions, the economic systems and the religions of Europe through the last twenty-five centuries. For the preliterate societies with which anthropology is concerned, it is not possible to study the details of long processes of change of type. The one kind of change which the anthropologist can observe is the disintegration of social structures. Yet even here we can observe and compare spontaneous movements towards reintegration. We have, for instance, in Africa, in Oceania, and in America the appearance of new religions which can be interpreted on a functional hypothesis as attempts to relieve a condition of social dysnomia produced by the rapid modification of the social life through contact with white civilisation.

The concept of function as defined above constitutes a "working hypothesis" by which a number of problems are formulated for investigation. No scientific enquiry is possible without some such formulation of working hypotheses. Two remarks are necessary here. One is that the hypothesis does not require the dogmatic assertion that everything in the life of every community has a function. It only requires the assumption that it *may* have one, and that we are justified in seeking to discover it. The second is that what appears to be the same social

---

[2] To avoid misunderstanding it is perhaps necessary to observe that this distinction of eunomic and dysnomic social conditions does not give us any evaluation of these societies as "good" or "bad." A savage tribe practising polygamy, cannibalism, and sorcery can possibly show a higher degree of functional unity or consistency than the United States. This objective judgment, for such it must be if it is to be scientific, is something very different from any judgment as to which of the two social systems is the better, the more to be desired or approved.

usage in two societies may have different functions in the two. Thus the practice of celibacy in the Roman Catholic Church of today has very different functions from those of celibacy in the early Christian Church. In other words, in order to define a social usage, and therefore in order to make valid comparisons between the usages of different peoples or periods, it is necessary to consider not merely the form of the usage but also its function. On this basis, for example, belief in a Supreme Being in a simple society is something different from such a belief in a modern civilised community.

The acceptance of the functional hypothesis or point of view outlined above results in the recognition of a vast number of problems for the solution of which there are required wide comparative studies of societies of many diverse types and also intensive studies of as many single societies as possible. In field studies of the simpler peoples it leads, first of all, to a direct study of the social life of the community as the functioning of a social structure, and of this there are several examples in recent literature. Since the function of a social activity is to be found by examining its effects upon individuals, these are studied, either in the average individual or in both average and exceptional individuals. Further, the hypothesis leads to attempts to investigate directly the functional consistency or unity of a social system and to determine as far as possible in each instance the nature of that unity. Such field studies will obviously be different in many ways from studies carried out from other points of view, e.g. the ethnological point of view that lays emphasis on diffusion. We do not have to say that one point of view is better than another, but only that they are different, and any particular piece of work should be judged in reference to what it aims to do.

The "functionalist" point of view here presented does imply that we have to investigate as thoroughly as possible all aspects of social life, considering them in relation to one another, and that an essential part of the task is the investigation of the individual and of the way in which he is moulded by or adjusted to the social life.

There is not, and cannot be, any conflict between the functional hypothesis and the view that any culture, any social system, is the end-result of a unique series of historical accidents. The process of development of the race-horse from its five-toed ancestor was a unique series of historical accidents. This does not conflict with the view of the physiologist that the horse of today and all the antecedent forms conform or conformed to physiological laws, i.e. to the necessary conditions of organic existence. Palaeontology and physiology are not in conflict. One "explanation" of the race-horse is to be found in its history—how it came to be just what it is and where it is. Another and entirely independent "explanation" is to show how the horse is a special exemplification of physiological laws. Similarly one "explanation" of a social system will be its history, where we know it—the detailed account of how it came to be what it is and where it is. Another "explanation" of the same system is obtained by showing (as the functionalist attempts to do) that it is a special exemplification of laws of social physiology or social functioning. The two kinds of explanation do not conflict, but supplement one another.

CHAPTER 10

Associations

———————◆◗◗——————

THE FAMILY AS A PRIMARY SOCIAL GROUP

BY

GEORGE F. VINCENT AND ALBION W. SMALL

THE family is the simplest permanent group which is discoverable in society. It is for this reason, and not because it is historically the original social structure, that we call the family the primary combination, or, to borrow a term from physical science, the molecule of society.

In the family we find certain psychical bonds of union between individuals, and certain relations between these individuals and the land and wealth. These bonds are formed by the satisfaction of certain desires, which we have found to be characteristic of human nature, and the relations with the land and wealth are required by certain other wants, which are equally a part of man's life. A man and a woman together form the personal nucleus of this structure, to which are added children, and other relatives in varying degrees of consanguinity, as well as domestic servants. While the personal element of the family may be made to include a very wide circle of more or less related individuals, it is usual to describe by the term that group which, with some degree of permanence, occupies the same abode, and practices a single domestic economy.

Not only do we discover in the family these related personalities, but

Abridged from: Vincent, George F., and Small, Albion W., *An Introduction to the Study of Society*, New York: American Book Company, 1894.

we find also various forms of wealth which have been appropriated by the family and made essential parts of its organization. Very much as a plant, taking materials from soil and air, builds them into its own organism, does the family possess itself of material goods, and give them place in its structure. Having thus sketched in outline the general arrangement of social factors in the family, let us examine in detail the relations, personal and material, which we discover.

The real bond which permanently unites a man and a woman must be distinguished from the mere outward ceremony by which the union is given a conventional sanction or legal existence. The actual tie is formed by satisfactions which range from simple animalism to high types of psychical sympathy and altruistic devotion. The bond never consists wholly of one element of desire. It is a complex of many, but its general nature is determined by that factor which predominates and thus gives character to the whole. Again, we must remember that there are two personalities here involved, and that the uniting influence has, therefore, two subjective aspects. On the one side, certain desires may be in the ascendency, on the other quite different preeminent wants may seek satisfaction. We may remark, in general, that the bond of union is strong in proportion as these two sets of desires coincide with each other, and approximate to the highest ideal.

The relation of husband to wife in old countries, and even in new, has in it a certain element of authority, more or less recognized by law and custom, which must be regarded as of some significance in a study of family structure. The average husband is to be thought of as in a real sense the head of the family. The question as to how these two personalities react upon each other and produce modifications in both belongs properly to Social Psychology, and need not be discussed at this point.

Attention should be called to one influence which decidedly affects the bond between husband and wife, i.e. parenthood. The physical necessity of caring for children, as well as the exigencies of propagation, may be designated as a peculiar cohesive force of the family group.

Another influence which tends to preserve the stability of the marriage relation is the external coercion of conventionality and public opinion. When other ties lose their power, this pressure from without often serves to perpetuate at least the appearance of union.

We come next to an examination of the ties which unite father and mother with their offspring. The most obvious and primary bond is that of physical dependence of children upon parents. It is necessary that the young should be nourished and protected from the early period of their helplessness up to the time that they assume quasi-independent relations of one kind or another. This dependence is not only physical, but psychical. Natural affection, the chief bond of union in the family, has, as it exists between parent and child, two aspects—from the one side, authority, from the other, docility. The relation is best expressed by the Latin terms *auctoritas* and *pietas*. Both qualities originate in the natural superiority of the parents. In actual society, we find the exercise of parental authority varying from virtual tyranny to the most lax and vacillating policy of control; filial docility also ranges from trembling obedience to open impudence. On the whole, however, the parent and child are united by a bond of natural affection, which is characterized on the one hand by some degree of beneficence, discipline, and encouragement, on the other, by a certain measure of gratitude, obedience, and confidence.

The relations of parents and children give rise to a variety of combinations. Thus the relations of father to son, of father to daughter, of mother to son, and of mother to daughter, all present phenomena of a more or less peculiar character. The father usually exerts an influence of a kind quite different from that of the mother. The former has more of the master in his tone and manner, if not in his heart; the latter, as a rule, admonishes and persuades in a gentler spirit. So also the father can sometimes manage a son whom the mother cannot control. Again, just the reverse is true, and the maternal influence is the stronger. Thus we see that, while the bonds between parents and children may be described in terms of wide generalization, they do, in fact, present countless variations in degree and in the proportion of elements.

The number of personal elements which may be connected with the nucleus of the family by relationships of blood and by the intermarriage of children with the members of other families is capable of various degrees of expansion. The ties thus formed may reach over great distances, and ramify in peculiar ways through the structure of a whole society. Other things being equal, these bonds will be strong in proportion to nearness of relationship, frequency and permanency of actual contact, and congeniality of tastes.

These conditions, however, vary in influence and are further modified by the psychical peculiarities of different families. We may here repeat that a limitation of the family, as a personal social structure, to that group of individuals who live together in the same domicile is important for the sake of clearness of view. When children have assumed other social relations permanently, they have, by so much, become parts of other structural groups or families. In such circumstances, the ties of consanguinity and marriage lose their distinctive character as family bonds, and become forces which unite family with family into a more complex structure. We may conceive of these relationships, then, as among the secondary influences of social cohesion in distinction from the primary forces which insure the solidarity of the family.

The functional many-sidedness of the primary social combination, the family, is of great significance. In comparative isolation, when a measure of self-sufficiency is unavoidable, the family performs, in a more or less rudimentary way, all primary social functions, which, as differentiation and integration advance, are gradually shared with special social organs, or almost entirely surrendered to them. In other words, the family displays in *microcosm* all the activities of the village, city, or nation. This is not to be construed into an assertion that the nation is merely a larger structure of the family type, or that modern government corresponds to parental authority. Nor is the student to infer that the functions performed by the family in a state of approximate isolation are all of a definitely developed form. Most of them are comparatively primitive, while many are potential rather than actually exercised.

In conditions generally recognized as normal, propagation is exclusively a function of the family, which therefore serves as a connecting link between physical life and that of the social organism. It is the peculiar service of the family to produce the new individuals who take the places of those that perish. Thus the elements of society are constantly renewed and social existence is perpetuated. The biological laws which govern this function of propagation are, as we have already seen, of great structural importance. The complete dependence of children upon parents during a long period of infancy necessitates a corresponding permanence of the family relation and gives rise to new psychical bonds, which reënforce the original tie between husband and wife. In normal circumstances, the family thus gains coherence from the performance of its peculiar function, which, in turn, renders necessary many other activities.

In order that a society may attain a high degree of organization and stability, it is necessary that its individual members should be brought into orderly relations with the land. This service is rendered by the family, which has for one of its chief aims the establishment and maintenance of a permanent abode, under such conditions as afford sufficient area for the successful accomplishment of domestic tasks, and opportunities for normal family life.

The prevailing system of private property in land has gradually established itself largely as a result of this function of settlement which demands both definiteness of area and permanency of tenure.

From earliest times, defense has been an all-important function of the individual, and because of the relation which individuals sustain to collective life, this same activity has been more and more exercised by society, and is especially characteristic of the family. This function of defense includes broadly (1) shelter and protection against external nature, (2) prevention and cure of disease, (3) defense against animals and unsocial individuals.

The relation of the family to the production of wealth varies with different stages of social organization. In contemporary society, to which we are confining our examination, differentiation and inter-dependence have advanced so far that a wholly self-sufficient family is well-nigh inconceivable. Although production in general has been largely surrendered to special social agencies, yet each family, as such, carries on some measure of domestic production. The transformation of raw supplies into edible food is a conspicuous productive function which is still performed by the family. Various minor domestic activities of the same order are also carried on. The fact that vast numbers of families are concerned in the production of wealth, and thereby retain their appropriate places in the whole social organism, should not mislead the student as to the extent of domestic production, as such, which is limited to the function actually performed within the family group.

Each family, by virtue either of some service rendered to society or of some conventional economic arrangement, receives, through the channels of transportation and exchange, a certain volume of wealth measured and generally represented by money. The distribution or apportionment of this wealth among members of the household is an important family function. It is a function of the family, therefore, to supply means of physical sustenance to its members until such time as children are mature enough to assume independent economic relations with society, or to become dependent members of other families.

In what are recognized as normal conditions, the family income is received in return for the social service of its head, the husband, through whom wife and children obtain their shares. Thus the family has an essential work to do in apportioning the aggregate wealth of society among its individual members. Again, the family not only distributes wealth, but it also accumulates property of different kinds in the form of capital. It is manifestly essential to individual and social progress that these accumulations should be handed on, in a definite and orderly way, from one generation to the next. This important function of transmission, by means of gift, bequest, and inheritance, is chiefly performed by the family, which bestows upon children the wealth that has been inherited or accumulated by the parents.

It is quite as essential to social life and progress that accumulations of knowledge should be transmitted from one generation to another as that material wealth should be so handed down. The systematic teaching of the young has become so largely a social activity in contemporary society that the family function in this regard is virtually limited to the early period of children's lives, and even this much of instruction is being gradually surrendered to the kindergarten. The family performs an all-important educational function, if education be used in its widest sense, but on the whole, the average family, as such, does not direct specifically the intellectual development of its young members—a service which is performed by the kindergarten, the school, the academy, the college, and the university.

The development of æsthetic capacities in children is a task which the family shares with social organs. Home decoration, music, and art are important factors which cooperate with other agencies in cultivating an appreciation of the beautiful.

In order that society may preserve its efficiency, and advance to higher types of organization, it is necessary that the individuals composing it should possess and exercise certain capacities for subordination, cooperation, self-control, and altruism. Man may always have been a gregarious animal, but it has required ages of struggle and stress, of hard discipline and cruel suffering, of groping blindly toward lofty ideals, to make him a social person. It it manifestly of vital importance that the experiences of the race represented in the common wisdom of any generation should guide the training of the next.

Next to propagation itself, to fit the young for social life in its broadest aspects is the chief function of the family. Howsoever this activity may be shared with other institutions, in final analysis the responsibility of preparing children to take part effectively and harmoniously in the life of society rests upon the family.

The structure of the family held together by a common bond of affection, with relations of authority and docility betweeen parents and children, and of virtual equality among the latter, affords admirable means for the exercise of this function. The organized household with its system of government and its domestic economy forms a miniature society, a school of discipline. Parental affection supplies care, patience, and loving persistence by which alone the best results can be secured. Children are trained to prompt instinctive habits which are often more useful than reasoned conduct; they learn to practice subordination and obedience, which are so necessary in social tasks of cooperation; in their relations with brothers, sisters, and parents, they are taught principles of justice, and sentiments of courtesy and kindness, which make true social life possible; they are specially trained, usually with the aid of schools and other institutions, to perform certain of the tasks which society imposes upon its members, and thus are prepared to take their places in the social organism. The several specific functions of the family which we have enumerated may be regarded as together constituting one great service, *i.e.* the preservation of generational continuity, physical and psychical. The family bridges the gap between one generation and the next. It transmits physical life, material wealth, and psychical resources. In this broad view the family assumes new importance, and its general function is clearly recognized as fundamental, in the present order.

Society, having its life in a common body of thought and belief, exhibits growth, *i.e.* readjustments of structures and activities in correspondence with modified ideals; and displays certain general functions, all of which are performed, at least rudimentarily, by the isolated family; but, as organization advances, these are shared in greater or less degree with social institutions or organs.

POLITICAL AND ECONOMIC ASSOCIATIONS
IN COMPLEX SOCIETIES

B Y

ROBERT M. MACIVER

IN all the more complex societies the organizations of the political and economic order become the comprehensive framework of the social structure. They ramify everywhere, creating an ever wider and ever more intricate scheme of relationships. They link land with land over all the earth, often outstripping in their advance the associations of the cultural order. They link the savage to the civilized man. They ignore in large measure differences of creed or nationality or color. This condition arises out of the peculiar character of political and economic interests. We have already classified them as "secondary interests," constituting, as it were, neutral means to which all other interests of men are related and through which all other interests may be pursued. Consequently, given the technological basis of communication, they are capable of unlimited expansion. Together they constitute the great mechanism which men must use to obtain the objects of their desire. In their development they establish great forms of social order which both liberate and limit the expression of all our primary interests.

Abridged from: MacIver, Robert M., *Society: A Textbook of Sociology*, New York: Farrar and Rinehart, 1937. Reprinted by permission of Rinehart and Company, Inc.

The state and the community.—When we call the state an association we mean that it is a specific organization of society. We distinguish
it thereby from the country or the nation on the one hand, from the
unity of the social structure on the other. The confusion is still a
prevalent one. It is encouraged by language, since we use the same
terms, *the United States, England, Germany,* and so forth, to denote
both the country and its people or the state and its government. We
say "the United States makes a treaty"—and here we mean the state—
or we say "the United States has a standard of living"—and here we
mean the people. It is fostered by the tradition of old theories which
regarded the state, contrary to definite evidences, as a *universal* partnership. It is a mistaken inference from the fact that the state does
actually control or regulate a great part of our social activities and relationships and that it is *constitutionally* competent to control a still
greater part. It is consequently maintained that if the state lets other
aspects of social life alone "it is none the less dealing with them—it
only lets them alone in a certain way and on certain terms." [1] But
even if we accepted this position it does not follow that the regulator
is to be identified with that which is regulated. Moreover, there are
various social codes which are distinct from and only in small part
controlled by the code of the state. And there are many associations
to which we belong which are in no sense merely divisions or branches
of the great association of the state. As social beings, we are more than
merely citizens of a state. We enter into many relationships, we carry
on many social activities, not as members of a state, not as citizens, but
as social beings, as friends or lovers, as members of families, of
churches, of clubs or other groups. The real problem, that of the relation of the state to the inclusive community, is only obscured if we
begin by identifying the two. Most modern constitutions set limits to
the things the state can do. Generally, for example, it forbids the state
to require the profession of any religion of its citizens or to discriminate between citizens with respect to their religion. We say it forbids
the state and not simply the government. For it proclaims—or rather
the people proclaim through it—that laws of a certain nature shall
not be passed and that certain liberties shall not be abrogated, and to
this end it usually provides that a mere majority shall not suffice to
alter these constitutional guarantees. Whatever practical difficulties
may arise from such provisions they surely bear witness to the intention of "the people" or the community to set limits to the place and
power of the state itself.

The state then is an essential part, but never the whole, of the social

[1] Quotation from a letter to the author by the late Professor Bosanquet, who
asserted this point of view in his work, *The Philosophical Theory of the State.*

structure. It is best conceived of as an agency of the community with very broad and important functions, but nevertheless limited. It does not, and cannot, take the place of other agencies; these have their own functions, which they alone are fitted to perform. The family has its place, the church has its place, and so forth. How far the state *should* regulate other associations is a question admitting vast experimentation; how far the state *can* take over the functions of certain associations, particularly of the economic order, is another question of great significance.

The peculiar nature of the state.—The state is an organization with special attributes, special instruments, special powers. What primarily distinguishes it from all other associations is its instrument of political law. This kind of law differs from all other social laws in two ways, first, that there is attached to it the peculiar sanction of socialized and unconditional compulsion, second—a corollary from the first—that it applies without exception to everyone within a geographical area. In these respects the legal code has an advantage over all other codes, but it must pay a price for it. Because it applies to everyone, it can apply only where uniformity of control is felt to be desirable by those who uphold the state—it cannot apply to matters where its members claim the right to differ from one another. Because its sanction is force, its power of appeal is limited. Other associations, to which men freely belong, can on that very ground use means of persuasion with greater efficacy than can the state. They appeal to the free will which is automatically secured by voluntary membership. The state can appeal to its citizens and above all can control powerful engines of propagandism to influence them, but always behind the appeal there is the threat of compulsion. In other associations the malcontents have the alternative of leaving; if grave differences arise within them, the association itself can dissolve or split. But obviously these alternatives are for practical purposes ruled out in the case of the state. In earlier stages of civilization a group which disapproved the policy of the state might, with hardship and peril, secede and establish a new one, as did the Roman plebeians or the Pilgrim Fathers, but in the modern world this recourse is practically impossible. The state has thus a compulsive aspect which very definitely limits its control over the spirit of its people.

It follows that there are certain things which the state can do well, others it can do less well than the free associations, and others which it cannot do at all. What actions fall in these various categories depends in part on the particular conditions of individual states. The functions of the state vary greatly at different stages of its history. Sometimes the state has been mainly an exploitative power, controlling the rest of the population in the interest of a dominant class. As the basis of citizenship broadened, it assumed to a larger extent protective functions, and these must always remain an important aspect of its task. In quite recent times another aspect has begun to assume significance, that of the state as a positive agency of social welfare. Thus in some countries of Europe we see old strongholds, the seats of a former exploitative nobility, turned into employment offices and health insurance bureaus. The three aspects of the state exist together, with varying emphasis, in present-day democracy.

THE FUNCTIONS OF THE STATE IN A COMPLEX SOCIETY

The limits to the functions of the state.—Perennial controversy rages around the functions of the state. They are the issues of party warfare. They vary from state to state, from period to period, even from year to year. The capitalistic and the communistic state seem at opposite poles in their solutions of the question. The liberal state and the fascist state give contradictory answers. The totalitarian state would usurp all functions. One is tempted to think that the functions of the state are whatever functions the controlling power within any state cares to assume. And this view is supported by the traditional doctrine of state sovereignty. "The sovereign," said a characteristic exponent of this tradition, "has the complete disposal of the life, rights, and duties of the individual." [2] The sovereign, said the jurist Blackstone, is "a supreme, irresistible, uncontrollable authority." But in reality, whatever the legal or constitutional form may be, the state has limits to what it can do.

Functions peculiar to the state.—First, there are social functions which the state alone can perform. The state alone can establish an effective and basic order in a complex society. The state can maintain such an order because of the peculiar attributes which it and it alone possesses. On the one hand its law is binding on *all* who live within an entire geographical area; on the other hand it possesses the ultimate right of enforcement. The establishment and maintenance of a universal order is thus an essential function of the state, its function *par excellence.* The state alone can make rules of universal application. It alone can guarantee facilities which shall be equally available to all the members of a community. It alone can establish rights and obligations which admit of no exemptions. It alone can establish conditions of equal opportunity. It alone can ensure the universal validity of units and standards of measurement, weight, quality, and value. It alone can set up minimum standards requisite for decent living with

[2] Cornewall, Lewis, *The Use and Abuse of Political Terms* (Oxford, 1898), Chap. V.

the assurance that none shall be allowed to fall below them. It alone can define the areas and limits of subordinate powers. It alone can co-ordinate within one great social framework the various organizations of a society. The state, in short, is the guarantor and the guardian of the public order.

But the state cannot be content with the mere establishment of order. The order maintained by a tyranny or by a slave state or by an empire differs vastly from the order of a "free" or democratic state. Order is always based on some principle, and the state is vitally concerned with the broad social policy of which a given order is the expression. Order may rest on privilege and status, or it may be guided by the ideal of equal opportunity. It may be designed to keep the weak in subjection to the strong or to prevent the strong from encroachment on the weak. Some principle of *justice* is inevitably involved, and the attainment of justice is a far more difficult and more controversial function than the attainment of order. It is obviously not secured by the simple "rule of law" which makes everyone equally subject to its dictates, which, as Anatole France remarked, "in its majestic equality forbids the rich as well as the poor to sleep in the streets and to beg bread." One of the fundamentals of any order is a system of property rights, and since such rights are not given by "nature" they must be determined by authority. Justice, in the old phrase, is "to give every man his own" (*suum cuique tribuere*), but how to decide what a man's own may be is an ever-perplexing problem. The old individualistic notion, translated into modern economic terms in the "labor theory of value," that men gain legitimate titles to goods in terms of the toil they expend in transforming them from their natural state, becomes meaningless in the world of economic and social interdependence. Yet the state cannot fulfill its clear and inevitable function of maintaining order without involving itself in the further and infinitely harder task of securing justice. And in the last resort, so far as this end can be achieved it can be achieved only through the instrumentality of the state. Alone possessing jurisdiction over all the members of a community, it alone can represent the interests common to all of them as against the interests which divide them.

Functions for which the state is well adapted.—We turn next to those functions which the state, in virtue of the means at its command, is more fitted to perform than any other organization. In this category comes the conservation of natural resources. Against the competitive interests which seek immediate economic gain the state can uphold the interest of the whole and the interest of the future. Reluctantly and often belatedly the state has had to intervene to prevent the wasteful consumption of the community's resources, its forests, its fisheries, its wild life, its irreplaceable mineral assets. And if the state is needed to control the social dangers of competition it is also needed to check the domination of private monopoly. Wherever particular interests manifestly infringe the common interest, the state is called upon to uphold the latter, though often the political pressure exerted by those particular interests prevent or even pervert its function. It is not possible within our limits to specify the magnitude and the variety of this task. All so-called social legislation, the establishment by law of various forms of industrial protection and insurance, may be regarded as coming within this category.

The conservation and the development of the personal, no less than of the economic, resources of the community devolves in large measure on the state. Included in this function is the general provision of education. Every civilized state has found that this essential service cannot be left to private agencies, that to be at all adequate for the needs of the future as well as of the present the endowment and control of general education must be publicly established. Only thus can standards be maintained for the community as a whole, and the more glaring inequalities of opportunity, which more than anything else stand in the way of the discovery, evocation, and utilization of human potentialities, be substantially reduced.

As we have said, there is no *a priori* limit to what the state can do for the service of the community. In so far as, with its vast and comprehensive organization, it can support and stimulate other agencies providing noncontroversial services, there seems no reason why it should not do so if its aid is not out of proportion to the cost. The case for such support is particularly strong with respect to those cultural services, of which education itself is an example, which do not yield an immediate economic return proportionate to their cost. How far the state can and should go in this direction must depend on the cultural values of the community, but the more enlightened it becomes the more the state can contribute to the development of science, to the encouragement of art, and in general to the economic equipment of those services which yield to mankind the more enduring and less competitive satisfactions. Together with such functions we may include that of the provision of the means and opportunities for the study of the greater and more urgent questions of social policy and for the collection, as in the census, of statistical and other information bearing on the welfare of the people. Other agencies can perform these tasks in part, but none so efficiently and on so great a scale and with such authority as can the state.

Functions for which the state is ill adapted.—We pass thirdly to those social functions in the performance of which the state is at a disadvantage as compared with other agencies. These again must vary with the conditions, but in all societies there are limits to what the state can effectively do. The multitude of diverse associations in an advanced civilization witnesses to those particular needs and selective purposes which the state cannot adequately satisfy. The state is the agency of the *whole* community. There are more intensive, more specialized, and more limited interests which unite groups within it. There are divergent and conflicting interests which properly create their own associations. There are experimental objectives which are far better pursued by the smaller interested groups. There are also interests which unite men on a great scale, but not as members of the state. To this order belong the broader cultural interests, including the religious. The state is not well adapted, in the light of its nature as already described, to sponsor the more intimate or more personal interests, those which admit a variety of spontaneous and variant expressions. Voluntary associations have a flexibility, an initiative, a capacity for experiment, a liberation from the heavier responsibility of taking risks that the state rarely, if ever, possesses. They can thus foster, in ways not permissible to the state, the nascent interests of groups, and encourage enterprise, social and economic, at the growing points of a society. Even the role of arbiter is here not within the competence of the state. It is not qualified to decide the merits of artistic, literary, scientific endeavor or to abitrate, say, religious controversies.

Functions which the state is incapable of performing.—There is a thin border line between the things which the state is ill qualified to do and those which it cannot do at all. Can the state control people's opinions? Given a sufficient support, it can prevent nonconformist groups from expressing their opinion overtly. But it is not thereby meeting opinion on its own ground, it is using the alien instrument of compulsion. An opinion claims truth, and force is entirely irrelevant to this claim. Often the suppression of belief has been worse than futile; sometimes it has given a secret strength to the persecuted belief, but at all times it has prevented belief from meeting the only true test, that of frank examination and discussion.[3] Can the state control people's morality? It can, given sufficient support, control the external aspects of conduct, but if morality means a set of attitudes towards our fellows and towards life in general, again we have entered a sphere in which mere enforcement is foolish or futile and in which the appeal to the feelings of men comes with greater efficacy from the free associa-

[3] The excellent argument of Mill on this point, in Chapter III of the essay *On Liberty*, still holds good. For a fuller discussion see H. Laski, *Liberty in the Modern State* (New York, 1930).

tions which, if they claim authority at all, claim it on grounds to which the compulsive state cannot aspire. The history of the state's attempt to control religion is one of the longest and most tragic chapters in the record of man's stupidity, but at least it has revealed this lesson to those who can read and understand, that there are in human nature certain resistances to compulsion which it is beyond the power of tyranny to destroy. Again, when a German minister of education, addressing the universities of the country, declares that science has to be "National Socialist science" and "a specific accomplishment of the national spirit," he is trying in the name of the state to make of science something that is contrary to its very being and that the scientific spirit can never accept.[4] Nor is it only the deeper, more spiritual impulses which resist this control. There are, as we have seen, codes regulative of conduct which are largely independent of the legal code. Custom sets limits to law, and no less does the seemingly superficial code of fashion. In the latter sphere men—and women still more—accept dictation from the prestige-owning arbiters of dress which they would violently reject from the government of the state.[5] In short, the more intimate details of conduct as well as the more deeply cultural traits claim a freedom from compulsion which places them largely outside the region of state control. The trends of culture, of the arts and the sciences, may be affected by the activity of the state, but they owe their vitality and their direction to forces inherent in the community and beyond the capacity of the state to determine.

THE DISTINCTIVE CHARACTER OF ECONOMIC ORGANIZATION

In what sense economic and political organization fall within the same category.—The relation of the political to the economic system constitutes the most urgent, important, and controversial problem of modern social organization. The two are so closely interdependent as to create everywhere institutional complexes. At the same time each has its own distinctive principle and above all its own distinctive method. The manner in which they are combined and the range within which either method is accepted and given priority over the other are most significant characteristics of any social structure.

By contrast with the varieties of cultural associations, economic and political associations fall within the same broad category of social

[4] Address of Dr. Bernard Rust, as quoted in *The New York Times*, November 8, 1936.

[5] A government may sometimes, though rarely, prescribe a particular material or type of dress on economic or other national grounds, as Frederick William of Prussia prescribed the wearing of cotton clothes. The Turkish government could proscribe the wearing of the fez and the veil, but these were the insignia of a discarded civilization. In neither of these instances was fashion involved.

structures. It might be said of them that organization constitutes their very being. They are in effect sheer means to ends realized through but not within the association, whereas the ends of cultural associations are realized in large measure within them, directly in the very process of communication which they establish. But economic and political associations satisfy our social needs indirectly by the products they yield. They are agencies of control, of power, means of attaining certain products of organization—order, wealth, and so forth. The social participation they offer is purely incidental, accessory. It is not the specific social needs of fellowship, of communication, which bring them into being. They are essentially external to the inner social life, though of course every organization that men create is utilized in some measure to satisfy their social impulses. But these associations are rather conditions of the social life than aspects of it.

Since both economic and political associations are concerned with universal means to human purposes, means which may be applied to many varied and divergent ends, they are capable of great expansion. Apart from cultural resistances, there is no reason why they should not form a great, closely interwoven network covering the whole earth. The logic of order sets this consummation before the political system, and the logic of economy works to the same end with respect to the economic system. The broad trend of civilization is in this direction. It has freer range in the expansion of the economic structure, while in the political structure it is retarded by the identification of the state with the cultural unity of the nation. But the necessities of order and the extension of cultural likeness through the development of communications are bringing influences to bear which make towards the transcendence of the national state as the ultimate range of free political organization.

Moreover, the economic and the political systems are in large part different means of attaining the same ends. In a socialist state many objectives are sought by political methods which in the capitalist state are sought by economic methods. In no community is it possible to draw a hard-and-fast line between the functions of the two systems. Wages and working conditions, for example, are in part determined by economic agencies, and in part by political regulation. Industrial disputes may be settled by trade agreements or by the action of governments. The credit system depends on arrangements in which governments cooperate with public, semipublic, or private banks. Within the economic order men seek by means of private savings to provide against the contingencies of life, unemployment, sickness, accident, old age. Within the political order the same result is sought by social legislation. Even in waging war the state must resort to economic weapons, and under modern conditions it is upon these that victory or defeat seems finally to depend. The economic and the political order interlock at myriad points, even in the most individualistic society, and the old *laissez-faire* idea, that each can "mind its own business" without interference by the other, is an outworn illusion. *The distinction between the economic and the political organization is not so much a distinction between spheres of activity as between methods of action.* It is only a confusion to suppose that economic interests are or can be the exclusive concern of what we name economic associations. In some degree they are interests of every form of association. But the difference is that what we specifically name economic associations are primarily devoted to the acquisition of wealth, to money-making or at least the provision of the means of living, without reference to the uses to which these means are subsequently applied. The economic means is their end-result; the disposal of these means lies beyond their interest.

The economic method.—The method which associations so constituted pursue we may term the "economic method." It stands in significant contrast to the political method, and an analysis of the difference will serve as an introduction to the study of the nature of economic association.

The economic method is devoted to the exclusive or private control or possession of wealth. In the economic association men seek wealth in conjunction, but ultimately in order to gain individual control or possession. In the process of acquiring wealth, first the association and then its individual members alienate or appropriate means for exclusive use. The political method, on the other hand, socializes or communizes wealth. Having done so, the state may, of course, return this wealth to the economic system by a process of redistribution, but in so far as the state retains it, it assumes a public character. When, for example, the state establishes a national park, or the municipality a hospital or school, it withdraws these possessions from the processes of the economic system. They become subject to a new and very different kind of regulation. Socialized or communized goods are removed from the sphere of exchange and of the regulating economic forces of supply and demand. In so far as they are communized they arouse no longer the competitive economic interest, any more than do the winds and the clouds.

The economic method differs therefore from the political in that its principle is ultimately distributive. Political action, no matter what private interests may underlie it, is at least ostensibly in the name of, and for the sake of, the common welfare. It is therefore unicentered within the area of a whole community, whereas economic action is multicentered. No matter how far the integration of economic associations advances through amalgamations, trusts, cartels, and other unions, the economic system, by its very nature, remains an arena of competing forces. But the political method is anticompetitive and assumes a complete unification of interest. It may be mistaken or perverted, and even when it does seek the common well-being it may be opposed or thwarted by dissentient economic forces, but at least it preserves the form of unity, the conception of the whole, and thus its intervention is, and always has been, necessary to preserve that unity against the disruptive and partial interests of the economic arena.

The economic association as a specific type of organization.—Since the economic association as such is indifferent to the uses of the means which it seeks, it reaches its developed form only when these means themselves are entirely detachable from any particular uses. When this stage is reached, as under modern systems of currency and credit, the economic method becomes more clearly differentiated from the political method. Its results are expressed in abstract units of exchange. A dollar is a convertible good, and a good only because convertible, convertible at the will of its possessor into any one of innumerable specific goods. The economic method is the pursuit through an elaborate mechanism of production, distribution, and exchange of this free kind of buying power. It is the detachment of this power from specific embodiments in forms of property which has made it so formidable and so pervasive. This situation is an aspect of modern capitalism. In old days, for example, landownership was never a purely economic category. It had a special social status and a definite political significance. Land was not bought and sold freely in the market place. It was too closely bound up with sentiments and traditions and privileges to be a mere "economic good." It was the inheritance of a family, with all the personal and social attachments consequent thereon. In the process of industrialization it has lost this earlier significance and become, for the most part, a form of capital. Labor itself has undergone a similar and no less momentous revolution. It is now, under capitalism, a free contractual good; in other words, it is bought and sold, with certain limitations, on economic terms agreed upon between the buyers and the sellers. It has passed from a condition of status to one of contract. The laborer is no longer attached to the land nor is his work and pay determined by the local traditions of an ancient craft. He offers his labor power in the open market, by the hour or by the "piece." He seeks, through combination with his fellows, to affect in his favor the conditions of labor supply, and that is because his labor is now an economic category, so that his wages, and his employment or lack of employment, are immediately determined by the prevailing conditions of supply and demand.

THE OCCUPATIONAL GROUP

B Y

EMILE DURKHEIM

WHILE religion, the family and the nation are preservatives against egoistic suicide, the cause of this does not lie in the special sort of sentiments encouraged by each. Rather, they all owe this virtue to the general fact that they are societies and they possess it only in so far as they are well integrated societies; that is, without excess in one direction or the other. Quite a different group may, then, have the same effect, if it has the same cohesion. Besides the society of faith, of family and of politics, there is one other of which no mention has yet been made; that of all workers of the same sort, in association, all who cooperate in the same function, that is, the occupational group or corporation.

Its aptness for this role is proved by its definition. Since it consists of individuals devoted to the same tasks, with solidary or even combined interests, no soil is better calculated to bear social ideas and sentiments. Identity of origin, culture and occupation makes occupational activity the richest sort of material for a common life. Moreover, in the past the corporation has proved that it could form a collective personality, jealous, even excessively so, of its autonomy and its authority over its members; so there is no doubt of its capacity to be a moral environment for them. There is no reason for the corporative interest not acquiring in its workers' eyes the respectable character and supremacy always possessed by social interests, as contrasted with private interests, in a well-organized society. From another point of view, the occupational group has the three-fold advantage over all others that it is omnipresent, ubiquitous and that its control extends to the greatest part of life. Its influence on individuals is not intermittent, like that of political society, but it is always in contact with them by the constant exercise of the function of which it is the organ and in which they collaborate. It follows the workers wherever they go; which

Reprinted by permission of the publisher. The Free Press, Glencoe, Illinois. Copyright 1951 by The Free Press. A Corporation.
Abridged from: Durkheim, Emile. *Suicide: A Study in Sociology* (translated by George Simpson), Glencoe, Illinois: The Free Press, 1951.

the family cannot do. Wherever they are, they find it enveloping them, recalling them to their duties, supporting them at need. Finally, since occupational life is almost the whole of life, corporative action makes itself felt in every detail of our occupations, which are thus given a collective orientation. Thus the corporation has everything needed to give the individual a setting, to draw him out of his state of moral isolation; and faced by the actual inadequacy of the other groups, it alone can fulfil this indispensable office.

But for it to have this influence it must be organized on wholly different bases from those of today. First, it is essential that it become a definite and recognized organ of our public life, instead of remaining a private group legally permitted, but politically ignored. By this we do not mean that it must necessarily be made obligatory, but the important thing is for it to be so constituted as to play a social role instead of expressing only various combinations of particular interests. This is not all. For the frame not to remain empty, all the germs of life of such a nature as to flouish there must find their places in it. For this grouping to remain no mere label, it must be given definite functions, and there are some which it can fulfil better than any other agency.

At present, European societies have the alternative either of leaving occupational life unregulated, or of regulating it through the State's mediation, since no other organ exists which can play this role of moderator. But the State is too far removed from these complex manifestations to find the special form appropriate to each of them. It is a cumbersome machine, made only for general and clear-cut tasks. Its every uniform action cannot adapt and adjust itself to the infinite variety of special circumstances. It is therefore necessarily compressive and levelling in its action. On the other hand, we feel how impossible it is to leave unorganized all the life thus unattached. In so doing, by an endless series of oscillations we alternately pass from authoritarian regulation made impotent by its excessive rigidity to systematic abstention which cannot last because it breeds anarchy. Whether the question is one of hours of work, or health, or wages, or social insurance and assistance, men of good will constantly encounter the same difficulties. As soon as they try to set up some rules, they prove inapplicable to experience because they lack pliability; or at least, they apply to the matter for which they are made only by doing violence to it.

The only way to resolve this antinomy is to set up a cluster of collective forces outside the State, though subject to its action, whose regulative influence can be exerted with greater variety. Not only will our reconstituted corporations satisfy this condition, but it is hard to see what other groups could do so. For they are close enough to the facts, directly and constantly enough in contact with them, to detect all their nuances, and they should be sufficiently autonomous to be able to respect their diversity. To them, therefore, falls the duty of presiding over companies of insurance, benevolent aid and pensions, the need of which are felt by so many good minds but which we rightly hesitate to place in the hands of the State, already so powerful and awkward; theirs it should likewise be to preside over the disputes constantly arising between the branches of the same occupation, to fix conditions—but in different ways according to the different sorts of enterprise—with which contracts must agree in order to be valid, in the name of the common interest to prevent the strong from unduly exploiting the weak, etc. As labor is divided, law and morality assume a different form in each special function, though still resting everywhere on the same general principles. Besides the rights and duties common to all men, there are others depending on qualities peculiar to each occupation, the number of which increases in importance as occupational activity increasingly develops and diversifies. For each of these special disciplines an equally special organ is needed, to apply and maintain it. Of whom could it consist if not of the workers engaged in the same function?

Here, in broad outlines, is what corporations should be in order to render the services rightly to be expected of them. When their present state is considered, of course, it is somewhat hard to conceive of their ever being elevated to the dignity of moral powers. Indeed, they are made up of individuals attached to one another by no bond, with only superficial and intermittent relations, even inclined to treat each other rather as rivals and enemies than as cooperators. But when once they have so many things in common, when the relations between themselves and the group to which they belong are thus close and continuous, sentiments of solidarity as yet almost unknown will spring up, and the present cold moral temperature of this occupational environment, still so external to its members, would necessarily rise. And these changes would occur not only among the agents of economic life, as the above examples might lead one to believe. Every occupation in society would demand such an organization and be capable of receiving it. Thus the social fabric, the meshes of which are so dangerously relaxed, would tighten and be strengthened throughout its entire extent.

RELIGIOUS EXPERIENCE AND
RELIGIOUS ORGANIZATION

B Y

EMILE DURKHEIM

THE theorists who have undertaken to explain religion in rational terms have generally seen in it before all else a system of ideas, corresponding to some determined object. This object has been conceived in a multitude of ways: nature, the infinite, the unknowable, the ideal, etc.; but these differences matter but little. In any case, it was the conceptions and beliefs which were considered as the essential elements of religion. As for the rites, from this point of view they appear to be only an external translation, contingent and material, of these internal states which alone pass as having any intrinsic value. This conception is so commonly held that generally the disputes of which religion is the theme turn about the question whether it can conciliate itself with science or not, that is to say, whether or not there is a place beside our scientific knowledge for another form of thought which would be specifically religious.

But the believers, the men who lead the religious life and have a direct sensation of what it really is, object to this way of regarding it, saying that it does not correspond to their daily experience. In fact, they feel that the real function of religion is not to make us think, to enrich our knowledge, nor to add to the conceptions which we owe to science others of another origin and another character, but rather, it is to make us act, to aid us to live. The believer who has communicated with his god is not merely a man who sees new truths of which the unbeliever is ignorant; he is a man who is *stronger*. He feels within him more force, either to endure the trials of existence, or to conquer them. It is as though he were raised above the miseries of the world, because he is raised above his condition as a mere man; he believes that he is saved from evil, under whatever form he may conceive this evil. The first article in every creed is the belief in salvation by faith. But it is hard to see how a mere idea could have this efficacy. An idea is in reality only a part of ourselves; then how could it confer upon us

Reprinted by permission of the publisher, The Free Press, Glencoe, Illinois. Abridged from: Durkheim, Emile, *The Elementary Forms of the Religious Life* (translated by Joseph W. Swaine), London, 1915.

powers superior to those which we have of our own nature? Howsoever rich it might be in affective virtues, it could add nothing to our natural vitality; for it could only release the motive powers which are within us, neither creating them nor increasing them. From the mere fact that we consider an object worthy of being loved and sought after, it does not follow that we feel ourselves stronger afterwards; it is also necessary that this object set free energies superior to these which we ordinarily have at our command and also that we have some means of making these enter into us and unite themselves to our interior lives. Now for that, it is not enough that we think of them; it is also indispensable that we place ourselves within their sphere of action, and that we set ourselves where we may best feel their influence; in a word, it is necessary that we act, and that we repeat the acts thus necessary every time we feel the need of renewing their effects. From this point of view, it is readily seen how that group of regularly repeated acts which form the cult get their importance. In fact, whoever has really practised a religion knows very well that it is the cult which gives rise to these impressions of joy, of interior peace, of serenity, of enthusiasm which are, for the believer, an experimental proof of his beliefs. The cult is not simply a system of signs by which the faith is outwardly translated; it is a collection of the means by which this is created and recreated periodically. Whether it consists in material acts or mental operations, it is always this which is efficacious.

As we have progressed, we have established the fact that the fundamental categories of thought, and consequently of science, are of religious origin. The same is true for magic and consequently for the different processes which have issued from it. On the other hand, it has long been known that up until a relatively advanced moment of evolution, moral and legal rules have been indistinguishable from ritual prescriptions. In summing up, then, it may be said that nearly all the great social institutions have been born in religion.[1] Now in order that these principal aspects of the collective life may have commenced by being only varied aspects of the religious life, it is obviously necessary that the religious life be the eminent form and, as it were, the concentrated expression of the whole collective life. If religion has given birth to all that is essential in society, it is because the idea of society is the soul of religion.

[1] Only one form of social activity has not yet been expressly attached to religion: that is economic activity. Sometimes processes that are derived from magic have, by that fact alone, an origin that is indirectly religious. Also, economic value is a sort of power or efficacy, and we know the religious origins of the idea of power. Also, richness can confer *mana;* therefore it has it. Hence it is seen that the ideas of economic value and of religious value are not without connection. But the question of the nature of these connections has not yet been studied.

Religious forces are human forces, moral forces. It is true that since collective sentiments can become conscious of themselves only by fixing themselves upon external objects, they have not been able to take form without adopting some of their characteristics from other things: they have thus acquired a sort of physical nature; in this way they have come to mix themselves with the life of the material world, and then have considered themselves capable of explaining what passes there. But when they are considered only from this point of view and in this role, only their most superficial aspect is seen. In reality, the essential elements of which these collective sentiments are made have been borrowed by the understanding. It ordinarily seems that they should have a human character only when they are conceived under human forms; but even the most impersonal and the most anonymous are nothing else than objectified sentiments.

It is only by regarding religion from this angle that it is possible to see its real significance. If we stick closely to appearances, rites often give the effect of purely manual operations: they are anointings, washings, meals. To consecrate something, it is put in contact with a source of religious energy.

But, it is said, what society is it that has thus made the basis of religion? Is it the real society, such as it is and acts before our very eyes, with the legal and moral organization which it has laboriously fashioned during the course of history? This is full of defects and imperfections. In it, evil goes beside the good, injustice often reigns supreme, and the truth is often obscured by error. How could anything so crudely organized inspire the sentiments of love, the ardent enthusiasm and the spirit of abnegation which all religions claim of their followers? These perfect beings which are gods could not have taken their traits from so mediocre, and sometimes even so base a reality.

But, on the other hand, does someone think of a perfect society, where justice and truth would be sovereign, and from which evil in all its forms would be banished for ever? No one would deny that this is in close relations with the religious sentiment; for, they would say, it is towards the realization of this that all religions strive. But that society is not an empirical fact, definite and observable; it is a fancy, a dream with which men have lightened their sufferings, but in which they have never really lived. It is merely an idea which comes to express our more or less obscure aspirations towards the good, the beautiful and the ideal. Now these aspirations have their roots in us; they come from the very depths of our being; then there is nothing outside of us which can account for them. Moreover, they are already religious in themselves; thus it would seem that the ideal society pre-supposes religion, far from being able to explain it.

But, in the first place, things are arbitrarily simplified when religion is seen only on its idealistic side: in its way, it is realistic. There is no physical or moral ugliness, there are no vices or evils which do not have a special divinity. There are gods of theft and trickery, of lust and war, of sickness and of death. Christianity itself, howsoever high the idea which it has made of the divinity may be, has been obliged to give the spirit of evil a place in its mythology. Satan is an essential piece of the Christian system; even if he is an impure being, he is not a profane one. The anti-god is a god, inferior and subordinated, it is true, but nevertheless endowed with extended powers; he is even the object of rites, at least of negative ones. Thus religion, far from ignoring the real society and making abstraction of it, is in its image; it reflects all its aspects, even the most vulgar and the most repulsive. All is to be found there, and if in the majority of cases we see the good victorious over evil, life over death, the powers of light over the powers of darkness, it is because reality is not otherwise. If the relation between these two contrary forces were reversed, life would be impossible; but, as a matter of fact, it maintains itself and even tends to develop.

But if, in the midst of these mythologies and theologies we see reality clearly appearing, it is none the less true that it is found there only in an enlarged, transformed and idealized form. In this respect, the most primitive religions do not differ from the most recent and the most refined. The question now raises itself of whence this idealiza-tion comes.

The explanation of religion which we have proposed has precisely this advantage, that it gives an answer to this question. For our defini-tion of the sacred is that it is something added to and above the real: now the ideal answers to this same definition; we cannot explain one without explaining the other. In fact, we have seen that if collective life awakens religious thought on reaching a certain degree of intensity, it is because it brings about a state of effervescence which changes the conditions of psychic activity. Vital energies are over-excited, passions more active, sensations stronger; there are even some which are pro-duced only at this moment. A man does not recognize himself; he feels himself transformed and consequently he transforms the environ-ment which surrounds him. In order to account for the very particular impressions which he receives, he attributes to the things with which he is in most direct contact properties which they have not, exceptional powers and virtues which the objects of every-day experience do not possess. In a word, above the real world where his profane life passes he has placed another which, in one sense, does not exist except in thought, but to which he attributes a higher sort of dignity than to the first. Thus, from a double point of view it is an ideal world.

The formation of the ideal world is therefore not an irreducible fact which escapes science; it depends upon conditions which observation can touch; it is a natural product of social life. For a society to become conscious of itself and maintain at the necessary degree of intensity the sentiments which it thus attains, it must assemble and concentrate itself. Now this concentration brings about an exaltation of the mental life which takes form in a group of ideal conceptions where is portrayed the new life thus awakened; they correspond to this new set of psychical forces which is added to those which we have at our disposition for the daily tasks of existence. A society can neither create itself nor recreate itself without at the same time creating an ideal. This creation is not a sort of work of supererogation for it, by which it would complete itself, being already formed; it is the act by which it is periodically made and remade. Therefore when some oppose the ideal society to the real society, like two antagonists which would lead us in opposite directions, they materialize and oppose abstractions. The ideal society is not outside of the real society; it is a part of it. Far from being divided between them as between two poles which mutually repel each other, we cannot hold to one without holding to the other. For a society is not made up merely of the mass of individuals who compose it, the ground which they occupy, the things which they use and the movements which they perform, but above all is the idea which it forms of itself. It is undoubtedly true that it hesitates over the manner in which it ought to conceive itself; it feels itself drawn in divergent directions. But these conflicts which break forth are not between the ideal and reality, but between two different ideals, that of yesterday and that of to-day, that which has the authority of tradition and that which has the hope of the future. There is surely a place for investigating whence these ideals evolve; but whatever solution may be given to this problem, it still remains that all passes in the world of the ideal.

Thus the collective ideal which religion expresses is far from being due to a vague innate power of the individual, but it is rather at the school of collective life that the individual has learned to idealize. It is in assimilating the ideals elaborated by society that he has become capable of conceiving the ideal. It is society which, by leading him within its sphere of action, has made him acquire the need of raising himself above the world of experience and has at the same time furnished him with the means of conceiving another. For society has constructed this new world in constructing itself, since it is society which this expresses. Thus both with the individual and in the group, the faculty of idealizing has nothing mysterious about it. It is not a sort of luxury which a man could get along without, but a condition of his very existence. He could not be a social being, that is to say, he could not be a man, if he had not acquired it. It is true that in incarnating themselves in individuals, collective ideals tend to individualize themselves. Each understands them after his own fashion and marks them with his own stamp; he suppresses certain elements and adds others. Thus the personal ideal disengages itself from the social ideal in proportion as the individual personality develops itself and becomes an autonomous source of action. But if we wish to understand this aptitude, so singular in appearance, of living outside of reality, it is enough to connect it with the social conditions upon which it depends.

In showing that religion is something essentially social, we do not mean to say that it confines itself to translating into another language the material forms of society and its immediate vital necessities. It is true that we take it as evident that social life depends upon its material foundation and bears its mark, just as the mental life of an individual depends upon his nervous system and in fact his whole organism. But collective consciousness is something more than a mere epiphenomenon of its morphological basis, just as individual consciousness is something more than a simple efflorescence of the nervous system. In order that the former may appear, a synthesis *sui generis* of particular consciousnesses is required. Now this synthesis has the effect of disengaging a whole world of sentiments, ideas and images which, once born, obey laws all their own. They attract each other, repel each other, unite, divide themselves, and multiply, though these combinations are not commanded and necessitated by the condition of the underlying reality. The life thus brought into being even enjoys so great an independence that it sometimes indulges in manifestations with no purpose or utility of any sort, for the mere pleasure of affirming itself. This is often precisely the case with ritual activity and mythological thought.

But if religion is the product of social causes, how can we explain the individual cult and the universalistic character of certain religions? If it is the work of definite and individualized societies, how has it been able to detach itself from them, even to the point of being conceived as something common to all humanity?

We have shown how the religious force which animates the clan particularizes itself, by incarnating itself in particular consciousnesses. Thus secondary sacred beings are formed; each individual has his own, made in his own image, associated to his own intimate life, bound up with his own destiny; it is the soul, the individual totem, the protecting ancestor, etc. These beings are the object of rites which the individual can celebrate by himself, outside of any group; this is the first form of the individual cult. To be sure, it is only a very rudimentary cult; but since the personality of the individual is still only slightly marked, and but little value is attributed to it, the cult which expresses it could hardly be expected to be very highly developed as yet. But as individuals have differentiated themselves more and more and the value of an individual has increased, the corresponding cult has taken a relatively greater place in the totality of the religious life and at the same time it is more fully closed to outside influences.

Thus the existence of individual cults implies nothing which contradicts or embarrasses the sociological interpretation of religion; for the religious forces to which it addresses itself are only the individualized forms of collective forces. Therefore, even when religion seems to be entirely within the individual conscience, it is still in society that it finds the living source from which it is nourished. We are now able to appreciate the value of the radical individualism which would make religion something purely individual: it misunderstands the fundamental conditions of the religious life. If up to the present it has remained in the stage of theoretical aspirations which have never been realized, it is because it is unrealizable. A philosophy may well be elaborated in the silence of the interior imagination, but not so a faith. For before all else, a faith is warmth, life, enthusiasm, the exaltation of the whole mental life, the raising of the individual above himself. Now how could he add to the energies which he possesses without going outside himself? How could he surpass himself merely by his own forces? The only source of life at which we can morally reanimate ourselves is that formed by the society of our fellow beings; the only moral forces with which we can sustain and increase our own are those which we get from others. Let us even admit that there really are beings more or less analogous to those which the mythologies represent. In order that they may exercise over souls the useful direction which is their reason for existence, it is necessary that men believe in them. Now these beliefs are active only when they are partaken by many. A man cannot retain them any length of time by a purely personal effort; it is not thus that they are born or that they are acquired; it is even doubtful if they can be kept under these conditions. In fact, a man who has a veritable faith feels an invincible need of spreading it: therefore he leaves his isolation, approaches others and seeks to convince them, and it is the ardour of the convictions which he arouses that strengthens his own. It would quickly weaken if it remained alone.

It is the same with religious universalism as with this individualism. Far from being an exclusive attribute of certain very great religions, we have found it, not at the base, it is true, but at the summit of the Australian system.

If sacred beings are formed which are connected with no geographically determined society, that is not because they have an extrasocial origin. It is because there are other groups above these geographically determined ones, whose contours are less clearly marked: they have no fixed frontiers, but include all sorts of more or less neighbouring and related tribes. The particular social life thus created tends to spread itself over an area with no definite limits. Naturally the mythological personages who correspond to it have the same character; their sphere of influence is not limited; they go beyond the particular tribes and their territory. They are the great international gods.

There is no people and no state which is not a part of another society, more or less unlimited, which embraces all the peoples and all the States with which the first comes in contact, either directly or indirectly; there is no national life which is not dominated by a collective life of an international nature. In proportion as we advance in history, these international groups acquire a greater importance and extent. Thus we see how, in certain cases, this universalistic tendency has been able to develop itself to the point of affecting not only the higher ideas of the religious system, but even the principles upon which it rests.

Thus there is something eternal in religion which is destined to survive all the particular symbols in which religious thought has successively enveloped itself. There can be no society which does not feel the need of upholding and reaffirming at regular intervals the collective sentiments and the collective ideas which make its unity and its personality.

THE ORGANIZATION OF EFFORT

B Y

EDWARD A. ROSS

ORGANIZATION is an effective way of combining the efforts of many for the achievement of a common end. From planless, haphazard co-operation—settlers fighting a prairie fire or lynchers storming a jail—organization is approached by a number of steps. One is the submitting of like efforts to direction, as when planters fortify a levee against a flood or citizens come together as a sheriff's posse. Another is the combining, under direction, of unlike efforts, as in a barn-raising, a rabbit-drive, or road-building. When, as in railway operation, a military enveloping movement, or a fleet maneuver, the several diverse efforts must be very precisely timed and adjusted to one another, direction will be very minute and authoritative. If the work is difficult, an authority will be needed to assign tasks according to individual aptitude or skill, and, if the organization is permanent, to provide that individuals are especially trained for the performance of their special functions. In large organizations there appear subheads, deputies, and supervisors, so that a hierarchy of authority grows up, uniting the apex of the pyramid with the base. Finally, organizations may, with or without modification, be combined into larger organizations, and these, in turn, enter into still more comprehensive schemes.

The chief determinant of the character of organization is *the nature of the task*. If it is something to be *done,* say erect a building or move trains, an organization is called for, the parts of which work smoothly together like the wheels and levers of a machine. But if the purpose sought is the beneficial influence which members may exert upon one another, organization is merely a means of promoting association and fellowship.

Again, is the effect aimed at *physical* or *psychic*? In an organization dealing with brute matter, like a plantation or a factory, the spirit of the workers is by no means as important as in the case of a newspaper staff, an associated charities, a propagandist society, or the soliciting force of a life-insurance company—all of them working in the realm

Abridged from: Ross, Edward A., "The Organization of Effort," *American Journal of Sociology*, 1916, 22, 1–18. Reprinted by permission of the University of Chicago Press.

of *mind*. Sullen men who hate their work may still cut sugar cane or tend machines, but no one who feels himself to be a slave, a drudge, or a cogwheel can teach, persuade, or inspire. All organizations, therefore, which work on *people* rather than on *things* have to pay heed to the *morale* of their force. Obliged to rely on hope rather than dread to call forth the best powers of their workers, they must appease the demands of the latter to the point of contentment and supply motives which arouse the higher faculties to their tasks.

When life and death are at stake, responsibility must be definite, and strict obedience will be exacted even from an intelligent personnel. Still greater is the subordination required in dealing with tasks which are subject to crisis. When tremendous consequences for weal or woe hinge on what is done in a few hours, or even a few minutes, mistake and failure must be eliminated at all costs. A fighting force, then— whether it is to cope with foes, mobs, fires, surf, floods, or epidemics —tends toward a military organization. Not only is literal and prompt obedience enforced by severe penalties, but, in order that the right thing may be done in the emergency, it must be ingrained as habit. Hence, all organizations which are subject to *crisis* make much of *drill*.

Military organization, just because it reached a high development as early as the middle of the eighteenth century, has unfortunately served as pattern for later types of organization which are not subject to the strain of crisis. Hence, in government bureaus and in business administration has prevailed the false idea that the usefulness of the subordinate to his superior consists in executing orders and furnishing reports. It is irrational, however, to repress the natural doubts, queries, or remonstrances of the intelligent and loyal subordinate in a non-fighting organization. The higher may well consult with the lower, while retaining the power to decide. Question or criticism or demur from the intelligent under-man, with reference to orders or policies that seem unworkable, ought not to be treated as if it were the murmur of a soldier under fire against the commands of his officer.

In sharpest contrast to the discipline imposed by crisis stands monastic discipline, which is imposed not by the needs of a common task but by the difficulty of realizing the religious life. Under the Rule of St. Benedict, the disobedient and unruly monk should secretly be warned by the deacon once, and again. If this warning prove fruitless, he should be shut off from the common table or from common prayer. In the case of a serious misdeed the monk is also forbidden intercourse with the other monks; but, in order that no offender should be driven into obstinacy, the elder monks, with the permission of the abbot, should sometimes approach him to comfort him and try to move him to repentance. A monk hardened in wickedness should suffer bodily punishment; if this is unavailing, the abbot with all the monastery should pray for his recovery. If he remains obstinate, he should be turned out of the monastery. If a monk who has been turned out sees his fault and prays penitently to be taken in again, his wish should be granted to him, even to three times; but the fallen monk should prove his humility by taking the lowest place.

No working organization could afford to be so patient with a recalcitrant.

Again, does or does not the task in hand put a great strain on ordinary human nature? The more it does so the stricter will be the discipline, the harsher the penalties for disobedience. This is the culminating reason why military discipline is more methodical than any other, why rigid training is so insisted on for a man of so little skill as the common soldier. To build a habit that shall hold him steady before the cannon's mouth and cold steel—this is the reason for the endless drill, the rhythmic regularity, the automatic obedience exacted by the makers of armies.

The monk like the soldier is under a strain, but the end sought is utterly different. Military organization has in view physical action, while monastic organization is for the sake of the spiritual life. Hence, the rules of the former are clear-cut, to be carried out without hesitation; while the rules of the latter, though in their effects on personality far more gripping than military rules, are undefined in outline, fluid, subtle, complicated by particular circumstances, as one would expect when it is the soul that is to be controlled and not simply the body.

Finally, a distinction is to be made between a working group the members of which from long practice have gained a smooth team play and one in which each man may readily be replaced. When, as in a football team or an orchestra, the members of an organization have become mutually adapted to one another, the dismissal of one hurts the whole, so that discipline will be milder than in an organization of interchangeable parts.

Another determinant of organization is *the character of the organized*. Men who appreciate the indispensableness of plan and order in great undertakings will, without in the least lowering their self-respect, render due obedience to their superiors. The more intelligent, therefore, the rank and file of an organization the less is the need of prestige and severity in order to uphold the authority of the superior. An army can never be a mass meeting or a debating society, but democrats may be organized into a well-disciplined fighting force without losing their sense of civic equality. Likewise the head of a school system, a hospital, or a bureau, while he must command the confidence of his teachers, nurses, and agents, is not obliged to inspire them with fear or awe in order to get his plans carried out.

Unpaid workers cannot be disciplined by the crude methods of reprimand, fine, lay-off, demotion, or dismissal, but must be reached through *esprit de corps* or conscience. The means of discipline—entreaty, rebuke, isolation, prayer, warning, and suspension—are not punishments so much as appeals to conscience. The contrast between exacted and volunteer service is so broad that the executive who has conducted with success military or industrial organization may fail ignominiously when directing a body of scholars, missionaries, or social workers.

A third determinant of organization is the *spacing between the organized*. Men fall more readily into the grades imposed by the technique of associated effort if they are already spaced. Thus the relation of superior to subordinate chafes little if the former is older. Sex reinforces age in making it easy for the male school superintendent to direct the work of young women teachers and for the male doctor to hold in obedience young women nurses.

Special knowledge and training set apart their possessor.

Finally, it makes a difference whether the controlling purpose in an organization is *the doing of a worth-while work* or *the maximizing of profits*. As a rule, capable workers become interested in some concrete aspect of what they are doing.

THE BENEFITS OF ORGANIZATION

The benefits of organization are unmistakable. Among them are:

1. The accomplishment of ends which are quite unattainable by means of unorganized efforts becomes possible.

2. A common interest cared for intermittently by all—such as fire-fighting, thief-catching, levee-mending, or road-making—may be turned over to the continuous efforts of a few who have gained skill from experience or fitted themselves by a preliminary training.

3. The division of a work into its natural parts and the assignment of these to different individuals permit the utmost advantage to be taken of special aptitude, knowledge, or training. Conversely, men with particular weak points may keep to lines of work in which they are not handicapped by them.

4. Narrowing the field of attention is favorable to the attainment of a higher degree of expertness. Thus we see a deliberative body resolve itself into committees, each to study and report upon a particular class of questions. Not public bodies alone, but civic, commercial, and scientific bodies as well, organize themselves on the committee plan.

5. Many distinct efforts are fitted into a single comprehensive, intelligent plan. Ordinarily those who plan a work direct its execution, but there is a tendency to form a thinking and planning branch of the administrative body, which advises but does not execute. This is the "general staff," a device used first in the army, but suitable for other kinds of organization.

6. Co-ordination into a larger whole ends that needless duplication of effort which often shows itself among agencies which are striving for the same end.

7. Elimination of the wastes of competition is possible.

8. Serving as a useful part in a great beneficent, permanent organization supplies some men with a large superpersonal end which appeals to their imagination and sustains them in their life work.

9. Not all men are fit for solitary work. Many a man finds in working on a team an inspiration and a stimulus he can find nowhere else. The fellowship of his mates, the leadership of his superior, the spur of rivalry, and the hope of promotion provide powerful incentives which he would miss as an isolated worker.

THE WASTES OF ORGANIZATION

But the gains through organization are subject to deduction on account of the wastes to which it gives rise:

1. In a team or gang, the man who directs is also a doer, but, as the group becomes larger, there comes a time when he drops his tools, and from that moment begins the burden of "overhead expense."

2. In an organization that has not outgrown the powers of one man, the manager's eye checks waste of time and material, and his memory holds the records by which the competent worker is promoted or the poor worker dismissed. But in the big concern there must be installed an elaborate system of record, check, and audit which constitutes another deduction from the operative force. In extended organization the subordinate with his heart in his task chafes under the necessity of making entries, filling out forms, filing memoranda, and writing reports which do not in the least advance the work he has in hand.

3. Not without loss is energy transmitted through a series of shafts, belts, or cogwheels; nor is it possible for the intelligent purposes of the heads of elaborate organizations to be carried out without waste through friction between the parts. The center forms no true picture of the situation confronting the extremities. Orders are misunderstood or lose in force as they descend in the chain of authority.

4. A tendency to formalism and red tape is to be noted.

5. There is, finally, the relative inflexibility of all machinery composed of numerous correlated parts. No complex organization is

prompt to adapt itself to rapidly changing conditions. Individuals who by themselves might quickly change their activities or their methods find themselves locked, as it were, in an iron system.

THE ABUSES OF ORGANIZATION

Organization is furthermore liable to be abused in various ways:

1. Executives may misapply for personal ends the power which has been given them for the good of the work. Nepotism may govern appointments and promotions. The head of a central organization may encroach on the local chapters under pretext of efficiency, but really from craving for power. Superior may misuse his authority over subordinate to gratify his lust of domination, to exact a tribute of flattery, to indulge a personal spite, to keep down a possible rival, or to cover up his own shortcomings.

2. When an executive attempts to keep everything under his hat-band, he comes to lean too much upon his immediate helpers. The result is that his chief clerk handles communications to department heads who are his official superiors, and matters of moment may hinge on the decision of a mere office subordinate. This tendency of executives to assume responsibility for more matters than one man can cope with amounts, in fact, to an evasion of responsibility. The local mine manager justifies himself by showing that during the labor war he was continually reporting to his distant chief, while this over-burdened chief pleads ignorance of the lawless policies pursued by his subordinate. Between the two stools real responsibility comes to the ground.

3. It is pleasanter to be near the apex of the pyramid than the base. There is, therefore, a constant tendency for organizations to become top-heavy—too many officers for the privates, too many planners and supervisors and too few doers, too many dawdlers about headquarters or the main office and too few at the front, on the road, on the firing-line, at the railhead, behind the crowbar, or before the mast.

4. Men in different departments of a large organization may become too specialized to take one another's viewpoint or to work smoothly together. The staff officer becomes eccentric and overbearing, while the line officer is too busy getting things done to think out the principles underlying his work or to originate better methods. Over-specialization may be prevented by rotating men through related functions.

5. The organization becomes an end in itself rather than a means. In general, it is outside, not inside, forces which keep an organization in proper relation to its work and to other interests of society.

THE SACRIFICES ORGANIZATION REQUIRES

Human nature shaped by a primitive life in the woods does not easily meet the conditions of technical efficiency. Night duty, monotonous toil, and sedentary work are to most of us made tolerable only by habit. Still greater is the strain of being a cog in some intricate machine. Unquestioning obedience, for instance—how revolting it is at first to any intelligent person! Team harness may be cruelly galling to such as are not quick at personal adjustment. Punctuality, schedule, method, regularity of stroke, standardized performance—these surely go against the native grain. Machinery should be built of metal, not of living, plastic beings.

Hence, there ought always to be reserved a large place for those who in organization feel like squirrels in cages, those to whom freedom and spontaneity are the breath of life. Society should leave a broad footing for the solitary worker who labors when and where and as he pleases. Under excess of routine we tend to become wooden and unresponsive, so that the artist type, that depends on mood and whim, that waits for the moment of inspiration, will be needed to revive and freshen us as the system of group labor extends.

INTERNAL PROBLEMS

Organization in general has been so little considered philosophically that it abounds in unsettled problems. Only a few of them can be stated here:

1. As regards the selection and placement of men, it is not always best that the man in charge of a work should pick his helpers unaided. The master of a technique may be a poor judge of men. Not only is it costly to "tryout" the unfit man, but often the man who has failed in one post would succeed in some other place in the organization. The difficulty of getting the round peg into the round hole and the square peg into the square hole is so great that some organizations, in adding to their personnel, call in the experimental psychologist or the character expert.

2. A vacancy to be filled raises the question: "New blood or promotion?" The shortsighted executive imports a seasoned outsider "who can do the work." This policy deadens the force and in the long run deters the capable from joining. To the more enterprising in an organization the prospect of rising is the only thing in it which lends interest to the future. Otherwise the years stretch away in full view to retirement, pension, and death. A cut-and-dried future is revolting to the high-spirited, although it may attract the plodder. Chance of advancement introduces that element of adventure, of surprise, which

induces the ambitious young man to enter army, navy, public service, or corporate service, instead of carving out a career for himself.

In a well-built organization there will be no "blind-alley" or "dead-end" jobs, leading to nothing. Normal promotion routes—with short cuts for the very exceptional man and cross-paths for one who changes his goal—should be worked out for every position, and posted charts showing such routes should vizualize to each worker his path of possible advancement. The prick of the spur will be sharpest when selection for advancement is made on merit as revealed in carefully kept records of each man's performance. In order to dispense with the need of calling in the outsider—except to start a new line of work—each man should train his best subordinate into an understudy for himself, and his own promotion should hinge in part on his producing a man competent to fill his shoes.

3. The isolated worker has the natural incentive to growth, but in a fixed system the supplying of incentive has to be carefully considered. The appeal to fear is the first resource of the dull, unimaginative manager. Hence, in keying up performance, much more has been made of punishment than of attraction. Yet the low productiveness of all slave labor in comparison with free labor ought to have made it clear that the normal man can be led at a faster pace than he can be driven.

Graduated reward lures one to do his utmost. Pay, in addition to a fixed element, should include an element varying with one's efficiency or with one's length of service. Insurance, permanency of employment, and retiring allowance after a term of service leave good men free to do their best work.

Since honor is coveted as well as money, honor should be as carefully graduated and as punctually paid. A non-discriminating treatment of those on different rungs of the organization ladder flings away a precious means of stimulation. In order to whet the eagerness to earn advancement, something, however slight, should be used to distinguish men of each grade from those below. It may be a uniform, a stripe, a band of gold braid, a cap, or a button. It may be the right of precedence, of dining at a reserved table, entering by a special door, sitting on a higher seat, or having one's desk behind a railing or on a raised floor. It may be the privilege of sitting in the presence of the top man, of being addressed as "Mr." or "Sir," of receiving a certain salute, or of donning a certain robe. Whatever be the mark of honor, it should be patent without being conspicuous, its value should be symbolic rather than intrinsic, it should be certain to him who is entitled to it, and it should be consistently withheld from all others.

Pitting a man against his record or pitting gang against gang, shop against shop, branch office against branch office, school against school, battleship against battleship, rouses the spirit of emulation.

4. In contrast to the fostering of loyalty and *esprit de corps* the earliest authorities made little use of "imponderables." "Hear, tremble, and obey" was supposed to provide every incentive. But as we learn more about human nature more heed is given to the spirit of the rank and file.

It is something if the body to which one belongs is believed to render a valuable service to society. It is better yet if this value is openly recognized so that one feels himself a member of a popular and honorable organization. When the soldier's uniform commands respect, when a university is old and famous, *esprit de corps* comes of itself. Even street sweepers develop it after the public has been taught to appreciate the work of the street-cleaning department.

If the chiefs keep all the glory that comes from the achievement of their organization, the underlings have the deadening sense of being mere instruments.

The rivalry of one organization with another soon kindles *esprit de corps*.

CENTRALIZATION

In extended organization it is a problem how far the local body should be subordinated to the general body. History shows a marked drift of authority from the local toward the general.

Owing to chance, circumstances, and faults of leaders, any local association for general objects is subject to vagary and fatuousness unless it is steadied by membership in a general organization, which of necessity has attained to clear-cut aims and rational methods. Possessing the advantages of experience, breadth of view, and able leaders, the general organization may well exercise control over the local.

Although, as we have seen, the characteristics of an organization flow primarily from the nature of the task, there is, nevertheless, a tendency for organizations to agree in pattern. The principle of the dominant organization or organizations is likely to reappear in all the rest. Thus if, in government, the relation of superior to subordinate is purely authoritative, this spirit may be expected to prevail in family, school, church, business, industry, and voluntary associations. If, on the other hand, government admits into this relation a consultative element, something like it will be found in most other organizations in society.

We have seen that the requirements of combined effort go rather against the native grain. As organization comes to embrace more of us, certain adjustments are necessary if human beings are not to become painfully warped. The more one's work conforms to plan, or pattern, or orders the more one's manner of life and one's disposal of leisure time must be relied on to nourish and to express an individuality. This is why that unity in moral and religious ideas and in ground pattern of life which has sometimes worked out quite well among a peasant or fisher folk is an utterly impossible and undesirable ideal for a people subject to the trying discipline of modern organization.

CHAPTER 11

Community

———————•◦•———————

STRUCTURE AND PROCESS IN THE CITY

BY

ROBERT E. PARK

THE city, from the point of view of this paper, is something more than a congeries of individual men and of social conveniences—streets, buildings, electric lights, tramways, and telephones, etc.; something more, also, than a mere constellation of institutions and administrative devices—courts, hospitals, schools, police, and civil functionaries of various sorts. The city is, rather, a state of mind, a body of customs and traditions, and of the organized attitudes and sentiments that inhere in these customs and are transmitted with this tradition. The city is not, in other words, merely a physical mechanism and an artificial construction. It is involved in the vital processes of the people who compose it; it is a product of nature, and particularly of human nature.

The city has been studied, in recent times, from the point of view of its geography, and still more recently from the point of view of its ecology. There are forces at work within the limits of the urban community—within the limits of any natural area of human habitation, in fact—which tend to bring about an orderly and typical grouping of its population and institutions. The science which seeks to isolate these factors and to describe the typical constellations of

Abridged from: Park, Robert E., "The City: Suggestions for the Investigation of Human Behavior in the Urban Environment," *American Journal of Sociology*, 1916, 20, 577–612. Reprinted by permission of the University of Chicago Press.

persons and institutions which the co-operation of these forces produces, is what we call human, as distinguished from plant and animal, ecology.

Transportation and communication, tramways and telephones, newspapers and advertising, steel construction and elevators—all things, in fact, which tend to bring about at once a greater mobility and a greater concentration of the urban populations—are primary factors in the ecological organization of the city.

The city is not, however, merely a geographical and ecological unit; it is at the same time an economic unit. The economic organization of the city is based on the division of labor. The multiplication of occupations and professions within the limits of the urban population is one of the most striking and least understood aspects of modern city life. From this point of view, we may, if we choose, think of the city, that is to say, the place and the people, with all the machinery and administrative devices that go with them, as organically related; a kind of psychophysical mechanism in and through which private and political interests find not merely a collective but a corporate expression.

Much of what we ordinarily regard as the city—its charters, formal organization, buildings, street railways, and so forth—is, or seems to be, mere artifact. But these things in themselves are utilities, adventitious devices which become part of the living city only when, and in so far as, through use and wont they connect themselves, like a tool in the hand of man, with the vital forces resident in individuals and in the community.

The city is, finally, the natural habitat of civilized man. It is for that reason a cultural area characterized by its own peculiar cultural type.

Anthropology, the science of man, has been mainly concerned up to the present with the study of primitive peoples. But civilized man is quite as interesting an object of investigation, and at the same time his life is more open to observation and study. Urban life and culture are more varied, subtle, and complicated, but the fundamental motives are in both instances the same.

We are mainly indebted to writers of fiction for our more intimate knowledge of contemporary urban life. But the life of our cities demands a more searching and disinterested study than even Émile Zola has given us in his "experimental" novels and the annals of the Rougon-Macquart family.

We need such studies, if for no other reason than to enable us to read the newspapers intelligently. The reason that the daily chronicle of the newspaper is so shocking, and at the same time so fascinating, to the average reader is because the average reader knows so little about the life of which the newspaper is the record.

The observations which follow are intended to define a point of view and to indicate a program for the study of urban life: its physical organization, its occupations, and its culture.

I. THE CITY PLAN AND LOCAL ORGANIZATION

The city, particularly the modern American city, strikes one at first blush as so little a product of the artless processes of nature and growth, that it is difficult to recognize it as a living entity. The ground plan of most American cities, for example, is a checkerboard. The unit of distance is the block. This geometrical form suggests that the city is a purely artificial construction which might conceivably be taken apart and put together again, like a house of blocks.

The fact is, however, that the city is rooted in the habits and customs of the people who inhabit it. The consequence is that the city possesses a moral as well as a physical organization, and these two mutually interact in characteristic ways to mold and modify one another. It is the structure of the city which first impresses us by its visible vastness and complexity. But this structure has its basis, nevertheless, in human nature, of which it is an expression. On the other hand, this vast organization which has arisen in response to the needs of its inhabitants, once formed, imposes itself upon them as a crude external fact, and forms them, in turn, in accordance with the design and interests which it incorporates. Structure and tradition are but different aspects of a single cultural complex which determines what is characteristic and peculiar to city, as distinguished from village, life and the life of the open fields.

The city plan.—It is because the city has a life quite its own that there is a limit to the arbitrary modifications which it is possible to make (1) in its physical structure and (2) in its moral order.

The city plan, for example, establishes metes and bounds, fixes in a general way the location and character of the city's constructions, and imposes an orderly arrangement, within the city area, upon the buildings which are erected by private initiative as well as by public authority. Within the limitations prescribed, however, the inevitable processes of human nature proceed to give these regions and these buildings a character which it is less easy to control. Under our system of individual ownership, for instance, it is not possible to determine in advance the extent of concentration of population which is likely to occur in any given area. The city cannot fix land values, and we leave to private enterprise, for the most part, the task of determining the city's limits and the location of its residential and industrial districts. Personal tastes and convenience, vocational and economic interests, infallibly tend to segregate and thus to classify the populations of great cities. In this way the city acquires an organization and distribution of population which is neither designed nor controlled.

Physical geography, natural advantages and disadvantages, including means of transportation, determine in advance the general outlines of the urban plan. As the city increases in population, the subtler influences of sympathy, rivalry, and economic necessity tend to control the distribution of population. Business and industry seek advantageous locations and draw around them certain portions of the population. There spring up fashionable residence quarters from which the poorer classes are excluded because of the increased value of the land. Then there grow up slums which are inhabited by great numbers of the poorer classes who are unable to defend themselves from association with the derelict and vicious.

In the course of time every section and quarter of the city takes on something of the character and qualities of its inhabitants. Each separate part of the city is inevitably stained with the peculiar sentiments of its population. The effect of this is to convert what was at first a mere geographical expression into a neighborhood, that is to say, a locality with sentiments, traditions, and a history of its own. Within this neighborhood the continuity of the historical processes is somehow maintained. The past imposes itself upon the present, and the life of every locality moves on with a certain momentum of its own, more or less independent of the larger circle of life and interests about it.

The organization of the city, the character of the urban environment and of the discipline which it imposes is finally determined by the size of the population, its concentration and distribution within the city area. For this reason it is important to study the growth of cities, to compare the idiosyncrasies in the distribution of city populations.

The neighborhood.—Proximity and neighborly contact are the basis for the simplest and most elementary form of association with which we have to do in the organization of city life. Local interests and associations breed local sentiment, and, under a system which makes residence the basis for participation in the government, the neighborhood becomes the basis of political control. In the social and political organization of the city it is the smallest local unit.

The neighborhood exists without formal organization. The local improvement society is a structure erected on the basis of the spontaneous neighborhood organization and exists for the purpose of giving expression to the local sentiment in regard to matters of local interest.

Under the complex influences of the city life, what may be called the normal neighborhood sentiment has undergone many curious and interesting changes, and produced many unusual types of local communities. More than that, there are nascent neighborhoods and neighborhoods in process of dissolution.

It is important to know what are the forces which tend to break up the tensions, interests, and sentiments which give neighborhoods their individual character. In general these may be said to be anything and everything that tends to render the population unstable, to divide and concentrate attentions upon widely separated objects of interest.

On the other hand, certain urban neighborhoods suffer from isolation. Efforts have been made at different times to reconstruct and quicken the life of city neighborhoods and to bring them in touch with the larger interests of the community. Such is, in part, the purpose of the social settlements. These organizations and others which are attempting to reconstruct city life have developed certain methods and a technique for stimulating and controlling local communities. We should study, in connection with the investigation of these agencies, these methods and this technique, since it is just the method by which objects are practically controlled that reveals their essential nature, that is to say, their predictable character (*Gesetzmässigkeit*).

Colonies and segregated areas.—In the city environment the neighborhood tends to lose much of the significance which it possessed in simpler and more primitive forms of society. The easy means of communication and of transportation, which enable individuals to distribute their attention and to live at the same time in several different worlds, tend to destroy the permanency and intimacy of the neighborhood. On the other hand, the isolation of the immigrant and racial colonies of the so-called ghettos and areas of population segregation tend to preserve and, where there is racial prejudice, to intensify the intimacies and solidarity of the local and neighborhood groups. Where individuals of the same race or of the same vocation live together in segregated groups, neighborhood sentiment tends to fuse together with racial antagonisms and class interests.

Physical and sentimental distances reinforce each other, and the influences of local distribution of the population participate with the influences of class and race in the evolution of the social organization. Every great city has its racial colonies. In addition to these, most cities have their segregated vice districts, their rendezvous for criminals of various sorts. Every large city has its occupational suburbs, and its residential enclaves, each of which has the size and character of a complete separate town, village, or city, except that its population is a selected one.

In the older cities of Europe, where the processes of segregation have gone farther, neighborhood distinctions are likely to be more marked than they are in America. East London is a city of a single class, but within the limits of that city the population is segregated again and again by racial, cultural, and vocational interests. Neighborhood sentiment, deeply rooted in local tradition and in local custom, exercises a decisive selective influence upon the populations of the older European cities and shows itself ultimately in a marked way in the characteristics of the inhabitants.

II. INDUSTRIAL ORGANIZATION AND THE MORAL ORDER

The ancient city was primarily a fortress, a place of refuge in time of war. The modern city, on the contrary, is primarily a convenience of commerce, and owes its existence to the market place around which it sprang up. Industrial competition and the division of labor, which have probably done most to develop the latent powers of mankind, are possible only upon condition of the existence of markets, of money, and other devices for the facilitation of trade and commerce.

An old German adage declares that "city air makes men free" (*Stadt Luft macht frei*). This is doubtless a reference to the days when the free cities of Germany enjoyed the patronage of the emperor, and laws made the fugitive serf a free man if he succeeded for a year and a day in breathing city air. Law, of itself, could not, however, have made the craftsman free. An open market in which he might sell the products of his labor was a necessary incident of his freedom, and it was the application of the money economy to the relations of master and man that completed the emancipation of the serf.

Vocational classes and vocational types.—The old adage which describes the city as the natural environment of the free man still holds so far as the individual man finds in the chances, the diversity of interests and tasks, and in the vast unconscious co-operation of city life the opportunity to choose his own vocation and develop his peculiar individual talents. The city offers a market for the special talents of individual men. Personal competition tends to select for each special task the individual who is best suited to perform it.

The difference of natural talents in different men is, in reality, much less than we are aware of; and the very different genius which appears to distinguish men of different professions, when grown up to maturity, is not upon many occasions so much the cause, as the effect of the division of labour. The difference between the most dissimilar characters, between a philosopher and a common street porter, for example, seems to arise not so much from nature, as from habit, custom, and education. When they came into the world, and for the first six or eight years of their existence, they were perhaps very much alike, and neither their parents nor playfellows could perceive any remarkable difference. About that age, or soon after, they come to be employed in different occupations. The difference of talents comes then to be taken notice of, and widens by degrees, till at last the vanity of the philosopher is willing to acknowledge scarce any resemblance. But without the disposition to truck, barter, and exchange, every man must have procured to himself every necessary and conveniency of life which he wanted. All must have had the same duties to perform, and the same work to do, and there could have been no such difference of employment as could alone give occasion to any great difference of talent. . . .

As it is the power of exchanging that gives occasion to the division of labour, so the extent of this division must always be limited by the extent of that power, or, in other words, by the extent of the market. . . . There are some sorts of industry, even of the lowest kind, which can be carried on nowhere but in a great town.[1]

Success, under conditions of personal competition, depends upon concentration upon some single task, and this concentration stimulates the demand for rational methods, technical devices, and exceptional skill. Exceptional skill, while based on natural talent, requires special preparation, and it has called into existence the trade and professional schools, and finally bureaus for vocational guidance. All of these, either directly or indirectly, serve at once to select and emphasize individual differences.

Every device which facilitates trade and industry prepares the way for a further division of labor and so tends further to specialize the tasks in which men find their vocations.

The outcome of this process is to break down or modify the older social and economic organization of society, which was based on family ties, local associations, on culture, caste, and status, and to substitute for it an organization based on occupation and vocational interests.

In the city every vocation, even that of a beggar, tends to assume

[1] Adam Smith, *The Wealth of Nations*, pp. 28–29.

the character of a profession and the discipline which success in any vocation imposes, together with the associations that it enforces, emphasizes this tendency—the tendency, namely, not merely to specialize, but to rationalize one's occupation and to develop a specific and conscious technique for carrying it on.

The effect of the vocations and the division of labor is to produce, in the first instance, not social groups, but vocational types: the actor, the plumber, and the lumber-jack. The organizations, like the trade and labor unions which men of the same trade or profession form, are based on common interests. In this respect they differ from forms of association like the neighborhood, which are based on contiguity, personal association, and the common ties of humanity. The different trades and professions seem disposed to group themselves in classes, that is to say, the artisan, business, and professional classes. But in the modern democratic state the classes have as yet attained no effective organization. Socialism, founded on an effort to create an organization based on "class consciousness," has never succeeded, except, perhaps, in Russia, in creating more than a political party.

The effects of the division of labor as a discipline, i.e., as means of molding character, may therefore be best studied in the vocational types it has produced. Among the types which it would be interesting to study are: the shopgirl, the policeman, the peddler, the cabman, the nightwatchman, the clairvoyant, the vaudeville performer, the quack doctor, the bartender, the ward boss, the strikebreaker, the labor agitator, the school teacher, the reporter, the stockbroker, the pawnbroker; all of these are characteristic products of the conditions of city life; each, with its special experience, insight, and point of view determines for each vocational group and for the city as a whole its individuality.

News and the mobility of the social group.—The division of labor, in making individual success dependent upon concentration upon a special task, has had the effect of increasing the interdependence of the different vocations. A social organization is thus created in which the individual becomes increasingly dependent upon the community of which he is an integral part. The effect, under conditions of personal competition, of this increasing interdependence of the parts is to create in the industrial organization as a whole a certain sort of social solidarity, but a solidarity based, not on sentiment and habit, but on community of interests.

In the sense in which the terms are here used, sentiment is the more concrete, interest the more abstract, term. We may cherish a sentiment for a person, a place, or any object whatsoever. It may be a sentiment of aversion, or a sentiment of possession. But to possess or to be possessed by a sentiment for, or in regard to, anything means that we are incapable of acting toward it in a thoroughly rational way. It means that the object of our sentiment corresponds in some special way to some inherited or acquired disposition. Such a disposition is the affection of a mother for her child, or even the feeling she may have for the child's empty cradle.

The existence of a sentimental attitude indicates that there are motives for action of which the individual who is moved by them is not wholly conscious; motives over which he has only a partial control. Every sentiment has a history, either in the experience of the individual, or in the experience of the race, but the person who acts on that sentiment may not be aware of the history.

Interests are directed less toward specific objects than toward the ends which this or that particular object at one time or another embodies. Interests imply, therefore, the existence of means and a consciousness of the distinction between means and ends. Our sentiments are related to our prejudices, and prejudices may attach to anything—persons, races, as well as inanimate things. Prejudices are related also to taboos, and so tend to maintain "social distances" and the existing social organization. Sentiment and prejudice are elementary forms of conservatism. Our interests are rational and mobile, and make for change.

Money is the cardinal device by which values have become rationalized and sentiments have been replaced by interests. It is just because we feel no personal and no sentimental attitude toward our money, such as we do toward, for example, our home, that money becomes a valuable means of exchange. We will be interested in acquiring a certain amount of money in order to achieve a certain purpose, but provided that purpose may be achieved in any other way we are likely to be just as well satisfied. It is only the miser who becomes sentimental about money, and in that case he is likely to prefer one sort of money, say gold, to another, irrespective of its value. In this case the value of gold is determined by personal sentiment rather than by reason.

An organization which is composed of competing individuals and of competing groups of individuals is in a state of unstable equilibrium, and this equilibrium can be maintained only by a process of continuous readjustment. This aspect of social life and this type of social organization are best represented in the world of business which is the special object of investigation of political economy.

The extension of industrial organization, which is based on the impersonal relations defined by money, has gone forward hand in hand with an increasing mobility of the population. The laboring man and the artisan fitted to perform a specific task are compelled, under the conditions created by city life, to move from one region to another in search of the particular kind of employment which they are fitted to perform. The tide of immigration which moves back and forth between Europe and America is to some extent a measure of this same mobility.

On the other hand, the tradesman, the manufacturer, the professional man, the specialist in every vocation, seeks his clients as the difficulties of travel and communication decrease over an ever widening area of territory. This is another way in which the mobility of the population may be measured. However, mobility in an individual or in a population is measured, not merely by change of location, but rather by the number and variety of the stimulations to which the individual or the population responds. Mobility depends, not merely upon transportation, but upon communication. Education and the ability to read, the extension of the money economy to an ever increasing number of the interests of life, in so far as it has tended to depersonalize social relations, has at the same time vastly increased the mobility of modern peoples.

The term "mobility," like its correlative, "isolation," covers a wide range of phenomena. It may represent at the same time a character and a condition. As isolation may be due to the existence of purely physical barriers to communication, or to a peculiarity of temperament and a lack of education, so mobility may be a consequence of the natural means of communication or of an agreeable manner and a college education.

It is now clearly recognized that what we ordinarily call a lack of intelligence in individuals, races, and communities is frequently a result of isolation. On the other hand, the mobility of a population is unquestionably a very large factor in its intellectual development.

There is an intimate connection between the immobility of the primitive man and his so-called inability to use abstract ideas. The knowledge which a peasant ordinarily possesses, from the very nature of his occupation, is concrete and personal. He knows individually and personally every member of the flock he tends. He becomes in the course of years so attached to the land he tills that the mere transposition from the strip of soil on which he has grown up to another with which he is less intimately acquainted is felt by him as a personal loss. For such a man the neighboring valley, or even the strip of land at the other end of the village is in a certain sense alien territory. A large part of the peasant's efficiency as an agricultural laborer depends upon this intimate and personal acquaintance with the idiosyncrasies of a single plot of land to the care of which he has been bred. It is apparent that, under conditions like these, very little of the peasant's practical knowledge will take the abstract form of scientific generalization. He thinks in concrete terms because he knows and needs no other.

On the other hand, the intellectual characteristics of the Jew and his generally recognized interests in abstract and radical ideas are unquestionably connected with the fact that the Jews are, before all else, a city folk. The "Wandering Jew" acquires abstract terms with which to describe the various scenes which he visits. His knowledge of the world is based upon identities and differences, that is to say, on analysis and classification. Reared in intimate association with the bustle and business of the market place, constantly intent on the shrewd and fascinating game of buying and selling, in which he employs that most interesting of abstractions, money, he has neither opportunity nor inclination to cultivate that intimate attachment to places and persons which is characteristic of the immobile person.[2]

Concentration of populations in cities, the wider markets, the division of labor, the concentration of individuals and groups on special tasks, have continually changed the material conditions of life, and in doing this have made readjustments to novel conditions increasingly necessary. Out of this necessity there have grown up a number of special organizations which exist for the special purpose of facilitating these readjustments. The market which brought the modern city into existence is one of these devices. More interesting, however, are the exchanges, particularly the stock exchange and the board of trade, where prices are constantly being made in response to changes, or rather the reports of changes, in economic conditions all over the world.

These reports, so far as they are calculated to cause readjustments, have the character of what we call news. It is the existence of a critical situation which converts what were otherwise mere information into news. Where there is an issue at stake, where, in short, there is crisis, there information which might affect the outcome one way or another becomes "live matter," as the newspaper men say. Live matter is news; dead matter is mere information.

The stock exchanges and the mob.—The exchanges, upon which we may watch the fluctuation of prices in response to the news of

[2] Cf. W. I. Thomas, *Source Book of Social Origins*, p. 169.

economic conditions in different parts of the world, are typical. Similar readjustments are taking place in every department of social life, where, however, the devices for making these readjustments are not so complete and perfect. For example, the professional and trade papers, which keep the professions and the trades informed in regard to new methods, experiences, and devices, serve to keep the members of these trades and professions abreast of the times, which means that they facilitate readjustments to changing conditions.

There is, however, this important distinction to be made: Competition in the exchanges is more intense; changes are more rapid and, as far as the individuals directly concerned, more momentous. In contrast with such a constellation of forces as we find on the exchanges, where competing dealers meet to buy and sell, so mobile a form of social organization as the crowd and the mob exhibits a relative stability.

It is a commonplace that decisive factors in the movements of crowds, as in the fluctuations of markets, are psychologic. This means that among the individuals who make up the crowd, or who compose the public which participates in the movements reflected in the market, a condition of instability exists which corresponds to what has been defined elsewhere as crisis. It is true of the exchanges, as it is of crowds, that the situation they represent is always critical, that is to say, the tensions are such that a slight cause may precipitate an enormous effect. The current euphemism, "the psychological moment," defines such a critical condition.

Psychological moments may arise in any social situation, but they occur more frequently in a society which has acquired a high state of mobility. They occur more frequently in a society where education is general, where railways, telegraph, and the printing press have become an indispensable part of the social economy. They occur more frequently in cities than in smaller communities. In the crowd and the public every moment may be said to be "psychological."

Crisis may be said to be the normal condition on the exchanges. What are called financial crises are merely an extension of this critical condition to the larger business community. Financial panics which sometimes follow upon financial crises are a precipitate of this critical condition.

The fascinating thing about the study of crises, as of crowds, is that in so far as they are in fact due to psychological causes, that is, in so far as they are the result of the mobility of the communities in which they occur, they can be controlled. The evidence for this is the fact that they can be manipulated, and there is abundant evidence of manipulation in the transactions of the stock market. The evidence for the manipulation of crowds is less accessible. Labor organizations have, however, known how to develop a pretty definite technique for the instigation and control of strikes. The Salvation Army has worked out a book of tactics which is very largely devoted to the handling of street crowds; and professional revivalists have an elaborate technique for conducting their revivals.

Under the title of collective psychology much has been written in recent years in regard to crowds and kindred phenomena of social life. Most that has been written thus far has been based upon general observation and almost no systematic methods exist for the study of this type of social organization. The practical methods which practical men like the political boss, the labor agitator, the stock-exchange speculator, and others have worked out for the control and manipulation of the public and the crowd furnish a body of materials from which it is possible to make a more detailed, a more intimate study of what may be called, in order to distinguish it from that of more highly organized groups, collective behavior.

The city, and particularly the great city, in which more than elsewhere human relations are likely to be impersonal and rational, defined in terms of interest and in terms of cash, is in a very real sense a laboratory for the investigation of collective behavior. Strikes and minor revolutionary movements are endemic in the urban environment. Cities, and particularly the great cities, are in unstable equilibrium. The result is that the vast casual and mobile aggregations which constitute our urban populations are in a state of perpetual agitation, swept by every new wind of doctrine, subject to constant alarms, and in consequence the community is in a chronic condition of crisis.

III. SECONDARY RELATIONS AND SOCIAL CONTROL

Modern methods of urban transportation and communication—the electric railway, the automobile, the telephone, and the radio—have silently and rapidly changed in recent years the social and industrial organization of the modern city. They have been the means of concentrating traffic in the business districts, have changed the whole character of retail trade, multiplying the residence suburbs and making the department store possible. These changes in the industrial organization and in the distribution of population have been accompanied by corresponding changes in the habits, sentiments, and character of the urban population.

The general nature of these changes is indicated by the fact that the growth of cities has been accompanied by the substitution of indirect, "secondary," for direct, face-to-face, "primary" relations in the associations of individuals in the community.

Touch and sight, physical contact, are the basis for the first and most elementary human relationships. Mother and child, husband and wife, father and son, master and servant, kinsman and neighbor, minister, physician, and teacher—these are the most intimate and real relationships of life, and in the small community they are practically inclusive.

The interactions which take place among the members of a community so constituted are immediate and unreflecting. Intercourse is carried on largely within the region of instinct and feeling. Social control arises, for the most part spontaneously, in direct response to personal influences and public sentiment. It is the result of a personal accommodation, rather than the formulation of a rational and abstract principle.

The church, the school, and the family.—In a great city, where the population is unstable, where parents and children are employed out of the house and often in distant parts of the city, where thousands of people live side by side for years without so much as a bowing acquaintance, these intimate relationships of the primary group are weakened and the moral order which rested upon them is gradually dissolved.

Under the distintegrating influences of city life most of our traditional institutions, the church, the school, and the family, have been greatly modified. The school, for example, has taken over some of the functions of the family. It is around the public school and its solicitude for the moral and physical welfare of the children that something like a new neighborhood and community spirit tends to get itself organized.

The church, on the other hand, which has lost much of its influence since the printed page has so largely taken the place of the pulpit in the interpretation of life, seems at present to be in process of readjustment to the new conditions.

It is probably the breaking down of local attachments and the weakening of the restraints and inhibitions of the primary group, under the influence of the urban environment, which are largely responsible for the increase of vice and crime in great cities. It would be interesting in this connection to determine by investigation how far the increase in crime keeps pace with the increasing mobility of the population and to what extent this mobility is a function of the growth of population. It is from this point of view that we should seek to interpret all those statistics which register the disintegration of the moral order, for example, the statistics of divorce, of truancy, and of crime.

Crisis and the courts.—It is characteristic of city life that all sorts of people meet and mingle together who never fully comprehend one another. The anarchist and the club man, the priest and the Levite, the actor and the missionary who touch elbows on the street still live in totally different worlds. So complete is the segregation of vocational classes that it is possible within the limits of the city to live in an isolation almost as complete as that of some remote rural community.

In the immigrant colonies which are now well established in every large city, foreign populations live in isolation. Each one of these little colonies has a more or less independent political and social organization of its own, and is the center of a more or less vigorous nationalist propaganda.

Under these conditions the social ritual and the moral order which these immigrants brought with them from their native countries have succeeded in maintaining themselves for a considerable time under the influences of the American environment. Social control, based on the home mores, breaks down, however, in the second generation.

We may express the relation of the city to this fact in general terms by saying that the effect of the urban environment is to intensify all effects of crisis.

> The term "crisis" is not to be understood in a violent sense. It is involved in any disturbance of habit. There is a crisis in the boy's life when he leaves home. The emancipation of the Negro and the immigration of the European peasant are group crises. Any strain of crisis involves three possible changes: greater fitness, reduced efficiency, or death. In biological terms, "survival" means successful adjustment to crisis, accompanied typically by a modification of structure. In man it means mental stimulation and greater intelligence, or mental depression, in case of failure.[3]

Under the conditions imposed by city life in which individuals and groups of individuals, widely removed in sympathy and understanding, live together under conditions of interdependence, if not of intimacy, the conditions of social control are greatly altered and the difficulties increased.

The problem thus created is usually characterized as one of "assimilation." It is assumed that the reason for rapid increase of crime in our large cities is due to the fact that the foreign element in our population has not succeeded in assimilating American culture and does not conform to the American mores. This would be interesting, if true, but the facts seem to suggest that perhaps the truth must be sought in the opposite direction.

What we do observe, as a result of the crisis, is that control that was

[3] William I. Thomas, "Race Psychology: Standpoint and Questionnaire with Particular Reference to the Immigrant and Negro," *American Journal of Sociology*, XVII (May, 1912), 736.

formerly based on mores was replaced by control based on positive law. This change runs parallel to the movement by which secondary relationships have taken the place of primary relationships in the association of individuals in the city environment.

It is characteristic of the United States that great political changes should be effected experimentally under the pressure of agitation or upon the initiative of small but militant minorities. There is probably no other country in the word in which so many "reforms" are in progress as at the present time in the United States. Reform has, in fact, become a kind of popular "indoor sport." The reforms thus effected, almost without exception, involve some sort of restriction or governmental control over activities that were formerly "free" or controlled only by the mores and public opinion.

The effect of this extension of what is called the police power has been to produce a change, not merely in the fundamental policy of the law, but in the character and standing of the courts.

The juvenile and morals courts illustrate a change which is perhaps taking place elsewhere. In these courts the judges have assumed something of the functions of administrative officers, their duties consisting less in the interpretation of law than in prescribing remedies and administering advice intended to restore delinquents brought before them to their normal place in society.

A similar tendency to give judges a wide discretion and to impose upon them a further responsibility is manifest in those courts which have to deal with the technical affairs of the business world, and in the growth in popularity of commissions in which judicial and administrative functions are combined, for example, the Interstate Commerce Commission.

In order to interpret in a fundamental way the facts in regard to social control it is important to start with a clear conception of the nature of corporate action.

Corporate action begins when there is some sort of communication between individuals who constitute a group. Communication may take place at different levels; that is, suggestions may be given and responded to on the instinctive, senso-motor, or ideo-motor levels. The mechanism of communication is very subtle, so subtle, in fact, that it is often difficult to conceive how suggestions are conveyed from one mind to another. This does not imply that there is any special form of consciousness, any special sense of kinship or consciousness of kind, necessary to explain corporate action.

In fact, it has recently been shown that in the case of certain highly organized and static societies, like that of the well-known ant, probably nothing that we would call communication takes place.

Individuals not only react upon one another in a reflex way, but they inevitably communicate their sentiments, attitudes, and organic excitements, and in doing so they necessarily react, not merely to what each individual actually does, but to what he intends, desires, or hopes to do. The fact that individuals often betray sentiments and attitudes to others of which they are themselves only dimly conscious makes it possible for individual A, for example, to act upon motives and tensions in B as soon, or even before, B is able to do so. Furthermore, A may act upon the suggestions that emanate from B without himself being clearly conscious of the source from which his motives spring. So subtle and intimate may the reactions be which control individuals who are bound together in a social-psychological process.

It is upon the basis of this sort of instinctive and spontaneous control that every more formal sort of control must be based in order to be effective.

Party politics and publicity.—There is everywhere at present a disposition to increase the power of the executive branch of the government at the expense of the legislative. The influence of state legislatures and of city councils has been diminished in some instances by the introduction of the referendum and the recall. In others they have been largely superseded by the commission form of government. The ostensible reason for these changes is that they offer a means for overthrowing the power of the professional politicians. The real ground seems to me the recognition of the fact that the form of government which had its origin in the town meeting and was well suited to the needs of a small community based on primary relations is not suitable to the government of the changing and heterogeneous populations of cities of three or four millions.

For one thing, the problems of city government have become, with the growth and organization of city life, so complicated that it is no longer desirable to leave them to the control of men whose only qualification for handling them consists in the fact that they have succeeded in gaining office through the ordinary machinery of ward politics.

Another circumstance which has made the selection of city officials by popular vote impractical under the conditions of city life is the fact that, except in special cases, the voter knows little or nothing about the officials he is voting for; knows little or nothing about the functions of the office to which that official is to be elected; and, besides all the rest, is too busy elsewhere to inform himself about conditions and needs of the city as a whole.

At a recent election in Chicago, for example, voters were called upon to select candidates from a ballot containing 250 names, most of them unknown to the voters. Under these circumstances the citizen who wishes to vote intelligently relies on some more or less interested organization or some more or less interested advisor to tell him how to vote.

To meet this emergency, created primarily by conditions imposed by city life, two types of organization have come into existence for controlling those artificial crises that we call elections. One of these is the organization represented by the political boss and the political machine. The other is that represented by the independent voters' leagues, taxpayers' associations, and organizations like the bureaus of municipal research.

It is an indication of the rather primitive conditions in which our political parties were formed that they sought to govern the country on the principle that the remedy for all sorts of administrative evils was to "turn the rascals out," as the popular phrase expressed it, a change of government. The political machine and the political boss have come into existence in the interest of party politics. The parties were necessarily organized to capture elections. The political machine is merely a technical device invented for the purpose of achieving this end. The boss is the expert who runs the machine. He is as necessary to the winning of an election as a professional coach is necessary to success at football.

It is characteristic of the two types of organization which have grown up for the purpose of controlling the popular vote that the first, the political machine, is based, on the whole, on local, personal, that is to say, primary, relationships. The second, the good-government organizations, make their appeal to the public, and the public, as we ordinarily understand that expression, is a group based on secondary relationships. Members of a public are not as a rule personally acquainted.

The political machine is, in fact, an attempt to maintain, inside the formal administrative organization of the city, the control of a primary group. The organizations thus built up, of which Tammany Hall is the classic illustration, appear to be thoroughly feudal in their character. The relations between the boss and his ward captain seem to be precisely that, of personal loyalty on one side and personal protection on the other, which the feudal relation implies. The virtues which such an organization calls out are the old tribal ones of fidelity, loyalty, and devotion to the interests of the chief and the clan. The people within the organization, their friends and supporters, constitute a "we" group, while the rest of the city is merely the outer world, which is not quite alive and not quite human in the sense in which the members of the "we" group are. We have here something approaching the conditions of primitive society.

The conception of "primitive society" which we ought to form is that of small groups scattered over a territory. The size of the groups is determined by the conditions of the struggle for existence. The internal organization of each group corresponds to its size. A group of groups may have some relation to each other (kin, neighborhood, alliance, *connubium,* and *commercium*) which draws them together and differentiates them from others. Thus a differentiation arises between ourselves, the we-group or in-group, and everybody else or the others-groups, out-groups. The insiders in a we-group are in a relation of peace, order, law, government, and industry, to each other. Their relation to all outsiders, or others-groups, is one of war and plunder, except so far as agreements have modified it.

The relation of comradeship and peace in the we-group and that of hostility and war toward others-groups are correlative to each other. The exigencies of war with outsiders are what make peace inside, lest internal discord should weaken the we-group for war. These exigencies also make government and law in the in-group, in order to prevent quarrels and enforce discipline.[4]

Advertising and social control.—In contrast with the political machine, which has founded its organized action on the local, personal, and immediate interests represented by the different neighborhoods and localities, the good-government organizations, the bureaus of municipal research, and the like have sought to represent the interests of the city as a whole and have appealed to a sentiment and opinion neither local nor personal. These agencies have sought to secure efficiency and good government by the education of the voter, that is to say, by investigating and publishing the facts regarding the government.

In this way publicity has come to be a recognized form of social control, and advertising—"social advertising"—has become a profession with an elaborate technique supported by a body of special knowledge.

It is one of the characteristic phenomena of city life and of society founded on secondary relationships that advertising should have come to occupy so important a place in its economy.

As a source of social control public opinion becomes important in societies founded on secondary relationships, of which great cities are a type. In the city every social group tends to create its own milieu and, as these conditions become fixed, the mores tend to accommodate

Sumner, *Folkways*, p. 12.

themselves to the conditions thus created. In secondary groups and in the city fashion tends to take the place of custom, and public opinion, rather than the mores, becomes the dominant force in social control.

In any attempt to understand the nature of public opinion and its relation to social control it is important to investigate first of all the agencies and devices which have come into practical use in the effort to control, enlighten, and exploit it.

The first and the most important of these is the press, that is, the daily newspaper and other forms of current literature, including books classed as current.

After the newspaper, the bureaus of research which are now springing up in all the large cities are the most interesting and the most promising devices for using publicity as a means of control.

The fruits of these investigations do not reach the public directly, but are disseminated through the medium of the press, the pulpit, and other sources of popular enlightenment.

In addition to these there are the educational campaigns in the interest of better health conditions, the child-welfare exhibits, and the numerous "social advertising" devices which are now employed, sometimes upon the initiative of private societies, sometimes upon that of popular magazines or newspapers, in order to educate the public and enlist the masses of the people in the movement for the improvement of conditions of community life.

The newspaper is the great medium of communication within the city, and it is on the basis of the information which it supplies that public opinion rests. The first function which a newspaper supplies is that which formerly was performed by the village gossip.

In spite, however, of the industry with which newspapers pursue facts of personal intelligence and human interest, they cannot compete with the village gossips as a means of social control. For one thing, the newspaper maintains some reservations not recognized by gossip, in the matters of personal intelligence. For example, until they run for office or commit some other overt act that brings them before the public conspicuously, the private life of individual men or women is a subject that is, for the newspaper, taboo. It is not so with gossip, partly because in a small community no individual is so obscure that his private affairs escape observation and discussion; partly because the field is smaller. In small communities there is a perfectly amazing amount of personal information afloat among the individuals who compose them.

The absence of this in the city is what, in large part, makes the city what it is.

IV. TEMPERAMENT AND THE URBAN ENVIRONMENT

Great cities have always been the melting-pots of races and of cultures. Out of the vivid and subtle interactions of which they have been the centers, there have come the newer breeds and the newer social types. The great cities of the United States, for example, have drawn from the isolation of their native villages great masses of the rural populations of Europe and America. Under the shock of the new contacts the latent energies of these primitive peoples have been released, and the subtler processes of interaction have brought into existence not merely vocational, but temperamental, types.

Mobilization of the individual man.—Transportation and communication have effected, among many other silent but far-reaching changes, what I have called the "mobilization of the individual man." They have multiplied the opportunities of the individual man for contact and for association with his fellows, but they have made these contacts and associations more transitory and less stable. A very large part of the populations of great cities, including those who make their homes in tenements and apartment houses, live much as people do in some great hotel, meeting but not knowing one another. The effect of this is to substitute fortuitous and casual relationship for the more intimate and permanent associations of the smaller community.

Under these circumstances the individual's status is determined to a considerable degree by conventional signs—by fashion and "front"—and the art of life is largely reduced to skating on thin surfaces and a scrupulous study of style and manners.

Not only transportation and communication, but the segregation of the urban population tends to facilitate the mobility of the individual man. The processes of segregation establish moral distances which make the city a mosaic of little worlds which touch but do not interpenetrate. This makes it possible for individuals to pass quickly and easily from one moral milieu to another, and encourages the fascinating but dangerous experiment of living at the same time in several different contiguous, but otherwise widely separated, worlds. All this tends to give to city life a superficial and adventitious character; it tends to complicate social relationships and to produce new and divergent individual types. It introduces, at the same time, an element of chance and adventure which adds to the stimulus of city life and gives it, for young and fresh nerves, a peculiar attractiveness. The lure of great cities is perhaps a consequence of stimulations which act directly upon the reflexes. As a type of human behavior it may be explained, like the attraction of the flame for the moth, as a sort of tropism.

The attraction of the metropolis is due in part, however, to the fact that in the long run every individual finds somewhere among the varied manifestations of city life the sort of environment in which he expands and feels at ease; finds, in short, the moral climate in which his peculiar nature obtains the stimulations that bring his innate dispositions to full and free expression. It is, I suspect, motives of this kind which have their basis, not in interest nor even in sentiment, but in something more fundamental and primitive which draw many, if not most, of the young men and young women from the security of their homes in the country into the big, booming confusion and excitement of city life. In a small community it is the normal man, the man without eccentricity or genius, who seems most likely to succeed. The small community often tolerates eccentricity. The city, on the contrary, rewards it. Neither the criminal, the defective, nor the genius has the same opportunity to develop his innate disposition in a small town that he invariably finds in a great city.

Fifty years ago every village had one or two eccentric characters who were treated ordinarily with a benevolent toleration, but who were regarded meanwhile as impracticable and queer. These exceptional individuals lived an isolated existence, cut off by their very eccentricities, whether of genius or of defect, from genuinely intimate intercourse with their fellows. If they had the making of criminals, the restraints and inhibitions of the small community rendered them harmless. If they had the stuff of genius in them, they remained sterile for lack of appreciation or opportunity. Mark Twain's story of *Pudd'n Head Wilson* is a description of one such obscure and unappreciated genius. It is not so true as it was that

> Full many a flower is born to blush unseen
> And waste its fragrance on the desert air.

Gray wrote the "Elegy in a Country Churchyard" before the rise of the modern metropolis.

In the city many of these divergent types now find a milieu in which, for good or for ill, their dispositions and talents parturiate and bear fruit.

The moral region.—It is inevitable that individuals who seek the same forms of excitement, whether that excitement be furnished by a horse race or by grand opera, should find themselves from time to time in the same places. The result of this is that in the organization which city life spontaneously assumes the population tends to segregate itself, not merely in accordance with its interests, but in accordance with its tastes or its temperaments. The resulting distribution of the population is likely to be quite different from that brought about by occupational interests or economic conditions.

Every neighborhood, under the influences which tend to distribute and segregate city populations, may assume the character of a "moral region." Such, for example, are the vice districts, which are found in most cities. A moral region is not necessarily a place of abode. It may be a mere rendezvous, a place of resort.

In order to understand the forces which in every large city tend to develop these detached milieus in which vagrant and suppressed impulses, passions, and ideals emancipate themselves from the dominant moral order, it is necessary to refer to the fact or theory of latent impulses of men.

The fact seems to be that men are brought into the world with all the passions, instincts, and appetites, uncontrolled and undisciplined. Civilization, in the interests of the common welfare, demands the suppression sometimes, and the control always, of these wild, natural dispositions. In the process of imposing its discipline upon the individual, in making over the individual in accordance with the accepted community model, much is suppressed altogether, and much more finds a vicarious expression in forms that are socially valuable, or at least innocuous. It is at this point that sport, play, and art function. They permit the individual to purge himself by means of symbolic expression of these wild and suppressed impulses.

No doubt many other social phenomena such as strikes, wars, popular elections, and religious revivals perform a similar function in releasing the subconscious tensions. But within smaller communities, where social relations are more intimate and inhibitions more imperative, there are many exceptional individuals who find within the limits of the communal activity no normal and healthful expression of their individual aptitudes and temperaments.

The causes which give rise to what are here described as "moral regions" are due in part to the restrictions which urban life imposes; in part to the license which these same conditions offer. We have, until very recently, given much consideration to the temptations of city life, but we have not given the same consideration to the effects of inhibitions and suppressions of natural impulses and instincts under the changed conditions of metropolitan life. For one thing, children, which in the country are counted as an asset, become in the city a liability. Aside from this fact it is very much more difficult to rear a family in the city than on the farm. Marriage takes place later in the city, and sometimes it doesn't take place at all. These facts have consequences the significance of which we are as yet wholly unable to estimate.

Temperament and social contagion.—What lends special importance to the segregation of the poor, the vicious, the criminal, and exceptional persons generally, which is so characteristic a feature of city life, is the fact that social contagion tends to stimulate in divergent types the common temperamental differences, and to suppress characters which unite them with the normal types about them. Association with others of their own ilk provides also not merely a stimulus, but a moral support for the traits they have in common which they would not find in a less select society. In the great city the poor, the vicious, and the delinquent, crushed together in an unhealthful and contagious intimacy, breed in and in, soul and body, so that it has often occurred to me that those long genealogies of the Jukes and the tribes of Ishmael would not show such a persistent and distressing uniformity of vice, crime, and poverty unless they were peculiarly fit for the environment in which they are condemned to exist.

We must then accept these "moral regions" and the more or less eccentric and exceptional people who inhabit them, in a sense, at least, as part of the natural, if not the normal, life of a city.

It is not necessary to understand by the expression "moral region" a place or a society that is either necessarily criminal or abnormal. It is intended rather to apply to regions in which a divergent moral code prevails, because it is a region in which the people who inhabit it are dominated, as people are ordinarily not dominated, by a taste or by a passion or by some interest which has its roots directly in the original nature of the individual. It may be an art, like music, or a sport, like horse-racing. Such a region would differ from other social groups by the fact that its interests are more immediate and more fundamental. For this reason its differences are likely to be due to moral, rather than intellectual, isolation.

Because of the opportunity it offers, particularly to the exceptional and abnormal types of man, a great city tends to spread out and lay bare to the public view in a massive manner all the human characters and traits which are ordinarily obscured and suppressed in smaller communities. The city, in short, shows the good and evil in human nature in excess. It is this fact, perhaps, more than any other, which justifies the view that would make of the city a laboratory or clinic in which human nature and social processes may be conveniently and profitably studied.

CHAPTER 12

Social Class

———————•••———————

CLASS AND CASTE

B Y

CHARLES HORTON COOLEY

SPEAKING roughly, we may call any persistent social group, other than the family, existing within a larger group, a class. And every society, except possibly the most primitive, is more or less distinctly composed of classes. Even in savage tribes there are, besides families and clans, almost always other associations: of warriors, of magicians and so on; and these continue throughout all phases of development until we reach the intricate group structure of our own time. Individuals never achieve their life in separation, but always in cooperation with a group of other minds, and in proportion as these cooperating groups stand out from one another with some distinctness they constitute social classes.

We may say of this differentiation, speaking generally, that it is useful. The various functions of life require special influences and organization, and without some class spirit, some speciality in traditions and standards, nothing is well performed. Thus, if our physicians were not, as regards their professional activities, something of a psychological unit, building up knowledge and sentiment by communication, desiring the approval and dreading the censure of their colleagues, it would

be worse not only for them but for the rest of us. There are no doubt
class divisions that are useless or harmful, but something of this nature
there should be, and I have already tried to show that our own society
suffers considerably from a lack of adequate group differentiation in
its higher mental activities.

Fundamental to all study of classes are the two principles, of inheritance and of competition, according to which their membership is
determined. The rule of descent, as in the hereditary nobility of England or Germany, gives a fixed system, the alternative to which is some
kind of selection—by election or appointment as in our politics; by
purchase, as formerly in the British army and navy; or by the informal
action of preference, opportunity and endeavor, as in the case of most
trades and professions at the present day.

Evidently these two principles are very much intermingled in their
working. The hereditary distinctions must have a beginning in some
sort of selective struggle, such as the military and commercial competition from which privileged families have emerged in the past, and
never become so rigid as not to be modified by similar processes. On
the other hand, inherited advantages, even in the freest society, enter
powerfully into every kind of competition.

Another consideration of much interest is that the strict rule of
descent is a biological principle, making the social organization subordinate to physical continuity of life, while selection or competition
brings in psychical elements, of the most various qualities to be sure,
but capable at the best of forming society on a truly rational method.

Finally it is well to recognize that there is a vast sum of influences
governed by no ascertainable principle at all, which go to assign the
individual his place in the class system. After allowing for inheritance
and for everything which can fairly be called selection (that is, for all
definite and orderly interaction between the man and the system),
there remains a large part which can be assigned only to chance. This
is particularly true in the somewhat tumultuous changes of modern
life.

When a class is somewhat strictly hereditary, we may call it a caste—
a name originally applied to the hereditary classes of India, but to
which it is common, and certainly convenient, to give a wider meaning.

Perhaps the best way to understand caste is to open our eyes and
note those forces at work among ourselves which might conceivably
give rise to it.

On every side we may see that differences arise, and that these tend
to be perpetuated through inherited associations, opportunities and

culture. The endeavor to secure for one's children whatever desirable thing one has gained for oneself is a perennial source of caste, and this endeavor flows from human nature and the moral unity of the family.

Such intangible advantages as culture, manners, good associations and the like, whether associated with wealth or not, are practically heritable, since they are chiefly derived by children from a social environment determined by the personality and standing of their parents.

Indeed, irrespective of any intention toward or from inheritance, there is a strong drift toward it due to mere familiarity. It is commonly the line of least resistance. The father knows much about his own trade and those closely related to it, little about others; and the son shares his point of view. So when the latter comes to fix upon a career he is likely, in the absence of any decided individuality of preference, to take the way that lies most open to him. Of course he may lack the ability to carry the paternal function; but this, though common enough, does not affect the majority of cases. The functions that require a peculiar type of natural ability, while of the first importance, since they include all marked originality, are not very numerous, sound character and training, with fair intelligence, being ordinarily sufficient. Even in the learned professions, such as law, medicine, teaching and the ministry, the great majority of practitioners hold their own by common sense and assiduity rather than by special aptitude. To the best of my observation, there are many men serving as foremen in various sorts of handicraft, or as farmers, who have natural capacity adequate for success in law, commerce or politics. A man of good, all-round ability will succeed in that line of work which he finds ready to his hand, but only a few will break away from their antecedents and seek a wholly different line. And if their work affords them health, thought and mastery, why should they wish to change it if they could?

I would not have it supposed, however (because I dwell thus upon opportunity), that I agree with those whose zeal for education and training leads them to depreciate natural differences. I do not know how to talk with men who believe in native equality: it seems to me that they lack common sense and observation.

The two variables of personality, "nature and nurture," are without doubt of equal diversity and importance, and they must work together to bring about any notable achievement. Natural ability is essential; but, no matter how great, it cannot know or develop its power without opportunity. Indeed, great natural faculty is often more dependent on circumstance than is mediocrity—because of some trait, like extreme sensitiveness, that unfits it for miscellaneous competition. Opportunity, moreover, means different things in different cases, and is not to be identified with wealth or facile circumstances of any sort. Some degrees and kinds of difficulty are helpful, others not.

And yet, leaving out, on the one hand, unusual talent or energy, and, on the other, decided weakness or dulness, the mass of men are guided chiefly by early surroundings and training, which determine for them, in a general way, what sort of life they will take up, and contribute much to their success or failure in it. Society, even in a comparatively free country, is thus vaguely divided into hereditary strata or sections, from which the majority do not depart.

If the transmission of function from father to son has become established, a caste spirit, a sentiment in favor of such transmission and opposed to the passage from one class into another, may arise and be shared even by the unprivileged classes. The individual then thinks of himself and his family as identified with his caste, and sympathizes with others who have the same feeling. The caste thus becomes a psychical organism, consolidated by community of sentiment and tradition.

CONDITIONS FAVORING OR OPPOSING THE GROWTH OF CASTE

There seem to be three conditions which, chiefly, make for the increase or diminution of the caste principle. These are, first, likeness or unlikeness in the constituents of the population; second, the rate of social change (whether we have to do with a settled or a shifting system), and, finally, the state of communication and enlightenment. Unlikeness in the constituents, a settled system and a low state of communication and enlightenment favor the growth of caste, and *vice versa*. The first provides natural lines of cleavage and so makes it easier to split into hereditary groups; the second gives inheritance time to consolidate its power, while the third means the absence of those conscious and rational forces which are its chief rivals.

The most important sorts of unlikeness in the constituents of the population are perhaps three: differences in race, differences, apart from race, due to immigration or conquest, and unlikeness due to the gradual differentiation of social functions within a population originally homogeneous.

Two races of different temperament and capacity, distinct to the eye and living side by side in the same community, tend strongly to become castes, no matter how equal the social system may otherwise be. The difference, as being hereditary, answers in its nature to the idea of caste, and the external sign serves to make it conscious and definite.

The race caste existing in the Southern United States illustrates the impotence of democratic traditions to overcome the caste spirit when fostered by obvious physical and psychical differences. This spirit is immeasurably strong on the part of the whites, and there is no apparent prospect of its diminution.

The specially caste nature of the division—as distinguished from those personal differences which democratic tradition recognizes—is seen in the feeling, universal among the whites, that the Negro must be held apart and subordinate not merely as an individual, or any number of individuals, but as a race, a social whole. That is, the fact that many individuals of this race are equal, and some superior, to the majority of whites does not, in the opinion of the latter, make it just or expedient to treat them apart from the mass of their race. To dine with a Negro, to work or play by his side, or to associate in any relation where superiority cannot be asserted, is held to be degrading and of evil example, no matter what kind of Negro he may be. It is the practice and policy of the dominant race to impress upon the Negro that he belongs by birth to a distinct order out of which he can in no way depart. There or nowhere he must find his destiny. If he wishes to mingle with whites it must be as an acknowledged inferior. As a servant he may ride in the same railway car, but as a citizen he may not do so.

Thoughtful whites justify this attitude on the ground, substantially, that a race *is* an organic whole—bound together by heredity and social connection—and that it is practically necessary to recognize this in dealing with race questions. The integrity of the white race and of white civilization, they say, requires Negro subordination (separation being impracticable), and the only available line of distinction is the definite one of color. A division on this line is even held to be less invidious—as involving no judgment of individuals—as well as more feasible, than one based on personal traits. Particular persons cannot, in practice, be separated from their families and other antecedents, and if they could be the example of mixture on an equal footing would be demoralizing.

This argument is probably sound in so far as it requires the recognition of the two races as being, for some purposes, distinct organisms. In this regard it is perhaps better sociology than the view that every one should be considered solely on his merits as an individual.

At the same time it is only too apparent that our application of this doctrine is deeply colored with that caste arrogance which does not recognize in the Negro a spiritual brotherhood underlying all race difference and possible "inferiority." The matter of unequal ability, in races as in individuals, is quite distinct from that sharing in a common spirit and service from which no human being can rightly or Christianly be excluded. The idea that he is fundamentally a man like the rest of us cannot and should not be kept from the Negro any more than from other lowly orders of people. Science, religion and the democratic spirit all give him a right to it; and the white man cannot deny it to him without being false to his own best self. Anything in our present attitude which does deny it we must hope to be transitory, since it is calculated, in a modern atmosphere, to generate continuing disquiet and hatred. It belonged with slavery and is incongruous with the newer world.

These may be subtleties, but subtlety is the very substance of the race question, the most vital matter being not so much what is done as the spirit in which it is done.

When peoples of the same race mingle by migration, the effect, as regards classes, depends chiefly on their states of civilization and the character of the migration, as hostile or friendly. Much depends, of course, upon the special character of the institutions and traditions that thus come into contact. Some societies are rigid and repellent in their structure, while others, like the United States, are almost ideally constituted to invite and hasten assimilation.

Conquest has been one of the main sources of caste the world over. The hostile tradition it leaves may continue indefinitely; servile functions are commonly forced upon the conquered, and the consciousness of superiority leads the conquerors to regard intermarriage as shameful.

The unlikeness out of which caste grows may not be original, as in the case of race difference or conquest, but may arise gradually by the differentiation of a homogeneous people. Any distinct social group, having its special group sympathies and traditions, has some tendency to pass on its functions and ideas to the children of its members, promoting association and intermarriage among them, and thus taking on a caste character.

Accordingly, any increase in the complexity of social functions— political, religious, military or industrial—such as necessarily accompanies the enlargement of a social system, may have a caste tendency, because it separates the population into groups corresponding to the several functions; and this alone may without doubt produce caste if the conditions are otherwise favorable.

A settled state of society is favorable, and change hostile, to the growth of caste, because it is necessary that functions should be continuous through several generations before the principle of inheritance can become fixed. Whatever breaks up existing customs and traditions tends to abolish hereditary privilege and throw men into a rough struggle, out of which strong, coarse natures emerge as victors, to found, perhaps, a new aristocracy.

That a low state of communication and of enlightenment are favorable to caste, while intelligence—especially political intelligence—and facility of intercourse antagonize it, becomes evident when we consider what, psychologically speaking, caste is. It is an organization of the social mind on a biological principle. That functions should follow the line of descent instead of adjusting themselves to individual capacity and preference, evidently means the subordination of reason to convenience, of freedom to order. The ideal principle is not biological but moral, based, that is, on the spiritual gifts of individuals without regard to descent. Caste, then, is something which, we may assume, will give way to this higher principle whenever the conditions are such as to permit the latter to work successfully; and this will be the case when the population is so mobilized by free training and institutions that just and orderly selection is practicable.

The diffusion of intelligence, rapid communication, the mobilization of wealth by means of money, and the like, mark the ascendency of the human mind over material and biological conditions. Popular government becomes possible, commercial and industrial functions—other things equal—come under more open competition, and free personal development of all sorts is fostered. The general sentiment also, perceiving the superiority of free organization to caste, becomes definitely hostile to the latter and antagonizes it by public educational and other opportunities. The most effective agent in keeping classes comparatively open is an adequate system of free training for the young, tending to make all careers accessible to those who are naturally fit for them. In so far as there is such a system early education becomes a process of selection and discipline which permits ability to serve its possessor and the world in its proper place.

But before this mobility is achieved, caste is perhaps the only possible basis for an elaborate social structure; the main flow of thought is then necessarily in local channels. The people cannot grasp the life of which they are a part in any large way, or have a free and responsible share in it, but are somewhat mechanically held in place by habit and tradition. Those special relations to the system of government, religion or industry which are implied in classes, since they cannot be determined by rational selection, must be fixed in some traditional way, and the most available is the inheritance of functions.

OPEN CLASSES

With the growth of freedom classes come to be more open, that is, more based on individual traits and less upon descent. Competition comes actively into play and more or less efficiently fulfils its function of assigning to each one an appropriate place in the whole. The theory of a free order is that every one is born to serve mankind in a certain way, that he finds out through a wise system of education and experiment what that way is, and is trained to enter upon it. In following it he does the best possible both for the service of society and his own happiness. So far as classes exist they are merely groups for the furtherance of efficiency through cooperation, and their membership is determined entirely by natural fitness.

This ideal condition is never attained on a large scale. In practice the men who find work exactly suited to them and at the same time acceptable to society are at the best somewhat exceptional—though habit reconciles most of us—and classes are never wholly open or wholly devoted to the general good.

The problem of finding where men belong, of adapting personal gifts to a complex system, is indeed one of extreme difficulty, and is in no way solved by facile schemes of any sort. There are, fundamentally, only two principles available to meet it, that of inheritance or caste and that of competition. While the former is a low principle, the latter is also, in many of its phases, objectionable, involving waste of energy and apt to degenerate into anarchy. There are always difficulties on either hand, and the actual organization of life is ever a compromise between the aspiration toward freedom and the convenience of status.

We may assume, then, that in contemporary life we have to do with a society in which the constitution of classes, so far as we have them, is partly determined by inheritance and partly by a more or less open competition, which is, again, more or less effective in placing men where they rightly belong.

If classes are open and men make their way from one into another, it is plain that they cannot be separate mental wholes as may be the case with castes. The general state of things becomes one of facile intercourse, and those who change class will not forget the ideas and associations of youth. Non-hereditary classes may have plenty of solidarity and class spirit—consider, for instance, the mediæval clergy —and their activity may also be of a special and remote sort, like that of an astronomical society, but after all there will be something democratic about them; they will share the general spirit of the whole in which they are rooted. They mean only specialization in consciousness, where caste means separation.

Where classes do not mean separate currents of thought, as in the case of caste, but are merely differentiations in a common mental whole, there are likely to be several kinds of classes overlapping one another, so that men who fall in the same class from one point of view are separated in another. The groups are like circles which, instead of standing apart, interlace with one another so that several of them may pass through the same individual. Classes become numerous and, so to speak, impersonal; that is, each one absorbs only a part of the life of the individual and does not sufficiently dominate him to mould him to a special type.

It is, then, easy to see why different classifiers discover different class divisions in our society, according to their points of view; namely, because there are in fact an indefinite number of possible collocations. This would not have been the case anywhere in the Middle Ages, nor is it nearly as much the case in England at the present time as in the United States.

We might, to take three of the most conspicuous lines of division, classify the people about us according to trade or profession, according to income, and according to culture. The first gives us lawyers, grocers, plumbers, bankers and the like, and also, more generally, the hand-laboring class, skilled and unskilled, the mercantile class, the professional class and the farming class. The division by income is, of course, related to this, though by no means identical. We might reckon paupers, the poor, the comfortable, the well-to-do and the rich. Culture and refinement have with us no very close or essential connection with occupation or wealth, and a classification based upon the former would show a very general rearrangement.

Class animosity by no means increases in proportion to the separation of classes. On the contrary, where there is a definite and recognized class system which no one thinks of breaking down, a main cause of arrogance and jealousy is absent. Every one takes his position for granted and is not concerned to assert or improve it. In Spain, it is said, "you may give the inch to any peasant; he is sure to be a gentleman, and he never thinks of taking the ell." So in an English tale, written about 1875, I find the following: "The peasantry and little people in country places like to feel the gentry far above them. They do not care to be caught up into the empyrean of an equal humanity, but enjoy the poetry of their self-abasement in the belief that their superiors are indeed their betters." So at the South there was a kind of fellowship between the races under slavery which present conditions make more difficult. A settled inequality is the next best thing, for intercourse, to equality.

But where the ideal of equality has entered, even slight differences may be resented, and class feeling is most bitter, probably, where this ideal is strong but has no regular and hopeful methods of asserting itself. In that case aspiration turns sour and generates hateful passions. Caste countries are safe from this by lacking the ideal of equality, democracies by partly realizing it. But in Germany, for instance, where there is a fierce democratic propaganda on the one hand, and a stone wall of military and aristocratic institutions on the other, one may feel a class bitterness that we hardly know in America. And in England also, at the present time, when classes are still recognized but very ill-defined, there seems to be much of an uneasy preoccupation about rank, and of the elbowing, snubbing and suspicion that go with it. People appear to be more concerned with trying to get into a set above them, or repressing others who are pushing up from below, than with us. In America social position exists, but, having no such definite symbols as in England, is for the most part too intangible to give rise to snobbery, which is based on titles and other externalities which men may covet or gloat over in a way hardly possible when the line is merely one of opinion, congeniality and character.

THE BASES OF THE LEISURE CLASS

B Y

THORSTEIN VEBLEN

IN the sequence of cultural evolution the emergence of a leisure class coincides with the beginning of ownership. This is necessarily the case, for these two institutions result from the same set of economic forces. In the inchoate phase of their development they are but different aspects of the same general facts of social structure.

Wherever the institution of private property is found, even in a slightly developed form, the economic process bears the character of a struggle between men for the possession of goods. It has been customary in economic theory, and especially among those economists who adhere with least faltering to the body of modernised classical doc-

Abridged from: Veblen, Thorstein, *The Theory of the Leisure Class,* New York: The Macmillan Co., 1899.

trines, to construe this struggle for wealth as being substantially a struggle for subsistence. Such is, no doubt, its character in large part during the earlier and less efficient phases of industry. Such is also its character in all cases where the "niggardliness of nature" is so strict as to afford but a scanty livelihood to the community in return for strenuous and unremitting application to the business of getting the means of subsistence. But in all progressing communities an advance is presently made beyond this early stage of technological development. Industrial efficiency is presently carried to such a pitch as to afford something appreciably more than a bare livelihood to those engaged in the industrial process. It has not been unusual for economic theory to speak of the further struggle for wealth on this new industrial basis as a competition for an increase of the comforts of life,—primarily for an increase of the physical comforts which the consumption of goods affords.

The end of acquisition and accumulation is conventionally held to be the consumption of the goods accumulated—whether it is consumption directly by the owner of the goods or by the household attached to him and for this purpose identified with him in theory. This is at least felt to be the economically legitimate end of acquisition, which alone it is incumbent on the theory to take account of. Such consumption may of course be conceived to serve the consumer's physical wants —his physical comfort—or his so-called higher wants—spiritual, æsthetic, intellectual, or what not; the latter class of wants being served indirectly by an expenditure of goods, after the fashion familiar to all economic readers.

But it is only when taken in a sense far removed from its naive meaning that consumption of goods can be said to afford the incentive from which accumulation invariably proceeds. The motive that lies at the root of ownership is emulation; and the same motive of emulation continues active in the further development of the institution to which it has given rise and in the development of all those features of the social structure which this institution of ownership touches. The possession of wealth confers honour; it is an invidious distinction. Nothing equally cogent can be said for the consumption of goods, nor for any other conceivable incentive to acquisition, and especially not for any incentive to the accumulation of wealth.

It is of course not to be overlooked that in a community where nearly all goods are private property the necessity of earning a livelihood is a powerful and ever-present incentive for the poorer members of the community. The need of subsistence and of an increase of physical comfort may for a time be the dominant motive of acquisition for those classes who are habitually employed at manual labour, whose subsistence is on a precarious footing, who possess little and ordinarily accumulate little; but it will appear that even in the case of these impecunious classes the predominance of the motive of physical want is not so decided as has sometimes been assumed. On the other hand, so far as regards those members and classes of the community who are chiefly concerned in the accumulation of wealth, the incentive of subsistence or of physical comfort never plays a considerable part.

With the growth of settled industry the possession of wealth gains in relative importance and effectiveness as a customary basis of repute and esteem. Not that esteem ceases to be awarded on the basis of other, more direct evidence of prowess; not that successful predatory aggression or warlike exploit ceases to call out the approval and admiration of the crowd, or to stir the envy of the less successful competitors; but the opportunities for gaining distinction by means of this direct manifestation of superior force grow less available both in scope and frequency. At the same time opportunities for industrial aggression, and for the accumulation of property by the quasi-peaceable methods of nomadic industry, increase in scope and availability. And it is even more to the point that property now becomes the most easily recognised evidence of a reputable degree of success as distinguished from heroic or signal achievement. It therefore becomes the conventional basis of esteem. Its possession in some amount becomes necessary in order to any reputable standing in the community. It becomes indispensable to accumulate, to acquire property, in order to retain one's good name. When accumulated goods have in this way once become the accepted badge of efficiency, the possession of wealth presently assumes the character of an independent and definitive basis of esteem. The possession of goods, whether acquired aggressively by one's own exertion or passively by transmission through inheritance from others, becomes a conventional basis or reputability. The possession of wealth, which was at the outset valued simply as an evidence of efficiency, becomes, in popular apprehension, itself a meritorious act. Wealth is now itself intrinsically honourable and confers honour on its possessor. By a further refinement, wealth acquired passively by transmission from ancestors or other antecedents presently becomes even more honorific than wealth acquired by the possessor's own effort.

Prowess and exploit may still remain the basis of award of the highest popular esteem, although the possession of wealth has become the basis of commonplace reputability and of a blameless social standing. The predatory instinct and the consequent approbation of predatory efficiency are deeply ingrained in the habits of thought of those peoples who have passed under the discipline of a protracted predatory culture. According to popular award, the highest honours within human reach may, even yet, be those gained by an unfolding of extraordinary predatory efficiency in war, or by a quasi-predatory efficiency in state-craft; but for the purposes of a commonplace decent standing in the community these means of repute have been replaced by the acquisition and accumulation of goods. In order to stand well in the eyes of the community, it is necessary to come up to a certain, somewhat indefinite, conventional standard of wealth; just as in the earlier predatory stage it is necessary for the barbarian man to come up to the tribe's standard of physical endurance, cunning, and skill at arms. A certain standard of wealth in the one case, and of prowess in the other, is a necessary condition of reputability, and anything in excess of this normal amount is meritorious.

Those members of the community who fall short of this, somewhat indefinite, normal degree of prowess or of property suffer in the esteem of their fellow-men; and consequently they suffer also in their own esteem, since the usual basis of self-respect is the respect accorded by one's neighbours. Only individuals with an aberrant temperament can in the long run retain their self-esteem in the face of the disesteem of their fellows. Apparent exceptions to the rule are met with, especially among people with strong religious convictions. But these apparent exceptions are scarcely real exceptions, since such persons commonly fall back on the putative approbation of some supernatural witness of their deeds.

So soon as the possession of property becomes the basis of popular esteem, therefore, it becomes also a requisite to that complacency which we call self-respect. In any community where goods are held in severalty it is necessary, in order to his own peace of mind, that an individual should possess as large a portion of goods as others with whom he is accustomed to class himself; and it is extremely gratifying to possess something more than others. But as fast as a person makes new acquisitions, and becomes accustomed to the resulting new standard of wealth, the new standard forthwith ceases to afford appreciably greater satisfaction than the earlier standard did. The tendency in any case is constantly to make the present pecuniary standard the point of departure for a fresh increase of wealth; and this in turn gives rise to a new standard of sufficiency and a new pecuniary classification of one's self as compared with one's neighbours. So far as concerns the present question, the end sought by accumulation is to rank high in comparison with the rest of the community in point of pecuniary strength. So long as the comparison is distinctly unfavourable to himself, the normal, average individual will live in chronic dissatisfaction with his present lot; and when he has reached what may be called the normal pecuniary standard of the community, or of his class in the community, this chronic dissatisfaction will give place to a restless straining to place a wider and ever-widening pecuniary interval between himself and this average standard. The invidious comparison can never become so favourable to the individual making it that he would not gladly rate himself still higher relatively to his competitors in the struggle for pecuniary reputability.

In the nature of the case, the desire for wealth can scarcely be satiated in any individual instance, and evidently a satiation of the average or general desire for wealth is out of the question. However widely, or equally, or "fairly," it may be distributed, no general increase of the community's wealth can make any approach to satiating this need, the ground of which is the desire of every one to excel every one else in the accumulation of goods. If, as is sometimes assumed, the incentive to accumulation were the want of subsistence or of physical comfort, then the aggregate economic wants of a community might conceivably be satisfied at some point in the advance of industrial efficiency; but since the struggle is substantially a race for reputability on the basis of an invidious comparison, no approach to a definitive attainment is possible.

What has just been said must not be taken to mean that there are no other incentives to acquisition and accumulation than this desire to excel in pecuniary standing and so gain the esteem and envy of one's fellow-men. The desire for added comfort and security from want is present as a motive at every stage of the process of accumulation in a modern industrial community; although the standard of sufficiency in these respects is in turn greatly affected by the habit of pecuniary emulation. To a great extent this emulation shapes the methods and selects the objects of expenditure for personal comfort and decent livelihood.

Besides this, the power conferred by wealth also affords a motive to accumulation. That propensity for purposeful activity and that repugnance to all futility of effort which belong to man by virtue of his character as an agent do not desert him when he emerges from the naive communal culture where the dominant note of life is the unanalysed and undifferentiated solidarity of the individual with the group with which his life is bound up. When he enters upon the predatory stage, where self-seeking in the narrower sense becomes the dominant note, this propensity goes with him still, as the pervasive trait that shapes his scheme of life. The propensity for achievement and the repugnance to futility remain the underlying economic motive. The propensity changes only in the form of its expression and in the proximate objects to which it directs the man's activity. Under the régime of individual ownership the most available means of visibly achieving a purpose is that afforded by the acquisition and accumulation of goods; and as the self-regarding antithesis between man and man reaches fuller consciousness, the propensity for achievement—the instinct of workmanship—tends more and more to shape itself into a straining to excel others in pecuniary achievement. Relative success, tested by an invidious pecuniary comparison with other men, becomes the conventional end of action. The currently accepted legitimate end of effort becomes the achievement of a favourable comparison with other men; and therefore the repugnance to futility to a good extent coalesces with the incentive of emulation. It acts to accentuate the struggle for pecuniary reputability by visiting with a sharper disapproval all shortcoming and all evidence of shortcoming in point of pecuniary success. Purposeful effort comes to mean, primarily, effort directed to or resulting in a more creditable showing of accumulated wealth. Among the motives which lead men to accumulate wealth, the primacy, both in scope and intensity, therefore, continues to belong to this motive of pecuniary emulation.

In making use of the term "invidious," it may perhaps be unnecessary to remark, there is no intention to extol or depreciate, or to commend or deplore any of the phenomena which the word is used to characterise. The term is used in a technical sense as describing a comparison of persons with a view to rating and grading them in respect of relative worth or value—in an æsthetic or moral sense—and so awarding and defining the relative degrees of complacency with which they may legitimately be contemplated by themselves and by others. An invidious comparison is a process of valuation of persons in respect of worth.

*   *   *

If its working were not disturbed by other economic forces or other features of the emulative process, the immediate effect of such a pecuniary struggle as has just been described in outline would be to make men industrious and frugal. This result actually follows, in some measure, so far as regards the lower classes, whose ordinary means of acquiring goods is productive labour. These lower classes can in any case not avoid labour, and the imputation of labour is therefore not greatly derogatory to them, at least not within their class. Rather, since labour is their recognised and accepted mode of life, they take some emulative pride in a reputation for efficiency in their work, this being often the only line of emulation that is open to them. For those for whom acquisition and emulation is possible only within the field of productive efficiency and thrift, the struggle for pecuniary reputability will in some measure work out in an increase of diligence and parsimony. But certain secondary features of the emulative process, yet to be spoken of, come in to very materially circumscribe and modify emulation in these directions among the pecuniarily inferior classes as well as among the superior class.

But it is otherwise with the superior pecuniary class, with which we are here immediately concerned. For this class also the incentive to diligence and thrift is not absent; but its action is so greatly qualified by the secondary demands of pecuniary emulation, that any inclination in this direction is practically overborne and any incentive to diligence tends to be of no effect. The most imperative of these secondary demands of emulation, as well as the one of widest scope, is the requirement of abstention from productive work.

In order to gain and to hold the esteem of men it is not sufficient merely to possess wealth or power. The wealth or power must be put in evidence, for esteem is awarded only on evidence. And not only does the evidence of wealth serve to impress one's importance on others and to keep their sense of his importance alive and alert, but it is of scarcely less use in building up and preserving one's self-complacency.

This direct, subjective value of leisure and of other evidences of wealth is no doubt in great part secondary and derivative. It is in part a reflex of the utility of leisure as a means of gaining the respect of others, and in part it is the result of a mental substitution. The performance of labour has been accepted as a conventional evidence of inferior force; therefore it comes itself, by a mental short-cut, to be regarded as intrinsically base.

Abstention from labour is not only a honorific or meritorious act, but it presently comes to be a requisite of decency. The insistence on property as the basis of reputability is very naive and very imperious during the early stages of the accumulation of wealth. Abstention from labour is the conventional evidence of wealth and is therefore the conventional mark of social standing; and this insistence on the meritoriousness of wealth leads to a more strenuous insistence on leisure. *Nota notæ est nota rei ipsius.* According to well-established laws of human nature, prescription presently seizes upon this conventional evidence of wealth and fixes it in men's habits of thought as something that is in itself substantially meritorious and ennobling; while productive labour at the same time and by a like process becomes in a double sense intrinsically unworthy. Prescription ends by making labour not only disreputable in the eyes of the community, but morally impossible to the noble, freeborn man, and incompatible with a worthy life.

So much of the honourable life of leisure as is not spent in the sight of spectators can serve the purposes of reputability only in so far as it leaves a tangible, visible result that can be put in evidence and can be measured and compared with products of the same class exhibited by competing aspirants for repute. Some such effect, in the way of leisurely manners and carriage, etc., follows from simple persistent abstention from work, even where the subject does not take thought of the matter and studiously acquire an air of leisurely opulence and mastery. Especially does it seem to be true that a life of leisure in this way persisted in through several generations will leave a persistent, ascertainable effect in the conformation of the person, and still more in his habitual bearing and demeanour. But all the suggestions of a cumulative life of leisure, and all the proficiency in decorum that comes by the way of passive habituation, may be further improved upon by taking thought and assiduously acquiring the marks of honourable leisure, and then carrying the exhibition of these adventitious marks of exemption from employment out in a strenuous and systematic discipline. Plainly, this is a point at which a diligent application of effort and expenditure may materially further the attainment of a decent proficiency in the leisure-class proprieties. Conversely, the greater the degree of proficiency and the more patent the evidence of a high degree of habituation to observances which serve no lucrative or other directly useful purpose, the greater the consumption of time and substance impliedly involved in their acquisition, and the greater the resultant good repute. Hence, under the competitive struggle for proficiency in good manners, it comes about that much pains is taken with the cultivation of habits of decorum; and hence the details of decorum develop into a comprehensive discipline, conformity to which is required of all who would be held blameless in point of repute. And hence, on the other hand, this conspicuous leisure of which decorum is a ramification grows gradually into a laborious drill in deportment and an education in taste and discrimination as to what articles of consumption are decorous and what are the decorous methods of consuming them.

In this connection it is worthy of notice that the possibility of producing pathological and other idiosyncrasies of person and manner by shrewd mimicry and a systematic drill have been turned to account in the deliberate production of a cultured class—often with a very happy effect. In this way, by the process vulgarly known as snobbery, a syncopated evolution of gentle birth and breeding is achieved in the case of a goodly number of families and lines of descent. This syncopated gentle birth gives results which, in point of serviceability as a leisure-class factor in the population, are in no wise substantially inferior to others who may have had a longer but less arduous training in the pecuniary proprieties.

Much of the courtesy of everyday intercourse is of course a direct expression of consideration and kindly good-will, and this element of conduct has for the most part no need of being traced back to any

underlying ground of reputability to explain either its presence or the
approval with which it is regarded; but the same is not true of the code
of proprieties. These latter are expressions of status. It is of course
sufficiently plain, to any one who cares to see, that our bearing towards menials and other pecuniarily dependent inferiors is the bearing
of the superior member in a relation of status, though its manifestation
is often greatly modified and softened from the original expression of
crude dominance. Similarly, our bearing towards superiors, and in
great measure towards equals, expresses a more or less conventionalised
attitude of subservience. Witness the masterful presence of the high-
minded gentleman or lady, which testifies to so much of dominance
and independence of economic circumstances, and which at the same
time appeals with such convincing force to our sense of what is right
and gracious. It is among this highest leisure class, who have no superiors and few peers, that decorum finds its fullest and maturest
expression; and it is this highest class also that gives decorum that
definitive formulation which serves as a canon of conduct for the classes
beneath. And here also the code is most obviously a code of status and
shows most plainly its incompatibility with all vulgarly productive
work. A divine assurance and an imperious complaisance, as of one
habituated to require subservience and to take no thought for the
morrow, is the birthright and the criterion of the gentleman at his
best; and it is in popular apprehension even more than that, for this
demeanour is accepted as an intrinsic attribute of superior worth, before which the base-born commoner delights to stoop and yield.

THE PECUNIARY STANDARD OF LIVING

For the great body of the people in any modern community, the
proximate ground of expenditure in excess of what is required for
physical comfort is not a conscious effort to excel in the expensiveness
of their visible consumption, so much as it is a desire to live up to the
conventional standard of decency in the amount and grade of goods
consumed. This desire is not guided by a rigidly invariable standard,
which must be lived up to, and beyond which there is no incentive to
go. The standard is flexible; and especially it is indefinitely extensible,
if only time is allowed for habituation to any increase in pecuniary
ability and for acquiring facility in the new and larger scale of expenditure that follows such an increase. It is much more difficult to
recede from a scale of expenditure once adopted than it is to extend
the accustomed scale in response to an accession of wealth. Many items
of customary expenditure prove on analysis to be almost purely wasteful, and they are therefore honorific only, but after they have once
been incorporated into the scale of decent consumption, and so have

become an integral part of one's scheme of life, it is quite as hard to give up these as it is to give up many items that conduce directly to one's physical comfort, or even that may be necessary to life and health. That is to say, the conspicuously wasteful honorific expenditure that confers spiritual well-being may become more indispensable than much of that expenditure which ministers to the "lower" wants of physical well-being or sustenance only. It is notoriously just as difficult to recede from a "high" standard of living as it is to lower a standard which is already relatively low; although in the former case the difficulty is a moral one, while in the latter it may involve a material deduction from the physical comforts of life.

But while retrogression is difficult, a fresh advance in conspicuous expenditure is relatively easy; indeed, it takes place almost as a matter of course. In the rare cases where it occurs, a failure to increase one's visible consumption when the means for an increase are at hand is felt in popular apprehension to call for explanation, and unworthy motives of miserliness are imputed to those who fall short in this respect. A prompt response to the stimulus, on the other hand, is accepted as the normal effect. This suggests that the standard of expenditure which commonly guides our efforts is not the average, ordinary expenditure already achieved; it is an ideal of consumption that lies just beyond our reach, or to reach which requires some strain. The motive is emulation—the stimulus of an invidious comparison which prompts us to outdo those with whom we are in the habit of classing ourselves. Substantially the same proposition is expressed in the commonplace remark that each class envies and emulates the class next above it in the social scale, while it rarely compares itself with those below or with those who are considerably in advance. That is to say, in other words, our standard of decency in expenditure, as in other ends of emulation, is set by the usage of those next above us in reputability; until, in this way, especially in any community where class distinctions are somewhat vague, all canons of reputability and decency, and all standards of consumption, are traced back by insensible gradations to the usages and habits of thought of the highest social and pecuniary class—the wealthy leisure class.

It is for this class to determine, in general outline, what scheme of life the community shall accept as decent or honorific; and it is their office by precept and example to set forth this scheme of social salvation in its highest, ideal form. But the higher leisure class can exercise this quasi-sacerdotal office only under certain material limitations. The class cannot at discretion effect a sudden revolution or reversal of the popular habits of thought with respect to any of these ceremonial requirements. It takes time for any change to permeate the mass and change the habitual attitude of the people; and especially it takes time to change the habits of those classes that are socially more remote from the radiant body. The process is slower where the mobility of the population is less or where the intervals between the several classes are wider and more abrupt. But if time be allowed, the scope of the discretion of the leisure class as regards questions of form and detail in the community's scheme of life is large; while as regards the substantial principles of reputability, the changes which it can effect lie within a narrow margin of tolerance. Its example and precept carries the force of prescription for all classes below it; but in working out the precepts which are handed down as governing the form and method of reputability—in shaping the usages and the spiritual attitude of the lower classes—this authoritative prescription constantly works under the selective guidance of the canon of conspicuous waste, tempered in varying degree by the instinct of workmanship. To these norms is to be added another broad principle of human nature—the predatory animus—which in point of generality and of psychological content lies between the two just named. The effect of the latter in shaping the accepted scheme of life is yet to be discussed.

The canon of reputability, then, must adapt itself to the economic circumstances, the traditions, and the degree of spiritual maturity of the particular class whose scheme of life it is to regulate. It is especially to be noted that however high its authority and however true to the fundamental requirements of reputability it may have been at its inception, a specific formal observance can under no circumstances maintain itself in force if with the lapse of time or on its transmission to a lower pecuniary class it is found to run counter to the ultimate ground of decency among civilised peoples, namely, serviceability for the purpose of an invidious comparison in pecuniary success.

It is evident that these canons of expenditure have much to say in determining the standard of living for any community and for any class. It is no less evident that the standard of living which prevails at any time or at any given social altitude will in its turn have much to say as to the forms which honorific expenditure will take, and as to the degree to which this "higher" need will dominate a people's consumption. In this respect the control exerted by the accepted standard of living is chiefly of a negative character; it acts almost solely to prevent recession from a scale of conspicuous expenditure that has once become habitual.

A standard of living is of the nature of habit. It is an habitual scale and method of responding to given stimuli. The difficulty in the way of receding from an accustomed standard is the difficulty of breaking a habit that has once been formed. The relative facility with which an advance in the standard is made means that the life process is a process of unfolding activity and that it will readily unfold in a new direction whenever and wherever the resistance to self-expression decreases. But when the habit of expression along such a given line of low resistance has once been formed, the discharge will seek the accustomed outlet even after a change has taken place in the environment whereby the external resistance has appreciably risen. That heightened facility of expression in a given direction which is called habit may offset a considerable increase in the resistance offered by external circumstances to the unfolding of life in the given direction. As between the various habits, or habitual modes and directions of expression, which go to make up an individual's standard of living, there is an appreciable difference in point of persistence under counteracting circumstances and in point of the degree of imperativeness with which the discharge seeks a given direction.

The accepted standard of expenditure in the community or in the class to which a person belongs largely determines what his standard of living will be. It does this directly by commending itself to his common sense as right and good, through his habitually contemplating it and assimilating the scheme of life in which it belongs; but it does so also indirectly through popular insistence on conformity to the accepted scale of expenditure as a matter of propriety, under pain of disesteem and ostracism. To accept and practise the standard of living which is in vogue is both agreeable and expedient, commonly to the point of being indispensable to personal comfort and to success in life. The standard of living of any class, so far as concerns the element of conspicuous waste, is commonly as high as the earning capacity of the class will permit—with a constant tendency to go higher. The effect upon the serious activities of men is therefore to direct them with great singleness of purpose to the largest possible acquisition of wealth, and to discountenance work that brings no pecuniary gain. At the same time the effect on consumption is to concentrate it upon the lines which are most patent to the observers whose good opinion is sought; while the inclinations and aptitudes whose exercise does not involve a honorific expenditure of time or substance tend to fall into abeyance through disuse.

CLASS CONSERVATISM

The leisure class is in great measure sheltered from the stress of those economic exigencies which prevail in any modern, highly organised industrial community. The exigencies of the struggle for the means of life are less exacting for this class than for any other; and as a consequence of this privileged position we should expect to find it one of the least responsive of the classes of society to the demands which the situation makes for a further growth of institutions and a readjustment to an altered industrial situation. The leisure class is the conservative class. The exigencies of the general economic situation of the community do not freely or directly impinge upon the members of this class. They are not required under penalty of forfeiture to change their habits of life and their theoretical views of the external world to suit the demands of an altered industrial technique, since they are not in the full sense an organic part of the industrial community. Therefore these exigencies do not readily produce, in the members of this class, that degree of uneasiness with the existing order which alone can lead any body of men to give up views and methods of life that have become habitual to them. The office of the leisure class in social evolution is to retard the movement and to conserve what is obsolescent. This proposition is by no means novel; it has long been one of the commonplaces of popular opinion.

The prevalent conviction that the wealthy class is by nature conservative has been popularly accepted without much aid from any theoretical view as to the place and relation of that class in the cultural development. When an explanation of this class conservatism is offered, it is commonly the invidious one that the wealthy class opposes innovation because it has a vested interest, of an unworthy sort, in maintaining the present conditions. The explanation here put forward imputes no unworthy motive. The opposition of the class to changes in the cultural scheme is instinctive, and does not rest primarily on an interested calculation of material advantages; it is a revulsion at any departure from the accepted way of doing and of looking at things—a revulsion common to all men and only to be overcome by stress of circumstances. All change in habits of life and of thought is irksome. The difference in this respect between the wealthy and the common run of mankind lies not so much in the motive which prompts to conservatism as in the degree of exposure to the economic forces that urge a change. The members of the wealthy class do not yield to the demand for innovation as readily as other men because they are not constrained to do so.

This conservatism of the wealthy class is so obvious a feature that it has even come to be recognised as a mark of respectability. Since conservatism is a characteristic of the wealthier and therefore more reputable portion of the community, it has acquired a certain honorific or decorative value. It has become prescriptive to such an extent that an adherence to conservative views is comprised as a matter of course in our notions of respectability; and it is imperatively incumbent on all who would lead a blameless life in point of social repute.

The fact that the usages, actions, and views of the well-to-do leisure class acquire the character of a prescriptive canon of conduct for the rest of society, gives added weight and reach to the conservative influence of that class. It makes it incumbent upon all reputable people to follow their lead. So that, by virtue of its high position as the avatar of good form, the wealthier class comes to exert a retarding influence upon social development far in excess of that which the simple numerical strength of the class would assign it. Its prescriptive example acts to greatly stiffen the resistance of all other classes against any innovation, and to fix men's affections upon the good institutions handed down from an earlier generation.

CLASS, STATUS AND PARTY

B Y

MAX WEBER

ECONOMICALLY DETERMINED POWER AND THE SOCIAL ORDER

LAW exists when there is a probability that an order will be upheld by a specific staff of men who will use physical or psychical compulsion with the intention of obtaining conformity with the order, or of inflicting sanctions for infringement of it.[1] The structure of every legal order directly influences the distribution of power, economic or otherwise, within its respective community. This is true of all legal orders and not only that of the state. In general, we understand by "power" the chance of a man or of a number of men to realize their own will in a communal action even against the resistance of others who are participating in the action.

"Economically conditioned" power is not, of course, identical with "power" as such. On the contrary, the emergence of economic power may be the consequence of power existing on other grounds. Man does not strive for power only in order to enrich himself economically. Power, including economic power, may be valued "for its own sake." Very frequently the striving for power is also conditioned by the social

Abridged from: Weber, Max, "Class, Status, Party," *From Max Weber: Essays in Sociology* (translated by H. H. Gerth and C. Wright Mills), New York: Oxford University Press, 1946. Reprinted by permission of Oxford University Press, Inc.

[1] *Wirtschaft und Gesellschaft,* part III, chap. 4, pp. 631–40. The first sentence in paragraph one and the several definitions in this chapter which are in brackets do not appear in the original text. They have been taken from other contexts of *Wirtschaft und Gesellschaft.* [Tr.]

"honor" it entails. Not all power, however, entails social honor: The typical American Boss, as well as the typical big speculator, deliberately relinquishes social honor. Quite generally, "mere economic" power, and especially "naked" money power, is by no means a recognized basis of social honor. Nor is power the only basis of social honor. Indeed, social honor, or prestige, may even be the basis of political or economic power, and very frequently has been. Power, as well as honor, may be guaranteed by the legal order, but, at least normally, it is not their primary source. The legal order is rather an additional factor that enhances the chance to hold power or honor; but it cannot always secure them.

The way in which social honor is distributed in a community between typical groups participating in this distribution we may call the "social order." The social order and the economic order are, of course, similarly related to the "legal order." However, the social and the economic order are not identical. The economic order is for us merely the way in which economic goods and services are distributed and used. The social order is of course conditioned by the economic order to a high degree, and in its turn reacts upon it.

Now: "classes," "status groups," and "parties" are phenomena of the distribution of power within a community.

DETERMINATION OF CLASS-SITUATION BY MARKET-SITUATION

In our terminology, "classes" are not communities; they merely represent possible, and frequent, bases for communal action. We may speak of a "class" when (1) a number of people have in common a specific causal component of their life chances, in so far as (2) this component is represented exclusively by economic interests in the possession of goods and opportunities for income, and (3) is represented under the conditions of the commodity or labor markets. [These points refer to "class situation," which we may express more briefly as the typical chance for a supply of goods, external living conditions, and personal life experiences, in so far as this chance is determined by the amount and kind of power, or lack of such, to dispose of goods or skills for the sake of income in a given economic order. The term "class" refers to any group of people that is found in the same class situation.]

COMMUNAL ACTION FLOWING FROM CLASS INTEREST

According to our terminology, the factor that creates "class" is unambiguously economic interest, and indeed, only those interests involved in the existence of the "market." Nevertheless, the concept of "class-interest" is an ambiguous one: even as an empirical concept it is ambiguous as soon as one understands by it something other than the factual direction of interests following with a certain probability from the class situation for a certain "average" of those people subjected to the class situation. The class situation and other circumstances remaining the same, the direction in which the individual worker, for instance, is likely to pursue his interests may vary widely, according to whether he is constitutionally qualified for the task at hand to a high, to an average, or to a low degree. In the same way, the direction of interests may vary according to whether or not a *communal* action of a larger or smaller portion of those commonly affected by the "class situation," or even an association among them, e.g. a "trade union," has grown out of the class situation from which the individual may or may not expect promising results. [Communal action refers to that action which is oriented to the feeling of the actors that they belong together. Societal action, on the other hand, is oriented to a rationally motivated adjustment of interests.] The rise of societal or even of communal action from a common class situation is by no means a universal phenomenon.

The class situation may be restricted in its effects to the generation of essentially *similar* reactions, that is to say, within our terminology, of "mass actions." However, it may not have even this result. Furthermore, often merely an amorphous communal action emerges. The degree in which "communal action" and possibly "societal action," emerges from the "mass actions" of the members of a class is linked to general cultural conditions, especially to those of an intellectual sort. It is also linked to the extent of the contrasts that have already evolved, and is especially linked to the *transparency* of the connections between the causes and the consequences of the "class situation." For however different life chances may be, this fact in itself, according to all experience, by no means gives birth to "class action" (communal action by the members of a class). The fact of being conditioned and the results of the class situation must be distinctly recognizable. For only then the contrast of life chances can be felt not as an absolutely given fact to be accepted, but as a resultant from either (1) the given distribution of property, or (2) the structure of the concrete economic order. It is only then that people may react against the class structure not only through acts of an intermittent and irrational protest, but in the form of rational association.

TYPES OF "CLASS STRUGGLE"

Thus every class may be the carrier of any one of the possibly innumerable forms of "class action," but this is not necessarily so. In any case, a class does not in itself constitute a community. To treat "class" conceptually as having the same value as "community" leads to distortion. That men in the same class situation regularly react in mass actions to such tangible situations as economic ones in the direction of those interests that are most adequate to their average number is an important and after all simple fact for the understanding of historical events.

Yet, if classes as such are not communities, nevertheless class situations emerge only on the basis of communalization. The communal action that brings forth class situations, however, is not basically action between members of the identical class; it is an action between members of different classes. Communal actions that directly determine the class situation of the worker and the entrepreneur are: the labor market, the commodities market, and the capitalistic enterprise. But, in its turn, the existence of a capitalistic enterprise presupposes that a very specific communal action exists and that it is specifically structured to protect the possession of goods *per se,* and especially the power of individuals to dispose, in principle freely, over the means of production. The existence of a capitalistic enterprise is preconditioned by a specific kind of "legal order." Each kind of class situation, and above all when it rests upon the power of property *per se,* will become most clearly efficacious when all other determinants of reciprocal relations are, as far as possible, eliminated in their significance. It is in this way that the utilization of the power of property in the market obtains its most sovereign importance.

STATUS HONOR

In contrast to classes, *status groups* are normally communities. They are, however, often of an amorphous kind. In contrast to the purely economically determined "class situation" we wish to designate as "status situation" every typical component of the life fate of men that is determined by a specific, positive or negative, social estimation of *honor.* This honor may be connected with any quality shared by a plurality, and, of course, it can be knit to a class situation: class distinctions are linked in the most varied ways with status distinctions. Property as such is not always recognized as a status qualification, but in the long run it is, and with extraordinary regularity. But status honor need not necessarily be linked with a "class situation." On the contrary, it normally stands in sharp opposition to the pretensions of sheer property. Both propertied and propertyless people can belong to the same status group, and frequently they do with very tangible consequences. This "equality" of social esteem may, however, in the long run become quite precarious.

GUARANTEES OF STATUS STRATIFICATION

In content, status honor is normally expressed by the fact that above all else a specific *style of life* can be expected from all those who wish to belong to the circle. Linked with this expectation are restrictions on "social" intercourse (that is, intercourse which is not subservient to economic or any other of business's "functional" purposes). These restrictions may confine normal marriages to within the status circle and may lead to complete endogamous closure. As soon as there is not a mere individual and socially irrelevant imitation of another style of life, but an agreed-upon communal action of this closing character, the "status" development is under way.

The development of status is essentially a question of stratification resting upon usurpation. Such usurpation is the normal origin of almost all status honor. But the road from this purely conventional situation to legal privilege, positive or negative, is easily traveled as soon as a certain stratification of the social order has in fact been "lived in" and has achieved stability by virtue of a stable distribution of economic power.

"ETHNIC" SEGREGATION AND "CASTE"

Where the consequences have been realized to their full extent, the status group evolves into a closed "caste." Status distinctions are then guaranteed not merely by conventions and laws, but also by *rituals*. This occurs in such a way that every physical contact with a member of any caste that is considered to be "lower" by the members of a "higher" caste is considered as making for a ritualistic impurity and to be a stigma which must be expiated by a religious act. Individual castes develop quite distinct cults and gods.

In general, however, the status structure reaches such extreme consequences only where there are underlying differences which are held to be "ethnic." The "caste" is, indeed, the normal form in which ethnic communities usually live side by side in a "societalized" manner. These ethnic communities believe in blood relationship and exclude exogamous marriage and social intercourse. Such a caste situation is part of the phenomenon of "pariah" peoples and is found all over the world. These people form communities, acquire specific occupational traditions of handicrafts or of other arts, and cultivate a belief in their ethnic community. They live in a "diaspora" strictly segregated from all personal intercourse, except that of an unavoidable sort, and their situation is legally precarious. Yet, by virtue of their economic indispensability, they are tolerated, indeed, frequently privileged, and they live in interspersed political communities.

A "status" segregation grown into a "caste" differs in its structure from a mere "ethnic" segregation: the caste structure transforms the horizontal and unconnected coexistences of ethnically segregated groups into a vertical social system of super- and subordination. Correctly formulated: a comprehensive societalization integrates the ethnically divided communities into specific political and communal action. In their consequences they differ precisely in this way: ethnic coexistences condition a mutual repulsion and disdain but allow each ethnic community to consider its own honor as the highest one; the caste structure brings about a social subordination and an acknowledgment of "more honor" in favor of the privileged caste and status groups. This is due to the fact that in the caste structure ethnic distinctions as such have become "functional" distinctions within the political societalization (warriors, priests, artisans that are politically important for war and for buildings, and so on). But even pariah people who are most despised are usually apt to continue cultivating in some manner that which is equally peculiar to ethnic and to status communities: the belief in their own specific "honor."

Only with the negatively privileged status groups does the "sense of dignity" take a specific deviation. A sense of dignity is the precipitation in individuals of social honor and of conventional demands which a positively privileged status group raises for the deportment of its members. The sense of dignity that characterizes positively privileged status groups is naturally related to their "being" which does not transcend itself, that is, it is to their "beauty and excellence." Their kingdom is "of this world." They live for the present and by exploiting their great past. The sense of dignity of the negatively privileged strata naturally refers to a future lying beyond the present, whether it is of this life or of another.

Incidentally, the development of status groups from ethnic segregations is by no means the normal phenomenon. On the contrary, since objective "racial differences" are by no means basic to every subjective sentiment of an ethnic community, the ultimately racial foundation of status structure is rightly and absolutely a question of the concrete individual case.

PARTIES

Whereas the genuine place of "classes" is within the economic order, the place of "status groups" is within the social order, that is, within the sphere of the distribution of "honor." From within these spheres, classes and status groups influence one another and they influence the legal order and are in turn influenced by it. But "parties" live in a house of "power."

Their action is oriented toward the acquisition of social "power," that is to say, toward influencing a communal action no matter what its content may be. In principle, parties may exist in a social "club" as well as in a "state." As over against the actions of classes and status groups, for which this is not necessarily the case, the communal actions of "parties" always mean a societalization. For party actions are always directed toward a goal which is striven for in planned manner. This goal may be a "cause" (the party may aim at realizing a program for ideal or material purposes), or the goal may be "personal" (sinecures, power, and from these, honor for the leader and the followers of the party). Usually the party action aims at all these simultaneously. Parties are, therefore, only possible within communities that are societalized, that is, which have some rational order and a staff of persons available who are ready to enforce it. For parties aim precisely at influencing this staff, and if possible, to recruit it from party followers.

In any individual case, parties may represent interests determined through "class situation" or "status situation," and they may recruit their following respectively from one or the other. But they need be neither purely "class" nor purely "status" parties. In most cases they are partly class parties and partly status parties, but sometimes they are neither. They may represent ephemeral or enduring structures.

PART V

The Persistence of Social Structures

SOCIOLOGICAL THEORY MUST ACCOUNT FOR THE PERSISTENCE OF society and of social structures just as it must account for their development and their changes. The body of theory concerned with social stability has appeared under different names, among which social control and conformity are, perhaps, most common. Although the term social control is frequently rejected because it may imply a dualism between society and the individual, it is still a useful concept when taken in the context of socialization and the maintenance of patterns of behavior consonant with established social expectations. Likewise, the pressure to conform may be viewed as the complement of social control. These points of view underlie the materials selected for Part V.

Georg Simmel's article on "The Persistence of Social Groups" is probably the most extensive theoretical consideration of this subject which has appeared, and constitutes our Chapter 13. Simmel's examination of the subject—ostensibly to illustrate what he means by a distinctively sociological analysis—proceeds from the more external conditions which yield persistence to the most subtle integrating forces at work within the group. Without yielding to the temptation to assign exclusive or even critical influence to any one factor, Simmel's analysis nevertheless achieves a remarkable theoretical unity.

The processes by which social stability is achieved are the subject matter of Chapter 14. The selection from *Suicide* by Durkheim characterizes the power of collective tendencies to produce social regularities. The selections by William I. Thomas— the first from *The Unadjusted Girl* and the second from his earlier *Source Book for Social Origins*—emphasize the power which the perceived norms, or definitions of the situation, exercise over behavior. More systematically, Edward A. Ross, in a selection from his *Social Control,* considers some of the processes by which social stability is maintained and analyzes the influence of types of groups, norms, and codes on social behavior. The excerpt from William McDougall's *Introduction to Social Psychology* uses the concept of "imitation," made popular by the French sociologist Gabriel Tarde, to mean the process whereby traditions are preserved and innovations shared, and emphasizes that social stability and social change are complementary.

The stable components of society may be felt by the individual as pressures to conform. The selections from Charles Horton Cooley's *Social Organization* in Chapter 15 explore these pressures as they appear in the social self. Conscience is viewed as the personal reflection of the social expectation to conform, and nonconformity is analyzed by reference to what Cooley calls "remoter conformity." The result for society is order and continuity on the one hand and adaptability and change on the other. The part which the personal model plays for the individual in achieving this continuity is suggested in the second selection in this chapter by Edward A. Ross, "The Personal Ideal and Social Control." A. R. Radcliffe-Brown's consideration of social sanctions views the problem of societal persistence in its broadest context. Society persists through the exercise of sanctions. Sanctions appear as motives in the individual regulating his conduct toward conformity and as organized power through which the group enforces its own survival insofar as its membership is concerned. This viewpoint, consistent with that of Cooley and Ross, systematizes the underlying point of view which this chapter and, indeed, the whole of Part V presents.

CHAPTER 13

The Persistence of Groups

———•••———

THE PERSISTENCE OF SOCIAL GROUPS

BY

GEORG SIMMEL

THE subject-matter of sociology is the forms or ways in which human beings exist beside, for, and with each other. The purposes for the sake of which these socializations come into being—economic and social, religious and criminal, sexual and military, political and ethical, etc. —will be treated by other sciences. Since now socialization only occurs among human beings for the sake of such purposes, we shall discover the laws of social forms only by collecting such societary phenomena of the most diverse contents, and by ascertaining what is common to them in spite of their diversity. In this way the diverse contents of the forms of socialization nullify each other, and that which is formally the same, the societary form as such, must clearly appear. By this method we discover, for example, as such forms, superiority and inferiority, the erection of hierarchies, competition, division of labor, imitation, representation, and countless other types of human socialization. Only after all their separate forms, from their most primitive to their most developed types, have been inductively determined and psychologically interpreted, can we gradually solve the riddle: "What is society in its essence?" For society is surely not a structure so unitary that a single exhaustive definition is possible. Society consists rather of

Abridged from: Simmel, Georg, "The Persistence of Social Groups (translated by Albion W. Small), *American Journal of Sociology*, 1897, 3, 662–698, 829–836, and 1898, 4, 35–50.

the sum of all the ways and means of combination that appear among its elements. It cannot be said that "society" must exist before all these separate relations make their appearance in society. Any single relation may be eliminated, to be sure, since in the societies known to us there are always enough remaining relations. If we try to project our thought beyond all these relations, however, there remains no society at all.

Merely as an example of this method I shall attempt in the following to exhibit the specific ways in which society as such maintains itself. In this attempt I use the term "society" not in the now usual sense of the whole great complex of all the individuals and groups held together by common nationality or common culture. I see society rather wherever a number of human beings come into reciprocity and form a transient or permanent unity. In each such unification the phenomenon emerges which also determines the life of the individuals, viz., that at every moment destructive forces attack the life both from within and from without, and, if these alone operated, the unity would soon be resolved into its elements or transformed into other combinations. But opposed to these destructive forces there are preservative influences which hold the individual parts together by maintaining reciprocity between them, from which comes cohesion of parts, and hence a unity of the whole. This unity is of longer or shorter duration, until, like everything earthly, it at last yields to decomposing forces.

At this point the justification must appear for speaking of the society as a special unity over and above its individual elements. These phenomena of the self-preservation of societies are by no means identical with the instinct of self-preservation in the individual members. The latter, on the contrary, calls for quite different treatment; it employs quite different forces from those that preserve the group to which the individual belongs; so that the self-preservation of the individuals may be complete while that of the group is weakened and destroyed, or, on the contrary, the latter may show itself still in full force after the self-sustaining power of the individuals is in decadence. These facts have done the most to recommend the idea that the society, the unified group, is a structure of independent reality, which leads its life after peculiar laws and by virtue of peculiar forces, independent of all its individual components. In fact, when we consider the development and the characteristics of language, morals, church, law, political and social organization, that conception seems inevitable. All these seem to be products and functions of an impersonal structure. They seem to belong to all in common, as a piece of public property belongs to the community, yet in such a way that no individual could be named as the sufficient cause or the determining purpose of the same, nor could the precise share of any single individual in its creation be distinguished. These products stand rather over against the individual as something objective, absolved from the limitations of personal life. On the other hand, it is certain that in the last analysis only individuals exist, that there are human products apart from human beings themselves only in the case of material things; that, on the other hand, spiritual structures like those just mentioned have their existence only in personal minds. Every attempt to think of them outside of persons is a mysticism like the conceptual realism which made independent substantial entities of human ideas. How, then, if we hold fast to the existence of individuals only, shall we explain the super-individual character of those structures, the objectivity and independence of societary forces and organizations?

So far as I can see, this antinomy can be resolved in only one way. From the view point of completed knowledge we must hold unconditionally to the fact that there are only spiritual individuals. An all-penetrating vision would peremptorily resolve that appearance which seems to announce a new independent unity above the individuals into the reciprocity which plays between the individuals, and it would see that, if this reciprocity were actually separated from the individuals, nothing of it could remain. But this completed knowledge is denied to men. The relations of human beings to each other are so complex, so ramified, and so compact that it would be a wholly hopeless task to resolve them into their elements, and we are consequently compelled to treat them as unities rather than as self-existing structures. It is, therefore, only a methodological device to speak of the essence and the development of the state, of law, of institutions, of fashion, etc., as if each of these were a unified entity. We cannot resolve the unitary aspect which they present to us into its components, and it is, therefore, a scientific interim-filler if we treat this aspect as a something that has an independent existence. This provisional convenience is like our treatment of the "life processes" as though they were a proper entity, although we assume that they are merely the complex of the endlessly complicated mechanical reciprocities of the minutest parts of the organic body. In like manner is the conflict to be adjusted between the individualistic and, as we may term it, the monistic conception of the social structure. The former corresponds with the fact, the latter with the limited power of analysis; the former is the ideal of intelligence, the latter the stage of understanding actually attained. In our knowledge of physical organisms we have succeeded in thinking beyond the idea of a vital power that seemed to sway over the separate organs, and to compose a new entity in addition to them. We have, in part at least, substituted for this conception the reciprocal action of the organs. In like manner we must attempt in the social sciences to approach nearer and nearer to the individual operations which produce the social structure, however far we may be obliged to stop short of complete analysis. In the case of our particular subject-matter the question might be formulated in this way: When we see that the most manifold socializations betray the operation of apparently specific efficient forces, in behalf of self-maintenance, into what more primary processes may these phenomena be resolved? Although the continuance of the group, after it is once in existence, seems to declare at the same time a special vital force, a stability having a unified source, all this is nevertheless the consequence, or rather summation (*Zusammenfassung*), of a collection of separate and manifold fragmentary processes of a social nature. Our task, therefore, is to search these out.

The most general case in which the persistence of the group presents itself as a problem occurs in the fact that, in spite of the departure and the change of members, the group remains identical. We say that it is the same state, the same association, the same army, which now exists that existed so and so many decades or centuries ago. This, although no single member of the original organization remains. Here is one of the cases in which the temporal order of events presents a marked analogy with the spatial order. Out of individuals existing side by side, that is, apart from each other, a social unity is formed. The inevitable separation which space places between men is nevertheless overcome by the spiritual bond between them, so that there arises an appearance of unified interexistence. In like manner the temporal separation of individuals and of generations presents their union in our conceptions as a coherent, uninterrupted whole. In the case of persons spatially separated this unity is effected by the reciprocity maintained between them across the dividing distance. The unity of complex beings means nothing else than the cohesion of elements which is produced by the reciprocal exercise of forces. In the case of temporally separated persons, however, unity cannot be effected in this manner, because reciprocity is lacking. The earlier may influence the later, but the later cannot influence the earlier. Hence the persistence of the social unity in spite of shifting membership presents a peculiar problem which is not solved by explaining how the group came to exist at a given moment.

*   *   *

The first and most obvious element of the continuity of group unity is the continuance of the locality, of the place and soil on which the group lives. The state, still more the city, and also countless other associations, owe their unity first of all to the territory which constitutes the abiding substratum for all change of their contents. To be sure, the continuance of the locality does not of itself alone mean the continuance of the social unity, since, for instance, if the whole population of a state is driven out or enslaved by a conquering group, we speak of a changed civic group in spite of the continuance of the territory. Moreover, the unity of whose character we are speaking is psychical, and it is this psychical factor itself which makes the territorial substratum a unity. After this has once taken place, however, the locality constitutes an essential point of attachment for the further persistence of the group. But it is only one such element, for there are plenty of groups that get along without a local substratum. On the one hand, there are the very small groups, like the family, which continue precisely the same after the residence is changed. On the other hand, there are the very large groups, like that ideal community of the "republic of letters," or the other international associations in the interest of culture, or the groups conducting international commerce. Their peculiar character comes from entire independence of all attachment to a definite locality.

In contrast with this more formal condition for the maintenance of the group, of incomparably greater importance to the same end is the physiological connection of the generations—in general the whole concatenation of blood relationships. Community of stock is not always enough to insure unity of coherence for a long time. In many cases the local unity must be added. On the other hand, when other bonds of union fail, the physiological is the last recourse to which the self-maintenance of the group resorts.

The physiological coherence of successive generations is of incomparable significance for the maintenance of the unitary self of the group, for the special reason that the displacement of one generation by the following *does not take place all at once.* By virtue of this fact it comes about that a continuity is maintained which conducts the vast majority of the individuals who live in a given moment into the life of the next moment. The change, the disappearance and entrance of persons, affects in two contiguous moments a number relatively small compared with the number of those who remain constant. Another element of influence in this connection is the fact that human beings are not bound to a definite mating season, but that children are begotten at any time. It can never properly be asserted of a group, therefore, that at any given moment a new generation begins. The departure of the older and the entrance of the younger elements proceed so gradually and continuously that the group seems as much like a unified self as an organic body in spite of the change of its atoms. If the substitution of elements took place all at once and suddenly, in such a way as to affect the group throughout, it could scarcely be said that in spite of the disappearance of individuals the group maintains its unitary selfhood. Since at each moment those who were members of the groups in earlier moments constitute a vast majority over the entering members, the identity of the group is saved, in spite of the fact that moments far separated from each other may have no common elements.

The foregoing is one of the few cases in which the fact that change is gradual furnishes a real explanation of the change. In general, care must be taken not to imagine that a change from one condition into another quite different is explained when it is described as "gradual." When we use that formula, we are apt to think of a multitude of inter-mediate stages interposed between the two extremes in question. We assume that the difference between any two contiguous stages was so minute as to be a negligible quantity, so that no great spiritual force was demanded to make the transition, but, on the contrary, the mind could glide over easily from the earlier stage to the later. This too frequent attempt to get rid of the problem and its difficulties by simple reference to the gradualness of the change or development is a self-deception as seductive as it is fatal. We are justified in extreme in-credulity whenever "gradualness" is alleged as basis of explanation. Even in the case before us, the change itself, the ultimate substitution of wholly different group elements, is not to be explained by the for-mula of gradualness. The form of gradualness in which the alteration actually occurs explains rather how it happens that we regard the group as persistent in spite of the shifting membership. This form is the vehicle of the group unity throughout the succession of members, somewhat as the form of reciprocity performs the same function for contemporaneous members. This form of gradualness, moreover, is obviously operative, not merely when the unity of the group is to be preserved in spite of the change of membership. It works, also, in cases where change affects other elements of group unity. For instance, where the political forms, the law, the customs, the entire culture of a group change to such an extent that after a time the group presents a wholly altered aspect, our right to speak of it as the identical group depends upon the fact that the alterations did not affect all the vital forms of the group simultaneously. If the change were instantaneous, it is doubtful if we should be justified in calling the group "the same" after the critical moment as before. The circumstance alone that the transi-tion affected in a given moment only a minimum of the total life of the group makes it possible for the group to retain its selfhood through the change. We may express this schematically as follows: If the totality of individuals or other conditions of the life of the group be repre-

sented by *a, b, c, d, e;* in a later moment by *m, n, o, p, q;* we may nevertheless speak of the persistence of identical selfhood if the development takes the following course: *a, b, c, d, e—m, b, c, d, e—m, n, c, d, e
—m, n, o, d, e—m, n, o, p, e—m, n, o, p, q.* In this case each stage is
differentiated from the contiguous stage by only one member, and at
each moment it shares the same chief elements with its neighboring
moments.

This continuity in change of the individuals who are the vehicles of
the group unity is most immediately and thoroughly visible when it
rests upon procreation. The same form is found, however, in cases
where this physical agency is excluded, as, for example, within the
Catholic clerus. Here the continuity is secured by provision that
enough persons always remain in office to initiate the neophytes. This
is an extremely important sociological fact. It makes bureaucracies so
tenacious, and causes their character and spirit to endure in spite of all
shifting of individuals. The physiological basis of self-maintenance
here gives place to a psychological one. To speak exactly, the preservation of group identity in this case depends, of course, upon the amount
of invariability in the vehicles of this unity, but, at all events, the
whole body of members belonging in the group at any given moment
only separate from the group after they have been associated with their
successors long enough to assimilate the latter fully to themselves, *i. e.,*
to the spirit, the form, the tendency of the group. The immortality of
the group depends upon the fact that the change is sufficiently slow
and gradual.

The fact referred to by the phrase "immortality of the group" is of
the greatest importance. The preservation of the identical selfhood of
the group through a practically unlimited period gives to the group a
significance which, *ceteris paribus,* is far superior to that of the individual. The life of the individual, with its purposes, its valuations, its
force, is destined to terminate within a limited time, and to a certain
extent each individual must start at the beginning. Since the life of
the group has no such *a priori* fixed time limit, and its forms are really
arranged as though they were to last forever, the group accomplishes
a summation of the achievements, powers, experiences, through which
it makes itself far superior to the fragmentary individual lives.

On this account special arrangements are necessary so soon as the life
of the group is intimately bound up with that of a leading, commanding individual. What dangers to the integrity of the group are concealed in this sociological form may be learned from the history of all
interregnums—dangers which, of course, increase in the same ratio in
which the ruler actually forms the central point of the functions

through which the group preserves its unity, or, more correctly, at each moment creates its unity anew.

The objectification of the coherence of the group may, also, do away with the personal form to such an extent that it attaches itself to a material symbol. In view of the destructibility of a material object, since too this disadvantage cannot be offset, as in the case of a person, by the continuity of heredity, it is very dangerous for the group to seek such a support for its self-preservation. When, however, the social coherence is lost in this way, it is safe to say that it must have suffered serious internal disorder before, and that in this case the loss of the external symbol representing the unity of the group is itself only the symbol that the social elements have lost their coherence. Where this last is not the case, the loss of the group symbol not only has no disintegrating effect, but it exerts a direct integrating influence. While the symbol loses its corporal reality, it may as mere thought, longing, ideal, work much more powerfully, profoundly, indestructibly. The destruction of the group symbol works in two directions upon the persistence of the group: destructively where the integrating reciprocal action of the members is already weak, and constructively where these reciprocal influences are so strong in themselves that they can replace the lost tangible symbol by its spiritualized and idealized representation.

The significance of a material symbol for the persistence of a society is much heightened when the symbol, besides its suggestive use, is a real social possession in itself, that is, when the centralizing functions of the society depend upon it, or are facilitated by it, when the material interests of all the members of the group converge in this symbol. In this case it will be of peculiar importance for the maintenance of the group to secure this common possession against destruction, somewhat as is done in the case of the personal group center by the fiction that the king does not die. The most frequent means to this end is "the dead hand," the provision that the property of corporations, which as such should be permanent, shall not be alienable. As the transitoriness of the individual is reflected in the destructibility of his property, so the indestructibility of the association is mirrored in its inalienable and non-assignable tenure of possessions. In contrast with all movable property, especially with money, property in land has a stability, an indestructibility, a fixity which renders it the most appropriate content for the "dead hand" form of tenure. Moreover, the local definiteness and precision of this tenure bring it about that those who enjoy its benefits have in it the fixed point by means of which they can always keep their reckoning and, at the same time, either directly or indirectly in their interests, can unite without confusion. This significance which the continuance of landed property has for the maintenance of a social form has found expression in the hypothesis that landed possession on a large scale was one of the origins of hereditary monarchy. Superior riches secure, at all events, a leading position in a group. So long, however, as wealth consists only in herds, it is very insecure and may easily die out. Only when it has become immobile is there good chance that it may remain in the hands of one person or family. The stable character of landed property, even if only in the hands of the leader, is favorable to the stability of the constitutional form. It secures for the above discussed hereditary principle a basis that is at once adequate and of corresponding form.

Thus the "dead hand" was by no means merely a matter of material advantage. It was rather a subtle agency of preserving the form and substance of the group. This very fact, however, often entangles the group in a conflict of typical sociological significance, and for the reason that the group thus assisted in its self-preservation is only a portion of a larger civic society containing it. Almost all sorts of human association, whatever be their specific content and character, have to work to secure the cooperation in social unity of certain parts that persist in following a certain egoistic impulse. The form and tendency of these parts duplicate in miniature those of the group of which they are members, with which however they are often, for this very reason, in disagreement. The role appropriate to them as part and member of a comprehensive whole does not comport with the part they are trying to play as egoistic wholes. I shall return presently to the principles involved in this tragic relation, which recurs within all large societies. At this point I merely observe how prominently it impresses itself in the case of the "dead hand." While, as above indicated, it is of extreme importance for the status of a close corporation that it has its own territorial foundation as firm basis of its unity, and as means of delimitation, it is also highly critical if a portion of such society demands the same for itself. The conflict of interest thus arising between the part and the whole appeared immediately in the fact that the "dead hand," as a rule, demanded and obtained exemption from taxation. Indirectly, but still more significantly, the antithesis appeared in the injury to national industry from withdrawal of such properties from the stream of commerce. The firmness of social structure that comes from indestructibility and inalienability of property works as a thorn in the flesh so soon as it comes to be an attribute of a distinct portion of a large group. In that case the state of things which promotes the persistence of the fractional group is, from the standpoint of the larger containing group, directly antagonistic, because it leads to the benumbing and finally the excision of an organic member.

The sociological technique of self-preservation operates again in higher potency in the regulation of certain associations that, even in case of the dissolution of the association, its property shall not be distributed among its members, but shall revert to some union for similar purposes. Self-maintenance is concerned in such case, not with the physical existence of the group, but with its idea, which is incarnated in the group that becomes its heir, the continuity of which is just as well provided for through the transference of its property to that group.

I come now to a further type of means for social maintenance. It may be described as both ideal and concrete. It constitutes, in fact, a peculiar species beyond this antithesis, and finds its most efficient example in *honor*. The sociological significance of honor, as a form of cohesion which reappears as formally the same in the most diverse socializations, is extraordinarily great, and can be understood only after extended observation. In general, it may be said that, through the appeal to honor, society secures from its members the kind of conduct conducive to its own preservation, particularly within the spheres of conduct intermediate between the purview of the criminal code, on the one hand, and the field of purely personal morality, on the other. If we place these three forms of imperative in a series—morality, honor, criminal law—each earlier member of the series covers the range of the remaining, but the scope of a latter member does not cover that of a predecessor. Complete morality contains what honor and law can only command and forbid. Fulfilled honor prohibits of itself what the law lays under penalty, but honor does not assure everything which morality demands, nor does the criminal law secure everything that morality and honor decree. From this series we may immediately conclude that honor corresponds, as a social requisite, to the needs of a somewhat contracted circle, between those of the largest civic group, which coerces its members by penal law, and those of purely personal life, which finds its norms only in the autonomy of the individual. In the executive action of these three sorts of law the intermediate position of honor also shows itself. While civic law employs physical force as its sanction, while personal morality has no other recourse than the approval or disapproval of conscience, the laws of honor are guarded by penalties which have neither the pure externality of the former nor the pure subjectivity of the latter. This peculiar intermediary position of honor points to the perception which arises from the most general observation of the workings of honor, viz.:

that honor is originally a class standard (*Standesehre*); *i. e.*, an appropriate life-form of smaller circles contained within a larger whole. By the demands upon its members contained in the group standard of honor the group preserves its unified character and its distinctness from the other groups within the same inclusive association. That which we think of as honor in a larger sense than this, as human honor in general, or, otherwise expressed, as purely individual honor, is an abstract idea made possible by effacing the boundaries of the class (*Stand*). It is, indeed, impossible to name any single procedure which assails human honor as such, *i. e.*, every human being's sense of honor without exception. It is a matter of honor with the ascetic to let himself be spit upon; with the girls of a certain African tribe to have as many sexual relations as possible. Accordingly the essential thing is the specific idea of honor in narrow groups—family honor, officers' honor, mercantile honor, yes, even the "honor among thieves." Since the individual belongs to various groups, the individual may, at the same time, be under the demands of several sorts of honor which are independent of each other. Thus honor consists in the relation of the individual to a particular circle, which in this respect manifests its separateness, its sociological distinctness from other groups.

So far as its content is concerned, honor seems to me to get its character as duty of the individual from the circumstance that, in preserving his own honor, the individual preserves at the same time the honor of his own social circle. This is the enormous advantage which society derives from the honor of its members, and for the sake of which society permits the individual to do things which are otherwise both by ethics and law positively forbidden.

When the social group intrusts to each of its elements its total honor *pro rata,* it confides to the individual at the same time a good of extraordinary value, something that the individuals are, as a rule, not in a position to gain for themselves, something that they have simply to keep from losing. Since the honor of the whole circle becomes thus at the same time the private possession of the individual, and in this individualization becomes his honor, it thereby demonstrates a unique and extremely close coalescence of individual and social interest. The latter has taken in this case, for the consciousness of the individual, a completely personal form. Herewith the enormous service is manifest which honor renders to the self-maintenance of the group, for what I called the honor of the group, represented by the honor of the individual, proves, on close examination, to be nothing else than the stability, the unity, and the durable character of the group. Honor demands from the individual those kinds of conduct which promote these ends of his society. Since conformity to this demand acquires, on the one hand, an ideal worth, so ideal and so powerful at the same time that honor is preferred to life; since the preservation of honor, on the other hand, has very sensible pleasurable effects upon the individual, and its loss produces equally keen pains, it comes about that honor constitutes an extraordinarily close bond between the whole group and its elements. Accordingly honor is one of the most thorough means of maintaining the existence and specific significance of the group.

*   *   *

From such recourse of social self-preservation to individual persons, to a material substance, to an ideal conception, we pass now to the cases in which social persistence takes advantage of an organ composed of a number of persons. The objective principle in which unity manifests itself again exhibits societary character. The structure of such organs is the result of sociological division of labor. The reciprocity between individuals in which all socialization consists, and the special form of which determines the character of the group as such, goes on at first immediately between the separate members of the society as such. The unification of operations comes about from direct agreement or from mutual adjustment of interests; the unity of the religious community through the common longing of the religious sentiment for union; the military constitution of the group through the interest of every man capable of military service in being strong for offense and defense; the administration of justice through immediate judgment by the community as a whole; the organization of leaders and led through the personal superiority of certain members over the rest; the economic system through direct exchange between producers.[1]

These functions, at first exercised by the persons immediately interested, presently pass over to special functional groups. The previous reciprocities of the elements give place to a condition in which each element comes into relations with the newly developed organ. Otherwise expressed, while previously, where there was no structure of organs, the individual primary elements alone had a substantial existence, and its coherence was merely functional, now the coherence of organs gets an existence of its own, and, more than this, an existence not merely apart from all the members of the group in which the new organ belongs, but even separate from those individuals who are the

---

[1] I will not assert that this logically primary condition has everywhere been the historical starting point of the further social development, yet in order to make clear the essential meaning of the division of labor among social organs the assumption of this primitive condition is permissible, even if it is only a fiction. In numberless cases it surely is not fiction.

immediate constituents of the organ itself. In short, what was once erroneously assumed to be true of physical life, viz., that it is something maintained by a peculiar vital spirit, instead of being, as we now know, a sort of reciprocity between certain physical atoms—this, or something closely corresponding with it, is true of social life. In origin it is a direct reciprocity. Presently it is maintained by a special self-existing structure. These structures represent the idea or the power which holds the group together in this particular respect, and they, at the same time, consolidate the group coherence so that it passes from a mere functional to a substantial character.

It is one of the profoundest facts about humanity, and of most specific application to human conditions, that individuals as well as groups have derived considerable powers and advantages from structures which they have themselves endowed with the energies and qualities from which these reinforcements come. The effective energies of an actor, with which he secures his maintenance and development, exhibit themselves very often in the roundabout way of first producing an apparently objective structure, from which they then flow back upon the actor. Think, for instance, of the idea of the gods, whom men first endowed with all sorts of qualities, worthinesses, and excellencies reflected from human souls. Then the same men used these gods as a source of moral laws and of power to enforce them. Think again how we endow a fine country in which we live with meanings taken from our own feelings, and then draw from contemplation of the same comfort, earnestness, and impulse. Think again how often friend or wife seems to enrich us in thought and feeling, until we perceive that all this spiritual content came from ourselves, and is only reflected back upon us by these helpers. If in all such occurrences a deep self-deception is concealed, it is surely not without profound utility. Without question many powers of our nature require such extension, transformation, and projection in order to reach their highest use. We must set them at a certain distance from ourselves in order for them to work upon us with maximum force. Illusion about their actual source is evidently very advantageous in preventing intereference with this influence.

Social elaboration of differentiated organs for special purposes occurs in many ways under the form-type just discussed. The group forces are concentrated in a special structure, which, in turn, with its own status and character, places itself in antithesis with the group as a whole. Since this organ promotes the purposes of the group, it appears as though independent energies proceeded from it. They are, in fact, nothing but the transformed energies of the same elements upon which the organ now reacts.

The specialized organ permits greater flexibility of movement in the social body. So soon as it is necessary for the whole group to put itself in action for a single purpose, such as political determinations, judicial judgments, administrative measures, etc., the group will suffer from clumsiness, and that in two different ways: first, physically or locally. In order that the group as a whole may take action, it must needs assemble. It is so hard, and it takes so much time, and it is so often impossible to bring the whole group together, that many movements are altogether prevented, and others are so long impeded that they are at last too late. But if this external difficulty of assemblage is overcome, the difficulty of psychical approach arises—the task of bringing a great mass to unanimity. Every farsighted action of a large body must overcome the force of doubts, objections, antagonistic interests, and especially the indifference of individuals. The social organ that exists exclusively for this purpose, and which is composed of relatively few persons, is free from a large proportion of these obstructions. Such organs of the group promote its persistence, therefore, through an increased quickness and precision of social action, in contrast with which the movements of a whole group have an inflexible and dilatory character. These physical and psychological difficulties, so to speak, may dispose a mass to appoint representatives, even in case no technical difficulties of the tasks make it inevitable to do so. There are innumerable cases of representation of a large number to reach this external factor—agreement. A group of smaller number has merely for that reason, and without qualitative superiority, the advantage of easier mobility, of greater rapidity of assemblage, and of more precise determination, as compared with a multitude. The local difficulty appears, moreover, not alone in cases requiring the congregation of the whole group. It emerges in connection with economic exchanges. So long as exchange and purchase take place only when producers and consumers are actually in each other's presence, the transactions are evidently clumsy and imperfect, and the difficulties of these local limitations must be contended with continually. So soon, however, as the trader intervenes, and finally a mercantile class systematizes exchange and brings into existence every sort of relationship between people with economic interests, the whole coherence of the group becomes immeasurably closer and stronger.

In case the whole group of equally privileged and equally stationed elements must exert itself for a specific purpose, there inevitably arise within the group counter efforts, each of which has a priori equal weight, and for which there is no decisive court of appeal. The most adequate expression of this condition is the case in which not even a majority may decide, but each dissenter either defeats the decision altogether or at least is personally not bound by it. This danger, not only for the external purposeful action, but also for the internal form and unity of the group, is met by the development of social organs, at least in two directions. First, an administrative agency (*Amt*), a commission, a delegation, etc., will have more special knowledge than the aggregate of other persons. By resort to these substitutes those frictions and oppositions will be avoided which come from pure ignorance of the things involved. The group will be the more able to maintain such unity of action as comes from knowledge of the conditions concerned, and from exclusion of the vascillations due to mere subjective influences, the more the direction of its special plans is committed to an organ separately designated for the purpose. The significance of a second and related factor is not so obvious. The absence of adaptations to the circumstances, which so often prevents unity in the actions of the mass (for subjective errors are numberless, while in the case of objectively correct representations all must at last come to the same result), is not always the consequence of mere ignorance of the subject, but often also of the very important sociological fact that the factions, which, in connection with any important subject, always divide the group, stand for mental differences upon matters far removed from and wholly unrelated to the question in hand. These differences are evidence that accord is radically impossible. The party divisions that have arisen from any cause whatsoever are preserved throughout the whole range of interests, and bring it to pass that, for example, political parties must occupy hostile camps, even about religious, æsthetic, personal, and culture questions of every sort, even in cases where the content of the new party programmes has no real connection with that which caused the original division. The line which divides parties in any vital matter is produced through affairs of every possible sort, from generalities to particularities, and simply because opponents upon the important subject will not cooperate upon any other. The mere fact that the one party has taken sides upon any open question is sufficient to make the opposing party take the other side. This power of party, as a mere form which shows itself in unbroken continuance throughout the most heterogeneous kinds of interests, is one of the weightiest obstacles to the unification of a group, and even to the performance of any group action at all. This production of the line of hostility occurs also not merely where it separates whole divisions of groups. It appears as well in the relations of individuals with each other. The mere fact that *A* votes for the measure *m* is often enough to make his enemy vote against it. The factionalism and obstruction that follow should promote the transference of group business to special organs. Since these are constituted with sole reference to the definite purpose in view, the latter is set farther apart psychologically from the other interests and opinions of the person to whom the purpose is intrusted. This purpose, therefore, receives on behalf of the members of the group an emphasis which would be lessened or lost if it were naively jumbled together with essentially unrelated tendencies. When social action is thus freed from the oppositions, entanglements, and centrifugal movements which spring from the association of special issues with other personal and party positions, this action becomes much more unified, animated, and purposeful (*zielbewusster*). The power of persistence in the group gains in the ratio in which that waste of energy ceases, which is involved in the above noted confusions and consequent paralyzing of forces, and which is unavoidable in the neglect of group tasks that is sure to exist if the group as a group tries to do its needed work.

While these advantages of social organs over the group as a whole in promoting the persistence of the group thus fall in with the *tempo* and rhythm of the powers or process that preserve the group, they extend furthermore to certain qualitative conditions. In the first place, it is decisive that the total action of the group will always be on a relatively low intellectual level. This is due to the fact that the particular point about which a large number of individuals agree must always be close to the level occupied by that one of them who stands lowest. This is evident from the fact that those who stand higher can descend, but not everyone on a lower intellectual level can ascend. The latter sort, therefore, and not the former, determine the level which may be occupied in common.

In cases of agitation and expression of feelings this rule does not hold, because in an actually assembled mass of people there develops a certain collective irritability, a rapture (*Mitgerissen-werden*) of emotion, a reciprocal stimulation, so that there may follow a momentary elevation of the individuals above the average intensity of their feelings. This in no wise prejudges the appropriateness or inappropriateness of these feelings, nor the wisdom or foolishness of their content. In this respect the sentiments of the mass will remain on that level below the average which is accessible to lower and higher alike. That level may be raised sometimes, as experience shows, in respect of feeling and willing, but not in respect of intelligence.

While now the persistence of the group rests, on the one side, upon the immediate relations of individuals to individuals, and in so far the individual may unfold all the powers of intellect with which he is endowed, this is not absolutely true in those matters in which the group has to act as a unity. We may call the former the molecular action of the group, the latter the molar action. In the former kind of action representation of the individual is, in principle, neither possible nor desirable. In the latter it is both possible and desirable. When a group of any considerable size conducts its affairs directly, the group is shut up to relatively trivial actions by the inexorable condition that each member must in some degree comprehend and approve each group measure. Only when the guidance of group action is intrusted to an organization consisting of relatively few persons can specific talent be enlisted for its direction. Within a group acting as an undifferentiated mass such endowment and special knowledge as only the few may possess must at best fight their way to influence in each particular case. Within a differentiated organ, on the other hand, such endowment and knowledge have, in principle at least, uncontested influence.[2]

Therein lies the superiority of the parliamentary system over the plebiscite. It has been observed that direct popular votes seldom show a majority for original and bold measures. The popular majority is rather on the side of caution, convenience, and triviality. The single representative, whom the mass chooses, possesses still other personal qualities besides those which—especially during the epochs of purely partisan choices—are in the consciousness of the electing multitude.

---

[2] To be sure, contrasted phenomena occur. Within an official bureau jealousy sometimes prevents talent from exerting its proper influence, while on the other hand the masses may sometimes easily follow a talented individual even when he leads contrary to their judgment. It is impossible for an abstract science like sociology to exhaust the whole abundance and complications of historical action when it exhibits the separate typical relationships. For, however correct may be the assertion of relationship, and however influential, the concrete occurence will always contain a number of elements beside this, and in the final, visible, aggregate effect the influence of the typal form may be concealed. The science of physics is analogously made up in part of certain regular relationships of movements which never appear in the actual world just as they work out mathematically, or as they can be produced in the laboratory. Nevertheless, the demonstrated relations of force are real and operative in all those cases in which science has discovered their participation. Only their *visible* action is not entirely in accordance with the scientific schedule in which it is formulated, because beside them a number of other forces and conditions operate upon the same substance. In the resultant of both the former and the latter, which constitutes the actual event, the share of the formulated influence may be concealed from immediate observation. It may have contributed only an insensible and indistinguishable part. This inadequacy, which is exhibited by every sort of cognition through types, when compared with the concrete actuality, evidently reaches its culmination in the psychical sciences. In their territory not only the factors of the particular occurrence mix in almost inextricable complexity, but even the fate of a given element, that may be analyzed out of the confusion, is beyond determination by mathematics and experiment. No matter what correlation of cause and effect may be looked upon as the normal form by which to interpret historical events and psychological probabilities, there will be many cases in which the conditions of that type seem to be present, but the type itself does not emerge. This need not shake confidence in the correctness of the abstraction. It shows only that other, perhaps contrary, forces have worked upon the individuals in question, and that these latter have outweighed the former in the total or visible effect.

He brings to his post something in addition to that which was really chosen in selecting him. Hence in parliaments personal talents and intellectual shadings, such as are found only in single persons, may win a high degree of influence. They may even be able to promote the stability of the group by exerting influence that reaches over the gaps between parties which so often threaten group unity. To be sure, the effectiveness of the personal principle in parliaments is modified by new levelings; in the first place, because the parliament to which the single person speaks is itself a relatively large body. It includes extremely diverse parties and individuals, so that the points of common and reciprocal understanding can lie only very low in the intellectual scale. In the second place, because the individual belongs to a party which, as such, stands not on an individual but on a social plane, by which its parliamentary activities are *a priori* reduced to an average level. In the third place, because the individual speaks, indirectly but intentionally, to the whole country. These subtractions from the intellectual advantages of constituting organs are necessary only in the case of parliaments. They do not equally affect other forms. Indeed, these very disadvantages give proof, as the higher developments of parliamentarism show, that the differentiation of organs is necessary.

On the other hand, the persistence of the group depends on the fact that the organ thus differentiated does not attain *absolute* independence. Rather must the idea remain ever operative (although by no means always conscious) that the organ is in fact only a corporealized abstraction of the reciprocal action within the group itself. The group remains always the foundation. Its powers, developments, purposes, only receive a peculiarly practical form in the organs. The latter only exhibit the mode in which the directly reciprocating primary elements of the group may work out their latent energies most completely and efficiently. So soon as the differentiation of the organ releases it from dependence upon the aggregate movements of the group, its preservative action may be turned into a destructive influence. I suggest two types of grounds for this: First, when the organ gains too vigorous independent life, and does not place the emphasis of its importance upon the worth of its service to the group, but upon its value to itself, the persistence of the organ may come into conflict with the persistence of the group. A relatively harmless case, but for that very reason one that quite clearly represents the type, is the bureaucracy. The bureaucratic body, a formal organization for exercising an extended administration, constitutes in itself a scheme which frequently clashes with the variable requirements of practical social life. This, on the one hand, because the departmental work of the bureaucratic system is not adjusted with reference to very individual and complicated cases, which none the less must be disposed of by means of the bureaucratic machinery; on the other hand, because the *tempo* in which the bureaucratic wheels must revolve is often in striking contrast with the urgency of the particular case. If now a structure with such functional inadequacies forgets its role as merely servitor of the group, and deports itself as though its own existence were its ultimate purpose, the difference between its life forms and those of the whole group must eventuate in positive harm to the latter. The persistence of both is no longer compatible. In this respect we might compare bureaucratic with logical schematism. The latter bears about the same relation to knowledge of reality in general that the former bears to civic administration. Each is a tool and a form, indispensable in connection with the content which it is called to order, but the whole meaning and purpose of each lie in this content. When logic poses, however, as independent knowledge, and, without reference to the real content of which it is a mere form, presumes to construct of itself a separate intelligence, it makes for itself a world which usually presents marked contrasts with the real universe. The logical forms abstracted and organized into a science are merely an organ for comprehension of the totality of things. So soon, however, as logic declines this role and strives after complete self-sufficiency, so soon as logic attempts to be the conclusion rather than the medium of understanding, it becomes as obstructive to the preservation, extension, and unification of knowledge as bureaucratic schematism may be to the aggregate interests of the group.

Even the law does not always avoid this sociological complication. The law is aboriginally that form of reciprocal relationship between the group members which has approved itself as most necessary for the stability of the group. The form which the law defines is not sufficient of itself to assure this stability or the progress of the society in which it is in force. The law of any group is the minimum, which must be preserved as the foundation of the existence of that group. The elaboration of organs is, in this connection, double. From transactions actually demanded, and as a rule really customary, there differentiates itself "the law," the abstracted form and norm of just these transactions, logically connected and completed, which then remains as a standard to which real action shall conform. This group-preserving organ, being composed of ideas, needs still further a concrete organ in order that it may be effective against opposition. Technical relations brought about the destruction of that original unit in which either the *pater familias* or the assembled group rendered judgment. A special class became necessary to assure the integrity of the legal norms in the acts of the group elements. But useful and necessary as are both these developments—the abstraction of group conduct with arrangement into a completed system of laws, and the incarnation of the law in a judicial class—yet from both comes unavoidably the danger that the very necessary firmness and completeness (*innere Geschlossenheit*) of these structures may some time come into collision with the demands of group progress or with the requirements of cases containing specific complications. Through the logical cohesion of its structure and the dignity of its administrators, the law attains not only an independence which is actual, and for its purpose necessary to a very great extent, but it derives from within itself—by a *circulus vitiosus,* to be sure—a claim to unlimited and irresponsible independence. Since now the concrete circumstances of the group sometimes demand other conditions for its maintenance, situations occur which have been expressed in the words *fiat justitia pereat mundus,* and *summum jus summa injuria.* The attempt is made to give the law that flexibility and adaptability which are appropriate to its character as an organ, by leaving to the judge a certain scope in the application and interpretation of statutes. On the borders of this territory within judicial discretion occur those cases of collision between the persistence of the law and that of the group which may here serve as illustrations of the fact. The group must allow its organs to acquire a certain staunchness and independence, or they could not promote the maintenance of the group. Precisely this necessary stability of the organ may efface its organic character. The autonomy and rigidity of the organ that acts as though it were an independent whole may turn into an injury of group unity.

In the case of bureaucracy, as in that of legal formalism, this conversion of an organ into a self-governing totality is the more dangerous because it takes the appearance and offers the pretext of being always for the sake of the whole.

But not alone the possible antagonism between the whole and the parts, between the group and its organ, should hold the independence of the latter within certain bounds; but the same is desirable in order that, in case of necessity, the differentiated function may revert to the group. There is this peculiarity about the evolution of society, that its preservation sometimes calls for temporarily throwing out of service organs that have already been differentiated. This is not to be regarded as closely analogous with those structural degenerations which take place in animal organisms from changes in the conditions of life, as for example in visual organs that have become rudimentary after the habitat has long been in the dark. In these cases the function itself becomes superfluous, and for that reason the organ performing the function gradually dies away. In the social developments now in mind, on the contrary, the function is indispensable, and on that account, when the organ proves unequal to its performance, recourse must be had to that unmediated reciprocity between primary group elements as a substitute for which the organ was originally developed.

In many cases the structure of the group is from the beginning adjusted to such alternation between functions immediately discharged by the group and those that are performed by an organ. It follows as a matter of course that not every group can adapt itself to such reversion of type. In very large groups, or in those that live under very complicated conditions, the assumption of administrative functions by the group directly is a simple impossibility. The structure of organs is not to be recalled, and their flexibility and vital interdependence with the elements can at most show themselves in the ability of the elements to change the *persons* who at a given moment compose the organ, and replace them with more suitable persons. Nevertheless it is continually happening, even in cases of rather high development, that the group power flows back from the organs to its original source, though this may be but a process of transition to the formation of new organs.

*   *   *

The elaboration of differentiated organs is, so to speak, a substantial aid to social self-preservation. Thereby a new member grows upon the structure of society. We must treat quite apart from this the question how the impulse of self-preservation affects the life of the group in functional respects. The question whether this group life progresses in undifferentiated unity or with specialized organs is for this purpose secondary. The question is rather with reference to the general form or *tempo* in which the life processes of the group proceed. We meet here two chief possibilities. The group may be preserved, (1) by conserving with the utmost tenacity its firmness and rigidity of form, so that the group may meet approaching dangers with substantial resistance, and may preserve the relation of its elements through all change of external conditions; (2) by the highest possible variability of its form, so that adaptation of form may be quickly accomplished in response to change of external conditions, so that the form of the group may adjust itself to any demand of circumstances. This duality of possibilities obviously arises from a quite general demeanor of the group. Analogies may be found in every possible realm, even the physical. A body is protected against destruction from stress and shock either by rigidity and unyielding cohesion of its elements, so that the attacking force makes no impression; or by pliability and elasticity, by virtue of which it gives way before every onset, to be sure, but after each attack ceases it recovers its previous form. We have now to discuss these two ways of social preservation.

Persistence by means of the conservative policy seems to be the method indicated wherever the aggregate consists of very diverse elements with latent or potent antipathies, so that every attack, no matter of what sort, is dangerous, and even measures for maintenance and for positive usefulness must be avoided if they entail agitation. Accordingly a state that is very complex, and must perpetually balance a somewhat unstable equilibrium, will, on the whole, be strongly conservative because any disturbance might produce an irreparable disarrangement of the equilibrium. This consequence attaches itself in general to the form of heterogeneity of the component elements in a large group, unless this diversity leads to the harmonious interlacing of interests that comes from essential unity. The danger to the maintenance of the social *status quo* lies here in the fact that every disturbance must produce very different sorts of consequences in the different strata of the group, because they are the repositories of highly contrasted energies. The smaller the amount of essential compatibility between the elements of the group, the more probable is it that new agitations, new stimulations of consciousness, new occasions for resolves and for developments will force the contrasted elements still further apart. There are countless ways in which people may be estranged from each other, but often only a single way of approach. Consequently it makes no difference how useful the changes might be in themselves, their effects upon the elements will bring the entire heterogeneity of the latter to expression, and to heightened expression, just as the mere lengthening of divergent lines makes the divergence more evident.[3] The avoidance of every innovation, of every departure from the previous way, a severe and rigid conservatism, is here indicated, therefore, in order to hold the group in its existing form.

But without a divergence of group elements to the extent of enmity, the same conservative character will be favorable to the maintenance

---

[3] It sometimes looks as though the very shocks of a foreign war serve to reconcile elements of the state that were drawing apart, to establish the equilibrium that was threatened, and so to preserve the forms of the state. This, however, is only an apparent exception which really proves the rule. War really appeals to those energies which are common to the discordant elements of the community. These are vital and fundamental in their nature. War brings them so forcibly into consciousness that its disturbances actually nullify the differences. Thus the condition which, so far as our present thought is concerned, makes war dangerous disappears in the presence of war. In case the attack is not sharp enough to overcome the enmities present in the group, war produces the above asserted effects. How often has war given the last blow to a state system suffering from internal disruption! How often political groups, torn by internal dissensions, have faced the alternative of war against others, which might either cause domestic quarrels to be forgotten, or might on the contrary aggravate them beyond reconciliation!

of the group whenever the divergence, of whatever sort, is considerable. Where the social differences are very marked, and where they do not merge into each other through intermediate gradations, any sudden movement and disturbance of the structure of the whole must be much more dangerous than when many intermediate strata are present. This follows from the fact that evolution always affects at first a portion of the group exclusively or with especial energy. Accordingly, in the case last considered, the consequences or extension of the evolution will appear but gradually, while in the first case the movement will be much more violent and will take sudden hold of portions of the group that are most distant and most opposed. The intermediate classes act then as buffers. In the event of sudden developments, or unavoidable disturbance of the structure of the whole, they graduate, mollify, and distribute the shock.

It is most necessary to preserve at all hazards the social peace, stability, and conservative character of the group life in those instances in which the group structure is discontinuous and characterized by sharp internal differences. For that reason we notice, as a matter of fact, that in groups containing tremendous and irreconcilable class contrasts, peace and persistence of the forms of social life are more apt to prevail than in cases of approach and mediation and commingling between the extremes of the social scale. In the latter case preservation of the whole in the *status quo ante* is much more likely to be along with unstable conditions, sudden developments, and progressive tendencies.

This connection between stability of the social character and width of distances between social elements betrays itself in the opposite direction. In case the preservation of the group, by means of stability, is mechanically forced, abrupt social differences often take shape with that end in view.

A further instance in which the self-preservation of the group makes for all possible stability and rigidity of its forms is evident in the case of outlived structures which have no longer an inherent right of existence, and whose elements really belong in other relations and social formations. Every quantitative extension of a group requires certain qualitative modifications and adaptations. An obsolete structure cannot go through these changes without collapse. The social form is in very close dependence upon the numerical definiteness of its elements. That structure of a society which is appropriate for a given number of members is no longer appropriate when a certain increase has occurred. The process of transformation into the new form demanded force, the assimilation and disposition of the new elements consume force. Structures which have lost their essential meaning have no strength left for this task. They must rather use all the energy remaining to protect the still surviving form against internal and external dangers. That rigid exclusion of new associates, which later characterizes the outlived *Zunft* organizations, signified immediately, therefore, that the group was confirming its stability by the exclusion which confined it to its once acquired members and their descendants. It signified still further, however, an avoidance of those reconstructions which are necessary with every quantitative extension of the group, modifications for which a structure that has outlasted its usefulness has no longer the requisite strength. The instinct of self-preservation will consequently lead such a group to measures of rigid conservatism. In general, structures that are unfit for competition will incline to these means, for in the degree in which their form is variable, in which it passes through different stages and accomplishes new adaptations, occasion is given to competitors for dangerous attacks. The most assailable stage for societies as for individuals is that between two periods of adjustment. Whoever is in motion cannot at every moment be so guarded on all sides as he may be who is in a position of stability and repose. A group which has a feeling of insecurity with reference to its competitors will on that account for the sake of its self-preservation avoid all variation, and will live in accordance with the principle *quieta non movere.*

This rigid self-limitation is especially to the purpose whenever competition is not yet present, but the aim is to prevent its appearance, because of conscious inability to cope with it. Rigorous measures of exclusion alone will in this case maintain the status, because if new relationships arise, if new points of connection with parties outside the group are offered, the group will be drawn into a wider sphere, in which it might encounter competition that could not be overcome. This sociological norm may be operative very widely in the following connection. An irredeemable paper currency has the peculiarity, in contrast with redeemable paper money, that it circulates only within the territory of the government that issues it, and cannot be exported. This is proclaimed as its greatest advantage. It remains in the country. It is ready at hand for all enterprises. It does not take part in that equalization of precious metal with other states which immediately produces importation of foreign goods and the outflow of money, if there is a superfluity of money and consequent rise of prices. Consequently, if the circulating power of currency is limited to the country of issue, the circulating medium becomes an inner bond of unity for that country, and a means by which it maintains its social form, since it shuts the country off from the great competition of the world's markets. A country that is industrially strong and equal to any competitive enterprise would not need this means. It would rather be sure that it would increase the strength of its essential form in the variability of exchange, and in the developments of reciprocal dependence.

The precisely contrary picture, namely, the most extreme ductility and exchangeability of the sociological forms as a condition of self-preservation, is shown for example by groups that maintain their existence within larger groups either by tolerance or it may be purely *par nefas*. Only by means of the most complete elasticity can such a society combine firmness of coherence with the constant necessity of defense or with the necessity of rapid shifting from defense to offense. Such a group must be able, so to speak, to crawl into every hole. It must be able, according to circumstances, to expand or to contract. Like a fluid body it must be able to take on any form that offers itself. Thus bands of rogues and conspirators must acquire capacity to divide instantly and to act in separate groups; to follow without restriction now this and now that leader; whether in direct or indirect contact, to preserve the same group spirit; after each disruption to reorganize themselves at once in any form that is possible at the moment, etc. They arrive in this way at that power of self-maintenance in consequence of which the Gipsies are wont to say of themselves: "It would be useless to hang us, for we never die."

Through their relations to further sociological concepts of more capital rank these two ways of social persistence come into especially characteristic antithesis. When, for instance, the preservation of a group is very closely bound up with maintenance of a particular stratum in its existence and peculiarities—for example, the highest, the broadest, or the middle stratum—the first two cases demand more rigidity of the social-life form, the last more elasticity. Aristocracies are in general conservative. If they are in reality what the name asserts, they are the most adequate expression of the actual inequality between men. In this case—with reference to which I do not here inquire whether the presumed condition is ever more than partially realized —the spur is lacking for revolutionary movements, viz., non-correspondence between the inherent qualifications of the people and their social situation. Such lack of correspondence is the point of departure both for the most important and heroic of human deeds and for the most senseless undertakings. Given then this most favorable case of an aristocracy, the whole aristocratic class is bound to punctilious insistence upon the conditions which are essential to its preservation; for every experimental disturbance might threaten that fine and rare proportion between qualification and position, either in reality or in the feelings of the persons concerned, and thus might furnish an impulse for radical transformation.

The real occasion for such change of an aristocracy, however, will be that such absolute justification of the regulating system scarcely ever exists. The lordship of the few over the many is likely to rest rather on a totally different basis, and not on the ideal appropriateness of this relation. Under these circumstances the ruling class will have the utmost interest in affording the least occasion for movements toward disturbance and innovation, for every movement of that sort would stimulate the rightful or supposed claims of the ruled. There is danger in this case that not the persons merely, but the whole constitution, might be changed, and this is the decisive period for our course of thought. The very fact that violent changes in the personnel of the ruling class have often been brought about with the assistance of the masses calls attention to the possibility, which has not seldom become a reality, that on such an occasion the whole aristocratic principle may be overturned. Because of this connection the aristocratic form of constitution will maintain itself best through the utmost immobility of its status. This by no means holds good for political purposes alone. It is true also for ecclesiastical, family, and social groupings into which the aristocratic form may enter. In general, so soon as this form has once established itself, a severe conservatism will be most favorable, not merely for the momentary personal standing of the regulating system, but also for its preservation in form and principle.

This often appears clearly enough in the history of reformatory movements in aristocratic constitutions. That adaptation to newly emerging social forces or ideals, such as takes place through diminution of exploitation and subjection, through legal definition of rights in place of arbitrary interpretation, through increase of the rights and of the shares of goods assigned to the lower classes—such adaptation is not wont, so far as it is a voluntary concession, to find its ultimate purpose in that which is changed by the concession, but rather in that which may be preserved by means of such concession. The limitation of the aristocratic prerogative is only the *conditio sine qua non* of saving the aristocratic régime at all. If the movement is allowed to go so far, however, these concessions no longer suffice. Each reform is likely to uncover new points demanding reform, and the movement which was inaugurated for the confirmation of the existing order leads, as though on an inclined plane, either to the overthrow of that order or, if the new demands cannot prevail, to a radical reaction which may reverse the changes already made. This danger which threatens at every modification and compliance of an aristocratic constitution, viz., that the concession made for the sake of self-preservation may by sheer forces of its own specific gravity lead to a complete overthrow, exhibits conservatism, at the start, and the form of defense which is invariably rigid and unyielding, as most favorable for the aristocratic social form.

In case the form of the group is determined, not by the eminence of a numerically small stratum, but by the most extensive stratum and its autonomy, the self-preservation of the group will likewise be promoted by stability and unshaken firmness. An immediate influence in this direction is the fact that the great mass, in so far as it functions as the permanent vehicle of a social unity, is very rigid and immovable in its temper. The mass is in this respect very sharply distinguished from any multitude that may actually assemble. The latter is highly variable in its moods and acts, and may change its attitude from one extreme to another upon the most casual impulse. In case the mass is not roused by direct physical excitement and in consequence of stimulations and suggestions from opposite sides, nervous vacillation begins in place of firm direction, thus putting the mass at the mercy of every actual impulse; in case its deep and permanent character operates rather, the mass follows the law of inertia. It does not change its condition from rest *or movement* by its own initiative, but only as a result of the cooperation of new positive forces. Hence it is equally the case that movements which are carried on by great masses, and are left to themselves, move on consistently to their extreme, and on the other hand a once attained equilibrium of conditions is not easily abandoned, so far as the change depends on the mass. It corresponds better with the healthy instinct of the mass to guard itself against change of circumstances and agitations by substantial firmness and rigidity of form rather than by pliable adaptation and quickly effected alteration of attitudes.

In the case of political constitutions, an additional element of essential importance is that the foundation of their social form upon that stratum which is most extensive and in which rights are most equal occurs chiefly among agricultural peoples—the old Roman peasant class and the old German community of free men are cases in point. Here the action of the social form is prejudiced by content of social interests. The cultivator of the soil is *a priori* conservative. His occupation requires long terms, abiding arrangements, resolute persistency. The uncertainties of the weather, upon which his fortunes hang, incline him to a certain fatalism, which shows itself, with respect to external powers, rather in enduring than in evading. His processes cannot be made to confront changes of conjunctions with such quick qualitative modifications as those of manufacturer or merchant. The technical conditions, therefore, create for groups whose form-maintenance is identical with that of a chiefly agricultural mass the disposition to procure this maintenance by firmness and persistence, not by variability of their life processes.

It is quite otherwise in case the middle class has undertaken leadership and the social form of the group stands or falls with the predominance of this middle class. This middle class alone has both an upper and a lower boundary. This is of such a sort that individuals are constantly brought within it both from the higher and from the lower class, and other individuals go from the middle class in either direction. The character of fluctuation is impressed on this stratum, therefore, and the appropriateness of its attitude will, therefore, be in large measure an appropriateness of adaptations, variations, concessions, through which the inevitable movement of the whole may be at least so guided or opposed that the essential form and force of the group may remain throughout all change of conditions. We may designate the sociological form of a group which is characterized by the extension and prevalence of a middle class as that of *continuity.* Such a form coexists neither with an actual ungraded equality of individuals throughout the group, nor if the group consists of an upper and a lower class separated from each other by no intervening medium. The middle class, in fact, adds an entirely new sociological element. It is not only a third in addition to the two. It does not merely have somewhat the same, that is, quantitative, relation to each of these that they have to each other. The new element is rather that this third stratum itself has an upper and a lower boundary, that upon these boundaries an exchange with the other two strata is constantly taking place, and that through this continual fluctuation effacement of boundaries and continual transitions are produced.

An actual continuity of social life does not arise from the fact that individuals are built into positions one above another, with never so slight gradations. This would still produce discontinuous structure. Continuity exists only when single individuals circulate through higher and lower positions. Only thus is the separateness of strata changed over into an actually uninterrupted structure. In the fortune of the individuals the upper and the lower situation must first meet, in order that the sociological picture may show an actual mediation between the upper and the lower. Precisely this, and not a simple intermediate position, is secured by a middle class. It requires little reflection to discern that this closeness of gradation must characterize also the grades within the middle class. The continuity of stations with reference to repute, possessions, activity, culture, etc., rests not merely in the minuteness of the differences which are coordinated in an objective scale, but rather in the frequency of the change which leads one and the same person through a number of such situations, and thus produces at the same time perpetual and varying personal unions of objectively different situations. Under these circumstances the social aspect, as a whole, will be that of *elasticity*. The dominant middle class affords the medium of easy interchangeability of the elements, so that the self-preservation of the group throughout the change of external or internal circumstances and assaults is accomplished not so much because of fixity and rigidity in the cohesion of its elements as because of facile yielding and quick transformation.

In the same way it may be shown, in the opposite direction, that a group with very many positions, built the one above another in close gradation, must have the character of decided fluidity and variability, if the greatest perplexities and disturbances are to be avoided. When a great multiplicity of situations is possible, it is from the outset less probable that each will at once fall into the right position than in the case of a fixed social system which assigns each a place within the great group comprehending many forms of action. Where a group contains only a few sharply distinguished stations, the individuals are there, as a rule, from the beginning carefully trained for their sphere. Such constitutions may secure harmony between the dispositions and the station of individuals through the fact that the separate life spheres are relatively broad, and their demands and opportunities are extensive enough to offer appropriate places for the individuals, diverse as they may be from variations of heredity, education, and example. A class constitution, consequently, provides for a preestablished harmony between the qualities or dispositions of the individual and his position in the social whole. In case, however, on account of the existence of an extensive middle class, the clearly defined classes have given place to a great number of graduated stations, the forces named cannot with certainty predispose the individual to the situation to which he belongs. What was in the other case preestablished harmony must in this case be reached *a posteriori*, empirically; the individual must have the possibility of passing from an inappropriate to an appropriate position. In this case, therefore, the self-preservation of the group form demands that there shall be easy shifting of boundaries, constant correction and interchangeability of situations, and likewise a ready constructibility of the latter, so that special individuals may find special positions. Thus, in order to maintain its integrity, a group with a predominant middle class needs a policy quite different from that of a group under aristocratic leadership, or one entirely without class divisions.

The following, however, is to be added: What instability and variability of the group form are in succession, that the division of labor is
in coexistence. In the former case the group has to adapt itself by
various modifications of its form to the different life conditions which
emerge one after another. In the latter case the problem of the group
is to adjust its varying individual members to satisfaction of the
diverse coexisting demands. The whole diversity and gradation in
callings and positions to which we have referred is evidently possible
only through division of labor. Consequently this division of labor,
like its counterpart, variability of social life form, is a characteristic
of the middle class and of its predominance. Neither the aristocracy
nor the class of free peasant citizens tends to any large degree of
division of labor. The aristocracy has no such tendency, because every
division of labor brings with it gradation of rank, and this is repugnant
to the class consciousness and inimical to its unity. The peasant class
does not have it, because it is not required or permitted by its technique. It is peculiar, however, that variability and division of labor,
much as they essentially and in their personal agents depend on each
other, with respect to the self-maintenance of the group, often work
in direct opposition to each other. This results, on the one hand, from
the fact, emphasized above, that multiplicity and easy gradation of
positions which arise from division of labor lead to all sorts of difficulties and perplexities, unless there be added easy mobility and
transferability of the social elements. These tend to offset the dangers
that come from extreme division of labor, viz., disintegration
(Zersplitterung), one-sidedness, discrepancy between the talent and
the station of individuals. On the other hand, the complementary relation of division of labor and variability in respect to maintenance of
the group is manifest in the following manner. There will be many
cases in which the inconstancy of the middle station produces uncertainty, indefiniteness, and uprooting. This is prevented by division
of labor, since it binds the elements of the group wonderfully close
together. Petty groups of nature peoples, however centralized their
organization may be, are easily disrupted, because each little component of the group is equally capable of separate existence. Each
can do just what the other can. Owing to the hardships of their lot
in external relations they are thrown upon each other. No particular
qualifications of these instinctive allies are involved, however. They
can associate quite at will.

The cohesion of a great civilized group, on the other hand, rests
on its division of labor. The one is absolutely dependent on the
others. The disruption of the group would leave each individual quite
helpless. Thus division of labor, with its linking of individuals to each

other, works against variability in case this would harmfully affect
the maintenance of the group. This will be observable even in small
groups. A band of settlers will be on the whole very pliable and
variable. It will dispose itself now in centralized form, now in very
free fashion, according as it is under pressure from without or has
plenty of scope for action. It will confide leadership according to
changing interests to frequently changing persons. It will seek prosperity now in attachment to other groups, now in exercise of the
largest autonomy. These variations of their sociological form will
be sure in certain cases to promote self-preservation. On the whole,
however, they will give occasion for conflicts, uncertainties, and
divisions; all this is energetically counterbalanced by developed division of labor. On the one hand, this puts the individual into dependence upon the group; on the other hand, it gives the group a lively
interest in holding fast to the individual.

* * *

In all the cases considered thus far, the easy changeability of group
life, its inclination to transfers of both formal and personal sorts, has
been an adaptation to the necessities of life; a bending necessary to
avoid breaking, whenever there is a lack of that substantial firmness
which, in any event, would defeat every exertion of destructive force.
By its variability the group responds to the change of circumstances,
and accommodates it so that the result is its own confirmation. But
it may now be asked whether such changeability, such persistence
through changing and often contradictory conditions, actually promotes the maintenance of the group merely as a reaction against the
change of external conditions, or whether the most immanent principle
of the group existence may not urge the same demand. Quite apart
from the question, what external or internal occasions call forth the
variations of its attitude, may not the force and health of the life
process of the group, as development of purely inherent energies, be
bound up with a certain change of its poise, a shifting of its interests,
a somewhat frequent reconstruction of its form? Of the individual
we know that varying stimulations are necessary for maintenance.
The force and unity of his existence are not preserved by unbroken
mechanical sameness of external and internal condition and action.
On the contrary, the individual is likewise naturally adapted to preservation of his unity in change, not merely of what he does and endures,
but also in change within each of these factors of his experience. It is
consequently not impossible that the bond which holds the group
together needs varying stimulation in order to remain in consciousness
and force. A hint of such relation of things is contained in certain

phenomena which manifest an intimate mixture (*Verschmelzung*) between social unity in general and a definite content or equipment of
the unity. A case in point occurs, as may easily be understood, when
a condition that is definite either in content or otherwise remains long
unchanged, and there is danger that the condition disturbed presently
by some outward circumstance may drag down the social unity itself
in its fall. Just as religious conceptions are often, by long reciprocal
relationship, closely interwoven with moral feelings, and by virtue of
this association the removal of the feeling by enlightenment results in
uprooting the ethical norms at the same time, so a formerly rich family
often goes to pieces on losing its property, and likewise many a poor
family when it suddenly becomes rich. In a similar way a state that
has always been free may be torn by factions and dissensions after it
loses its freedom (I call to mind Athens after the Macedonian period),
and likewise a state formerly under despotic rule so soon as it suddenly
becomes free. The history of revolutions presents the latter case often
enough. It appears, therefore, as though a certain changeability in the
conditions and formations of the group protects it against too rigid
combination of the essential unity of the group with a particular form
of the unity. In case this close combination exists in a group, the occurrence of a change, in spite of the rigid form, threatens the very life
principle of the group. Against this danger frequent change seems
to act like a sort of inoculation. The bond between the most essential
and the less vital relationships remains looser, and a disturbance of
the latter opposes less danger to the preservation of the group in its
essential unity.

We are easily inclined to regard peace, harmony of interests, concord, as the essence of social self-preservation; all antagonism, on the
other hand, as destructive of the unity which it is the essential aim to
preserve, and as the fruitless consumption of force which might be
used for the positive up-building of the group organism. Yet it seems
more correct to interpret a certain rhythm between peace and strife
as the preservative life form. This interpretation may be applied
equally in two directions. It is true both of struggle between the group
as a whole and external foes, in alternation with peaceful epochs, and
also of the strife of competitors, parties, opposing tendencies of every
sort, by the side of the facts of community and of harmony. The one
is an alternative between harmonious and discordant phenomena in
a series, the latter in coexistence. The motive of both is in the last
analysis one and the same. It realizes itself in different ways. The
struggle against a power standing outside the group brings the unity
of the group and the necessity of maintaining it unshaken to most
lively consciousness. It is a fact of the greatest social significance, one

of the few which are true almost without exception of group formations of every sort, that common antagonism against a third party under all circumstances tends to consolidate the combining group, and with much greater certainty than community in friendly relationships toward a third party. There is scarcely a group—domestic, ecclesiastic, economic, political, or whatever—that can dispense entirely with this cement. In the purest reciprocity there develops here the consciousness of existing unity and practical reinforcement of it, each growing and working on the basis of the other.

It appears to be necessary for us human beings, whose whole psychical nature is built upon our sensitiveness of difference, that a feeling of separateness should always exist alongside of the feeling of unity to make this latter perceptible and tangible. Now this process may, as suggested, proceed within the group itself. Aversions and antagonism between group elements may bring the actual unity of the whole, existing in spite of them, to keener effectiveness. Since these oppositions shorten the social binding cords, they tighten them at the same time and thus make them more perceptible. This is also the way to snap them, to be sure. But before that occurs, these counter-movements, which are possible only on the basis of fundamental coherence and closeness of relationship, will have brought these oppositions into more and more energetic functioning. Nor is it essential whether the adjustment is accompanied by correspondingly sharpened consciousness of the adaptation or not. Thus attacks and violence among the members of a community have had as a consequence the enactment of laws in defense against such assaults. Although these laws were measures in opposition to the hostile egoism of individuals, yet they brought the community as a whole to consciousness and expression of its totality, its coherence, its solidarity, and its unity of interest. In like manner economic competition is a highly intimate reciprocal relationship which brings the competitors and their customers closer together. It makes the former more dependent upon the latter and upon each other than they would be if it had not existed. Accordingly, this wish to anticipate hostilities and to minimize their consequences has led to unifications (for example, industrial and political compacts), to all sorts of usages in economic and other transactions, which, although they grew up solely on the ground of actual or possible antagonism, nevertheless have resulted in positive promotion of the coherence of the whole.

This double role of opposition as related to social self-preservation —with reference to external and to internal relations, as antithesis between the whole group and an external power, and as antithesis between the elements of the group among themselves—is reproduced as genuine sociological life form in the narrower relationships between individual people. These also plainly need the stimulus of difference in order to retain and protect their unity. Now this difference may reside either within the relationship itself, in the different characteristics of its temporal divisions, or in the difference which appears between the relationship as a whole and, on the other hand, experiences and emotions quite outside of it. Thus it is often remarked that friendship, love, and marriage need occasional interruptions in order to get a true realization of their meaning and intimacy (*Festigkeit*), after reconciliation. Similar relationships are to be distinguished which do not require this internal difference, but rather, along with more even internal character, become conscious of their own weal through the difference from that which the world otherwise affords, and that which is otherwise known of it. The last form surely stands higher in the scale, and gives evidence of stronger, positive motives of coherence. The first form, in its turn, stands lower, according to the degree of frequency in the alternation between the divergent and the convergent periods. The lowest grade is represented by the formula: "One minute blows, the next agreement (*Pack schlägt sich, Pack verträgt sich*)." This marks a condition in which the essential and permanent relationships have only a slight value in consciousness; the disposition being rather determined at each moment by external stimuli, which work in accidental alternation, now in attraction, now in repulsion. For that very reason, however, there is in all this a deep utility in connection with the promotion of coherence. For wherever the occasion to be conscious of precisely this coherence is in itself slight, and the capability of appreciating it is itself not particularly developed, there will be needed, in order to arouse it, constantly renewed psychological impulses and rude stimulation from contrasts. These cannot be furnished better than in the form of constantly renewed agreements after constantly repeated disagreements. This at the same time affords the background from which unity at last appears.

I come back, herewith, to the starting point of this discussion. Enmities and strifes are, in their significance for the self-preservation of the group, the characteristic examples for the value which variability of group life, change of its forms of activity, possess for this purpose. For, although antagonism, in general, never entirely and universally dies out, yet it accords with its nature to build only a spatially and temporally limited section between the operations of the forces that make for coherence and unified harmony. In its peculiar nature, antagonism presents one of those contrast-stimuli, evidently demanded by the innermost needs of the unifying social bond, because there, as elsewhere, the permanent can emerge and come to conscious force only as a function of the changeable. Social unity is the abiding form, or element, or whatever we may call it, which asserts itself as the substantial in all changes of its peculiar, special shape, its content, its relations to the social interests and destinies; and asserts itself the more, the livelier the change of these factors. The depth (*Vertiefung*), intensiveness (*Festigkeit*), and unity of the marriage relationship, for example, is surely, *ceteris paribus,* a function of the manifoldness and changeableness of the destinies, the experience of which stands out in distinction from the unchangeability of the matrimonial communion.

It is the essence of the human that the condition of the existence of its separate factors is the existence of their opposites. The manifoldness of formations, of changes, of contents, is so essential for the self-preservation of the group, not only because in each limited period the unity of the group stands out in contrast with the passing variations, but especially because the unity always recurs as the same, while the formations, the changes, the contents, from which it is distinguished are each time different. It therefore gains thereby, as against all interruptions, those chances of confirmation and effectiveness which truth possesses over error. Little as the truth, in and of itself, in the isolated case, possesses an advantage, or a mystic power of prevalence, over error, yet its ultimate victory is probable for the reason that truth is only one, while errors about the same subject are countless. It is therefore to be assumed from the start that the truth will more frequently reappear in the see-saw of opinions, *not than error in general, to be sure, but than any given error.* So the unity of the social group has the chance to preserve, to strengthen, and to deepen itself against all interruptions and fluctuations, because these are always of different sorts, while the group unity at each reappearance is the same. By virtue of this fact, the above discussed favorable consequences of social variability for the maintenance of the group may exist without the necessity that the fact of change in general shall enter into serious competition with the principle of unity.

CHAPTER 14

Processes of Social Control

————◆•◆————

THE EXTERNAL REALITY OF SOCIETY

BY

EMILE DURKHEIM

COLLECTIVE tendencies have an existence of their own; they are forces as real as cosmic [1] forces, though of another sort; they, likewise, affect the individual from without, though through other channels. The proof that the reality of collective tendencies is no less than that of cosmic forces is that this reality is demonstrated in the same way, by the uniformity of effects. When we find that the number of deaths varies little from year to year, we explain this regularity by saying that mortality depends on the climate, the temperature, the nature of the soil, in brief on a certain number of material forces which remain constant through changing generations because independent of individuals. Since, therefore, moral acts such as suicide are reproduced not merely with an equal but with a greater uniformity, we must likewise admit that they depend on forces external to individuals. Only, since these forces must be of a moral order and since, except for individual men, there is no other moral order of existence in the world but society, they must be social. But whatever they are called, the important thing is to recognize their reality and conceive of them as a totality of forces which cause us to act from without, like the physico-

Reprinted by permission of the publisher, The Free Press, Glencoe, Illinois. Copyright 1951 by The Free Press, A Corporation.
Abridged from: Durkheim, Emile, *Suicide: A Study in Sociology* (translated by George Simpson), Glencoe, Illinois: The Free Press, 1951.

[1] Ed. Note: Durkheim uses this term to mean the physical environment.

chemical forces to which we react. So truly are they things *sui generis* and not mere verbal entities that they may be measured, their relative sizes compared, as is done with the intensity of electric currents or luminous foci. Thus, the basic proposition that social facts are objective, a proposition we have had the opportunity to prove in another work [2] and which we consider the fundamental principle of the sociological method, finds a new and especially conclusive proof in moral statistics and above all in the statistics of suicide. Of course, it offends common sense. But science has encountered incredulity whenever it has revealed to men the existence of a force that has been overlooked. Since the system of accepted ideas must be modified to make room for the new order of things and to establish new concepts, men's minds resist through mere inertia. Yet this understanding must be reached. If there is such a science as sociology, it can only be the study of a world hitherto unknown, different from those explored by the other sciences. This world is nothing if not a system of realities.

But just because it encounters traditional prejudices this conception has aroused objections to which we must reply.

First, it implies that collective tendencies and thoughts are of a different nature from individual tendencies and thoughts, that the former have characteristics which the latter lack. How can this be, it is objected, since there are only individuals in society? But, reasoning thus, we should have to say that there is nothing more in animate nature than inorganic matter, since the cell is made exclusively of inanimate atoms. To be sure, it is likewise true that society has no other active forces than individuals; but individuals by combining form a psychical existence of a new species, which consequently has its own manner of thinking and feeling. Of course the elementary qualities of which the social fact consists are present in germ in individual minds. But the social fact emerges from them only when they have been transformed by association since it is only then that it appears. Association itself is also an active factor productive of special effects. In itself it is therefore something new. When the consciousness of individuals, instead of remaining isolated, becomes grouped and combined, something in the world has been altered. Naturally this change produces others, this novelty engenders other novelties, phenomena appear whose characteristic qualities are not found in the elements composing them.

It is not true that society is made up only of individuals; it also includes material things, which play an essential role in the common life. The social fact is sometimes so far materialized as to become an element of the external world. For instance, a definite type of architec-

[2] See *Règles de la méthode sociologique,* ch. II.

ture is a social phenomenon; but it is partially embodied in houses and buildings of all sorts which, once constructed, become autonomous realities, independent of individuals. It is the same with the avenues of communication and transportation, with instruments and machines used in industry or private life which express the state of technology at any moment in history, of written language, etc. Social life, which is thus crystallized, as it were, and fixed on material supports, is by just so much externalized, and acts upon us from without. Avenues of communication which have been constructed before our time give a definite direction to our activities, depending on whether they connect us with one or another country. A child's taste is formed as he comes into contact with the monuments of national taste bequeathed by previous generations. At times such monuments even disappear and are forgotten for centuries, then, one day when the nations which reared them are long since extinct, reappear and begin a new existence in the midst of new societies. This is the character of those very social phenomena called Renaissances. A Renaissance is a portion of social life which, after being, so to speak, deposited in material things and remained long latent there, suddenly reawakens and alters the intellectual and moral orientation of peoples who had had no share in its construction. Doubtless it could not be reanimated if living centers of consciousness did not exist to receive its influence; but these individual conscious centers would have thought and felt quite differently if this influence were not present.

The same remark applies to the definite formulae into which the dogmas of faith are precipitated, or legal precepts when they become fixed externally in a consecrated form. However well digested, they would of course remain dead letters if there were no one to conceive their significance and put them into practice. But though they are not self-sufficient, they are none the less in their own way factors of social activity. They have a manner of action of their own. Juridical relations are widely different depending on whether or not the law is written. Where there is a constituted code, jurisprudence is more regular but less flexible, legislation more uniform but also more rigid. Legislation adapts itself less readily to a variety of individual cases, and resists innovations more strongly. The material forms it assumes are thus not merely ineffective verbal combinations but active realities, since they produce effects which would not occur without their existence. They are not only external to individual consciousness, but this very externality establishes their specific qualities. Because these forms are less at the disposal of individuals, individuals cannot readily adjust them to circumstances, and this very situation makes them more resistant to change.

Of course it is true that not all social consciousness achieves such externalization and materialization. Not all the aesthetic spirit of a nation is embodied in the works it inspires; not all of morality is formulated in clear precepts. The greater part is diffused. There is a large collective life which is at liberty; all sorts of currents come, go, circulate everywhere, cross and mingle in a thousand different ways, and just because they are constantly mobile are never crystallized in an objective form. Today, a breath of sadness and discouragement descends on society; tomorrow, one of joyous confidence will uplift all hearts. For a while the whole group is swayed towards individualism; a new period begins and social and philanthropic aims become paramount. Yesterday cosmopolitanism was the rage, today patriotism has the floor. And all these eddies, all these fluxes and refluxes occur without a single modification of the main legal and moral precepts, immobilized in their sacrosanct forms. Besides, these very precepts merely express a whole sub-jacent life of which they partake; they spring from it but do not supplant it. Beneath all these maxims are actual, living sentiments, summed up by these formulae but only as in a superficial envelope. The formulae would awake no echo if they did not correspond to definite emotions and impressions scattered through society. If, then, we ascribe a kind of reality to them, we do not dream of supposing them to be the whole of moral reality. That would be to take the sign for the thing signified. A sign is certainly something; it is not a kind of supererogatory epiphenomenon; its role in intellectual development is known today. But after all it is only a sign.[3]

But because this part of collective life has not enough consistency to become fixed, it none the less has the same character as the formulated precepts of which we were just speaking. *It is external to each average individual taken singly.* Suppose some great public danger arouses a gust of patriotic feeling. A collective impulse follows, by virtue of which society as a whole assumes axiomatically that private interests, even those usually regarded most highly, must be wholly effaced before the common interest. And the principle is not merely uttered as an *ideal;* if need be it is literally applied. Meanwhile, take a careful look at the average body of individuals. Among very many of them you will recapture something of this moral state of mind, though infinitely attenuated. The men who are ready to make freely

---

[3] We do not expect to be reproached further, after this explanation, with wishing to substitute the exterior for the interior in sociology. We start from the exterior because it alone is immediately given, but only to reach the interior. Doubtless the procedure is complicated; but there is no other unless one would risk having his research apply to his personal feeling concerning the order of facts under investigation, instead of to this factual order itself.

so complete a self-abnegation are rare, even in time of war. *Therefore there is not one of all the single centers of consciousness who make up the great body of the nation, to whom the collective current is not almost wholly exterior, since each contains only a spark of it.*

Observation thus confirms our hypothesis. The regularity of statistical data, on the one hand, implies the existence of collective tendencies exterior to the individual, and on the other, we can directly establish this exterior character in a considerable number of important cases. Besides, this exteriority is not in the least surprising for anyone who knows the difference between individual and social states of consciousness. By definition, indeed, the latter can reach none of us except from without, since they do not flow from our personal predispositions. Since they consist of elements foreign to us they express something other than ourselves. To be sure in so far as we are solidary with the group and share its life, we are exposed to their influence; but so far as we have a distinct personality of our own we rebel against and try to escape them. Since everyone leads this sort of double existence simultaneously, each of us has a double impulse. We are drawn in a social direction and tend to follow the inclinations of our own natures. So the rest of society weighs upon us as a restraint to our centrifugal tendencies, and we for our part share in this weight upon others for the purpose of neutralizing theirs. We ourselves undergo the pressure we help to exert upon others. Two antagonistic forces confront each other. One, the collective force, tries to take possession of the individual; the other, the individual force, repulses it. To be sure, the former is much stronger than the latter, since it is made of a combination of all the individual forces; but as it also encounters as many resistances as there are separate persons, it is partially exhausted in these multifarious contests and reaches us disfigured and enfeebled. When it is very strong, when the circumstances activating it are of frequent recurrence, it may still leave a deep impression on individuals; it arouses in them mental states of some vivacity which, once formed, function with the spontaneity of instinct; this happens in the case of the most essential moral ideas. But most social currents are either too weak or too intermittently in contact with us to strike deep roots in us; their action is superficial. Consequently, they remain almost completely external. Hence, the proper way to measure any element of a collective type is not to measure its magnitude within individual consciences and to take the average of them all. Rather, it is their sum that must be taken. Even this method of evaluation would be much below reality, for this would give us only the social sentiment reduced by all its losses through individuation.

THE REGULATION OF THE WISHES

B Y

WILLIAM I. THOMAS

ONE of the most important powers gained during the evolution of animal life is the ability to make decisions from within instead of having them imposed from without. Very low forms of life do not make decisions, as we understand this term, but are pushed and pulled by chemical substances, heat, light, etc., much as iron filings are attracted or repelled by a magnet. They do tend to behave properly in given conditions—a group of small crustaceans will flee as in a panic if a bit of strychnia is placed in the basin containing them and will rush toward a drop of beef juice like hogs crowding around swill —but they do this as an expression of organic affinity for the one substance and repugnance for the other, and not as an expression of choice or "free will." There are, so to speak, rules of behavior but these represent a sort of fortunate mechanistic adjustment of the organism to typically recurring situations, and the organism cannot change the rule.

On the other hand, the higher animals, and above all man, have the power of refusing to obey a stimulation which they followed at an earlier time. Response to the earlier stimulation may have had painful consequences and so the rule or habit in this situation is changed. We call this ability the power of inhibition, and it is dependent on the fact that the nervous system carries memories or records of past experiences. At this point the determination of action no longer comes exclusively from outside sources but is located within the organism itself.

Preliminary to any self-determined act of behavior there is always a stage of examination and deliberation which we may call *the definition of the situation*. And actually not only concrete acts are dependent on the definition of the situation, but gradually a whole life-policy and the personality of the individual himself follow from a series of such definitions.

But the child is always born into a group of people among whom

Abridged from: Thomas, William I., *The Unadjusted Girl*, Boston: Little, Brown and Company, 1927. Reprinted by permission of the Social Science Research Council. In connection with the writings of W. I. Thomas, see: Thomas, W. I., *Social Behavior and Personality*. Contributions of W. I. Thomas to Theory and Social Research. Edited by Edmund H. Volkart, New York: Social Science Research Council, 1951.

all the general types of situation which may arise have already been defined and corresponding rules of conduct developed, and where he has not the slightest chance of making his definitions and following his wishes without interference. Men have always lived together in groups. Whether mankind has a true herd instinct or whether groups are held together because this has worked out to advantage is of no importance. Certainly the wishes in general are such that they can be satisfied only in a society. But we have only to refer to the criminal code to appreciate the variety of ways in which the wishes of the individual may conflict with the wishes of society. And the criminal code takes no account of the many unsanctioned expressions of the wishes which society attempts to regulate by persuasion and gossip.

There is therefore always a rivalry between the spontaneous definitions of the situation made by the member of an organized society and the definitions which his society has provided for him. The individual tends to a hedonistic selection of activity, pleasure first; and society to a utilitarian selection, safety first. Society wishes its members to be laborious, dependable, regular, sober, orderly, self-sacrificing; while the individual wishes less of this and more of new experience. And organized society seeks also to regulate the conflict and competition inevitable between its members in the pursuit of their wishes. The desire to have wealth, for example, or any other socially sanctioned wish, may not be accomplished at the expense of another member of the society,—by murder, theft, lying, swindling, blackmail, etc.

It is in this connection that a moral code arises, which is a set of rules or behavior norms, regulating the expression of the wishes, and which is built up by successive definitions of the situation. In practice the abuse arises first and the rule is made to prevent its recurrence. Morality is thus the generally accepted definition of the situation, whether expressed in public opinion and the unwritten law, in a formal legal code, or in religious commandments and prohibitions.

The family is the smallest social unit and the primary defining agency. As soon as the child has free motion and begins to pull, tear, pry, meddle, and prowl, the parents begin to define the situation through speech and other signs and pressures: "Be quiet", "Sit up straight", "Blow your nose", "Wash your face", "Mind your mother", "Be kind to sister", etc. This is the real significance of Wordsworth's phrase, "Shades of the prison house begin to close upon the growing child." His wishes and activities begin to be inhibited, and gradually, by definitions within the family, by playmates, in the school, in the Sunday school, in the community, through reading, by formal instruction, by informal signs of approval and disapproval, the growing member learns the code of his society.

In addition to the family we have the community as a defining agency. At present the community is so weak and vague that it gives us no idea of the former power of the local group in regulating behavior. Originally the community was practically the whole world of its members. It was composed of families related by blood and marriage and was not so large that all the members could not come together; it was a face-to-face group. I asked a Polish peasant what was the extent of an *"okolica"* or neighborhood—how far it reached. "It reaches," he said, "as far as the report of a man reaches—as far as a man is talked about." And it was in communities of this kind that the moral code which we now recognize as valid originated. The customs of the community are "folkways," and both state and church have in their more formal codes mainly recognized and incorporated these folkways.

From the foregoing it appears that the face-to-face group (family-community) is a powerful habit-forming mechanism. The group has to provide a system of behavior for many persons at once, a code which applies to everybody and lasts longer than any individual or generation. Consequently the group has two interests in the individual,—to suppress wishes and activities which are in conflict with the existing organization, or which seem the starting point of social disharmony, and to encourage wishes and actions which are required by the existing social system. And if the group performs this task successfully, as it does among savages, among Mohammedans, and as it did until recently among European peasants, no appreciable change in the moral code or in the state of culture is observable from generation to generation. In small and isolated communities there is little tendency to change or progress because the new experience of the individual is sacrificed for the sake of the security of the group.

But by a process, an evolution, connected with mechanical inventions, facilitated communication, the diffusion of print, the growth of cities, business organization, the capitalistic system, specialized occupations, scientific research, doctrines of freedom, the evolutionary view of life, etc., the family and community influences have been weakened and the world in general has been profoundly changed in content, ideals, and organization.

Young people leave home for larger opportunities, to seek new experience, and from necessity. Detachment from family and community, wandering, travel, "vagabondage" have assumed the character of normality. Relationships are casualized and specialized. Men meet professionally, as promoters of enterprises, not as members of families, communities, churches. Girls leave home to work in factories, stores, offices, and studios. Even when families are not separated they leave home for their work.

Every new invention, every chance acquaintanceship, every new environment, has the possibility of redefining the situation and of introducing change, disorganization or different type of organization into the life of the individual or even of the whole world. Thus, the invention of the check led to forgery; the sulphur match to arson; at present the automobile is perhaps connected with more seductions than happen otherwise in cities altogether; an assassination precipitated the World War; motion pictures and the *Saturday Evening Post* have stabilized and unstabilized many existences, considered merely as opportunity for new types of career. The costly and luxurious articles of women's wear organize the lives of many girls (as designers, artists, and buyers) and disorganize the lives of many who crave these pretty things.

In the small and spatially isolated communities of the past, where the influences were strong and steady, the members became more or less habituated to and reconciled with a life of repressed wishes. The repression was demanded of all, the arrangement was equitable, and while certain new experiences were prohibited, and pleasure not countenanced as as end in itself, there remained satisfactions, not the least of which was the suppression of the wishes of others. On the other hand the modern world presents itself as a spectacle in which the observer is never sufficiently participating. The modern revolt and unrest are due to the contrast between the paucity of fulfillment of the wishes of the individual and the fullness, or apparent fullness, of life around him. All age levels have been affected by the feeling that much, too much, is being missed in life. This unrest is felt most by those who have heretofore been most excluded from general participation in life,—the mature woman and the young girl. Sometimes it expresses itself in despair and depression, sometimes in breaking all bounds. Immigrants form a particular class in this respect. They sometimes repudiate the old system completely in their haste to get into the new. There are cases where the behavior of immigrants, expressing natural but random and unregulated impulses, has been called insane by our courts.

Formerly the fortunes of the individual were bound up with those of his family and to some degree with those of the community. He had his security, recognition, response, and new experience in the main as group member. He could not rise or fall greatly above or below the group level. Even the drunkard and the "black sheep" had respect in proportion to the standing of his family. And correspondingly, if a family member lost his "honor," the standing of the whole family was lowered.

Individualism, on the other hand, means the personal schematization of life,—making one's own definitions of the situation and determining one's own behavior norms. Actually there never has been and never will be anything like complete individualization, because no one lives or can live without regard to a public. Anything else would be insanity. But in their occupational pursuits men have already a degree of individualization, decide things alone and in their own way. They take risks, schematize their enterprises, succeed or fail, rise higher and fall lower. A large element of individualism has entered into the marriage relation also. Married women are now entering the occupations freely and from choice, and carrying on amateur interests which formerly were not thought of as going with marriage. And this is evidently a good thing, and stabilizes marriage. Marriage alone is not a life, particularly since the decline of the community type of organization.

CONTROL AND ATTENTION

B Y

WILLIAM I. THOMAS

THERE is a useful concept into which all activity can be translated, or to which it can at least be related, namely, *control*. Control is not a social force, but is the object, realized or unrealized, of all purposive activity. Food and reproduction are the two primal necessities, if the race is to exist. The whole design of nature with reference to organic life is to nourish the individual and provide a new generation before the death of the old, and the most elementary statement, as I take it, which can be made of individual and of social activity is that it is designed to secure that control of the environment which will assure these two results. I will illustrate my meaning by applying the concept of *control* to some of the steps in organic and social development.

The animal differs from the plant primarily in its superior control

Abridged from: Thomas, William I., *Source Book for Social Origins*, Chicago: The University of Chicago Press, 1909.
Reprinted by permission of the Social Science Research Council. In connection with the writings of W. I. Thomas, see: Thomas, W. I., *Social Behavior and Personality*, Contributions of W. I. Thomas to Theory and Social Research, Edited by Edmund H. Volkart, New York: Social Science Research Council, 1951.

of the environment, secured through the power of motion. It does not wait for food, but goes after it. In man the principle of motion and consequent control is extended through the use of animals and the various means of mechanical transportation which he has developed. With the use of free hands man immensely increased his control, through the ability to make and use weapons and tools. Fire is a very precious element in control, since through its use man was able to transform inedible into edible materials, to smelt and forge iron, and to enlarge the habitable world by regulating the temperature of the colder regions. Mechanical invention is to be viewed as control. It utilizes new forces or old forces in new ways, making them do work, and assist man in squeezing out of nature values not before suspected, not within reach, or not commonly enjoyed. The gregariousness of animals and the associated life of men are modes of control, because numbers and co-operation make life more secure. Language is a powerful instrument of control, because through it knowledge, tradition, standpoint, ideals, stimulations, copies, are transmitted and increased. Forms of government are aids to control, by providing safety and fair play within the group and organized resistance to intrusions from without. Religion assists control, reinforcing by a supernatural sanction those modes of behavior which by experience have been determined to be moral, i. e., socially advantageous. Art aids control by diffusing admirable copies for imitation, with the least resistance and the maximum of contagion. Play is an organic preparation and practice for control. Marriage secures better provision and training to children than promiscuity. Medicine keeps the organism in order or repairs it. Liberty is favorable to control, because with it the individual has opportunity to develop ideas and values by following his own bent which he would not develop under repression. The human mind is preeminently the organ of manipulation, of adjustment, of control. It operates through what we call knowledge. This in turn is based on memory and the ability to compare a present situation with similar situations in the past and to revise our judgments and actions in view of the past experience. By this means the world at large is controlled more successfully as time goes on. Knowledge thus becomes the great force in control, and those societies are the most successful and prosperous in which the knowledge is most disseminated, most reliable, and most intensive. This is the sense in which knowledge is power. And as to morality, if we should single out and make a catalogue of actions which we are accustomed to call laudable and virtuous, we should see that they can all be stated from the control standpoint. But I will not multiply instances, and I need not point out that all conflict, exploitation, showing off, boasting, gambling, and violation of the decalogue, are designed to secure control, however unsuccessful in the end.

There is, however, a still more serviceable standpoint for the examination of society and of social change, and that is *attention*. This is by no means in conflict with the category of *control*. Control is the end to be secured and attention is the means of securing it. They are the objective and subjective sides of the same process. Attention is the mental attitude which takes note of the outside world and manipulates it; it is the organ of accommodation. But attention does not operate alone; it is associated with habit on the one hand and with crisis on the other. When the habits are running smoothly the attention is relaxed; it is not at work. But when something happens to disturb the run of habit the attention is called into play and devises a new mode of behavior which will meet the crisis. That is, the attention establishes new and adequate habits, or it is its function to do so.

Such conditions as the exhaustion of game, the intrusion of outsiders, defeat in battle, floods, drought, pestilence, and famine illustrate one class of crisis. The incidents of birth, death, adolescence, and marriage, while not unanticipated, are always foci of attention and occasions for control. They throw a strain on the attention, and affect the mental life of the group. Shadows, dreams, epilepsy, intoxication, swooning, sickness, engage the attention and result in various attempts at control. Other crises arise in the conflict of interests between individuals, and between the individual and the group. Theft, assault, sorcery, and all crimes and misdemeanors are occasions for the exercise of attention and control. To say that language, reflection, discussion, logical analysis, abstraction, mechanical invention, magic, religion, and science are developed in the effort of the attention to meet difficult situations through a readjustment of habit, is simply to say that the mind itself is the product of crisis. Crisis also produces the specialized occupations. The medicine-man, the priest, the law-giver, the judge, the ruler, the physician, the teacher, the artist and other specialists, represent classes of men who have or profess special skill in dealing with crises. Among the professions whose connection with crisis is least obvious are perhaps those of teacher and artist. But the teacher is especially concerned with anticipating that most critical of periods in the life of the youth when he is to enter manhood and be no longer supported by others; and art always arises as the memory of crisis.

Of course a crisis may be so serious as to kill the organism or destroy the group, or it may result in failure or deterioration. But crisis, as I am employing the term, is not to be regarded as habitually violent. It is simply a disturbance of habit, and it may be no more than an incident, a stimulation, a suggestion. It is here that imitation plays a

great role. But it is quite certain that the degree of progress of a people
has a certain relation to the nature of the disturbances encountered,
and that the most progressive have had a more vicissitudinous life.
Our proverb "Necessity is the mother of invention" is the formulation
in folk-thought of this principle of social change.

The run of crises encountered by different individuals and races is
not of course, uniform, and herein we have a partial explanation of
the different rate and direction of progress in different peoples. But
more important than this in any explanation of the advanced and
backward races is the fact that the same crisis will not produce the
same effect uniformly. And in this connection I will briefly indicate
the relation of attention and crisis to (1) the presence of extraordinary
individuals in the group, (2) the level of culture of the group, and
(3) the character of the ideas by which the group-mind is prepossessed:

1. Whatever importance we may attach to group-mind and mass-
suggestion, the power of the attention to meet a crisis is primarily an
individual matter, or at least the initiative lies with the individual.
The group, therefore, which possesses men of extraordinary mental
ability is at an advantage. The fleeing animal, for instance, is always
a problem, and the resilience of wood is probably always observed, but
the individual is not always present to relate the two facts, and invent
the bow and arrow. If he is present he probably, as Lewis Morgan
suggests, raises his group to a higher level of culture by producing a
new food epoch. The relation of the "great man" to crisis is indeed
one of the most important points in the problem of progress. Such
men as Moses, Mohammed, Confucius, Christ, have stamped the whole
character of a civilization.

2. The level of culture of the group limits the power of the mind to
meet crisis and readjust. If the amount of general knowledge is small
and the material resources scanty, the mind may find no way out of
an emergency which under different conditions would be only the occasion for further progress. If we could imagine a group without
language, numbers, iron, fire, and without the milk, meat, and labor
of domestic animals, and if this group were small, as it would necessarily be under those conditions, we should have also to imagine a very
low state of mind in general in the group. The individual mind cannot
rise much above the level of the group-mind, and the group-mind will
be simple if the outside environmental conditions and the antecedent
racial experiences are simple. On this account it is just to attribute
important movements and inventions to individuals only in a qualified
sense. The extraordinary individual works on the material and psychic
fund already present, and if the situation is not ripe neither is he ripe.
From this standpoint we can understand why it is almost never pos-

sible to attribute any great modern invention to any single person. When the state of science and the social need reach a certain point a number of persons are likely to solve the same problem.

3. The character of the accommodations already made affects the character of the accommodation to the new crisis. When our habits are settled and running smoothly they much resemble the instincts of animals. And the great part of our life is lived in the region of habit. The habits, like the instincts, are safe and serviceable. They have been tried, and they are associated with a feeling of security. There consequently grows up in the folk-mind a determined resistance to change. And there is a degree of sense in this, for while change implies possibilities of improvement it also implies danger of disaster, or a worse condition. It must also be acknowledged that a state of rapid and constant change implies loss of settled habits and disorganization. As a result, all societies view change with suspicion, and the attempt to revise certain habits is even viewed as immorality. Now it is possible under these conditions for a society to become stationary, or to attempt to remain so. The effort of the attention is to preserve the present status rather than to reaccommodate. This condition is particularly marked among the savages. In the absence of science and a proper estimation of the value of change, they rely on ritual and magic, and a minute, conscientious, unquestioning and absolute adhesion to the past. Change is consequently introduced with a maximum of resistance. Indeed, the only world in which change is at a premium and is systematically sought is the modern scientific world. It is plain therefore that the nature of the reaction of attention to crisis is conditioned by the ideas which prepossess the mind.

SOME ASPECTS OF SOCIAL CONTROL

B Y

EDWARD A. ROSS

SUCCESSFUL *cooperation* bespeaks a high grade of social order, inasmuch as each of the cooperators must unfold specific activities within precise limits, and the results therefrom are enjoyed or shared according to some recognized principle. *Hierarchical organization* is still more a test of orderliness, inasmuch as in the sharing of unlike burdens and

Abridged from: Ross, Edward A., *Social Control*, New York: The Macmillan Co., 1901.

the division of unequal benefits men are more apt to fall afoul of one another.

In general, the absence of hostile encounter is a mark of social order, since it implies that interferences are adjusted according to some rule. But extreme division of social labor and high organization is the surest sign of order, since it requires the nice adjustment of multifarious activities according to some prearranged plan.

The readiness of men to disturb the peace or to violate rules in the pursuit of their personal interests depends upon their mental make-up. The peaceable turn aside from collision, while the pugnacious welcome it. The easily contented readily accommodate their desires and actions to the customary restrictions, but the enterprising are always pressing against and trampling upon barriers. The passive strive only to satisfy old wants, and are therefore much stronger in resistance than in offence. The aggressive are insatiate and put forth as much energy to seize what they have not, as to keep what they have.

Most of us take order for granted, and are hardly more aware of it than we are of the air we breathe. Order being the universal and indispensable condition of all our social structures, we give no more thought to it than to the force of cohesion that keeps our machinery from flying into bits.

But it would be, in truth, much juster to assume a state of disorder. We ought to take for granted that men living in propinquity will continually fall afoul of one another. We ought to expect in the normal person not, it is true, the malice, lust, or ferocity of the born criminal, but certainly a natural unwillingness to be checked in the hot pursuit of his ends. Whenever men swarm in new places,—Dutch Flat, Kimberly, Siberia, Skagway,—the man-to-man struggle stands out naked and clear, and the slow emergence of order out of disorder and violence presents itself as the attainment of a difficult and artificial condition.

THE NEED OF SOCIAL CONTROL

So far as the fruits of a common enterprise can be reaped in full by the participants, cooperation may be left entirely free; but when the benefits of a cooperation will redound to the group as a whole and be enjoyed by all alike, it is necessary that all be required to assume their due share of the burden. Among the earliest signs of collective pressure is the endeavor to make kickers, cowards, and shirkers take part in joint undertakings which benefit all.

In complex cooperation even the willing need an authority over them, for success implies such a delicate poise of numerous individual performances that the Word must go forth and with power. Even in peaceful communities, the greater propinquity that comes with social growth and the greater intimacy of men in their dealings and relations subjects the natural order to a breaking strain. Friction wears away the good-will that prevails when men live "in open order." Disputes multiply and with them occasions for disturbance of the peace.

In every cluster there are predatory persons who can no more put themselves in the place of another, than the beast can enter into the anguish of its prey, or the parasite sympathize with his host. Even in a free and fluid association like the mining camp, there were "mean" and "low-lived" men; but in an old society these degenerates, "sports," and men of prey constitute a formidable fraction. Now greater propinquity and growing complexity of relation give this class more power to do harm. Just as when men form a line for passing water at a fire, the man who spills or pours out some of the contents of each bucket he passes does more harm than when each man handles a bucket of his own; so when men who have been working apart enter into intricate cooperations, the mean man finds it easier to prey and inflict damage upon the others, and the individual reaction is less able to hold him in check. The development of mutual aid and higher forms of organization, therefore, necessarily thrusts upon society the problem of controlling the delinquent class.

In the struggle for order the group is not always pitted against the person, the social against the individual interest. It is often the big group against the little group, society against the sect or clan. Furthermore our institutions are not shaped by any one simple ethical principle that appeals to all men who are not bad. They are called into being to balance warring forces, and hence they enclose hopeless contradictions. Unless the all-inclusive group finds means to assimilate and reconcile its members and weaken the ties that bind men into minor groups, the social order will be disrupted.

THE DIRECTION OF SOCIAL CONTROL

As toward every deed there are three possible attitudes,—that of the doer, that of the sufferer, and that of the disengaged spectator,—so there are three bodies of feeling and opinion that work together in shaping social control; namely, that of those who wish to follow a certain line of conduct, that of those who are injured by such conduct, and that of the rest of the community. The second and third *impose* control, the first *limits* it.

In trying to make a man do or desist from something, society may be acting either as indignant bystander or as irate victim. Its policy may be inspired by moral disapprobation or by self-interest. We can account for the volume of existing constraint only by keeping in view *both* these factors. Neither factor by itself can generate all the control there is. Time and again thinkers have sought to interpret the imperatives and ideals in force at a given moment in terms of common sentiment. Time and again thinkers have been fain to interpret them in terms of social utility. But each of these mutually exclusive explanations has about it something strained and arbitrary. The fact is that society interferes with the course of the individual in some cases from sentiment and in other cases from self-interest.

The first service of sentiments like sympathy and the sense of justice is to enable a man to control himself. Their next service is to stir him up to control others. But in the soical field this latter service is much the greater, seeing it employs far more of the total moral sentiment abroad in the community. Rare is the strength that can single-handed overcome temptation; but common enough is that mild predilection for the right which is equal to supporting some one else under temptation.

Far from meriting sarcasm, the faculty of apprehending my neighbor's case so much better than my own deserves to be spoken well of. For the fact that the role of the referee is far easier than that of the principal, renders available for social control a vast amount of correct sentiment which is too weak to be effective for self-control.

When men constrain one another, conduct comes to be determined less by the individual as *agent* and more by the individual as *bystander*. And the views of the man standing by have the same moral superiority over the feelings of the man acting that the verdict of the reflective self has over that of the acting self. Moralists love to see the original fount of all goodness in the voice of the reflective, onlooking self, *i.e. the conscience,* and to make public opinion the unison of many such consciences. But it is more likely that the onlooking fellow-man had his say before the "spectator within the breast," and that conscience is the reflection of public opinion rather than public opinion the reflection of conscience.

In what may be called *the sympathetic functioning of the sense of injustice* we have a motive to disinterested intereference which is of the highest importance in the evolution of order. Sympathy alone makes for *helpfulness*. The sense of injury makes for *retaliation*. But their *interaction* yields that "moral indignation" which leads a community to interfere in quarrels or aggressions that in no way harm it. To this force is due, in a measure, that gradual encroachment of society on private action which is registered in the progressive transformation of wrongs or torts into crimes.

But in giving collective sentiment its full due we have not therewith supplied the clew to the direction of control. For the key to the interpretation of social pressure is, after all, not righteous impulse but utility. Though the surface is troubled by the cross-currents of senti-ment, the tidal movements in the struggle of the many with the one betray the influence of self-interest. The man on Mars who should undertake to forecast the contents of our terrestrial codes would do better to deduce from interests than to work out from sentiments. An acquaintance with the conditions that favor the smooth running of social machinery would be of more use to him than a knowledge of the human heart.

Like the hypothesis that storks bring babies, the theory that the moral instincts beget control has a distressing lack of finality. But how the mystery lights up when we reach the idea of *society*,—a some-thing distinct from a bunch of persons! For we can regard this society as a living thing, actuated, like all the higher creatures, by the instinct of self-preservation. Social control, then, appears as one of the ways in which this living thing seeks to keep itself alive and well. Or, we can regard this society as a person having its good and its evil and a knowledge of this good and evil. And social control would be the limitation that the social ego for its own sake imposes upon the free-dom of the individual ego. In either view society is seen to take action not as bystander but as interested party. The conduct it frowns on is that which in the long run hurts it; the conduct it smiles on is that which in the long run helps it. Laws and imperatives would be—as in fact we find them—neither uniform nor immutable, but adapted to the situation in which society happens to find itself.

There are several reasons why the practical nature of most control does not show on the surface. Since the exercise of social discipline is often attended with much heat and emotion, the sentiment that effects a particular reaction frequently hides from us the origin and meaning of that class of social reactions. Again, society in managing the indi-vidual assumes a disinterested air, and speaks to him with the language of sentiment rather than with the language of interest; for it would be bad policy openly to pit its interest against his. In the third place, ignorance and superstition adapt requirements not to the real, but to the supposed, interests of society.

Furthermore, as social commands are adapted to social needs not so much by conscious thought as by a slow and hidden process in the deeps of the folk mind, they frequently outlive the conditions that called them into being. Retaining their authority after their usefulness has utterly departed, they confuse the observer and hide from him the real meaning of social control.

Finally, the tenor of control changes from time to time. The life of a given society reveals a bewildering series of metamorphoses in laws, moral standards, and personal ideals. And one might well hesitate to connect the changes in the legality or morality of slavery, insolvency, usury, heresy, or polygamy, with changes in the requisites of the social welfare.

*　　*　　*

Let us now review the shares of sentiment and interest in the various codes.

Of all the controls that impinge upon the individual that of the Crowd is the most aimless, arbitrary, and capricious. The crowd stands for the common man in his most unreasonable mood, and hence its rule is marked by impatience of contradiction, contempt for individual rights, and destruction of personal freedom.

In purpose and sanity the Moral Code, which embodies the injunctions of public opinion, stands far higher than the behests of the crowd. The Public is the people organized about natural centres of influence, and hence guided in a measure by time and wisdom. Its control is therefore less emotional and better fitted to protect common interests against particular interests.

The norms comprised under Custom possess a certain presumptive fitness, seeing they have been winnowed by time and slowly shaped by social needs. But the needs they serve are those of the past, and if society comes into new situations the norms of custom may prove exceedingly ill-adapted. Moreover, the dictates of custom are enforced by veneration of the time-hallowed and horror of the new, perhaps of all the sentiments that inspire control the ones most remote from any rational purpose.

Quite apart in its purport stands the Religious Code. In some respects religion is well qualified to be the custodian of the obscure and permanent interests of society. Often those requirements of the religious code which outrun the common moral sentiment are directed to the preservation of fundamental institutions—such as the relations of the sexes, marriage, paternal authority, property, etc.—which do not appeal immediately to the feelings of the public. The reason is that a church, even when it is lay and democratic, gives more weight to the superior few and sets more store by the garnered wisdom of the ages than does the public. At its best, then, the church shows a truly statesmanlike intuition of the laws of collective life.

Of all the controls, that of the State is the least sentimental because the state is an organization that puts the wise minority in the saddle. In spite of the not infrequent ascendency of the class interest over the social interest, the state aims more steadily at a rational safeguarding of the collective welfare than any organ society has yet employed. Prescribed as they are by a special body and enforced by special agents, the rules of the law differ in no small degree from the rules of morality. When the legal code refuses to go with the moral code, it is usually because the state sees no social harm in personal vices that common sentiment condemns.

When, on the other hand, the legal code extends beyond the moral code, it will be found that the insight of picked men has descried evils and dangers to the general weal, not yet realized in the common consciousness. Law being the most progressive department of control, conduct that harms society in new ways is made crime before it has had time to become wrong or sin; and fine and imprisonment is visited upon an offence that brings, as yet, neither blame nor shame.

THE SYSTEM OF SOCIAL CONTROL

In respect to their fundamental character, it is possible to divide most of the supports of order into two groups. Such instruments of control as public opinion, suggestion, personal ideal, social religion, art, and social valuation draw much of their strength from the primal moral feelings. They take their shape from sentiment rather than utility. They control men in many things which have little to do with the welfare of society regarded as a corporation. They are aimed to realize not merely a social order but what one might term a *moral* order. These we may call *ethical.*

On the other hand, law, belief, ceremony, education, and illusion need not spring from ethical feelings at all. They are frequently the means deliberately chosen in order to reach certain ends. They are likely to come under the control of the organized few, and be used, whether for the corporate benefit or for class benefit, as the tools of policy. They may be termed *political,* using the word "political" in its original sense of "pertaining to policy."

Now, the prominence of the one group or the other in the regulative scheme depends uopn the constitution of the society. The *political* instruments operating through prejudice or fear will be preferred:—

1. In proportion as the population elements to be held together are antipathetic and jarring.

2. In proportion to the subordination of the individual will and welfare by the scheme of control.

3. In proportion as the social constitution stereotypes differences of status.

4. In proportion as the differences in economic condition and opportunity it consecrates are great and cumulative.

5. In proportion as the parasitic relation is maintained between races, classes, or sexes.

On the other hand the *ethical* instruments, being more mild, enlightening, and suasive, will be preferred:—

1. In proportion as the population is homogeneous in race.

2. In proportion as its culture is uniform and diffused.

3. In proportion as the social contacts between the elements in the population are many and amicable.

4. In proportion as the total burden of requirement laid upon the individual is light.

5. In proportion as the social constitution does not consecrate distinctions of status or the parasitic relation, but conforms to common elementary notions of justice.

Again, the instruments of control may be distinguished in respect to the functions that devolve upon them. There is a tendency to assign to each form of control that work for which it is best fitted. Law represses that undesirable conduct which is at once important and capable of clear definition. Central positive qualities—courage or veracity in man, chastity in woman—are taken in charge by the sense of honor or self-respect. The supernatural sanction is ordinarily reserved for those acts and abstinences requiring the utmost backing. Religion mounts guard over the ancient, unvarying fundamentals of group life, but takes little note of the temporary adjustments required from time to time. In its code, as well as in its ritual and creed, religion betrays its archaic character.

In morals as well as in microscopes there is provided a major and a minor adjusting apparatus. In adaptability public opinion stands at one end of a series of which religion constitutes the other extreme. Connected with these there is a gradation in the nature of the sanction. Public opinion bans many things not unlawful, law may require much more than self-respect, and self-respect may be wounded by that which is not regarded as sinful. But the universality of the sanction widens as the scope of prohibition narrows. In the first case the offender encounters the public here and now, in the second the crystallized disapproval of society, in the third the opinion of generations of men who have conspired to frame a standard or ideal, and in the last case the frown of the Ruler of the Universe.

IMITATION, STABILITY AND CHANGE

B Y

WILLIAM McDOUGALL

IN the development of individual human beings, imitation, as we have seen, is the great agency through which the child is led on from the life of mere animal impulse to the life of self-control, deliberation, and true volition. And it has played a similar part in the development of the human race and of human society.

The mental constitution of man differs from that of the highest animals chiefly in that man has an indefinitely greater power of learning, of profiting by experience, of acquiring new modes of reaction and adjustment to an immense variety of situations. This superiority of man would seem to be due in the main to his possession of a very large brain, containing a mass of plastic nervous tissue which exceeds in bulk the sum of the innately organised parts and makes up the principal part of the substance of the cerebral hemispheres. This great brain, and the immense capacity for mental adaptation and acquisition implied by it, must have been evolved hand in hand with the development of man's social life and with that of language, the great agent and promoter of social life. For to an individual living apart from any human society the greater part of this brain and of this capacity for acquisition would be useless and would lie dormant for lack of any store of knowledge, belief, and custom to be acquired or assimilated. Whereas animal species have advanced from lower to higher levels of mental life by the improvement of the innate mental constitution of the species, man, since he became man, has progressed in the main by means of the increase in volume and improvement in quality of the sum of knowledge, belief, and custom, which constitutes the tradition of any society. And it is to the superiority of the moral and intellectual tradition of his society that the superiority of civilised man over existing savages and over his savage forefathers is chiefly, if not wholly, due. This increase and improvement of tradition has been effected by countless steps, each relatively small and unimportant, initiated by the few original minds of the successive generations and

Abridged from: McDougall, William, *An Introduction to Social Psychology,* Boston: J. W. Luce and Company, 1909 (2nd Edition).
From *An Introduction to Social Psychology* by William McDougall. By permission of Bruce Humphries, Inc.

incorporated in the social tradition through the acceptance or imitation of them by the mass of men. All that constitutes culture and civilisation, all, or nearly all, that distinguishes the highly cultured European intellectually and morally from the men of the stone age of Europe, is then summed up in the word "tradition," and all tradition exists only in virtue of imitation; for it is only by imitation that each generation takes up and makes its own the tradition of the preceding generation; and it is only by imitation that any improvement, conceived by any mind endowed with that rarest of all things, a spark of originality, can become embodied within the tradition of his society.

Imitation is, then not only the great conservative force of society, it is also essential to all social progress. We may briefly glance at its social operations, under these two heads.[1]

IMITATION AS A CONSERVATIVE AGENCY

The similarities obtaining between the individuals of any one country, any one county, social class, school, university, profession, or community of any kind, and distinguishing them from the members of any other similar community, are in the main due to the more intimate intercourse with one another of the members of the one community, to their consequent imitation of one another, and to their acceptance by imitation of the same tradition. Under this head fall similarities of language, of religious, political, and moral convictions, habits of dressing, eating, dwelling, and of recreation, all those routine activities which make up by far the greater part of the lives of men.[2]

There is widely current a vague belief that the national characteristics of the people of any country are in the main innate characters. But there can be no serious question that this popular assumption is erroneous and that national characteristics, at any rate all those that distinguish the peoples of the European countries, are in the main the expressions of different traditions. There are innate differences of mental constitution between the races and sub-races of men and between the peoples of the European countries; and these innate peculiarities are very important, because they exert through long periods of time a constant bias or moulding influence upon the growth of

[1] The following summary account of the social operations of imitation is in large part extracted from M. Tarde's well-known treatise, "Les Lois de l'Imitation."

[2] The last century has seen a great change in respect to the force with which his immediate social environment bears upon the individual; but, that the form of each man's religious belief is determined for him by the tradition of his society, was strictly true almost without exception in all earlier ages, and still remains true as regards the mass of men. There has been a similar weakening as regards the influence of political tradition, but still it is roughly true that "every little boy and girl that's born into this world alive is either a little liberal or else a little conservative," and for the most part continues so throughout life.

national cultures and traditions. But, relatively to the national peculiarities acquired by each individual in virtue of his participation in
the traditions of his country, the innate peculiarities are slight and
are almost completely obscured in each individual by these superim-
posed acquired characters. If the reader is inclined to doubt the truth
of these statements, let him make an effort of imagination and suppose
that throughout a period of half a century every child born to English
parents was at once exchanged (by the power of a magician's wand)
for an infant of the French, or other European, nation. Soon after the
close of this period the English nation would be composed of individuals of French extraction, and the French nation of individuals of
English extraction. It is, I think, clear that, in spite of this complete
exchange of innate characters between the two nations, there would be
but little immediate change of national characteristics.

It is a general law of imitation that modes of doing persist more
obstinately than modes of thinking and feeling. Hence the many remarkable instances of survival of former stages of culture generally
take the form of practices whose meanings and original purposes have
been long forgotten or completely transformed.

This tendency of practices to survive by continued imitation, long
after their original significance has been forgotten, has had far more
important effects than that of preserving vestiges as curiosities for the
anthropologists. There can be no doubt that practices so surviving the
memory of their significance have in many cases been interpreted and
been given a new meaning by the generations that found themselves
performing them in blind obedience to tradition; although, from the
nature of the case, it can seldom be possible to attain more than a
speculative probability in regard to such transformations and developments.

IMITATION AS AN AGENT OF PROGRESS

If imitation, maintaining customs and traditions of every kind, is
the great conservative agency in the life of societies, it plays also a
great and essential part in bringing about the progress of civilisation.
Its operation as a factor in progress is of two principal kinds: (1) the
spread by imitation throughout a people of ideas and practices gen-
erated within it from time to time by its exceptionally gifted members;
(2) the spread by imitation of ideas and practices from one people to
another. There are certain features or laws of the spreading by imitation that are common to these two forms of the process.

The spread of any culture element, a belief, an art, a convention, a
sentiment, a habit or attitude of mind of any kind, tends to proceed in

geometrical progression, because each individual or body of individuals that imitates the new idea and embodies it in practice becomes an additional centre of radiation of that idea to all individuals and groups that come in contact with it; and also because, with each step of the spread of the idea over a wider area and to larger numbers of persons, the power of mass-suggestion grows in virtue of mere numbers.

The rapidity of the spreading of a culture-element by imitation among any people depends in great measure upon two conditions: first, the density of population; secondly, the degree of development of means of communication and the degree of use made of these means. These propositions are so obviously true that we need not dwell upon them. We have only to look around us to see how, in our own country at the present time, the rapid development of the means of communication during the latter part of the nineteenth century has so facilitated spread by imitation among our dense population as to bring about a very high degree of uniformity in many respects. In almost all such cases imitation and contra-imitation work strongly together; each victim is moved not only by the prestige of those whom he imitates, but also by the desire to be different from the mass who have not yet adopted the fashion. And it is owing to this strong element of contra-imitation that these trivial fashions are usually so fleeting; for, as soon as the fashion has spread to a certain proportion of the total population, the operation of contra-imitation is reversed and begins to make for the abolition of the fashion and its supplanting by some other—the mistress cannot possibly continue to wear the new shape of hat, however becoming to her, because her maids and her humbler neighbours have begun to imitate it.

These trivial fashions generally pass away completely. But all new ideas that spread by imitation must first become fashions, before they can become embodied in tradition as customs; and the easy catching-on and rapid spread of new fashions are sure indications that the culture of a people is mobile and plastic, that it is ready and likely to embody new features in its customs, beliefs, and institutions, and so to undergo change; though such change is not necessarily or always progress towards a better state of civilisation or of social organisation.

Imitation modifies a people's civilisation in one of two ways—by substitution or by accumulation; that is to say, the new culture-element, spreading by imitation among a people, either conflicts with, drives out, and supplants some older traditional element, or constitutes an extension, complication, and enrichment of the existing tradition. Thus a language or a religious system may be imitated by one people from another, and may completely supplant the indigenous language or religion. But more commonly it becomes worked up with the indigenous language, or religion, enriching it and rendering it more complex and more adequate to the needs of the people.

An idea or practice that has once begun to be imitated by a people tends to spread to the maximum extent possible under the given conditions of society; and then the custom or institution in which it has become embodied tends to persist indefinitely with this maximum degree of intensity and diffusion; and it only recedes or disappears under the influence of some newly introduced antagonistic rival. It is when imitation of any idea has reached this saturation point or degree of maximum diffusion, that the statistician shows numerically the constancy of the occurrence of its external manifestations, and cites his figures to prove that the actions of man are as completely determined and as predictable as the motions of the heavenly bodies.

The imitation of peoples follows the fundamental law of all imitation—the law, namely, that the source from which the impression comes is one enjoying prestige, is an individual or collective personality that is stronger, more complex, or more highly developed, and therefore to some extent mysterious, not completely ejective, to the imitators. Whether the ideas of an individual shall be accepted by his fellow-countrymen depends not so much upon the nature of those ideas as upon the degree of prestige which that individual has or can secure.

But originality is a very rare quality, and still more rarely is it combined with the moral and physical and social advantages necessary for the acquisition of high prestige; hence, if the progress of each nation took place only by the acceptance of the ideas of its own great men, progress would have been very much slower than it actually has been.

The imitation of one people by another has been a principal condition of the progress of civilisation in all its stages, but more especially in its later stages. The people that is imitated by another is always one of more highly evolved civilisation or of greater skill and power in the use of the particular idea or institution that is imitated.

CHAPTER 15

The Pressure to Conform

———•◦•———

THE SOCIAL ASPECT OF CONSCIENCE

B Y

CHARLES HORTON COOLEY

I AGREE with those moralists who hold that what we judge to be the right is simply the rational, in a large sense of that word. The mind is the theatre of conflict for an infinite number of impulses, variously originating, among which it is ever striving to produce some sort of unification or harmony. This endeavor to harmonize or assimilate includes deliberate reasoning, but is something much more general and continuous than that. It is mostly an unconscious or subconscious manipulation of the materials presented, an unremitting comparison and rearrangement of them, which ever tends to organize them into some sort of a whole. The right, then, is that which stands this test; the sanction of conscience attaches to those thoughts which, in the long run, maintain their places as part of that orderly whole which the mental instinct calls for, and which it is ever working with more or less success to build up. That is right which presents itself, after the mind has done its full work upon the matter, as the mentally necessary, which we cannot gainsay without breaking up our mental integrity.

According to this view of the matter, judgments of right and wrong are in no way isolated or radically different in kind from other judg-

ments. Such peculiarity as they have seems to come chiefly from the
unusual intensity of the mental conflict that precedes them. The
slightest scrutiny of experience shows, it seems to me, that the sharp
and absolute distinction often assumed to exist between conscience
and other mental activities does not hold good in life. There are
gradual transitions from judgments which no one thinks of as peculiarly moral, through others which some would regard as moral and
others would not, to those which are universally so regarded; and likewise moral feeling or sentiment varies a good deal in different individuals, and in the same individual under different conditions.

The class of judgments which every one considers as moral is perhaps
limited to such as follow an exciting and somewhat protracted mental
struggle, involving an imaginative weighing of conflicting personal
ideas. A line of conduct has to be chosen; alternatives present themselves, each of which is backed by strong impulses, among which are
some, at least, of sympathetic origin; the mind is intensely, even painfully, aroused, and when a decision is reached, it is accompanied by a
somewhat peculiar sort of feeling called the sense of obligation, duty,
or right. There would be little agreement, however, as to what sort of
situations evoke this feeling. We are apt to feel that any question in
regard to which we are much in earnest is a question of right and
wrong.

The fact that the judgment of right is likely to present itself to people of emotional temperament as an imagined voice, admonishing
them what they ought to do, is an illustration of that essentially social
or interlocutory character of thought. Our thoughts are always, in
some sort, imaginary conversations; and when vividly felt they are
likely to become distinctly so. On the other hand, people whose moral
life is calm perceive little or no distinction, in this regard, between the
conclusions of conscience and other judgments.

Of course, the view that the right is the rational would be untrue, if
by rational were meant merely the result of formal reasoning. The
judgment of right and the conclusion of formal thought are frequently
opposed to each other, because, I take it, the latter is a comparatively
narrow, partial, and conventional product of the mind. The former is
rational and mentally authoritative in a larger sense; its premises are
immeasurably richer; it deals with the whole content of life, with instincts freighted with the inarticulate conclusions of a remote past, and
with the unformulated inductions of individual experience. To set the
product of a superficial ratiocination over the final output, in conscience, of our whole mental being, is a kind of pedantry. I do not
mean to imply that there is usually an opposition between the two—
they should work harmoniously together—but only to assert that when

there is, conscience must be regarded as of a profounder rationality.

On the other hand, the wrong, the immoral, is, in a similar sense, the irrational. It is that which, after the mind has done its full work upon the matter, presents itself as the mentally isolated, the inharmonious, that which we cannot follow without having, in our more collected moods, a sense of having been untrue to ourselves, of having done ourselves a harm. The mind in its fullest activity is denied and desecrated; we are split in two. To violate conscience is to act under the control of an incomplete and fragmentary state of mind; and so to become less a person, to begin to disintegrate and go to pieces. An unjust or incontinent deed produces remorse, apparently because the thought of it will not lie still in the mind, but is of such a nature that there is no comfortable place for it in the system of thought already established there.

The main significance of the view that the right is the rational is to deny that there is any sharp distinction in kind between the question of right and wrong and other mental questions; the conclusion of conscience being held to be simply a more comprehensive judgment, reached by the same process as other judgments. It still leaves untouched the remoter problems, mental and social, underlying all judgments; as, for instance, of the nature of impulses, of what determines their relative intensity and persistence, of the character of that process of competition and assimilation among them of which judgments are the outcome; and of the social order as determining impulses both indirectly, through its action upon heredity, and directly through suggestion.

And behind these is that problem of problems, to which all the roads of thought lead, that question of organization or vital process, of which all special questions of society or of the mind are phases. From whatever point of view we look at life, we can see something going on which it is convenient to call organization, development, or the like; but I suppose that all who have thought much about the matter feel that we have only a vague notion of what the fact is that lies behind these words.

It is useless to look for any other or higher criterion of right than conscience. What is felt to be right *is* right; that is what the word means. Any theory of right that should turn out to be irreconcilable with the sense of right must evidently be judged as false. And when it is urged that conscience is variable, we can only answer that, for this very reason, the right cannot be reduced to a universal and conclusive formula. Like life in all its phases, it is a progressive revelation out of depths we do not penetrate.

For the individual considering his own conduct, his conscience is the only possible moral guide, and though it differ from that of every one else, it is the only right there is for him; to violate it is to commit moral suicide. Speculating more largely on conduct in general he may find the right in some collective aspect of conscience, in which his own conscience appears as member of a larger whole; and with reference to which certain particular consciences, at variance with his own, like those of certain sorts of criminals, may appear as degenerate or wrong —and this will not surprise him, because science teaches us to expect degenerate variations in all forms of life. But, however broad a view he takes, he cannot do otherwise than refer the matter to his conscience; so that what *I* think, or—to generalize it—what *we* think, must, in one form or another, be the arbiter of right and wrong, so far as there can be any. Other tests become valid only in so far as conscience adopts them.

It would seem that any scientific study of the matter must consist essentially in investigating the conditions and relations of concrete right—the when, where, and why of what people *do* think is right. Social or moral science can never be a final source or test of morality; though it can reveal facts and relations which may help conscience in making its authoritative judgment.

The view that the right is the rational is quite consistent with the fact that, for those who have surplus energy, the right is the *onward*. The impulse to act, to become, to let out the life that rises within from obscure springs of power, is the need of needs, underlying all more special impulses; and this onward *Trieb* must always count in our judgments of right: it is one of the things conscience has to make room for. There can be no harmony in a mental life which denies expression to this most persistent and fundamental of all instinctive tendencies: and consequently the equilibrium which the active mind seeks, and a sense of which is one with the sense of right, is never a state of rest, but an *equilibrium mobile*.

When we say that right is largely determined by habit, we only emphasize the other aspect of that progressive mingling of continuity with change, which we see in mental life in all its phases. Habit, we know, makes lines of less resistance in thought, feeling, and action; and the existence of these tracks must always count in the formation of a judgment of right, as of any other judgment. It ought not, apparently, to be set over against novel impulses as a contrary principle, but rather thought of as a phase of all impulses, since novelty always consists, from one point of view, in a fresh combination of habits. It is much the same question as that of suggestion and choice, or of invention and imitation. The concrete fact, the real thing, in each case, is not one of these as against the other, or one modified by the other, but a single, vital act of which these are aspects, having no separate existence.

Whether a person's life, in its moral or any other aspect, is obviously changeful, or, on the contrary, appears to be merely repetitive or habitual, depends upon whether the state of his mind, and of the conditions about it, are favorable to rapid changes in the system of his thought. Thus if he is young and vigorous, and if he has a natural open-mindedness and keenness of sensibility, he will be so much the more likely, other things equal, to incorporate fresh elements of thought and make a new synthesis, instead of running on habit. Variety of life in the past, preventing excessive deepening of the mental ruts, and contact with strong and novel influences in the present, have the same tendency.

What is called principle appears to be simply a habit of conscience, a rule formed originally by a synthesis of various impulses, but become somewhat mechanical and independent of its origin—as it is the nature of habit to do. As the mind hardens and matures there is a growing inaptitude to take in novel and powerful personal impressions, and a corresponding ascendancy of habit and system; social sentiment, the flesh and blood of conduct, partly falls away, exposing a skeleton of moral principles. The sense of duty presents itself less and less as a vivid sympathetic impulse, and more and more as a sense of the economy and restfulness of a definite standard of conduct. When one has come to accept a certain course as duty he has a pleasant sense of relief and of lifted responsibility, even if the course involves pain and renunciation. It is like obedience to some external authority; any clear way, though it lead to death, is mentally preferable to the tangle of uncertainty.

Actions that appear memorable or heroic are seldom achieved at the moment of decisive choice, but are more likely to come after the habit of thought which produces the action has become somewhat mechanical and involuntary. It is probably a mistake to imagine that the soldier who braves death in battle, the fireman who enters the burning building, the brakeman who pursues his duty along the icy top of a moving train, or the fisherman who rows away from his vessel into the storm and mist, is usually in an acute state of heroism. It is all in the day's work; the act is part of a system of thought and conduct which has become habitual and would be painful to break. Death is not imagined in all its terrors and compared with social obligation; the case is far simpler. As a rule there is no time in a crisis for complicated mental operations, and whether the choice is heroic or cowardly it is sure to be simple. If there is any conflict of suggestions it is brief, and the one that gains ascendancy is likely to be followed mechanically, without calculation of the future.

One who studies the "sense of oughtness" in children will have no difficulty in seeing that it springs largely from a reluctance to break habits, an indisposition, that is, to get out of mental ruts. It is in the nature of the mind to seek a principle or unifying thought—the mind is a rule-demanding instinct—and in great part this need is met by a habit of thought, inculcated perhaps by some older person who proclaims and enforces the rule, or perhaps by the unintended pressure of conditions which emphasize one suggestion and shut out others. However the rule originates, it meets a mental want, and, if not too strongly opposed by other impulses, is likely to be adopted and felt as obligatory just because it is a consistent way of thinking.

Those who think as I do will reject the opinion that the right is, in any general sense, the social as opposed to the individual. As already stated, I look upon this antithesis as false when used to imply a radical opposition. All our human thought and activity is either individual or social, according to how you look at it, the two being no more than phases of the same thing, which common thought, always inclined to confuse words with things, attempts to separate. This is as true in the ethical field as in any other. The consideration of other persons usually enters largely into questions of right and wrong; but the ethical decision is distinctly an assertion of a private, individualized view of the matter. Surely there is no sound general principle in accordance with which the right is represented by the suggestions of the social environment, and the wrong by our more private impulses.

The individual and the group are related in respect to moral thought quite as they are everywhere else; individual consciences and the social conscience are not separate things, but aspects of one thing, namely, the moral Life, which may be regarded as individual by fixing our attention upon a particular conscience in artificial isolation, or as general, by attending to some collective phase, like public opinion upon a moral question. Suppose, for instance, one were a member of the Congress that voted the measure which brought on the war with Spain. The question how he should vote on this measure would be, in its individual aspect, a matter of private conscience; and so with all other members. But taking the vote as a whole, as a synthesis, showing the moral drift of the group, it appears as an expression of a social conscience. The separation is purely artificial, every judgment of an individual conscience being social in that it involves a synthesis of social influences, and every social conscience being a collective view of individual consciences. The concrete thing, the moral Life, is a whole made up of differentiated members. If this is at all hard to grasp, it is only because the fact is a large one. We certainly cannot get far unless we can learn to *see* organization, since all our facts present it.

Because of its dependence upon personal suggestion, the right always reflects a social group; there is always a circle of persons, more or less extended, whom we really imagine, and who thus work upon our impulses and our conscience; while people outside of this have not a truly personal existence for us. The extent of this circle depends upon many circumstances, as for instance upon the vigor of our imaginations, and the reach of the means of communication through which personal symbols are impressed upon them.

In these days of general literacy, many get their most potent impressions from books, and some, finding this sort of society more select and stimulating than any other, cultivate it to the neglect of palpable persons. This kind of people often have a very tender conscience regarding the moral problems presented in novels, but a rather dull one for those of the flesh-and-blood life about them. In fact, a large part of the sentiments of imaginative persons are purely literary, created and nourished by intercourse with books, and only indirectly connected with what is commonly called experience. Nor should it be assumed that these literary sentiments are necessarily a mere dissipation. Our highest ideals of life come to us largely in this way, since they depend upon imaginative converse with people we do not have a chance to know in the flesh. Indeed, the expansion of conscience that is so conspicuous a fact of recent years, the rise of moral sentiment regarding international relations, alien races, and social and industrial classes other than our own, could not have taken place without the aid of cheap printing and rapid communication.

Not to pursue this line of thought too far, it is enough for our purpose to note that conscience is always a group conscience, however the group may be formed, so that our moral sentiment always reflects our time, our country, and our special field of personal imagination. On the other hand, our sense of right ignores those whom we do not, through sympathy, feel as part of ourselves, no matter how close their physical contiguity.

In minds capable of constructive imagination the social factor in conscience may take the form of ideal persons, whose traits are used as a standard of behavior.

Idealization, of this or any other sort, is not to be thought of as sharply marked off from experience and memory. It seems probable that the mind is never indifferent to the elements presented to it, but that its very nature is to select, arrange, harmonize, idealize. That is, the whole is always acting upon the parts, tending to make them one with itself. What we call distinctively an ideal is only a relatively complex and finished product of this activity. The past, as it lives in our minds, is never a mere repetition of old experience, but is always colored by our present feeling, is always idealized in some sense; and it is the same with our anticipation of the future, so that to wholesome thought expectation is hope.

An ideal, then, is a somewhat definite and felicitous product of imagination, a harmonious and congenial reconstruction of the elements of experience. And a *personal ideal* is such a harmonious and congenial reconstruction of our experience of persons. Its active function is to symbolize and define the desirable, and by so doing to make it the object of definite endeavor.

Probably the phrase "ideal person" suggests something more unified and consistent than is actually present in the minds of most people when they conceive the desirable or good in personal character. Is it not rather ideal traits or sentiments, fragments of personal experience, phases of past intercourse returning in the imagination with a new emphasis in the presence of new situations? We have at times divined in other people courage, generosity, patience, and justice, and judged them to be good. Now, when we find ourselves in a situation where these traits are called for, we are likely to be reminded by that very fact of our previous experience of them; and the memory of it brings these sentiments more vividly to life and gives them more authority in conscience.

This building up of higher personal conceptions does not lend itself to precise description. It is mostly subconscious; the mind is continually at work ordering and bettering its past and present experiences, working them up in accordance with its own instinctive need for consistency and pleasantness; ever idealizing, but rarely producing clean-cut ideals. It finds its materials both in immediate personal intercourse and through books and other durable media of expression.

CONFORMITY AND NON-CONFORMITY

B Y

CHARLES HORTON COOLEY

CONFORMITY may be defined as the endeavor to maintain a standard set by a group. It is a voluntary imitation of prevalent modes of action, distinguished from rivalry and other aggressive phases of emulation by being comparatively passive, aiming to keep up rather than to excel, and concerning itself for the most part with what is outward and formal. On the other hand, it is distinguished from involuntary imitation by being intentional instead of mechanical. Thus it is not conformity, for most of us, to speak the English language, because we have practically no choice in the matter, but we might choose to conform to particular pronunciations or turns of speech used by those with whom we wish to associate.

The ordinary motive to conformity is a sense, more or less vivid, of the pains and inconveniences of non-conformity. Most people find it painful to go to an evening company in any other than the customary dress; the source of the pain appearing to be a vague sense of the depreciatory curiosity which one imagines that he will excite. His social self-feeling is hurt by an unfavorable view of himself that he attributes to others. This example is typical of the way the group coerces each of its members in all matters concerning which he has no strong and definite private purpose. The world constrains us without any definite intention to do so, merely through the impulse, common to all, to despise peculiarity for which no reason is perceived.

It would seem that the repression of non-conformity is a native impulse, and that tolerance always requires some moral exertion. We all cherish our habitual system of thought, and anything that breaks in upon it in a seemingly wanton manner, is annoying to us and likely to cause resentment. So our first tendency is to suppress the peculiar, and we learn to endure it only when we must, either because it is shown to be reasonable or because it proves refractory to our opposition. The innovator is nearly as apt as any one else to put down innovation in others. Words denoting singularity usually carry some reproach with them; and it would perhaps be found that the more settled the social system is, the severer is the implied condemnation. In periods of disorganization and change, such as ours is in many respects, people are educated to comparative tolerance by unavoidable familiarity with conflicting views—as religious toleration, for instance, is the outcome of the continued spectacle of competing creeds.

Conformity is a sort of co-operation: one of its functions is to economize energy. The standards which it presses upon the individual are often elaborate and valuable products of cumulative thought and experience, and whatever imperfections they may have they are, as a whole, an indispensable foundation for life: it is inconceivable that any one should dispense with them. If I imitate the dress, the manners, the household arrangements of other people, I save so much mental energy for other purposes. It is best that each should originate where he is specially fitted to do so, and follow others where they are better qualified to lead. It is said with truth that conformity is a drag upon genius; but it is equally true and important that its general action upon human nature is elevating. We get by it the selected and systematized outcome of the past, and to be brought up to its standards is a brief recapitulation of social development: it sometimes levels down but more generally levels up. It may be well for purposes of incitement to goad our individuality by the abuse of conformity; but statements made with this in view lack accuracy. It is good for the young and aspiring to read Emerson's praise of self-reliance, in order that they may have courage to fight for their ideas; but we may also sympathize with Goethe when he says that "nothing more exposes us to madness than distinguishing us from others, and nothing more contributes to maintaining our common sense than living in the universal way with multitudes of men."

There are two aspects of non-conformity: first, a rebellious impulse or "contrary suggestion" leading to an avoidance of accepted standards in a spirit of opposition, without necessary reference to any other standards; and, second, an appeal from present and commonplace standards to those that are comparatively remote and unusual. These two usually work together. One is led to a mode of life different from that of the people about him, partly by intrinsic contrariness, and partly by fixing his imagination on the ideas and practices of other people whose mode of life he finds more congenial.

In its second aspect non-conformity may be regarded as a remoter conformity. The rebellion against social influence is only partial and apparent; and the one who seems to be out of step with the procession is really keeping time to another music. As Thoreau said, he hears a different drummer. If a boy refuses the occupation his parents and friends think best for him, and persists in working at something strange and fantastic, like art or science, it is sure to be the case that his most vivid life is not with those about him at all, but with the masters he has known through books, or perhaps seen and heard for a few moments. Environment, in the sense of social influence actually at work, is far from the definite and obvious thing it is often assumed to be. Our real environment consists of those images which are most present to our thoughts, and in the case of a vigorous, growing mind, these are likely to be something quite different from what is most present to the senses. The group to which we give allegiance, and to whose standards we try to conform, is determined by our own selective affinity, choosing among all the personal influences accessible to us; and so far as we select with any independence of our palpable companions, we have the appearance of non-conformity.

All non-conformity that is affirmative or constructive must act by this selection of remoter relations; opposition, by itself, being sterile, and meaning nothing beyond personal peculiarity. There is, therefore, no definite line between conformity and non-conformity; there is simply a more or less characteristic and unusual way of selecting and combining accessible influences.

THE PERSONAL IDEAL AND
SOCIAL CONTROL

BY

EDWARD A. ROSS

FROM the fact that self-esteem exhilarates and shame depresses, the normal person aspires to that which he deems precious and worthy. Be it trophy or title, grace or dexterity, wit or erudition, it remains true that what he admires he strives to acquire. Admiration has, therefore, a transforming power, because its object becomes the goal of endeavor. In the field of character the admired becomes a personal ideal toward which one strives. Hence, to control personal ideals is to control character.

Abridged from: Ross, Edward A., *Social Control*, New York: The Macmillan Co., 1901.

To this end are elaborated various patterns of conduct and of character, which may be termed *social types*. These types may become in the course of time *personal ideals,* each for that category of persons for which it is intended. By keeping distinct these two stages in the process, it is easy for us to perceive that the presence of self-control, fidelity, or courage in the types held up for imitation in a community by no means proves that these are the leading qualities of its members. It is perfectly possible for the pattern evolved by a community of grasping men to embrace fair play and respect for ownership. It is just because the type held before the average man is *above* him, that it is able to lift him once he comes to love it and lay hold on it.

The analysis of fit character in all manner of positions so as to discover uniformities which are erected into virtues and made the reigning ideals for individual life is a real master stroke. Its economy is that of the alphabet. There, by analyzing spoken words into their simplest sound elements, we are enabled to reduce the number of written characters from thousands to a little over a score; these, in turn, must be variously combined in order to form the multitude of written words required. Here, by analyzing social characters into their ultimate elements, we can make a few virtues do the work of many concrete types; but these virtues must be combined in varying degrees and proportions, in order to give the variety of guidance needed in the social system. Vast, indeed, is the gain from this moral alphabet. In all early societies that reached a settled order, we find elaborate codes specifying what is standard conduct for all the chief places and functions. The bringing up of each person in the highly specific ethic of his particular status and calling tended to confirm caste, lessen mobility, and discourage variation. Such societies had to throttle progress, for with change in the number, strength, or relation of the orders of men in society, the elaborate patterns ceased to fit, and morality collapsed. It is the bringing people up to love and imitate *generalized* social qualities and *generalized* social character that has given control the elasticity necessary to progress.

But there remain certain concrete types that affect us all. One of these is the elementary type of "man" or "woman" which is embraced as a personal ideal by the common workaday millions. Everybody knows that to "be a man" means not to whimper, to face danger that is unavoidable, to keep promises, to deal fairly, to support one's wife, and to be considerate of a woman. Everybody knows, too, that a woman cannot "be a woman" unless she is modest in demeanor, ministers to her children, and stands by her husband through thick and thin. So much are these the guiding ideals for the common folk of our race that there is not one male out of ten who will not redden or bridle if told that he is "no man at all" or "half a man"; while the female who is not distressed at the charge of being "unwomanly" is properly considered very far gone indeed.

Another concrete socializing type is that of the "gentleman" (or "lady"). This type, which grew up in a military-religious order constituting but a small fraction of the population, conquered first the upper class, and later the middle and lower classes.

It might at first blush seem strange that the aspiring millions of our democracy should embrace an ideal worked out among professional fighters, and neglect ideals like that of the Quaker or the Puritan or the Moravian, which sprang up among men of peace, and are more suitable to a pacific industrial society. But it is to be remembered that people will adopt as ideal only that type which charms and fascinates them. Our experience, as well as that of Japan, shows that an upper-class ideal, with its halo of luxury, romance, and feats of arms, is more apt to take by storm the hearts of plain people than one that springs from the soul of the prophet or reformer.

There are two other types which, though they are not set before everybody, are noteworthy, on account of the social energy that has gone to perfect and glorify them. These are the *soldier* and the *priest*.

They have been the concern of society partly because religious and military functions have seemed to be of highest moment of the common welfare, but still more because the demands of these professions go so much against the grain. To develop the courage, obedience, and fortitude of the warrior, or the self-denial, chastity, and piety of the priest, human nature has to be overlaid with an artificial nature. As the task is difficult, the means have to be powerful, and thus it is that these types have been worked out to a distinctness and backed up with an authority we find nowhere else. The most powerful known agencies—poetry, song, eloquence, applause—are summoned to uphold and commend them. So deeply and durably is the type stamped upon the individual, that he betrays in his thought and feeling a certain arrest of development. The thought of the soldier or the priest cannot wander much beyond the range marked out by his type. Either can do scientific detail work, but very rarely does either do first-class thinking on social, religious, or philosophical subjects—those, namely, about which he has been trained to think and feel in a particular way.

Besides these chief types carefully constructed and strongly fortified, we find many subordinate types serving to effect the minor adjustments of the individual to the group. The framing of these is the work not of society but of the minor group most immediately conversant with the function regulated—usually the trade or profession. The lawyers in their intercourse, their papers and discussions, their legal

books and periodicals, their bar associations, and their law schools arrive at a professional ethics which sketches out the type that becomes
the ideal of those lawyers imbued with the "professional" spirit. So
teachers, clergymen, physicians, civil engineers, artists, or actors, by
agreeing among themselves as to what is praiseworthy and what disreputable, control the feelings and consequently the endeavor of
the individual. Likewise conductors, typesetters, glass-blowers, or
pilots communicate to each other standards of excellence which become trade types. Every "service"—military, naval, hospital, revenue,
police, life saving, detective, or missionary—acquires in time traditions,
stories, anecdotes, precedents, maxims, and sayings which conspire to
delineate and glorify its type. It is this power to subdue the initiate
to its standards that marks the bureaucracy. When a service is originated, say the Franciscan Order or the Salvation Army, the inspiration
of its members comes from the magnetic charm and the ascendant
personality of its founder. But with age the vitality of the order comes
to reside in its models or ideals which each member has accepted for
himself and seeks to communicate to the novice.

Every party, labor union, guild, lodge, surveying corps, or athletic
team will, in the course of time, develop for its special purposes appropriate types of character or observance, which exert on its members
an invisible pressure subordinating them to the welfare or aims of
the association. In other words, the minor groups of men resemble
the great social group in needing to control their units and in the
means they employ for this purpose. We have pointed out the need
of a succession of generations for perfecting a social type and giving
it prestige. So of minor groups it is only the stabler ones with a succession of memberships that are able to create a distinctive atmosphere.

SOCIAL SANCTIONS

B Y

A. R. RADCLIFFE-BROWN

IN any community there are certain modes of behaviour which are
usual and which characterise that particular community. Such modes
of behaviour may be called usages. All social usages have behind them

Abridged from: Radcliffe-Brown, A. R., "Social Sanctions," *Encyclopedia of the
Social Sciences.* New York: The Macmillan Co., 1933. Reprinted by permission of
The Macmillan Company.

the authority of the society, but among them some are sanctioned and others are not. A sanction is a reaction on the part of a society or of a considerable number of its members to a mode of behaviour which is thereby approved (positive sanctions) or disapproved (negative sanctions). Sanctions may further be distinguished according to whether they are diffuse or organised; the former are spontaneous expressions of approval or disapproval by members of the community acting as individuals, while the latter are social actions carried out according to some traditional and recognised procedure. It is a significant fact that in all human societies the negative sanctions are more definite than the positive. Social obligations may be defined as rules of behaviour the failure to observe which entails a negative sanction of some sort. These are thus distinguished from non-obligatory social usages, as, for example, customary technical procedures.

The sanctions existing in a community constitute motives in the individual for the regulation of his conduct in conformity with usage. They are effective, first, through the desire of the individual to obtain the approbation and to avoid the disapprobation of his fellows, to win such rewards or to avoid such punishment as the community offers or threatens; and, second, through the fact that the individual learns to react to particular modes of behaviour with judgments of approval and disapproval in the same way as do his fellows, and therefore measures his own behaviour both in anticipation and in retrospect by standards which conform more or less closely to those prevalent in the community to which he belongs. What is called conscience is thus in the widest sense the reflex in the individual of the sanctions of the society.

It is convenient to begin a discussion of sanctions by a consideration of the diffuse negative sanctions, comprising reactions toward the particular or general behaviour of a member of the community which constitute judgments of disapproval. In such reactions there are not only differences of degree—for disapproval is felt and expressed with different degrees of intensity—but also differences of kind. Such differences are difficult to define and classify. In the English language, for example, there are a large number of words which express disapproval of individual behaviour; these vary from discourteous, unmannerly, unseemly and unworthy, through improper, discreditable, dishonourable and disreputable, to outrageous and infamous. Every society or culture has its own ways of judging behaviour, and these might conveniently be studied in the first instance through the vocabulary. But until comparative study of societies of different types has proceeded further no systematic classification of the kinds of diffuse negative sanction is possible. Provisionally the negative moral or ethical sanction may be defined as a reaction of reprobation by the community toward a person whose conduct is disapproved; moral obligations may thus be considered as rules of conduct which, if not observed, bring about a reaction of this kind. Another distinguishable sanction is that whereby the behaviour of an individual is met with ridicule on the part of his fellows; this has been called the satirical sanction. The varieties of diffuse positive sanctions, being less definite than negative sanctions, are therefore still more difficult to classify.

From the diffuse sanctions already described there should be distinguished what may be called (by a wide extension of the term) religious sanctions; these have also been named supernatural sanctions and mystic sanctions, but both these terms have unsatisfactory connotations. The religious sanctions are constituted in any community by the existence of certain beliefs which are themselves obligatory; it is therefore only within a religious community that these sanctions exist. They take the form that certain deeds by an individual produce a modification in his religious condition, in either a desirable (good) or an undesirable (evil) direction. Certain acts are regarded as pleasing to gods or spirits or as establishing desirable relations with them, while others displease them or destroy in some way the desirable harmonious relations. The religious condition of the individual is in these instances conceived to be determined by his relation to personal spiritual beings. The change in the religious condition may elsewhere be regarded as the immediate effect of the act itself, not mediated by its effects on some personal god or spirit, a view common not only in many of the simpler societies, but also found in a special form in Buddhism and in other advanced Indian religions. Sin may be defined as any mode of behaviour which falls under a negative religious sanction; there is no convenient term for the opposite of sin, that is an action which produces religious merit or a desirable ritual condition.

The religious sanctions involve the belief that most unsatisfactory ritual or religious conditions (pollution, uncleanness, sinfulness) can be removed or neutralised by socially prescribed or recognised procedures, such as lustration, sacrifice, penance, confession and repentance. These expiatory rites are also considered to act either immediately, or mediately through their effects on gods or spirits, depending upon whether the sin is regarded as acting in the one way or the other.

While in modern western civilisation a sin is usually regarded as necessarily a voluntary action or thought, in many simple societies an involuntary action may fall within the given definition of sin. Sickness—for example, leprosy among the Hebrews—is often regarded as similar to ritual or religious pollution and as therefore requiring expiation or ritual purification. A condition of ritual or religious impurity is normally considered as one of immediate or ultimate danger to the individual; it may be believed that he will fall sick and perhaps die unless he can be purified. In some religions the religious sanction takes the form of a belief that an individual who sins in this life will suffer some form of retribution in an after-life. In many instances an individual who is ritually unclean is looked upon as a source of danger not only to himself but also to those with whom he comes in contact or to the whole community. He may therefore be more or less excluded for a time or even permanently from participation in the social life of the community. Frequently, if not always, an obligation therefore rests upon the sinner, or unclean person, to undertake the necessary process of purification.

Thus the religious sanctions differ from the other diffuse sanctions by reason of the beliefs and conceptions indicated above, which cannot be defined or described in any simple way. Somewhat similar beliefs underlie magical practices and procedure in relation to luck, but whereas religious observances and the beliefs associated with them are obligatory within a given religious community, the former are comparable with technical procedures, customary but not obligatory.

Organised sanctions are to be regarded as special developments of the diffuse sanctions, frequently under the influence of the beliefs belonging to religion. Organised positive sanctions, or premial sanctions, are rarely developed to any great extent. Honours, decorations, titles and other rewards for merit, including monetary rewards such as special pensions, given to individuals by a community as a whole, are characteristic of modern societies. In preliterate societies a man who has slain an enemy may be given the right to distinguish himself by wearing some special decoration or in other ways.

Organised negative sanctions, important among which are the penal sanctions of criminal laws, are definite recognised procedures directed against persons whose behaviour is subject to social disapproval. There are many varieties of such procedures, the most important and widespread being the following: subjection to open expression of reprobation or derision, as, for example, through forcible public exposure by confinement in stocks; partial exclusion, permanent or temporary, from full participation in social life and its privileges, including permanent or temporary loss of civil or religious rights; specific loss of social rank, or degradation, the exact contrary of the positive sanction of promotion; infliction of loss of property by imposition of a fine or by forcible seizure or destruction; infliction of bodily pain; mutilation or branding in which pain is incidental to permanent exposure to reprobation; permanent exclusion from the community, as by exile; imprisonment; and punishment by death. These sanctions are legal sanctions when they are imposed by a constituted authority, political, military or ecclesiastic.

In any given society the various primary sanctions form a more or less systematic whole which constitutes the machinery of social control. There is an intimate relation between the religious sanctions and the moral sanctions, which varies, however, in different societies, and cannot be stated in any brief formula. The primary legal sanctions of criminal law, in all societies except the highly secularised modern states, show a close connection with religious beliefs.

Besides these primary social sanctions and resting upon them there are certain sanctions which may be termed secondary; these are concerned with the actions of persons or groups in their effects upon other persons or groups. In modern civil law, for example, when an individual is ordered by a court to pay damages, the primary sanction behind the order is the power of the court to make forcible seizure of his property or to imprison or otherwise punish him for contempt of court if he fails to obey. Thus secondary sanctions consist of procedures carried out by a community, generally through its representatives, or by individuals with the approval of the community, when recognised rights have been infringed. They are based upon the general principle that any person who has suffered injury is entitled to satisfaction and that such satisfaction should be in some way proportioned to the extent of the injury.

One class of such procedures consists of acts of retaliation, by which is meant socially approved, controlled and limited acts of revenge. Thus in an Australian tribe when one man has committed an offence against another, the latter is permitted by public opinion, often definitely expressed by the older men, to throw a certain number of spears or boomerangs at the former or in some instances to spear him in the thigh. After he has been given such satisfaction he may no longer harbour ill feelings against the offender. In many preliterate societies the killing of an individual entitles the group to which he belongs to obtain satisfaction by killing the offender or some member of his group. In regulated vengeance the offending group must submit to this as an act of justice and must not attempt further retaliation. Those who have received such satisfaction are felt to have no further grounds for ill feeling.

Satisfaction for injury may be obtained also through the duel, a recognised and controlled combat between individuals, or through similar combats between two groups. Among Australian tribes duelling with spears, boomerangs, clubs and shields or stone knives, with the bystanders ready to interfere if they think things are going too far, is a frequently adopted alternative to one-sided retaliation. In these same tribes there are similar regulated combats between two groups, sometimes in the presence of other groups who see that there is fair play. It is often difficult to draw a dividing line between such group combats and warfare; in fact they may possibly be regarded as a special kind of warfare characteristic of primitive rather than of civilised societies. Frequently, therefore, war may be regarded as a secondary social sanction similar to the duel. A political group maintains recognition of its rights by the threat of war if those rights should be infringed. Even in the simplest societies it is recognised that certain acts are right in war and others are wrong and that a declaration of war may be just in certain circumstances and in others unjust, so that the conduct of warfare is to some extent controlled by diffuse sanctions.

Indemnification is often found as an alternative to retaliation as a means of giving and receiving satisfaction. An indemnity is something of value given by a person or group to another person or group in order to remove or neutralise the effects of an infringement of rights. It may be distinguished from a propitiatory gift by the fact that it is obligatory (i.e. subject to a negative sanction, diffuse or organised) in the particular circumstances. A payment made in anticipation of an invasion of rights with the consent of the person or persons receiving it may be regarded as an indemnity. Thus in many societies taking a woman in marriage is regarded as an invasion of the rights of her family and kin, so that before they consent to part with her they must receive an indemnity or the promise of such. In these cases the process of indemnification bears some similarity to that of purchase, which is a transfer of rights of property for a consideration.

In many preliterate societies procedures of indemnification are carried out under the diffuse sanction of public opinion, which compels an individual to indemnify one whose rights he has infringed. In some societies there is a recognised right of an injured person to indemnify himself by forcible seizure of the property of the offender. When society becomes politically organised, procedures of retaliation and indemnification, backed by diffuse sanctions, give place to legal sanctions backed by the power of judicial authorities to inflict punishment. Thus arises civil law, by which a person who has suffered an infringement of rights may obtain reparation or restitution from the person responsible.

In a consideration of the functions of social sanctions it is not the effects of the sanction upon the person to whom they are applied that are most important but rather the general effects within the community applying the sanctions. For the application of any sanction is a direct affirmation of social sentiments by the community and thereby constitutes an important, possibly essential, mechanism for maintaining these sentiments. Organised negative sanctions in particular, and to a great extent the secondary sanctions, are expressions of a condition of social dysphoria brought about by some deed. The function of the sanction is to restore the social euphoria by giving definite collective expression to the sentiments which have been affected by the deed, as in the primary sanctions and to some extent in the secondary sanctions, or by removing a conflict within the community itself. The sanctions are thus of primary significance to sociology in that they are reactions on the part of a community to events affecting its integration.

PART VI

Social Change

THE FACT OF CHANGE, IN SOCIETY AS IN ALL NATURE, IS UNIVER-sally recognized. The task of sociological theory is to define the special character of social change and to describe and account for the processes which bring it about. Part VI brings together a variety of approaches to this problem. Implicit in them is the notion that social change is not capricious. Deliberate control of social processes and forms therefore becomes a real possibility.

There are many ways in which social change may occur, and the distinctions necessarily require different terms. Nowhere is such a consideration of processes of change better stated than in Robert M. MacIver's *Society,* from which a brief conceptual analysis is presented in Chapter 16. Change has implicit in it the notion of time, so that it is not strange that most considerations of change have been historically stated. In the passage from Karl Mannheim's *Ideology and Utopia* change is viewed in terms of the prevailing ideas. Those ideas held by the group in the dominant position are identified as "ideologies," and those which compete or challenge such domination are called "utopias." What is seen to underlie social change is a struggle between ideas in which the historical circumstance defines the arena of struggle and determines whether the eventual outcome constitutes a change from what previously existed. From a different standpoint, the forms of social behavior are related to the level of the arts of survival, and the selection by Lewis H. Morgan from his *Ancient Society* considers the problem of change in relation to the status of property and technology. In keeping with the evolutionary perspective which he attained, Morgan sees technological change as progressively accelerating, and social change as a process of development to higher forms. In this view, each higher form must have its antecedent, and implicit in the evolutionary process is the differentiation and unfolding of social forms. The final section of Chapter 10 presents a passage from the *Theory of the Leisure Class* in which Thorstein Veblen describes institutional change as a process of selection and adaptation to changing external circumstances.

Instituting a social change may not be a simple matter, and ways of introducing changes may vary greatly. In Chapter 17 some of the processes through which social change is actuated are presented. Sir Henry S. Maine's discussion of legal fictions, taken from his *Ancient Law*, indicates the distinction between the prescribed norm and the actual practice. But it does more than this. It involves an analysis of the operation of the legal system, of control of changes within a social system, and of the rationalizing adaptive behavior. His analysis focuses directly (a) on the distinction between that which is said to exist and that which exists in actuality, i.e., in modern parlance, between ideal and real culture, and (b) on the distinction between changes in form and function, i.e., forms may persist in a society while the function the form plays in regard to the operation of society may change. William I. Thomas and Florian Znaniecki, in their monumental work, *The Polish Peasant in Europe and America,* considered many problems of change. One of their clearest identifications was of the process of "ordering and forbidding" through which a change required in crisis is effected by decreeing the disappearance of the undesirable or decreeing the creation of the desirable, and then enforcing the decree arbitrarily. In another section included in this chapter, Thomas and Znaniecki present a conception of "disorganization" as one side of a dynamic process of reorganization. No social form is so stable that the influence of rules on the social behavior of members is unvarying, and the variation of adherence to rules around some equilibrium point may be considered as the process of organization and reorganization. When a new social form thus occurs, it may be accepted or rejected. Acceptance suggests the enlargement of the sphere of knowledge about the social form, and the spread of knowledge may be viewed as diffusion. Ralph Linton's discussion of diffusion, which is taken from *The Study of Man,* considers such problems as contact, communication, and compatibility. As a final section in Chapter 17 we have included Thomas and Znaniecki's consideration of the relationship of science to social practice. When scientific knowledge becomes available, it appears logical that it should be accepted and integrated into social practice in order to achieve deliberate change in society. But this is by no means an automatic consequence, as Thomas and Znaniecki indicate in their analysis of what happens when scientific knowledge conflicts with social practice.

The selections which make up Chapter 18 deal with the problem of conflicting values and their relationship to social integration and change in society. Like the conception of disorganization proposed by Thomas and Znaniecki, a sophisticated theory of social problems is used by Willard Waller in his analysis of conflicting values and social change. But conflict of values essential to social change exists not only in the generalized social sense, but also in the internalization of the values in the person. In a perceptive essay, Josiah Royce deals clearly with the development of self-consciousness and anomalies in self-consciousness. Emile Durkheim's analysis of *Suicide* in relationship to the integration of society is a reflection of both the psychological and the sociological approach. This context thus enhances the viewpoints to be found both in Waller's essay and in that of Royce in the course of interpreting the specific phenomenon of suicide. Finally, the fact that conflicts exist among values in a society and among societies is

a truism. That the process of change is tied to the existence of conflicting values is also simple to see. But how conflicts are resolved
is a more difficult problem for sociology. Some forms of resolution
may be favored by the values themselves, although they may not be
the dominant forms of resolution. The ideal which a society has of
itself is not unrelated to the direction and modes of change in the
society. A problem of this order is the concern of George H. Mead
in the selection on the ideal of social integration taken from *Mind,
Self and Society.*

CHAPTER 16

The Character of Social Change

————•◦•————

PATTERNS OF SOCIAL CHANGE

B Y

ROBERT M. MACIVER

Different modes of change: Type One.—There are many modes of change which respectively characterize different subjects of change. Take an invention, for example. It seems to be born suddenly, but before it is proclaimed there is generally a long series of preparatory steps, and once it reaches the stage of practicality and exploitation, there commences another long series of cumulative improvements. This process is illustrated by the history of the telephone, the automobile, the airplane, the radio, and so forth. What is distinctive of this mode of change is not its suddenness but the continuous cumulative development of a utilitarian device, until perhaps it is discarded altogether by some new device that has also undergone a similar process. As we have seen, this continuity of direction is characteristic of technological change in general. Somewhat similar is the type of change which a science undergoes. The area of knowledge constantly increases and the science tends towards greater coherence and integration, partially disturbed from time to time by revolutionary discoveries or theories that prepare the way for a completer synthesis of its material. The growth of the science of biology in the nineteenth century, for the most part gradual but suddenly accelerated by the theories of Darwin and by the discoveries of Mendel, may serve as an example.

Abridged from: MacIver, Robert M., *Society: A Textbook of Sociology*, New York: Farrar and Rinehart, 1937. Reprinted by permission of Rinehart and Company, Inc.

Type Two.—The mode of change just mentioned can be represented graphically by a line that always slopes upwards, though with constantly varying angles of ascent. Its relative permanence of direction distinguishes it from another mode of change which traces an upward line for a time but which is liable to reversals of direction. This mode of change is characteristic of economic phenomena and over longer periods of the phenomena of population. Cities grow and then decline, international trade advances and falls off, business activity rises, booms, and then slumps. In the first mode of change there is a practical certainty that, at whatever pace, the same direction at least will be maintained, both over long and over short periods. In the second mode there is no such assurance.

Type Three.—Somewhat similar to the second is a third mode of change. Seeking to represent it we resort to a wavelike curve. Many phenomena, alike of nature and of human society, are thought of as following a cyclical course. The variations of business activity are frequently referred to as the economic cycle. The illustrations offered by nature herself are perhaps more convincing—the orbital motions of atoms and of planets, the regular sequence of the seasons, the precession of the equinoxes, the succession of barometric "highs" and "lows," and so forth. Sometimes the term "cyclical" is applied to the process that the individual organism reveals from birth through to maturity and then to decline and death—and there have been many thinkers who have regarded societies and civilizations as pursuing a similar course. Sometimes it is applied to the rhythm of successive ups and downs that repeats itself without definite beginning or ending, like that of the waves, and this pattern, too, many thinkers have thought they discovered in human affairs, in political movements of conservatism and radicalism, in long-range changes of population, in the tides of fashion, in the mores that are by turns more repressive and more free, and so forth.

These three types of change may therefore be represented as follows:

TYPE ONE

Patterns of technological change, scientific advance, etc.

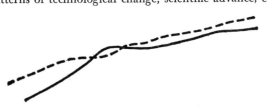

There are, of course, many types of change that cannot be represented by such simple diagrams. There are qualitative changes of various kinds that are not measurable in quantitative units, and these become more important as we pass from technology to culture. Even in the technological field the invasion of the cultural element complicates the processes of change. Thus a new invention mimics at first the older device that it replaces—as the automobile imitated the horse-drawn carriage—and then gradually establishes its own type. If

TYPE TWO

Patterns of economic activity, population movements, etc.

TYPE THREE

Patterns of fashion change, cultural movements, etc.

the device belongs to the class of "consumers' goods," then style changes will accompany, and sometimes interfere with, advances in efficiency. Wherever cultural values enter in, the way of change becomes complex and objectively indeterminate. Those parts of our civilization which are remote from final valuations move in a different way from those which are more subject to their influence. The science of electrical engineering has a simpler path to follow than the art of politics, and that art in turn goes through a more limited series of changes than the art of writing novels or of composing music.

Terms signifying modes of change.—We must next distinguish various terms which connote a mode or quality of change. The term "change" itself is wholly neutral, implying nothing but a difference through time in the object to which it is applied. When we speak of social change, we suggest so far no law, no theory, no direction, even no continuity. The idea of continuity is introduced when we refer to a social change as a *process*. A process means continuous change taking place in a definite manner through the operation of forces present from the first within the situation. Thus we speak of the "group process," or the manner in which the relations of the members of a group, once brought together, acquire a certain distinctive character. In a process we observe a series of transitions between one state of being and another. There is no necessary implication as to the relative quality of the two states of being, or as to the direction followed. A process may be up or down, forward or backward, towards integration or disintegration. All that is meant by process is the definite step-by-step manner through which one state or stage merges into another.

Another set of terms is needed when we express not only continuity but direction of change, and for scientific purposes the most important of these is *evolution*. The idea of evolution is in other sciences, and especially the biological, the grand key to the comprehension of change. It would hardly be too much to say that where we cannot discover an evolutionary element in change, there the past belongs to the historian and not to the scientist. Evolution means more than growth. The latter term does connote a direction of change but only one of a quantitative character. Evolution, as we shall presently see, involves something more intrinsic, a change not merely in size but at least in structure also. So do the associated terms "development," "regression," "retrogression." The suggestion of "forward" or "backward," of "higher" or "lower" with respect to some scale is present in them all.

Here another distinction, of supreme importance to the student of society, must be introduced. When we speak of "higher" and "lower," of "more" or "less advanced," on the evolutionary scale, we do not, or certainly should not, impute any standard of valuation. We do not mean "better" or "worse" in any ethical sense. We should beware of confusing the *concept* of evolution and the *concept* of progress. When we speak of progress we imply not merely direction, but direction towards some final goal, some destination determined ideally, not simply by objective consideration of the forces at work. What defines this goal is the value-judgment of the spectator, not the inevitability of causation. It may be that the evolutionary process moves in accord with our conception of desirable change, but there is no *logical* necessity that it should, and in any event the judgment of final value varies with the mentality and experience of the individual and the group, whereas the process of evolution is objectively given, waiting only to be discovered and understood. If the process so revealed satisfies also *our* sense of values, if the direction of evolutionary change brings also a fuller realization of the values we cherish, then *for us* it is also progress.

There remains a group of terms which signify not the change of one object or system in itself but the changing relation of two or more objects or systems to one another. These terms are often wrongly equated with the terms of the last two groups. They are "adaptation," "adjustment," "accommodation," "assimilation," and their negatives. To these we may add such vaguer terms as "harmony." We have already dwelt on their meaning. We should note, however, that the positive terms cannot as such *mean* either evolution or progress. They signify merely that the two objects conform to one another within a common process, but whether that process should be named evolution or progress or something else altogether remains thereby undetermined. There is not the slightest reason to regard the lowest forms of life as less adapted to their environment than the highest forms. The amoeba can certainly claim to be as well adjusted to its life conditions as civilized man to his.

We may now sum up these preliminary distinctions as follows:

TERMS SIGNIFYING MODES OF CHANGE

I. Determinate continuous change

Process
Movement, etc.

II. Determinate continuous change in a specific direction

(a) quantitatively defined, with respect to size

Growth
Accumulation, etc.

(b) qualitatively defined, with respect to structural or functional differentiation

Evolution
Development
Regression
Retrogression

(c) qualitatively defined, with respect to its conformity to a standard of value

Progress
Decline
Decay
Decadence
Degeneration

(d) defined by reference to some other object or system, with respect to their compatibility within a common process

Adaptation
Adjustment
Accommodation
Assimilation
Harmony and their contradictories

APPLICATION TO SOCIETY OF VARIOUS CONCEPTS OF CHANGE

Social change as cyclical process.—In every society there are numerous processes of change occurring simultaneously. Here adjustment is established and here conflict breaks down adjustment. Here dominance is attained, and here overthrown. Here there is revolution and here quiescence. Here men aspire to new goals, and here they return to old ones. In all this change can we discover any movement of the whole, of society conceived as a unity, whether in terms of a nation, or culture area, or a large civilization? Does society itself, however we define its limits, undergo any processes of change, and if so, have they any specific character or direction? This is a question many thinkers have sought to answer, and we shall here indicate briefly the nature of the answers that have most frequently been offered. Perhaps the oldest is that which conceives social change as following, over sufficiently large periods, a cyclical course.

It is a common reflection that all life, in fact all being, exhibits recurrent rhythmic movement. Many illustrations lie near to us, the beat of the heart, the intake and exhalation of the breath, the recurrent appetites, the succession of the seasons, and the processes of organic growth and decline. Our mechanisms mimic the pulsations of the organism. The skies themselves move in rhythmic periods of the day, the year, and the mightier cycles of the outer cosmos. At the other extreme the scientist conceives the atom as a dance of electrons. The pulsations which thus permeate the universe seem to have their counterpart in social phenomena, in the seasonal rhythms of the volume of employment, the frequency of crime, the number of marriages, births, and deaths, and in the longer, less predictable oscillations of prosperity, population growth, fashion trends, political attitudes, and so forth. And if this rhythmic movement affects the particular phenomena of social life, may it not also be revealed in the total being of society?

The most impressive of these rhythms is that which has a definite beginning and ending, the closed cycle of birth and death forever repeated within the life of the species. This theme is renewed on the vast scale of the cosmos.

> Worlds on worlds are rolling ever
> From creation to decay.

A rhythm so momentous to human beings, themselves manifestations of it, has a peculiar attraction for the interpreter of social change. In all ages men have found a correspondence between the course of the individual life and that of the group, the nation, the empire, the civilization. "Sceptre and crown must tumble down" in fulfillment of the like destiny of all that lives. Generally this principle is merely a form of the inadequate organic analogy, and as such we have dealt with it elsewhere. But sometimes other concepts of a more fruitful nature are combined with it, as we shall see later when we take up the cultural conditions of social change.

Social change as evolutionary process.—In recent times the evolutionary concept has been applied in diverse ways to the interpretation of social change, sometimes rather superficially and sometimes in a more penetrating and revealing fashion. Even in the ancient world the idea that society evolved occasionally caught the imagination of men, as is witnessed to, for example, by the account of the rise of humanity given in the *Prometheus* of Sophocles and in the remarkable poem by Lucretius, *On the Nature of Things*. But it was after the triumphant advance of evolutionary biology led by Darwin in the middle of the nineteenth century that the evolutionary clue began to be persistently followed by students of society. Herbert Spencer was a leader in this movement, although his somewhat hasty generalizations have not, for the most part, stood the test of time. This fact has led to a revulsion among sociologists that unduly depreciates the social significance of the evolutionary principle.

Evolution is literally "unrolling," a process in which hidden or latent aspects or characters of a thing reveal themselves. It is an order of change which unfolds the variety of aspects belonging to the nature of the changing object, in which potentialities lying within it are made actual. Evolution cannot properly be predicated of anything whose nature is already completely revealed in the present. Nor can we speak of evolution when an object or system is changed merely by forces acting on it from without. The change must occur within the changing unity, as the manifestation of forces operative within it, so as to constitute a fuller revelation through time of its own capacities. Since, however, nothing is independent of the universe about it, evolution is a process involving at the same time a changing adaptation of the object to its environment and a further manifestation of its own nature. Consequently it is a change permeating the whole character of the object, a sequence in which the equilibrium of its entire structure undergoes modification.

We have not yet stated the basic moment of the evolutionary process, the essential criterion of its presence. The term "evolution" is often loosely used to signify any process of becoming, the series of transitions between two stages of the existence of anything. In more scientific usage it is still applied with somewhat varying significance to different types of object, though with a common core of meaning. Thus we speak of the evolution of an individual organism, of the evolution of a species, and of the evolution of life through different species. We speak also of the evolution of the earth, or the solar system, or the cosmos itself. We speak again of the evolution of any established system, though here the term loses its sharpness, for generally we mean no more than the process by which it has become established.

The concept of evolution gained its wide modern vogue as a result of its successful application in the field of biology. When Charles Darwin wrote of "the evolution of species" he traced a process by which the multiplicity of organic types emerged from earlier, fewer, less differentiated forms of life. The particular mechanistic explanation of this process which Darwin offered may or may not be valid, but the scheme of evolution which he so clearly traced does not stand or fall with any theory of the manner in which it has come about. The scheme itself is corroborated by myriad evidences; the scientific issue is no more the reality of biological evolution but the causal interpretation of it. The basis of the scheme is the correlation of the time-order with the order of appearance of more complex or more differentiated species. Many divergences occur, many collateral variations which do not exemplify this primary correlation, but it remains the nucleus of the grand plan of organic evolution. It is not, of course, implied that the later in appearance is necessarily the more evolved, but only that the more evolved is later in appearance than the less evolved and proceeds from it by means of the variations somehow emerging in the interplay of heredity and environment. The kernel of organic evolution is therefore differentiation, the process in which latent or rudimentary characters take on distinct and variable forms within the unity of the organism, giving rise to new and more complex types of life. We shall find that the differentiation of structure must be related to the differentiation of function.

In this quest we shall not follow the dangerous method of analogy. Reliance on this method has impaired the contribution of Herbert Spencer and other sociologists who have followed the evolutionary clue. There are many unities or systems which reveal a process of differentiation, but the process itself varies with the nature of the subject which undergoes it. Thus differentiation occurs (a) where the subject is the whole organic world, branching into its genera and species, (b) where the subject is a particular species, revealing *either* a modification of its type in this direction *or* the emergence of several varieties from an earlier type, (c) where the subject is an individual organism, in the course of its development from the germ to the full-grown being, and (d) where the subject is any unity or system which comes to assume a more determinate form or a variety of forms through the operation of inherent forces. Society falls in the last of these groups, and there has been a constant danger of confusing it with one—or all at the same time—of the other three. For example, it is often treated as if it fell at the same time into both group (b) and group (c), a confusion appearing in the pages of Spencer and many other writers. We should observe particularly the difference between these two groups as subjects of evolution. Group (b) exhibits an evolutionary process which has no determinate limits, whereas the process in group (c) is bounded by the life of the individual organism. A species maintains its existence by the reproduction of its members, an individual organism is not self-perpetuating but only a factor in race-perpetuation. An individual organism therefore grows old and is always at some stage in the process from youth to age; its evolution is the expression of an initial life-energy within it. None of these statements can properly be predicated of a species, and it is only a hazardous guess which asseverates that they are true of other self-perpetuating unities, such as communities or even the social systems which they create.

All organisms grow old and die, and though life has flowed on some species have become extinct. We have found in differentiation the clue to the evolutionary order, but when the process of decline towards death or extinction sets in, differentiation ceases and some counterprocess takes its place. Or again, a species, once self-maintaining, becomes parasitic, like the duckweeds in the vegetable kingdom, and some of its evolved organs degenerate. Shall we then include within the meaning of evolution those reverse tendencies? It seems simpler to do so. Decay and parasitism, whether in a species or in a society, are never simple reversals of a former trend, mere returns to an earlier stage. Age is never, literally, second childhood. From the beginning to the end new aspects of the nature of the organic being appear. We find in differentiation the clue to evolution and we can therefore also call evolutionary any process which comprises both differentiation and some sequel of differentiation, which includes an "upward" and a consequent "downward" course. When it is desirable to specify an "upward" course only, a process, that is, of increasing differentiation, we can use the appropriate term "development."

We are now in a position to see what evolution means in its social reference. Wherever in the history of society we find an increasing specialization of organs or units within the system or serving the life of the whole, we can speak of social evolution. Observe that such specialization does not mean simply more complexity and is not equivalent to the appearance of mere novelty, for to meet our sense of differentiation such complexity or novelty must be integrated within the social structure, or—what we shall see is here another aspect of the same principle—must contribute to the interrelation of function between the whole and the parts. A diseased condition of the organism may involve additional complexity and introduce new phenomena, but no one would call this an evolutionary process.

Often it is said that evolution is a process of differentiation *and* integration, but the term "differentiation," properly understood, connotes integration. In a society it manifests itself in such ways as the following: (a) a greater division of labor, so that the energy of more individuals is concentrated on more specific tasks and so that thereby a more elaborate system of co-operation, a more intricate nexus of functional relationships, is sustained within the group; (b) an increase in the number and the variety of functional associations and institutions, so that each is more defined or more limited in the range or character of its service; and (c) a greater diversity and refinement in the instruments of social communication, perhaps above all in the medium of language. We may regard the last of these conditions as rather a mark than a mode of differentiation, but as the history of language can often be more accurately traced than the life history of those who spoke it, it is obviously a record of very great importance for the study of the earlier evolution of different peoples and of the same people at different stages.

Various sociologists have laid stress on one or another of these aspects of evolution. Thus Durkheim has insisted on the pre-eminent importance of the social division of labor as a criterion of social development. Other writers have taken the various aspects together and sought to show that society passes through a definite series of evolutionary stages.

IDEOLOGICAL BASIS OF SOCIAL CHANGE

B Y

KARL MANNHEIM

THE emergence of the problem of the multiplicity of thought-styles which have appeared in the course of scientific development and the perceptibility of collective-unconscious motives hitherto hidden, is only one aspect of the prevalence of the intellectual restiveness which

From *Ideology and Utopia* by Karl Mannheim. Reprinted by permission of Harcourt, Brace and Company, Inc.
Abridged from: Mannheim, Karl, *Ideology and Utopia: An Introduction to the Sociology of Knowledge* (Translated by L. Wirth and E. A. Shils), New York: Harcourt, Brace and Company, 1936.

characterizes our age. In spite of the democratic diffusion of knowledge, the philosophical, psychological, and sociological problems have been confined to a relatively small intellectual minority. This intellectual unrest came gradually to be regarded by them as their own professional privilege, and might have been considered as the private preoccupation of these groups had not all strata, with the growth of democracy, been drawn into the political and philosophical discussion.

The breakdown of the objective view of the world, of which the guarantee in the Middle Ages was the Church, was reflected even in the simplest minds. What the philosophers fought out among themselves in a rational terminology was experienced by the masses in the form of religious conflict.

When many churches took the place of one doctrinal system guaranteed by revelation with the aid of which everything essential in an agrarian-static world could be explained—when many small sects arose where there had formerly been a world religion, the minds of simple men were seized by tensions similar to those which the intellectuals experienced on the philosophical level in terms of the co-existence of numerous theories of reality and of knowledge.

At the beginning of modern times, the Protestant movement set up in the place of revealed salvation, guaranteed by the objective institution of the Church, the notion of the subjective certainty of salvation. It was assumed in the light of this doctrine that each person should decide according to his own subjective conscience whether his conduct was pleasing to God and conducive to salvation. Thus Protestantism rendered subjective a criterion which had hitherto been objective, thereby paralleling what modern epistemology was doing when it retreated from an objectively guaranteed order of existence to the individual subject. It was not a long step from the doctrine of the subjective certainty of salvation to a psychological standpoint in which gradually the observation of the psychic process, which developed into a veritable curiosity, became more important than the harkening to the criteria of salvation which men had formerly tried to detect in their own souls.

Nor was it conducive to the public belief in an objective world-order when most political states in the period of enlightened absolutism attempted to weaken the Church by means which they had taken over from the Church itself, namely, through attempting to replace an objective interpretation of the world guaranteed by the Church, by one guaranteed by the State. In doing this, it advanced the cause of the Enlightenment which at the same time was one of the weapons of the rising bourgeoisie. Both the modern state and the bourgeoisie achieved success in the measure that the rationalistic naturalistic view of the world increasingly displaced the religious one. This took place, however, without the permeation into the broadest strata of that fullness of knowledge required for rational thinking. Furthermore, this diffusion of the rationalistic world-view was realized without the strata involved in it being brought into a social position which would have allowed an individualization of the forms of living and thinking.

Without, however, a social life-situation compelling and tending toward individualization, a mode of life which is devoid of collective myths is scarcely bearable. The merchant, the entrepreneur, the intellectual, each in his own way occupies a position which requires rational decisions concerning the tasks set by everyday life. In arriving at these decisions, it is always necessary for the individual to free his judgments from those of others and to think through certain issues in a rational way from the point of view of his own interests. This is not true for peasants of the older type nor for the recently emerged mass of subordinate white-collar workers who hold positions requiring little initiative, and no foresight of a speculative kind. Their modes of behaviour are regulated to a certain extent on the basis of myths, traditions or mass-faith in a leader. Men who in their everyday life are not trained by occupations which impel toward individualization always to make their own decisions, to know from their own personal point of view what is wrong and what is right, who from this point on never have occasion to analyse situations into their elements and who, further, fail to develop a self-consciousness in themselves which will stand firm even when the individual is cut off from the mode of judgment peculiar to his group and must think for himself—such individuals will not be in a position, even in the religious sphere, to bear up under such severe inner crises as scepticism. Life in terms of an inner balance which must be ever won anew is the essentially novel element which modern man, at the level of individualization, must elaborate for himself if he is to live on the basis of the rationality of the Enlightenment. A society which in its division of labour and functional differentiation cannot offer to each individual a set of problems and fields of operation in which full initiative and individual judgment can be exercised, also cannot realize a thoroughgoing individualistic and rationalistic *Weltanschauung* which can aspire to become an effective social reality.

Although it would be false to believe—as intellectuals easily tend to do—that the centuries of the Enlightenment actually changed the populace in a fundamental way, since religion even though weakened lived on as ritual, cult, devotion, and ecstatic modes of experience, nonetheless their impact was sufficiently strong to shatter to a large extent the religious world-view. The forms of thought characteristic of industrial society gradually penetrated into those areas which had any contact whatever with industry and sooner or later undermined one element after another of the religious explanation of the world.

The absolute state, by claiming as one of its prerogatives the setting forth of its own interpretation of the world, took a step which later on with the democratization of society tended more and more to set a precedent. It showed that politics was able to use its conception of the world as a weapon and that politics was not merely a struggle for power but really first became fundamentally significant only when it infused its aims with a kind of political philosophy, with a political conception of the world. We can well dispense with sketching in detail the picture of how, with increasing democratization, not only the state but also political parties strove to provide their conflicts with philosophical foundation and systematization. First liberalism, then haltingly following its example conservatism, and finally socialism made of its political aims a philosophical credo, a world-view with well established methods of thought and prescribed conclusions. Thus to the split in the religious world-view was added the fractionalization of political outlooks. But whereas the churches and sects conducted their battles with diverse irrational articles of faith and developed the rational element in the last analysis only for the members of the clergy and the narrow stratum of lay intellectuals, the emergent political parties incorporated rational and if possible scientific arguments into their systems of thought to a much greater degree and attributed much more importance to them. This was due in part to their later appearance in history in a period in which science as such was accorded a greater social esteem and in part to the method by which they recruited their functionaries, since in the beginning, at least, these were chosen largely from the ranks of the above-mentioned emancipated intellectuals. It was in accord with the needs of an industrial society and of these intellectual strata for them to base their collective actions not on a frank enunciation of their creed but rather on a rationally justifiable system of ideas.

The result of this amalgamation of politics and scientific thought was that gradually every type of politics, at least in the forms in which it offered itself for acceptance, was given a scientific tinge and every type of scientific attitude in its turn came to bear a political colouration.

This amalgamation had its negative as well as its positive effects. It so facilitated the diffusion of scientific ideas that ever broader strata in the whole of their political existence had to seek theoretical justifications for their positions. They learned thereby—even though frequently in a very propagandistic manner—to think about society and politics with the categories of scientific analysis. It was also helpful to political and social science in that it gained a concrete grip on reality and in so doing gave itself a theme for stating its problems, which furnished a continuous link between it and that field of reality within which it had to operate, namely, society. The crises and the exigencies of social life offered the empirical subject-matter, the political and social interpretations, and the hypotheses through which events became analysable. The theories of Adam Smith as well as those of Marx —to mention only these two—were elaborated and extended with their attempts to interpret and analyse collectively experienced events.

The principal liability, however, in this direct connection between theory and politics lies in the fact that while knowledge always has to retain its experimental character if it wishes to do justice to new sets of facts, thinking which is dominated by a political attitude can not allow itself to be continuously readapted to new experiences. Political parties, because of the very fact of their being organized, can neither maintain an elasticity in their methods of thought nor be ready to accept any answer that might come out of their inquiries. Structurally they are public corporations and fighting organizations. This in itself already forces them into a dogmatic direction. The more intellectuals became party functionaries, the more they lost the virtue of receptivity and elasticity which they had brought with them from their previous labile situation.

The other danger which arises from this alliance between science and politics is that the crises affecting political thinking also become the crises of scientific thought. Out of this complex we will concentrate on only one fact which, however, became significant for the contemporary situation. Politics is conflict and tends increasingly to become a life-and-death struggle. The more violent this struggle became, the more tightly did it grip the emotional undercurrents which formerly operated unconsciously but all the more intensively, and forced them into the open domain of the conscious.

Political discussion possesses a character fundamentally different from academic discussion. It seeks not only to be in the right but also to demolish the basis of its opponent's social and intellectual existence. Political discussion, therefore, penetrates more profoundly into the existential foundation of thinking than the kind of discussion which thinks only in terms of a few selected "points of view" and considers only the "theoretical relevance" of an argument. Political conflict, since it is from the very beginning a rationalized form of the struggle for social predominance, attacks the social status of the opponent, his public prestige, and his self-confidence. It is difficult to decide in this case whether the sublimation or substitution of discussion for the older weapons of conflict, the direct use of force and oppression, really constituted a fundamental improvement in human life. Physical repression is, it is true, harder to bear externally, but the will to psychic annihilation, which took its place in many instances, is perhaps even more unbearable. It is therefore no wonder that particularly in this sphere every theoretical refutation was gradually transformed into a much more fundamental attack on the whole life-situation of the opponent, and with the destruction of his theories one hoped also to undermine his social position. Further, it is not surprising that in this conflict, in which from the very start one paid attention not only to what a person said but also the group for which he was the spokesman and with what action in view he set forth his arguments, one viewed thought in connection with the mode of existence to which it was bound. It is true that thought has always been the expression of group life and group action (except for highly academic thinking which for a time was able to insulate itself from active life). But the difference was either that in religious conflicts, theoretical issues were not of primary significance or that in analysing their adversaries, men did not get to an analysis of their adversaries' groups because the social elements in intellectual phenomena had not become visible to the thinkers of an individualistic epoch.

In political discussion in modern democracies where ideas were more clearly representative of certain groups, the social and existential determination of thought became more easily visible. In principle it was politics which first discovered the sociological method in the study of intellectual phenomena. Basically it was in political struggles that for the first time men became aware of the unconscious collective motivations which had always guided the direction of thought. Political discussion is, from the very first, more than theoretical argumentation; it is the tearing off of disguises—the unmasking of those unconscious motives which bind the group existence to its cultural aspirations and its theoretical arguments. To the extent, however, that modern politics fought its battles with theoretical weapons, the process of unmasking penetrated to the social roots of theory.

The discovery of the social-situational roots of thought at first, therefore, took the form of unmasking. In addition to the gradual dissolution of the unitary objective world-view, which to the simple man in the street took the form of a plurality of divergent conceptions of the world, and to the intellectuals presented itself as the irreconcilable plurality of thought-styles, there entered into the public mind the tendency to unmask the unconscious situational motivations in group thinking. This final intensification of the intellectual crisis can be characterized by two slogan-like concepts "ideology and utopia."

The concept "ideology" reflects the one discovery which emerged from political conflict, namely, that ruling groups can in their thinking become so intensively interest-bound to a situation that they are simply no longer able to see certain facts which would undermine their sense of domination. There is implicit in the word "ideology" the insight that in certain situations the collective unconscious of certain groups obscures the real condition of society both to itself and to others and thereby stabilizes it.

The concept of *utopian* thinking reflects the opposite discovery of the political struggle, namely that certain oppressed groups are intellectually so strongly interested in the destruction and transformation of a given condition of society that they unwittingly see only those elements in the situation which tend to negate it. Their thinking is incapable of correctly diagnosing an existing condition of society. They are not at all concerned with what really exists; rather in their thinking they already seek to change the situation that exists. Their thought is never a diagnosis of the situation; it can be used only as a direction for action. In the utopian mentality, the collective unconscious, guided by wishful representation and the will to action, hides certain aspects of reality. It turns its back on everything which would shake its belief or paralyse its desire to change things.

The collective unconscious and the activity impelled by it serve to disguise certain aspects of social reality from two directions. It is possible, furthermore, to designate specifically the source and direction of the distortion.

At first those parties which possessed the new "intellectual weapons," the unmasking of the unconscious, had a terrific advantage over their adversaries. It was stupefying for the latter when it was demonstrated that their ideas were merely distorted reflections of their situation in life, anticipations of their unconscious interests. The mere fact that it could be convincingly demonstrated to the adversary that motives which had hitherto been hidden from him were at work must have filled him with terror and awakened in the person using the weapon a feeling of marvellous superiority. It was at the same time the dawning of a level of consciousness which mankind had hitherto always hidden from itself with the greatest tenacity. Nor was it by chance that this invasion of the unconscious was dared only by the attacker while the attacked was doubly overwhelmed—first, through the laying bare of the unconscious itself and then, in addition to this, through the fact that the unconscious was laid bare and pushed into prominence in a spirit of enmity. For it is clear that it makes a considerable difference whether the unconscious is dealt with for purposes of aiding and curing or for the purpose of unmasking.

To-day, however, we have reached a stage in which this weapon of the reciprocal unmasking and laying bare of the unconscious sources of intellectual existence has become the property not of one group among many but of all of them. But in the measure that the various groups sought to destroy their adversaries' confidence in their thinking by this most modern intellectual weapon of radical unmasking, they also destroyed, as all positions gradually came to be subjected to analysis, man's confidence in human thought in general. The process of exposing the problematic elements in thought which had been latent since the collapse of the Middle Ages culminated at last in the collapse of confidence in thought in general. There is nothing accidental but rather more of the inevitable in the fact that more and more people took flight into scepticism or irrationalism.

Two powerful currents flow together here and reinforce one another with an overwhelming pressure: one, the disappearance of a unitary intellectual world with fixed values and norms; and, two, the sudden surge of the hitherto hidden unconscious into the bright daylight of consciousness. Man's thought had from time immemorial appeared to him as a segment of his spiritual existence and not simply as a discrete objective fact. Reorientation had in the past frequently meant a change in man himself. In these earlier periods it was mostly a case of slow shifts in values and norms, of a gradual transformation of the frame of reference from which men's actions derived their ultimate orientation. But in modern times it is a much more profoundly disorganizing affair. The resort to the unconscious tended to dig up the soil out of which the varying points of views emerged. The roots from which human thought had hitherto derived its nourishment were exposed. Gradually it becomes clear to all of us that we cannot go on living in the same way once we know about our unconscious motives as we did when we were ignorant of them. What we now experience is more than a new idea, and the questions we raise constitute more than a new problem. What we are concerned with here is the elemental perplexity of our time, which can be epitomized in the symptomatic question "How is it possible for man to continue to think and live in a time when the problems of ideology and utopia are being radically raised and thought through in all their implications?"

It is possible, of course, to escape from this situation in which the plurality of thought-styles has become visible and the existence of collective-unconscious motivations recognized simply by hiding these processes from ourselves. One can take flight into a supra-temporal logic and assert that truth as such is unsullied and has neither a plurality of forms nor any connection with unconscious motivations. But in a world in which the problem is not just an interesting subject for discussion but rather an inner perplexity, someone will soon come forth who will insist against these views that "our problem is not truth as such; it is our thinking as we find it in its rootedness in action in the social situation, in unconscious motivations. Show us how we can advance from our concrete perceptions to your absolute definitions. Do not speak of truth as such but show us the way in which our statements, stemming from our social existence, can be translated into a sphere in which the partisanship, the fragmentariness of human vision, can be transcended, in which the social origin and the dominance of the unconscious in thinking will lead to controlled observations rather than to chaos." The absoluteness of thought is not attained by warranting, through a general principle, that one has it or by proceeding to label some particular limited viewpoint (usually one's own) as suprapartisan and authoritative.

Nor are we aided when we are directed to a few propositions in which the content is so formal and abstract (e.g. in mathematics, geometry, and pure economics) that in fact they seem to be completely detached from the thinking social individual. The battle is not about these propositions but about that greater wealth of factual determinations in which man concretely diagnoses his individual and social situation, in which concrete interdependences in life are perceived and in which happenings external to us are first correctly understood. The battle rages concerning those propositions in which every concept is meaningfully oriented from the first, in which we use words like conflict, breakdown, alienation, insurrection, resentment—words which do not reduce complex situations for the sake of an externalizing, formal description without ever being able to build them up again and which would lose their content if their orientation, their evaluative elements, were dropped out.

The development of modern science led to the growth of a technique of thought by means of which all that was only meaningfully intelligible was excluded. Behaviourism has pushed to the foreground this tendency towards concentration on entirely externally perceivable reactions, and has sought to construct a world of facts in which there will exist only measurable data, only correlations between series of factors in which the degree of probability of modes of behaviour in certain situations will be predictable. It is possible, and even probable, that sociology must pass through this stage in which its contents will undergo a mechanistic dehumanization and formalization, just as psychology did, so that out of devotion to an ideal of narrow exactitude nothing will remain except statistical data, tests, surveys, etc., and in the end every significant formulation of a problem will be excluded. All that can be said here is that this reduction of everything to a measurable or inventory-like describability is significant as a serious attempt to determine what is unambiguously ascertainable and, further, to think through what becomes of our psychic and social world when it is restricted to purely externally measurable relationships. There can no longer be any doubt that no real penetration into social reality is possible through this approach. Let us take for example the relatively simple phenomenon denoted by the term "situation." What is left of it, or is it even at all intelligible when it is reduced to an external constellation of various reciprocally related but only externally visible patterns of behaviour? It is clear, on the other hand, that a human situation is characterizable only when one has also taken into account those conceptions which the participants have of it, how they experience their tensions in this situation and how they react to the tensions so conceived. Or, let us take some milieu; for instance, the milieu in which a certain family exists. Are not the norms which prevail in this family, and which are intelligible only through meaningful interpretation, at least as much a part of the milieu as the landscape or the furniture of the household? Still further, must not this same family, other things being equal, be considered as a completely different milieu (e.g. from the point of the training of the children) if its norms have changed? If we wish to comprehend such a concrete phenomenon as a situation or the normative content of a milieu, the purely mechanistic scheme of approach will never suffice and there must be introduced in addition concepts adequate for the understanding of meaningful and nonmensurative elements.

But it would be false to assume that the relations between these elements are less clear and less precisely perceivable than those that obtain between purely measurable phenomena. Quite on the contrary, the reciprocal interdependence of the elements making up an event is much more intimately comprehensible than that of strictly external formalized elements. Here that approach which, following Dilthey, I should like to designate as the understanding of the primary interdependence of experience (*das verstehende Erfassen des "ursprünglichen Lebenszusammenhanges"* [1]) comes into its own. In this approach, by use of the technique of understanding, the reciprocal functional interpenetration of psychic experiences and social situations becomes immediately intelligible. We are confronted here with a realm of existence in which the emergence of psychic reactions from within becomes evident of necessity and is not comprehensible merely as is an external causality, according to the degree of probability of its frequency.

It has become clear that the principal propositions of the social sciences are neither mechanistically external nor formal, nor do they represent purely quantitative correlations but rather situational diag-

[1] Here I use Dilthey's expression, leaving unsettled the question as to how his use of the term is different from that above.

noses in which we use, by and large, the same concrete concepts and thought-models which were created for activistic purposes in real life. It is clear, furthermore, that every social science diagnosis is closely connected with the evaluations and unconscious orientations of the observer and that the critical self-clarification of the social sciences is intimately bound up with the critical self-clarification of our orientation in the everyday world. It is precisely in the degree in which one participates evaluationally (sympathetically or antagonistically) in the struggle for ascendancy of the lower strata, in the degree that he evaluates resentment positively or negatively, that he becomes aware of the dynamic significance of social tension and resentment. "Lower class," "social ascendancy," "resentment" instead of being formal concepts are meaningfully oriented concepts. If they were to be formalized, and the evaluations they contain distilled out of them, the thought-model characteristic of the situation, in which it is precisely resentment which produced the good and novel fruitful norm, would be totally inconceivable. The more closely one examines the word "resentment" the more clear it becomes that this apparently non-evaluative descriptive term for an attitude is replete with evaluations. If these evaluations are left out, the idea loses its concreteness.

In order to work in the social sciences one must participate in the social process, but this participation in collective-unconscious striving in no wise signifies that the persons participating in it falsify the facts or see them incorrectly. Indeed, on the contrary, participation in the living context of social life is a presupposition of the understanding of the inner nature of this living context. The type of participation which the thinker enjoys determines how he shall formulate his problems. The disregard of qualitative elements and the complete restraint of the will does not constitute objectivity but is instead the negation of the essential quality of the object.

But, at the same time, the reverse—the greater the bias, the greater the objectivity—is not true. In this sphere there obtains a peculiar inner dynamic of modes of behaviour in which, through the retention of the *élan politique*, this *élan* subjects itself to an intellectual control. There is a point at which the *élan politique* collides with something, whereupon it is thrown back upon itself and begins to subject itself to critical control. There is a point where the movement of life itself, especially in its greatest crisis, elevates itself above itself and becomes aware of its own limits. This is the point where the political problem-complex of ideology and utopia becomes the concern of the sociology of knowledge, and where the scepticism and relativism arising out of the mutual destruction and devaluation of divergent political aims becomes a means of salvation. For this relativism and scepticism compel self-criticism and self-control and lead to a new conception of objectivity.

What seems to be so unbearable in life itself, namely, to continue to live with the unconscious uncovered, is the historical prerequisite of scientific critical self-awareness. In personal life, too, self-control and self-correction develop only when in our originally blind vital forward drive we come upon an obstacle which throws us back upon ourselves. In the course of this collision with other possible forms of existence, the peculiarity of our own mode of life becomes apparent to us. Even in our personal life we become masters of ourselves only when the unconscious motivations which formerly existed behind our backs suddenly come into our field of vision and thereby become accessible to conscious control. Man attains objectivity and acquires a self with reference to his conception of his world not by giving up his will to action and holding his evaluations in abeyance but in confronting and examining himself. The criterion of such self-illumination is that not only the object but we ourselves fall squarely within our field of vision. We become visible to ourselves, not just vaguely as a knowing subject as such but in a certain role hitherto hidden from us, in a situation hitherto impenetrable to us, and with motivations of which we have not hitherto been aware. In such moments the inner connection between our role, our motivations, and our type and manner of experiencing the world suddenly dawns upon us. Hence the paradox underlying these experiences, namely the opportunity for relative emancipation from social determination, increases proportionately with insight into this determination. Those persons who talk most about human freedom are those who are actually most blindly subject to social determination, inasmuch as they do not in most cases suspect the profound degree to which their conduct is determined by their interests. In contrast with this, it should be noted that it is precisely those who insist on the unconscious influence of the social determinants in conduct, who strive to overcome these determinants as much as possible. They uncover unconscious motivations in order to make those forces which formerly ruled them more and more into objects of conscious rational decision.

This illustration of how the extension of our knowledge of the world is closely related to increasing personal self-knowledge and self-control of the knowing personality is neither accidental nor peripheral. The process of the self-extension of the individual represents a typical example of the unfolding of every kind of situationally determined knowledge, i.e. of every kind of knowledge which is not merely the simple objective accumulation of information about facts and their causal connections, but which is interested in the understanding of an inner interdependence in the life process. Inner interdependence can be grasped only by the understanding method of interpretation, and the stages of this understanding of the world are bound at every step to the process of individual self-clarification. This structure, in accordance with which self-clarification makes possible the extension of our knowledge of the world about us, obtains not only for individual self-knowledge but is also the criterion of group self-clarification. Although here, too, it should again be emphasized that only individuals are capable of self-clarification (there is no such thing as a "folk mind" and groups as wholes are as incapable of self-clarification as they are of thinking), it makes a powerful difference whether an individual becomes conscious of those quite special unconscious motivations which have characterized particularly his previous thinking and acting or whether he is made aware of those elements in his motivations and outlook which tie him to the members of a particular group.

It is a problem in itself as to whether the sequence which the stages of self-clarification follow is entirely a matter of chance. We are inclined to believe that individual self-clarification occupies a position in a stream of self-clarification, the social source of which is a situation common to the different individuals. But whether we are here concerned with the self-clarification of individuals or of groups, one thing is common to both, namely, their structure. The centrally important feature of this structure is that in so far as the world does become a problem it does not do so as an object detached from the subject but rather as it impinges upon the fabric of the subject's experiences. Reality is discovered in the way in which it appears to the subject in the course of his self-extension (in the course of extending his capacity for experience and his horizon).

What we have hitherto hidden from ourselves and not integrated into our epistemology is that knowledge in the political and social sciences is, from a certain point on, different from formal mechanistic knowledge; it is different from that point where it transcends the mere enumeration of facts and correlations, and approximates the model of situationally determined knowledge.

Once the interrelationship between social science and situationally bound thinking, as it is for instance found in political orientation, becomes evident, we have reason to investigate the positive potentialities as well as the limits and dangers of this type of thinking. It is furthermore important that we take our point of departure in that state of crisis and uncertainty in which were disclosed the dangers of this sort of thinking as well as those new possibilities of self-criticism through which it was hoped that a solution could be found.

If the problem is attacked from this point of view, the uncertainty which had become an ever more unbearable grief in public life becomes the soil from which modern social science gains entirely new insights. These fall into three main tendencies: first, the tendency towards the self-criticism of collective-unconscious motivations, in so far as they determine modern social thinking; second, the tendency towards the establishment of a new type of intellectual history which is able to interpret changes in ideas in relation to social-historical changes; and, third, the tendency towards the revision of our epistemology which up to now has not taken the social nature of thought sufficiently into account. The sociology of knowledge is, in this sense, the *systematization* of the doubt which is to be found in social life as a vague insecurity and uncertainty.

Nothing is simpler than to maintain that a certain type of thinking is feudal, bourgeois or proletarian, liberal, socialistic, or conservative, as long as there is no analytical method for demonstrating it and no criteria have been adduced which will provide a control over the demonstration. Hence the chief task in the present stage of research is to elaborate and concretize the hypotheses involved in such a way that they can be made the basis of inductive studies. At the same time, the segments of reality with which we deal must be analysed into factors in a much more exact manner than we have been accustomed to do in the past. Our aim then is, first, to refine the analysis of meaning in the sphere of thought so thoroughly that grossly undifferentiated terms and concepts will be supplanted by increasingly exact and detailed characterizations of the various thought-styles; and, second, to perfect the technique of reconstructing social history to such an extent that, instead of scattered isolated facts, one will be able to perceive the social structure as a whole, i.e. the web of interacting social forces from which have arisen the various modes of observing and thinking through the existing realities that presented themselves at different times.

PROPERTY, TECHNOLOGY AND
SOCIAL CHANGE

B Y

LEWIS H. MORGAN

SOME of the ancient poets and philosophers recognized the fact, that mankind commenced in a state of extreme rudeness from which they had risen by slow and successive steps. They also perceived that the course of their development was registered by a progressive series of inventions and discoveries, but without noticing as fully the more conclusive argument from social institutions.

Human progress, from first to last, has been in a ratio not rigorously but essentially geometrical. This is plain on the face of the facts; and it could not, theoretically, have occurred in any other way. Every item of absolute knowledge gained became a factor in further acquisitions, until the present complexity of knowledge was attained. Consequently, while progress was slowest in time in the first period, and most rapid in the last, the relative amount may have been greatest in the first, when the achievements of either period are considered in their relations to the sum. It may be suggested, as not improbable of ultimate recognition, that the progress of mankind in the period of savagery, in its relations to the sum of human progress, was greater in degree than it was afterwards in the three sub-periods of barbarism; and that the progress made in the whole period of barbarism was, in like manner, greater in degree than it has been since in the entire period of civilization.

What may have been the relative length of these ethnical periods is also a fair subject of speculation. An exact measure is not attainable, but an approximation may be attempted. On the theory of geometrical progression, the period of savagery was necessarily longer in duration than the period of barbarism, as the latter was longer than the period of civilization. If we assume a hundred thousand years as the measure of man's existence upon the earth in order to find the relative length of each period,—and for this purpose, it may have been longer or shorter,—it will be seen at once that at least sixty thousand years must be assigned to the period of savagery. Three-fifths of the life of the most advanced portion of the human race, on this apportionment, were spent in savagery. Of the remaining years, twenty thousand, or one-

---

Abridged from: Morgan, Lewis H., *Ancient Society,* Chicago: Kerr, 1887.

fifth, should be assigned to the Older Period of barbarism. For the Middle and Later Periods there remain fifteen thousand years, leaving five thousand, more or less, for the period of civilization.

The relative length of the period of savagery is more likely under than overstated. Without discussing the principles on which this apportionment is made, it may be remarked that in addition to the argument from the geometrical progression under which human development of necessity has occurred, a graduated scale of progress has been universally observed in remains of ancient art, and this will be found equally true of institutions.

The most advanced portion of the human race were halted, so to express it, at certain stages of progress, until some great invention or discovery, such as the domestication of animals or the smelting of iron ore, gave a new and powerful impulse forward. While thus restrained, the ruder tribes, continually advancing, approached in different degrees of nearness to the same status; for wherever a continental connection existed, all the tribes must have shared in some measure in each other's progress. All great inventions and discoveries propagate themselves; but the inferior tribes must have appreciated their value before they could appropriate them. In the continental areas certain tribes would lead; but the leadership would be apt to shift a number of times in the course of an ethnical period. The destruction of the ethnic bond and life of particular tribes, followed by their decadence, must have arrested for a time, in many instances and in all periods, the upward flow of human progress.

Savagery was the formative period of the human race. Commencing at zero in knowledge and experience, without fire, without articulate speech and without arts, our savage progenitors fought the great battle, first for existence, and then for progress, until they secured safety from the ferocious animals, and permanent subsistence. Out of these efforts there came gradually a developed speech, and the occupation of the entire surface of the earth. But society from its rudeness was still incapable of organization in numbers. The earliest inventions were the most difficult to accomplish because of the feebleness of the power of abstract reasoning. Each substantial item of knowledge gained would form a basis for further advancement; but this must have been nearly imperceptible for ages upon ages, the obstacles to progress nearly balancing the energies arrayed against them. The achievements of savagery are not particularly remarkable in character, but they represent an amazing amount of persistent labor with feeble means continued through long periods of time before reaching a fair degree of completeness.

*   *   *

If men in savagery had not been left behind, in isolated portions of the earth, to testify concerning the early condition of mankind in general, it would have been impossible to form any definite conception of what it must have been. An important inference at once arises, namely, that the institutions of mankind have sprung up in a progressive connected series, each of which represents the result of unconscious reformatory movements to extricate society from existing evils. The wear of ages is upon these institutions, for the proper understanding of which they must be studied in this light. It cannot be assumed that the Australian savages are now at the bottom of the scale, for their arts and institutions, humble as they are, show the contrary; neither is there any ground for assuming their degradation from a higher condition, because the facts of human experience afford no sound basis for such an hypothesis. Cases of physical and mental deterioration in tribes and nations may be admitted, for reasons which are known, but they never interrupted the general progress of mankind. All the facts of human knowledge and experience tend to show that the human race, as a whole, have steadily progressed from a lower to a higher condition. The arts by which savages maintain their lives are remarkably persistent. They are never lost until superseded by others higher in degree. By the practice of these arts, and by the experience gained through social organizations, mankind have advanced under a necessary law of development, although their progress may have been substantially imperceptible for centuries. It was the same with races as with individuals, although tribes and nations have perished through the disruption of their ethnic life.

*   *   *

The earliest ideas of property were intimately associated with the procurement of subsistence, which was the primary need. The objects of ownership would naturally increase in each successive ethnical period with the multiplication of those arts upon which the means of subsistence depended. The growth of property would thus keep pace with the progress of inventions and discoveries. Each ethnical period shows a marked advance upon its predecessor, not only in the number of inventions, but also in the variety and amount of property which resulted therefrom. The multiplicity of the forms of property would be accompanied by the growth of certain regulations with reference to its possession and inheritance. The customs upon which these rules of proprietary possession and inheritance depend, are determined and modified by the condition and progress of the social organization. The growth of property is thus closely connected with the increase of inventions and discoveries, and with the improvement of social institutions which mark the several ethnical periods of human progress.

I. *Property in the Status of Savagery.*

In any view of the case, it is difficult to conceive of the condition of mankind in this early period of their existence, when divested of all they had gained through inventions and discoveries, and through the growth of ideas embodied in institutions, usages and customs. Human progress from a state of absolute ignorance and inexperience was slow in time, but geometrical in ratio. Mankind may be traced by a chain of necessary inferences back to a time when, ignorant of fire, without articulate language, and without artificial weapons, they depended, like the wild animals, upon the spontaneous fruits of the earth. Slowly, almost imperceptibly, they advanced through savagery, from gesture language and imperfect sounds to articulate speech; from the club, as the first weapon, to the spear pointed with flint, and finally to the bow and arrow; from the flint-knife and chisel to the stone axe and hammer; from the ozier and cane basket to the basket coated with clay, which gave a vessel for boiling food with fire; and, finally, to the art of pottery, which gave a vessel able to withstand the fire.

Before the close of this period, mankind had learned to support themselves in numbers in comparison with primitive times; they had propagated themselves over the face of the earth, and come into possession of all the possibilities of the continents in favor of human advancement. In social organization, they had advanced from the consanguine horde into tribes organized in gentes, and thus became possessed of the germs of the principal governmental institutions. The human race was now successfully launched upon its great career for the attainment of civilization, which even then, with articulate language among inventions, with the art of pottery among arts, and with the gentes among institutions, was substantially assured.

But the property of savages was inconsiderable. Their ideas concerning its value, its desirability and its inheritance were feeble. Rude weapons, fabrics, utensils, apparel, implements of flint, stone and bone, and personal ornaments represent the chief items of property in savage life. A passion for its possession had scarcely been formed in their minds, because the thing itself scarcely existed. It was left to the then distant period of civilization to develop into full vitality that "greed of gain" (*studium lucri*), which is now such a commanding force in the human mind. Lands, as yet hardly a subject of property, were owned by the tribes in common, while tenement houses were owned jointly by their occupants. Upon articles purely personal which were increasing with the slow progress of inventions, the great passion was nourishing its nascent powers. Those esteemed most valuable were deposited in the grave of the deceased proprietor for his continued use in the spirit-land. What remained was sufficient to raise the question of its inheritance. Of the manner of its distribution before the organization into gentes, our information is limited, or altogether wanting. With the institution of the gens came in the first great rule of inheritance, which distributed the effects of a deceased person among his gentiles. Practically they were appropriated by the nearest of kin; but the principle was general, that the property should remain in the gens of the decedent, and be distributed among its members. This principle was maintained into civilization by the Grecian and Latin gentes. Children inherited from their mother, but took nothing from their reputed father.

II. *Property in the Lower Status of Barbarism.*

From the invention of pottery to the domestication of animals, or, as an equivalent, the cultivation of maize and plants by irrigation, the duration of the period must have been shorter than that of savagery. With the exception of the art of pottery, finger weaving and the art of cultivation, in America, which gave farinaceous food, no great invention or discovery signalized this ethnical period. It was more distinguished for progress in the development of institutions. Finger weaving, with warp and woof, seems to belong to this period, and it must rank as one of the greatest of inventions; but it cannot be certainly affirmed that the art was not attained in savagery. The principles of this great invention, which has since clothed the human family, were perfectly realized; but they were unable to extend it to the production of the woven garment. Picture writing also seems to have made its first appearance in this period. If it originated earlier, it now received a very considerable development. It is interesting as one of the stages of an art which culminated in the invention of a phonetic alphabet. The series of connected inventions seem to have been the following: 1. Gesture Language, or the language of personal symbols; 2. Picture Writing, or idiographic symbols; 3. Hieroglyphs, or conventional symbols; 4. Hieroglpyhs of phonetic power, or phonetic symbols used in a syllabus; and 5, a Phonetic Alphabet, or written sounds. Since a language of written sounds was a growth through successive stages of development, the rise of its antecedent processes is both important and instructive.

The cultivation of maize and plants gave the people unleavened bread, the Indian succotash and hominy. It also tended to introduce a new species of property, namely, cultivated lands or gardens. Although lands were owned in common by the tribe, a possessory right to cultivated land was now recognized in the individual, or in the group, which became a subject of inheritance. The group united in a common household were mostly of the same gens, and the rule of inheritance would not allow it to be detached from the kinship.

The variety and amount of property were greater than in savagery, but still not sufficient to develop a strong sentiment in relation to inheritance. In the mode of distribution, the germ of the second great rule of inheritance, which gave the property to the agnatic kindred, to the exclusion of the remaining gentiles. Agnation and agnatic kindred, as now defined, assume descent in the male line; but the persons included would be very different from those with descent in the female line. The principle is the same in both cases, and the terms seem as applicable in the one as in the other. With descent in the female line, the agnates are those persons who can trace their descent through females exclusively from the same common ancestor with the intestate; in the other case, who can trace their descent through males exclusively. It is the blood connection of persons within the gens by direct descent, in a given line, from the same common ancestor which lies at the foundation of agnatic relationship.

III. *Property in the Middle Status of Barbarism.*

The condition of mankind in this ethnical period has been more completely lost than that of any other. It was exhibited by the Village Indians of North and South America in barbaric splendor at the epoch of their discovery. Their governmental institutions, their religious tenets, their plan of domestic life, their arts and their rules in relation to the ownership and inheritance of property, might have been completely obtained; but the opportunity was allowed to escape. All that remains are scattered portions of the truth buried in misconceptions and romantic tales.

This period opens in the Eastern hemisphere with the domestication of animals, and in the Western with the appearance of the Village Indians, living in large joint-tenement houses of adobe brick, and, in some areas, of stone laid in courses. It was attended with the cultivation of maize and plants by irrigation, which required artificial canals, and garden beds laid out in squares, with raised ridges to contain the water until absorbed. When discovered, they were well advanced toward the close of the Middle Period, a portion of them having made bronze, which brought them near the higher process of smelting iron ore. The joint-tenement house was in the nature of a fortress, and held an intermediate position between the stockaded village of the Lower, and the walled city of the Upper Status. There were no cities, in the proper sense of the term, in America when discovered.

To maize, beans, squashes and tobacco, were now added cotton, pepper, tomato, cacao, and the care of certain fruits. A beer was made by fermenting the juice of the maguey. The Iroquois, however, had produced a similar beverage by fermenting maple sap. Earthen vessels of capacity to hold several gallons, of fine texture and superior ornamentation were produced by improved methods in the ceramic art.

Bowls, pots and water-jars were manufactured in abundance. The discovery and use of the native metals first for ornaments, and finally for implements and utensils, such as the copper axe and chisel, belong to this period. The melting of these metals in the crucible, with the probable use of the blow-pipe and charcoal, and casting them in moulds, the production of bronze, rude stone sculptures, the woven garment of cotton, the house of dressed stone, ideographs or hieroglyphs cut on the grave-posts of deceased chiefs, the calendar for measuring time, and the solstitial stone for marking the seasons, cyclopean walls, the domestication of the llama, of a species of dog, of the turkey and other fowls, belong to the same period in America. A priesthood organized in a hierarchy, and distinguished by a costume, personal gods with idols to represent them, and human sacrifices, appear for the first time in this ethnical period. Two large Indian pueblos, Mexico and Cusco, now appear, containing over twenty thousand inhabitants, a number unknown in the previous period. The aristocratic element in society began to manifest itself in feeble forms among the chiefs, civil and military, through increased numbers under the same government, and the growing complexity of affairs.

Turning to the Eastern hemisphere, we find its native tribes, in the corresponding period, with domestic animals yielding them a meat and milk subsistence, but probably without horticultural and without farinaceous food. When the great discovery was made that the wild horse, cow, sheep, ass, sow and goat might be tamed, and, when produced in flocks and herds, become a source of permanent subsistence it must have given a powerful impulse to human progress. But the effect would not become general until pastoral life for the creation and maintenance of flocks and herds became established. Europe, as a forest area in the main, was unadapted to the pastoral state; but the grass plains of high Asia, and upon the Euphrates, the Tigris and other rivers of Asia, were the natural homes of the pastoral tribes. Thither they would naturally tend; and to these areas we trace our own remote ancestors, where they were found confronting like pastoral Semitic tribes. The cultivation of cereals and plants must have preceded their migration from the grass plains into the forest areas of Western Asia and of Europe. It would be forced upon them by the necessities of the domestic animals now incorporated in their plan of life. There are reasons, therefore, for supposing that the cultivation of cereals by the Aryan tribes preceded their western migration, with the exception perhaps of the Celts. Woven fabrics of flax and wool, and bronze implements and weapons appear in this period in the Eastern hemisphere.

Such were the inventions and discoveries which signalized the Middle Period of barbarism. Society was now more highly organized, and its affairs were becoming more complex. Differences in the culture of the two hemispheres now existed in consequence of their unequal endowments; but the main current of progress was steadily upward to a knowledge of iron and its uses. To cross the barrier into the Upper Status, metallic tools able to hold an edge and point were indispensable. Iron was the only metal able to answer these requirements. The most advanced tribes were arrested at this barrier, awaiting the invention of the process of smelting iron ore.

From the foregoing considerations it is evident that a large increase of personal property had now occurred, and some changes in the relations of persons to land. The territorial domain still belonged to the tribe in common; but a portion was now set apart for the support of the government, another for religious uses, and another and more important portion, that from which the people derived their subsistence, was divided among the several gentes, or communities of persons who resided in the same pueblo. That any person owned lands or houses in his own right, with power to sell and convey in fee-simple to whomsoever he pleased, is not only unestablished but improbable. Their mode of owning their lands in common, by gentes, or by communities of persons, their joint-tenement houses, and their mode of occupation by related families, precluded the individual ownership of houses or of lands. A right to sell an interest in such lands or in such houses, and to transfer the same to a stranger, would break up their plan of life. The possessory right, which we must suppose existed in individuals or in families, was inalienable, except within the gens, and on the demise of the person would pass by inheritance to his or her gentile heirs. Joint-tenement houses, and lands in common, indicate a plan of life adverse to individual ownership.

The Spanish writers have left the land tenure of the southern tribes in inextricable confusion. When they found a community of persons owning lands in common, which they could not alienate, and that one person among them was recognized as their chief, they at once treated these lands as a feudal estate, the chief as a feudal lord, and the people who owned the lands in common as his vassals. At best, it was a perversion of the facts. One thing is plain, namely, that these lands were owned in common by a community of persons; but one, not less essential, is not given; namely, the bond of union which held these persons together. If a gens, or a part of a gens, the whole subject would be at once understood.

Descent in the female line still remained in some of the tribes of Mexico and Central America, while in others, and probably in the larger portion, it had been changed to the male line. The influence of property must have caused the change, that children might participate as agnates in the inheritance of their father's property. Among the Mayas, descent was in the male line, while among the Aztecs, Tezcucans, Tlacopans and Tlascalans, it is difficult to determine whether it was in the male or the female line. It is probable that descent was being changed to the male line among the Village Indians generally, with remains of the archaic rule manifesting themselves, as in the case of the office of Teuctli. The change would not overthrow gentile inheritance. It is claimed by a number of Spanish writers that the children, and in some cases the eldest son, inherited the property of a deceased father; but such statements, apart from an exposition of their system, are of little value.

Among the Village Indians, we should expect to find the second great rule of inheritance which distributed the property among the agnatic kindred. With descent in the male line, the children of a deceased person would stand at the head of the agnates, and very naturally receive the greater portion of the inheritance. It is not probable that the third great rule, which gave an exclusive inheritance to the children of the deceased owner, had become established among them. The discussion of inheritances by the earlier and later writers is unsatisfactory, and devoid of accurate information. Institutions, usages and customs still governed the question, and could alone explain the system. Without better evidence than we now possess, an exclusive inheritance by children cannot be asserted.

*   *   *

The earliest laws of the Greeks, Romans and Hebrews after civilization had commenced, did little more than turn into legal enactments the results which their previous experience had embodied in usages and customs. Having the final laws and the previous archaic rules, the intermediate changes, when not expressly known, may be inferred with tolerable certainty.

At the close of the Later Period of barbarism, great changes had occurred in the tenure of lands. It was gradually tending to two forms of ownership, namely, by the state and by individuals. But this result was not fully secured until after civilization had been attained. Lands among the Greeks were still held, as we have seen, some by the tribes in common, some by the phratry in common for religious uses, and some by the gens in common; but the bulk of the lands had fallen under individual ownership in severalty. In the time of Solon, while Athenian society was still gentile, lands in general were owned by individuals, who had already learned to mortgage them; but individual ownership was not then a new thing. The Roman tribes, from their first establishment, had a public domain, the *Ager Romanus;*

while lands were held by the *curia* for religious uses, by the gens, and by individuals in severalty. After these social corporations died out, the lands held by them in common gradually became private property. Very little is known beyond the fact that certain lands were held by these organizations for special uses, while individuals were gradually appropriating the substance of the national areas.

These several forms of ownership tend to show that the oldest tenure, by which land was held, was by the tribe in common; that after its cultivation began, a portion of the tribe lands was divided among the gentes, each of which held their portion in common; and that this was followed, in course of time, by allotments to individuals, which allotments finally ripened into individual ownership in severalty. Unoccupied and waste lands still remained as the common property of the gens, the tribe and the nation. This, substantially, seems to have been the progress of experience with respect to the ownership of land. Personal property, generally, was subject to individual ownership.

Our principal information concerning the kinds of property, that existed among the Grecian tribes in this period, is derived from the Homeric poems, and from the early laws of the period of civilization which reflect ancient usages. Mention is made in the Iliad of *fences* around cultivated fields, of an *enclosure of fifty acres,* half of which was fit for vines and the remainder for tillage; and it is said of Tydeus that he lived in a mansion rich in resources, and had corn-producing fields in abundance. There is no reason to doubt that lands were then fenced and measured, and held by individual ownership. It indicates a large degree of progress in a knowledge of property and its uses. Breeds of horses were already distinguished for particular excellence. Herds of cattle and flocks of sheep possessed by individuals are mentioned, as "sheep of a rich man standing countless in the fold." Coined money was still unknown, consequently trade was by barter of commodities, as indicated by the following lines: "Thence the long-haired Greeks bought wine, some for brass, some for shining iron, others for hides, some for the oxen themselves, and some for slaves." Gold in bars, however, is named as passing by weight and estimated by talents. Manufactured articles of gold, silver, brass and iron, and textile fabrics of linen and woolen in many forms, together with houses and palaces, are mentioned. It will not be necessary to extend the illustrations. Those given are sufficient to indicate the great advance society had attained in the Upper Status of barbarism, in contrast with that in the immediately previous period.

After houses and lands, flocks and herds, and exchangeable commodities had become so great in quantity, and had come to be held by individual ownership, the question of their inheritance would press upon human attention until the right was placed upon a basis which satisfied the growing intelligence of the Greek mind. Archaic usages would be modified in the direction of later conceptions. The domestic animals were a possession of greater value than all kinds of property previously known put together. They served for food, were exchangeable for other commodities, were usable for redeeming captives, for paying fines, and in sacrifices in the observance of their religious rites. Moreover, as they were capable of indefinite multiplication in numbers, their possession revealed to the human mind its first conception of wealth. Following upon this, in course of time, was the systematical cultivation of the earth, which tended to identify the family with the soil, and render it a property-making organization. It soon found expression, in the Latin, Grecian and Hebrew tribes, in the family under paternal power, involving slaves and servants. Since the labor of the father and his children became incorporated more and more with the land, with the production of domestic animals, and with the creation of merchandise, it would not only tend to individualize the family, now monogamian, but also to suggest the superior claims of children to the inheritance of the property they had assisted in creating. Before lands were cultivated, flocks and herds would naturally fall under the joint ownership of persons united in a group, on a basis of kin, for subsistence. Agnatic inheritance would be apt to assert itself in this condition of things. But when lands had become the subject of property, and allotments to individuals had resulted in individual ownership, the third great rule of inheritance, which gave the property to the children of the deceased owner, was certain to supervene upon agnatic inheritance. There is no direct evidence that strict agnatic inheritance ever existed among the Latin, Grecian or Hebrew tribes, excepting in the reversion, established alike in Roman, Grecian and Hebrew law; but that an exclusive agnatic inheritance existed in the early period may be inferred from the reversion.

When field agriculture had demonstrated that the whole surface of the earth could be made the subject of property owned by individuals in severalty, and it was found that the head of the family became the natural center of accumulation, the new property career of mankind was inaugurated. It was fully done before the close of the Later Period of barbarism. A little reflection must convince any one of the powerful influence property would now begin to exercise upon the human mind, and of the great awakening of new elements of character it was calculated to produce. Evidence appears, from many sources, that the feeble impulse aroused in the savage mind had now become a tremendous passion in the splendid barbarian of the heroic age. Neither archaic nor later usages could maintain themselves in such an advanced condition. The time had now arrived when monogamy, having assured the paternity of children, would assert and maintain their exclusive right to inherit the property of their deceased father.[1]

During the Later Period of barbarism a new element, that of aristocracy, had a marked development. The individuality of persons, and the increase of wealth now possessed by individuals in masses, were laying the foundation of personal influence. Slavery, also, by permanently degrading a portion of the people, tended to establish contrasts of condition unknown in the previous ethnical periods. This, with property and official position, gradually developed the sentiment of aristocracy.

In the Upper Status of barbarism, the office of chief in its different grades, originally hereditary in the gens and elective among its members, passed, very likely, among the Grecian and Latin tribes, from father to son, as a rule. That it passed by hereditary right cannot be admitted upon existing evidence; but the possession of either of the offices of *archon, phylo-basileus,* or *basileus* among the Greeks, and of *princeps* and *rex* among the Romans, tended to strengthen in their families the sentiment of aristocracy. It did not, however, become strong enough to change essentially the democratic constitution of the early governments of these tribes, although it attained a permanent existence. Property and office were the foundations upon which aristocracy planted itself.

Whether this principle shall live or die has been one of the great problems with which modern society has been engaged through the intervening periods.

Some of the principles, and some of the results of the growth of the idea of property in the human mind have now been presented. Although the subject has been inadequately treated, its importance at least has been shown.

With one principle of intelligence and one physical form, in virtue of a common origin, the results of human experience have been substantially the same in all times and areas in the same ethnical status.

The principle of intelligence, although conditioned in its powers within narrow limits of variation, seeks ideal standards invariably

---

[1] The German tribes when first known historically were in the Upper Status of barbarism. They used iron, but in limited quantities, possessed flocks and herds, cultivated the cereals, and manufactured coarse textile fabrics of linen and woolen; but they had not then attained to the idea of individual ownership in lands. According to the account of Caesar, elsewhere cited, the arable lands were allotted annually by the chiefs, while the pasture lands were held in common. It would seem, therefore, that the idea of individual property in lands was unknown in Asia and Europe in the Middle Period of barbarism, but came in during the Later Period.

the same. Its operations, consequently, have been uniform through all the stages of human progress. No argument for the unity of origin of mankind can be made, which, in its nature, is more satisfactory. A common principle of intelligence meets us in the savage, in the barbarian, and in civilized man. It was in virtue of this that mankind were able to produce in similar conditions the same implements and utensils, the same inventions, and to develop similar institutions from the same original germs of thought. There is something grandly impressive in a principle which has wrought out civilization by assiduous application from small beginnings; from the arrow head, which expresses the thought in the brain of a savage, to the smelting of iron ore, which represents the higher intelligence of the barbarian, and, finally, to the railway train in motion, which may be called the triumph of civilization.

It must be regarded as a marvelous fact that a portion of mankind five thousand years ago, less or more, attained to civilization. And yet civilization must be regarded as an accident of circumstances. Its attainment at some time was certain; but that it should have been accomplished when it was, is still an extraordinary fact. The hindrances that held mankind in savagery were great, and surmounted with difficulty.

INSTITUTIONAL ADAPTATION

B Y

THORSTEIN VEBLEN

THE life of man in society, just like the life of other species, is a struggle for existence, and therefore it is a process of selective adaptation. The evolution of social structure has been a process of natural selection of institutions. The progress which has been and is being made in human institutions and in human character may be set down, broadly, to a natural selection of the fittest habits of thought and to a process of enforced adaptation of individuals to an environment which has progressively changed with the growth of the community and with the changing institutions under which men have lived. Institutions are not only themselves the result of a selective and adaptive process which shapes the prevailing or dominant types

Abridged from: Veblen, Thorstein, *The Theory of the Leisure Class*, New York: The Macmillan Co., 1899.

of spiritual attitude and aptitudes; they are at the same time special methods of life and of human relations, and are therefore in their turn efficient factors of selection. So that the changing institutions in their turn make for a further selection of individuals endowed with the fittest temperament, and a further adaptation of individual temperament and habits to the changing environment through the formation of new institutions.

The forces which have shaped the development of human life and of social structure are no doubt ultimately reducible to terms of living tissue and material environment; but proximately, for the purpose in hand, these forces may best be stated in terms of an environment, partly human, partly non-human, and a human subject with a more or less definite physical and intellectual constitution. Taken in the aggregate or average, this human subject is more or less variable; chiefly, no doubt, under a rule of selective conservation of favourable variations. The selection of favourable variations is perhaps in great measure a selective conservation of ethnic types. In the life history of any community whose population is made up of a mixture of divers ethnic elements, one or another of several persistent and relatively stable types of body and of temperament rises into dominance at any given point. The situation, including the institutions in force at any given time, will favour the survival and dominance of one type of character in preference to another; and the type of man so selected to continue and to further elaborate the institutions handed down from the past will in some considerable measure shape these institutions in his own likeness. But apart from selection as between relatively stable types of character and habits of mind, there is no doubt simultaneously going on a process of selective adaptation of habits of thought within the general range of aptitudes which is characteristic of the dominant ethnic type or types. There may be a variation in the fundamental character of any population by selection between relatively stable types; but there is also a variation due to adaptation in detail within the range of the type, and to selection between specific habitual views regarding any given social relation or group of relations.

For the present purpose, however, the question as to the nature of the adaptive process—whether it is chiefly a selection between stable types of temperament and character, or chiefly an adaptation of men's habits of thought to changing circumstances—is of less importance than the fact that, by one method or another, institutions change and develop. Institutions must change with changing circumstances, since they are of the nature of an habitual method of responding to the stimuli which these changing circumstances afford. The development of these institutions is the development of society. The institutions are, in substance, prevalent habits of thought with respect to particular relations and particular functions of the individual and of the community; and the scheme of life, which is made up of the aggregate of institutions in force at a given time or at a given point in the development of any society, may, on the psychological side, be broadly characterised as a prevalent spiritual attitude or a prevalent theory of life. As regards its generic features, this spiritual attitude or theory of life is in the last analysis reducible to terms of a prevalent type of character.

The situation of to-day shapes the institutions of tomorrow through a selective, coercive process, by acting upon men's habitual view of things, and so altering or fortifying a point of view or a mental attitude handed down from the past. The institutions—that is to say the habits of thought—under the guidance of which men live are in this way received from an earlier time; more or less remotely earlier, but in any event they have been elaborated in and received from the past. Institutions are products of the past process, are adapted to past circumstances, and are therefore never in full accord with the requirements of the present. In the nature of the case, this process of selective adaptation can never catch up with the progressively changing situation in which the community finds itself at any given time; for the environment, the situation, the exigencies of life which enforce the adaptation and exercise the selection, change from day to day; and each successive situation of the community in its turn tends to obsolescence as soon as it has been established. When a step in the development has been taken, this step itself constitutes a change of situation which requires a new adaptation; it becomes the point of departure for a new step in the adjustment, and so on interminably.

It is to be noted then, although it may be a tedious truism, that the institutions of to-day—the present accepted scheme of life—do not entirely fit the situation of to-day. At the same time, men's present habits of thought tend to persist indefinitely, except as circumstances enforce a change. These institutions which have so been handed down, these habits of thought, points of view, mental attitudes and aptitudes, or what not, are therefore themselves a conservative factor. This is the factor of social inertia, psychological inertia, conservatism.

Social structure changes, develops, adapts itself to an altered situation, only through a change in the habits of thought of the several classes of the community; or in the last analysis, through a change in the habits of thought of the individuals which make up the community. The evolution of society is substantially a process of mental adaptation on the part of individuals under the stress of circumstances which

will no longer tolerate habits of thought formed under and conforming to a different set of circumstances in the past. For the immediate
purpose it need not be a question of serious importance whether this
adaptive process is a process of selection and survival of persistent
ethnic types or a process of individual adaptation and an inheritance
of acquired traits.

Social advance, especially as seen from the point of view of economic
theory, consists in a continued progressive approach to an approximately exact "adjustment of inner relations to outer relations"; but
this adjustment is never definitively established, since the "outer relations" are subject to constant change as a consequence of the progressive change going on in the "inner relations." But the degree of
approximation may be greater or less, depending on the facility with
which an adjustment is made. A readjustment of men's habits of
thought to conform with the exigencies of an altered situation is in
any case made only tardily and reluctantly, and only under the coercion
exercised by a situation which has made the accredited views un-
tenable. The readjustment of institutions and habitual views to an
altered environment is made in response to pressure from without;
it is of the nature of a response to stimulus. Freedom and facility of
readjustment, that is to say capacity for growth in social structure,
therefore depends in great measure on the degree of freedom with
which the situation at any given time acts on the individual members
of the community—the degree of exposure of the individual members
to the constraining forces of the environment. If any portion or class
of society is sheltered from the action of the environment in any
essential respect, that portion of the community, or that class, will
adapt its views and its scheme of life more tardily to the altered general
situation; it will in so far tend to retard the process of social transformation. The wealthy leisure class is in such a sheltered position
with respect to the economic forces that make for change and readjustment. And it may be said that the forces which make for a readjustment of institutions, especially in the case of a modern industrial
community, are, in the last analysis, almost entirely of an economic
nature.

Any community may be viewed as an industrial or economic mechanism, the structure of which is made up of what is called its economic
institutions. These institutions are habitual methods of carrying on
the life process of the community in contact with the material environment in which it lives. When given methods of unfolding human
activity in this given environment have been elaborated in this way,
the life of the community will express itself with some facility in these
habitual directions. The community will make use of the forces of

the environment for the purposes of its life according to methods learned in the past and embodied in these institutions. But as population increases, and as men's knowledge and skill in directing the forces of nature widen, the habitual methods of relation between the members of the group, and the habitual method of carrying on the life process of the group as a whole, no longer give the same result as before; nor are the resulting conditions of life distributed and apportioned in the same manner or with the same effect among the various members as before. If the scheme according to which the life process of the group was carried on under the earlier conditions gave approximately the highest attainable result—under the circumstances —in the way of efficiency or facility of the life process of the group; then the same scheme of life unaltered will not yield the highest result attainable in this respect under the altered conditions. Under the altered conditions of population, skill, and knowledge, the facility of life as carried on according to the traditional scheme may not be lower than under the earlier conditions; but the chances are always that it is less than might be if the scheme were altered to suit the altered conditions.

The group is made up of individuals, and the group's life is the life of individuals carried on in at least ostensible severalty. The group's accepted scheme of life is the consensus of views held by the body of these individuals as to what is right, good, expedient, and beautiful in the way of human life. In the redistribution of the conditions of life that comes of the altered method of dealing with the environment, the outcome is not an equable change in the facility of life throughout the group. The altered conditions may increase the facility of life for the group as a whole, but the redistribution will usually result in a decrease of facility or fulness of life for some members of the group. An advance in technical methods, in population, or in industrial organisation will require at least some of the members of the community to change their habits of life, if they are to enter with facility and effect into the altered industrial methods; and in doing so they will be unable to live up to the received notions as to what are the right and beautiful habits of life.

Any one who is required to change his habits of life and his habitual relations to his fellow-men will feel the discrepancy between the method of life required of him by the newly arisen exigencies, and the traditional scheme of life to which he is accustomed. It is the individuals placed in this position who have the liveliest incentive to reconstruct the received scheme of life and are most readily persuaded to accept new standards; and it is through the need of the means of livelihood that men are placed in such a position. The pressure ex-

erted by the environment upon the group, and making for a readjustment of the group's scheme of life, impinges upon the members of
the group in the form of pecuniary exigencies; and it is owing to this
fact—that external forces are in great part translated into the form
of pecuniary or economic exigencies—it is owing to this fact that we
can say that the forces which count toward a readjustment of institutions in any modern industrial community are chiefly economic forces;
or more specifically, these forces take the form of pecuniary pressure.
Such a readjustment as is here contemplated is substantially a change
in men's views as to what is good and right, and the means through
which a change is wrought in men's apprehension of what is good
and right is in large part the pressure of pecuniary exigencies.

Any change in men's views as to what is good and right in human
life makes its way but tardily at the best. Especially is this true of
any change in the direction of what is called progress; that is to say,
in the direction of divergence from the archaic position—from the
position which may be accounted the point of departure at any step
in the social evolution of the community. Retrogression, reapproach
to a standpoint to which the race has been long habituated in the
past, is easier. This is especially true in case the development away
from this past standpoint has not been due chiefly to a substitution
of an ethnic type whose temperament is alien to the earlier standpoint.

CHAPTER 17

Processes in Social Change

———————

LEGAL FICTIONS

B Y

HENRY S. MAINE

WHEN primitive law has once been embodied in a Code, there is an
end to what may be called its spontaneous development. Henceforward
the changes effected in it, if effected at all, are effected deliberately
and from without. It is impossible to suppose that the customs of any
race or tribe remained unaltered during the whole of the long—in
some instances the immense—interval between their declaration and
their publication in writing. It would be unsafe too to affirm that no
part of the alteration was effected deliberately. But from the little we
know of the progress of law during this period, we are justified in
assuming that set purpose had the very smallest share in producing
change. Such innovations on the earliest usages as disclose themselves
appear to have been dictated by feelings and modes of thought which,
under our present mental conditions, we are unable to comprehend.
A new era begins, however, with the Codes. Wherever, after this epoch,
we trace the course of legal modification we are able to attribute it to
the conscious desire of improvement, or at all events of compassing
objects other than those which were aimed at in the primitive times.

It may seem at first sight that no general propositions worth trusting
can be elicited from the history of legal systems subsequent to the
codes. The field is too vast. We cannot be sure that we have included

Abridged from: Maine, Henry S., *Ancient Law,* 1861. (Currently available in an
edition published by the Oxford University Press, 1933.)

a sufficient number of phenomena in our observations, or that we accurately understand those which we have observed. But the undertaking will be seen to be more feasible, if we consider that after the epoch of codes the distinction between stationary and progressive societies begins to make itself felt. It is only with the progressive societies that we are concerned, and nothing is more remarkable than their extreme fewness. In spite of overwhelming evidence, it is most difficult for a citizen of western Europe to bring thoroughly home to himself the truth that the civilization which surrounds him is a rare exception in the history of the world. The tone of thought common among us, all our hopes, fears, and speculations, would be materially affected, if we had vividly before us the relation of the progressive races to the totality of human life. It is indisputable that much the greatest part of mankind has never shown a particle of desire that its civil institutions should be improved since the moment when external completeness was first given to them by their embodiment in some permanent record. One set of usages has occasionally been violently overthrown and superseded by another; here and there a primitive code, pretending to a supernatural origin, has been greatly extended, and distorted into the most surprising forms, by the perversity of sacerdotal commentators; but, except in a small section of the world, there has been nothing like the gradual amelioration of a legal system.

The difference between the stationary and progressive societies is, however, one of the great secrets which inquiry has yet to penetrate. It may be remarked that no one is likely to succeed in the investigation who does not clearly realize that the stationary condition of the human race is the rule, the progressive the exception.

I confine myself in what follows to the progressive societies. With respect to them it may be laid down that social necessities and social opinion are always more or less in advance of Law. We may come indefinitely near to the closing of the gap between them, but it has a perpetual tendency to reopen. Law is stable; the societies we are speaking of are progressive. The greater or less happiness of a people depends on the degree of promptitude with which the gulf is narrowed.

I employ the word "fiction" in a sense considerably wider than that in which English lawyers are accustomed to use it, and with a meaning much more extensive than that which belonged to the Roman "fictiones." Fictio, in old Roman law, is properly a term of pleading, and signifies a false averment on the part of the plaintiff which the defendant was not allowed to traverse; such, for example, as an averment that the plaintiff was a Roman citizen, when in truth he was a foreigner. The object of these "fictiones" was, of course, to give juris-

diction, and they therefore strongly resembled the allegations in the
writs of the English Queen's Bench and Exchequer, by which those
Courts contrived to usurp the jurisdiction of the Common Pleas:—
the allegation that the defendant was in custody of the king's marshal,
or that the plaintiff was the king's debtor, and could not pay his debt
by reason of the defendant's default. But I now employ the expression
"Legal Fiction" to signify any assumption which conceals, or affects
to conceal, the fact that a rule of law has undergone alteration, its
letter remaining unchanged, its operation being modified. The words,
therefore, include the instances of fictions which I have cited from
the English and Roman law, but they embrace much more, for I
should speak both of the English Case-law and of the Roman Responsa
Prudentum as resting on fictions. Both these examples will be examined presently. The *fact* is in both cases that the law has been
wholly changed; the *fiction* is that it remains what is always was. It is
not difficult to understand why fictions in all their forms are particularly
congenial to the infancy of society. They satisfy the desire for improvement, which is not quite wanting, at the same time that they do not
offend the superstitious disrelish for change which is always present.
At a particular stage of social progress they are invaluable expedients
for overcoming the rigidity of law, and, indeed, without one of them,
the Fiction of Adoption which permits the family tie to be artificially
created, it is difficult to understand how society would ever have
escaped from its swaddling-clothes, and taken its first steps towards
civilization. We must, therefore, not suffer ourselves to be affected by
the ridicule which Bentham pours on legal fictions wherever he meets
them. To revile them as merely fraudulent is to betray ignorance of
their peculiar office in the historical development of law. But at the
same time it would be equally foolish to agree with those theorists
who, discerning that fictions have had their uses, argue that they
ought to be stereotyped in our system. They have had their day, but
it has long since gone by. It is unworthy of us to effect an admittedly
beneficial object by so rude a device as a legal fiction. I cannot admit
any anomaly to be innocent, which makes the law either more difficult
to understand or harder to arrange in harmonious order. Now legal
fictions are the greatest of obstacles to symmetrical classification. The
rule of law remains sticking in the system, but it is a mere shell. It
has been long ago undermined, and a new rule hides itself under its
cover. Hence there is at once a difficulty in knowing whether the
rule which is actually operative should be classed in its true or in its
apparent place, and minds of different casts will differ as to the
branch of the alternative which ought to be selected. If the English
law is ever to assume an orderly distribution, it will be necessary to

prune away the legal fictions which, in spite of some recent legislative improvements, are still abundant in it.

The next instrumentality by which the adaptation of law to social wants is carried on I call Equity, meaning by that word any body of rules existing by the side of the original civil law, founded on distinct principles and claiming incidentally to supersede the civil law in virtue of a superior sanctity inherent in those principles. The Equity whether of the Roman Prætors or of the English Chancellors, differs from the Fictions which in each case preceded it, in that the interference with law is open and avowed. On the other hand, it differs from Legislation, the agent of legal improvement which comes after it, in that its claim to authority is grounded, not on the prerogative of any external person or body, not even on that of the magistrate who enunciates it, but on the special nature of its principles, to which it is alleged that all law ought to conform. The very conception of a set of principles, invested with a higher sacredness than those of the original law and demanding application independently of the consent of any external body, belongs to a much more advanced stage of thought than that to which legal fictions originally suggested themselves.

Legislation, the enactments of a legislature which, whether it take the form of an autocratic prince or of a parliamentary assembly, is the assumed organ of the entire society, is the last of the ameliorating instrumentalities. It differs from Legal Fictions just as Equity differs from them, and it is also distinguished from Equity, as deriving its authority from an external body or person. Its obligatory force is independent of its principles. The legislature, whatever be the actual restraints imposed on it by public opinion, is in theory empowered to impose what obligations it pleases on the members of the community. There is nothing to prevent its legislating in the wantonness of caprice. Legislation may be dictated by equity, if that last word be used to indicate some standard of right and wrong to which its enactments happen to be adjusted; but then these enactments are indebted for their binding force to the authority of the legislature and not to that of the principles on which the legislature acted; and thus they differ from rules of Equity, in the technical sense of the word, which pretend to a paramount sacredness entitling them at once to the recognition of the courts even without the concurrence of prince or parliamentary assembly. It is the more necessary to note these differences, because a student of Bentham would be apt to confound Fictions, Equity, and Statute law under the single head of legislation. They all, he would say, involve *law-making;* they differ only in respect of the machinery by which the new law is produced. That is perfectly true, and we must never forget it; but it furnishes no reason why we should deprive ourselves of so convenient a term as Legislation in the special sense. Legislation and Equity are disjoined in the popular mind and in the minds of most lawyers; and it will never do to neglect the distinction between them, however conventional, when important practical consequences follow from it.

ORDERING AND FORBIDDING

B Y

WILLIAM I. THOMAS AND
FLORIAN ZNANIECKI

ONE of the most significant features of social evolution is the growing importance which a conscious and rational technique tends to assume in social life. We are less and less ready to let any social processes go on without our active interference and we feel more and more dissatisfied with any active interference based upon a mere whim of an individual or a social body, or upon preconceived philosophical, religious, or moral generalizations.

The marvelous results attained by a rational technique in the sphere of material reality invite us to apply some analogous procedure to social reality. Our success in controlling nature gives us confidence that we shall eventually be able to control the social world in the same measure. Our actual inefficiency in this line is due, not to any fundamental limitation of our reason, but simply to the historical fact that the objective attitude toward social reality is a recent acquisition.

While our realization that nature can be controlled only by treating it as independent of any immediate act of our will or reason is four centuries old, our confidence in "legislation" and in "moral suasion" shows that this idea is not yet generally realized with regard to the social world. But the tendency to rational control is growing in this field also and constitutes at present an insistent demand on the social sciences.

Abridged from: Thomas, William I., and Znaniecki, Florian, *The Polish Peasant in Europe and America,* Chicago: The University of Chicago Press, 1918.
Reprinted by permission of the Social Science Research Council. In connection with the writings of W. I. Thomas, see: Thomas, W. I., *Social Behavior and Personality,* Contributions of W. I. Thomas to Theory and Social Research, Edited by Edmund H. Volkart, New York: Social Science Research Council, 1951.

This demand for a rational control results from the increasing rapidity of social evolution. The old forms of control were based upon the assumption of an essential stability of the whole social framework and were effective only in so far as this stability was real. In a stable social organization there is time enough to develop in a purely empirical way, through innumerable experiments and failures, approximately sufficient means of control with regard to the ordinary and frequent social phenomena, while the errors made in treating the uncommon and rare phenomena seldom affect social life in such a manner as to imperil the existence of the group; if they do, then the catastrophe is accepted as incomprehensible and inevitable.

But when, owing to the breakdown of the isolation of the group and its contact with a more complex and fluid world, the social evolution becomes more rapid and the crises more frequent and varied, there is no time for the same gradual, empirical, unmethodical elaboration of approximately adequate means of control, and no crisis can be passively borne, but every one must be met in a more or less adequate way, for they are too various and frequent not to imperil social life unless controlled in time. The substitution of a conscious technique for a half-conscious routine has become, therefore, a social necessity, though it is evident that the development of this technique could be only gradual, and that even now we find in it many implicit or explicit ideas and methods corresponding to stages of human thought passed hundreds or even thousands of years ago.

The oldest but most persistent form of social technique is that of "ordering-and-forbidding"—that is, meeting a crisis by an arbitrary act of will decreeing the disappearance of the undesirable or the appearance of the desirable phenomena, and using arbitrary physical action to enforce the decree. This method corresponds exactly to the magical phase of natural technique. In both, the essential means of bringing a determined effect is more or less consciously thought to reside in the act of will itself by which the effect is decreed as desirable and of which the action is merely an indispensable vehicle or instrument; in both, the process by which the cause (act of will and physical action) is supposed to bring its effect to realization remains out of reach of investigation; in both, finally, if the result is not attained, some new act of will with new material accessories is introduced, instead of trying to find and remove the perturbing causes. A good instance of this in the social field is the typical legislative procedure of today.

It frequently happens both in magic and in the ordering-and-forbidding technique that the means by which the act of will is helped are really effective, and thus the result is attained, but, as the process of causation, being unknown, cannot be controlled, the success is always more or less accidental and dependent upon the *stability of general conditions;* when these are changed, the intended effect fails to appear, the subject is unable to account for the reasons of the failure and can only try by guesswork some other means. And even more frequent than this accidental success is the result that the action brings some effect, but not the desired one.

There is, indeed, one difference between the ordering-and-forbidding technique and magic. In social life an expressed act of will may be sometimes a real cause, when the person or body from which it emanates has a particular authority in the eyes of those to whom the order or prohibition applies. But this does not change the nature of the technique as such.

SOCIAL REORGANIZATION THROUGH DISORGANIZATION

B Y

WILLIAM I. THOMAS AND FLORIAN ZNANIECKI

THE concept of social disorganization refers primarily to institutions and only secondarily to men. Just as group-organization embodied in socially systematized schemes of behavior imposed as rules upon individuals never exactly coincides with individual life-organization consisting in personally systematized schemes of behavior, so social disorganization never exactly corresponds to individual disorganization. Even if we imagined a group lacking all internal differentiation, *i.e.,* a group in which every member would accept all the socially sanctioned and none but the socially sanctioned rules of behavior as schemes of his own conduct, still every member would systematize these schemes differently in his personal evolution, would make a different life-organization out of them, because neither his temperament nor his life-history would be exactly the same as those of other

Abridged from: Thomas, William I., and Znaniecki, Florian, *The Polish Peasant in Europe and America,* Chicago: The University of Chicago Press, 1918.
Reprinted by permission of the Social Science Research Council. In connection with the writings of W. I. Thomas, see: Thomas, W. I., *Social Behavior and Personality,* Contributions of W. I. Thomas to Theory and Social Research. Edited by Edmund H. Volkart, New York: Social Science Research Council, 1951.

members. As a matter of fact, such a uniform group is a pure fiction; even in the least differentiated groups we find socially sanctioned rules of behavior which explicitly apply only to certain classes of individuals and are not supposed to be used by others in organizing their conduct, and we find individuals who in organizing their conduct use some personal schemes of their own invention besides the traditionally sanctioned social rules. Moreover, the progress of social differentiation is accompanied by a growth of special institutions, consisting essentially in a systematic organization of a certain number of socially selected schemes for the permanent achievement of certain results. This institutional organization and the life-organization of any of the individuals through whose activity the institution is socially realized partly overlap, but one individual cannot fully realize in his life the whole systematic organization of the institution since the latter always implies the collaboration of many, and on the other hand each individual has many interests which have to be organized outside of this particular institution.

We can define social disorganization briefly as a *decrease of the influence of existing social rules of behavior upon individual members of the group*. This decrease may present innumerable degrees, ranging from a single break of some particular rule by one individual up to a general decay of all the institutions of the group. Now, social disorganization in this sense has no unequivocal connection whatever with individual disorganization, which consists in a decrease of the individual's ability to organize his whole life for the efficient, progressive and continuous realization of his fundamental interests. An individual who breaks some or even most of the social rules prevailing in his group may indeed do this because he is losing the minimum capacity of life-organization required by social conformism; but he may also reject the schemes of behavior imposed by his milieu because they hinder him in reaching a more efficient and more comprehensive life-organization. On the other hand also, the social organization of a group may be very permanent and strong in the sense that no opposition is manifested to the existing rules and institutions; and yet, this lack of opposition may be simply the result of the narrowness of the interests of the group-members and may be accompanied by a very rudimentary, mechanical and inefficient life-organization of each member individually. Of course, a strong group organization may be also the product of a conscious moral effort of its members and thus correspond to a very high degree of life-organization of each of them individually. It is therefore impossible to conclude from social as to individual organization or disorganization, or vice versa. In other words, social organization is not coextensive with individual morality, nor does social disorganization correspond to individual demoralization.

Social disorganization is not an exceptional phenomenon limited to certain periods or certain societies; some of it is found always and everywhere, since always and everywhere there are individual cases of breaking social rules, cases which exercise some disorganizing influence on group institutions and, if not counteracted, are apt to multiply and to lead to a complete decay of the latter. But during periods of social stability this continuous incipient disorganization is neutralized by such activities of the group as reinforce with the help of social sanctions the power of existing rules. The stability of group institutions is thus simply a dynamic equilibrium of processes of disorganization and *reorganization*. This equilibrium is disturbed when processes of disorganization can no longer be checked by any attempts to reinforce the existing rules. A period of prevalent disorganization follows, which may lead to a complete dissolution of the group. More usually, however, it is counteracted and stopped before it reaches this limit by a new process of reorganization which in this case does not consist in a mere reinforcement of the decaying organization, but in a production of new schemes of behavior and new institutions better adapted to the changed demands of the group; we call this production of new schemes and institutions *social reconstruction*. Social reconstruction is possible only because, and in so far as, during the period of social disorganization a part at least of the members of the group have not become individually disorganized, but, on the contrary, have been working toward a new and more efficient personal life-organization and have expressed a part at least of the constructive tendencies implied in their individual activities in an effort to produce new social institutions.

DIFFUSION

BY

RALPH LINTON

THE comparatively rapid growth of human culture as a whole has been due to the ability of all societies to borrow elements from other cultures and to incorporate them into their own. This transfer of

Abridged from: Linton, Ralph, *The Study of Man*, New York; Appleton-Century, 1936. Reprinted by permission of Appleton-Century-Crofts, Inc.

culture elements from one society to another is known as *diffusion*.
It is a process by which mankind has been able to pool its inventive
ability. By diffusion an invention which has been made and socially
accepted at one point can be transmitted to an ever-widening group
of cultures until, in the course of centuries, it may spread to practically
the whole of mankind.

A real understanding of the dynamics of diffusion can be arrived
at only by observing the process in actual operation. A thorough study
of the current spread of any new culture element, the factors responsible for this spread, the reactions which the new element has evoked
in different societies, and the adaptations which the acceptance of
the new trait into various cultures has entailed would do more to put
diffusion studies on a sound basis than twenty studies of trait distribu-
tions at a given point in time. Unfortunately there is hardly a single
study of this sort extant. In the discussion which follows we must,
therefore, raise far more questions than we can answer. Nevertheless,
there are a few generally recognized principles of diffusion, and we
may begin our investigation with these.

The first of these is that, *other things being equal, elements of culture will be taken up first by societies which are close to their points
of origin and later by societies which are more remote or which have
less direct contacts.* This principle derives from the fact that the diffusion of any element obviously requires both contact and time. It is
impossible for any trait to spread to a culture unless there is contact
with some other culture which already has it. Thus if we have three
tribes, A, B, and C, with the territory of B intervening between that
of A and C and preventing any direct contact between them, no new
culture trait which A may develop can reach C until after it has been
accepted by B. From this it also follows that the trait will be received
later by C than by B.

From this principle of the diffusion of traits to more and more
remote localities a second principle emerges, that of *marginal survivals.* Let us suppose that a new appliance has been developed by a
particular society and is spreading to the neighboring societies in an
ever-widening circle. At the same time it may very well be undergoing
changes and improvements at its point of origin. These improvements
will, in turn, be diffused to the neighboring societies, but since this
diffusion will begin at a later point in time, the improved appliance
will have a tendency to lag behind the original one in its spread.
Long after the new appliance has completely supplanted the ancestral
one at its point of origin, the ancestral one will continue in use about
the margins of the diffusion area.

A group which is reluctant to take over a new trait interposes a bar between the origin point of that trait and more remote groups which might be quite willing to accept it if given the opportunity. Even if the reluctance of the intermediary culture is finally broken down, much time will have been lost. Because of this varying coefficient of receptivity, traits always spread from their origin points irregularly and certain traits may be diffused with amazing speed while others diffuse slowly, if at all.

No simple mechanistic interpretation of diffusion will prove adequate to the needs of even the rather limited field of historic reconstruction. Diffusion required not only a donor but also a receiver, and the role of this receiver is certainly the more important. Diffusion really includes three fairly distinct processes: presentation of the new culture element or elements to the society, acceptance by the society, and the integration of the accepted element or elements into the preexisting culture. Each of these is influenced by a large number of variable factors most of which still require study.

The presentation of new elements to a society always presupposes contact. The society with which this contact is established may, of course, be either the originator of the new culture element or simply an intermediary in its spread. This factor can have little influence on the process. However, the nature of the contact is of tremendous importance. Such contacts vary from those in which two societies and cultures are brought into a close relationship as wholes to sporadic trade contacts or those in which a single individual from one society settles in another society. Complete contacts are decidedly rare. It is difficult to find examples of them except in the case of conquering groups who settle among and exploit the conquered or in that of immigrant groups such as we still have in many parts of America. Such contacts have a somewhat different quality from those involved in the ordinary diffusion process, and the process of culture change under these conditions is usually termed *acculturation*. Apparently the use of this term, which was first applied to the study of changes in immigrant groups, is based on the rather naïve belief that one of the societies thus brought into contact completely abandons its former culture and completely accepts that of the other. Actually, such close and complete contacts always result in an exchange of culture elements. In the long run both the originally diverse societies and their cultures will fuse to form a new society and culture. In this final product elements from both will be represented, although they may be represented in widely varying proportions.

Taking the world as a whole, the type of contact which makes acculturation possible is more likely to arise through conquest and the settlement of the conquering groups among the vanquished than through anything else. In such cases the normal numerical superiority of the conquered is likely to be balanced to a considerable extent by the superior prestige of the conquerors, so that the two cultures stand on fairly equal terms in their contribution to the new culture which always arises under such conditions. Such hybrid cultures usually present the aspects of a chemical rather than a mechanical mixture. In addition to traits drawn from both the parent cultures they possess qualities foreign to both. However, we must return to the more normal forms of culture contact and the dissemination of culture elements which these make possible.

It goes without saying that contacts between cultures can only be established through the medium of individuals. We have pointed out in a previous chapter that no individual participates completely in the culture of his own society. This means that under ordinary conditions the full culture of the donor society is never offered to the receiving society. The only elements made available to them are those with which the contact individuals are familiar. Thus if a trade relation exists between two tribes, the trade being carried on by men, the product of the women's industries in one tribe may become familiar to the other tribe, but the techniques will not be transmitted with it. The men who do the trading, even if they do not guard these techniques as valuable commercial secrets, will have only a vague idea of how the things are made. If the receiving tribe becomes accustomed to the use of this product and then finds the supply suddenly cut off, it may develop quite different techniques for the manufacture of equivalent articles.

The differential which is introduced into diffusion by this varying participation of individuals in their own culture is just as strongly operative when the contact-individuals from the donor group settle among the receiving group. The trader, missionary, or government official can transmit no more of his culture than he himself knows. If the contact-individual is a male, he usually can transmit very little from the female half of his own culture, and the female elements which he can transmit are likely to be heterogeneous and to bear little functional relation to each other.

When two societies are in long-continued contact, as in the case of two tribes who live side by side and are generally on friendly terms, sooner or later the entire culture of each will be made available to the other. The long series of contacts with individuals, each of whom is a partial participant, will have a cumulative effect. When, on the other hand, the contacts of one society are exclusively with selected groups of individuals from the other society, the receiving group may never be exposed to the totality of the donor group's culture.

A second factor which exercises a strong influence upon diffusion is what, for lack of a better term, may be called the inherent communicability of the culture elements themselves. This has nothing to do with the attitudes of the receiving group or with its preexisting culture configurations. Although this aspect of the diffusion problem has never been studied, it seems probable that we are dealing here with something which is fairly constant. We have pointed out that culture is itself a socio-psychological phenomenon and that the various forms of behavior which we are able to observe and record are simply its overt expressions. Certain elements of culture can be much more readily expressed than others, whether this expression takes the form of ordinary acts or verbalizations. Since it is only through the observation of these overt expressions that culture elements can be transmitted from one individual to another or from one society to another, it follows that those culture elements which can be most readily and completely expressed will be those which are the most readily available for acceptance. Among the varied elements which go to make up the totality of a culture, the techniques for food-getting and manufacturing take precedence in this respect. These can be made clear to a bystander without the medium of speech. If he wishes to acquire such techniques, all he has to do is to imitate the worker's movements carefully and exactly. Although he may lack the proper muscular control at first, this can be acquired through practice. The same holds for manufactured objects. Even when the techniques have not been observed, the members of the receiving culture can fix the details of the object firmly in their memory and proceed to reproduce it at leisure.

As soon as we pass from such simple culture elements as techniques and their material products, we encounter increasing difficulties in communication. Although it is quite possible to describe such an element of culture as the ideal pattern for marriage and even to express it in non-verbal behavior, this expression is much less complete than that which is possible with regard to such a culture element as basket-making. The most thorough verbalization has difficulty in conveying the series of associations and conditioned emotional responses which are attached to this pattern and which give it meaning and vitality within our own culture configuration. In all our overt expressions of such a pattern these things are taken for granted, but the individual to whom we are attempting to convey a sense of the pattern can know nothing of them. Even when language difference has ceased to be a serious barrier to the conveyance of such patterns, it is extremely difficult to put them across. This is even more true of those concepts which, while a part of culture, find no direct expression in behavior aside from verbalizations.

Lastly, we have in all cultures those vital attitudes and values which lie largely below the level of individual consciousness and which the average member of a society rarely tries to verbalize even to himself. The practical impossibility of making such elements available for borrowing by the members of some other society is obvious. This part of any culture simply is not susceptible to diffusion. It can never be presented in sufficiently concrete and objective terms. Such things as religious or philosophical concepts can be communicated after a fashion, although probably never in their entirety. Patterns of social behavior can also be transmitted in the same uncertain way, but the associations which give them genuine potentialities for function cannot be transmitted. A borrowing group may imitate their outward forms, but it will usually be found that it has introduced new elements to replace those which could not be genuinely communicated to it.

Our discussion hitherto has dealt with donor cultures and the qualities of culture elements. Let us turn now to what is the real core of the problem of diffusion, the reactions of the accepting group to the elements presented to it. In its acceptance or rejection of these elements a society exercises free will. There may be a few exceptions to this in cases in which a socially dominant group seeks to impose its culture forcibly upon a subject society, but these are less important than they might appear. In the first place, such a dominant group rarely, if ever, attempts to impose its culture as a whole. It is content with the imposition of a few selected elements, such as outward adherence to its religion or the custom of wearing trousers. Obviously no amount of force can introduce into another culture any element which is not constantly and directly reflected in overt behavior. The conquered can be forced to attend church regularly, and it may even become a habit with them, something which produces no emotional response, but they cannot be forced to accept the new faith emotionally or be prevented from praying to their own gods alone and in private. At the same time, the very use of force makes the proscribed elements of the native culture symbols of revolt and this inspires a stronger attachment to them. Under a veil of superficial compliance a persecuted group can maintain its own ideals and values intact for generations, modifying and reinterpreting the superficial elements of culture which are forced upon it in such a way that they will do these no violence.

With very few exceptions, therefore, every new element which a society incorporates into its culture, it accepts of its own free will. This acceptance, in turn, is controlled by a large number of variable factors. The only constant in the situation is that such elements are always taken at their face value. A society can apprehend only those parts of a total complex which can be communicated to it plainly and directly. There is no perception of the modifications in preexisting patterns which the adoption of the new element will entail. In fact it is doubtful whether any mind is ever able to foresee any but the most immediate of these. Even in our own culture no one could have foretold the profound changes which have come in the wake of the acceptance of the automobile, changes which have affected our social patterns even more deeply than they have affected our economic ones.

The factors which control the receptivity of a society toward any new element of culture are, after all, very much the same whether this element originates inside or outside of their culture, i.e., whether it comes to them through invention or through diffusion. The main difference between these two processes lies in the fact that, if society rejects an invention, that addition to the sum total of culture is permanently lost, while if it rejects an element presented by diffusion this element is not lost but remains in the hands of the donor culture and may crop up at a later time when the society's reaction to it may be quite different.

New traits are accepted primarily on the basis of two qualities, utility and compatibility: in other words, on the basis of what they appear to be good for and how easily they can be fitted into the existing culture configuration. Both these qualities are, of course, relative to the receiving culture and are influenced by such a long series of factors that an outsider can hardly ascertain all of them. We have mentioned elsewhere that culture change is mainly a matter of the replacement of old elements by new ones and that every culture normally includes adequate techniques for meeting all the conscious needs of the society's members. When a new trait presents itself its acceptance depends not so much on whether it is better than the existing one as on whether it is enough better to make its acceptance worth the trouble. This in turn must depend upon the judgment of the group, their degree of conservatism, and how much change in existing habits the new appliance will entail. Even in the simplest form of diffusion, that of mechanical appliances, superiority cannot be judged simply in terms of increased output.

Very much the same situation holds with regard to the problem of compatibility. The acceptance of any new culture element entails certain changes in the total culture configuration. Although the full extent of these changes can never be forecast, certain of them are usually obvious. If the new trait is of such a sort that its acceptance will conflict directly with important traits already present in the culture, it is almost certain to be rejected.

Most conflicts between new elements and preexisting elements are less direct and obvious. In the matter of compatibility as in that of utility there is a broad zone of uncertainty. There are new elements which may be recognized as slightly superior to existing ones and other elements which may be seen to be somewhat incompatible, but not enough so as to make their acceptance impossible. Very often the advantages and disadvantages are so evenly balanced that the acceptance of the new trait may seem desirable to certain members of the society and undesirable to others. The ultimate acceptance or rejection of elements which fall within this zone is controlled by still another series of variable factors about which we know very little. One of the most important of these is certainly the particular interests which dominate the life of the receiving group. A new trait which is in line with these interests will be given more serious consideration and has a better chance of adoption than one which is not. A slight gain along the line of these interests is felt to be more important than a larger one in some other line in which the group takes little interest.

There are other factors beside those of the receiving group's interests and evaluations which may help to weight the scales for or against a new element of culture. One of the most important of these is the prestige of the donor group. There are many different grades and kinds of prestige. Occasionally one encounters a society which seems to have a genuine inferiority complex with regard to some other and to consider everything which this admired society has superior to the corresponding elements in its own culture. Such a group will borrow almost anything from its model that it has an opportunity to borrow.

Such a condition is unusual. Donor prestige is usually of a much more limited type, referring only to certain aspects of culture. The average society believes in its general superiority to the rest of mankind, but at the same time admits that some other society or societies are superior in particular respects.

A further factor which influences the acceptance of new culture elements is the prestige of the individuals under whose auspices the new thing is presented to the society. In diffusion as in invention, acceptance of a new trait begins with a single individual or at most a small group of individuals. It makes a great deal of difference who these innovators happen to be. If they are persons whom the society admires and is accustomed to imitate, the way for the general acceptance of the new trait is smoothed from the start. If the innovators happen to be personally unpopular or of low social status, the new element immediately acquires undesirable associations which may outweigh any intrinsic advantages.

Lastly, there is the factor of what can only be termed "faddism." It is an observed fact that certain new elements of culture will be eagerly accepted by groups when there are no discernible reasons of either utility or prestige. Major elements are unlikely to be introduced into any culture in this way, but a whole series of minor ones may be.

SCIENCE AND SOCIAL PRACTICE

B Y

WILLIAM I. THOMAS AND FLORIAN ZNANIECKI

ASSUMING that social theory fulfils its task satisfactorily and goes on discovering new laws which can be applied to regulate social becoming, what will be the effect of this on social practice? First of all, the limitations with which social practice has struggled up to the present will be gradually removed. Since it is theoretically possible to find what social influences should be applied to certain already existing attitudes in order to produce certain new attitudes, and what attitudes should be developed with regard to certain already existing social values in order to make the individual or the group produce certain new social values, there is not a single phenomenon within the whole sphere of human life that conscious control cannot reach sooner or later. There are no objective obstacles in the nature of the social world or in the nature of the human mind which would essentially prevent social practice from attaining gradually the same degree of efficiency as that of industrial practice. The only obstacles are of a subjective kind.

There is, first, the traditional appreciation of social activity as meritorious in itself, for the sake of its intentions alone. There must, indeed, be some results in order to make the good intentions count, but, since anything done is regarded as meritorious, the standards by which the results are appreciated are astonishingly low. Social practice must cease to be a matter of merit and be treated as a necessity. If the theorician is asked to be sure of his generalizations before trying to apply them in practice, it is at least strange that persons of merely good will are permitted to try out on society indefinitely and irresponsibly their vague and perhaps sentimental ideas.

Abridged from: Thomas, William I., and Znaniecki, Florian, *The Polish Peasant in Europe and America*, Chicago: University of Chicago Press, 1918. Reprinted by permission of the Social Science Research Council. In connection with the writings of W. I. Thomas, see: Thomas, W. I., *Social Behavior and Personality*, Contributions of W. I. Thomas to Theory and Social Research, Edited by Edmund H. Volkart, New York: Social Science Research Council, 1951.

The second obstacle to the development of a perfect social practice is the well-known unwillingness of the common-sense man to accept the control of scientific technique. Aganist this unwillingness there is only one weapon—success. This is what the history of industrial technique shows. There is perhaps not a single case where the first application of science to any field of practice held by common sense and tradition did not provoke the opposition of the practitioner. It is still within the memory of man that the old farmer with his common-sense methods laughed at the idea that the city chap could teach him anything about farming, and was more than skeptical about the application of the results of soil-analysis to the growing of crops. The fear of new things is still strong even among cultivated persons, and the social technician has to expect that he will meet at almost every step this old typical hostility of common sense to science. He can only accept it and interpret it as a demand to show the superiority of his methods by their results.

But the most important difficulty which social practice has to overcome before reaching a level of efficiency comparable to that of industrial practice lies in the difficulty of applying scientific generalizations. The laws of science are abstract, while the practical situations are concrete, and it requires a special intellectual activity to find what are the practical questions which a given law may help to solve, or what are the scientific laws which may be used to solve a given practical question. In the physical sphere this intellectual activity has been embodied in technology, and it is only since the technologist has intervened between the scientist and the practitioner that material practice has acquired definitely the character of a self-conscious and planfully developing technique and ceased to be dependent on irrational and often unreasonable traditional rules. And if material practice needs a technology in spite of the fact that the generalizations which physical science hands over to it have been already experimentally tested, this need is much more urgent in social practice where the application of scientific generalizations is their first and only experimental test.

We cannot enter here into detailed indications of what social technology should be, but we must take into account the chief point of its method—the general form which every concrete problem of social technique assumes. Whatever may be the aim of social practice—modification of individual attitudes or of social institutions—in trying to attain this aim we never find the elements which we want to use or to modify isolated and passively waiting for our activity, but always embodied in active practical *situations,* which have been formed independently of us and with which our activity has to comply.

The situation is the set of values and attitudes with which the individual or the group has to deal in a process of activity and with regard to which this activity is planned and its results appreciated. Every concrete activity is the solution of a situation. The situation involves three kinds of data: (1) The objective conditions under which the individual or society has to act, that is, the totality of values—economic, social, religious, intellectual, etc.—which at the given moment affect directly or indirectly the conscious status of the individual or the group. (2) The pre-existing attitudes of the individual or the group which at the given moment have an actual influence upon his behavior. (3) The definition of the situation, that is, the more or less clear conception of the conditions and consciousness of the attitudes. And the definition of the situation is a necessary preliminary to any act of the will, for in given conditions and with a given set of attitudes an indefinite plurality of actions is possible, and one definite action can appear only if these conditions are selected, interpreted, and combined in a determined way and if a certain systematization of these attitudes is reached, so that one of them becomes predominant and subordinates the others. It happens, indeed, that a certain value imposes itself immediately and unreflectively and leads at once to action, or that an attitude as soon as it appears excludes the others and expresses itself unhesitatingly in an active process. In these cases, whose most radical examples are found in reflex and instinctive actions, the definition is already given to the individual by external conditions or by his own tendencies. But usually there is a process of reflection, after which either a ready social definition is applied or a new personal definition worked out.

Now, while the task of science is to analyze by a comparative study the whole process of activity into elementary facts, and it must therefore ignore the variety of concrete situations in order to be able to find laws of causal dependence of abstractly isolated attitudes or values on other attitudes and values, the task of technique is to provide the means of a rational control of concrete situations. The situation can evidently be controlled either by a change of conditions or by a change of attitudes, or by both, and in this respect the role of technique as application of science is easily characterized. By comparing situations of a certain type, the social technician must find what are the predominant values or the predominant attitudes which determine the situation more than others, and then the question is to modify these values or these attitudes in the desired way by using the knowledge of social causation given by social theory.

To be sure, it may happen that, in spite of an adequate scientific knowledge of the social laws permitting the modification of those factors which we want to change, our efforts will fail to influence the situation or will produce a situation more undesirable than the one we wished to avoid. The fault is then with our technical knowledge. That is, either we have failed in determining the relative importance of the various factors, or we have failed to foresee the influence of other causes which, interfering with our activity, produce a quite unexpected and undesired effect. And since it is impossible to expect from every practitioner a complete scientific training and still more impossible to have him work out a scientifically justified and detailed plan of action for every concrete case in particular, the special task of the social technician is to prepare, with the help of both science and practical observation, thorough schemes and plans of action for all the various *types* of situations which may be found in a given line of social activity, and leave to the practitioner the subordination of the given concrete situation to its proper type. This is actually the role which all the organizers of social institutions have played, but the technique itself must become more conscious and methodically perfect, and every field of social activity should have its professional technicians. The evolution of social life makes necessary continual modifications and developments of social technique, and we can hope that the evolution of social theory will continually put new and useful scientific generalizations within the reach of the social technician; the latter must therefore remain in permanent touch with both social life and social theory, and this requires a more far-going specialization than we actually find.

But, however efficient this type of social technique may become, its application will always have certain limits beyond which a different type of technique will be more useful. Indeed, the form of social control outlined above presupposes that the individual—or the group—is treated as a passive object of our activity and that we change the situations for him, from case to case, in accordance with our plans and intentions. But the application of this method becomes more and more difficult as the situations grow more complex, more new and unexpected from case to case, and more influenced by the individual's own reflection. And, indeed, from both the moral and the hedonistic standpoints and also from the standpoint of the level of efficiency of the individual and of the group, it is desirable to develop in the individuals the ability to control spontaneously their own activities by conscious reflection. To use a biological comparison, the type of control where the practitioner prescribes for the individual a scheme of activity appropriate to every crisis as it arises corresponds to the tropic or reflex type of control in animal life, where the activity of the individual is controlled mechanically by stimulations from without, while the reflective and individualistic control corresponds to the type of activity characteristic of the higher conscious organism, where the control is exercised from within by the selective mechanism of the nervous system. While, in the early tribal, communal, kinship, and religious groups, and to a large extent in the historic state, the society itself provided a rigoristic and particularistic set of definitions in the form of "customs" or "mores," the tendency to advance is associated with the liberty of the individual to make his own definitions.

We have assumed throughout this argument that if an adequate technique is developed it is possible to produce any desirable attitudes and values, but this assumption is practically justified only if we find in the individual attitudes which cannot avoid response to the class of stimulations which society is able to apply to him. And apparently we do find this disposition. Every individual has a vast variety of wishes which can be satisfied only by his incorporation in a society. Among his general patterns of wishes we may enumerate: (1) the desire for new experience, for fresh stimulations; (2) the desire for recognition, including, for example, sexual response and general social appreciation, and secured by devices ranging from the display of ornament to the demonstration of worth through scientific attainment; (3) the desire for mastery, or the "will to power," exemplified by ownership, domestic tyranny, political despotism, based on the instinct of hate, but capable of being sublimated to laudable ambition; (4) the desire for security, based on the instinct of fear and exemplified negatively by the wretchedness of the individual in perpetual solitude or under social taboo. Society is, indeed, an agent for the repression of many of the wishes in the individual; it demands that he shall be moral by repressing at least the wishes which are irreconcilable with the welfare of the group, but nevertheless it provides the only medium within which any of his schemes or wishes can be gratified. And it would be superfluous to point out by examples the degree to which society has in the past been able to impose its schemes of attitudes and values on the individual.

CHAPTER 18

Conflicting Values
and Social Integration

——————◄•►——————

CONFLICT OF VALUES

B Y

WILLARD WALLER

IF we are to treat social problems scientifically, we must try to understand why we consider them problems. We must subject to analysis our judgments of value as well as the social phenomena upon which these judgments are passed. We may do this by applying the concept of the mores to the problem of social problems as we have defined it. Social problems exist within a definite moral universe. Once we step out of our circle of accustomed moralities, social problems cease to exist for us. Likewise, if we consider the possibility of revolutionary change, social problems lose most of their complexity. A simple formulation of our standpoint, which we advance as roughly accurate for most social problems, rests upon the assumption of two conflicting sets of mores. Social problems result from the interaction of these two groups of mores, which we may call the *organizational* and the *humanitarian* mores.[1]

Abridged from: Waller, Willard, "Social Problems and the Mores," *American Sociological Review*, 1936, 1, 922–933. Reprinted by permission of the American Sociological Society.

[1] I have limited the present paper to a discussion of the interaction of these mores at the present time. A lengthier treatment of the subject would have to pay considerable attention to the historical interrelations of these sets of mores.

The organizational, or basic, mores, are those upon which the social order is founded, the mores of private property and individualism, the mores of the monogamous family, Christianity, and nationalism. Conditions of human life which we regard as social problems emanate from the organizational mores as effective causes. Indeed, the fact that a certain condition is in some sense humanly caused is an unrecognized but essential criterion of the social problem. We are all, as Galsworthy remarked, under sentence of death, but death is not a social problem; death becomes a social problem only when men die, as we think, unnecessarily, as in war or by accident or preventable disease. Not all the miseries of man kind are social problems. Every condition which we regard as a social problem is in some sense a result of our institutions or we do not concern ourselves with it.

Alongside the organizational mores there exists a set of humanitarian mores; those who follow the humanitarian mores feel an urge to make the world better or to remedy the misfortunes of others.[2] Probably the humanitarian impulse has always existed, but it has apparently attained group-wide expression at a relatively late period in our history, following the breakdown of primary group society. Social problems in the modern sense did not exist when every primary group cared for its own helpless and unfortunate. Social problems as we know them are a phenomenon of secondary group society, in which the primary group is no longer willing and able to take care of its members. It was this breakdown which called group wide humanitarianism into existence; it was this situation which brought it about that we were asked to feel sympathy for those whom we had never seen. Humanitarian mores are frequently expressed, for they are highly verbal, and they command the instant assent of almost any group.

The formula which crystallizes in our minds as we approach social problems from the angle of the mores is this: Social problems are social conditions of which some of the causes are felt to be human and moral. Value judgments define these conditions as social problems. Value judgments are the formal causes of social problems, just as the law is the formal cause of crime. Value judgments originate from the humanitarian mores, which are somewhat in conflict with the organizational mores. Social problems are moral problems; they are like the problems of a problem play. The existence of some sort of moral problem is the single thread that binds all social problems together. Any important social problem is marked by moral conflict in the individual and social

---

[2] While an explanation in terms of psychopathology would account for the fact that certain persons rather than certain others are the ones to pass value judgments, we must assume humanitarian mores in order to account for the fact that anyone passes them.

conflict in the group. It is thus that the strain for consistency in the mores expresses itself.[3]

When someone has expressed a value judgment upon some condition of human life which originates from the organizational mores, and begins to reflect upon possible courses of action, he is at last in a position to understand the sense in which social problems are complex. For the same mores from which the deplored conditions originate continue to operate to limit any action which one takes in order to remedy them. Frank illustrates this limiting action of the organizational mores by showing how difficult it would be to explain our housing problem to a man from Mars.

We should have to delegate an economist, a lawyer, a political scientist, a sociologist, and a historian to explain about the system of private property, the price system, popular government, congestion of population, transportation, and so on. And when they had severally and jointly expounded the complexities of the situation, pointing out that we cannot just build houses, but must rely upon individual initiative and private enterprise to enter the field of building construction, that we must use the "price system" to obtain the needed land which is someone's private property, to buy the necessary materials and to hire the skilled labor, that we must borrow capital on mortgages to finance these expenditures, paying a bonus to induce someone to lend that capital and also pay interest on the loan, together with amortization quotas and then we must contrive to rent these dwellings in accordance with a multiplicity of rules and regulations about leases and so on—after all these sundry explanations showing that to get houses built we must not infringe anyone's rights of private property or freedom to make a profit, and that what we want is to find a way of getting houses without interefering with anyone's customary activities, our visitor would suddenly exclaim, "Yes, I begin to see; have you any other such difficult problems, for this is exceedingly interesting?" [4]

[3] I should not like to be understood as making a claim for the originality of this conception of social problems. My interpretation is apparently not very far from Sumner's. L. K. Frank, in the paper quoted and in some other writings, appears to have anticipated my statement almost completely (L. K. Frank, *Social Problems; Amer. Jour. Sociol.*, 30, Jan. 1925, 463.) Throughout this paper I have drawn heavily upon Frank's fundamental discussion. Burgess makes use of a similar conception in one of his papers. (See E. W. Burgess, "Social Planning and the Mores," *Pub. Amer. Sociol. Soc.*, 29, 3, 1–18.) In numerous writings Woodard has attacked the same problem by means of a different type of analysis; I have in fact borrowed some terminology and certain interpretations from him. The Marxian conception of dialectic seems closely related to my interpretation; so, I am informed, are certain passages of Bergson. It appears, then, that a great many thinkers have converged upon what is essentially the same interpretation, a fact which should serve, at any rate, to give the interpretation a certain added cogency.

[4] L. K. Frank, *op. cit.*, pp. 465–466.

In every social problem seek the moral problem; try to discover the complex processes of conflict, supplementation, and interference in our own moral imperatives. That is the principle which should guide the sociologist as he seeks to study social problems scientifically. Let us attempt to sketch the outlines of this conflict of mores with regard to a few typical social problems. Poverty is a social problem, when it exists in the midst of plenty, or in a world in which universal plenty is a technological possibility. The value judgment passed on poverty defines it as at least in part socially caused and as something which ought to be remedied. A simpleton would suggest that the remedy for poverty in the midst of plenty is to redistribute income. We reject this solution at once because it would interfere with the institution of private property, would destroy the incentive for thrift and hard work and disjoint the entire economic system. What is done to alleviate poverty must be done within the limits set by the organizational mores.

A slightly different type of conflict appears when a value judgment is passed, not upon the conditions of someone's life, but upon his behavior. An unmarried girl has a baby; her family and community take harsh and unreasoned action against her. The humanitarian comes in to save the pieces, but he cannot make things too easy for the girl or try to convince her family and community that she is not guilty of moral turpitude for fear of encouraging illegitimacy and injuring the morality upon which the monogamous family is founded. Likewise, venereal disease becomes a social problem in that it arises from our family institutions and also in that the medical means which could be used to prevent it, which would unquestionably be fairly effective, cannot be employed for fear of altering the mores of chastity. The situation is similar when it is a question of adjusting family relationships.

Confusing conflicts of mores appear in those situations, frequent enough in unemployment relief, in which human misery and misbehavior are intermingled. When people suffer privation, the humanitarian mores dictate relief. If these people are willing to work, if the old live in strict monogamy and the young do not contract marriage until they are off the relief rolls, if they obey the law, if they do not conceal any assets, if they spend absolutely nothing for luxuries, if they are grateful and not demanding, if the level of relief does not approach the income of the employed, relatively few objections are raised to the giving of relief. But let any of the above violations of the organizational mores defining the situation of the recipient of charity arise, and the untrained investigator will quite possibly cut off relief in a storm of moral indignation. Herein he is in agreement with the moral sense of the greater part of the community. The trained social worker attempts at this point to bring the investigator over to a more broadly humanitarian point of view.

It is necessary to remember that in all this the humanitarian is simply following his own mores, which he has received irrationally and which he obeys without reflection, being supported in this by the concurrence of his own group. When the social worker says, "One must not make moral judgments," she means that one must not make moral judgments of the conventional sort, but that it is perfectly all right to pass a moral judgment on the cruel judge or to hate the man who hates the negro. Often the humanitarian has all the prejudices of his society upside down, and one who talks to him is reminded that there is still "a superstition in avoiding superstition, when men think to do best when they go furthest from the superstition formerly received." Among the sociologists, those who teach so-called "attitudes courses" are particularly likely to fall into this type of confusion.

A few further complications may be noted. The humanitarian often argues for his reforms on the basis of considerations which are consonant with the organizational mores but alien to the spirit of humanitarianism; he advocates a new system of poor relief, saying that it will be cheaper, while really he is hoping that it will prove more humane. As all of us must do sometimes, in order to communicate truth he has to lie a little. Great confusion is caused in the field of criminology by shuttling back and forth between practical and humanitarian universes of discourse. Orthodox economists have recognized the humanitarian impulse in an almost perverted manner; they owlishly assure us that prevalent economic practices are not what they seem to be, but are in the long run ultra-humanitarian.

Certain implications of this interpretation of social problems on the basis of conflict in the mores seem very clear. I should venture to suggest the following points:

(1) The notion of conflict of mores enables us to understand why progress in dealing with social problems is so slow. Social problems are not solved because people do not want to solve them. From a thousand scattered sources the evidence converges upon this apparently unavoidable conclusion, from the history of reform movements, from the biographies and autobiographies of reformers, from politics, from the records of peace conferences, from the field of social work, from private discussions, and even from the debates of so-called radical groups. Even those who are most concerned about social problems are not quite at one with themselves in their desire to solve them. Solving social problems would necessitate a change in the organizational mores from which they arise. The humanitarian, for all his allegiance to the humanitarian mores, is yet a member of our society and as such is

under the sway of its organizational mores. He wishes to improve the condition of the poor, but not to interfere with private property. Until the humanitarian is willing to give up his allegiance to the organizational mores, and in some cases to run squarely against them, he must continue to treat symptoms without removing their causes.[5]

Frequently the liberal humanitarian is brought squarely up against the fact that he does not really want what he says he wants. The difficulty which he faces is that the human misery which he deplores is a necessary part of a social order which seems to him good. A cruel person may amuse himself at the expense of humanitarians by suggesting simple and effective means to secure the ends which they believe they value above all others, or a cynical person may use this device to block reform. The means suggested, if adequate to the ends, are certain to involve deep changes in our society, and their cost terrifies the humanitarian so that he feels compelled to make excuses.

When one considers the conditions under which the humanitarian impulse comes to expression, he must realize that the urge to do something for others is not a very important determinant of change in our society, for any translation of humanitarianism into behavior is fenced in by restrictions which usually limit it to trivialities. The expression of humanitarian sentiments must remain almost wholly verbal, and because of this situation which is inherent in our acquisitive and possessive society: No one loses by giving verbal expression to humanitarianism or by the merely verbal expression of another, but many would lose by putting humanitarianism into practice, and someone would certainly lose by any conceivable reform. From the powerful someone who is certain to lose comes opposition to reform.

For the person who makes his living by practicing humanitarianism, the professional social worker, there is small opportunity to participate in social change in any important or fundamental way. The private agency depends for its support upon voluntary contributions, and the contributions of the rich greatly outweigh those of everyone else. The social worker earnestly follows the humanitarian mores, and passes value judgments upon conditions of human life which originate from the organizational mores, but he dares not attack those organizational mores directly and effectively, for the people who pay his salary and in

---

[5] Frank makes his intelligent Martian say: "If it is not indelicate of me to remark, every social problem you describe seems to have the same characteristics as every other social problem, namely, the crux of the problem is to find some way of avoiding the undesirable consequences of your established laws, institutions, and social practices, without changing those established laws, etc. In other words, you appear to be seeking a way to cultivate the flower without the fruit, which, in a world of cause and effect is somewhat difficult, to say the least." (*Op. cit.,* p. 467.)

countless ways assist him in his work of mercy are the persons who
profit from the continuation of things as they are.

(2) The conflict of motives with which we face social problems produces a lack of wholeness in our mental processes concerning them.
Although sociologists have studied social problems for many years, they
have produced astonishingly little systematic thought concerning them.
Sociologists have displayed a considerable tendency to take over the
formulations of social workers. Let us attempt a brief critical analysis
of the mental product of the social worker. The mental processes of
social workers as a group may perhaps be described as aim-inhibited.
The profession lacks a philosophy, and lacks it precisely because some
generations of social workers have defined their task narrowly in terms
of a half-understood interaction of conflicting sets of mores. When one
has accustomed himself to the thought that he can carry any proposed
scheme only a certain distance, when one has formed the habit of
breaking off any action, or speech, or thought, when it reaches a point
where it may offend someone important, he loses the faculty of carrying mental processes through to completion. The task determines the
content and organization of the mind to a considerable degree; the
task which the social worker sets for his intelligence is to work for
social amelioration and yet remain within the bounds of the basic
mores. He must, therefore, keep his mental processes fragmentary.
Other characteristics betray the useful inability of even very intelligent
social workers to draw obvious conclusions. There is overemphasis of
the individual causes of poverty. There is the tendency to regard social
problems as the problems of poor people exclusively. Euphemisms be-
cloud the premises and the conclusions of the social worker to an
amazing degree, and only a few of the boldest escape the tendency to
speak in riddles. The function of these euphemisms is of course to
prevent another from drawing for the social worker the conclusion
which he so carefully avoids stating. Following those fads which always
flourish where a basic philosophy is lacking, social workers seize upon
various harmless proposals—case work, psychiatry, social security, and
other assorted brands of salvationism—and magnify their importance
until they seem like things worth dying for.

(3) The humanitarian and organizational mores are somewhat in
conflict with one another, but they are also related in another way.
These two sets of mores are complementary parts of the same culture
configuration, related parts of a single organic whole. The organizational mores produce conditions which call the humanitarian spirit
into activity; at the same time humanitarianism takes care of certain
exigencies in such a way as to decrease the probability of sudden, vio-

lent changes in the organizational mores; the "pathos manipulation," to employ the phraseology of a colleague, of the social worker and the reformer enables the existing culture configuration to persist unbroken. Here we are brought sharply up against the inescapable problems of value which are implicit in the evolution-revolution antithesis.

*   *   *

Almost everything that has been said or written concerning social problems has been oriented from the point of view of the humanitarian mores. Making use of one verbal trick or another, sociologists have found excuses for importing into our science almost the whole of the humanitarian ideology with all its self-contradictions and illogicalities. Such practices give color to the belief that sociologists are "fake professors of a pretended science." Pretended scientists have lost themselves in the mazy interrelations of the humanitarian and the organizational mores, when they should have been following a third set of mores, the scientific. The duty of one who wishes to adhere to the scientific morality is clear enough. He must study the processes of social change of which the struggles to deal with social problems are a part. The scientist must completely eschew all moral judgments, those which emanate from humanitarianism as well as others.[6] He must completely subordinate all other values to that of intellectual and scientific integrity.

The urge for social betterment is itself a part of the dialectic of social change which the sociologist sets out to study. The sociologist must investigate the growth and functioning of the humanitarian mores, as well as the operation of those mores from which the conditions which we call social problems result. He must trace the complex patterns of facilitation and interference which characterize the interaction of these mores. He must discover the long run as well as the short run interactions of humanitarianism and individualism, and ascertain to what extent they tend to interpenetrate. He must study the cultural and psychological background of reformers. He must attempt to forge a really comprehensive theory of social change; he must

[6] I am inclined to agree with Woodard that this formulation does not exclude all evaluations. Woodard argues that the scientist should not pass moral judgments (and this includes judgments emanating from the humanitarian mores), but points out that in a functional science some sort of judgment of value is not only appropriate but altogether unavoidable. He suggests that the sociologist may essay "inductive appraisals of functional appropriateness," based upon his special knowledge of social processes, of the interrelations of human beings and institutions, and his grasp of the organismic unity of society; such judgments are non-moral in nature, and are in fact the best possible safeguard against moral judgments. Cf. James W. Woodard, "Critical Notes on the Nature of Sociology as a Science," *Social Forces,* 11, Oct. 1932, 28–43.

do more fundamental thinking than has yet been done as to the relative importance of compromise and of intransigent struggle in social change.

ANOMALIES OF SELF-CONSCIOUSNESS

B Y

JOSIAH ROYCE

IN its inner aspects and relations, what we mean by self-consciousness, in any one man, is an enormously complex function or rather a little world of functions. But this world of functions is centred about certain well known habits and experiences which at once serve, not to explain it, but in a measure to begin for us the definition of our problem. There are, namely, in any mature person, certain established motor habits, which, according as they appear to be intact or not, enable us at once to test, from without, the relative normality of whatever belongs to that which one may call the mere routine of an individual's self-consciousness. There are also certain inner experiences, in terms of which the normal individual himself, from moment to moment, can feel assured of the apparent naturalness of his own notion or estimate of himself. A mature man whose self-consciousness is normal, if his means of expressing himself are intact, must be able to explain "who he is," *i. e.*, he must be able to tell his name, his business, his general relations in life, and whatever else would be essential to the practical purpose of identifying him. Furthermore, his account of himself must be able to show an estimate by no means adequate or infallible, but at least not too wildly absurd, of his actual degree of social dignity, of his personal importance and of his physical capacity. He will to be sure quite normally estimate his value, his prowess, or even his social rank, not, in general, precisely as his fellows do. But this sort of estimate has its normal, if rather wide, limits of error. If these limits are passed, the man's account of himself proves the presence of a derangement of self-consciousness. Finally, as to this account which the normal man can give of himself, he must show a certain degree of correctness as to what he can tell us of his body and of its present state. Here, of course, the limits of error are very wide, but are still pretty definite. A man is normally a very poor judge of his internal bodily states. But if he says

Abridged from: Royce, Josiah. "Some Observations on the Anomalies of Self-consciousness." *Psychological Review*, 1895, 2, 433–457.

he is made of glass, or that he is aware that he is a mile high, or that he is conscious of having no body at all, we recognize a disorder involving alterations of self-consciousness.

Within his own mind, meanwhile, and from his own point of view, a man normally self-conscious is more or less aware of a great deal about himself of which it is notoriously hard for him to give any exact account whatever. Yet this internally normal self-consciousness has, at any time, a definitive, if not easily definable content, which, in its relatively inexpressible complexity of constitution, far transcends what one expresses when he tells you his name, his place in life, his degree, or his notion of his bodily condition. This normal inner self-consciousness involves, in the first place, what we are now accustomed to call, from a psychological point of view, masses of somewhat vaguely localized bodily sensations, which, just in so far as they affect our general consciousness, are not sharply differentiated from one another. Moreover, the visual perception of the body, the auditory experiences of the sound of one's own voice, and yet other sensory contents, including the more general sensations of bodily movement, obviously determine, now more, and now less, the content or the coloring of normal self-consciousness. If any of these masses of sensory contents are suddenly altered, our immediate self-consciousness may be much changed thereby. Dizziness, sensations of oppression in the head, a general sense of bodily ill-being, a flushed face, a ringing in the ears,—any of these may involve what we primarily take to be a general alteration of our feeling of self, and only secondarily distinguish from the self as a separate and localized group of experiences. In general, the more sharply we localize our sensations, and the more we refer them to external objects, the less do these sensory experiences blend into our total immediate feeling of ourselves. The localized or objectified sensory state appears as something foreign, as coming to us, as besetting us, or as otherwise affecting us, but not as being a part of the self; and only a relatively philosophical reflection regards even our perceptions as part of ourselves. Our more naive self-consciousness tends to regard the sensory or immediate self as a vague whole, from which one separates one's definite experiences of this place on the skin, of this color or tone, or of this outer object.

Yet our inner notion of the self of self-consciousness is by no means confined to this cruder apperception of massive sensory contents. In addition, our normal mature awareness of who and what we are means what one may call a collection of feelings of inner control, of self-possession, or, as many would say, of spontaneity. If such feelings begin to be altered or lost, one complains of confusion, of a sense of self-estrangement, of helplessness, of deadness, of mental automatism, or of a divided personality. As a fact, since the associative processes always depend upon the conditions of which we are not conscious, our sense that we can and do rule our whole current train of conscious states is, as it is ordinarily felt, a fallacious sense. But if we cannot really predetermine, in consciousness, what idea shall next come to consciousness, but are dependent, even in the clearest thinking, upon the happy support of our associative mechanism, it is still normal to feel as if, on the whole, our inner process were, in certain respects, relatively spontaneous, i. e., as if it were controlled by our ruling interests and by our volition. This sense of inner self-possession is, to be sure, an extremely delicate and unstable affair, and is constantly interfered with, in the most normal life, not only by a series of uncontrollable sensory novelties, due to the external world, but by baffling variations, either in the play of our impulses and ideal associations, or in the tone of our emotions, or in both. Yet, when we are alert, these little interferences continually arise only to be subordinated. If this rule no longer holds of our inner life, then our self-consciousness begins to vary, and we suffer from confusion or from other forms of the sense of lost inner control.

Thus the self of ordinary self-consciousness appears at once as a relatively stable group of unlocalized sensory contents or contents of feeling, and as the apparent controller of the train of associated ideas, impulses, and acts of attention or of choice. Of course these two aspects of the self are closely related. It is the associative potency of the ruling feelings and interests that most secures the fact and the sense of inner self-control. But meanwhile the self also seems, or may seem, to its possessor, much larger than any group of facts or of functions now present. One notoriously regards the present self as only the representative of a self which has been present, in the remembered past of our lives, and which will be present in the expected future to which we look forward. Nor does self-consciousness usually cease with this view. The characters, attributes, functions, or other organic constituents of the self commonly extend, from our own point of view, decidedly beyond anything that can be directly presented in any series of our isolated inner experiences, however extended. When one is vain, one's self-consciousness involves the notion that one's self really exists, in some way or other, for the thoughts and estimates of others, and is at least worthy, if not the possessor, of their praise or of their envy. When one feels guilty, one does not and cannot abstract from the conceived presence of one's self in and for the experience of a real or ideal judge of one's guilt. In all such cases the self of self-consciousness thus appears as something that it would not and could not be were there not others in the world to behold, or to estimate it, to be led or otherwise influenced by it, or to appeal to it. It is now from such points of view that the self of self-consciousness comes, in the end, to get form as a being who takes himself to have a social position, an office, a profession,—in brief, a vast group of functions without which the self would appear itself to be, relatively speaking, a mere cipher, while these functions are at once regarded as organically joined to the self, and centered in it, and, nevertheless, are unintelligible unless one goes beyond one's private consciousness, and takes account of the ideas and estimates of other people.

Every normal man thus knows what it means to be a person with a social position, or a dignity, or a place in the world, or a character, a person vain of himself, or ashamed of himself, or socially confident or timid about himself, or otherwise disposed to view himself either as others seem to view him, or as he fancies that they ought to view him, or as he has faith that God views him. And such a view of one's self cannot be satisfied with any group of inner facts, however extensive, as containing within it the whole of one's ego. This view conceives the office, calling, dignity, worth, position, as at once a possession, or a real aspect, of the self, and as a possession or an aspect that would vanish from the world were not the self conceived as existing for others besides itself, in other words, were not the self conceived as having an exterior as well as an interior form of existence.

The self of normal self-consciousness, then, is felt at any moment as this relatively stable group of inner states; it is also felt or conceived as the supposed spontaneous controller of the general or of the principal current of successive conscious states; it is remembered or expected as the past or future self, which is taken to be somehow more or less precisely the same as the present self; and finally, it is viewed as having a curious collection of exterior functions that involve its actual value, potency, prowess, reputation, or office, in its external social relations to other actual or ideal selves, e. g., to its neighbors, to humanity at large, or, in case one's faith extends so far, to God.

And, now, just as the immediate self of the mass of inner sensations and feelings can vary, or just as the self of the sense of self-control can be more or less pathologically altered; so too the identical or persistent self of memory can be confused, divided, or lost, in morbid conditions; and so too finally, the self of the social type of self-consciousness is subject to very familiar forms of diseased variation. The social self above all can come to be the object of a morbidly depressed or exalted inner estimate. One's social prowess, position, office and other relations can be conceived in the most extravagantly false fashions. And furthermore, as I wish at once to point out, the most noteworthy alterations of self-consciousness, in insanities involving delusions of suspicion, of

persecution and of grandeur, appear upon their very surface as pathological variations of the social aspect of self-consciousness. Note at once
the possible significance of this fact. However you explain delusions of
guilt, of suspicion, of persecution and of grandeur, however much you
refer their source to altered sensory or emotional states, they stand before you, when once they are well developed, as variations of the
patient's habits of estimating his relations to other selves. They involve, then, *maladies of the social consciousness.* The theoretical significance of this fact surely seems worthy of a closer consideration than
it customarily receives.

In the foregoing sketch, I have been simply reporting familiar psychological phenomena. That our human self-consciousness involves all
these various elements, is, one may say, agreed. The problem is, how
have all these elements come thus to hang together? And so we next
have to attack the central problem just mentioned, *i. e.,* we have to
ask, in a purely psychological sense: How does this elaborate mental
product called self-consciousness get formed out of these numerous
elements and why, when once formed, is it so variable, and, finally,
why, when it varies, does it vary in the directions so frequently re-
ported?

It is here that our theoretical knowledge is at present so poor. The
collection of observed facts is, to be sure, at present, considerable.
Readers of Ribot's book on the "Diseases of Personality," know of the
general types of varying self-consciousness to which attention has been
most attracted. Loss of the sense of personality; or again, the delusion
that one is dead, or is lost, or is an automaton; or the feeling or idea
that there is a foreign or other self within one; or the attribution of
one's own thoughts, or acts, to another and wholly external person or
persons; or the alternation or the apparently actual multiplication of
one's own personality; or the refusal to regard one's present self as
identical with one's past self: such are some of the variations to which
self-consciousness is subject, in addition to the before-mentioned alterations of the obviously social type of self-consciousness. But when we
ask why any of these alterations takes place, we have so far only one
unquestionable, but theoretically inadequate answer, viz.: In all such
cases there are alterations of the common sensibility, or of the memory,
or of both. Now one sees, without doubt, that self-consciousness involves the common sensibility, in the sense before indicated. One sees
then that if this core of normally stable, vaguely localized sensory conditions and feelings gets altered, one's notion of one's self may also
naturally change. And, not to leave the limits of ordinary experience,
one knows and understands what it means to say, when these central
masses of feeling do more or less change: "I feel queer; I feel altered; I

am no longer quite myself; I am not my old self." By a little stretch of imagination one can also understand such a delusion as "I am made of glass," quite as well as one can understand any other delusion. For here our dreams help us to see our way, and we have only to suppose that a certain association of ideas, whereby a partial anæsthesia gets interpreted, becomes fixed, and exclusive, in order to see how the delusions as to bodily condition or constitution, present in a measure in all hypochondriacs, can assume such extreme forms. Just so too the mere assertion "I am lost," or "I am dead," is, on the face of it, just an insistent verbal statement, or at best an inner judgment whose exclusive presence in consciousness is due merely to morbid habit, and whose meaning or logical consequences we often need not suppose the patient to develop in any delusionally definite form at all. These phenomena involve, where they are alone, or are segregated from the rest of the patient's life, rather pathological simplifications of the contents of consciousness, morbid associations of sensations with simple groups of words or of ideas, than any other processes. So far, then, we see some light.

But now the case is otherwise when one says: "There are two of me," and proceeds actively to develop the consequences of this inner variety of self. Here, to be sure, the phenomena of dreams, and of the commoner forms of transient delirium, as in fevers, bring this sort of doubleness within the remembered experience of very many persons; and familiar moral and poetical statements about the two selves or more that dwell in one's breast, assimilate such experiences to those of normal people. But one's consciousness, in such cases, throws little direct light upon how the phenomena arise. Sometimes, to be sure, in delirium their basis is plainly hallucinatory, as when a fever patient sees himself, in bodily presence, standing at a distance, or lying in the bed. But even then one wishes for more light as to the question whether and how such a tendency to pathological duplication has any natural foundation in the understood habits of normal life. This problem seems even the more insistent when one observes that the sense of the inwardly doubled personality often arises without any obvious basis in hallucinations of the special senses. But in such cases, our present theories often fall back again upon the variations of the common sensibility. Yet here one fails to see how any easily conceivable alteration in the contents of the central core of the sensory self is by itself sufficient to explain a tendency to apperceive that self as double. One does not doubt the existence, in such cases, of an altered common sensibility; what one fails to follow is the link between such alteration, and the new habits, of judgment, or of apperception, which tend to get formed upon this basis.

But I do not wish to burden you with a mere enumeration of problems, and I will not here further dwell upon the inadequacies of the current theories of the factors of self-consciousness, whether these theories lay stress upon the common sensibility, or upon the memory, as the principal factor in their explanations of the variations of the ego. It is only necessary to show that, while both the common sensibility and the memory are certainly largely concerned in the constitution of the self, the problem of self-consciousness is not thus to be fully solved. One must look to other factors as well. One has in fact only to remember that some large alterations of the common sensibility seem to involve very little change of self-consciousness at all, in order to see how complex the problem is.

And now, as to the real problem itself, it is surely one relating to the origin, to the nature and to the variations, of a certain important collection of mental habits. What are these habits? How do they arise?

If a man regards himself, as this individual Ego, he always sets over against his Ego something else, viz.: some particular object represented by a portion of his conscious states, and known to him as his then present and interesting non-Ego. This psychological non-Ego, represented in one's conscious states, is of course very seldom the universe, or anything in the least abstract. And, for the rest, it is a very varying non-Ego. And now, it is very significant that our mental habits are such that the Ego of which one is conscious varies with the particular non-Ego that one then and there consciously seems to encounter. If I am in a fight, my consciously presented non-Ego is my idea of my opponent. Consequently I am then conscious of myself as of somebody fighting him. These two contents of consciousness, then, are psychologically linked. Alone, I am so far not myself. My consciousness of my Ego is a consciousness colored by my conceived relations to my endlessly changing consciousness of a non-Ego. Here, I think, lies the real key to all the variations of Self-consciousness, whether their conditions involve the common sensibility or not.

One must ask: How has one come to form all these habits of drawing a boundary, in one's consciousness, between mental states that represent a non-Ego, and mental states that clump themselves together into the central object called the Ego? One must also ask: Whence comes all this material for variation, whereby the content called the Ego shifts endlessly as the content called the non-Ego alters? And one must further inquire: How do the constitution and the variations of the Ego get that intimate relation to the sensations of the common sensibility upon which we have laid stress from the start?

Now to all these questions, as I hold, the recent study of childhood has tended to suggest at least a plausible answer. The substantial basis for the answer that I shall suggest has been reached, pretty independently, by my friend Professor Baldwin, of Princeton, and by myself. Professor Baldwin has given to some aspects of the matter, so far as concerns child life, a much fuller working out than I have done, both in his earlier papers and in his recently published book called *Mental Development in the Child and the Race*. On the other hand, in a recent discussion in the *Philosophical Review* (of Cornell) I have stated my own notions as to certain philosophically important aspects of the growth of self-consciousness. But the application of these theoretical considerations to the study of the pathological variations of self-consciousness in the present paper is, I think, new.

The early intellectual life of the child is lost to us in obscurity, despite numerous recent observations. But we are clear that the infant, in the first months of life, has nothing that we should call self-consciousness. But the first clear evidence that we get of the presence of a form of self-consciousness intelligible to us comes when the infant begins to be observantly imitative of the acts, and later of the words, of the people about it. In other words, the first Ego of the child's intelligible consciousness appears to be, in its own mind, set over against a non-Ego that, to the child, is made up of the perceived fascinating, and to its feeling more or less significant, deeds of the persons in its environment. From this time on, up to seven or eight years of age, any normal child remains persistently, although perhaps very selectively, imitative, of deeds, of habits, of games, of customs, and often of highly ideal and perhaps quite imaginary models, such as are suggested to it by fairy-stories and other such material. As one follows the growth of these imitative tendencies, from their initial and quite literal stages, through those stages of elaborate impersonation and of playful, originally colored, often enormously insistent games, in which the child follows all sorts of real and fantastic models, one is struck by the fact that any normal child leads, relatively speaking, two lives, one naive, intensely egoistic from our point of view, but relatively free from any marked self-consciousness in the child's own mind, while his other life is the life in which he develops his conscious ideas and views of himself as a person. The relatively naive life is the life of his childish appetites and passions; the relatively self-conscious life is the life of his imitations and dramatic impersonations, of his poses and devices, of his games, and of his proudly fantastic skill, and of the countless social habits and attitudes that spring up from this source. The two lives mingle and cross in all sorts of ways. But the child who merely eats, cries, and enjoys his physical well-being, is not just then self-conscious as is the child who plays horse, or hero, or doctor, or who carefully tries to follow a model as he draws, or to invent a trick as good as one that he has seen. The latter child, however, is essentially imitative, first of persons, then of ideas, then of the facts of the physical world as such. But the former child is simply the creature of natural impulses and passions, and would never come to self-consciousness, in our sense, if his life were not gradually moulded by the elaborate habits which the imitative child constantly introduces.

Now the psychological importance of imitation lies largely in the fact, that in so far as a child imitates, he gets ideas about the inner meaning or intent of the deeds that he imitates, and so gets acquainted with what he early finds to be the minds of other people. The child that repeats your words, slowly learns what they mean. The child that uses scissors, pencil, or other tools after you, learns, as he imitates, what cutting means, and what drawing, or other such doings. And as he thus learns, he gets presented to his own consciousness contents, which he regards as standing for those of your mind. The experienced interesting outcome of an imitated deed, is for the child the obvious meaning of that deed, for you, as you did it. But he does not get these contents,—these glimpses of your meaning,—he does not get them, at first, very easily. He gets them by persistently watching you, listening to you, playing with you, trying to be like you, all activities that for him involve muscular sensations, emotional concerns, and still other variations of his common sensibility. These efforts of his to grasp your meaning are marked and often delightful incidents of his consciousness. He returns over and over to his favorite games with you. He encounters every time your meaning, and he sets over against it those experiences of his own doings, whereby he comes to participate in your meaning. Here now the child always has present to him two sets of contents, both fascinating, each setting the other off sharply by contrast, while the contrast itself establishes the boundary between them. The first set of contents are his perceptions of your deeds, and his representation of your discovered meaning in these deeds. The second set of contents are his own imitative acts themselves, as perceived by himself, these acts, and his delights in them. The first set of contents depend upon you. The child feels them to be uncontrollable. As perceptions, and as representations, these contents do not get closely linked to the child's common sensibility. They stand off as external although welcome intruders. On the other hand, the other set of contents, the child's own newly discovered powers, due to his imitation, are closely centred about his common sensibility, are accompanied with all the feelings which make up the sense of control, and get remembered, thenceforth, accordingly. The first set of contents form the psychological non-Ego of this particular phase of consciousness. The second set of contents form the psychological Ego corresponding

thereto. One sees why the Ego-part of this sort of consciousness includes the common sensibility, and the sense of voluntary control, and
why the non-Ego here involves contents that are set off by the contrast as uncontrollable, and as not closely linked to the common sensibility. And it is in this contrast that the source of true self-consciousness lies. We do not observe a given group of mental contents as such
unless they are marked off by contrast from other contents. One could
have all the common sensibility you please, and all the feelings of
voluntary control, without ever coming to take note of this totality of
united or centralized mental contents as such, and as clearly different
from the rest of one's field of consciousness. Even now we all of us tend
to lose clear self-consciousness so soon as we get absorbed in any activity, such as rowing, hill-climbing, singing, whistling, looking about
us at natural scenery,—any activity I say, whose object does not, by the
sharp contrast between its own external meaning and our efforts, call
our attention to our specific relation to some non-Ego. Yet in lonely
rowing and hill-climbing the common sensibility is as richly present as
it is in many of our most watchfully self-conscious states. On the other
hand, when I work hard to make my meaning clear to another man,
or to make out what he means, I am self-conscious, just in so far as I
contrast my idea of his ways and thoughts, with my own effort to conform to his ways and thoughts. And just such an effort, just such a
contrast, seems to mediate the earliest self-consciousness of the imitative
child, and to secure the tendency of the self to be built up about the
common sensibility, while the not self gets sundered therefrom. So
then one sees the rule:—If one is keenly self-conscious, the common
sensibility must be central. But, on the other hand, one may have a
rich common sensibility without any keen self-consciousness. It is the
contrast of Ego and non-Ego that is essential to self-consciousness.

But of course the child's relations to the varying non-Ego of consciousness do not remain merely imitative. When once he has other
minds in his world, the function whose essence is the contrast between
his conceptions of these minds and his view of his own response to
them, can take as many forms as his natural instincts determine. His
naive life of appetites gets gradually infected by his conscious relations
to other people. He wants good things, and perhaps must feign affection or show politeness, or invent some other social device, to get what
he wants. Here again is an activity depending upon and bringing to
light, the contrast between his own intention, and the conceived or
perceived personal traits and whims to which he conforms his little
skill. He learns to converse, and gets a new form of the contrast between the sayings of others (which he interprets by listening), and his
own ideas and meanings. He reaches the questioning age, and now he

systematically peers into the minds of others as into an endlessly wealthy non-Ego, in whose presence he is by contrast self-conscious as an inquirer. Here, every time one has the essential element of contrast upon which all self-consciousness depends. Argument and quarreling later involve similar contrasts. As to the external physical world,—what the child shall most care for in that, is largely determined for him by his social relations. Whatever habit he has acquired by social imitation, he can, therefore, in the end, apply to things as well as to persons. As a fact he is notoriously often animistic, directly transferring social habits to physical relations, and regarding things as alive. And here again he becomes self-conscious, by contrasting his own activities with the conceived natures and meanings of external things. I do not at all suppose that the child regards all natural things in an animistic way; but I am of opinion, for reasons which I have set forth elsewhere, that our whole tendency to distinguish as sharply, as we all now do, between the self and the external physical world, is a secondary tendency, due in the child's case, to social influences. It is language, it is the accounts that people give to us of things, it is the socially acquired questioning habit,—it is such things that extend the contrast between Ego and non-Ego, at first mainly a social contrast, to the relations between one's own mind and one's physical environment.

But, to return to the explicitly social relations, there is still another factor to note in our early relations to our conceived social non-Ego. And this is the fact that, by our instinctive mental constitution as moulded by our social habits, we are early subject to a vast number of more or less secondary emotions, each one of which involves large alterations of the common sensibility, while all of these particular emotions arise under circumstances which make explicit the contrast between one's self, and one's idea of one's fellow's mind. Such emotions we get as children when people praise us, blame us, caress us, call us pet names, stare at us, call us by name, ask us questions, and otherwise appeal to us in noteworthy ways. Such emotions too we get again, in novel forms, in youth, when the subtle coloring of the emotions of sex begins to pervade our whole social life. Such emotions are shame, love, anger, pride, delight in our own bodily seeming as displayed before others, thrills of social expectation, fears of appearing ill in the eyes of others. Such emotions involve blushing, weeping, laughter, inner glow, visceral sensations of the most various kinds, and feelings of the instinctive muscular tensions related to our countless expressive social deeds. These experiences are, however, aroused by situations all of which essentially involve the aforesaid contrast between our own ideas, wishes, or meanings, and the conceived states of other minds. Hence these emotional states associate themselves, as variations of the common-sensibility, first, with social situations, *i. e.,* with cases where Ego and non-Ego are sharply contrasted; and then especially with the Ego-member of the relation of contrast. And so, altogether by the force of habit, these emotions, which if primarily aroused would be mere content, belonging neither to Ego nor to non-Ego, come to be the specific emotions of self-consciousness, so that now whenever we have just these emotions, from any cause whatever, we are at once keenly self-conscious, —and that merely because the emotions in question faintly or keenly suggest particular social situations. Emotions that have had no such constant relation to social situations, involve no such marked states of self-consciousness. Fear of physical dangers tends to diminish our self-consciousness; shame intensifies it. Yet keen physical fear, as the more primitive emotion, involves vaster commotions of the common sensibility than does shame. Were then the marked presence or variation of the common sensibility in consciousness the sole and sufficient cause of the presence or of the variation of one's immediate or sensory Ego, physical terror would make one more self-conscious than does shame. But panic fear, in its intensest conscious forms, involves rather a destruction than a positive alteration of self-consciousness; while the most abject shame grows the more intensely self-conscious as it gets the more marked. Why? Because shame, habitually associated only with social situations, suggests them even where it is pathological and is not due to them; and so it brings to consciousness the contrast of Ego and non-Ego.

Thus, then, it is that I propose to explain what the current theories of self-consciousness usually seem unable to deal with, viz., the before-mentioned fact that certain pathological variations of the common sensibility profoundly alter the tone or constitution of a patient's self-consciousness, while others, equally intimate and vast, either leave self-consciousness relatively intact, or simply put it wholly out of sight without first tampering with its integrity. When a man has the colic he does not say, "My Ego is deranged." His account of the case is far less metaphysical. But when, as in the depression after the grip, he has certain very much dimmer and more subtle alterations of the common sensibility, he may complain of precisely such a sense of alienation from himself. Why? Well, as I should say, the colic suggests no social situation; the vague depression after the grip may dimly suggest, by habit, situations of social failure, or confusion, or powerlessness, such as, from sensitive childhood until now, have played their part in one's life. The suggestion may be very faint, and utterly abstract. No particular failure, no special case of social helplessness, comes to mind. But our nascent associations can be present in all degrees of faintness; and here I maintain are associations dimly involving social contrasts between Ego and non-Ego. Here, then, are conditions for the function of self-consciousness.

Since the emotional alteration of the common sensibility has thus the most various habitual relations, now with our unsocial physical states as such, now with social activities, one sees how it is possible for a nervous sufferer to say, on one day, that he personally feels his very being wrecked, and his self-hood lost or degraded, while on another day he may simply declare that he suffers keenly, but regards the affair as a mere physical infliction, external to his central self-hood. In the physical sufferings of sensitive women this shifting of the enemy's ground from the region of the physical or psychical pain felt as a mere brute fact, hateful but still bearable, to the region where the sufferer complains of an intolerable loss of self-possession, is notoriously a common and, to the sufferer herself, a puzzling incident. Both times the common sensibility is deeply affected, often in ways not subjectively localizable; the difference, I think, must be due to the nascent associations of the common sensibility now with ideas of social situations, now with ideas of unsocial bodily events. There are some chronic neurasthenic sufferers who, despite headaches, spinal pains, and other distorted sensations innumerable, preserve for years a marvelous self-possession in face of their disorder; very many other such nervous sufferers, of the same general type, are throughout self-consciously cowardly and abject. One cannot assert that the latter class are more deranged in common sensibility than are the former. But many a neurasthenic man has really little to complain of *except* the unspeakable wretchedness of his deranged self-consciousness. How can one explain such phenomena without resort to the principles of habit and association? The social habits, however, of the type now defined, at once furnish a *vera causa* for the interpretation of some sensory disturbances as alterations of self-consciousness, while other disturbances, equally great and vague, get interpreted by the sufferer as merely external events. To be sure we cannot yet give an exhaustive classification of the variations of the common sensibility into those closely associated with social situations, and those not associated, or but slightly associated, yet the contrast of physical fear and of shame has already shown us that such a classification might, with care, be more or less worked out. We know, for instance, that the sexually tinged emotions normally have very complex social associations. Consequently, we may expect to find self-consciousness especially deranged in disorders involving the sexual functions. This expectation seems to be abundantly verified, even in ordinary cases of disorder, such as the teacher of youth may sometimes see as well as the doctor; and if one wants more verification, one may get it at will from the monumental records that fill

Krafft-Ebing's too well-known and ghastly book. On the other hand, a sufferer from the emotional states accompanying ordinary physical exhaustion, or from some forms even of grief, or from a severe cold that does not give the form of depression now associated with the grip, or from some forms of even violent headache, often wonders how much pain and emotional alteration he can endure without any proportionate alteration of self-consciousness. And these states are precisely such forms of consciousness as are not so closely associated with social situations. Finally, the emotions connected with laughter furnish an almost perfect natural experiment for our purpose. There are three principal sorts of laughter: the laughter of mere physical gleefulness, such as appears much in children, less in adults; the laughter of scorn, and the laughter of the sense of humor. The first is not an especially self-conscious affair; but the laughter of scorn and of a sense of humor are both of them always keenly self-conscious, involving what Hobbes called "sudden glory in him that laugheth." The emotions of the two latter types involve social situations, present or suggested. I shall find no time to point out at any length the application of the foregoing analysis to the study of the associative alterations of the socially tinged self-consciousness in true melancholia, in mania, or in the exaltation of general paralysis. But the mention of such alteration of the self brings us at once to the next and final stage of our inquiry.

I have so far spoken of self-consciousness as it appears in more or less explicitly social relations. But, one may reply, "Are we not, at pleasure, self-conscious when we are quite alone? Does not one reflect, does not one judge one's self? Is lonely meditation free from self-consciousness? Is not conscience a self-conscious affair? And yet in such cases does one contrast an Ego with any literal non-Ego? In such processes is not the Ego explicitly related to just the Ego, alone by itself? And are there not, in the phenomena of insanity, many alterations of this sort of purely internal self-consciousness?" I reply at once that my theory is precisely *that habits once acquired in social intercourse can and do hold over when we are alone, and can then apply within the content of one's own mind.* The transition is simple. First I can dramatically remember my actually past imitative deeds, my quarrels, my successful social feats, my chagrins, my questionings, my criticisms of others, and the bearings of others towards me. In all such cases I am self-conscious over again in memory, by virtue of our now familiar contrast-effect. Further, as just seen, my emotions can vaguely suggest social situations, indefinite in character to any degree. By coalescence, a vast group of social habits of judging others, and of feeling myself judged by them, can get woven into a complex product such as is now my conscience. Conscience is a well-knit system of socially acquired habits of estimating acts—a system so constituted as to be easily aroused into conscious presence by the coming of the idea of any hesitantly conceived act. If conscience is aroused in the presence of such a hesitant desire to act, one has, purely as a matter of social habit, a disposition to have present both the tendency to the action, and the disposition to judge it, standing to one another in the now familiar relation of Ego and non-Ego. Which one of them appears as the Ego, which the non-Ego, depends upon which most gets possession, in the field of consciousness, of the common sensibility. If the tendency to the estimated act is a passionate tendency, a vigorous temptation, and if the conscientious judgment is a coldly intellectual affair, then the situation dimly reminds me of cases where other people, authoritative and dignified rather than pleasing, have reproved my wishes. Conscience is then the colder non-Ego, the voice of humanity, or of God. My common sensibility merges with my passion. The reproof perhaps shames me; yet *I* want to have my way; only that other, that authoritative inner non-Ego, my conscience, will not let me go free. But if, on the other hand, the conceived act is less keenly desired, and if my conscientious plans are just now either fervently enthusiastic or sternly resolute in my mind, then it is my conscience which merges with my common sensibility, and I myself am now, in presence of the conceived act, as if judging another. I feel then secure in my righteousness, and I look with disdain upon that which would tempt me if I were weaker, but which now is a mere non-Ego. It is in a similar fashion, by a dramatic imitation not of actual, but of abstractly possible social relations, that I can question myself, and wait for an answer, can reflect upon my own meaning, can admire myself, love myself, hate myself, laugh at myself, in short do or suffer in presence of my own states and processes whatever social life has taught me to do or to suffer in presence of the states and processes of others. In every such case the central Ego is so much of my conscious process as tends more to merge with the common sensibility. My inner, but more peripheral, relative non-Ego is so much of my conscious process as tends more to resemble, in interest, in general tone or in uncontrollable unexpectedness, the experiences which, in ordinary social life, are due to other people. Yet since all these inner contrasts are constantly corrected by my habits of external perception and of memory, which remind me all the while of a literal non-Ego outside of all these processes, this inner sundering normally remains only, as Professor Ladd has called it, dramatic—a sort of metaphor, which I can correct at pleasure, saying at any moment, "but all this is merely Ego, after all. The real non-Ego is the world of live other people yonder."

Thus the normal inner life of reflection, of conscience, of meditation, and of the so-called "spiritual Ego" in general, is simply, in us human beings, an imitation, a brief abstract and epitome, of our literal social life. We have no habits of self-consciousness which are not derived from social habits, counterparts thereof. Where the analogy of our relations to our fellows ceases, reflection ceases also. And this is precisely what constitutes the limitation of our reflective processes in philosophy and in psychology.

But surely, if this summarizes the conditions of our normal self-consciousness, when we are thinking alone, it also gives room for indefinitely numerous abnormal variations. Suppose that there appear in the conscious field hallucinations of the muscular sense, of the sort so well described in Cramer's noted monograph. Let these be motor speech hallucinations. Then the patient may observe the puzzling phenomenon that, whenever he thinks, there is some mysterious tendency present that aims to objectify his thoughts, in spoken words. Somebody or something either takes his own thoughts away from him and speaks them, or forces him, willy nilly, to speak them himself. The thoughts are his own. The sounding of them forth, in this way, is not his. His thoughts run off his tongue, get spoken in his stomach, creak out in his shoes as he walks, are mockingly echoed or in the end commented upon by another power. This other power, this stealing of his thoughts, involves of course a deep disturbance of his self-consciousness, which tends gradually to pass over into a regular system of delusions. Yet what does the process mean? It means, at first, merely the appearance of uncontrollable elements of consciousness, which by virtue of the habits connected with the uncontrollable in general cannot get merged in the common sensibility, and which are yet in a problematic and painfully intimate relation to what he does recognize as his own. This foreign power need not for a good while behave *enough* like the true voice of another to become a genuine hallucinatory comrade or enemy, as it would do and does if the patient hears his voices without of himself recognizing their close relation to his stream of thought. But in this uncontrollable hallucinatory thinking aloud there is enough suggestion of the foreign to make the patient feel that his own thoughts are getting somehow estranged from him. That these are his own thoughts he at first knows, by virtue of the general contrasts between real Ego and real non-Ego still present to him. That they are getting estranged he knows, for that is to any one a relative non-Ego which behaves more or less as one's original social non-Ego, one's fellow in society, behaves. His behaviour is relatively uncontrollable; and so is here that of the patient's thoughts.

Or again, suppose that one's depressed emotional condition, as in melancholia, or at the outset of a delirium of suspicion or of persecution, contains emotions resembling the normal emotions of conscientious guilt, or the feeling of social dread. Then these feelings tend to assimilate in one's actual surroundings, or in one's memories, data which suggest, to one patient an actually believed social condemnation of his deeds, or an actual judgment of his inner conscience passed upon his sinfulness, while to another patient his own sorts of emotion suggest an especially hostile scrutiny of his appearance by the passers by, or an inner sense that he must hide from possible scrutiny. On the other hand, feelings quite the reverse of these suggest to the exalted general paralytic whatever remembered or fancied social relations, expressing his vast powers, the fragments of left-over social habits which still survive in his chaos permit him, in passing, to express.

Or, once more, another patient has present to consciousness two or more streams of feelings, impulses, thoughts, which are sharply contrasted with one another, while the portions of each stream more or less hang together, by virtue of common contents or tone. All of these streams belong to his general Ego,—this he recognizes by the normal contrast with the actual external world. But meanwhile they have their inner contrast, which is no longer, like the just mentioned contrasts in normal consciousness, a source of merely dramatic metaphor. This abnormal contrast is intense, uncontrollable, continuous. Now let the reflections or the context of these streams be such as in any fashion to remind the patient of any social relation, contest, rivalry, quarrel, criticism, pity, questioning, discussion; and then the patient can only say: "There are in me two or more selves, I am divided." If one of the streams involves more of the common sensibility than does the others, or more of the sense of control, the patient may speak of the less favored streams as other selves, or as the "Other Fellow" without having any full-fledged delusions of a real outside oppressor. And in all this there will be mere associations of ideas, mere socially acquired habits,—no new mysteries of self-hood whatever.

SOCIAL INTEGRATION AND SUICIDE

B Y

E M I L E   D U R K H E I M

WE have successively set up the three following propositions:

Suicide varies inversely with the degree of integration of religious society.

Suicide varies inversely with the degree of integration of domestic society.

Suicide varies inversely with the degree of integration of political society.

This grouping shows that whereas these different societies have a moderating influence upon suicide, this is due not to special characteristics of each but to a characteristic common to all. Religion does not owe its efficacy to the special nature of religious sentiments, since domestic and political societies both produce the same effects when strongly integrated. This, moreover, we have already proved when studying directly the manner of action of different religions upon suicide. Inversely, it is not the specific nature of the domestic or political tie which can explain the immunity they confer, since religious society has the same advantage. The cause can only be found in a single quality possessed by all these social groups, though perhaps to varying degrees. The only quality satisfying this condition is that they are all strongly integrated social groups. So we reach the general conclusion: suicide varies inversely with the degree of integration of the social groups of which the individual forms a part.

But society cannot disintegrate without the individual simultaneously detaching himself from social life, without his own goals becoming preponderant over those of the community, in a word without his personality tending to surmount the collective personality. The more weakened the groups to which he belongs, the less he depends on them, the more he consequently depends only on himself and recognizes no other rules of conduct than what are founded on his private interests. If we agree to call this state egoism, in which the

Abridged from: Durkheim, Emile, *Suicide: A Study in Sociology* (translated by George Simpson), Glencoe, Illinois: The Free Press, 1951.

individual ego asserts itself to excess in the face of the social ego and at its expense, we may call egoistic the special type of suicide springing from excessive individualism.

But how can suicide have such an origin?

First of all, it can be said that, as collective force is one of the obstacles best calculated to restrain suicide, its weakening involves a development of suicide. When society is strongly integrated, it holds individuals under its control, considers them at its service and thus forbids them to dispose wilfully of themselves. Accordingly it opposes their evading their duties to it through death. But how could society impose its supremacy upon them when they refuse to accept this subordination as legitimate? It no longer then possesses the requisite authority to retain them in their duty if they wish to desert; and conscious of its own weakness, it even recognizes their right to do freely what it can no longer prevent. So far as they are the admitted masters of their destinies, it is their privilege to end their lives. They, on their part, have no reason to endure life's sufferings patiently. For they cling to life more resolutely when belonging to a group they love, so as not to betray interests they put before their own. The bond that unites them with the common cause attaches them to life and the lofty goal they envisage prevents their feeling personal troubles so deeply. There is, in short, in a cohesive and animated society a constant interchange of ideas and feelings from all to each and each to all, something like a mutual moral support, which instead of throwing the individual on his own resources, leads him to share in the collective energy and supports his own when exhausted.

But these reasons are purely secondary. Excessive individualism not only results in favoring the action of suicidogenic causes, but it is itself such a cause. It not only frees man's inclination to do away with himself from a protective obstacle, but creates this inclination out of whole cloth and thus gives birth to a special suicide which bears its mark. This must be clearly understood for this is what constitutes the special character of the type of suicide just distinguished and justifies the name we have given it. What is there then in individualism that explains this result?

It has been sometimes said that because of his psychological constitution, man cannot live without attachment to some object which transcends and survives him, and that the reason for this necessity is a need we must have not to perish entirely. Life is said to be intolerable unless some reason for existing is involved, some purpose justifying life's trials. The individual alone is not a sufficient end for his activity. He is too little. He is not only hemmed in spatially; he is also strictly limited temporally. When, therefore, we have no other object than ourselves we cannot avoid the thought that our efforts will finally end in nothingness, since we ourselves disappear. But annihilation terrifies us. Under these conditions one would lose courage to live, that is, to act and struggle, since nothing will remain of our exertions. The state of egoism, in other words, is supposed to be contradictory to human nature and, consequently, too uncertain to have chances of permanence.

In this absolute formulation the proposition is vulnerable. If the thought of the end of our personality were really so hateful, we could consent to live only by blinding ourselves voluntarily as to life's value. For if we may in a measure avoid the prospect of annihilation we cannot extirpate it; it is inevitable, whatever we do. We may push back the frontier for some generations, force our name to endure for some years or centuries longer than our body; a moment, too soon for most men, always comes when it will be nothing. For the groups we join in order to prolong our existence by their means are themselves mortal; they too must dissolve, carrying with them all our deposit of ourselves. Those are few whose memories are closely enough bound to the very history of humanity to be assured of living until its death. So, if we really thus thirsted after immortality, no such brief perspectives could ever appease us. Besides, what of us is it that lives? A word, a sound, an imperceptible trace, most often anonymous,[1] therefore nothing comparable to the violence of our efforts or able to justify them to us. In actuality, though a child is naturally an egoist who feels not the slightest craving to survive himself, and the old man is very often a child in this and so many other respects, neither ceases to cling to life as much or more than the adult; indeed we have seen that suicide is very rare for the first fifteen years and tends to decrease at the other extreme of life. Such too is the case with animals, whose psychological constitution differs from that of men only in degree. It is therefore untrue that life is only possible by its possessing its rationale outside of itself.

Indeed, a whole range of functions concern only the individual; these are the ones indispensable for physical life. Since they are made for this purpose only, they are perfected by its attainment. In everything concerning them, therefore, man can act reasonably without thought of transcendental purposes. These functions serve by merely serving him. In so far as he has no other needs, he is therefore self-sufficient and can live happily with no other objective than living. This

---

[1] We say nothing of the ideal protraction of life involved in the belief in immortality of the soul, for (1) this cannot explain why the family or attachment to political society preserves us from suicide; and (2) it is not even this belief which forms religion's prophylactic influence, as we have shown above.

is not the case, however, with the civilized adult. He has many ideas, feelings and practices unrelated to organic needs. The roles of art, morality, religion, political faith, science itself are not to repair organic exhaustion nor to provide sound functioning of the organs. All this supra-physical life is built and expanded not because of the demands of the cosmic environment but because of the demands of the social environment. The influence of society is what has aroused in us the sentiments of sympathy and solidarity drawing us toward others; it is society which, fashioning us in its image, fills us with religious, political and moral beliefs that control our actions. To play our social role we have striven to extend our intelligence and it is still society that has supplied us with tools for this development by transmitting to us its trust fund of knowledge.

Through the very fact that these superior forms of human activity have a collective origin, they have a collective purpose. As they derive from society they have reference to it; rather they are society itself incarnated and individualized in each one of us. But for them to have a raison d'etre in our eyes, the purpose they envisage must be one not indifferent to us. We can cling to these forms of human activity only to the degree that we cling to society itself. Contrariwise, in the same measure as we feel detached from society we become detached from that life whose source and aim is society. For what purpose do these rules of morality, these precepts of law binding us to all sorts of sacrifices, these restrictive dogmas exist, if there is no being outside us whom they serve and in whom we participate? What is the purpose of science itself? If its only use is to increase our chances for survival, it does not deserve the trouble it entails. Instinct acquits itself better of this role; animals prove this. Why substitute for it a more hesitant and uncertain reflection? What is the end of suffering, above all? If the value of things can only be estimated by their relation to this positive evil for the individual, it is without reward and incomprehensible. This problem does not exist for the believer firm in his faith or the man strongly bound by ties of domestic or political society. Instinctively and unreflectively they ascribe all that they are and do, the one to his Church or his God, the living symbol of the Church, the other to his family, the third to his country or party. Even in their sufferings they see only a means of glorifying the group to which they belong and thus do homage to it. So, the Christian ultimately desires and seeks suffering to testify more fully to his contempt for the flesh and more fully resemble his divine model. But the more the believer doubts, that is, the less he feels himself a real participant in the religious faith to which he belongs, and from which he is freeing himself; the more the family and community become foreign to the individual, so much the more does he become a mystery to himself, unable to escape the exasperating and agonizing question: to what purpose?

If, in other words, as has often been said, man is double, that is because social man superimposes himself upon physical man. Social man necessarily presupposes a society which he expresses and serves. If this dissolves, if we no longer feel it in existence and action about and above us, whatever is social in us is deprived of all objective foundation. All that remains is an artificial combination of illusory images, a phantasmagoria vanishing at the least reflection; that is, nothing which can be a goal for our action. Yet this social man is the essence of civilized man; he is the masterpiece of existence. Thus we are bereft of reasons for existence; for the only life to which we could cling no longer corresponds to anything actual; the only existence still based upon reality no longer meets our needs. Because we have been initiated into a higher existence, the one which satisfies an animal or a child can satisfy us no more and the other itself fades and leaves us helpless. So there is nothing more for our efforts to lay hold of, and we feel them lose themselves in emptiness. In this sense it is true to say that our activity needs an object transcending it. We do not need it to maintain ourselves in the illusion of an impossible immortality; it is implicit in our moral constitution and cannot be even partially lost without this losing its raison d'etre in the same degree. No proof is needed that in such a state of confusion the least cause of discouragement may easily give birth to desperate resolutions. If life is not worth the trouble of being lived, everything becomes a pretext to rid ourselves of it.

But this is not all. This detachment occurs not only in single individuals. One of the constitutive elements of every national temperament consists of a certain way of estimating the value of existence. There is a collective as well as an individual humor inclining peoples to sadness or cheerfulness, making them see things in bright or sombre lights. In fact, only society can pass a collective opinion on the value of human life; for this the individual is incompetent. The latter knows nothing but himself and his own little horizon; thus his experience is too limited to serve as a basis for a general appraisal. He may indeed consider his own life to be aimless; he can say nothing applicable to others. On the contrary, without sophistry, society may generalize its own feeling as to itself, its state of health or lack of health. For individuals share too deeply in the life of society for it to be diseased without their suffering infection. What it suffers they necessarily suffer. Because it is the whole, its ills are communicated to its parts. Hence it cannot disintegrate without awareness that the regular conditions of general existence are equally disturbed. Because society is the end on which our better selves depend, it cannot feel us escaping it without a simultaneous realization that our activity is purposeless. Since we are its handiwork, society cannot be conscious of its own decadence without the feeling that henceforth this work is of no value. Thence are formed currents of depression and disillusionment emanating from no particular individual but expressing society's state of disintegration. They reflect the relaxation of social bonds, a sort of collective asthenia, or social malaise, just as individual sadness, when chronic, in its way reflects the poor organic state of the individual. Then metaphysical and religious systems spring up which, by reducing these obscure sentiments to formulae, attempt to prove to men the senselessness of life and that it is self-deception to believe that it has purpose. Then new moralities originate which, by elevating facts to ethics, commend suicide or at least tend in that direction by suggesting a minimal existence. On their appearance they seem to have been created out of whole cloth by their makers who are sometimes blamed for the pessimism of their doctrines. In reality they are an effect rather than a cause; they merely symbolize in abstract language and systematic form the physiological distress of the body social.[2] As these currents are collective, they have, by virtue of their origin, an authority which they impose upon the individual and they drive him more vigorously on the way to which he is already inclined by the state of moral distress directly aroused in him by the disintegration of society. Thus, at the very moment that, with excessive zeal, he frees himself from the social environment, he still submits to its influence. However individualized a man may be, there is always something collective remaining—the very depression and melancholy resulting from this same exaggerated individualism. He effects communion through sadness when he no longer has anything else with which to achieve it.

Hence this type of suicide well deserves the name we have given it. Egoism is not merely a contributing factor in it; it is its generating cause. In this case the bond attaching man to life relaxes because that attaching him to society is itself slack. The incidents of private life which seem the direct inspiration of suicide and are considered its determining causes are in reality only incidental causes. The individual yields to the slightest shock of circumstance because the state of society has made him a ready prey to suicide.

Several facts confirm this explanation. Suicide is known to be rare among children and to diminish among the aged at the last confines of life; physical man, in both, tends to become the whole of man. Society is still lacking in the former, for it has not had the time to

[2] This is why it is unjust to accuse these theorists of sadness of generalizing personal impressions. They are the echo of a general condition.

form him in its image; it begins to retreat from the latter or, what amounts to the same thing, he retreats from it. Thus both are more self-sufficient. Feeling a lesser need for self-completion through something not themselves, they are also less exposed to feel the lack of what is necessary for living. The immunity of an animal has the same causes. We likewise see that, though lower societies practice a form of suicide of their own, the one we have just discussed is almost unknown to them. Since their social life is very simple, the social inclinations of individuals are simple also and thus they need little for satisfaction. They readily find external objectives to which they become attached. If he can carry with him his gods and his family, primitive man, everywhere that he goes, has all that his social nature demands.

THE IDEAL OF SOCIAL INTEGRATION

B Y

GEORGE H. MEAD

A HIGHLY developed and organized human society is one in which the individual members are interrelated in a multiplicity of different intricate and complicated ways whereby they all share a number of common social interests,—interests in, or for the betterment of, the society—and yet, on the other hand, are more or less in conflict relative to numerous other interests which they possess only individually, or else share with one another only in small and limited groups. Conflicts among individuals in a highly developed and organized human society are not mere conflicts among their respective primitive impulses but are conflicts among their respective selves or personalities, each with its definite social structure—highly complex and organized and unified —and each with a number of different social facets or aspects, a number of different sets of social attitudes constituting it. Thus, within such a society, conflicts arise between different aspects or phases of the same individual self (conflicts leading to cases of split personality when they are extreme or violent enough to be psychopathological), as well as between different individual selves. And both these types of individual conflict are settled or terminated by reconstructions of the particular social situations, and modifications of the given framework

Abridged from: Mead, George H. (edited by Charles W. Morris), *Mind, Self and Society,* Chicago: University of Chicago Press, 1934. Reprinted by permission of the University of Chicago Press.

of social relationships, wherein they arise or occur in the general human social life-process—these reconstructions and modifications being performed, as we have said, by the minds of the individuals in whose experience or between whose selves these conflicts take place.

Mind, as constructive or reflective or problem-solving thinking, is the socially acquired means or mechanism or apparatus whereby the human individual solves the various problems of environmental adjustment which arise to confront him in the course of his experience, and which prevent his conduct from proceeding harmoniously on its way, until they have thus been dealt with. And mind or thinking is also— as possessed by the individual members of human society—the means or mechanism or apparatus whereby social reconstruction is effected or accomplished by these individuals. For it is their possession of minds or power of thinking which enables human individuals to turn back critically, as it were, upon the organized social structure of the society to which they belong (and from their relations to which their minds are in the first instance derived), and to reorganize or reconstruct or modify that social structure to a greater or less degree, as the exigencies of social evolution from time to time require. Any such social reconstruction, if it is to be at all far-reaching, presupposes a basis of common social interests shared by all the individual members of the given human society in which that reconstruction occurs; shared, that is, by all the individuals whose minds must participate in, or whose minds bring about, that reconstruction. And the way in which any such social reconstruction is actually effected by the minds of the individuals involved is by a more or less abstract intellectual extension of the boundaries of the given society to which these individuals all belong, and which is undergoing the reconstruction—an extension resulting in a larger social whole in terms of which the social conflicts that necessitate the reconstruction of the given society are harmonized or reconciled, and by reference to which, accordingly, these conflicts can be solved or eliminated.

The changes that we make in the social order in which we are implicated necessarily involve our also making changes in ourselves. The social conflicts among the individual members of a given organized human society, which, for their removal, necessitate conscious or intelligent reconstructions and modifications of that society by those individuals, also and equally necessitate such reconstructions or modifications by those individuals of their own selves or personalities. Thus the relations between social reconstruction and self or personality reconstruction are reciprocal and internal or organic; social reconstruction by the individual members of any organized human society entails self or personality reconstruction in some degree or other by each of these individuals, and vice versa, for, since their selves or personalities are constituted by their organized social relations to one another, they cannot reconstruct those selves or personalities without also reconstructing, to some extent, the given social order, which is, of course, likewise constituted by their organized social relations to one another. In both types of reconstruction the same fundamental material of organized social relations among human individuals is involved, and is simply treated in different ways, or from different angles or points of view, in the two cases, respectively; or in short, social reconstruction and self or personality reconstruction are the two sides of a single process—the process of human social evolution. Human social progress involves the use by human individuals of their socially derived mechanism of self-consciousness, both in the effecting of such progressive social changes, and also in the development of their individual selves or personalities in such a way as adaptively to keep pace with such social reconstruction.

Ultimately and fundamentally societies develop in complexity of organization only by means of the progressive achievement of greater and greater degrees of functional, behavioristic differentiation among the individuals who constitute them; these functional, behavioristic differentiations among the individual members implying or presupposing initial oppositions among them of individual needs and ends, oppositions which in terms of social organization, however, are or have been transformed into these differentiations, or into mere specializations of socially functional individual behavior.

The human social ideal—the ideal or ulitmate goal of human social progress—is the attainment of a universal human society in which all human individuals would possess a perfected social intelligence, such that all social meanings would each be similarly reflected in their respective individual consciousnesses—such that the meanings of any one individual's acts or gestures (as realized by him and expressed in the structure of his self, through his ability to take the social attitudes of other individuals toward himself and toward their common social ends or purposes) would be the same for any other individual whatever who responded to them.

One may say that the attainment of functional differentiation and social participation in the full degree is a sort of ideal which lies before the human community. The present stage of it is presented in the ideal of democracy. It is often assumed that democracy is an order of society in which those personalities which are sharply differentiated will be eliminated, that everything will be ironed down to a situation where everyone will be, as far as possible, like everyone else. But of course that is not the implication of democracy: the implication of democracy is rather that the individual can be as highly developed as lies within the possibilities of his own inheritance, and still can enter into the attitudes of the others whom he affects. There can still be leaders, and the community can rejoice in their attitudes just in so far as these superior individuals can themselves enter into the attitudes of the community which they undertake to lead.

How far individuals can take the roles of other individuals in the community is dependent upon a number of factors. The community may in its size transcend the social organization, may go beyond the social organization which makes such identification possible. The most striking illustration of that is the economic community. This includes everybody with whom one can trade in any circumstances, but it represents a whole in which it would be next to impossible for all to enter into the attitudes of the others. The ideal communities of the universal religions are communities which to some extent may be said to exist, but they imply a degree of identification which the actual organization of the community cannot realize. We often find the existence of castes in a community which make it impossible for persons to enter into the attitude of other people although they are actually affecting and are affected by these other people. The ideal of human society is one which does bring people so closely together in their interrelationships, so fully develops the necessary system of communication, that the individuals who exercise their own peculiar functions can take the attitude of those whom they affect. The development of communication is not simply a matter of abstract ideas, but is a process of putting one's self in the place of the other person's attitude, communicating through significant symbols. Remember that what is essential to a significant symbol is that the gesture which affects others should affect the individual himself in the same way. It is only when the stimulus which one gives another arouses in himself the same or like response that the symbol is a significant symbol. Human communication takes place through such significant symbols, and the problem is one of organizing a community which makes this possible. If that system of communication could be made theoretically perfect, the individual would affect himself as he affects others in every way. That would be the ideal of communication, an ideal attained in logical discourse wherever it is understood. The meaning of that which is said is here the same to one as it is to everybody else. Universal discourse is then the formal ideal of communication. If communication can be carried through and made perfect, then there would exist the kind of democracy to which we have referred, in which each individual would carry just the response in himself that he knows he calls out in the community. That is what makes communication in the significant sense the organizing process in the community. It is not simply a process of transferring abstract symbols; it is always a gesture in a social act which calls out in the individual himself the tendency to the same act that is called out in others.

What we call the ideal of a human society is approached in some sense by the economic society on the one side and by the universal religions on the other side, but it is not by any means fully realized. Those abstractions can be put together in a single community of the democratic type. As democracy now exists, there is not this development of communication so that individuals can put themselves into the attitudes of those whom they affect. There is a consequent leveling-down, and an undue recognition of that which is not only common but identical. The ideal of human society cannot exist as long as it is impossible for individuals to enter into the attitudes of those whom they are affecting in the performance of their own peculiar functions.

EPILOGUE

B Y

EMILE DURKHEIM

SOCIOLOGY APPEARS DESTINED TO OPEN A NEW WAY TO THE SCI-ence of man. Up to the present, thinkers were placed before this double alternative: either explain the superior and specific faculties of men by connecting them to the inferior forms of his being, the reason to the senses, or the mind to matter, which is equivalent to denying their uniqueness; or else attach them to some super-experimental reality which was postulated, but whose existence could be established by no observation. What put them in this difficulty was the fact that the individual passed as being the *finis naturæ*—the ultimate creation of nature; it seemed that there was nothing beyond him, or at least nothing that science could touch. But from the moment when it is recognized that above the individual there is society, and that this is not a nominal being created by reason, but a system of active forces, a new manner of explaining men becomes possible. To conserve his distinctive traits it is no longer necessary to put them outside experience. At least, before going to this last extremity, it would be well to see if that which surpasses the individual, though it is within him, does not come from this super-individual reality which we experience in society. To be sure, it cannot be said at present to what point these explanations may be able to reach, and whether or not they are of a nature to resolve all the problems. But it is equally impossible to mark in advance a limit beyond which they cannot go. What must be done is to try the hypothesis and submit it as methodically as possible to the control of facts.

Reprinted by permission of the publisher, The Free Press, Glencoe, Illinois. Abridged from: Durkheim, Emile, *The Elementary Forms of the Religious Life* (translated by Joseph W. Swaine), London, 1915.

INDEX

OF AUTHORS AND TITLES

A NOTE ON THE TYPE

The text of this book was set on the Linotype in a face called Baskerville, named for John Baskerville (1706–75), of Birmingham, England, who was a writing master with a special renown for cutting inscriptions in stone. About 1750 he began experimenting with punch-cutting and making typographical material, which led, in 1757, to the publication of his first work, a Virgil in royal quarto, with great primer letters, in which the types throughout had been designed by him. This was followed by his famous editions of Milton, the Bible, the Book of Common Prayer, and several Latin classic authors. His types fore-shadowed what we know today as the "modern" group of type faces, and these and his printing became greatly admired. After his death Baskerville's widow sold all his punches and matrices to the SOCIÉTÉ PHILOSOPHIQUE, LIT-TÉRAIRE ET TYPOGRAPHIQUE (totally embodied in the person of Beaumarchais, author of THE MARRIAGE OF FIGARO and THE BARBER OF SEVILLE), which used some of the types to print the seventy volume edition, at Kehl, of Voltaire's works. After a checkered career on the Continent, where they dropped out of sight for some years, the punches and matrices finally came into the possession of the distin-guished Paris type-founders, Deberney & Peignot, who, in singularly generous fashion, returned them to the Cam-bridge University Press in 1953.

Composed, printed, and bound by KINGSPORT PRESS, INC., Kingsport, Tennessee. Paper manufactured by S. D. WAR-REN COMPANY, Boston, Massachusetts. Designed by HARRY FORD.